The Tagalog Language

CANSTANTINO LENDOYRO

Jno. F. Finley

Oct - 31st 1906

THE TAGALOG LANGUAGE.

IMPORTANT NOTICE.

Special attention is called to what is said in the note on the last page of this book with regard to the most peculiar orthographical character in Tagalog. Students are particularly recommended to read such note carefully before their going into the Grammar, so that, from the start, they may not get accustomed to write it in the wrong manner it will be found printed throughout the work.

THE TAGALOG LANGUAGE.

A comprehensive grammatical Treatise adapted to self-instruction

and particularly designed for use of those engaged in Government

service or in business or trade in the Philippines,

by

CONSTANTINO LENDOYRO,

for twenty years intimately connected with trade and commerce

in these Islands.

FIRST EDITION.

Imprenta de "EL MERCANTIL,"

Manila (P. I.)

1902

The Tagalog Language.

FREFACE.

The great practical advantages enjoyed by one who speaks a native language or dialect over him who knows not a word uttered by those with whom he comes in daily contact are too obvious to require mention. The belief that Americans who look forward to a permanent or long residence in these Islands will be quick to perceive the benefits to be derived from a knowledge of the most widely spoken native language in the Philippines was the inspiring cause of the author's undertaking this work. It is offered as a practical aid to the acquisition of a thorough knowledge of the Tagalog language.

The method of instruction followed throughout this work is in accordance with the system which seems to be easiest for learners, whatever their age, to grasp a new language, namely, that of explaining its grammatical construction, as far as possible, in the same phraseology and on the same lines as they have been accustomed to in learning their own and other languages.

It was at first intended to avoid any unnecessary philological investigations or scientific theories of the language as being beyond the scope of a practical Grammar, but when such language as the Tagalog, so dissimilar in construction to those of the western world, is to be considered, some scientifical remarks showing its peculiar character can hardly be dispensed with. This has been done, to some extent, in the "Introduction" and occasionally in the text, mainly in the explanatory notes generally preceding every lesson and part of speech.

As it will be difficult at the outset, that the student should divest himself of the notion that Tagalog can be learnt or taught on identically the same lines as modern languages, it may, perhaps, appear to him, at first sight, that too much space has been devoted in this Grammar to explanations of this kind and that repetition of and frequent reference to them may, in some

cases, render the style somewhat prolix. This, if we under—
stand it rightly, is only seeming and the apparent deficiency is
accounted for by the nature of the language and the age of the
persons probably undertaking it.

As Tagalog is not a modern language and necessary, like
others, for common professional purposes or scientifical research,
it is not for children, but for persons of mature years,
(especially for those who trade and fill official duties in the Philippines) to learn it. Now, it would hardly be desirable to teach
such persons as will probably study Tagalog in the Islands, in
the same manner as children are taught. Reason being to Ma-
turity what Memory is to Infancy, a method grounded on a mere
exposition of English words or sentences coupled to their counterparts in Tagalog, as is usual in a dictionary or a vocabulary, would be a complete failure, as most of such learners would
have the opportunity of a better teaching derived from the
natives in the midst of whom they live. It is believed that
theory and a frequent reference to those rules which more directly
show the fundamental principles the language rests upon, conjointly with the practice of such words and idioms as are used
in common topics for all requirements of every-day life will best
accomplish the learner's end. It is in this way that the student
of mature years for whom the task of committing the lessons to
memory is so difficult will be able to acquire the language by merely
reading the grammar over from time to time as he may find it necessary to do. When adequate illustrations have been given on a
special point; a rule, as comprehensive as it may be, immediately follows: when the matter is treated of as a heading, the rule
precedes and the illustrations follow.

Great care has been taken in noting, either in the text or in
foot-notes, every word of Spanish origin and in tracing it back
to its original and simple spelling in the language so as to show
clearly the change undergone in its adaptation to Tagalog. If
such words appear combined with any Tagalog suffixes or prefixes
so as to impart some special sense, the various elements have
been separated and explained, when this has been deemed necessary. But above all, we have endeavoured to explain as fully
as we could, a matter which, it may be said, constitutes the very
pith of the language, that is to say, the particles and their use in
word—building. Every one of them has been fully treated of,
both as it occurs in the first lessons and in the closing part of
the book, when all the imparting senses and combinations they
are susceptible of have been brought together and thoroughly
reconsidered.

Besides the reading exercises given in the last three lessons
every other lesson is provided with an exercise in which the
words and phrases given in such lesson or in the previous ones
have a free play. In considering the matter offered for train-
ing in such exercises, the student must bear in mind that,
religious thoughts excepted, abstract ideas, which form so large

a part of our topics in conversation, have but little place in that of natives, and that the expressions resorted to, puerile or strange as they may appear to our minds, constitute however the conversational ground with that part of the native population with which, most probably, those for whom this work is intended have to deal. The exercises are arranged in questions and answers for the teacher (if there be one) and the pupil to engage in dialogues and the same may be extended to similar topics or read aloud as many times as may be necessary to acquire fluency. The exercises should, of course, be written without any other assistance than the vocabulary in the lessons and the mistakes made should, then, be corrected by comparison with the key which is given at the end of the book.

The author is, however, conscious of many imperfections in his work, but when it is considered that this is the first English-Tagalog grammar ever published and that the Tagalog language differs so widely in its structure and idioms from all modern languages, the great difficulties to be encountered in compiling even the simplest treatise of this kind will be better perceived and appreciated. It is hoped that this effort of the author will be found a useful and profitable source for better qualified persons to pursue the subject more deeply and in a more scientific and successful manner, and that the work, despite its imperfections, will be welcomed and appreciated by Americans both in these Islands and at home,

INTRODUCTION.

Tagalog is one ot the many dialects derived from the Malay language and can hardly be spoken of without reference being made to the trunk or fountain from which it originally sprung. Malay is not the language of a nation, but of tribes and communities widely scattered from the eastern coast of the Bay of Bengal to the Malay Peninsula, Sumatra, Sunda, Java, Borneo, Celebes, Flores, Timor, the Moluccas and the Philippines.

The similarity of the dialects used by the inhabitants of the above-mentioned countries with their stem the Malay as spoken in the west coast of the Malay Peninsula, was first noticed by Europeans in the sixteenth century when Magellan's Malay interpreter was found to be understood from one end of the Malay Archipelago to the other.

Tagalog has received the influence of Sanskrit, and of the Arabic and some other Semitic languages, but in a smaller degree than the other Malay dialects. It has, however, been influenced by Spanish in a much larger proportion than either Javanese or the Malay of the Straits of Malacca have been, respectively, influenced by Dutch, English or Portuguese.

The earliest Aryan influence came from Sanskrit in an epoch not yet accurately determined. It seems to be the prevailing theory that inmigrant tribes coming from Mid-Assia settled along the shores and spread themselves over the Peninsula, Sumatra. Java, Borneo and Celebes, but their further progress over the many islands more to the north and east appears to have been checked by older and less conquerable races. In one way or another these tribes must have made the island of Java their favorite abode or the court or focus from which Hinduism irradiated with a force decreasing proportionally with the distance to the countries it endeavoured to reach. This is proven by the fact of Javanese having become the recipient of a larger number of Sanskrit words and in a greater degree of purity than any other dialect of Malay derivation, their number decreasing as we recede from Java. Further research as to the comparative number of Sanskrit terms passing into Javanese and Tagalog will show that while in the former the proportion may be rated at the eleven per cent, it scarcely reaches in Tagalog one and a half per cent of the whole aggregate of words. This percentage, as may naturally be inferred, is somewhat, but not much larger, in the southern *Filipino* dialects, Bicol and Bisayan and still more in those spoken in the Sulu islands and in Borneo, but yet the proportion is not such as to constitute any of them a composite language on this sole account.

We subjoin a table of words of Sanskrit origin, which are, among others, made use of in Tagalog. This is mainly done to show what deviations both in meaning and in spelling, the words have undergone in their adaptation to the language, and at the same time, to instruct pupils as to the general way of Tagalizing words when they may have recourse to English words to express some new idea, a thing which they cannot help but do occasionally in Tagalog.

Sanskrit.	Signification.	Tagalog.	Signification,
Kastûrî (1)	Musk	Castoli	Musk.
Angâra	Charcoal	Oling	Charcoal.
Argha	Price	Halagá	Price
Laksha	(100,000)	Lacsà	(10,000)
Ayuta	(10,000)	Yota, sangyota	(100,000)
Tâmra	Copper	Tumbaga	Ore.
Tivra	Tin	Ting-ga	Tin or lead.
Caja	Elephant	Gadia	Elephant.
P râpatî	Pigeon	Palapati	Pigeon.
Chandana	Sandal-wood	Sandana	Sandal-wood.
Kusumbha	Sawfflower	Gasubha	A kind of saffron.
Chinta	Thought, care, anxiety	Sintà	Love.
Kuta	Fort	Cota	Wall, stronghold.
Vâna	Arrow	Pana	Bow, arrow.
Krit	To cut, to kill	Calis	A kind of sword.
Sâkshin	Witness	Sacsì	Witness.
Mridh	To pardon	Maharlica	Free, liberated,

It should be noticed that the very miscellaneous character of words imported into Tagalog from Sanskrit and the absence of many terms incidental to the ethical and religious Hindu institutions will tend to prove the small degree of influence Hinduism had in moulding the character and customs of the inhabitants of these Islands at those times.

* *

The influence coming next to that of Sanskrft came later with the irruption of the Arabs and added a Semitic element to the language. While it put a stop to the flowing into the vernacular of any new terms of Sanskrit origin, it, however, retained those already in general use, supplementing them with those appropriate to the ideas of a new and more advanced civilization, and above all with those relating to the Mohamedan religion introduced to the partial displacement of the worship of Budha. But the greatest revolution to the language came to Malay

---

(1) Sanskrit words are here transliterated into Roman characters, as few students would be acquainted with the Sanskrit ones.

2

through the introduction of the Arabic character in general writing, especially in Literature, which is still preserved in the Straits Settlements and elsewhere. (1) This revolution did not travel far into the different parts of the Malay Archipelago and the same causes which opposed the advancement of Hinduism in the Philippines, but chiefly the strong check which Mohammedanism encountered in comparatively recent times on the part of Spaniards after the conquest, prevented its adoption by the inhabitants of the Islands, who continued to write in their ancient rudimentary characters. This fact and the introduction of the Spanish alphabet, so simple and rational in structure, must be noted to the advantage of the learner of Tagalog. While a student of Malay must determine beforehand whether he intends to speak or to write the language or whether both things are aimed at, and in the latter case, the difficulty of obtaining any fluency in reading a new character often appears so great as even the discourage him from making a beginning, the learner of Tagalog will enjoy the inmense advantage of learning at once both the speaking and the writing, and on account of a fairly strict correspondence between Spanish Prosody and Orthography, he will be easily led to write any Tagalog word he has not been previously acquainted with, if it is distinctly uttered to him.

The Arabic element in Malay is not accurately determinable, for new words and expressions are constantly being introduced. In Tagalog, however, the same has had but little influence and perhaps does not number one per cent of all the words, it having besides put a stop to by the introduction of the Spanish element. Some Arabic terms are still pouring into the Moorish dialects of Mindanao and Sulu Islands where Mohammedan rites prevail yet to some extent.

We subjoin a set of words of Arabic origin, used in Tagalog.

Arabic.	Signification.	Tagalog.	Signification.
Utar	Nerve	Utac	Brains.
Inkiyad	Submission, obedience.	Paningcayad, tingcayad	To sit cross-ledged, (the respectful posture in church.)
Apium	Opium	Ampion	Opium.
Arak	Liquor	Alac	Wine, liquor.
Ilahi	Divine	Lahi	Nobility.
Taksir	Sluggish	Tacsil	Dull, stupid.
Ribu	(1,000)	Libò	(1,000)
Lezat	Savory	Lasap	To relish.

(1) The scholar will derive more valuable philological information from the words of Marsden, Crawford, Abbé Favre and Maxwell on Malay, from which, but especially from the latter's some of the ideas set forth in this sketch are taken.

VII.

Arabic.	Signification.	Tagalog.	Signification.
Sípat	Measuring-string or rule	Sípat	To mark out with a line.
Surat	Writing	Súlat	Writing.
Sujud	To prostrate	Lohor	To kneel down.
Salám	Amen, peace be to you (a salutation)	Salámat	Thanks.
Selúar	Trousers	Salaual	Trousers.
Hukum	Judge, judgement	Hócom	Judge.
Heyá	Timidity	Hiya	Blush, ashamed.
Zauj	Married party	Asáua	Married party.
Alimun	Occult science	Alimoan	Awful, dark place.

*
* *

Chinese is another element added to Tagalog through a long and close intercourse of Chinese with native people. Opinions have been expressed to the effect of Malay being of a primitive Mongolic origin. As for Tagalog, it might perhaps be true that Chinese was the earliest influence the language of the aborigines and first settlers received and that which it was moulded after, for although actual Tagalog is mainly dissyllabic, there is not wanting evidence of a monossyllabic tendency, but if so, the primitive Chinese element has been so far either assimilated or corrupted as to be hardly recognisable in the language of a now-a-days.

The easily determinable portion of Chinese is that which has come to Tagalog since the discovery and falls short of the amount that one would be led to infer from the fact of Chinese influence in other respects.

This may be due partly to difficulties of compenetration in the character of the two languages and to the conquest having given rise to a necessary preference for Spanish; but chiefly to that inbred disposition on the part of the Chinese race to shut others out from acquaintance with their national institutions and racial characteristics and to the natural reluctance of the Islanders to adopt the manners and speech of a class of people whom they saw despised and held aloof, and whose religion, practices, and even dressing, on the other hand, they were forbidden to imitate. Thus, a race of people, who, from the remotest epoch, have been so widely scattered throughout the Archipelago, and, in many other respects, so connatural to its native population, could only leave behind in the language, such terms as generally designate those tools and sorts of food which natives soon adopted and partook of; or kindred names, the latter mostly confined to the use of a particular class of people, as shown in the following table.

Chinese.	Signification.	Tagalog.	Signification.
Tchà	Tea	Cha or sa	Tea.
Pi–sau	Knife	Pisáo	Small knife.
Liu	To propel a boat by wielding an oar at the stern	Lio-lio	To propel a boat by wielding an oar at the stern.
Tient–sim	(A loosely twisted pith of a tree used as wick for cocoa–nut oil lamps)	Tientsín	(Pith of a tree serving as wick for cocoa-nut oil lamps.)
Tan–hun	(A kind of paste made into a slender worm-like form, used for soup)	Sotanjón	A kind of Chinese vermicelli.
Mi–ki	(A kind of vermicelli used for a sort of pastry)	Míquí	Do. do. do.
Mi–soan	Do. do.	Misuá	Do. do. do.
Pan–sit	(A kind of cake or relish made of *miquí, misuá,* etc.)	Pansit	A kind of cake thus called.
So–si	Key	Susi	Key.

Terms used only in some districts, especially by chinese mestizos.

Int–tian	His or their father	Intià	Father.
In–ma	Godmother	Imá	Mother.
In–pó	Aunt.	Impó	(Grandmother, the grandmother's sister and extensively any old woman.)
In–kong	Their grandfather	Ingcong	(The grandfather's brother and extensively any old man)
Ing–so	Sister-in-law	Insó	(Sister-in-law; more properly, the wife of the first-born brother.)
Sam–ko	Third brother	Samcó	The brother, third in age.
San–chi	Third sister.	Sansí	The sister third in age.

⁂

As has been hinted elsewhere in this outline, Spanish is by far the largest Aryan element introduced in Tagalog and that which supplies its many deficiencies and imparts to it its comparative efficiency and comprehensiveness.

The aboriginal dialect previous to the admixture of Spanish is but the poor vocabulary of men hardly raised above savage life. The purely native element in Tagalog profusively furnishes all the requisitive terms to express the physical objects surrounding men leading a primitive life in the forest and all that has to do with their food, dwellings, agriculture, fishing, hunting and domestic affairs. As soon as the analysis reaches moral ideas or conceptions in science the lack of appropriate terms commences to be felt, and it will be seen that their sense its to be conveyed to the native mind either by metaphors and round-about expressions or by having recourse to Spanish. Hence many Spanish words, unaltered or distorted, passed into the language to express those things or ideas that natives were not and could not be acquainted with in their isolated condition of life before the conquest. From this it will easily be inferred that a previous knowledge of Spanish is of assistance in the study of Tagalog, not only on account of the numerous Spanish a words that found their way into the language, but chiefly on account of the orthographical frame which is wholly Spanish. On the other hand, natives prided and they still, to some extent, pride themselves, on using such Spanish terms and expressions as may best command the belief of their being conversant with the latter, and this in a way that is sometimes destructive of the Tagalog syntax.

It is not here intended either to exhaust the number of Spanish words made use of in Tagalog or to go deeper into a matter that is treated more at length in the part devoted to Grammar, where every Spanish word has been noted and explained. It is only as an illustration that we give hereafter a table of some terms borrowed from Spanish.

Spanish	Signification	Tagalog	Signification
Dios.	God.	Dios.	God.
Virgen.	The Holy Virgin.,	Virgen.	The Holy Virgin.
Espíritu-Santo.	Holy Ghost	Espíritu-Santo.	Holy Ghost.
Manzana.	Apple.	Mansana.	Apple.
Topar.	To butt.	Topa.	Sheep, ram.
Caballo.	Horse.	Cabayò.	Horse.
Chapín.	Clog. (a kind of shoe worn by people in 16th century)	Sapín.	Shoe.
Confesarse.	To confess to the priest.	Compisal.	To confess to the priest.
Filosofía.	Philosophy.	Pilosopía.	Philosophy.
Vaso.	Glass, tumbler.	Baso or vaso.	Glass, tumbler.
Misa.	Mass.	Misa.	Mass.
Español.	Spaniard, Spanish.	Castila. (Corruption of the Sp. word *Castilla*).	Spaniard, Spanish.
Peso·	Dollar.	Pisos, misos.	Dollar.
Tabaco,	Tobacco.	Tabaco.	Tobacco.
Padre.	Father, priest.	Pare.	Father, priest.
Cura.	Curate.	Cura.	Curate.
Padrón.	Census.	Padrón.	Census.

***

Having thus sketched the strange elements of which Tagalog is made up, it only remains for us to give a brief account of the character and peculiarities of the language.

Tagalog is the most important dialect of the Philippines. This is not on account of its being spoken by the largest proportion of the inhabitants in the Islands, for Bisayans are in greater number than Tagals; but on account of Tagalog having become predominant and becoming more so every day. as the language of the most cultured part of the whole population and that which any average–educated native from other Districts must soon learn on his coming to Manila for instruccion.

The similarity between Tagalog and the other dialects spoken about the Islands is such as to make it easy for natives from different parts to understand each other by using their respective dialects for general conversational topics. The same must be the case with foreigners if they succeed in acquiring something more than a superficial knowledge of the language, as they can scarcely fail to understand and be understood at every corner of the Archipelago, if they speak Tagalog with some degree of fluency.

It will not appear irrelevant, now that the similary of the *Filipino* dialects is to be considered, to say something about what it consists in as regards Tagalog and the two dialects next to it in importance, Bisayan and Bicol. While the construction remains the same or nearly the same throughout them all, only some words vary from one to another dialect, as is even the case with any one of the dialects, from one place to another. In many an instance, words that are rarely, if ever, used in one dialect have a general use in the other with the same or analogous meaning; sometines terms of identical signification in both dialects, retain in spelling the same vowels while one or more consonants vary and are replaced by others according to certain rules. It is by studying this affinity and interchangeability of certain consonants that the scholar will be enabled to understand many words of the southern dialects. A change which, among others, does not fail to occur, is the softening of the *R* of Malay and the southern dialects into *L* or into *D* for Tagalog, as seen in the following table.

English.	Bisayan.	Bicol.	Tagalog.
Not to have or to be.	Uaráy.	Uará.	Ualá.
Letter, writting.	Súrat.	Súrat.	Súlat.
So carry, to take.	Dará.	Dará.	Dalà.
Bathing.	Carigos.	Carigos, parigos.	Maligo.
Sleeping.	Tórog.	Túrog.	Tólog.
Knowing.	Aram.	Aram.	Alam.
Sun, day.	Adláo.	Aldáo.	Arao,
Rain.	Urán.	Orán.	Ulán.
Shirt.	Bado.	Bado.	Baro.
Trousers.	Sarúal.	Saróal.	Salaual.
Maid.	Daraga.	Daraga.	Dalaga.

XI.

Many words are either equal or so similar as appears from the following table:

English.	Bisayan.	Bicol.	Tagalog.
Woman, female.	Babáy.	Babáy.	Babaye.
Man, male.	Lalaqui.	Lalaqui.	Lalaqui.
House.	Baláy.	Baláy or harong.	Báhay.
Sky, Heaven.	Lágnit.	Lángit.	Lángit.
Debt.	Otang.	Otang.	Utang.
To walk.	Lácao.	Lácao.	Lácad.
Bread.	Tinápay.	Tinápay.	Tinápay.
Ten.	Polo.	Polo.	Póuo. (1)

As regards the amount of effort necessary to acquire a knowledge of Tagalog that will be of practical advantage to the learner, it may be said that Tagalog is a language of which it is very easy to learn to speak a little; it is, however, very difficult to acquire the idioms of natives. Facility of expression and the accurate use of idioms can only be acquired by much practice in speaking with natives. Correctness cannot be entirely learnt from grammars, and instruction derived from books must be supplemented by constant practice.

Tagalog is thought to be a poor language and so it is, but not perhaps so much so as is generally supposed. That it often fails to furnish us with words for abstract ideas is a deficiency which it has in common with all uncultivated languages or rather with all races who have not yet risen to the height of our civilisation and development.

Tagalog as compared with Malay and the other dialects of Malay derivation is a great deal more free in construction and more concise. This is partly due to the influence of Spanish, but chiefly to Tagalog being richer in sense-modifying particles than any of those dialects. The flexible power of such particles and their manifold combinations with each other must be closely observed by the learner if he aims at something more than to clothe English sentences with Tagalog words.

One of greatest difficulties to be encountered is perhaps that regarding the right accentuation of Tagalog words and the best course to be recommended to the student in this respect, is to observe how natives pronounce and accentuate in the respective lacality.

The lack of uniformity of expression throughout the Tagalog region is such as to make it difficult to teach the colloquial language without imparting to the lesson the dis-

---

(1) Most of these terms are also common to the dialect of Ilocos, but it differs more from Tagalog in construction, than the latter from Bicol and Bisayan, and even from Malay.

tinct marks of a particular locality. The construction of the language and the general body of words remains, of course. the same or nearly the same, but in every Province or division of a Province there are peculiar words and expressions, and variations of accent and pronunciation which belong distinctively to it. Words common in one district sound strangely in another, or it may be they convey different meaning in the two places. It has been our aim to supply a work in which only such terms as are common to the whole body of Tagalog-speaking people appear, and the student may rest assured of his being understood everywhere in the Tagalog community if he makes use of them.

Natives speak more tersely than Europeans. but their abrupt sentences which seem rude to western ears convey no idea of impoliteness to the native mind.

The written language is more pompous and less idiomatic than the colloquial dialect. If, however, the subject of speech is carried away from common topics to the utterance of passionate feelings, the natives' imaginative power displays itself in an overflowing of metaphors, riddles and highflown expressions.

The advantages to be derived from acquiring a language so peculiar in character will be better appreciated by tradesmen and people filling official duties in the Philippines. when they perceive the ease with which they can transact their respective business by dealing directly with natives. As for the scholar, over and above the enlargement of mind, he will enjoy the benefit of getting deeply into the innermost character of a race of human beings whose proceedings, otherwise, defy explanation. Any other study which does not necessarily embody their manner of casting thoughts, however ethnological it may be, would fall short of the purpose.

We are not in a position to make any authoritative statement looking forward to a further development of the language or as to whether the political change in the Islands will promote or check its progress; but if Tagalog is to continue to be the vehicle of the thoughts of so many million people, a magnificent future may be anticipated for it. As receptivity, not originality, is the main feature of every tribe of the Malay race, so their language shows that capacity for the absorption and assimilation of foreign elements which has made English one of the most exhaustive languages ever spoken in the World.

———

ORTHOGRAPHY.

Tagalog is now written in the Roman character brought over by Spaniards and the Spanish alphabet, in its adoption, has been modified to suit the peculiarities of the language.

Although the introduction of the Spanish alphabet fully superseded and swept away the ancient rudimentary aboriginal character, the use of which is at present thoroughly discontinued in the Islands, the interest of the student may be promoted by giving him, before passing over to the modern orthography of the language, the following summary account of what characters the primitive alphabet consisted in, as still to be found in some European and Malay dictionaries.

The characters made use of in writing by natives previous to the arrival of Spaniards, were seventeen, viz:

INDEPENDENT VOWEL SIGNS.

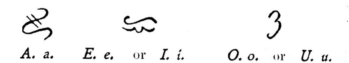

A. a.   E. e.   or   I. i.   O. o.   or   U. u.

CONSONANTS.

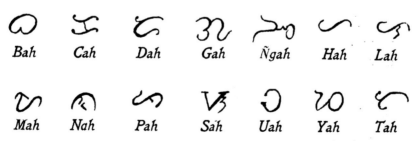

Bah   Cah   Dah   Gah   Ñgah   Hah   Lah

Mah   Nah   Pah   Sah   Uah   Yah   Tah

Every one of these consonants carried along with it the inherent vowel sound of (ah); a tittle placed above indicated

the sound of eh–ih thus, ⟨image⟩ beh–bih, and the same dot placed

2

under the consonant made it sound *oh–uh* 〰 *loh–luh*, and so

forth for the rest. Independent vowel characters were used only when a vowel came alone, or two vowels came together in the word to express the last of them in the diphthong, as,

for instance, in ☙ 𝓃 𝟥 *agáo*, "to snatch". It is easy to

conceive how deficient this system was to represent the Phonetic of all the vocables, as syllables in the composition of which, an inarticulate consonant, alone, or two, one articulate and the other not, entered, could not find adequate means of expression in writing. Thus, in many cases, the reader's mind was left to conjecture from the context, which word of those expressible by the same characters was meant, and the work of the writer ought to have consisted in his selecting such vocables as could less entail confusedness, thus narrowing the art into a profession, kept by a special rank of people, and drawing a line of separation between the spoken and written language.

This matter of the primitive alphabet having been outlined, we pass over to the practical part of it, and since Spanish Orthography has been so far introduced in Tagalog, the following remarks as to the sound of vowels, Spanish consonants used in Tagalog, and combinations with each other should be learnt by the student.

There are in Spanish, as well as in English, the five following vowels:

A-a,   E-e,   I-i,   O-o,   U-u,

the sound of which corresponds nearly with that of the same letters in the English words:

Far,   Bell,   Mill,   Off,   Bull,,

besides **Y-y**, which, when it comes at the end is considered as a vowel.

The same vowels are made use of in Tagalog; but the sound of **A-a** is independent; those of **E-e**, **I-i**; **O-o**, and **U-u** are, in the majority of cases, respectively, freely exchanged, to suit euphony or the taste of the speaker; so that, properly speaking, the fundamental vowel sounds in Tagalog are only three: **A-a, I-i, U-u**; **I-i**, or **E-e** having the broad expanded sounds lying between the vowel sound in "sheep" and in "bed" passing through the vowel sound in "bid" and somewhat in "first"; **O-o** or **U-u**, those between "Ball" and "Bull".

CONSONANTS.

All the Spanish consonants are made use of in Tagalog, but the peculiar to the latter are:

B-b,   C-c.   D-d,   G-g,   H-h,   L-l,   M-m,

N-n,   P-p,   Q-q,   R-r,   S-s,   T-t,   Y-y,

and sometimes, although improperly, *V-v* is used for B-b or for *U-u*. (1)

Over and above these consonants borrowed from Spanish and having, generally, the same sound they have therein, there is another, *Ñg-ñg*, peculiar to Tagalog and a very important one. The Tagalog alphabet consists, therefore, of the following twenty written characters.

A, B, C, D, E, G, H, I, L, M, N, Ñg, O, P, Q, R, S, T, U, and Y.

PRONUNCIATION.
VOWELS.

A-a, absolute vowel sound, always having that of the same letter in the English word "Far", example: *Aga* (pron. *áh-gah*) "to dawn"; *aso* (pron. *áh-soe*,) "dog"; *Abala*, (pron. *ah-báh-lah*) "occupation". *A*, is freely met with at any portion of the words.

E–e, variable vowel sound, generally exchangeable for *I-i*, having the sound of English *e* in "bed" or *i* in "bid. *E–e*, is but rarely met with at the middle or at the end, and never at the beginning of words (some not–altered Spanish words excepted.). It can be considered as a superflous vowel doomed to disappear and be replaced by *I-i* without detriment to the language. It is however still preserved in some words as in *maselán* or *mascilán*, (pron. *mah–seh–láhn* or *mah–say–láhn*,) "pru-

---

(1) Native pedantry, quite of late, has put in use *K–k*, *W–w* and other somewhat injudiciona novations, people formerly engaged in plotting against Spanish rule thus paying homage to the work carried out in their secret lodges or *Catiponans* and to its hieroglyphical writings. While there may be good reasons for the use of *K–k*, we fail to see what the reason may be for writing *Cawit* instead of *Cavite* and which other Orthography could better suit Tagalog, than the Spanish one. It is not that we consider the latter, in its application to Tagalog, as entirely irreformable, but that such needful changes as, no doubt, it requires, be done according to linguistic principles and not from political prejudice. In so far as the matter stands we do not favour these novations and the student is hereby informed that such words as *Kapatid*, "brother" or "sister"; *Gawá*, "work"; will always be spelt in this Grammar *Capatid*, *Gauá*.

dish"; "delicate"; *babáe, babaye* or *babáy*, (pron. *bah-báh-eh, bah-báh-yeh* or *bah-by*,) "woman", "female".

I-i, variable vowel sound, exchangeable for *E-e*, having for its principal sound that of *ea* in "meat". It is predominant and becomes more so every day for replacing that of *E-e*. *I-i*, can be found everywhere in words, but at the beginning is not so frequent as *A-a* and *O-o*. Examples: *Ibig* or *ybig*, (pron. *eé-big*) "to wish", "to love"; *Inà*, (pron. *ee-náh*,) "mother"; *Minsán*, (pron. *mean-sáhn*,) "once"; *Tahi*, (pron. *tah-heé*,) "to sew".

O-o, variable vowel sound, exchangeable for *U-u*, mainly sounding nearly as *O* in "Off". Example: *Otang* or *Utang* (pron. *áw-tang* or *oó-tang*.) "debt"; *Cocó* (pron. *Coh-cóe*,) "nail of the fingers". *O-o*, is much more frequently met with at the beginning than *U-u*; but in composition when the final *o* of a root-word is to be appended by some suffix, *o* is generally changed into *u*. Example: *Olò*, "head"; *Olohan* or better *Oluhan*, "big-headed" or "bolster".

U-u, variable vowel sound, exchangeable for *O-o*, sounding like *u* in "bull". Few words begin with this vowel; but is frequently met with at the middle and, although not so much, at the end. Examples: *Ualá*, (pron. *Ooah-láh*,) "nothing"; *Puti*, (pron. *Poo-teé*), "whiteness"; *pucáu* or *pocáo*, (pron. *poo-cáh-oo* or *paw-cáh-oh*,) "to wake". *U* generally replaces final *o* in root-words when the latter are recompounded by means of a suffix as said above.

What is said about the interchangeability of *E* and *I*, *O* and *U* must not be construed to mean that either of them have an equal phonetic value in writing. *E*, if written, should always be pronounced as *e* in "bed"; *I* as *i* in "mill"; *O*, as *o* in "roll" and *U*, as *u*, in "bull". Thus, natives, when they want to produce the vowel sound of "bed", write *e* and so forth for the other vowels. What is generally indifferent, especially in polysyllables, is to pronounce and write *E* or *I*, *O* or *U;* I and *U,* however, being prevalent; but if for reasons of taste, for the sake of euphony, or to suit the peculiar local manners of speaking, one of these interchangeable sounds is preferred, it should be written accordingly. The broad scope of the vowel sounds accounts for this expansion, as no misconception can arise from pronouncing one way or the other, there being, properly speaking, only three vowel sounds in Tagalog.

Looking further into the matter, a scientifical research will prove that natives pronounce the second and third vowels in a way sharing nearly equally of the sounds into which they can be expanded, somewhat after the manner that the vowel *e* is pronunced in the English word "pretty", for the former, and something as an intermediate sound between *o* in "roll" and *u* in "bull", for the latter.

CONSONANTS.

B-b, sounds as in English, no matter what part of the word it comes in. Examples: *Bata*, (pron. *bah-tah*,) "child": *Tabá*, (pron. *tah-báh*,) "fatness"; *Dibdib*, (pron. *deeb-deéb*,) "breast".

C-c, has the palatal sound it has in "cart". Examples: *cagat*, (pron. *cah-gátt*, "to bite"; *Bácal*, (pron. *báh-cahl*,) "iron"; *Palacol*, (pron. *pah-lah-cóll*) "axe"; *Itac*, (pron. *ee-táck*) "knife". This letter in modern Spanish, when coming before *e* or *i*, sounds like English *th* in "think". No such sound of *th* exists in Tagalog: thus, if any Spanish word in which *c* fulfils the above-mentioned conditions is made use of in Tagalog and it is preferred to preserve the letter, it should be pronounced *s*. For instance, *Cebólla*. (Sp.) "onion"; is to be pronounced *Sebolla*, (that is to say, *Seh-bóh-llah*, and not *theh-bóh-llah*, as it should have been); but it is much better to Tagalize the word by writing *Seboya*, *Siboya* or *Sibuya*, (pron. *Seh-bóh-yah*, or *See-bóh-yah See-boó-yah*, the last being the best Tagalized and pronounced of the three.

Owing to the palatal sound which this letter has before *a, o, u*, or a consonant and to the lack of fixedness in the orthography of the language, *C* is written by some people to represent the sound of *qu* in "conquer". Thus, *aquin*, "mine"; is written by some *acin*; but we consider this an improper manner of writting and it is only mentioned to acquaint the student with it and to enable him to understand such deviation when he may find it used in other books, for nothing of it will be found in this Grammar, where *aquin* and similar articulations are always written *qu*.

D-d. It is not so dental in Tagalog as it is in English. Its sound is so mild as to resemble that of *R* with which it is interchangeable in many cases. Examples: *Dugó*, (pron. *doo-góe*,) "blood"; *Bondoc* or *Bundoc*, (pron. *bohn-dóck* or *boon-dóck*,) "mountain"; *Capatid* or *Capatir* (pron. *Cah-pah-teéd* or *Cah-pa h-teér*,) "brother" or "sister". *D-d*. at the end of a word may be written *d* or *r* (the termination *d* being preferable) and the sound shares of both letters, somewhat as in English; but in rootwords, initial *d* is generally changed into mild *r* in compositions where any particle ending in a vowel is prefixed; for instance: *dami*, "much"; *caramihan*, instead of *cadamihan*, "majority". The same is the case at the end, when the writing with *d* is preferred, as from *pilad* or *pilar*, "lucky"; *capalaran* instead of *capaladan*, "happiness". In the middle of a root *d* is more used than *r* when a consonant precedes; *r*, on the contrary, is generally preceded by a vowel; *pandac*, (pron. *pan-dáck*), "dwarf"; *sira*, (pron. *seé-rah*), "to destroy".

G-g, sounds as in English in the words "get", "grave", "finger". Examples: *Gabi*, (pron. *Gah-bée*,) "night"; *pagod* or *pa-gor*, (pron. *pah-gód* or *pah-gór*,) "weariness"; *dalay* (pron. *dah–láhg*), "a kind. of fish". *G-g*, has in Spanish two sounds, a harsh guttural one, stronger than that of the English *h*, and another mild, according, respectively, to its coming before *e* and *i* or any other letter. In the Spanish syllables *gue gui*, *u* does not sound at all, (1) it being only a sign of pronunciation, indicating that *g* is not to be pronounced gutturally, but that it sounds as the same letter in "gate". This is sometimes disregarded in Tagalog, some people writing *gintó* instead of *guintó*, (pron. *geen-tóh*,) "gold", etc. Now, if the proper rules of the Spanish Prosody are to be applied here as elsewhere in Tagalog, *gintó* should be pronounced *heen-tóe*, while *guintó*, which is the correct term, should sound *geen-tóe*, as it should be. The student is warned that the articulations *ge* in "gelder" *gi* in "gift" will always be written in this. Gammar indifferently *gue, gui*, or *g-e g-i*, the hyphen being used, especially in composition, for the same purposes as the insertion of the *u*, as explained hereafter. *G-g*, when at the end of a particle should be distinctly pronounced in a very mild and particular way somewhat resembling the sound it has in the English word "dignity". Hearing it, however, pronounced by a native will convey a better idea of its sound. Any disregard on this point might lead to many misconceptions, for *madalí*, and *magdalí*, although both of them are compounds of *dalí*, "swiftness", differ broadly in sense. To what has been said about the insertion of *u*, the following is an exception. When any particle ending in *g* is to be prefixed to a root beginning with *i*, the *u* may or may not be inserted; but in the latter case, the *g* of the particle should be separated from the *i* by a hyphen, thus to denote that *g* has the mild sound which it would have, had *u* been inserted. Example: *Ibig*, "wish", "love"; *pag-íbig* or *paguíbig*, (pron. *pag-geé-beeg*,) "to wish", "to love"; and not *pah-heé-beeg* in the first of these cases. The hyphen may also be used when the root to which a particle ending with *g* is to be prefixed, begins with the same consonant, as in *gauá*, "work"; *pag-gauá* "working"; or when *h*, should be separated from any other consonant with which it might have a different sound, as *muc-há*, (pron. *moock-háh*), "face"; *duc-h,ú* (pron. *dook-háh*), "poor"; or to indicate that two consonants do not fuse into each other, as in *bulac-lac*, (pron. *booh-lack-láck*), "flower".

H-h, sounds exactly as in English. Examples: *Halagá*,

---

(1) There are some cases in which the *u* inserted between *g* and any of the vowels *e* or *i*, sounds, both in Spanish and in Tagalog; but then the crema (**) should be used. For instance, *uica* means "word" in Tagalog: if a particle ending in *g* is to be prefixed, (as *mag* is sometimes), thus forming *magüica*, "to pronounce"; (pron. *mag-ooeé-kah*), the crema is necessary, for otherwise the compound resulting would be *maguica* and it should have to be pronounced *mag-geé-kah*, destructive of the sound *uica*.

(pron. *hah-lah-gáh*), "price"; *halayháy*, (pron. *hah-li-hí*,) "to put linen to dry". *H-h*, is never a final consonant. (1).

L-l, sounds as in English. Examples: *Locsó*, (pron. *Locks-ó*) "jump", "leap"; *talabá*, (pron. *tah-lah-báh*,) "oyster"; *cambál*, (pron. *cam-báhl*,) "twin".

M-m. Its sound in Tagalog does not differ from that which it has in English. Example: *Mahal*, (pron. *Mah-háhl*,) "dear"; *salámat*, (pron. *sah-láh-matt*,) "thanks"; *gótom*, (pron. *góh-tom*.) "hunger". *M-m* and not *N-n* is generally used before *b* and *p* in root-words: *Sambit*, "to mourn"; *tampal*, "slap".

N-n, sounds as in English. Examples:: *Nácao* (pron. *náh-cah-oh*,) "stealing"; *tandá*, (pron. *tan-dáh*,) "oldness"; *dáan*, (pron. *dáh-ahn*,) "road"

Ñg-ñg, This is an exclusive Tagalog consonant and a very peculiar one, both in character and in sound. The latter is produced by expelling the breath towards the roof of the mouth so that a portion of the air should come forth through the nostrils. The student should have it pronounced by a native. Examples: *Ñgayón* (pron. *Ñgah-yóhn*,) "now", "at present"; *sañgà*, (pron. *sang-áh*,) "branch" of a tree". *Ñg*, is never a terminal consonant.

Ng-ng, at the end of a word may be a part thereof or a euphonic ligament; in either case, both letters have a nasal sound, *g* having the mild, but still perceptible sound it has in "dignity" as above said; but if *ng* belongs to the word and the latter is suffixed with any aditament beginning with a vowel, *ng* is changed into *ñg* and the sound is the nasal one peculiar to the latter; for instance: *Magaling*, "good", "sound"; *cagaliñgan*, "goodness", "soundness". *Ñg*, always comes before a vowel.

P.-p. It has the same sound as in English. Examples: *Para*. (pron. *Páh-rah*,) "like"; *pacpac*, (pron. *pack-páck*,) "wing"; *daquip*, (pron. *dah-keép*,) "to seize".

P.-p, replaces *f* in all Spanish words, in which the latter enters, when they have been Tagalized, the sound of *f* being exotic and of very difficult pronunciation for a native. Thus, for instance, *favor*, "favor", is Tagalized into *pavor* and so on.

Q-q, has the same sound as in French or in the English words "antique", "conquer", and should always be written *qu* (the *u* being soundless) with either *e* or *i* following. Examples: *quilala*, (pron. *kee-láh-lah*,) "to be acquainted with"; *que-*

---

(1) The fact that *h* is frequently met at the end in Malay words when written in the Roman character and that of the same consonant never being a final letter in Tagalog, constitutes a deficience in the latter imputable to those only who first adapted the Spanish alphabet and prosody to Tagalog. The importance of appending *h* to a final sharply-accented vowel does not seem to have appeared to their minds, nor they seemed to realize the simplicity resulting from writing *gandah*, *batoh*, etc, instead of *gandá*, *bató*, etc, to form the derivatives *cagandahan*, *batohin*, thus doing away with one of the greatest difficulties in the language.

braḍa, (pron. *kay-bráh-dah*,) "wreck". In inserting the *u* due attention is paid to Spanish ortographical rules which Tagalog has been built upon; but owing, however, to the same causes as explained for the misuse of *C* and *G* and to a different employing of *Q* when Tagalog began to be written, still *Q* alone and not *Qu* is found in some ancient books and even now some persons write *qibo* instead of *quibo* and so on for analogous articulations, a practice which is, on no account, to be recommended. *Q* is never a final letter.

R-r. The sound of this consonant is somewhat to be compared to that of the same in English when it comes at the middle of a word, as, for instance, in "very"; but in so far as it shares that of *D* with which it is frequently interchangeable, the student would do well to notice how it is pronounced by natives. *R-r* is never found at the beginning but at the middle or the end of words: at the end, however, *d* is preferable to *r*. Examples: *marahil*, (pron. *mah-ráh-heel*) "perhaps"; *lácar* or *lácad*, (pron. *Lih-car* or *láh-cadd*), "to walk"; *torᶁ*, (pron. *tor-óh*,) "to point out": As for its interchangeability with *D*, see this letter.

S-s, has the sound of English *s* in "same", "yes". Examples: *Siyá* (pron, *see-yáh*,) "he or she"; *lisan*, (pron' *leé-san*,) "to leave off": *labás*, (pron. *lah-báss*,) "outside". *S-s*, replaces *C* in the Spanish sillables *ce, ci, za, zo, zu*, (pron. *thay, thceh, thah, thoe, thoo*) (pron. *th* as in "think"), in all Spanish words made use of in Tagalog, this strong sound of *th* not existing in the language as above said. *Cebolla, Ciceron, zapato, Zoilo, zueco* are Tagalized into *sibuya, Siscron, sapato, Soilo, sueco*.

T-t, sounds as in English in "tea". Examples: *Tónay* or *túnay*, (pron. *tónn-i* or *toó-nnie*), "true"; *patáy*, (pron. *pah-tíe*,) "dead"; *at*, (pron. *at*,) "and".

Y-y, at the beginning of a word or a syllable and before a vowel, is considered as a consonant, and as a vowel at the end. Its sound is that which it bears in English in "yes", "day". Examples. *Yacap* (pron. *yah-cáhp*,) "to embrace"; *diyata*, (pron. *dee-yáh-tah*,) "therefore"; *baybáy*, (pron. *by-bíe*,) "beach". This letter is used for Spanish *Ll* as Tagalized in *cebolla, sibuya*. *Y* preceded by a consonant is never to be found at the end of words.

ESPECIAL REMARK.

Persons consulting Spanish-Tagalog dictionaries must be aware of the indiscriminate use of some letters: E and I, O and U, C and S or Q, D and R, Y and I, *Ll* and F, *gue gui* and *ge, gi, Qu* and Q, looking for the same word written in the various manners in which it can be, that they may get at it some way or other.

PROSODY.

Although Spanish Prosody could not be so fully applied to Tagalog, this has been however done in so far as its application is not destructive of the peculiar character of the latter. The student's work, therefore, may be advanced by his previously being acquainted with the following prosodical remarks.

COMPOSITION OF SYLLABLES.

A syllable in Tagalog may consist:

A) Of a single vowel, as *a* in *a-ca-la,* "to guess."

B) Of one vowel and one consonant or vice-versa, as *in,* in *in-sic,* "chinese;" *ha,* in *ha-bá,* "length."

C) Of one vowel between two consonants, as *pan* in *pan-hic,* "to go upstairs".

D) Of one vowel and two consonants, provided the latter be not fusible into each other, as *ang* in *ang-cam* "race", "ancestry".

E) Of one consonant, one vowel and two consonants under the same conditions as above, as *ling* in *ling-cod,* "to wait upon".

F) Of two consonants and one vowel, one of the former being a liquid one, as *clá* in *ba-clá,* "astonishment". (1) Words consisting of two similar portions are excepted, as in *bulac-lac,* "flower".

G) The same combinations as in *F*, followed by a consonant, as *clar* in *ba-clar,* (2) "reed-net for fish"; (fishing-enclosure), *crot* in *si-crot,* "a kind of play with pebbles".

H) Of one consonant, one vowel and two consonants under certain conditions to be explained hereafter, as *locs* in *locs-ò,* "to jump".

DIVISION OF SYLLABLES.

A consonant between two vowels joins the second vowel, (unless the last vowel should be separated for purposes of com-

---

(1) In this the language has been influenced by Spanish Prosody, for the liquid consonants were formerly, and are still, pronounced separately by some people, especially by those who have been kept aloof from intercourse with Spaniards. Thus, *baclá,* is pronounced by them *bac-lá* and so forth for similar articulations.

(2) Combinations *F* and *G* are not found in the first syllables of genuine Tagalog words.

position when the affixes *in* or *an* ought to be preceded by the aspirated sound of *h*, as explained further on.) Examples: *A-bá* "oh;" *ba-ta*, "child". Dissyllables consisting of two equal portions are excepted. Examples: *ac-ac*, "notch"; *ol-ol*, "mad". Combinations into which *l* or *r* enters with a consonant with which either of the former can be fused are considered as a single consonant in root-tagalog words, for the purposes of division, as in *i-cli*, "shortness"; *ha-blá*, "complaint", "charge". This is not generally applicable either to derivatives and contractions or to root-words ending in a gravely accented vowel (`), when the latter is to be separated for purposes of composition as above indicated. Examples: *Mag-la-bás*, "to take out"; *put-lin*, "cut it"; *pacl-à* "displeased".

When two consonants come between two vowels, to each vowel a consonant is joined. Examples: *Bun-tis*, "to be in family way"; *hin-hin*, "still, quiet".

When three consonants come between two vowels, the two first consonants join the first vowel, as in *Dang-cal*, "length measure from the thumb to the extremity of the little finger stretched out".

The case of three consonants coming between two vowels only occurs in cases as in the preceding example when *g* comes after *n* followed by a consonant, or in combinations in which *l* enters fused with some other consonant.

Every final consonant joins the preceding vowel to form a syllable therewith.

Every final vowel thus accented (`) should be considered as separated from the preceding letters and forming a syllable by itself. This is of the utmost importance as serving to distinguish many words which are written alike and only differ in the accent. Thus, *ba-ta*, means "child"; but *bat-à*, means "to suffer"; *ba-sa*, means "to wet"; but *bas-à*, means "to read", and so on for many other words.

THE ACCENT.

The most difficult thing in Tagalog is perhaps to lay down proper rules on the accent, and those follow but a vain phantom who seek to prescribe exact modes of accentuation for vocables regarding which even native authorities are not agreed and of which the pronunciation may vary according to locality. The experience of Spanish friars and Tagalists sufficiently proves this; there are words in their dictionaries written in as many as three different ways.

The written Spanish accent indicative of the syllable upon which a particular stress is laid has been somewhat injudiciously applied to Tagalog. Some grammarians go so far as to admit of seven different manners of accentuation; some, four; and some others, three; which they represent by (´) acute;

(`) grave, and (ˆ), circumflex. There are even others who make use only, either of the first or the first two, while most writers do not seem to acknowledge any; for, whatever they may think thereof in theory, they, at least, use none in practice, leaving rather the reader's presupposed knowledge to pronounce in the proper manner or in the way that may better suit the local peculiarities. The fact is that the Spanish accent has been carried away from its province and that it was intended to make it explain linguist peculiarities which would have better means of expression by other orthographical signs. The matter stands however in such a way as hardly to be changed, and the adoption of a method being necessary, we have, for purposes of the teaching, adopted that which seems to be the simplest, and we admit and shall make use of two accents in this work: the acute (´), and the grave (`), the latter always bearing upon the final vowel, and this merely as indicative of words, the enlargement of which requires the insertion of *h* when any additament beginning with a vowel is to be suffixed thereto, and thus it may be that the student may not find it employed outside this work. (1) Nor should learners be discouraged by finding sometimes the same word either differently accented or unaccented. It is that in some cases the accentuation is influenced by the word preceding or following, or by the sense to be denoted, in a way which practice alone can teach.

To a thorough understanding of the matter the following rules are established.

Unaccented words ending in a vowel, or in *n* or *s* are grave. The stress in this case bears upon the penultimate syllable. Examples: *Acala*, "to think"; *bayan*, "town"; *gatas*, "milk". Pron. *acála, báyan, gátas*.

Unaccented words ending in a consonant (*n* and *s* excepted) are acute, (*ictus*). The stress here is on the last syllable. Examples: *Payat*, "lean, meagre"; *manoc*, "fowl. Pron. *payát, manóc*.

Words ending in a vowel thus accented (`), should be pronounced acute in a peculiar way: the last vowel should be pronounced separately from the rest, so as to constitute a syllable by itself and, moreover, the grave accent it bears is an indication that if the word is to be enlarged by *in* or *an* suffixed, *in* or *an* should be written and pronounced *hin, han*. Examples: *Gondà*, "beautiful"; *cagandahan*, "beauty"; *tubì*, "aside"; *tabihan*, "secluded place"; *tauò*, "man"; *catauohan*, "mankind". Any deviation from these rules will be marked by the accent. Thus, *bintí*, "calf of the leg"; *bucà*, "to lay open"; *canilá*, "their"; *tatló*, "three"; *tamís*, "sweet"; *salamín*, "looking-glass"; should be accented, for otherwise they would be grave, while *dápat*, "worthy". *útang*, "debt"; *lálim*, "depth"; on the contrary, are accented to indicate that they are to be pronounced grave instead of acute as they should be if no accent marks were used.

---

(1) See note. page XIX.

The accent serves in many cases to distinguish words which, although written alike, differ in meaning, as *gatas*, "milk"; and *gatás*, "path"; *gúling*, "source", "origin", "coming from": and *galing*, "fair", sound", healthy"; *sacá*, "afterwards"; and *sacà*, "to till", "to farm".

For the proper accentuation, care should be taken with regard to words ending in a vowel or in *n* when they, for reasons to be explained, receive the euphonic ligament of *g* or *ng*. Thus, for instance, *binti*, which is marked as an acute word will also be so marked in the phrase *binting matabá*, "big calf of the leg"; to indicate that it is the same word *binti* linked to the following one *tabá* for the sake of euphony. In the same manner and for the same purpose, the accent will or will not be employed respectively in *salaming mahal* "costly looking-glass"; *bayang malaquì*, "large town".

Words ending in *y* or in two vowels will always be accented on the vowel bearing the stress. *y* being sometimes a vowel, and sometimes a consonant, and the joining of two vowels not always constituting a diphthong for the effects of pronunciation.

By paying attention to the foregoing rules, students will be assisted in attaining a desirable pronunciation. They must, however, understand that the adoption of the two orthograhical signs of accentuation in this work is merely a matter of ex-expediency, as most books written in Tagalog are deprived of such characters.

DIPHTHONGS AND TRIPHTHONGS.

The joining together or two or three vowels is frequently met with in Tagalog words. For the purposes of pronunciation they to not constitute diphthongs or triphthongs in the English prosodical sense, as each vowel preserves its proper sound, *ua, uo, ui, iu*, sometimes forming syllables by themselves; *tiua*, "laughter"; *gauí*, "skill"; *gauá*, "work"; *iua*, "dagger", *bituín*, "star".

***

The accent in relation to the structure and meaning of words.

Some knowledge can be derived with regard to the accented syllable of a word by considering its structure and meaning. As general rules which, of course, admit of many exceptions, the following are laid down:

Acute *(ictus)* words are:

Root–words ending in a consonant, both syllables, or the last two syllables of which are equal or similar in structure. Examples: *camcam*, "to take away"; *tastás*, "to unsew"; *bulac-*

lae, "flower"; calisquis, "fin of fishes"; haloquipquip, "folding of the arms".

Root–words or derivatives the last two syllables of which end in ay; as baybáy, "sand"; talaytáy, "to circulate".

Root–words and derivatives ending in a consonant preceded by one vowel and two consonants; as tampal, "slap"; baloctot, "intermingled".

Grave words are:

Polysyllabic root–words ending in consonants and consisting of two equal dysyllabic parts; as gonamgónam, "to muse", galang-gálang, "reverence.

Dysyllabic root-words ending in vowels and consisting of two equal parts, as coco, "lukewarm"; caca, colloquial word for "eldest brother"; pipi, "mute", "dumb".

Derivatives from acute or grave root–words when they have been enlarged by a suffix, as from bató, "stone"; batohin, "made of stone; from samà, "accompanying"; samahan, "accompanied"; panhic, "going upstairs"; panhican, "staircase". To this rule some imperatives are an exception.
No rule can be laid down for words not comprised in the above divisions.

As for the meaning, generally words denoting celerity are acute; as tacbó, "to run"; lipad or lipar, "to fly"; those importing motion in quite a general sense are acute or grave according to the idea which is to be conveyed with regard to the degree of acceleration in the action. Thus, lácad is grave and means "to walk" in the natural way; while maglacad, which means "to walk much", "to walk" swiftly"; is acute. Words denoting slowness are generally grave in accent, as; tiguil, "to calm", "to refrain from"; tahan, "to stop".

PECULIARITIES.

Under certain conditions to be explained in the text, words having a particular mutual dependence are linked to each other by means of particles or connectives adhering thereto or placed between them, either to suit euphony or to impart a particular relation. The ligaments made use of for this purpose, are y, suffixed to words ending in n, when they should be linked to the following one; ng, affixed to those ending in one or two equal vowels, and na, placed between those ending in a consonant (n excepted) or two different vowels, and the following word to be linked thereto. Ay or ai, y or i is likewise a connective to be placed between words entailing a verbal relation.

The illustrations hereafter will convey to the student's mind the understanding which is required at this stage. Bayan, "town"; malaquì, "large"; bayang malaquì, "large town"; mabutì, "good": *tauó* "man", "person"; *mabuting tauó* or *tauóng mabuti*, "good fellow"; *malicot*, "naughty"; *anac*, son or or daughter"; *malicot na anac*, or *anac na malicot*, "naughty son or daughter"; *bundoc* "montain": *mataas*, "high"; *ang bundoc ay mataas*, "the" mountain is high".

At or *t* is sometimes a connective used between causal conjunctions and the word following, as in **Di** *acó paroróon, sapagca,t, acó,i, may gauá*, "I shall not go there, because I have business".

Some words undergo certain contractions on account of briefness or euphony. In *ay* and *at*, "and"; for instance, *a*, may be dropped when the word immediately preceding ends in a vowel. If it ends in *n*, both the *n* of the word and the *a* of ligaments may of the dropped, the fashion in such case having established the putting of the *t* or *y-i* remaining of the ligament between two commas; (1) as in *gabi,t, árao*, for *gabi at árao*, "night and day"; *carunu,gan,t, cabanalan* instead of *carunuñgan at cabanalan*, "wisdom and virtue"; **Si** *Pedro,i, mabuti*, instead of **Si Pedro** *ay mabuti*, "Petter is good"; *iy'i,i, mahaba*, instead of *iy:in ay mahaba*, "that is long".

READING and PRONOUNCING EXERCISE.

Reading in Tagalog is therefore as simple as in Spanish: it merely consists in reading and pronouncing every letter (except *u* when it is inserted between *g* or *q* and certain vowels as stated), according with the sound assigned to it, in the chapter devoted to Orthography in this work.

The student, before passing beyond to the Grammar, should try to comprehend as fully as he can the foregoing remarks and to read and pronounce correctly the following exercise:

Tagalog.	Malaquing	totoó	ang	catungculan	
Pron.	**M**ah-lah-king	toh-toh-óh	ang	cah-toong-coó-lahn	
Trans.	Great	indeed	the	obligation	

Tag.	natin	umíbig	at	gumálang	sa
Pron.	náh-teen	oo-meé-big	at	goo-máh-lang	sah
Trans.	our (of us)	to love	and	revere	(to)

Tag.	ating	amá	at	iná	para	nang
Pron.	áh-ting	ah-máh	at	ee-náh	páh-rah	nang
Trans.	our	father	and	mother	according	to

---

(1) This work not being reformatory in kind, we confine ourselves to the teaching of the language as it is at present written; but there is little doubt that Tagalog requires reformation in this and some other points.

Tag.	sinaysáy	co	sa	inyó	nang	is`ng
Pron.	*see-ni-si*	*coh*	*sah*	*in-gñióh*	*nang*	*ee-sáng*
Trans.	explained	of me	to	you	on	(other) last

Tag.	lingo:	datapóua	.t.	mauaualáng
Pron.	*lín-goe*	*dah-tah-p´ih-ooah*	*t*	*mah-ooah-ooah-láng*
Trans.	Sunday;	however (it)		(will not have)

Tag.	cabuluhan	ang	gayóng	pag-íbig.
Pron.	*cah-boo-loó-han*	*ang*	*gah-yóng*	*pag-eé-big*
Trans.	(any) value	the	such	loving

Tag.	cundí	langcapan	nang	mabubuti
Pron.	*coon-deé*	*lang-c´ih-pan*	*nang*	*mah-boo-boo-teé*
Trans.	if not	united (backed)	to	good

Tag.	at	caúcol	na	gauá;	cundí	bagá
Pron.	*·at*	*cah-oó-coll*	*nah*	*gah-ooáh;*	*coon-deé*	*bah-g´ih*
Trans.	and	corresponding	works,		if not	of course

Tag.	samahan	nang	magaling	na
Pron.	*sah-máh-han*	*nang*	*mah-gah-ling*	*nah*
Trans.	accompanied	by	(a) sound	

Tag.	pagsónod	natin	sa	mañga
Pron.	*pag-sóh-nodd*	*náh-teen*	*sah*	*máng-ah*
Trans.	obeying	of ours	to	the

Tag.	utos	niláng	matotouir
Pron.	*oó-toss*	*nee-láng*	*mah-toh-toh-oo-eer*
Trans.	commandments	of them	right,

Tag.	at	nang	magaling	paglilingcod
Pron.	*at*	*nang*	*mah-gah-ling*	*pag-lee-leeng-códd*
Trans.	and	by	fair	serving

Tag.	at	pag-aalila	natin	sa
Pron.	*at*	*pag-ah-ah-leé-lah*	*n´ih-tin*	*sah*
Trans.	and	devoting devotion)	of ours	towards

Tag.	canilà,	cun	silá,	i,	nahihírap
Pron.	*cah-nee-láh,*	*coon*	*see-láh*	*ee*	*nah-hee-heé-rap*
Trans.	them.	if	they	are	sick

Tag.	at	nasasalatan.
Pron.	*at*	*nah-sah-sah-láh-tan.*
Trans.	and	destitute.

FREE TRANSLATION.

———

Great, no doubt, is our duty to love and revere our parents,
as I have explained to you last Sunday; but such love and

respect will be to no purpose if the latter are not backed by good and conscious works, if not, I say, accompanied by a proper obedience on our part to their just injunctions, and by our assistance and attendance to them when they are sick and destitute.

GRAMMAR.

FIRST LESSON.

UNANG PAGARAL.

THE ARTICLE.

The definite article *the*, in the singular, is expressed in Tagalog by *ang*, which may be said to stand for the English definite article, though it is rather a particle capable of expressing many other relations. *Ang* is used only before common, abstract, and proper nouns of things. Proper nouns of persons (personal names) take in Tagalog, contrary to the English usage, their proper definite article *Si*. As for other proper nouns, natives say: *Ang Pasig, ang Pilipinas, ang Maynila, ang Cavite;* "The Pasig," "the "Philippines," "Manila," "Cavite." The indefinite article *a* or *an* may be expressed in Tagalog by the numeral adjective "one," *isd*.

The (sing.)	Ang.
Have you?	(¿Mayróon ca po? (indeterminate.)
	) ¿Na sa iyò bagá? (determinate.)
Yes Sir, I have.	(Oo, po, mayróon acó. (indet.)
	(Na sa aquin po. (det.)
I have (söme.)	Mayróon.
Sir.	Po.
Have you any hat?	¿Mayróon ca pong *sambalelo?* (1)
Yes, I have a hat.	Oo, mayróon acóng *sambalelo.*
Have you my bread?	¿Na sa iyò bagá and tinápay co?
Yes, I have your bread.	Oo, na sa aquin ang tinápay mo.

Common, abstract, and proper nouns of things in the singular, possessive pronouns and clauses serving as subject to a sentence, are generally preceded by the particle or article *ang*.

The subject of a sentence, whether a noun or pronoun, may be placed either before or after the verb it governs, the order being governed by considerations of euphony.

May. ó m and *may,* (its root) are constructed between two nominatives. *Mayróon* may be used alone, *ma*, always requires some object of possession following.

---

(1) Corruption of the Spanish word *sombrero,* "hat."

5

To have, as an active verb, followed by a noun in an indeterminate sense, is translated by *may* or *mayróon*. (1) If the noun refers to some specific or particular thing, it is translated with *na* and the objetive case (ablative of place) of the noun or personal pronoun which is the subject in English, the literal translation being "your bread is with me". *Sa* is sometimes used before *cay*.

Numeral adjectives are not considered as determinative, unless they themselves are otherwise determined by some word having a determinative character. Example: *Mayróon acóng dalauàng paco*, "I have two nails"; *ang dalauàng paco ang na sa aquin*, "I have the two nails". (Literally, the two nails are with me.).

Properly speaking, the interrogative sense is not indicated in Tagalog by any sign or particular manner of construction; but by the employment of such words as *bag í*, *cayá*, etc., their use being optional. The interrogative signs, taken from Spanish, are however, largely used. They should be placed both at the beginning and at the end of the sentence. The tone of the voice, alone, may sometimes mark the interrogation sufficiently.

Table.	*Lamesa* (2).
Meat, flesh.	Lamán, (Tag.); *carne*, (Span.).
Salt.	Asín.
Sugar.	*Asúcal* (corruption of Spanish word *azúcar*.).
Water.	Túbig.
Paper: { writing paper. { written upon.	Sulatan, (Tag.); *papel*, (Span.). Súlat.
My, mine, *or* of me. (possessive).	Aquin, co.
Thy, thine, *or* of thee (poss.); your, yours, *or* of you (poss.) (in the singular.).	Iyò, mo.
My hat.	Ang *sambalelo* co, or, ang aquing *sambalelo*.
My table	Ang *lamesa* co, or, ang aquing *lamesa*.
Your (sing.) bread.	Ang tinápay mo, *or*, ang iyòng tinápay.
Have you may hat?.	¿Na sa iyò bagá { ang *sambalelo* co? { ang aquing *sambalelo*?
Yes, Sir, I have your hat.	Oo, po, na sa aquin { ang sambalelo mo. { ang iyòng sambalelo.
Have you your table?	¿Na sa iyò bagá (or cayá) { ang lamesa mo? { ang iyòng lamesa?
I have my table.	Na sa aquin { ang lamesa co. { ang aquing lamesa.
The king.	Ang hari.
The bishop.	Ang *obispo* (Span.).
What.	¿Anò?; ¿anò bagá?
Which?, which one?	¿Alín?; ¿alín bagá?
Which hat have you?	¿Alíng sambalelo ang na sa iyò?.
I have my hat.	Ang sambalelo co ang na sa aquin.
Which one?	¿Ang alín?; ¿alín bagá?
What table have you?	¿Anòng lamesa ang na sa iyò?.
I have your table.	Ang lamesa mo. Ang iyòng lamesa } ang na sa aquin.
What? (nominative).	¿Anò?; ¿anò bagá.

---

(1) *May* and *mayróon* may be written *mey* and *meyróon* and pronounced accordingly.

(2) The Spanish word *mesa* used with the article.

The possessive pronouns and the possessive case of the personal pronouns are alike and have two forms, one prepositive and the other postpositive.

Interrogative pronouns take sometimes the article when they come alone in the sentence; but it is a practice which is not to be recommended.

Ang is likewise a relative pronoun standing for "what" or "that which", as in ¿*alíng sambalelo ang na sa iyò?* and similar cases.

FIRST EXERCISE.

Have you any bread? Yes, Sir, I have some bread. Have you my bread? I have your bread. Have you the meat? I have the meat. Have you your meat? I have my meat. Have you the salt? I have the salt. Have you my salt? I have your salt. Have you the sugar? I have the sugar. Have you the water? I have the water. Have you your water? I have my water. What paper have you? I have my paper.

SECOND LESSON.

YCALAUANG PAGARAL.

GENDER.

Inflexion for gender is unknown in Tagalog, and the sexes are generally distinguished by the addition of such words as *lalaqui*, "male"; *babaye*. "female", in the case of living things. In a few instances, the distinction in gender is expressed by different words, as in *amá*, "father"; *iná*, "mother". etc.

John.	Si Juan.
Ortiz.	Si ortiz.
Robinson.	Si Señor Robinson.
Mr. Branagan	{ Si Señor Branagan. { Ang Señor Branagan.
Dr. Martin.	{ Si Doctor Martín. { Ang Doctor Martín.

Christian names and surnames in the singular and nominative case require the particle *Si* before them. When used with titles, they may be preceded by the same particle or by that of common nouns, according to whether stress is laid on the name or on the title.

The father.	Ang amá.
The mother.	Ang iná.
The brother.	Ang capatid na lalaqui.
The sister.	Ang capatid na babaye, (1).
Eldest brother. (first born).	Coya, caca. } (colloquial names)
Eldest sister.	Ati, ate. }
My eldest brother.	Si coya, Si caca.
My eldest sister.	Si ate.
My father.	Si amá.
My mother.	Si iná.

The article *Si* of proper personal nouns may be also used before common nouns to indicate living beings unique in kind and pertaining to the speaker. When animals are named after persons or bear specific appellations by which they are known, such nouns may likewise take *Si* in the nominative. Thus, of a horse known as *Babieca*, may be said, *Si Babieca*. The use of *Si* in reference to a person who is not an intimate relation of the speaker is mockery.

---

(1) *Babaye*, "woman", „female" may be written *babayi, babōe batōy*.

Thou, you (sing.)	Icáo, ca; icáo po (polite.)
House.	Báhay.
Rice-field, farm.	Búquid, or, búquir.
Book.	Libro (Sp.)
Power, authority.	Capangyarihan.
Strength, force.	Cabagsican, calacasan.
God.	Dios, (Sp.); Bathala, (Tag.)
Leaf.	} Dahon, (Tag.); pohas, (corr. from Sp. word hoja, "leaf.")

Icáo, is used alone and precedes the verb; ca, follows it.

The house of John.	An cay Juang báhay.
John's house.	Ang báhay ni Juan.
The power of God.	Ang capangyarihan nang Dios.
God's power.	Ang sa Dios na capangyarihan.
The leaf of the book.	} Ang dahon nang libro. / Ang sa librong dahon.
Book-leaf.	Dahon libro.
Love.	Sintá.
Loving (pres. participle.)	Pag-íbig.

Common and proper nouns of persons in the possessive case are immediately preceded by the particles *nang* or *sa*, *ni* or *cay* respectively; *sa* and *cay* being used when the object of possession comes before the possessor.

In nouns common to both genders, the distinction in sex is made by adding *lalaqui* (male) for the masculine, *babaye* (female) for the feminine.

Dios is used as a common noun.

Compound nouns, in which one of the member qualifies the other, are generally formed in Tagalog in a manner contrary to that of English, viz.: by naming first the principal noun and second the qualifier. no ligament being employed if the first member ends in a consonant.

DECLENSIONS. (1)

The particles used in place of articles are declined thus:

Article for common, and proper nouns of things in the singular.

Nom.			The.	Ang.
Poss.			Of the.	} Sa, nang; nğ. (contract). (2)
	Dative.		To the.	Sa.
	{ Acc.		The.	Nang, sa.
Object.	} Abl.	{ Cause or place	In, by, at the.	Sa.
		(Instrument.	By, through, with the.	Nang.

---

(1) For a better understanding of this matter we consider the English objective case divided into *dative case* (indirect object), *accusative* (direct object) and *ablative* as in Latin, and the *ablative* case subdivided into *local* and *instrumental*

(2) *Nang* is contracted into *ng*. Such contraction, although frequently met with in other books will not be found in this grammar, as it will be destructive of the prosody and the student might be induced into a false pronunciation thereof.

Article for proper nouns of persons, in the singular.

Nom.	(1).	Si,.
Poss.	Of.	Cay, ni.
Object. (all its divisons).	To, at, in, by, with etc.	Cay.

Declension with a common noun.

Nom.		The.			Ang.		
Poss.		Of the.			Sa.....or nang.		
Object.	Dat.	To the		Weapon.	Sa.		Sandatà.
	Acc.	The.			Nang, sa.		
	Abl. local	In, at the.			Sa.		
	inst.	By, with the.			Nang.		

Declension with a proper noun of person.

Nom.	Peter.	Si Pedro.
Poss.	Peter's, of Peter.	Cay Pedroug.... ni Pedro.
Object. (all its divisions.)	Peter; by, to, etc. Peter.	Cay Pedro.

Not to have (active verb), not to possess; there is (or are) not. (indefinite).	Ualá.
To have (active verb.); there is (or are).	May, mayróon.
I have no table.	Ualá acóng lamesa. Acó,i, ualáng lamesa.
Have you not the meat?	¿Ualá bagá sa iyò ang lamán or lamangcati?
There is some salt.	May asín, mayróon asín.
There is no sugar.	Ualáng asúcal.
He or she.	Siyá.
Is there any paper on the table?	¿Mayróon bagáng papel sa lamesa?.
There is no sugar in the water.	Ualáng asúcal sa túbig.
Is there any house in the farm?	¿May báhay cayá sa búquid?
There is none.	Ualá.
Have you the leaf of the book?	¿Na sa iyò bagá ang dahon nang libro?
I have it.	Na sa aquin nga.
Have I any book-leaf?	¿Mayróon bagá acóng dahon libro?

May, is used without any ligament. As for *mayróon* and *ualá*, when they come before a pronoun, the nominative of a sentence, the ligament passes over to the pronoun. If the nominative comes before, the ligament may be employed. *¿Mayróon cang papel bagá,? Ualá acóng papel.* Otherwise: *¿Icaó,i, mayróong papel;? acó,i, ualáng papel.*

Nga, is a particle largely used in Tagalog, which carries the sense to its most complete expression, as in, *na sa aquin ñga;* "I have it indeed"; *Ualá ñga*, "There is absolutely none". It should be carefully distinguished from *na*.

---

(1) There is no equivalent in English.

When the subject in a sentence comes before the verb, the verbal ligament *ay-i* should be placed between. No ligament is used in the contrary case.

SECOND EXERCISE.

Has my father any salt? He has none. Have you a mother? I have. Has the king any sister? He has none Has the bishop any brother? He has. Has John any water? John has some water. Has he any house? Certainly, he has a house. Has God any power? Yes, indeed, He has power. Has your love any force? Yes, my love has force. Has God love for man? Yes, God has love for man. Is there any book at your house? Yes, at my house there is a book. Has your mother's love any force? Yes, indeed. Which book have you? I have Peter's book. What farm has your father? He has the king's farm.

THIRD LESSON.

YCATLONG PAG-ARAL.

NUMBER, AND THE ADJECTIVE.

A definite plural number is expressed in Tagalog by the use of the particle *mañga* or such collective numeral adjectives as *páua, lahat, dilán,* 'all." Sometimes, however, the number remains indefinite and should be gathered from the context. When there is nothing to show whether singular or plural is meant, the noun may generally be assumed to be in the plural or used in an indefinite sense.

The (plural).	Ang mañga; mga. (abb.) (1).
You (plural), ye.	Cayó; cayó po, (polite).
We.	Tayo, camí, quitá, catá.
They.	Silá.
No.	Hindí, ualá.
Not.	Di, hindí, dili.
Do not. (prohibitive).	Houag.
Clothes.	Damit.
Looking-glass.	Salamín (nang muc-há)
Money.	Salapí, pílac.
Understanding, judgment.	Bait, cabaitan.
Anything which is good, the idea of goodness.	} Buti. (root-word).
Good. (adj.).	Mabutì.
Anything bad, the idea of wickedness.	Samá. (root-word.).
Bad. (adj.)	Masamá.
Anything pretty, the idea of prettiness.	Diquit. (root-word.)
Pretty.	Mariquit.
Anything beautiful, the idea of beauty.	Gandà. (root-word.)
Beautiful. (adj.)	Magandà.
Ugly, wicked.	Páñgit, lupit.
Anything old.	Tandá. (root-word.)
Old (in age). (adj.)	Matandá.
Man, person, creature.	Tauò.
Dog.	Aso.
Child.	Bata.
Horse.	} Cabayò. (corr. from Span. word *caballo.)*
Mare.	Cabayong babaye.
Judicious, prudent.	Mabait.
The looking-glasses.	Ang mañga salamín.

---

(1) *Mañga,* will often be met with contracted into *mga;* but for the same reasons as explained for *ñg* in the second note of the preceding lesson, such contraction will not be used in this grammar,

The men, the persons, the people.	Ang mañga tauò.
My brethren.	Mañga capatid co.
The old person.	Ang tauòng matandá, and matandáng tauò.
The good (judicious) child.	Ang batang mabait, ang mabait na bata.
The good horse.	Ang cabayong mabuti, ang mabuting cabayo.
The beautiful woman.	Ang babayeng .magandà, ang magandàng babaye.
The pretty dogs.	Ang mañga asong mariquit. Ang mañga mariquit na aso. Ang maririquit na aso. Ang asong maririquit. Ang mañga asong maririquit. Ang mañga maririquit na aso.
The ugly mares.	Ang mañga cabayong babayeng páñgit. Ang mañga páñgit na cabayong babaye.

One.	Ysà.
Two.	Dalauà.
One person, a person.	Ysàng tauò.
Two children.	Dalauàng bata.

Common nouns and adjectives are put in the plural by using the particle *mañja*, to be placed between that which indicates the relation of case and the noun or any attribute thereof, unless the number is indicated by a numeral adjective. Nouns in the vocative case (nominative of address) or in apposition, drop *ang* in the plural.

The adjectives formed by a root-word and the prefix *ma*, may, also, be put in the plural by repeating the first syllable of the root if such syllable consists of one or two letters and the first two letters thereof if it consists of more, the use of *mañga* being optional.

The nominative case of the first person pronoun has three forms in the plural: *tayo, camí, quitá,*. *Tayo*, should be used when both the speaker and the person addressed are included in the notion; *camí*, when only the speaker is concerned. Thus, an American speaking to a native must say; *tayo;i, mamamatáy* ,'we are mortal"; *camíng mañga americano,i, mapuputí*, "we, americans, are white.

Quitá is exclusive or dual; as exclusive, it means, you (thou) and I alone; as dual, it is possessive with regard to the speaker and nominative for the person spoken to; it is somewhat as, *thou art... by me*.

Root is the term which denotes that the simplest idea of a thing, a quality or an action, and which requires some elaboration to express the various relations, the thing, quality or action is capable of. There are substantive, adjective and verbal roots. Roots possesing substantive force may be made to mean a quality by prefixing the particle *ma*, as seen in the above instances, they being thus converted into as many adjectives. Roots having an adjective force may be, and generally are, expressed without any elaboration.

Ma is the prefix most frequently used for making adjectives from substantive roots. Adjectives are also made from verbal roots by employing other affixes in several ways, to be explained in subsequent lessons.

The illustrations in the vocabulary show that adjectives in Tagalog may come before or after the nouns they qualify.

DECLENSIONS.

The article in the plural.

Nom.			The (plural).	Ang mañga.
Poss.			Of the "	Nang mañga, sa mañga.
Object.	Dat.		To the "	Sa mañga.
	Acc.		The "	Nang mañga, sa mañga.
	Abl.	local and causal.	In, at, from, etc. the.	Sa mañga.
		instrumental.	By, with, etc. the.	Nang mañga.

Declension of a common noun in the plural.

Nom.			The.	Ang.
Poss.			Of the.	Nang, sa.
Object.	Dat.		To the.	Sa.
	Acc.		The.	Nang, sa.
	Abl.	local and causal.	From, in, at, etc. the.	} Houses. } mañga báhay.
				Sa.
		instrumental.	With, by, from, the.	Nang.

Declension of a noun in the plural with an adjective,

Nom.			The.	Ang,
Poss.			Of the.	Nang, sa.
Object.	Dat.		To the.	Sa.
	Acc.		The.	Nang, sa.
	Abl.	local and causal.	In at, from, etc. the,	ugly dogs. } Sa. } mañga asong púñgit. mañga púñgit na aso.
		instrumental.	With, by, etc. the.	Nang.

Proper nouns have no plural. It is, however, a peculiarity of Tagalog that proper nouns of persons should be preceded by *Siná*, the plural of *Si*, not when persons bearing the same name are meant; but when the principal person, the one who is as head of the family or association is to be represented together with his or her intimate relations or with those connected with him in other respects. *Siná*, is declined as follows:

Nom.	Siná.
Poss.	Niná, caná.
Object. (all its divisions.)	Caná.

So, for instance, "Jane and her family" (or persons in any intimate connection with her), is declined as follows:

Nom.		Siná.
Poss.	Jane and her people.	Niná, caná.
Object. (all its divsions.)		Caná.

Juana.

Edward and his people.	Siná Eduardo.
The farm of Thomas' family.	(Ang búquid niná Tomás.
	(Ang caná Tomás na búquid.
Astor & Coy.	Siná Astor.
To Russell & Coy.	Caná Rusel.

THIRD EXERCISE.

Have we undertanding? Yes, we have. Have they any good clothes? No, they have none. Have you (plur.) any bad looking–glasses? Yes, we have some bad ones. Have I your pretty horses? Yes, you have them. Have the judicious children my beautiful dogs? Yes, they have your beautiful dogs. Have they my fine books? No. Which hats have we? You have Peter's hats. Has John my old brothers' good horses? He has none. Has Peter's father my children's old horses? He has them not. Have old people love for children? Yes, Sir, they have love for children. Have John's family any good houses? No, they have no good houses, but (1) they have some pretty farms. What farms have Peter's family? Peter's family have beautiful farms. Have they the ugly houses of John's family? They have not the ugly houses of John's family. Are there any books on the tables? There are no books on the lables. Have your sisters any old dogs? No, they have no old dogs.

---

(1) But, *cundi*.

FOURTH LESSON.

YCAAPAT NA PAGARAL.

THE LIGAMENTS, AND THE VERB *TO BE*.

As has been indicated in foregoing chapters, the Tagalog language is distinguished from other Malay dialects by the employment of certain endings or separate particles intended to link words, clauses and sentences to each other. The proper use of such *connectives* or linking-particles is more a matter of practice than of theory, as euphony, in many cases, determines whether they shall be used or not.

Hereafter we give such explanations as may be useful at this stage; but this matter being both so important and abstruse, we refer the student to the sixty ninth lesson, where some further rules are given on the subject.

The mutual relation between a substantive and its qualifying word should be indicated by a ligament added to, or following the first word, unless the second be a monosyllable. According as the first vocable, whether the substantive or the qualifying word, ends in *n*, one or two different vowels or a consonant (except *n*), the ligament employed should be *g*, *ng* or *na*, respectively. Examples: *batang malicot* or *malicot na bata*, "naughty boy"; *iyông báhay* or *báhay mo*, "your (sing.) house"; *itông isá*, "this other"; *iyáng dalauáng libro*, "those two books"; *¿anóng tauô?*, "what person?"; *árao na malínao*, "clear day".

The subject, be it a noun or a pronoun, of an active affirmative sentence should be linked to the verb by means of *ay-i* (1) if the subject precedes the verb; but not when this order is inverted. Examples: *Acó,i, pungmásoc, pungmásoc acó*, "I entered"; *ang ibon ay hungmuhuni, hungmuhuni ang ibon*, "the bird sings".

Two clauses having mutual connection should likewise be linked by *ay-i,*. Example: *Cun dumating si Pedro ay umalis ca*, "if Peter arrives, go away".

A clause serving as subject of an active affirmative sentence should be linked to the verb in the same way, when such clause precedes the verb, but, ordinarily, not when the order is inverted, as: *ang pag-íbig sa Dios ay nagpapapuri sa tauô*, or, *nagpapapuri sa tauô ang pag-íbig sa Dios*, "to love God ennobles man", or, "it ennobles man to love God". However, the ligament may be preserved even when the subject follows the verb, when for the sake of greater emphasis the verb is preceded by a relative pronoun or used in the participial sense in Tagalog, as: *ang nagpapapuri sa tauô ay ang pag-íbig sa Dios*, "what ennobles man is to love God".

In compound active sentences the principal and the secondary sentence are linked to each other by means of *at-t*, when a conjunction of

---

(1) The student is notified that *ay-i*, (pron. *ah'-e, ee*) is by some pronounced *eh,-a-ay*, or rather in a manner equally sharing of both sounds.

cause is used, as: *hiudí acó nacababasà sa pagca,t, ualá acóng salamín*, "I cannot read, because I have no spectacles".

When an interrogative word is used to start a sentence, the verbal ligament is replaced by the nominal one, which, in this case, stands for the article or the relative pronoun, as: *¿sinong nagnácao?*, "who stole?", *¿anóng sabi mo?* "what do you say?"; literally, "who is he who stole", "what is that which you say?", it being indifferent to say, *sinong* or *sino ang nagnácao?, anóng* or *anó ang sabi mo?*; the latter forms are however preferable as being both more idiomatic and emphatic.

The ligaments are not generally used before monosyllabic words or expletive particles, nor before the particles serving to establish the relation of case, for instance: *damit sa árao árao*, "daily wearing apparel"; *lalaqui man, babaye man*, "be it man or woman"; *ang caloualhatían ó gloria bagá*, "bliss, that is to say, glory"; *itò,i, caná Pedro*, "this is for Peter and his family".

The ligament is also dropped before the possessive pronouns if put after the nouns they qualify, as; *salapí niyà, caniyàng salapí*; "his or her money".

The numeral adjectives drop the ligament when they come before the restrictive prefix *ca*, as in *ápat catauò* "four persons only".

No ligament is used between the subject and the verb if the former is preceded by some negative or prohibitive particle; for instance: *Di acó cungmacáin*, "I do not eat"; *houag lumácad*, "don't walk"; *hindi camí magnanácao*, "we are not thieves".

The verbal ligament may also be dropped for euphony' sake if the word serving as the subjet ends in *i*. Ex. *Ang pantali napatid*; "the tying rope parted".

We have said elsewhere that the *a* of *ay* and *at* may be dropped when coming after words ending in a vowel, and that if they end in *n*, both the *n* and the *a* may be dropped. This is not, however, the case when *at* and *ay* are followed by a monosyllabic word, as, for instance, in *sa cagaliñgan at sa cabanalan*; "for goodness and virtue"; *ang calolóua, ay sa Dios*, "the soul is for God".

The preceding remarks refer to ligaments considered as euphonic characters; but they may, too, express by themselves essential and very important relations of other kind. Thus, *to be*, in its copulative sense, when it takes a noun or an adjective for predicate, is expressed by the ligament *ay-i*; and the endings *g*, *ng* or the particle *na* stand sometimes for relative pronouns and cannot, therefore, be dropped.

To be at, to be in, etc. (in the sense of to dwell, to reside, to live at, to find one's self at).	Na (and a name of place in the local abl. case). Na (and an adverb of place) Na cay (and a name of person). Na caná (and a collective personal name).
To be, (copulative verb).	Ay,i, ñga. bagá, g, ng, na.
At home.	Na sa búhay, sa búhay.
At church.	Na sa simbahan, sa simbahan.
At school.	Na sa *escuelà* (Sp.) or escuelahan.
Here.	Dini, ditò.
There. { indicating a place near the person spoken to.	} Diyán.
There. { indicating a place far away from both interlocutors.	} Dóon.
To be here.	Narini, naritò.
To be there (yonder).	Nariyán.
To be there (far away).	Naróon.
Where?	¿Sáan?

Where { is { he? she? it? } are { they? }	¿Nasáan?, naháan?, ¿sáan naróon?.
Where is my eldest brother?.	¿Nasáan bagá Si coya?.
He is at home.	Na sa báhay siyá. Siyá,i, na sa báhay.
Where is your mother?	¿Sáan naróon ang inà mo?.
She is with Henry.	Na cay Enrique siyá.
She is at church.	Na sa simbahan siyá.
She is at Docot family's.	Na caná Docot.
Not to be at.	Ualá sa.
Mamma.	Nanáy, nánay, inang. (colloquial).
Papa.	Tata, tátang, tátay, tatáy. (colloquial).
Is it you?	¿Icáo bagá?
Oh! yes, it is you.	Abáa!, icáo ñga; icáo ñga palá.
Is your papa at the farm (or country)?.	¿Na sa búquid bagá ang tátay mo?
No, Sir, he is not at the farm, he is in the forest.	Di po, ualá siyá sa búquid, na sa gúbat siyá.

"To be", whenever it asserts presence is translated by *na* and a noun of place in the local ablative case, or by prefixing *na* to any word demonstrative in character.

Gold.	Guintó,
Silver.	Pílac.
Steel.	Patalim, binalon.
Iron.	Bácal.
Wood, lumber.	Cáhoy or cáhuy.
Chrystal, glass (matter)	Búbog.
Cotton.	Bulac.
Ring.	Singsing.
Pen.	Panúlat, (Tag.); *pluma* (Sp.).
My father is good.	Ang amá co,i, mabuti. Mabuti ang amá co. (better) ang aquing amá.)
My sister is beautiful.	Ang aquing capatid na babaye ay magandà.
Is his brother bad?	¿Masamá bagá ang caniyàng capatid?
His brother is bad, but mine is good. (judicious).	Ang capatid niyà,i, masamá; ñguni,t, ang aqui,i, mabait.
Is their ring a gold one?	¿Guintó bagá ang canilàng singsing?
Yes, their ring is a gold one.	Oo, ang singsing nilá,i, guintó.

Whenever "to be" is the copula and has no other value than to assert some attribute of the noun is not translated in Tagalog by any specific word, but the meaning may be conveyed in several ways. If a noun or an adjective is used as the predicate of another noun or pronoun, it is enough to insert *ay–i* between them to indicate the copula. As *ay–i* is not generally used in interrogative sentences when the subject comes after the verb, the relation is then expressed by some expletive or completive particle. Sometimes the ligaments or the arrangement of words serve to express the same relation of copula, as when a relative pronoun is understood, for instance: *ang banal na tauo*, "the virtuous man", or, "the man who is virtuous".

FOURTH EXERCISE.

Where is your father? My father is at home. Where is my brother's son? He is at church. Where is their daughter? Their daughter is at church. Where is our son? Our son is at school. Is the child here? No, the child is not here, he is in the country. Are your sister's children there (yonder)? My sister's children are not there (yonder.). Where are they? They are at home. Is it he? It is he. Is it you? (plural) It is not we. Are my mother's brothers there? My mother's brothers are not there, they are at John's. Is the mountain over there? Yes, it is over there. Is your ring a gold one? No, it is a silver one. Is your table a wooden one? No, my table is a glass one. Have your bishops any iron rings? No, they have no iron rings; they have some gold rings. Are our looking-glasses made of silver? No, Sir, they are made of glass. Have you any steel books? No, I have paper books. Have your sisters any wood pens? No, they have no wood pens, they have some steel pens. Have I any wooden hat? No, I have no wooden hat, I have two cotton ones.

FIFTH LESSON.

YCALIMANG PAGARAL.

DEMONSTRATIVE PRONOUNS.

The demonstrative pronouns in Tagalog are those treated of in this lesson. They can be used either as adjectives or as true pronouns; when used as adjectives they generally precede the noun which they qualify.

Straw.

Thread.

Stocking.
Half.
Fork.
Leather.

Shoe, boot.

Wool, down.

Ribbon.

The Earth, (the world).

Earth, (matter).
Land·
Gun.
Something, anything.

Have you anything?

I have something.
Nothing, not anything.
I have nothing.
The cloth.
Soap.
What (what thing) have you?

I have your steel pen.

What (indet.) have you?
I have some bread.
Wine, any kind of liquor.
Coffee.
Tea.
Cheese.

My candlestick.

String.

Guiniican.
) Sinulid. (root-word, *sulir*, "to spin"; *si-*
(*nulid*, spun).
Medias, (Sp.) (plural).
Calahati.
Tenedor. (Sp).
Balat, (Tag.); *cuero* (Sp.).
) Sapín, (Tag.); *sapatos*. (corr. from Sp.
(w. *zapato*).
Balahibo, (Tag.); *lana* (Sp.).
) *Sintas*. (corr. from Sp. w. *cinta*); *galón*
((Sp.).
) Ang lupa, ang sangcalupáan, sang-
(daigdigan.
Lupa.
Catì, catihan.
Baril.
Anomán, bálang na.....
(¿Mayróon cang anomán?
(¿May anomán ca?
Mayróon, may anomán acó,
Ualá.
Ualá acóng anomán.
Ang cayo.
Sabón (corr. from Sp. word, *jabón*).
¿Anò bagá ang na sa iyò?
) Ang iyòng plumang patalim ang na
(sa aquin.
¿Anòng mayróon ca?
May tinápay acó.
Alac.
Café (Sp.), *capé* (corr. from Sp. *café*).
Sá (Chinese).
Quiso (corr. from Sp. word *queso*)
) Ang aquing *candelero* (Sp).
(Ang candelero co. (Tag.), sasañgán).
Lúbid, lúbir, tali.

Tying-string.	Panali (root-word, *tali*, "tying"); pantali.
Something good.	Banlá nang mabuti, anomán mabuti.
Anything good.	Anomán mabuti.
This.	Yarí, yerí, itò.
That (that near you).	Yyán, yan.
That (far from the interlocutors).	Yaón, yon.
This book.	Yaríng libro, yaríng librong yarí; itòng libro, itòng librong itò.
That table. (near you).	Yyáng lamesa, iyáng lamesang iyán.
That church (far away).	Yaóng simbahan, yaóng simbahang yaón.
The neighbour.	Ang caapidbáhay. (1)
Neighbours.	Magcaapidbáhay. (two).
Crown.	Pótong or pútong.
Palace.	*Palasio.* (corr. from Sp. word *palacio*).

The particle *in* prefixed to a root beginning with a vowel or inserted between the first consonant and vowel of those beginning with a consonant, or consonants, forms a new word which indicates the result of the action. Thus, from *sulid*, "to spin"; *sinulid*, "what has been spun", "the thread".

Sang, is a collective particle which if prefixed to a root indicative of a divisible thing, expresses, with the suffix *an*, the whole contents thereof. Thus. *lupa*, "earth;" *sanglupáin*, "the world," "all the inhabitants thereof."

When *may* is used for "to have" it must be followed by the thing possessed.

"No," in response to a question with the verb "to have" is generally translated by *walá*; in response to other questions, *hindí* is generally used.

Pan, prefixed to a root indicating a manual action, forms the instrument which serves to execute it. Thus, from *sílat*, "to write;" *panúlat*, "pen;" *tali*, "to tie;" *panali*, "tying-rope." The change of *s* and *t* into *n* will be explained in further lessons.

The Tagalog demonstrative pronouns are those in the vocabulary. *Yarí* or *yerí* and *itò* stand for "this;" *yarí-yerí* is dying away and being rapidly replaced by *itò*. *Yyán*, *yaón-yon*, stand for "that;" *iyán*, pointing out a thing lying near the person addressed, and *yaón-yon* pointing out objects far away from both interlocutors, The plural is formed by immediately preceding them with the pluralizing particle *mañga*. Tagalog employs the repetition of the demonstrative pronouns in the nominative to render them emphatic.

Ca, is one of the most important prefix particles and is used in several ways. When *ca* is prefixed to nouns or verbs denoting, respectively, persons or collective reciprocal actions, it denotes one of the corresponding parties. If the compound so formed is prefixed by *mag*, it is made plural without requiring the employment of *mañga*, which can, however, be used, and indicates two, at least, of the parties.

Declension of the demonstrative pronouns.

Nom.	This.	Yarí, yerí.	Ytò.
Poss.	Of this.	Dini sa, nirí.	Ditò sa, nitò.

(1). A compound from *apir* "to join", *báhay*, "house" and *ca*, particle indicating companionship and restricting the sense to one alone of the corresponding parties.

			To this.	Dinì sa.	Ditò sà.
	Dat.		To this.	Dinì sa.	Ditò sà.
	Acc.		This.	Dinì sa, nirí.	Ditò sa, nitò.
Object.	Abl.	local and causal.	At, in, upon, etc. this.	Dinì sa.	Ditò sa.
		instrum-ental.	By, with, etc. this.	Nirí.	Nitò.

			THAT.	NEAR.	FAR.	
Nom.			That.	Yyán.	Yaón.	Yon.
Poss			Of that.	Diyán sa, niyán.	Dóon sa, niyaón.	Niyóon.
Object.	Dat.		To that.	Diyán sa.	Dóon sa.	Niyóon.
	Acc.		That.	Diyán sa, niyún.	Dóon sa. niyaón.	Niyón or niyóon.
	Abl.	local and causal.	In, at, upon, etc. that.	Niyán sa.	Dóon sa.	
		instrum-ental.	By, with, etc. that.	Niyún.	Niyaón.	Niyóon or niyón.

In the possessive and direct object cases the particle *sa*, which precedes the nouns, follows the demonstrative pronouns, the reason being that it refers to the thing pointed out and not to the pronoun. The two forms of the possessive case should be used in the way and cases already explained for those of the personal pronouns.

This person.

Of that child, that child's.

To *or* for that bishop.

These men (persons).

Those dogs' meat.

To or for those children.

Those books (object.).

Ytòng tauò, itòng tauò itò (emphatic).

Niyáng bata, niyáng batang iyán. (emph.).

Dóon sa obispo, dóon sa obispong yon (emph.)

Ytòng mañga tauò.
Ytòng mañga tauòng itò. (emph.).

Diyán sa mañga asong carne.
Ang carne niyán mañga aso.

Dóon sa mañga bata.
Dóon sa mañga batang yaón.

Niyaón mañga libro.
Niyáon mañga librong yaón.

It should be noticed that owing to the inflective character of the demonstrative pronouns in their declension, the relation of case is expressed by the pronoun if it comes before the noun, and by the latter if coming first. Thus, "that boy's book," is rendered, *ang libro niyáng bata,* or, *ang libro nang bata iyán,* and so forth for the other cases.

FIFTH EXERCISE.

Have you my gold ribbon? I have it not. Have you anything? I have nothing. Have you my steel pen? I have it not. Which pen have you? I have my good silver pen. What have you? I have nothing. Have you my steel or my silver pen? I have your steel pen. Have you my soap?

I have it not. Have you my candlestick? I have it not. Which candlestick have you? I have my gold candlestick. Have you my string? I have it not. Have you my good wine? I have it not. Have you that book? I have it not. Have you that meat? I have it. Have you anything good? I have nothing good. What have you pretty? I have the pretty gold ribbon. Have you anything ugly? I have nothing ugly, I have something fine. What have you fine? I have the fine dog. Have you your glass pen? I have your fork. Has he this or that crown? He has this, he has not that. Have my sisters the clothes of these children? They have not these children's clothes, they have those of their brothers. Is that pen for that man? That pen is not for that man, it is for those women.

SIXTH LESSON.

YCAANIM NA PAGARAL.

INTERROGATIVE PRONOUNS.

The following are the interrogative pronouns in Tagalog: ¿*ano?*, "what"?, "which?"; ¿*alín,?* "which"?; (discriminative), and ¿*sino?*, "who?". The first two may be used as adjectives and may be preceded by the article *ang*; *sino* can neither be used as an adjective nor, as a general rule, takes the article.

The merchant, the tradesman.	Ang mapagcalácal, mañgañgalácal.(from *calácal*, "merchandise"); ang *comerciante* (Sp.)
The Frenchman.	Ang taga *Pransia, ang pransés* (corr. from Sp. word *Francia* and *francés*.)
Umbrella.	Páyong.
Corkscrew.	Panbucás nang prongo (Tag.); *tirabusón*. (corr. from Sp. word *tirabuzón*).
Carpenter.	Anloague.
Nail. (iron spike).	Paco.
Hammer.	Pamocpoc (root, *pocpoc*, "to strike").
Beer.	*Serbesa*. (corr. from Sp. word *cerveza*).
Ink.	*Tinta*. (Sp.)
Honey.	Polot, pulut.
Walking-stick.	Tongcod, tungcod or tungcor.
Thimble.	*Dedal*. (Sp.)
Needle.	Caráyom.
Pin.	*Aspiler* (corr. from Sp. word *alfiler*.)
Watch.	*Orasán* (corr. from Sp. word *horas* and *an* to denote the place where hours are marked.)
The Englishman.	Ang *inglés* (Sp.); ang taga *Ynglaterra*, (Sp.).
Sheep, ram.	*Tvpa* (from Sp. *topar*, "to butt.")
Mutton.	Lamán nang topa.
Butter, lard.	*Mantica* (corr. from Sp. word *manteca*.).
Button.	*Botón*. (Spanish) or *bitones*,
Bed-sheet, quilt,	Cómot.
Neither.....nor.	Man. (always postponed). Hindí man.....hindí man or rin. hindí.........hindí namán.
Neither I nor you.	Acó man, icáo man. Hindí man acó, icáo ay, hindí rin.
Have you the needle or the pin?	¿Na sa iyò bagá ang caráyom ó ang aspiler.?

I have neither the needle nor the pin. — Ualá sa aquin ang caráyom man, ang aspiler man.

Who (sing.). — ¿Sino? ¿sino bagá?.

Who has? (indet.). — { ¿Sinong mayróon?, ¿sino ang mayróon?; ¿sinong may?.

Who has? (det.). — ¿Na sa canino? (bagá).

Knife, cutlass. — Itac, (Tag.), *cuchillo* (Sp.).

Who has any knife? — { ¿Sino cayá ang may itac? ¿Sinong mayróon itac?

Who has the knife? — ¿Na sa canino ang itac?.

The man has a knife. — Ang tauò ay may itac.

The man has the knife. — Na sa tauò ang itac.

Purse. — Sòpot or súput.

Who has the purse? — ¿Na sa canino ang súput?

The woman has the purse. — Ang súput ay na sa babaye.

Who has it? — ¿Na sa canino bagá? (ang súput).

Peter and John have it. — Na cay Pedro,t, cay Juan. (ang súput).

Or. — *O,* (Sp.); *cun.* (Tag.) (little used).

Either.........or. — Maguín.........maguín.

Be it.........or. — Man............man.

Either by night or by day. — Maguín sa gabi, maguín sa árao.

Either at home or at church. — Maguín sa báhay, maguín sa simbahan.

Be it man or woman. — Lalaqui man, babaye man.

What countryman are you? / What is your country? — { ¿Taga sáan ca? (bagá)

I am a Spaniard. / My country is Spain. — Taga *España* acó; acó,i, taga *España*; Castila acó; acó,i, castila.

Spaniard. — { Español (Sp.); Castila (corr. from Sp. word *Castilla*)

Of what country are those people? — { ¿Taga sáan cayá yaón mañga tauòng yaón?

Those people are Chinese. — Yaóng mañga tauò ay mañga insic.

Those people's country is China. — { Yaóng mañga tauóng yaó,i, taga Song-song.

Glass. (tumbler). — Vaso (Sp.).

Rice. — Bigás.

Ganta { a measure about 1/25 of the / Peck. { English bushel. — { Salop.

The particle *mapag*, prefixed to a verbal or substantive root, forms the frequentative noun for what the root means; *man*, under the same conditions, forms a verbal noun indicative of what a person is engaged in customarily.

Taga, placed before s'*an* or the name of a place or country denotes origin.

An, affixed to a root denotes place, or the thing or person on which or on whom the action is accomplished.

The fashion is going on somewhere among natives to have the noun subject of an active sentence, again represented at the end by the third person pronoun. *Ang tauò ay may itac siyà,* "the man has a knife"; *yaóng mañga tauòng yaó,i, mañga insic silá,* "those people are Chinese". The student is hereby cautioned against this manner of expression which, although not entirely ungrammatical, should be used sparingly.

Wood house. — Báhay na cáhoy.

Gold ring. — Singsing na guintó.

Steel pen. — { Plumang patalim, *asero* (Sp. word *acero* corr.)

Compound English nouns one of which expresses the matter a thing is made of, are generally expressed in Tagalog by means of the ligaments, the thing preceding the matter as above.

One glass of water.	Ysàng vasong túbig.
Two gantas of rice.	Dalauàng salop na bigás.

The relation between continent and contents is likewise expressed by the linking particles.

Clothing for children.	Damit sa mañga bata.
Writing-table.	Lamesang sulatán, lamesa sa pagsúlat.

Compound nouns one member of which denotes the use for which the other is intended, are generally translated by inserting the particle *sa*, which is also used as a translation of the preposition "for".

Declension of interrogative pronouns.

Nom.		Who?	¿Sino?
Poss.		Of whom? / Whose?	¿Canino?, ¿nino?.
Object. (all its forms)		Whom?	¿Sa canino?

Nom.			What?	¿Anò?, ¿ang anò?
Poss.			Of what?	¿Sa anò?,..... ¿nang anò?
Object	Dat.		For or to what.?	¿Sa anò?
	Acc.		What?	¿Sa anò?, ¿nang anò?
	Abl.	local and causal.	In, at, etc. what?	¿Sa anò?
		instru-mental.	By, with, etc. what?	¿Nang anò?

Nom.,			Which?	¿Alín? ¿ang alín?.
Poss.			Of „	¿Sa alín?..... ¿nang alín?
Obj.	Dat.		For or to „	¿Sa alín.
	Acc.		„	¿Sa alín?, ¿nang alín?.
	Abl.	local and causal,	In, at, etc. which?	¿Sa alín?.
		instru-mental.	By, with, etc. which?	¿Nang alín?.

Sino, is used for persons, and is not generally preceded by the artícle. The second form of the possessive case should be used only when the question has not been heard or understood.

The plural is formed either by repeating the pronoun or by using the pluralizing particle before or after the noun to which it makes reference, if there be any, as is frequently the case when "to be" enters in English to put a question, as shown in the following illustrations:

Nom.	Who (plural) are those men? (people).	¿Sino-sino yaóng tauò? ¿Mañga sinong tauò yaón? (somewhat improper). ¿Sinong mañga tauò yaón?.

Poss.	Whose (plural) are those rings?.	¿Canicanino (1) iyán mañga sìngsìng?.
Dat.	For whom (plural) are those hats?.	¿Sa canicanino bagá yaón mañga sambalilong yaón?.

What papers are these?
¿Anò anòng papel itò?
¿Anòng mañga papel itò?.
¿Mañga anòng papel itò?. (somewhat improper).

What kind of houses are these nails of?
¿Nang anò anòng báhay, itòng mañga pacong itò?
¿Nang mañga anòng báhay, itòng mañga pacong itò?. (somewhat improper).
¿Nang anòng mañga báhay itò mañga pacong itò?

Of the wood houses.
Sa mañga Líhay na cáhoy. (nang, may also be used, although not so properly).

Which candlesticks have you?
¿Alín-alíng candelero ang na sa iyò?
¿Mañga alíng candelero ang na sa iyò?
¿Alíng mañga candelero ang na sa iyò?

I have the bishop's candlesticks.
Ang sa obispo mañga candelero ang na sa aquin.
Ang mañga candelero nang obispo ang na sa aquin.

For which kings are these crowns?
¿Sa alín-alíng mañga hari, itòng mañga pótong na itò?
¿Sa alíng mañga hari, itòng mañga pótong na itò?
¿Sa mañga alíng hari itòng mañga pótong na itò?

The posessive case with *sa* should preferably be used in answering a question.

Alín may serve for persons and things; *anò*, only for things.

Who are you? (sing.).	¿Sino ca? (bagá).
Who are they?	¿Sino-sino (bagá) silá?
What do you want? (sing.).	¿Anò ca?, ¿anò ca bagá?
What are you doing here?	¿Aanò ca ditò?, ¿anò ca ditò?, ¿nagaanò ca ritò?.
What is his business there?	¿Aanò siyá dóon?, ¿nagaanò siyá róon?
What do you wish?	¿Anòng íbig mo?
I wish.	Ybig co.
You (sing.) wish.	Ybig mo.
He or she wishes.	Ybig niyà.
We wish.	Ybig natin, íbig namin.
You (plural) wish.	Ybig ninyò.
They wish.	Ybig nilá.

Ybig, in this sense, is a passive and invariable verb for to "wish", "to desire."

Natives avoid as much as they can the employment of third person pronouns in reference to things. They generally repeat the noun or

---

(1) It is a general rule that repetitions of syllables or words for various purposes in Tagalog do not pass beyond, respectively, the second letter or second syllable thereof. Thus, *canicanino*, instead of *caninocanino*, since *canino* is a three-syllable word.

try to construct in such a manner as to render it unnecessary to use the pronoun. **Examples:** ¿*mabutì bagá ang libro?*, "is the book good?"; *mabutì ñga*, "it is good," "certainly, it is;" instead of *mabutì siyá.*

SIXTH EXERCISE

Has the king the glass or the steel pen? The king has neither the glass nor the steel pen. Which pen has the bishop? The bishop has the fine pen. Have you the stocking? You have neither the stocking nor the pin. Has the Englishman the corkscrew? The Englishman has neither the corkscrew nor the needle. Is the merchant here? No, he is not here. Has the Frenchman my umbrella? He has not your umbrella. Is the corkscrew on the table? The carpenter has it. Who has their hammer? The carpenter has neither the hammer nor the nail. Which merchant has any beer? The merchant of my town has two glasses of beer. Whose ink is that? It is my brother's. What honey have the Englishmen? The Englishmen have some good honey. Which walking-stick has your mother's daughter? My mother's daughter has no walking-stick at all, she has her thimble, her needle, her pin and my watch. Are there any sheep in Spain? Yes, there are some. Is mutton good? It is very good. Who has my mother's bed-sheets? Peter has them. Is my knife made of iron? No, it is made of steel. For which person is that purse? That purse is for my sisters. Are you Spaniards? Yes, we are Spaniards. Who have my rice? The Englishmen have it. Is that ganta yours or my son's? That ganta is neither yours nor his. Where is John? John is not here, he is either at church or at school. Is he not at home? He is at home. What is your (pl.) country? Our country is France. What countrymen are those people? They are from this country. Are those people Chinese? They are not Chinese. This house is not a wooden one. Those looking-glasses are not silver. These rings are not gold. What are you, gentlemen? We are carpenters.

SEVENTH LESSON.
YCAPITONG PAGARAL.

PERSONAL and POSSESSIVE PRONOUNS.

Declensions are given hereafter of all the Tagalog personal pronouns from which the possessive ones are derived. That of the third person has three dictions in the plural; *Tayo, Camí, Quitá or catá,* "we". *Tayo* is used when the person addressed is intended to be included. *Camí,* on the contrary, like the royal "WE" in English, excludes the person addressed and is therefore the correct pronoun to use in prayers addressed to the Deity. *Catá,* has very little use in the nominative case; it is rather dual and partakes of the possessive case. *Quitá,* is also used in this latter sense.

Declension of personal pronouns

FIRST FERSON.

SINGULAR.

Nom.	I.	Acó.
Poss.	Of me.	Aquin, (prep); co, (postp.).
Object. (all its divisions).	Me.	Sa aquín.

SECOND PERSON.

Nom.	Thou.	You.	Icáo, (prep.); ca, (postp.).
Poss.	Of thee.	Of you.	Iyò, (prep.); mo, (postp.).
Object. (all its divisions). Thee.		You.	Sa iyò.

THIRD PERSON.

Nom.	He, she, it. (1).	Siyá. (1).
Poss.	Of him, of her, of it.	Caniyà, (prep.); niyà, (postp.).
Object. (all its divisions). Him, her, it.		Sa caniyà.

(1) *Siyà,* "it", is not generally applied to inanimate things, unless the latter are personified as in fables, etc.

PLURAL.

FIRST PERSON.

ABSOLUTE PLURAL.

Nom.	We, (both, the speakers and the persons spoken to, included)	Tayo.
Poss.	Of us (of all of us)	Atin, (prep.); natin, (postp.).
Object.	(all its divisions). Us.	Sa atin.

RESTRICTIVE PLURAL.

Nom.	We (the persons spoken to not included).	Camí.
Poss.	Of us.	Amin, (prep.); namin, (postp.).
Object.	(all its divisions). Us.	Sa amin.

EXCLUSIVE & DUAL PLURAL.

Nom.	We, (thou and I alone).	Quitá.
Poss.	Of us.	Canitá, (prep.); ta, (postp.).
Object.	(all its divisions). Us.	Sa canitá.

ANOTHER DUAL PLURAL.

Nom.	We.	Catá.
Poss.	Of us.	Atà, (prep.); ta, (postp.).
Object.	(all its divisions). Us.	Sa atà.

SECOND PERSON.

Nom.	You. (ye).	Cayó.
Poss.	Of you.	Ynyò, (prep.); ninyò, (postp.).
Object.	(all its divisions). You.	Sa inyò.

THIRD PERSON.

Nom.	They.	Silá.
Poss.	Of them.	Canilà, (prep.); nilà, (postp.).
Object.	(all its divisions). Them.	Sa canilà.

Personal pronouns like possessive pronouns have two forms in the possessive case: *aquin, iyò, caniyà, amin, canitá, inyò, canilà,* are prepositive, that is to say; precede the verb in passive sentences; *co, mo, niyà, natin, namin, ninyò, ta, nilà* and the nominative *quitá* (as dual) follow it. The nominative *ca* is likewise put after the verb in active sentences. *Quitá,* and *catá* are used indiscriminately. They both have very little use in the nominative case.

Possessive adjective pronouns, as stated before, are expressed in Tagalog by the possessive case of the personal ones, those of the latter preceding the verb, also precede the noun when used as possessive pronouns, and the others follow it. Possessive pronouns may be, and generally are, preceded by the particles (articles) of common nouns and they are declined and made plural in a similar manner. The same restrictive and dual sense existing between *atin, amin,* and *canilà*; and *natin, namin, ta,* as personal pronouns exists too as possessive pronouns.

Our soul.	Ang atin calolóua. / Ang calolóua natin.
My house.	Ang aquin báhay. / Ang báhay co.
My hands.	Ang aquin mañga camáy. / Ang mañga camáy co.
Your (sing.) fingers.	Ang iyòng mañga daliri. / Ang mañga daliri mo.
His or her eyes,	Ang caniyàng mañga mata. / Ang mañga mata niyà.
Our teeth (those of the person addressed included.)	Ang ating mañga ñgipin. / Ang mañga ñgipin natin.
Our tongue (that of the person addressed, not included).	Ang aming dila. / Ang dila namin.
Your (plur.) clothes.	And inyòng damit. / Ang damit ninyò.
Their eyebrows.	Ang canilàng mañga quílay. / Ang mañga quílay nilà.

The possessive absolute pronouns are expressed by the prepositive forms of the possessive case preceded by the article.

Mine.	Ang aquin.
Yours, thine.	Ang iyò
His, hers, its.	Ang caniyà.
Ours.	Ang amin, ang atin.
Yours (plur).	Ang inyò.
Theirs.	Ang canilà.

The dative case with the article is also used for this purpose. Thus, *ang sa canilà* may be employed for "theirs", etc.

Girl, maid, lass.	Dalaga.
Youngman, bachelor, lad.	Binata, bagong tauò.
Tailor.	Mananahé, (Tag.); *sastre,* (Sp.).
Baker.	*Panadero,* (Sp.); magtitinápay, (Tag.).
Silk.	Sutlá, (Tag.); *seda,* (Sp.).
Gown.	Quimón, (Tag.); *bata,* (Sp.).
Chicken.	Sísiu, manóc na sísiu; *poyo,* (corr. from Sp. word *pollo.*)
Pencil.	*Lapis* (corr. from Sp. word, *lápiz*).
Friend.	Caibigan, catoto.
Intimate friend.	Casi.
Key.	Susi.
Chocolate.	*Sicolate.* (corr. from Sp. word *chocolate*).
Trunk, chest.	Cabán.
Bag, sack. basket.	Bayong, bácol.
Lady, younglady, mistress.	Maguinoó, guinoóng babaye.

Bottle.	*Bote.* (corr. from Sp. word, *botella*).
Peasant, countryman.	Magsasacà, magbubuquir.
Servant.	Alila, lingcod.
Kinsman, relation.	Camaganac.
There, thither	Dóon.
To go there, thither.	Paróon, (active and passive) (1)
To sit down.	Upó or opó (root); umupó. (active.)
To say, to tell. (something).	Sabì (root); sabihin. (passive).
To speak.	Osap (root); mañgósap. (active).
To speak, to pronounce.	Uica (root); magüica. (act.).
To do, to make. (something).	{ Gauá (root); gaoin. (contracted pass. form).

If *pa* is prefixed to an adverb of place, the verb of motion indicated by the adverb is formed; when prefixed to a noun of place, *sa* should be inserted between to form the verb of motion towards that place.

A verbal root only expresses the abstract idea of the action and should be associated to some particle to express the several tenses and meanings it is capable of in the active voice; in the passive, it may be prefixed by *y-i* over and above other prefixes it may admit of, and suffixed by *in* or *an* according to the sense etc.

Do not go there (sing.).	Houag cang paróon.
Do. (plur.)	Houag cayóng paróon.
To go to the farm, into the country.	Pasabúquid.
Sit down here. (sing.).	Ditò ca umupó.
Let them not go into the country.	Houag siláng pasabúquid.
Don't say it (sing.).	{ Houag mong sabihin (prohibiting). Di mo sabihin (negative in composition)
Don't do it (plur).	Houag ninyòng gaoin.
She is not my mother.	Hindí co inà siyá.
Are they not your relations?	¿Hindí ninyò bagá camaganac silá?.
Let John sit down there.	Umupó diyán Si Juan.

The subject, be it noun or pronoun, of an active sentence is put in the nominative case: if the sentence is a passive one the subject should be put in the possessive case.

In spite of what has been said before with regard to the position of the postpositive form of the possessive case of personal pronouns, these are, nevertheless, placed before the verb in sentences beginning with an adverb or a negative particle. The same may also be the case in interrogative sentences, as in:

What else should I say?	¿Anò pa ang súcat cong sabihin?

He and I (both of us)	Camí niyà.
You (sing.) and John. (both of you).	Cayó ni Juan.
He and their mother (both of them).	Silá nang canilàng inà.
You (sing.) and they.	Cayó nilá.
He and his master.	Silá nang caniyàng pañginóon.
Jesus and His mother.	Mag-inà ni Jesús.
Alfred and his children.	Si Alfredo nang caniyàng mañga anac.

When two personal pronouns or a pronoun and a noun join in an active sentence, the personal pronoun, be it singular or plural, may be put in the nominative case and in the plural, and the noun or the other pronoun, in the possessive case of the proper number. The orderly arrangement of first, second and third person should be kept, as it would be a fault to say: *silà mo,*

---

(1) In Tagalog, intransitive as well as transitive verbs have a passive voice.

instead of *cayò niyà*, to indicate "he and you". The same peculiarity exists when a collective or companionship noun formed with *mag* is coupled to a personal name, *may*, being always with the noun of the principal corresponding party.

These forms of construction peculiar to Tagalog are however obsolescent and being replaced by the more natural ones of the western languages.

From the demonstrative pronouns the following largely used adverbs of place are derived:

Here,	(indicating a place very near to the speaker).	Dinì.
Here	(indicating a place equidistant from both interlocutors).	Ditò.
There	(indicating a place nearer to the person spoken to than to the speaker).	Diyán.
There, thither.	(indicating a place far from both interlocutors.)	Dóon.
To come here.		Parinì, paritò.
To go there.	(motion to the place where the person addressed stands).	Pariyán.

SEVENTH EXERCISE.

Has this man the pencil? He has it not. Have I the chocolate? You have neither the chocolate nor the sugar. Has my friend your stick? He has not my stick, he has my umbrella. Is your house pretty? Our house is not pretty; but it is good. What is that you have in your hands? What I have in my hands is a pencil. What is that they have in their fingers? What they have in their fingers are rings. What have I on my eyes? It is spectacles that you have on your eyes. Have we any teeth? All of us have teeth. We, men, have a tongue? Yes, we, men, have a tongue. Are natives' noses beautiful? No, they are not beautiful. Are their eyebrows pretty? Their eyebrows are pretty. Where is the girl? The girl is at home. Who is the father of this youngman.? The father of this youngman is the tailor. Who has the baker's silk.? My sons have the baker's silk. Where are her chickens.? Her chickens are at the farm. Who has our friends' pencils.? Nobody. Are they our friends.? They are our intimate friends. Who has my relation's chocolate? His friend has it in the trunk. Where is the lady's? bag.? The lady's bag is not here. Where is the chest–key? The peasant has it. What are those bottles made of? Those bottles are made of glass. Have you any male-servant? I have no male–servant, what I have are two female-servants. Are your relations at church? No, my relations are not at church, they are in town. Where is the church? The church is on the mountain. Is that lady his mother? She is not his mother. Are we good friends? We are good friends. Who are your friends? I have no friends. Are John's relations your friends? They are my friends.

EIGHTH LESSON.
YCAUALONG PAGARAL.

THE SUBSTANTIVE.

Substantives are either primitive or derivative, the former being those which in their original signification are substantives. A difficulty which attends the classification of Tagalog words into various parts of speech, according to the system applied to European languages, consists in the number of words which, while yet unmodified by particles, are either verb or substantive, adjective or adverb, according to the context, or, more generally, according to particles which precede or are prefixed to them.

The noun, as a rule, undergoes no change to denote number, gender or case, the latter being expressed, as in English, by prepositions.

A root while still retaining a certain predominant character which renders it, to some extent, classifiable as nominal, adjectival, verbal, etc., expresses but the simplest idea of the thing, quality or action and hence, generally, it requires the association of certain particles to develop the various relations the idea is capable of.

The congeniality of these particles with the language is such as to cause sometimes a root having a definite nominal force to be combined with noun-building particles to form either secondary derivatives or substantive terms which differ but little from the original meaning, somewhat in the manner of the difference in significance in the English words. "reciprocation", "reciprocity", "reciprocalness"; "gratitude", "gratefulness", etc.

Substantives in Tagalog are formed from all parts of speech, but especially from adjectives (adjectival or quality roots) and verbs.

The present lesson is intended to illustrate some of the commonest ways to form nouns. Other ways are to be found in further chapters throughout the grammar, as it would be inconvenient to acquaint the pupil with them at this stage.

Substantives used in a general sense take the article in Tagalog. "Riches are mere vanity". *Ang cayamana,i, ualáng cabolohan.*

Went (thither).		Naparóon.
Came.		Naparitò, naparini.
Went there.	(to the place where the person addressed stands)	Napariyán.
Went home.		Napasabáhay.
To be going there.	(marking present motion to a distant place)	Napaparóon, or, naparoróon.
To be going into town.		Napapasabayan, or, napasasabayan.
To be coming on, here.		Napaparitò, or, naparirito. Napaparini, or, naparirini.

New.	Bagò.
Old, worn out.	Luma.
Crashed, broken into pieces.	Basag.
Entire, whole, sound.	Bcò
Cat.	Pusa.
Uncle.	Amaín.
Aunt.	Ali.
White thing.	Putí (root).
White (adj.).	Maputí.
Black thing.	Itim.
Black (adj.).	Maitim.
Great, large thing.	Laquì.
Great, large, grown up. (adj.).	Malaquì.
Great, excellent, remarkable, conspicuous.	Daquila.
Virtuous.	Banal.
Sound, healthy thing.	Galing.
Sound, healthy. (adj.)	Magaling.
Wise. (idea of wisdom).	Dúnong or dónong.
Wise. (adj.).	Marúnong or marónong.
Whiteness.	Caputían,
Blackness.	Caitimán.
Greatness, growth.	Calaquihán.
Greatness, excellence.	Cadaquiláan.
Virtue.	Cabanalan.
Soundness, health.	Cagaliñgan.
Wisdom.	Carunuñgan.

Abstract nouns may be formed by prefixing *ca* and suffixing *an-han* to the root.

Divinity.	Pagcadios.
Manhood, humanity.	Pagcatauò
Manhood, masculineness.	Pagcalalaqui.
Womanhood.	Pagcababaye.
Wisdom, learning. (in action)	Pagcadúnung.

The prefix *pagca*, may likewise form abstract nouns, especially of common and proper nouns or adjectival roots expressing attributes of mind, the nouns so formed partaking more or less of the verbal character.

Accompanying,	companion.	Samà,	casamà.
Embarking,	fellow-passenger.	Sacáy,	casacáy.
Aiding,	assistant.	Túlong,	catúlong.
Quarrelling.	quarrelling-person, enemy.	Auay,	caáuay.
Teaching.	school-mate.	Aral,	caáral.
Like.	similar, coequal.	Para,	capara.
Face,	face-resembling person.	Muc-há,	camuc-há.

If *ca* is prefixed to a root denoting and idea of association, fellowship, reciprocity or likelihood, a verbal noun indicating one of the mutual parties is thus formed. If two of the mutual associated parties are to be meant, *mag* should be prefixed to the verbal noun already formed.

Two companions.	Magcasamà.
Married couple. (husband and wife).	Magasáua.
Two brothers or sisters.	Magcapatid.

Two brothers-in-law.	Magbayáo.
Two sisters-in-law.	Maghípag.
Two friends.	Magcaibigan.

If three or more of the corresponding parties are to be expressed (this manner of expression being selected) *ca*, should be repeated if the noun is not dual in character; and the first syllable of the root if it is only formed with *mag*.

Three or more brothers or sisters.	Magcacapatid.
Three or more companions.	Magcacasamà.
Three or more brothers-in-law.	Magbabayáo,
Three or more married couples.	Magcaasàua.

In common nouns denoting correlation of consanguinity or mutual dependence, *mag*, is prefixed to that of the principal correlative party to express his or her association with the secondary corresponding party.

Father and son.	Magamá.
Mother and daughter.	Mag-inà.
Master and servant.	Magpañginóon.

If more than one of secondary associated parties are to be expressed, the first syllable of the principal one should be repeated.

Father and children.	Magaamá.
Mother and children.	Mag-iinà.

Mag, is also prefixed to one of the associated parties when it is coupled to a proper personal noun, but then the latter should be put in the possessive case.

Jesus and His mother.	Mag-inà ni Jesús.
George and his son.	Mag-amá ni Jorge.
Mary and her father.	Mag-amá ni María.

An-han, if suffixed to a substantive root indicative of a natural product, the noun of the place for such product to be found, is formed.

Paddy,	rice-field.	Pálay	palayan.
Cocoa-rut,	cocoa-nut-plantation.	Niog,	niogán.
Sugar-cane,	sugar-plantation.	Tubò,	tubohan.
Plant,	garden.	Halaman,	halamanan.
Stone,	quarry.	Batò,	batohán.

If *ca* is prefixed to these first derivatives, the second derivative thus formed will be more collective.

Rice–field,	Tract abounding with.	Palayan,	capalayan.
Plantation of plantain-trees	Do. do.	Saguiñgan,	casaguiñgan.

The same suffix forms the place of performance with a substantive root implying a verbal sense.

Bath,	bath-room.	Paligo,	paliguán.
Cell,	sleeping–chamber.	Silid,	siliran,
Dancing,	ball.	Sayào,	sayáuan.

Father-in-law or mother-in-law.	Bianán. (lalaqui or babaye).
Son or daughter-in-law.	Manúgang. do do.
Short, little, small.	Maliit, muntí.
Nobody, no one.	Ualá sinománi, hindí; isà ma,i, ualá.
Buffalo. (animal).	Calabáo, damúlag.

Bird.	Ybon.
Copper.	Tangsó.
Name.	Ñgalan, pañgalan.
Broom.	Ualís, pañgualís.
Foot.	Paà.
Mouth.	Bibig.
Somebody, some one, any body, any one, whoever, whosoever.	Sinomán, bálang na tauò.
Any, anything, whatever, whatsoever.	Anomán, anománg bágay.
Whichever, whichsoever.	Alín man, alín mang bágay.
How much?, how many? (when a number is inquired after).	¿Ilán?, ¿ilán bagà?.
How much?. (when measure is inquired after).	¿Gaanò?.

An interrogative pronoun followed or suffixed by the adverb *man* is thereby converted into an indefinite one.

EIGHTH EXERCISE.

Did your uncle go there? My uncle did not go there, it is my aunt who went there. Did your wife's friend come here? He did not come here, he went home. Did Alfred and his master go to your house? They both went to our house. Where are John's two companions? They went into town. Did they go there? Yes, they went there; but the three brothers *Cruz* are coming. Did not Peter and his father go to the country? Peter and his father did not go to the country, they went to church. Are the wife and the husband going there to the forest? They are going to the town. Is your clothing new or old? My clothing is old (worn out). Are their looking-glasses entire (sound) or broken? They are not broken, they are worn out. Are my mother's sister's cats white or black? My mother's sister's cats are neither white nor black. Is your sister's virtue great? My sister's virtue is great. Is the wisdom of God, great? The wisdom of Cod has no equal. Who are wise? The sound are wise. Is the whiteness of our souls a beautiful thing? The whiteness of our souls is a beautiful thing. How many fellow-passengers are they? Peter, John and Mary are fellow-passengers. How many companions are you? George and I are companions. How many enemies came here? No enemies came here. Are Mary and you alike in face? Yes, Mary and I are alike in face. How many brothers are they? They are two brothers. Are you master and servant? Yes, we are master and servant. Are you father and son? No, we are not father and son. Are they sisters-in-law? Yes, they are sisters-in-law. Are they friends? No, they are not friends. Did John and his brother go into the forest? John and his brother did not go into the forest, they are at school. Did the father and his children come here? The father and his children did not come here. Did Jane and her mother go to church (mass)? No, Jane and her mother went to Cavite. Who is at home? No one. Where did my uncle's buffalo go? Your uncle's buffalo went into the fields. Did his bird go into your father-in-law's house? No, it went into my son-in-law's. What is coin made of? Coin is made of gold, silver and copper. What is your name? My name is Anthony. Where have you my servant's broom? Your servant's broom is not here. Is your foot well? It is not well. Where are the teeth? The teeth are in the mouth. Has anybody gone to Iloilo? No one has gone there. How much bread has my sister? Any bread she may have, is little. For which man are those birds? For whichever man.

NINTH LESSON.
YCASIYAM NA PAGARAL.

RELATIVE PRONOUNS.

True relative pronouns, as well as the copulative verb, do not exist in Tagalog. The mere arrangement of words may dispense with them; but most frequently the article and the nominal ligament render the English relative, somewhat after the manner of English, where it is understood in phrases like "the man you saw" or is included in the present participle, as when we say, "the boy writing the letter"..... etc.

The illustrations in this lesson will convey to the student further information on the subject.

Street, road.	Lansañgan, dáan.
Way, thorouhgfare.	Dáan.
High, road.	*Carsada* (corr. from Sp. word *calzada*.)
Will, good–will, disposition, inward feeling.	Lóob, calooban.
Memory, recollection.	Alaala.
Gratitude, gratefulness, obligation.	Utang na lóob, (lit., debt from the heart).
Noble, precious, dear.	Mahal.
Rascal, impudent fellow, cruel.	Tampalasan.
Stone.	Batò.
Head.	Olò.
Cousin.	Pinsán.
Cook.	Tagapagsáing, *cosinero*, (corr. from Sp. word, *cocinero*).
Ox or cow.	*Baca* (corr. from Sp. word, *raca*.)
But. (conjunction).	Cundí, datapóua, ñguní, subali, alintana.
Other.	Ibà, isà.
Another, one more.	Isà pa, il à pa.
Foreigner.	Taga ibàng lupaín.
Stranger.	Taga ibàng bayan.
Sea.	Dágat.
Seaman.	Tagarágat, magdadágat.
Pocket–book, porfolio.	Tagóan nang súlat (lit., hiding-place for papers); *cartera*, (Sp.).
Garden, orchard.	Halamanan.
Plant.	Halaman, pananim.
Corn, Grain.	Bútil.
Granary.	Tambóbong, camálig.
Principal, head, leader, lord.	Guinoò.

Quarry, place full of stones.	Batohán.
Bolster, upper end of a bed.	Olohán, olonán.
Plantation.	Halamanán.
Aristocracy.	Caguinoohan.

Subtantive roots expressive of some kind of matter or of things not capable of being made abstract, are prefixed with *ca* and suffixed with *an* to denote place or assemblage, as already said.

Hair.	Buhoc.
Forehead.	Noò.
Lip.	Labi.
Neck.	Liig.¶
Shoulders.	Mañga balícat.
Orphan.	Olila.
Strong.	Malacás.
Feeble, weak.	Mahina.

That, which, who, whom. (relative. pronouns).	Na, ng, g, (linking-particles).
What, that which, the one which.	Ang........, ang na.
The man who is coming here is my father.	Ang tauòng napaparitò,i, ang aquing amá.
This woman whom you love is my sister.	Itóng babayeng sinisintá mo,i. capatid co.
The letter which you wrote to me.	Ang súlat *na* ysinúlat mo sa aquin.
What I have is my sister-in-law's umbrella.	*Ang na* sa aquin, ay ang páyong nang aquin hípag.
That (conjunction).	Na.
Tell John's son to go into the country.	Sabihin mo sa anac ni Juan na pasabúquid siyá.
Do not tell him that I am here.	Houag mong sabihin sa caniyà *na* acó,i, naritò.

In the preceding examples the English relative pronoun is expressed by the ligaments, which, in this case, cannot be suppressed.

Students must understand that the mere replacing of the verbal ligament by the nominal one or by *ang* with the objective case before a verb, is a sure indication of the existence of a relative pronoun. Attention should be paid to the difference of sense in the following phrases:

The man is coming here.	Ang tauò ay napaparitò.
The man that is coming here....	Ang tauòng napaparitò........
You love this woman.	Ytòng babayeng itò,i, sinisintá mo.
This woman whom you love.	Ytòng babayeng sinisintá mo.
You wrote the letter to me.	Sinulatan mo acó.
The letter that you wrote to me.	Ang súlat *na* ysinúlat mo sa aquin.
I have my sister-in-law's umbrella.	Na sa aquin ang páyong nang aquing hípag.
What I have is my sister-in-law's umbrella.	*Ang na* sa aquin ay ang páyong nang hípag co.

This one, this other.	Ytòng isà, itòng ibà.
That other, that over there.	Yyáng isà, iyáng ibà.

Ysà-itòng isà, circumscribes more the number of things among which the one pointed out is, than *itòng ibà etc.*

Is the stone for this house?	¿Ang batò,i, ditò sa báhay na itò bagá?
No, it is for that other, that over there.	Hindí, diyán sa isà.
Is this bread for that child?	¿Ytòng tin·pay na itò, dóon sa batang yaón?
It is for that other.	Dóon sa isà.
Before (adv.), a while ago.	Cañgina, nóon unà.
Afterwards, by and by.	Mameá, mamayá-mayá.
Yesterday.	Cahapon.
The day before yesterday.	Camacalauà.
Some days ago.	Camacailán.
Just this morning, before in the morning.	Cañginang umaga.
When?	¿Cailán?

Camaca is a plural prefix which indicates as many past days, as are expressed by the root it is joined to.

Three days ago.	Camacatatlò.
Ten days ago.	Camacapóuo.

"To be", not having a specific expression in Tagalog the relation of tense can only be conveyed by some adverb or term expressive of time if not otherwise inferred from the context.

We were yesterday at the country.	Cahapo,i, camí naróon sa búquid,
Were they here at our town some days ago?	¿Camacailá,i, naritò bagá silá sa ating bayan?
When was your father-in-law's father at your son-in-law's?	¿Cailán bagá ang amá nang iyòng bianáng lalaqui naróon sa báhay nang manúgang mong lalaqui?
He was there this morning.	Naróon siyá cañginang umaga.
Were you ever Mary's household servant?	¿Alila ca bagá nóong unà niná María?
Yes, I was formerly their servant.	Oo, acó,i, alila nilá nóon unà.
Shall you be at church?	¿Nariyán ca bagá sa simbahan mamaya-mayá?
I shall be there.	Acó,i, nariyán mameá.
He will soon be Mary's husband.	Siyá mameá ang cay Maríang asáua.

The preceding illustrations are merely illustrative, for any word is capable of being verbalized in Tagalog, and the same expressions will be better constructed by conjugating the nouns in a way which will not yet be understood at this stage.

NINTH EXERCISE

Whose are these trees? My father's. Whose do you say? My father's. Whose children are those? Mine. Which gun has he? He has his own. Was your wife on the street yerterday? She was there the day before yesterday. Was anybody on the road? Nobody was on the road. Has man a good disposition towards God? Yes, man has a good disposition towards God. What is memory? Memory is a power of our soul. Have we gratitude toward our parents? Yes, we have gratitude toward our parents. Are noblemen rascals? Noblemen are not rascals. What have you on your head? What I have on my head is a hat. Will my cousin soon be a cook? Your cousin will not be a cook but a tailor. Has my mother-in-law an ox? She has two oxen. Has the foreigner some of these plants in his garden? No, he has not any of these, but he has others. Is the sea large? The sea is large. Where are the seamen?

The seamen are at the garden of our neighbour.   Have they any grain in their pocket-books? They have no grain. Where are your granaries? My granaries are at the rice-fields.   Where are the aristocracy of this town? The aristocracy of this town are at church.   How many plants have you in his garden?   I have no plants in his garden.   Was his hair black? His hair was black.   Where are located the forehead, the lips and the neck? On the head. Are shoulders on the head? No, shoulders are not on the head.   Is the orphan-boy strong or weak?   He is weak.   Is that man coming here your brother?   My brother is the one going there. Are those letters for your father?   The letters for my father are those on the table.   Is that one the woman whom you love?   The woman whom I love is my mother. What shall I say to my sister?   Tell your sister not to go to Iloilo.   Shall I tell them to go into the country?   Don't say that. Which of these two books is for my cousin?   The new book is for your cousin, this other is for your son. Is that bottle for this child? No, it is for that other.   Did you go to the garden before? I did not go there. When did John come here? It is some days ago that John came here. Did your sister-in-law's mother go into town yesterday? She went there the day before yesterday.

TENTH LESSON.
YCAPOUONG PAGARAL.

ON INTENSIVES.

It is to be noted that besides other ways of intensification, there are quite a number of words in Tagalog, which may properly be called particles, intended to impart an intensive degree of sense to the preceding word; these corresponding closely in meaning to "certainly", "indeed", "most", "exceedingly" and similar English terms, though some of them may be considered as expletives and are sometimes untranslatable. Among them. *rin* or *diu*, may be parsed as the Tagalog reflective pronoun, the English "self", as in *siyá rin*, "he himself"; etc. *Sarili* is also used somewhat as a reflective pronoun and means "own". As to the signification and place in the sentence of such intensives the attention of the student is called to further explanations in this lesson.

Moon, month.	Bouán.
January.	*Enero.*
February.	*Febrero.*
March.	*Marzo,*
April.	*Abril.*
May.	*Mayo.*
June.	*Juñio.*
July.	*Julio.* } (Spanish).
August.	*Agosto.*
September.	*Septiembre.*
October.	*Octubre.*
November.	*Noviembre.*
December.	*Diciembre.*
The month of March.	Bouáng Marzo or bouán nang Marzo ang ñgalan.
Year.	Taón.
Have you the letter which my brother had?	¿Na sa iyò bagá ang súlat nang aquing capatid? or, na na sa aquing capatir?
I have not the letter which your brother had.	Ualá sa aquin ang súlat nang capatid mo, or, na na sa iyòng capatid.
Which horse has he?	¿Alíng cabayo ang na sa caniyà.?
I have that which they had.	Ang canilà ang na sa aquin.
Monday.	*Lunes.*
Tuesday.	*Martes.*
Wednesday.	*Miércoles.*
Thursday.	*Jueves.* } (Spanish).
Friday.	*Viernes.*
Saturday.	*Sábado.*
Sunday.	Lingo. (corr. from Sp. word, *Domingo*).
The beginning.	Ang mulá.
The middle.	Ang pag-itan, paguitan.

The end.	Ang catapusán, ang hangán.
The trunk of a tree.	Ang pono.
Branch.	Sañgà.
Color.	Cúlay.
Dark.	Madilim.
Yellow.	Madiláo.
Red.	Mapulà.
What?, what then?. (in a tone of surprise).	¿Ay anò?.

When possession is meant, the English personal pronouns in clauses of relative or discriminative sentences may be rendered in Tagalog by the possessive ones, the verb "to have" remaining untranslated as seen above.

Intensive particles are always placed after the words which they are intended to intensify. The principal are:

How?, how now?.	¿Cayá?, ¿bagá?.
Yes, indeed; most certainly.	Ñga, nañga, din, mandín, ñgani.
Of course.	Ay anò, mangyari.
Ah!, oh!.	¡Abáa!
Then, therefore.	Palá.

Cayá, bagá, have an interrogative and somewhat a dubitative sense, as "perchance" in English.

Why?, is it you?	¿Ycáo bagá?
It is I myself.	Acó ñga.
How!, was it the women who stole?	¿Ang mañga babaye bagá ang nagnácao?
Yes, the very women themselves.	Oo, ang mañga babaye din or ñga.
Even they themselves did.	Silá ñga, mandín.
It is you indeed, it is you yourselves.	Cayó ñga, cayó ñgani.
I myself.	Acó rin, acó din, acó ñga.
They themselves.	Silá rin, silá nañga.

Cayá may be used in the secondary clause or sentence as a coordinate causative conjunction. Except in this case, intensive particles are not used to start a sentence. They are to be put immediately after the monosyllabic pronouns and immediately before the polysyllabic ones, unless the latter begin the sentence in which case the particles should come after them.

He had to tell me something, that is the reason why he came.	May sasabihin siyá sa aquin, cayá naparitò, or, naparitò siyá ay may sasabihin sa aquin.

Nañga is generally used as the plural of *ñga*. *Abáa* is an interjection very largely in use to express astonishment, surprise, etc.

Bagá, may be used in an affirmative sense as an alternative conjunction, serving as explanatory to the preceding word or sentence, as in:

Bliss, that is to say, the glory of God.	Ang caloualhatían, gloria bagá nang Dios.

Bagá may likewise be used in a conditional or dubitative sentence, it being then an expletive term rendering the expression round and euphonic.

If you, then, love your parents.	Cun cayó ñga,i, sungmisintà sa iyòng mañga magúlang, or, cun cayó bagá...

All these and many other emphatic particles are very largely used by natives and account for their innate tendency to exaggerate and to carry words to their utmost degree of intensity.

Man is a postpositive particle which circumscribes the sense of the word preceding in an oppositive sense.

Though I, even I.	Acó man.
Though Peter came here.	Naparitò man Si Pedro.
Although a man be virtuous.	Banal man ang tauò.
Is it, by chance, their father that man who is coming here?	¿Canilàng amú cayá yaóng tauòng napaparitò.?
Yes, indeed, it is he himself.	¡Abáa!, siyá ñga. (palá).
Was it he....?	¿Siyá bagá ang....?
How!, how now, are they, then, here in town?	¿Ay anò, naritò ñga bagá silá sa bayan?
Most certainly,	Oo, ñgani; oo, ñga.
Is that true?	¿Totoò cayá iyán?
Yes, indeed, it is absolutely true.	Totoòng totoò, totoò ñga, totoò mandín.
Why!, is it you who say it?	¿Ay anò, cayó nañga bagá ang nagsasabì?
Of course, it is we.	Ay anò, camí ñga.
Is this your child?	¿Ytò palá ang anac mo?
It is.	Siyá ñga (palá).
Oh!, how tall!	¡Abáa!, malaquì ñga.
Is that the same woman you love?	¿Yyáng babayeng iyán ñga bagá ang sinisintà mo?
The very same.	Siyá rin, (ñga).
Seven.	Pitò.
Twelve,	Labìng dalauà.
Week, a week.	Ysàng lingo.

TENTH EXERCISE.

What tree is that? This tree is oak. (molauin). Are its leaves large and beautiful? Certainly. Whose sons are these children? They are my sons. And that one, whose son is he? He is my friend's. How many months are there in a year? There are twelve months in a year. Name them. January, etc.. How many days are there in a week? There are seven days in a week. Name them. Sunday, etc., What month is this? The month of April. Are you here in the month of April? I am not here in the month of April, I am here in the month of July. When do you go to the farm? I go (will go) to the farm on Thursday. Are you not in town on Tuesday? I am in town on Sunday. When do you (will you) go to Manila? I go to Manila on Saturday. Is he going to church on Monday? He is going to church on Sunday. What day is this? (to—day). It is Friday. When do they go to the garden? They go to the garden at the commencement of the week. What is the last day in the month? The end of the month is Wednesday. What month is at the end of the year? The month at the end of the year is December. What color is the trunk of that tree? The color of the trunk of this tree is red. Is it not yellow?. No, it is brown. Is the day dark? No, it is not dark. What day is at the middle of the week? Thursday is at the middle of the week. What then? Nothing at all. Why!, is it that there is no God here on Earth? Yes, indeed, there is one God here everywhere. Why!, is it the brother of Peter who went there?. It was he himself who went there. What!, are you here? Of course, I am here. Then, is God great? Of course, He is great. Is it you then, who are there? Of course, it is I. Is it you yourself who

Went to Manila in October? I myself went there. Who stole any books? It was the women who stole some books. Are Europeans white? Oh!, they are. Where is God? Wherever you go there is God. Who says so. Anybody says so. Is John at church? Although he may be in town he does not go church. Is that true? It is true.

ELEVENTH LESSON.
YCALABING ISANG PAGARAL.

NUMERAL ADJECTIVES.

CARDINAL AND ORDINAL NUMBERS.

The numerals in Tagalog are exceedingly simple. They always precede the noun.

Cardinal numbers from eleven to nineteen inclusive are formed from the digits by preceding the latter with the particle *labì*, "more"; used as a co-efficient. Multiples of ten up to ninety inclusive have the termination *póuo*, "ten"; (*polo*, the word for "ten" in "Bisayan" and "Bicol" dialects being also used in several places.). The intermediate numbers are formed simply by adding the units. Above "a hundred," "*isàng dáan*; and "a thousand", *isàng libò*; the numbers proceed with equal regularity: 326, *tatlòng dáan, dalauàng póuo,t, ánim*; 2,641, *dalauàng libò ánim na ráan, ápat na p. uo,t, isà*.

Certain terms for high numbers have been borrowed from the Sanskrit language and misapplied to Tagalog, namely: *lacsá*. (Sansk. *laksha*, 100.000.) and *yota*, (Sansk. *ayota*, 10.000.) The numbers represented by these words in Tagalog are *isáng lacsá–sang lacsá*, "ten thousand;" *isáng yota–sang yota*, "a hundred thousand;" *sangpóuong, yota* "one million."

To express a quantity which approaches what in English is called a round number, it is sometimes convenient to state the latter qualified by the figure in which it is deficient, using the word *cúlang-cólang*, "less," "save;" as is done in the old-fashioned phrase *forty stripes save one*. Thus, instead of *isáng dáan siyam na póuo,t, ualò* "one hundred ninety eight;" the phrase *cólang nang dalauà sá dalauàng dáan*, may be used.

The ordinal numbers are formed from the cardinals by means of the prefix *yca*, as seen in this lesson.

The student will do well in trying to acquaint himself with Spanish numerals, for they are largely made use of by natives in counting.

One.	Isà.
Two.	Dalauà.
Three.	Tatlò.
Four.	Apat.
Five.	Limà.
Six.	Anim.
Seven.	Pitò.
Eight.	Ualò.
Nine.	Siyam.
Ten.	Sangpóuo.
Eleven.	Labing isà.
Twelve.	Labing dalauà.
Thirteen.	Labing tatlò.

Fourteen.	Labing ápat.
Fifteen.	Labing limà,
Sixteen.	Labing ánim.
Seventeen.	Labing pitò
Eighteen.	Labing ualò.
Nineteen.	Labing siyam.
Twenty.	Dalauàng póuo.
Twenty-one.	Dalauàng póuo,t, isà.
Thirty.	Tatlong póuo.
Thirty two.	Tatlòng póuo.t, dalauà.
Forty.	Apat na póuo.
Forty three.	Apat na póuo,t, tatlò.
Fifty.	Limàng póuo.
Fifty four.	Limàng póuo,t, ápat.
Sixty.	Anim na póuo.
Sixty five.	Anim na póuo,t, limà.
Seventy.	Pitòng póuo.
Seventy six.	Pitòng póuo,t, ánim.
Eighty.	Ualòng póuo.
Eighty seven.	Ualòng póuo,t, pitò.
Ninety.	Siyam na póuo.
Ninety eight.	Siyam na póuo,t, ualò.
One hundred.	Sang dáan, isàng dáan.
One hundred and nine.	Sang dáa,t, siyam.
One hundred and twenty.	Sang dáa,t, dalauäng póuo.
Two hundred.	Dalauàng dáan.
Two hundred and fifty.	Dalauàng dáa,t, limàng póuo.
Three hundred.	Tatlòng dáan.
Three hundred and sixty nine.	Tatlòng dáa,t, ánim na póuo,t, siyam.
Four hundred.	Apat na dáan, ápat na ráan.
Five hundred.	Limàng dáan.
Six hundred.	Anim na dáan.
Seven hundred.	Pitòng dáan.
Eight hundred.	Ualòng dáan.
Nine hundred.	Siyam na dáan.
One thousand.	Sang libò, isàng libò.
Eleven hundred.	Isàng libò,t, isàng dáan.
Two thousand.	Dalauàng libò.
Nine thousand.	Siyam na libò.
Ten thousand.	Sang lacsá, isàng lacsá.
Thirty thousand.	Tatlòng lacsá.
Seventy thousand.	Pitòng lacsá.
One hundred thousand.	Sang yota, is`ng yota.
Two hundred thousand.	Dalauàng yota.
One million.	Sang póuong yota, sang añgao-añgao.
How much? (asking for price).	¿Magcanò.?
Price.	Halagá.
How much is the price of that?	¿Magcanò ang halagá niyán.?
Six dollars.	Anim na piso. (Sp. peso.).

Cardinal numerals may be preceded by the article in a determinate sense, as in English. *Ang tatlòng pisos na ybinigáy co sa iyò.* "the three dollars I gave you".

Labi, which precedes the digit numbers to form the first denary, means "more" and is linked to the number. In the same way the different parts which a number is composed of are linked to each other by means of the ligaments. *At-t,* comes before the last expression of the quantity, and not before the denaries as in English, except when the number is decimal.

——— ———

Only, but.	Lámang.
Only one.	Ysà lámang, iisà.
Only two.	Dalauà lámang, dadalauà.
Ten only.	Sang póuo lámang, sasangpóuo.
A hundred only.	Sang dáan lámang, sasangdáan.

A number may be restricted in sense in the common way by the adverb *lámang* or by repeating the first syllable or the first two letters thereof if consisting of more than two. *Lámang* should be used postponed to the word it affects.

ORDINAL NUMERALS.

Ordinal numerals are formed from the cardinal ones, by prefixing to the latter the particle *yca*, the first four being somewhat irregular in formation. Cardinal numerals beginning with *a* drop it to form the ordinal. Ordinal numerals are generally preceded by the article as in English.

To precede, to go before.	Onà, pañgonà.
The first.	Ang naonà, ang unà.
The second.	Ang ycalauà.
,, third.	,, ycatlò.
,. fourth.	,, ycápat.
,, fifth.	,, ycalimà.
,, sixth.	., ycánim.
,, seventh.	,, ycapitò.
,, eigth.	,, ycaualò.
,, ninth.	., ycasiyam.
,, tenth.	,, ycasangpóuo.
., eleventh.	., ycalabìng isà.
,, twelfth.	,, ycalabìng dalauà.
,, twentieth.	,, ycadalauàng póuo.
., thirtieth.	., ycatlòng póuo.
,, fiftieth.	.. ycalimàng póuo.
,, eighty–ninth.	., ycaualòng póuo,t, siyam.
., hundredth.	., ycasangdáan.
,, thousandth.	., ycasanglibò.
,, ten thousandth.	,, ycasanglacsá.
,, 3.843rd.	{ ,, ycatlòng libò, ualòng dáan, ápat na póuo,t, tatlò.

In complex numbers only the first and most embracing one is ordinalized in Tagalog, contrary to the English practice.

The very first.	Ang caonaonahan.
The last.	Ang huli.
The very last.	Ang cahulihulihan.
The very first man was Adam.	Ang caunaunahang tauò ay Si Adán.
Oh! my God! I, the very last among sinners.	{ ¡Ayá! ¡Dios co!, acó, ang cahulihulihan nang mañga macasalanan.

The extreme ordinal numerals may be superlativized in Tagalog by the prefix *ca*, the repetition of the root and by using the suffix *an*.

Much (num. adj.), many.	Maramì. (from damì).
Very much, a great deal, a great many.	Maramìng maramì.
The majority, the most.	Ang caramihan.
All.	Lahat, ang lahat.
Enough. (adv.).	{ Siyá na, *husto* (corr. from Sp. word, *justo*)

More than (a cardinal number following).	Labis sa, higuit sa.
More than eight.	Labis sa ualò, higuit sa ualò.
More (comparative).	Lalo, lalo pa.
More (adv.), still, even.	Pa. (always postponed).
All men are not virtuous.	Ang lahat na tauò ay hindí mañga banal.
You say enough.	Siyá na ang sabi mo.
Are you taller than his brother?	¿Lalo ca pang matáas sa caniyà ıg capatid na lalaqui?
I am taller than he.	Lalo acóng matáas sa caniyà.
Has their father any more chickens?	¿Ang canilàng amá, mayróon pang sísiu?
He has still more.	Siyá,i, mayróon pa.
Now. (at present).	Ñgayón.
Some, few.	Ylán.
Only a few.	Ylán lámang, iilán.

Ylán, may likewise be made ordinal by prefixing *yca*, as *quantième* in French.

What day of the month is to-day?	¿Ycailáng árao ñgayón ñg bouán?
To-day is the thirteenth.	Ycalabing tatlò ñgayón.
What place (in order) have they?	¿Ycailán bagá silá?

Mañga, preceding a cardinal numeral imparts a sense of indetermination.

How many bags have they?	¿Yláng bayong ang na sa canilà?
Some twenty of them, about twenty.	Mañga dalauàng póuo.

Mañga, alone, and not *ang mañga*, comes before nouns in the plural when they are used indefinitely or in a partitive sense.

Houses.	Mañga báhay.
Men, people.	Mañga tauò.

ELEVENTH EXERCISE.

63. — 128. — 215.—519.—631.—911.—1.342.—3.000.—7.894.—10.614.—25.813. — 37.018. — 70.800.—100.526.—362.214.—836.565.—1.232.036.—3.434.608. What is the price of that cheese? Three dollars. How many houses has your father? He has none. Has your sister many looking-glasses? She has twenty. Have your parents all the rings? They have not all. How many children has the brother of Anthony? He has seven. Are all of them pretty? Three are pretty, the others ugly. How many brothers has your uncle? My uncle has five brothers. How many of them are male? (1). Three of them are male, the others are female. Has my aunt many trees? She has some. Where are the two brothers-in-law? They are at Cebú. How many women were there yesterday? A great many. Are there no books at home? We have many at home. Are there many dogs over there? There are only a few. How many cats has my cousin? He has only one. Are there twenty birds at your house? There are more than twenty. Where are they? They are on the branches of trees. Who told you there are many churches in Manila? My friends told me so. How many souls have we? We have only one. How many fingers are there in your hand? There are only four. Where, then, is the other? Well, then, the other is hidden. How many trees (trunks) are there in

---

(1) In Tagalog, as heretofore explained, *capatid* includes both brothers and sisters.

this garden? There are a great many. How many of them have branches and how many have none? Those not having branches are only a few. Who was the first man? The first man was Adam. And the first woman? Eve. What place in order has your sister at school? She is the fifth in order. What number have you? I have the 638th. Are you noble? I am the last of men. Are all men bad (wicked)? No, only some of them are wicked. Are all women judicious? The majority are judicious. Have you more than three pens? I have more than sixty. Is your friend older than his brother? He is taller, but he is not older. Have you still more sons? I have two more. What day of the week is to-day? To-day is Tuesday. And what day of the month was yesterday? Yesterday was the 25th. How many dollars have you? I have some thirty dollars.

TWELFTH LESSON.
YCALABING DALAUANG PAGARAL.

NUMERAL ADJECTIVES (continued).

ADVERBIAL, PARTITIVE AND DISTRIBUTIVE NUMERALS.

The adverbial numerals are formed by prefixing *maca* to the cardinals, the first being altogether, and the second and third somewhat, irregular.

Once.	Minsán.
Twice.	Macalauà.
Thrice, three times.	Macaitlò, macatlò.
Four times.	Macaúpat.
Five "	Macalimà.
Six "	Macaánim.
Seven "	Macapitò.
Eight "	Macaualò.
Nine "	Macasiyam.
Ten "	Macasangpóuo.
Eleven "	Macalabìng isà.
Nineteen "	Macalabìng siyam.
A hundred "	Macasangdáan.
A thousand "	Macasanglibò.
How many times?, how often?	¿Macailán?

The restriction in sense may be made by repeating the first two letters for *minsán* and the first syllable of the particle for the others, besides the common way of using *lámang* or both *lámang* ang the repetition.

Once only, only once.	Miminsán.
Twice only, " twice.	Mamacalauà.
Ten times only.	Mamacasangpóuo.
A hundred times only.	Mamacasangdáan.

These same adverbial numerals are used in Tagalog in some districts, to denote multiplication, in the same way as the suffix "fold" in English; *macalauà lalong malaquì*, "two-fold (doubly) greater or large".

¿*Nacailán?*, is used by some people for ¿*macailán?*. Properly speaking, ¿*nacailán?*, expresses past time and ?*macailán?*, present or future: ¿*Nacailán cang nacasalá?*, "how many times did you commit sin"?; ¿*macailán cang paparóon?*, "how often will you go there". *Beses*, (corrupt Spanish word for *veces*) (times) is sometimes used. ¿*Yláng beses?*, "how many times?", "how often?".

DISTRIBUTIVE ABSTRACT NUMERALS.

These are formed by repeating the cardinal numeral or the two first syllables thereof, if consisting of more than two, without any ligament.

One by one.	Ysà-isà.
Two by two, two at a time.	Daladalauà.
Three by three, three at a time.	Tatlò tatlo.
Four " four, four " " "	Apat ápat.
Five " five, five " " "	Limà limà.
Ten " ten, ten " " "	Sangpóuo sangpóuo.
Dozen " dozen, a dozen" " "	Labı labìng dalauà.
How many at a time?	¿Ylán ylán?.
Thousand by thousand.	Sangli sanglibò.
Hundred by hundred.	Sangdú sangdáan.
Every day, daily.	Arao úrao.
Every hour, hourly.	Oras oras.
Every month, monthly.	Bouán bouán.
Every year, yearly.	Taón taón.
Every week, weekly.	Lingo lingo.
Every Sunday.	Do. do.
Every Tuesday.	Touíng Martes.
Every Saturday.	" Sábado

PARTITIVE NUMERALS.

"The half" is expressed either by *ang calahati*, or *ang ycalauàng bahagui*, the former being far more in use. The other partitive numerals in the singular are expressed by the ordinals with the article, the word *bahagui*, "share," "portion"; being optionally used at the end. For the plural, the cardinals are used; the partitive, in the nominative case, and that indicative of the parts into which the unity is considered divided, in the possessive, with *bahagui* following:

The half.	Ang calahati, ang ycalauàng bahagui.
The third.	Ang ycatlòng (bahagui).
The tenth.	Ang ycasangpóuong bahagui.
Three fourths.	Tatlò nang ápat na bahagui
The seven eighths.	Ang pitò nang ualòng bahagui.

How many times did you come here yesterday?	¿Nacailán-macailán naparitò ca cahapon?
Twice.	Macalauà.
How often does your sister go to mass?	¿Macailán bagáng magsimbà ang capatid mong babaye?
Every Sunday.	Lingo lingo.

DISTRIBUTIVE DETERMINATE NUMERALS.

These are formed by prefixing *tig* to the cardinals and by repeating the first syllable from five upwards.

One to each one, one each.	Tig-isà.
Two to every one.	Tigalauà.
Three " " "	Tigatlò.
Four " " "	Tigàpat.

Five to every one.	Tiglilim`.
Six ,, ,, ,,	Tigaánim.
Seven ,, ,, ,,	Tigpipitó.
Eight ,, ,, ,,	Tig-uaualó.
Nine ,, ,, ,,	Tigsisiyam.
Ten ,, ,, ,,	Tigsasangpóuo.
Eleven ,, ,, ,,	Tiglalabìng isà.
Twelve ,, ,, ,,	Tiglalabing dalauà.
A dozen ,, ,, ,,	Tig-isàng *dosena* (corr. from Sp. *docena*)
How many to every one, at how many every one?	¿Tig-iilán?
How?, in what manner?	¿Paanò?
How is, are?	¿Maanò?

Tig, may also come before cardinal plural numerals indicative of the fixed or stamped value of a thing, without any repetition of syllable. Thus, "five dollars coined piece" may be expressed, *salapíng tiglimàng piso*; "fifteen cents' stamp", *seyong tiglabìng limàng séntimos*; although *na* is more in use. In southern provinces *tig* serves to express the season anything occurs or is proper to be made: *tighapon*, "to do something in the afternoon."

The distributives for unities of price, measure, etc. are formed by prefixing *man* to the root-word of the standard unity, the first letter of the root undergoing changes as follows: If it is a vowel or *c*, the last letter of the particle and the first of the root change into *ñg*. If it is *t*, *s* or *d*, both are dropped. If it is *p*, this and the last letter of the particle change into *m*.

Bushell.	Cabán.
Twenty five cents' value.	Cahati.
Twenty five pounds weight.	*Aroba* (Sp. *arroba*).
One ounce's weight of gold.	Táhil.
Half a real, $ 0'06. ¼.	Sicolo.
One real.	Sicápat.
Half a dollar.	Salapí, isàng salapí.
Inch.	Sandali, sang dali.
Handbreadth measure.	Dangcal.
Dollar.	Piso.
Farthing.	*Belis*, (corr. from Sp. word *maravedí*).
At one bushell per head.	Mañgabán.
,, $ 0'25 ,, ,,	Mañgahati.
,, 25 pounds weight ,, ,,	Mañgaroba.
,, one ounce's gold weight ,, ,,	Manáhil.
,, half a real ,, ,,	Manicolo.
,, half dollar ,, ,,	Manalapí.
,, one real ,, ,,	Manicápat.
,, one inch ,, ,,	Manandali, mandali.
,, handbreadth ,, ,,	Manangcal, mandangcal.
,, one dollar. ,, ,,	Mamiso.
,, ,, farthing ,, ,,	Manbelis.

The body.	Ang cataouán.
Time, weather, occasion.	Panahón.
Opportunity, awaiting of an opportunity.	Capanahonan.
Fine weather.	Mabuting panahón.
Rough weather.	Masamáng panahón.
At dawn, morning; early in the morning,	Omaga.
To-morrow morning.	Bucas nang umaga.
In the morning.	Sa umaga.

Mouse.	Dagá, bulílit.
Rat.	Dagá.
Louse.	Cutò.
Louse, crablouse.	Toma.
Pig, swine.	Bábuy.
Sow.	Anacán, inahín.
Boar, wild boar.	Bábuy damó.
To give, give.	Magbigáy (indet)
Gave.	Nagbigáy (indet.).
The giving.	Ang pagbibigáy.
To give (some thing)	Ibigáy (det.)
How many times did you give bread?	¿Macailán nagbigáy ca nang tinápay?.
Seven times.	Macapitò.
How many at a time to be given?	¿Yláng ilán bagá ang pagbibigáy?
Five at a time.	Limà limà.
Do you go to church every day?	¿Napasasasimbahan ca bagá árao árao.
No, I go to church only once a week.	Hindí, napapasasimbahan acó miminsán lingo lingo.
Does he come here every Friday?.	¿Napaparitò siyá bagá touíng viernes?.
No, he comes here every Sunday.	Hindí, napaparitò siyá lingo lingo.
How many to be given each?	¿Tig-ilán bagá ang pagbibigáy?
Two dozen to every one.	Tigalauàng dosena.
Give (sing.) one bushell per head.	Mañgabún ang ybigáy mo.
Give (plur.) 25 cents per head.	Mañgahati ang ybigáy ninyò.
How much money shall I give to every one?	¿Tig-ilán bagá ang ybibigáy cong salapí?
Give one real per head.	Manicápat ang ybigáy mo.
Shall I not give at the rate of one dollar to each?	¿Hindí bagá mamiso ang ybibigáy co?
How is the weather to-day?	¿Maanò bagá ang panahón ñgayón?
The weather is fine.	Ang panahó,i; mabuti.
Is not the weather rough?	¿Ang panahó,i. hindí bagá masamá?
Certainly, it is rough.	Masamáng totoò.
When do you go to Parañaque?	¿Cailín ca pasasa Parañaque?
To-morrow morning.	Bucas nang omaga.
Does your father come here in the morning or in the evening?	¿Ang amá mo bagá,i, napaparitò sa umaga ó sa gabì?
In the evening.	Sa gabi.

TWELFTH EXERCISE.

Which book have you? I have the first. And where is the second?
My brother has it. Is not October the ninth month of the year? No, Sir,
October is the tenth. How many times did your child purloin.? Only once.
Did your uncle go three times to the garden? He went to the garden
only once. How do you give your books? I give them one by one, but
my master gives them three by three. Do you go to school every Thursday?
I go there every day. How many hours are you at school in the morning?
I stay there two hours. What day of the week do your children not go
to school? They do not go to school on Sundays. How many pens did
you give to every one? I gave seven pens to every one. How many
did you say? I did say seven pens. How much money do you give to
each of their children? I give one dollar each. How much rice does
their father give them? Their father gives one ganta each. And their
uncle? Their uncle does not give them even a farthing each; their aunt
gave them once 25 pounds weight each. What parts is man made of?

Man is made of two parts, body and soul. When shall I come here? Come at the end of the month and you will be here in good time. Is the weather fine in the month of October? The weather is rough in the month of October. When will you go to the garden? I shall go there to-morrow morning. Are there many mice in your house? There are very few. Are there rats at your farm? There are rats and birds. Has your son any lice in his head? He has none, but in his clothes there are crablice. Have you many swine? I have only a boar and a sow.

THIRTEENTH LESSON.
YCALABING TATLONG PAGARAL.

DEGREES OF COMPARISON.

COMPARATIVE OF EQUALITY.

There are several ways of forming the comparative of equality in Tagalog, according to its being of quantity, quality or thing. This lesson treats of the most usual manners of forming the comparative of equality, but the student should try first to become acquainted with the following words used for the purpose.

So..........as.	Para, sing, casing, macasing, ga, ganga, pares, capares.
As..........as.	Para....ni, parang; sing or casing, magcasing. (prefixed to the root).
So.... ....as.	Ga, (prefixed to the root of the thing and ca, prefixed to the root of the quality).
As much......as.	Capara, caparis, capantáy, magcasing.
As many......as.	Capara, capares, capantáy, parapara, magcapares.
As I.	Para co.
As my brother.	Para nang aquing capatid.
As he.	Para niyà.
As Alfred.	Para ni Alfredo.
As my cousin.	Para nang aquing pinsán.
As stone.	Para nang batò, parang batò.
As this.	Ganitò, gaitò, para nitò.
......as this.	Ganitò ca..., gaitò ca..., para nitò ca...
As that.	Ganiyán, ganóon, para niyán, para niyón.
......as that.	Ganiyán ca..., ganóon ca..., para niyán ca..., para niyón ca...
As these.	Ganga nitò, para nitòng manga itò.
......as these,	Ganga nitò ca...
As those.	Ganga niyán, ganga nóon.
......as those.	Ganga niyáng ca..., ganga nóon ca...
As much bread as wine.	Tinápay na casingdami nang álac. Tinápay na caparis nang alac ang dami.
As many knives as pens.	Ang manga itac casingdami nang manga panúlat, or, magcapara singdami. Ang manga itac at ang manga panúlat ay magcasingdami.

The comparative of equality may be formed in several ways in Tagalog. The comparison of quality is formed either by prefixing *sing* or *casing* to the root expresive of the quality or by placing *para* after the adjective in full, with the possessive case of the thing or person serving as standard, at the end.

Peter is as wise as John.	Si Pedro,i, singdúnong (or casingdúnong) ni Juan. Si Pedro,i, marúnong na para ni Juan.
This wood is as hard as stone.	Ytòng cáhoy na itò,i, singtigás (or casingtigás) nang batò. Ytòng cahoy na itò,i, matigás para nang batò.

If an idea of assemblage is to be expressed, *casing* with the prefix *mag* may be used. The same sense is expressed by *sing* and the repetition of the first syllable of the root.

Richard and his father are equally wise.	Ang magamá ni Ricardo,i, magcasing dúnong.
Richard is as wise as his father.	Singdudúnong ang magamá ni Ricardo.

Pares, capares, magcapares, may be used before the adjective when both objects compared have been previously expressed, the prefix *ca* imparting a sense of companionship or likeness.

My uncle's children are as tall as my cousins'.	Ang mañga bata nang amaín co at ang sa mañga aquing pinsán,i, magcacaparis nang táas.

Ga is prefixed to the nominative of the common noun with which anything is compared, the quality root following prefixed with *ca.*

It is as white as paper.	Gapapel caputí.

Ga is also prefixed to the possessive case of the demonstrative pronouns, thus forming adverbs or adverbial expressions; and if the comparison is made with an adjective, the latter takes *ca.*

So, in this manner; so, as this.	Ganitò, gaitò.
So, in that manmer, as that.	Ganiyán, ganóon.
As large as this.	Ganitò calaqui.
As old as that.	Ganiyán catandá.

Ga is also prefixed to the interrogative pronouns in the nominative when the extent of a quality is in question.

To what degree is she virtuous.?	¿Gaanò siyá cabanal?
To which (what) degree is it beautiful?	¿Gaalín cariquit?
It is pretty like that.	Ganiyán cariquit.

When *ga* is prefixed to a verb it imparts a sense of mockery or fictitious imitation of the action.

As if you were selling, you pretend you are selling.	Ganagbibili ca.
As if he were weeping hard. Feigning he was weeping a great deal.	Ganagtatañgís siyá.

Ganga may be employed as plural.

As these.	Ganga nitò.
As those.	Ganga niyán, ganga nóon.

...... as these. Ganga nitò ca......
...... as those. Ganga niyán ca..., ganga nóon ca....

The comparison of quantity may be made by expressing the two objects compared in the nomínative case with *magcapares, magcapantáy* and the root of quantity prefixed with *ca* at the end, the translation being literally "such a thing and such a thing are equal in quantity". The possessive case of a proper noun may be used for the possessive pronoun.

My brother has not so many books as these. Ang aquing capatid ay ualáng ganitò caraming libro.

My uncle has as much ink as my father. } Ang *tinta* nang aquing amaín at ang nang aquin amú magcaparis carami.

Capara may govern the possessive case or the nominative of a common noun. *Para-para* is generally used to denote plurality.

Jewel, jewelry. Hiyas, *alhaja* (Sp.).
Comb. Sucláy.
Ear. Taiñga.
Work. Gauá, pag-gauá.
Eyelash. Pilicmatá.
Wrist. Galang-galañgan.
Flower. Bulac-lac.
Ankle. Bocò nang paà, bóol.
Armpit. Quiliquili.
Rich, wealthy. Mayaman.
Riches, wealth. Cayamanan.
State, condition. Lagáy.
Is he well? ¿Mabuti bagá ang lagáy niyà?.

THIRTEENTH EXERCISE.

You and your son, are well? We are well. Has your male–cousin any flowers in his garden? Yes, Sir, he has many flowers. Has he any other plants? Yes, Sir, he has other plants. Who have some houses? The wealthy have houses. Are there any good houses in your town?. Yes, Sir, there are some good houses. What more have you? We have some oxen. Have you much more money? My baker has a great deal more. Has he more paper? He has more. Has the sailor as much coffee as tea? He has as much tea as coffee. Has this man as many friends as enemies? He has as many of the former as of the latter. Have they as many shoes as stockings? They have no stockings. Is my brother's hat as pretty as mine? Your brother's is as pretty as yours. Are you as wise as my uncle? I am not so wise as he. Is John as virtuous as my sister? They both are equally virtuous. Is that crystal as hard as stone? Stone is not so hard as this crystal. Is iron as white as silver? Iron is not as white as silver. Is ink as black as this? My ink is as black as that. Is my father's steel as good as our uncle's? Both of them are equally good. Are these dogs as beautiful as those? These are not so beautiful. Is bread thus made? Yes, in that manner. To what degree is my father old? Your father is as old as mine. To which degree is my aunt's servant wicked? He is as wicked as a thief. How pretty is my bird? It is pretty as a flower. Is Anthony as judicious as I? Both of you are judicious. What does he wish? He wishes to feign as if he were weeping hard. Are they as red as those? They are as red as these.

Is your jewelry as precious as my sister's? My jewelry is not so precious as your sister's. How many combs have you? I have two. Is your ear as black as my nose? It is as black as your wrist. Where have you your ankles and armpits? My ankles are at my feet, my armpits (at) under my shoulders. Are Cruz's family rich? They are rich. To what degree are they wealthy? They are wealthy as a king. Is your brother-in-law well? He is well.

FOURTEENTH LESSON.
YCALABING APAT NA PAGARAL.

DEGREES OF COMPARISON (continued).

SUPERIORITY, INFERIORITY AND SUPERLATIVE.

The simplest way of forming the comparative of superiority in Taga-log is to put the object with which the comparison is made in the abla-tive case (local ablative) by the use of the prepositions *sa* or *cay*. "Virtue is more precious than riches", *ang cabanala,i, mahal sa cayamanan*; "Peter is richer than John", *Si Pedro,i, mayaman cay Juan*; "my brother is taller than I", *ang capatir co,i, malaqui sa aquin*; but it is both more idiomatic and more emphatic to insert the adverbs *lalo*, "more"; *pa*, still"; or *lalo pa*, "more still"; between the things compared, with the same construction. Thus, *ang cabanala,i, lalong mahal sa cayamanan; Si Pedro,i, mayaman pa cay Juan* and *ang capatid co lalo pang malaqui sa aquin*, express better the comparative of superiority. *Labis* and *labis pa* may likewise be used instead of *lalo*. *Pa* is used only in comparing a quality.

More (and a substantive)... than.	Lalo... (the substantive) sa.
	Lalo pa (the substantive) sa.
	(The adjective)... ... ...sa.
More (and an adj.)....than.	Lalo (the adject.)........sa.
	Lalo pa (the adj.)........sa.
	(The adj.) pa sa.
	Lalo..............sa.
	Lalo pa ....sa.
-Er, -r.. ... .than.	Pa.... ....sa.
	Labis sa.
	Labis pa.. ...... sa.
More gold than silver.	Lalong guintó sa pílac.
More water than wine.	Lalo pang túbig sa álac.
The countrymen have more oxen than the villagers.	Ang mañga magsasacà,i, mayróon la-long baca sa mañga taga bayan.
My father has more bread than butter.	Ang amá co,i, mayróon lalo pang ti-nápay sa mantiquiya.
You have more money than I.	Ycáo,i, mayróon lalo pang pílac sa aquin.
But the Judge has more than either of us.	Ñguní,t, ang Hocom, ay mayróon pa sa ating lahat.
Virtue is more precious than wealth.	Lalong mahal ang cabanalan sa caya-yamanan.
Jane is younger than I.	Si Juana,i, lalo pang bata sa aquin. or, Si Juana,i, bata pa sa aquin.
My sisters are poorer than they.	Ang mañga capatid cong babaye,i, duc-há pa sa canilà.

I am shorter than my cousin.	Maliit pa acó sa aquing pinsán.
She is browner than her brother.	Siyá,i, lalo pang cayomangui sa caniyang capatid na lalaqui.
Men are stronger than women.	Ang mañga lalaqui malacás pa sa mañga babaye.
Women are more beautiful than men.	Lalo pang magandà ang mañga babaye sa mañga lalaqui.

The comparative of inferiority, both for quantity and quality, is generally formed by reversing the terms. The adverbs *cólang* "less"; and *alañ,án*, "insufficient"; may also be used in this respect, as seen in the following comparative sentences.

It should be noticed, however, that if the negative adverbs *di, hindí* are not used, *cólang* has the force of a direct negative, as: *cólang bait,* "unjudicious", "not judicious"; *cúlang pílac,* "penniless".

Natives are less industrious tan Americans.	Ang mañga americano,i, lalong masípag sa Tagalog, or, ang mañga Tagalog ay cúlang nang sipag sa mañga americano.
Natives' wealth is less than American.'.	Ang cayamanan nang mañga Tagalog ay alañgán sa cayamanan nang mañga americano.
Men are fewer than women.	Lalong marami ang mañga babaye sa mañga lalaqui, or, ang mañga lalaqui cúlang nang dami sa mañga babaye.

Relation, kinsman.	Hinlog, camagánac.
Kindred, relationship.	Camaganacan, cahinlogan.
Consanguineous relation.	Cadugó.
Relation by affinity.	Cabalaye.
The skies, Heaven.	Lángit.
Coal.	*Carbón* (Sp.); uling na batò (Tag.).
Charcoal.	Oling.
Star.	Bituín.
Custom, habit. temper.	Asal, ugali.
Sick.	Maysaquit.
Apple.	*Mansanas.* (corr. from Sp. word *uanzana.)*
Painter.	*Pintor* (Sp.); manhihibo, (Tag.).
Picture, painting, image.	Laráuan.
The roof.	Ang bubong.
The roof of the house.	Ang sa báhay na bubong.
The thatching straw.	Ang páuid.
The thatching straw plant.	Ang nipa, ang sasì.
Nipa-plantation.	Sasahán.
Cruel, bad-tempered.	Mabagsic.
Prayer.	Dasal.

THE SUPERLATIVE

The superlative relative degree is formed in the same way as the comparative of superiority, the word *lahat* or any other completive term closing the sentence.

Who are the richest?	¿Sino sino ang lalong mayaman?
	¿Sino sino ang mayaman sa lahat?
Which of us is the wisest?	¿Alín ang lalo pang marúnong sa atin?
	(Lit., the wiser of us).
Which of them is the most industrious?	¿Alín sa canilà ang masípag sa lahat?
	(Lit., the industrious over all.)
My son is the most.	Ang anac co, ang lalo sa canilà.
	(Lit. the more of them.)

Absolute superlatives are formed in several ways. The simplest is by using some of the following adverbs:

Very, much, exceedingly.	Lubhá, masáquit, labis, totoò.
Extremely.	Di sapala, di hámac, di palac.

Of these, those that are simple in structure may come before or after the word they qualify; the compound ones, after it.

Lub–há and *labis* have a sense of excess somewhat as the English "too" or "too much"; *masáquit*, a sense of plenty as when "hard" is used in English adverbially. *Totoò* is a term of assurance; the others are adverbial expressions, meaning "not paltry", "not calculable".

She is extremely virtuous.	Banal siyá { di hámac. di sapala. di palac.
	Si yá,i, banal na { lub-há. totoò. labis. } siyáng banal.
God is extremely wise.	Ang Dios ay totoòng marúnong.
Peter is very ill.	Lub-háng maysaquit Si Pedro.
Their daughter is very beautiful.	Ang canilàng anac na babaye ay labis nang gandà.
His master is very cruel.	Ang caniyàng pañginóon, ay mabagsic na masáquit.
Heaven is exceedingly high.	Ang láñgit ay matáas na di sapala.
The king's crown is very precious.	Ang pótong nang Hari ay mahal na di hámac.
Honesty is much esteemed.	Ang minamahal na di palac ay ang puri.

Another way to form the absolute superlative is by repeating the adjective in full and inserting the proper ligament between.

Very red.	Mapulàng mapulà.
Extremely black.	Maitim na maitim.

The plural number is formed by employing the pluralizing particle for simple adjectives; and either by using the particle or by repeating the first syllable of the root, for those prefixed by *ma*.

Most industrious maids!	¡Mañga masípag na masípag na dalaga!
	¡Masípag na masípag na dalaga!
Very ugly dogs.	Mañga asong páñgit na páñgit.
The extremely good apples.	Ang mañga mabutìng mabutìng mansanas.
	Ang mabubutìng mabubutìng mansanas.

The adjectives may also be superlativized by repeating the root (or the two first syllables thereof) *ca*, being prefixed, and *an* or *han* suffixed.

Deep, profound.	Malálim.
Very deep, deepest, most profound.	Calalimlaliman.

Sweet.	Matamís.
Very sweet, sweetest.	Catamistamisan.
Wholesome.	Maguinhauà.
Very wholesome.	{ Caguinhaguinhauahan, or, maguinha- / nàng maguinhauà.

Superlatives or superlative expressions may be formed in a less formal way, as by using a negative word and any comparative term denoting equality, contention or fellowship before the possessive case of the adjective, the literal translation being "matchless", "unrivalled".

Matchless.			Capara.	
			Capares.	
Unrivalled.	in.	Di, ualáng	Catulad. Cauañgis.	nang.
			Cahambing.	
Imcomparable.			Cahalimbáua	
			Capantáy.	

This flower is matchless in beauty. { Itòng bulac-lac na itò,i, ualáng capa- / ris nang gandà.

King Richard was unrivalled in bravery. { Si Haring Ricardo,i, ualáng naguing capantáy nang tápang nang unàng panahón.

Verbs may also be superlativized in Tagalog.

FOURTEENTH EXERCISE.

Has your servant a good broom? He has one. Have the husbandmen of these or of those bags? They have neither of these nor of those. Who has a good trunk? My brother has one. Has he a leather or a wooden trunk? He has a wooden one. Has the carpenter many iron nails? He has many. Who has some guns? The Americans have some. Have you the wooden hammer of the Frenchman or that of the Englishman? I have neither. What is more precious than wealth? Virtue. Who is the greatest of all? God. Who are younger than my brothers? Your uncle's children are younger. Who have more wealth than virtue? The rich. Who have more virtue than wealth? The poor. Am I shorter than Peter? Yes, he is taller than you. Which of these three flowers is the prettiest? The prettiest is that one on the roof. Who are stronger than women? Men. Are buffalos less swift than horses? They are less swift. Are Americans fewer than natives? They are more. Is the neighbour's brother your relation? He is not my consanguineous relation, but he is my relation by marriage. How many people is your kindred composed of? It consists of seven male and four female relations. ¿Do virtuous people get into Heaven? Only virtuous people get into Heaven. Is coal different from charcoal? Yes, coal is different from charcoal. Are there many stars in the sky by night-time? Yes, there are a great many. Is your male cousin good-tempered? No, he is cruel. Is your mother sick? No, she is well, but the painter is sick. How much is the dozen of those apples? Twenty cents. Has your aunt many pictures in her house? She has three pictures at her house. Of what material is the roof of your neighbor's house? The roof of the neighbor's house is of thatching straw. What is the plant of thatching straw. Nipa. Are there any nipa fields in your province? Yes, there are some. Where is your master? He is at church. Is he cruel? No, he is not cruel, he is kind. What prayer is that? Our Father. (The Lord's prayer.) How many persons are there? There are three; John, Alfred and Richard. Which is the wisest? The wisest is John. Which the eldest? The eldest is Alfred. Which is the whitest.? The whitest is Richard. Which of your sisters is the most beautiful? Jane is beautiful. Mary is more beautiful; but Clara is the most beautiful of the three, oh! Clara is very beautiful. Are Americans very industrious? They are extremely industrious. Is honey very sweet? Yes, honey is very sweet. Are buffalos ugly? Yes, indeed, they are exceedingly ugly. What animal is very swift? The horse is very swift. Are birds swifter that horses? Yes, birds are swifter than horses. Are natives very swarthy? No, they are not very swarthy. Are your eyelashes very black? They are very black. Is the sea deep? The sea is very deep. Are apples wholesome? They are very wholesome. The bird is matchless in swiftness. Is your father virtuous? My father is matchless for virtue.

FIFTEENTH LESSON.
YCALABING LIMANG PAGARAL.

DIMINUTIVES.

It has been said in the preceding lesson that the repeating of an adjective in full and the inserting of the proper ligament between, forms a kind of superlative. Well, then, the repeating of the root of a compound adjective without any ligament makes the diminutive.

Idle, lazy.	Matamad.
A little idle, somewhat lazy.	Matamadtamad.
Savory, tasteful.	Masarap.
A little savory.	Masarapsarap.
Sour.	Maasim.
Sourish.	Maasimasim.
Salt, salted.	Maálat.
Saltish, brackish.	Maálatálat.
Rapid, fleet.	Matulin.
Moderately speedy.	Matulintulin.
Rough, uneven.	Magaspang.
Rather rough.	Magaspanggaspang.
Is the Del Rosario family's servant industrious?	¿Masípag bagá ang alila ninà del Rosario?
No, he is rather lazy.	Hindí, siyá,i, matamartamar.
What is sourish?	¿Anò bagá ang maasimasim?
These oranges are sourish.	Itòng mañga dalandán ay maasimasim.
Do you wish to have a little water?	¿Ybig mo bagá nang cauntíng túbig?.
I do not wish to have any, because it is saltish.	Ayáo acó nang túbig, sa pagca,t, maalatálat.

The preceding is the inflective form to lessen the meaning of an adjective, but *munti*, *caunti*, "small", "little"; before or after the word, may likewise be used. *Caunti* is more used as an adverb.

A little cotton.	Cauntíng búlac.
A small book.	Isàng muntíng libro, isàng librong muntí.
This milk is pretty good.	Itòng gatas na itò,i, mabutibuti.

Common nouns may be made diminutive by repeating the root and using the affix *an* or *han*. The term thus resulting is not only a diminutive noun, but it is moreover applicable to any graphic representation of the thing, and, in many cases, the sense imparted is one of contempt or derision of the original meaning.

Little bird or painted figure of a bird.	Ibonibonan.
Little person, abject fellow, or painted representation thereof, manikin.	Tauotauohan.

Petty king, ringleader, one who in play personates a king,	Harihárían.
Physician, person who cures.	Mangagamot, (Tag.); *médico*. (Sp.).
Quack, medicaster.	Medimedicohan. (1).
Who has Mary's little prayer book?	¿Na sa canino bagá ang cay Maríang librong muntí na dasalan?
I have it.	Na sa aquin.

Colloquial pretty names of persons are largely in use among natives, and although, in some cases, the original name has been so distorted, as not to preserve a single letter of the simple, the commonest way is however to pronounce the last two syllables and to change the last vowel to *oy* for male and to *ay* for female persons.

Francis,	Frank.	Francisco.	Ysco,	Quicóy
Frederic.	Fred.	Pederico.		Icóy.
Mary.	Mag.	María.		Biangue.
Margaret.	Madge.	Margarita.		Titáy.

Monosyllabic and dys-syllabic personal names are not generally made diminutives.

There are other suppletory ways of lessening the meaning of substantives, one of which, especially for the abstract ones, is to precede *may* and postpone *din*.

He is pretty well off.	Siyá.i, may cayamanan din.
My mother is slightly recovering her strength.	Ang inà co,i, may calacasan din.

Verbs are very frequently diminutivized in Tagalog as will be seen in subsequent lessons.

But (adv.), only.	Lámang, bocor.
But (prep.).	Bocor, tañgi, liban.
I have but one friend.	Mayróon acóng isàng caibigan lámang.
All of them came here but me.	Naparitò siláng lahat tañgi sa aquin.
Too much, too many.	Labís, lubháng maramt.
You have too much wine.	Cayó.i, mayróon úlac na labís.
They have too many books.	Silá,i, may lub-háng maramìng libro.
Pepper.	Lara, *paminta*. (corr. from Sp. word *pimienta*).
Vinegar.	Suca.
Vein or root.	Ugat.
Throat.	Lalamunan (root-word, *lamon*, "to swallow").
Brains, marrow, pith.	Utac.
Nerves.	Mañga lítid.
Cocoa-nut oil.	Lañgís.
Tinaja, large earthen jar about 20 gallons in capacity.	Tapayan.
Well, any hole dug in the ground to get at fresh water.	Bal-on.
Shirt.	Baro.
Beast, an animal whatever.	Háyop.

---

(1) Be it, once for all, taken into account that in repeating a syllable or a word the repetition does not pass beyond, respectively, the second letter or second syllable thereof.

Dead.	Patáy, namatáy.
Deceased people.	. Nañgamatáy.
Priest, curate, parson.	Cura (Sp.); pare (corr. from Sp. word word padre, "father").
Priest, minister of God.	Cahalili nang Dios.
Baby, infant.	Sangol.
Impudent.	Mahálay.
Impudence.	Cahalayan.
To belong to, to agree to, to fit, to suit, to bear towards.	Ocol.
Our soul is to God, our body to earth.	Ang ating cálolóua ay sa Dios (din) naoocol; ang ating cataouá,i, sa lupa (naoocol).

FIFTEENTH EXERCISE

How many shoes has your wife? She has only two. Who is lazy? The female servant is a little lazy. What is the most savory fruit in The Philippines? The pine-apple; but the banana is somewhat tasteful, Are oranges sour? Oranges are only sourish. Is this water salt water? No, it is only saltish. Are chickens fleeter than hens? Chickens, while they are still small, are only a little fleet. Is that apple tasteful? It is rather insipid. Will you have some bread? I wish to have some. Do you not wish to go to school? I wish to go to church, but my friend Frank does not. Have you a good deal of money? I have only a little. How is that milk? This milk is sourish. What is that picture? That picture is that of a bird. Are there many figures in that picture? This picture has (bears) twenty figures. Is his brother a physician? He is only a quack. What is that painted in that picture? It is a house. Is your baker well? He is sick. To what degree is he sick? He is pretty nearly recovered. Did all of you go to church this morning? They all went there but me. How many Gods are there? There is only one. How much money has the priest? The priest has too much. What is that you have in that bag? It is paper. Does he wish to have some vinegar? He does not wish to have any, for he has a sore throat. Where are roots and veins? Roots of trees are in the earth, veins are throughout the body of animals. What are brains? Brains are the roots of nerves. Is there any cocoa–nut oil in that *tinaja*? There is none, this *tinaja* is empty. Where is there any water? There is water in the well. Is your father dead? Yes, my father is dead. Where are now the souls of dead persons? Those of virtuous people are in Heaven, those of the wicked are in Hell. What is a priest? A priest is a minister of God. What is impudent? There are many actions that are impudent. Is it proper for a man to make shirts? No, it is proper for women. Are beasts and men alike? No, beasts and persons are different, beasts bear towards earth, men bear towards God

SIXTEENTH LESSON.
YCALABING ANIM NA PAGARAL.

THE VERB.

Verbs in Tagalog are either primitive or derivative; the former are those which in their original signification are verbs; the latter are formed from primitive verbs, substantives, adjectives or any other parts of speech by the addition of prefixes, suffixes or both; or by the insertion of particles. The derivative verbs may be subdivided into primary or secondary according to whether the root is combined with one or several particles.

Primitive verbs are generally dyssyllabic in structure.

Primitive verbs may be either transitive as *cáin*, "to eat"; or intransitive as *tólog*, "to sleep"; but a transitive sense may be given to an intransitive verb and vice-versa by the application of particles.

Though the examples of primitive verbs given above are translated for the sake of convenience by the English infinitive, their signification is not necessarily rendered by that mood. The fact is, that the meaning of the radical or primitive is indefinite and depends for its precise signification on its position (with respect to other words) in the sentence or on the particles which may be prefixed, inserted or suffixed to it. Thus, the verb in its simple form is best considered as being in the imperative mood, second person, that being the part of the verb which can, in the majority of cases, be expressed without the use of a particle.

It is not proposed, in a work like the present, to go deeply into a scientific arrangement which, however well suited to the European languages, is adapted with less propriety to uncultivated ones like Tagalog. It is believed that paradigms showing the most common changes of which the verbal root is susceptible and an exhaustive consideration of the particles will be sufficient for the student to grasp the matter; but we can hardly dispense with impressing on him the importance of these particles, a right understanding of which will give him the mastery of the language.

The particle *to*, expressive of the English infinitive; the prefixes and suffixes *a, ab, ant, di, er, ee. en, or,* etc., and the terminations *ing, ed* which accompany verbs and verbal nouns in English, however sense-imparting they may be, fall far short of the significance of the Tagalog particles.

That the student may have an idea of the modifying power of these particles, we subjoin a paradigm showing the manifold meanings they impart to the verbal root *áral,* (idea of knowledge, teaching) which has been selected for the purpose.

ROOT—ARAL.

SENSE.	PARTICLE.	DERIVATIVE.	MEANING.
Action on others, (objective action).	Um.	Umáral.	To teach.
Do. on one's self, (subjective action).	Mag.	Magáral.	To learn, to study

SENSE.	PARTICLE.	DERIVATIVE.	MEANING.
Habitual or mercenary action, customary performance.	Man.	Mañgáral.	To preach.
Potential. (object. action)	Maca.	Macaáral.	To be able to teach.
Do. (subject. „)	„	Macapagáral.	„ „ „ „ study.
Do. (habitual „)	„	Macapañgáral.	„ „ „ „ preach.
Causative. (object. „)	Magpa.	Magpaáral.	„ order „ teach.
Do. (subject. „)	„	Magpapagáral.	„ „ „ „ learn, study
Do. (habit. „)	„	Magpapañgúral	„ „ „ „ preach.
Interference, meddling with. (object. action).	Maqui.	Maquiáral.	„ meddle with teaching
Do. do. (subject. act.)	„	Maquipagáral	„ „ „ studying.
Do. do. (hab. „)	„	Maquipañgáral.	„ „ „ preaching.
Craving. (object. „)	Pa.	Paáral.	„ ask for teaching.
Do. (subject. „)	„	Papagáral.	„ crave for study.
Do. (hab. „)	„	Papañgáral.	„ ask for preaching.
Multitude. (object. „)	Magsi.	Magsiáral.	„ teach by many.
„ (subject. „)	„	Magsipagáral.	„ learn „ „
„ (hab. „)	„	Magsipañgáral.	„ preach „ „
Earnestness. (obj. „)	Magpaca.	Magpacaáral.	„ teach earnestly.
„ (subj. „)	„	Magpacapagáral.	„ learn „
„ (hab. „)	„	Magpacapañgáral.	„ try to preach well.

Verbal nouns expressive of every shade of meaning, mood or tense of which the verb is susceptible, are also formed by applying the particles and should be added to the preceding verbs in the same way as above, with the article.

PARTICLES.	TAGALOG COMPOUNDS.	SIGNIFICATION.
Pag. (prefixed).	Ang pagáral.	The lesson. (looked upon as to the teacher).
Do. („) and the repetition of the first syllable of the root.	Ang pagaáral.	Do do. (looked upon as to the pupil).
An. (suffixed).	Ang aralán.	The person to whom instruction is given.
Y. (pref).	Ang yáral.	What is taught.
Ungm. (pref.).	Ang ungmaáral	The teacher.
Pag. (prefixed and repetition of the first syll.)	Ang pagaáral.	The learning, the studing.
Mag. (pref.).	Ang magáral.	What learned.
Pag. (prefixed and an suffixed).	Ang pagaralán.	The person or book from whom or which learning is derived.
Man. (and the first syllable repeated).	Ang mañgaáral.	The master, the professor.
Ypinañg. (prefixed and repetition of the first syllable),	Ang ypinañgaáral.	What is preached, the subject of a sermon.
Pinañg, repetition and an suffixed.	Ang pinañgañgaralán.	The pulpit or the person to whom something is preached, the audience.
Man. (prefixed to the particle of the habitual sense).	Ang mañgañgáral.	The preacher.

We might continue thus to exhaust the derivatives of which the objective, subjective, etc., actions are capable, but what has already been given will be enough to convey to the student a fair idea of the importance of these particles and to make clear for him that his being acquainted with but few roots will enable him to express many thoughts if he knows these particles and employs them understandingly.

Among many other verbalizing particles, the following three, deemed to be essential, should be first considered.

Um, for verbalizing transitively or intransitively, when the action is looked upon as being in progress or the act of the subject without special reference as to the object.

Mag, for verbalizing, generally transitively, when the action looks forward to a definite object, or when reflectiveness or reciprocalness, and, in the case of intransitive verbs, intensiveness is meant.

Ma, for verbalizing in an intransitive or involuntary sense.

CONJUGATION.

The fact should not be lost sight of, that in primitive verbs, in their primary sense, or when a special modification of the action is not to be denoted, the radical alone may stand for every tense, if the latter can be gathered from the context or is otherwise implied by some expression of time. In the case of a derivative verb or when, for a primitive one, a definitely stated tense is to be expressed, the following general rules are laid down as to the conjugation.

FIRST.   In every case in which the verbalizing particle begins with *m*, *m* is changed into *n* for the present and past tenses.

SECOND.   In almost every case, either the first syllable of the root or the second of the particle, if the latter consists of more than one, is repeated for the present and future tenses.

There not being true auxiliary verbs in Tagalog, the tenses are all simple in structure. Some grammarians, however, in a desire to assimilate the Tagalog conjugation to that of the western languages, have adopted the particle *maca*, itself a true verbalizing one, with the optionally used completive postpositive particle *na*, to express the past complete and future complete tenses, *maca* changing into *naca* for the past perfect, according to the general rule, as above-stated. This particle is here retained for purposes of expediency, but the student is already instructed with regard to its meaning.

UM PARTICLE.

When a root is to be conjugated by *um*, this particle should be prefixed to the root if the latter begins with a vowel, and inserted between the first consonant (or consonants) and the vowel if the root begins with a consonant. Thus, the definite infinitive and imperative of the verb are formed. To form the present tense, *um*, but better *ungm*, is prefixed or inserted in the manner above stated and the first syllable of the root is repeated.

The past tense (present perfect and past indefinite) in this conjugation, is formed by simply prefixing *um* (better *ungm*) without repeating the first syllable of the root.

The pluperfect is formed in the suppletory way already explained of prefixing *naca* to the root (in other conjugations to the root prefixed with the passive particle). *na* being optionally used at the end.

The simple future (future indefinite tense) in this conjugation, is formed by merely repeating the first syllable of the root without the particle.

The compound future (future perfect tense) is formed by prefixing *maca* to the root, what has been said as to the pluperfect being also applicable to this tense.

It is hardly necessary to say again here, that if the first syllable of a root consists of more than two letters, only the first two should be taken for repetition. If it consists of a vowel and a consonant only the vowel is repeated in the present and future tenses. For instance: *acyat* "to go up"; *ungmaac-yat siyá*, and not, *ungmacac-yat siyá*, "he goes up."

U if inserted between *g* and *c* or *i* to soften the sound of *g* is not reckoned as a letter for the effects of repetition, as in: *guinhauà*, "growing well"; *acó,i, yungmiguinhauà*, instead of, *gungmuiguinhauà*, "I am getting well". This applies also to the liquid consonants in the few cases in which they are met with combined with another consonant and a vowel in the first sllable of verbs: *trabajo*, for instance, makes *nagtatrabajo*, and not *nagtratrabajo*, although both ways are in use.

There is in Tagalog, as in English, no specific form to express the French or Spanish imperfect tense of the indicative, that which represents a past action as going on or simultaneous with some other past action. This tense, which is rendered in English by the past tense of the verb "to be" and the present participle of the principal verb, as: "I was writing when he came," is made in Tagalog by using the verb in the present coupled with some adverb of time as illustrated to indicate the same tense with *mayróon*.

Two roots, *áral* and *súlat*, are hereafter conjugated by *um* to fully illustrate the explanations given above.

ROOT.

—

ARAL. (idea of instruction.)

Infinitive.

To teach.   Umáral.

Present indefinite tense.

I teach.	Acó,	i,	ungmaáral. (1).	ungmaáral	acó.
Thou teachest.	Ycáo,	,,	,,	,,	ca.
He, she. it teaches.	Siyá,	,,	,,	,,	siyá.
We teach.	{ Tayo, { Camí.	} ,,	,,	,,	} tayo. } camí.
You. ye ,,	Cayó,	,,	,,	,,	cayó.
They ,,	Silá,	,,	,,	,,	silá.

Present perfect and past indefinite tenses.

I taught, have taught.	Acó,	i,	ungmáral,	ungmáral	acó.
Thou taughtest, hast ,,	Ycáo,	,,	,,	,,,	ca.
He, she, it taught; has ,,	Siyá,	,,	,,	,,	siyá
We ,, have ,,	{ Tayo, { Camí,	} ,,	,,	,,	} tayo. } camí.
You, ye ,, ,, ,,	Cayó,	,,	,,	,,	cayó.
They ,, ,, ,,	Silá,	,,	,,	,,	silá.

---

(1). The student is recommended to write *ungmaáral* in the present and *ungmáral* etc. in the past tenses, instead of *umaáral*, *umáral* as many do. By so doing distinction is made between those tenses and the imperative and infinitive of the verb.

Pluperfect tense.

I had taught.	Acó,	i, nacaáral,				nacaáral acó.		
	,,	,,	ungmáral na, ungmáral			na ..		
Thou hadst ,,	Ycáo,	,,	·.			..		ca.
	,,	,,	,,	,,	,,	,,	ca	na.
He, she, it had .,	Siyá,	,,	,,			,,		siyá.
	,,	,,	,,	..	,,	na	,,	
We ,, ,,	Tayo, / Camí, {	,,	,·			,,		tayo. / camí.
	Tayo, / Camí, {	,,	,,	,,	,,	,,	tayo. / camí.
You, ye ,, ,.	Cayó,	,,	,,			,,		cayó.
	,,	,,	,,	,,	,, ,,	,,	silá.
They ,, ,,	Silá,	,,	,,			,.		silá.
	,,	,,	,,	,,	,,	,,	,,

Future indefinite tense.

I shall teach.	Acó,	i,	aáral,	aáral	acó
Thou wilt ,,	Ycáo,	,,	,,	,,	ca.
He, she, it will ,,	Siyá,	,.	,,	,,	siyá.
We shall ,,	Tayo, / Camí, {	,,	,,	,,	tayo. / camí.
You, ye will ,.	Cayó,	,,	,,	,,	cayó.
They ,, ,,	Silá,	,,	,,	..	silá.

Future perfect tense.

I shall have taught.	Acó,	i, macaáral,				macaáral acó.		
	,,	,.	aáral na,			aáral na .,		
Thou wilt .. ,,	Ycáo.	,,	,,			,,		ca.
	,,	,,	,,	,,	,,	,,	na.
He, she, it will ,, ,,	Siyá.	,,	,,			,.		siyá.
	,,	,,	,,	,,	,,	na	,,	
We shall ,. ..	Tayo, / Camí, {	,,	,,			,,		tayo. / camí.
	Tayo, / Camí, {	,,	,,	,,	,,	,,	tayo. / camí.
You will .. ,,	Cayó,	,,	,.			,,		cayó.
	,,	,,	,,	,,	,,	,,	silá.
They ,, .. ,.	Silá.	,,	,,			..		silá.
	,,	,,	,,	,,	,,	,,	,,

Imperative.

Teach. (thou).	Umáral ca
Let him, her, it, teach.	,, siyá.
Let us ,, {	,, tayo. / camí.
Teach. (ye).	,, cayó.
Let them teach.	,, silá.

ROOT.

SULAT, writing.

Infinitive.

To write.   Sumúlat.

Present indefinite tense.

I write.	Acó,	i, sungmusúlat, sungmusúlat acó.
Thou writest.	Ycáo,	„ „ „ ca.
He, she, it writes.	Siyá,	„ „ „ siyá.
We write.	Tayo, / Camí, }	„ „ „ } tayo. camí.
You, ye „	Cayó,	„ „ „ cayó.
They „	Silá,	„ „ „ silá.

Present perfect and past indefinite tenses.

I wrote.	have	written.	Acó,	i, sungmúlat.	sungmúlat acó.
Thou wrotest,	hast	„	Ycáo,	„ „	„ ca.
He, she, it wrote,	has	„	Siyá,	„ „	„ siyá.
We „	have	„	Tayo, / Camí, }	„ „	} tayo. camí.
You, ye „	„	„	Cayó,	„ „	„ cayó.
They „	„	„	Silá,	„ „	„ silá.

Pluperfect tense.

I had written.	Acó,	i, nacasúlat.		nacasúlat acó.
	„	„	sungmúlat na, sungmúlat	na „
Thou hadst „	Ycáo	„	„	„ ca.
	„	„	„ „ „	„ na.
He, she, it had „	Siyá,	„	„	„ siyá.
	„	„	„ „ „	na „
We „ „	Tayo, Camí, Tayo, Camí,	„ „	„ „ „	} tayo. camí. tayo. camí.
You, ye „ „	Cayó	„ „		cayó.
They „ „	Silá	„ „		silá.

Future indefinite tense.

I	shall	write.	Acó,	i, susúlat, susúlat acó.
Thou	wilt	„	Ycáo,	„ „ „ ca.
He, she. it	will.	„	Siyá,	„ „ „ siyá.

Future indefinite tense. (continued)

We	shall	write.	{ Tayo, { Camí,	} i, susúlat,	susúlat	{ tayo. { camí.
You, ye	will	,,	Cayó,	,, ,,	,,	cayó.
They	,,	,,	Silá,	,, ,,	,,	silá.

Future perfect tense.

I	shall have writen.	{ Acó, { ,,	i, macasúlat, ,,	susúlat na,	macasúlat susúlat	na	acó. acó.		
Thou	wilt	,,	,,	{ Ycáo, { ,,	,,	,,	,,	,,	ca. ,, na.
He, she, it will	,,	,,	{ Siyá, { ,,	,,	,,	,,	,,	na	siyá. ,,
We	shall	,,	,,	{ Tayo, { Camí, { Tayo, { Camí,	,,	,,	,,	,,	{ tayo. { camí. { tayo. ,, { camí.
You, ye	will	,,	,,	{ Cayó,	,,	,,	,,	,,	cayó.
They	,,	,,	,,	{ Silá { ,,	,,	,,	,,	,,	silá.

Imperative.

Write (thou).	Sumúlat ca.
Let him, her, it, write.	,, siyá.
Let us ,,	} ,, { tayo. { camí.
Write (ye).	,, cayó.
Let them write.	,, silá.

The imperative lacks the first person singular and it requires the pronouns to be put after it.

Verbal nouns are formed (in roots verbalized with *um*) by prefixing *pag* to the root. Thus,

The teaching.	Ang pagáral.
The writing.	Ang pagsúlat.

The subjunctive mood is in Tagalog, as in English, merely a syntactical one, the conjunction or any other special particle, and not an inflection. expressing the mood. The following two postpositive particles are, among others, the fittest to express the conditional (future consequent tense) and the past tenses.

Should, would. (signs of the conditional tense).	} Sana, disín.
I should like to teach, but I have no opportunity.	Ybig co sana,i, umáral, ñguní,t, ualá acóng capanahonan.
If he would write, I should go there.	{ Cun siyá,i, susúlat disín ay paroróon { (sana) acó.

The following are likewise conditional particles and expressions used in connection with the subjunctive mood.

If, whether.	Cun.
Were it not for.	Dañgan, cundañgan.
As if it were.	Cun sana sa.
Provided.	Lámang.
Provided not, unless.	Houag lámang.

The following have an optative sense.

| Would to God. | Nauá, siyá nauá, cahimanauari, maanong. |
| It would be better. | Di ñga salámat, maháñgay-mahañga. |

The following particles have a dubitative sense.

It may be, may be, may hap.	Sacali, bagá sacali, cun bagá sacali.
Perhaps.	Maráhil.
Lest.	Macá, bacá.

The following have an adversative inconditional sense.

Though, although.	Man, bagamán, cahit, cahima,t, bistá, bistat.
In spite of, despite.	Man, matáy man.
Happen what may.	Sucdán.
In spite of, for all that.	Matáy, matáy man.
Although not.	Di man.

The student should conjugate by *um* the following roots.

To drink.	Ynom, inum, uminum.
To ask for.	Hiñgí, humiñgí.
To read.	Basà, bumasà.
To go in, to enter.	Pásoc, pumásoc.
Running, to run.	Tacbò, tumacbò.
Outside, to go out, to come out.	Labás, lumabás.
Purchase, to buy.	Bili, bumili.
Eating, to eat.	Cáin, cumáin.
Step, pace, to walk.	Lácad, lumácad.
Arrival, to arrive.	Dating, dumating.
Departure, to leave, to go away.	Alís, umalís.

SIXTEENTH EXERCISE.

Do you teach Tagalog? Yes, Sir, I teach Tagalog. What was it he was teaching yesterday? What he was teaching yesterday was English. Did we write any letters last Sunday? We wrote many. When have they written any prayers? They have written some these past days. When will their father write? He will write the day after to-morrow. Had you read any letter when my sister arrived? When your sister arrived I had already read a letter. What did they say to their children? They said to them, read. Would he drink some water had he any? He would not drink any, had he some wine. Has the tailor asked his mother for anything? He asked her for some bread. Had I some books, would you wish to read? Had you some books, it may be I should read some. If he should go into town, would he enter his aunt's house? If he should go into town, he would perhaps enter his aunt's house. Shall I run? Do not run in such a manner, lest your father come here. Would you go out if the weather were fine? Were not the weather bad, I should perhaps go out. Would you buy any pens even if your master come? Yes, I should buy some pens though my master come. Will you eat much boiled rice next Sunday?

Though I may have a great deal I shall not eat much. Which is better, to run or to walk? To walk is better than to run. When will the bishop arrive? The bishop's arrival is only once a year. Shall you go away? In spite of bad weather, I shall go away. Shall I already have read when my son arrives? Though he does not come, I shall read, whatever may happen.

SEVENTEENTH LESSON.
YCALABING PITONG PAGARAL.

VERBALIZING PARTICLE *MAG-PAG*.

The second important verbalizing particle is *mag* for the active, *pag* for the passive voice of the verb.

The frame of the conjugation is for this particle nearly the same as for the preceding, *um*. The *m* is changed into *n* for present and past tenses, the first syllable of the root being repeated in the present and the future according to the general rule. A verbalizing particle has a corresponding one, generally beginning with *p*, for the passive voice, with which it will be always coupled in this grammar; *um* and *pa* conjugations are excepted.

We have admitted, for method's sake, of *naca* and *maca* expressing the pluperfect and future perfect tenses. *Maca*, being also an independent verbalizing particle, and it being the rule that if two different particles join in composition with the same root, that which imparts the primary sense should be expressed in the passive form, *naca*, *maca*, then, are not to be prefixed to *mag*, but to *pag* in this and the following conjugations, thus making *nacapag*, *macapag* for those tenses. In this, and in the simple future tense retaining the particle before the repetition of the first syllable of the root, this and all the other conjugations differ from that of *um*.

A paradigm and two roots conjugated by *mag* are subjoined for illustration:

ROOT

Idea of bartering, exchanging commodities. } Bili.

PARADIGM.

To buy.	Bumili.
Thing bought.	Bilhin, nabili.
The money or thing with which something is bought. }	Ang ybili.
The person from whom something is or has been bought. }	Ang bilhán, nabilhán. (contractions.)
Buying, purchase.	Pagbili.
He who could buy.	Ang nacabili.
He who purchases many things or is customarily engaged in buying. }	Ang namimili.
The price, reason, or time in or by which something is or has been bought. }	Ang ypinabili.
Persons from whom, if many.	Ang mañga pinabilhan.
The buying of many things.	Ang pamimili.

To sell.	Magbilì.
The thing.	Ang ypagbilì.
The person to whom or the place where, and also the price.	Ang pagbibilihan.
What has been involuntarily sold.	Ang naypagbili.
The money drawn from what has been sold.	Ang napagbilhan.
Person with whom a purchase has been agreed upon.	Ang cabilì.
The two bargaining parties.	Ang magcabilihan.
The cost. (looked upon on the seller's part).	Ang pagcabilihan.

ROOT.

Idea of instruction.	Aral.

CONJUGATION.

Infinitive.

To learn, to study; to sell.	Magáral, magbilì.

Present indefinite tense.

I	learn,	sell.	Nagaáral,	nagbibilì	acó.
Thou	learnest,	sellest.	„	„	ca.
He, she, it	learns,	sells.	„	„	siyá.
We	learn,	sell.	„	„	{ tayo. / camí.
You, ye	„	„	„	„	cayó.
They	„	„	„	„	silá. (1)

Present perfect and past indefinite tenses.

I	learned, sold; have	learnt,	sold.	Nagáral,	nagbilì	acó		
Thou	learnedst, soldest; hast	„	„	„	„	ca.		
He, she, it	learned, sold; has	„	„	„	„	siyá.		
We	„ „ have	„	„	„	„	{ tayo. / camí.		
You, ye	„ „ „	„	„	„	„	cayó.		
They	„ „ „	„	„	„	„	silá.		

Pluperfect tense.

I	had learnt, sold.	Nacapagáral, nacapagbilì;	nagáral na,	nagbilì na acó.				
Thou	hadst „ „	„	„	„	„	„ ca „		
He, she, it	had „ „	„	„	„	„	„ na siyá.		
We	„ „ „ „	„	„	„	„	" „ { tayo. / camí.		
You, ye	„ „ „ „	„	„	„	„	„ „ cayó.		
They	„ „ „ „	„	„	„	„	„ „ silá.		

(I) The student is already instructed that the subject, be it a noun or a pronoun, may come before the verb, the verbal ligament being inserted between: *acó,i, nagaáral acó,i, nagbibilì*. Not to fill up too much space we only use the form in the illustration, which is, on the other hand, both the commonest and the most idiomatic.

Future indefinite tense

I	shall	learn,	sell.	Magaáral.	magbibilì	acó.
Thou	wilt	,,	,,	,,	,,	ca.
He, she, it	will	,,	,,	,,	,,	siyá.
We	shall	,,	,,	,,	,,	tayo. / camí.
You, ye	will	,,	,,	,,	,,	cayó.
They	,,	,,	,,	,,	,,	silá.

Future perfect tense.

I shall	have learnt, sold.	Macapagáral, Magaáral na,	macapagbilì. magbibilì na	acó. ca / ,, na.
Thou wilt	,, ,, ,,	,, ,, ,,	,, ,,	na ca / ,, na.
He, she, it will ,,	,, ,,	,, ,, ,,	,, ,, ,,	na siyá.
We shall	,, ,, ,,	,, ,, ,, ,,	,, ,, ,, ,,	tayo. camí.
You, ye will	,, ,, ,,	,, ,,	,, ,,	cayó.
They	,, ,, ,, ,,	,, ,, ,,	,, ,, ,,	silá.

Imperative.

Learn, sell. .(thou).	Magáral,	magbili	ca.
Let him, her, it learn. sell.	,,	,,	siyá.
Let us ,, ,,	,,	,,	tayo. / camí.
Learn, sell. (ye).	,,	,,	cayó.
Let them learn, sell.	,,	,,	silá.

Verbal nouns.

The verbal noun for this second particle is formed by prefixing *paq* to the root, and repeating the first syllable of the latter.

The learning, selling. Ang pagaáral, pagbibilì.

Students should be careful to distinguish *um* verbal nouns from those of *mag*, as the same difference extends itself to many other particles which may be combined with these two. Thus, *ang pagáral*, "the teaching"; *ang pagaáral*, "the learning"; *ang pagpaáral*, "the ordering to teach"; *ang pagpapagaáral*, "the ordering to study"; and so forth for other particles.

The following roots should be conjugated with *mag* by the student.

Account, consideration; to think.	Ysip, mag-ísip.
Gift, to give.	Bigáy, magbigáy.
Wish, to desire.	Nasa, magnasa.
Outside, to take out.	Labás, maglabás.
Departure, leave; to take away.	Alís, magalís.
Load, to carry, to bear.	Dalà, magdalà.
To bring.	Magdalà ditò.

To take to, to convey.	Magdalà { diyán. / dóon.
Remittance, to send.	Hatid, maghatid.
Conveying, to convey to.	
Order, to order.	Otos, magótos.
Situation, to place.	Lagáy, maglagáy.

Soon, forthwith.	Madalí, pagdaca.
Afterwards.	Sacá, maméa.
Who told you your friend was sick.	¿Sino bagáng nagsabi sa iyò na ang iyòng caibiga,i, maysaquit?
As..............so.	Cun gaanò..............ay siyà.
As much.........so	
As the master so is the servant.	Cun gaanò ang pañginóon, ay siyà rin ang alila.
As much you give, so you will be given.	Cun gaanò ang pagbibigáy mo ay siyá rin bibig-yán sa iyò, or, ang pag-bibigáy sa iyò.
Still, even, yet. (adv.).	Pa.
Already.	Na.
No longer.	Ualá na.
Have you still a grandfather?	¿Mayróon pa po cayóng nono?.
No, Sir, I have no longer a grand-father.	Hindí, po, ualá na acóng nono.
And have you still a father?	¿At amá, mayróon pa po bagá cayó?
No, Sir, neither have I a father.	Ualá po, ualá rin acóng amá.
Neither, not either. (adv.).	Hindí rin, ualá rin.
Why?	¿Báquit?, ¿baquin?, ¿anò at?
Because.	Sa pagca,t, at, dahil sa, ang.
Herb, grass.	Damó.
Scissors.	Gunting, pangopit.
Husk-rice, paddy.	Pálay.
Plate. (shallow vessel).	Pingán.
Several, few.	Yilán, cacauntí.
Dish. (plate).	Bandejado. (corr. from Sp. word bandeja, "salver").
Penknife.	Lanseta (corr. from Sp. lanceta)

SEVENTEENTH EXERCISE.

Does your baker buy or sell bread? He sells bread, but he buys wood. Does your master do anything in Manila? He is learning English and teaching Tagalog. Do you think (intend) to give something to the poor? I give them no money, because I have very little; but I desire to have a great deal and then I will give them bread and clothes. Why do our daughter-in-law's brothers desire to go out? They wish to go out, because they are going to their father to take out some plates. When do the Docot family think (intend) to leave? They all will leave to-morrow in the afternoon, for they wish to take away some husk-rice from their mother's farm. Where do you carry any money? I bring some here, because I intend to buy some masonry houses. How much of it does Peter take there? He does not bring any now, he has brought a thousand dollars some days ago. Does your neighbour take something to his children? He takes to them some rice. Why do you order John to go to mass every Sunday? Because I remember that to go to mass is a commandment of God. Where did they put my dish? They put it in the garden. What do you say? Do that immediately and then (afterwards) go into the garden and bring (fetch) some grass. What is Moll saying about John's household? She is saying, as the parents, so the children are. Do you still desire to go to sea to bring some sailors? I desire to go there to take some money to my friends. Have you still many friends? No, Sir, I have very few, because the majority of them are dead. What is that you have in your hand? It is a pair of scissors. Have you another pair? No, I have only a penknife.

EIGHTEENTH LESSON.
YCALABING UALONG PAGARAL.

VERBALIZING PARTICLE $MA-\frac{CA}{MA}$

The particle *ma*, (*ca* and *ma* in the passive) is the mark of a verb which expresses a state or condition of being and is therefore mainly used to form intransitive verbs. In many cases, however, *ma* expresses, not merely a state or condition, but has even a possessive force as in *mabúhay*, "living", "having life"; and hence many derivatives with *ma* are true adjectives as, *marúnung*, "having, possessing wisdom"; but it should be carefully taken into account that such state or condition of being as expressed by *ma* must be intrinsic, and not one to be arrived at by any conscious delibe-rate endeavour of an agent. On the other hand, transitive actions which are conjugated with other particles when deliberate or conscious acts of the agent are to be expressed, may be conjugated by *ma* if they result from chance, fortuity, or by unconsciousness on the part of the agent.

The conjugation is similar to that of *mag*, but *naca* and *maca* in the past perfect and future perfect tenses are replaced by the completive adverb *na* after the respective simple tenses, a way to denote completeness and, at the same time, to avoid any misconception arising from the use of those particles, on account of *ma* being one of the passive particles for *maca*.

PARADIGMS.

ROOT.

Dying, dead.	Matáy, patáy.

To die.	Mamatáy.
The dying, death.	Ang pagcamatáy, ang camatayan.
Cause or time of.	Ang ycamatáy.
Place where.	Ang camatayán, (1) ang quinamata-yan.
Person to whom other's death affects.	Ang mamatayán.
To feign, to pretend to die or to be dead.	Magmamatáymatayan.

ROOT.

Sleeping.	Tólog.

To sleep. (status)	Matólog.
To go to sleep, to sleep purposely, to go to rest.	Tumólog.

---

(1) Note carefully the accentuation; *camatayan*, "death"; *camatayán*, "dying-place".

To sleep a great deal.		Magtólog.
Sleeping.		Pagcatólog, pagcatotólog.
The cause or time.		Ang ycatólog, ypagtólog.
Dull, sleepy person, one who sleeps much.	}	Mapagtolog, matologuín.
Sleeping-room.		Tologán.
To allow to sleep.		Patólog.

CONJUGATION.

Infinitive.

To die. To sleep. Mamatáy. Matólog.

Present indefinite tense.

I	die, sleep.	Namamatáy, natotólog acó.
Thou	diest, sleepest.	,, ,, ca.
He, she, it	dies, sleeps.	,, ,, siyá.
We	die, sleep.	,, ,, { tayo. camí.
You, ye	,, ,,	,, ,, cayó.
They	,, ,,	,, ,, silá.

Present perfect and past indefinite tenses.

I	died, slept;	have died, slept.	Namatáy, natólog acó.
Thou	diedst, sleepedst;	hast ,, ,,	,, ,, ca.
He, she, it	died, slept;	has ,, ,,	,, ,, siyá.
We	,, ,,	have ,, ,,	,, ,, { tayo. camí.
You, ye	,, ,,	,, ,, ,,	,, ,, cayó.
They	,, ,,	,, ,, ,,	,, ,, silá.

Pluperfect tense.

I	had died, slept.	Namatáy na, natólog na acó.
Thou	hadst ,, ,,	,, ,, ,, ca na. (1).
He, she, it	had ,, ,,	,, ,, ,, na siyá.
We	,, ,, ,,	,, ,, ,, ,,- { tayo. camí.
You, ye	,, ,, ,,	,, ,, ,, ,, cayó.
They	,, ,, ,,	,, ,, ,, ,, silá.

Future indefinite tense.

I	shall die, sleep.	Mamamatáy, matotólog acó.
Thou	wilt ,, ,,	,, ,, ca.
He, she, it	will ,, ,,	,, ,, siyá.
We	shall ,, ,,	,, ,, { tayo. camí.
You, ye	will ,, ,,	,, ,, cayó.
They	,, ,, ,,	,, ,, silá.

---

(1) *Na*, should be placed after monosyllabic pronouns and before the pollysyllabic ones in affirmative sentences.

Future perfect tense.

I	shall	have	died,	slept.	Mamamatáy	na,	matotólog	na	acó.
Thou	wilt	„	.,	„	„	„	„		ca	na.
He, she, it	will	„	„	„	„	„	„	na	siyá.
We	shall	„	„	„	„	„	„	„	{ tayo. / camí.
You, ye	will	„	„	„	„	„	„	„	cayó.
They	„	„	„	„	.,	„	„	„	silá.

Imperative.

Die,		sleep. (thou).	Mamatáy,	matólog	ca.
Let him, her, it die,	„		„	„	siyá.
Let us	„	„		„	„	{ tayo. / camí.
Die,	„	(you, ye).	„	„	cayó.
Let them	die,	„	„	„	silú.

Verbal nouns.

The verbal nouns for this particle are generally formed by prefixing *pagca* to the root, *pag*, however, may be applied to some roots; *pagcaca* is also sometimes used.

The dying, death.	Ang pagcamatáy.
Sleeping, the sleep.	Ang pagcatólog, ang pagtólog.

The student should conjugate the following roots, by using the verbal particle *ma*.

Hunger,	to be hungry.	Gótom,	magótom.
Thirst,	to be thirsty.	Ohao,	maóhao.
Fear,	to be afraid.	Tácot,	matácot.
Shame,	to be ashamed.	Hiyá,	mahiyá.
Cold,	to be cold.	Guináo,	maguináo.
Heat,	to be warm.	Ynit,	maínit (an).
Joy,	to be glad.	Tóua,	matóua.
Sadness,	to be sad, sorry.	Hapis,	mahapis.
Burning, burn;	to burn away.	Sónog,	masónog.

It seems, it appears.	Tila, anaqui, díua.
It seems like a person.	Tila tauò, anaqui tauò, díua ay tauò.
It seems as if he is coming on.	Tila napaparitò siyá.
Tear, to tear.	Guisi, gumisi.
Cut, to cut.	Pótol, magpótol.
To break up { into pieces as glass ware.	Magbásag.
{ into splints as timber.	Magbali.
To break, to part. (active) (speaking of lines).	Magpatir, maglagot.
To mend.	Magtagpí.
To pick up, to find.	Magpólot.
To try to, to intend.	Magbantá, magacala, magtica.
To look for, to seek.	Humánap.
Path.	Landás.

Track, trace, vestige.	Bacás.
Mango.	Manga
Guava.	Bayabas.
It is warm.	Mainit.
It is cool.	Malamig, maguínao.
How old are you?	{ ¿Ylán ca nang taón?
	{ ¿Ycáo,i, mayróon ilán cayáng taón?.
How much is this stuff?	¿Ytòng cayo,i, magcar.ò?
At one dollar the yard.	{ Mamisos ang bara. (corr from Sp.
	{ word vara)
Good morning, good day.	Magandàng árao.
Good afternoon, good evening.	Magandàng hapon.
Good evening, good night.	Magandàng gabì.
At noon.	Sa tanghali.
At mid-night.	Sa hating gabì.
Banana.	Súguing.
Fruit.	Boñga.
Banana plantation.	Saguiñgan.
The fruit of the plane tree is tasteful.	{ Ang boñgang súguing ay masarap.
Bamboo-cane.	Caoayan.
Rice-ear.	Ohay.
Every one, each.	Báua,t, isà, bálang isà.
For the very reason that they are wealthy, they behave haughtily.	Sa pagca,t, silá,i, mayayaman palalo ang canilàng ásal.
All, every.	Tanán, dilán, páua, dilá-dilá na.
All mankind.	{ Ang sangcatauohan, or, ang tanáng
	{ tau).
Every kind of fruit.	Ang diláng boñga.
All of them white.	Páuang mapuputí silá.

Lahat, tanán, refer to individuals, ang di!á ι, to the kind. Páua is generally used in relation to an adjective.

Also, likewise, as well.	{ Namán. (always after the word it
	{ affects.)
Is it likewise you who spoke?.	{ ¿Ycáo bagá namán ang nagsalitá. or.
	{ nañgósap?
When. (referring to a past tense).	Nang.

EIGHTEENTH EXERCISE.

How is your friend? It seems as if he were sleeping, but I think he is dying. Had you slept this morning when my sister arrived? No, I had not yet slept. What does a person profoundly asleep look like? A person who is profoundly asleep looks like a cadaver. Who among you are hungry? Not even one among us is hungry, but everybody is thirsty. Why are your female neighbours afraid? They are afraid, because their father is very sick and they fear that he may die. What did you do then, that you are so ashamed? Sir, I am ashamed, because it is one month since I went to mass. Is Jane, the tailor's sister, cold? She is not cold, she seems to be cold, but, on the contrary, she is warm. Why are their children glad? They are glad, because their father tries to conduct them all to Manila. Is your curate sad? He is sad, because very few people go to mass on Sundays. Whose are the houses that burn away? The houses that are burning belong to your friend, Jane's uncle. Who tore away your shirt? Nobody tore away my shirt, it seems as if it were torn; but it is only cut. Will his aunt break into pieces all the plates, glasses, bottles and *tinajas*? No, Sir, she only wishes to break the *tinajas*, but

15

she did not think to break all the other things. Why does not the servant bring here the cane I gave him yesterday (last) night? He is afraid and ashamed to come here, because he broke the cane into splints. Who parted this string? John's servant's aunt parted that and many other strings. Are you mending something there? I am mending shirts and shoes. Why does not your son take up the needles? He does not wish either to pick up the needles or the mangoes. Does a virtuous man try to seek something? A virtuous man tries to seek the path (the way) to Heaven. Is the water in the sea warm or cool? The water in the sea is somewhat warm. How old is already your first-born sister? She passes already thirty six years. What price is rice sold at at present? It is sold at five dollars the bushel. What do you say to me? I say to you good morning, because it is morning now; when noon is past I shall bid you good afternoon, and then when night enters I shall say good evening until mid-night. Which do you consider as the best of all fruits? I consider the banana the best fruit; but some people say the mango is the best of all. What is the rice plant? Rice is a plant that has an ear. What has every man? Every man has his own clothes; for the very reason they have clothes, they fear to tear those of other people. Will man die? All mankind will die, all plants will be burnt (faded, dried) and all the stars will be extinguished.

NINETEENTH LESSON.
YCALABING SIYAM NA PAGARAL.

THE PASSIVE VOICE.

The forms of conjugation given in foregoing lessons are not the most usual in Tagalog. They are the vague expression of an action abstract in notion and somewhat indeterminate as to object, manner, place or purpose. When the action bears upon a determinate object or special purpose, Tagalog verbs generally assume other forms of conjugation called passives. Among them, that which is formed with the particle *in–hin* is prominent and should be considered as the true passive voice. *In* may be prefixed. inserted or suffixed; *hin* is always suffixed.

To form the passive voice in roots conjugated actively with the particle *um*, *in* is prefixed to the first vowel of the root or inserted between consonant and the first vowel, for the simple present and past tenses. *In* or *hin*, as the case may be, is suffixed to the root in the simple future and imperative, *hin* being only for roots ending in a sharply accented vowel. The first syllable of the root should be repeated for simple present and future tenses as already stated. The pluperfect and future perfect may be formed in two different ways: either by adding the completive particle *na* after the respective simple tenses or by prefixing *na* to the root in the pluperfect, and *ma* in the future perfect if this construction is preferred, *ma. na* being the passive particles for *maca–naca*.

It has already been stated that a passive sentence in Tagalog requires the agent to be put in the possessive case. Now, if the subject is a pronoun either form of the possessive case may be used; the prepositive, of course, before (without the verbal ligament). or the postpositive, after, (also without the verbal ligament) as seen in the examples following. The latter construction is, however, more idiomatic and far more in use. If the subject is a noun or a sentence, it should be put after the verb, for, *cay Pedrong iniíbig si Juana*, although not ungrammatical is little in fashion; as *iniíbig ni Pedro Si Juana*, "Jane is loved by Peter"; is far more in use.

As an illustration, two examples serving of a standard as to how verbs with *um* in the active should be conjugated in the *in-hin* passive, are given hereafter.

To wish, to want, to love.	Umíbig.
Wishing,.	Pag-íbig.
To be loved, to love some thing.	Ybig-in or ibiguin.
To reward.	Gumanti.
Rewarding.	Pag-ganti.
To be rewarded, to reward somebody.	Gantihin.

ROOT. YBIG.

Infinitive.

To be loved.	Ybig-in. ibiguin.

Present indefinite tense.

```
. . . . is or are loved by  me.          Aquing iníibig.  iníibig  co.
. . . .  „    „    „    „   thee, you.   Yyòng      „        „      mo.
. . . .  „    „    „    „   him, her it. Caniyàng   „        „      niyà.
                                       ⌠ Ating              ⌠ natin.
. . . .  „    „    „    „   us.         ⌡ Aming     „      „ ⌡ namin.
. . . .  „    „    „    „   ye, you.    Ynyòng     „        „      ninyò.
. . . .  „    „    „    „   them.       Canilàng   „        „      nilà.
```

Present perfect and past indefinite tenses.

```
. . was, were; has, hast, have been loved by  me.        Aquing iníbig, iníbig co.
. .  „    „    „    „     „     „    „   „  ⌠ thee,        Yyòng     „     „   mo.
                                           ⌡ you.
. .  „    „    „    „     „     „    „   „  ⌠ him,         Caniyàng „        „ niyá.
                                           ⌡ her, it.
. .  „    „    „    „     „     „    „   „    us.    ⌠ Ating    „      „ ⌠ natin·
                                                   ⌡ Aming          ⌡ namin.
. .  „    „    „    „     „     „    „   „  ⌠ ye,          Ynyòng    „     „ ninyò.
                                           ⌡ you.
. .  „    „    „    „     „     „    „   „    them.        Canilàng  „     „ nilá.
```

Pluperfect tense.

```
. . . . had been loved by  me.          Aquing naíbig, iníbig na; naíbig, iníbig co na.
. . . .  „    „    „   ⌠ thee,          Yyòng    „    „    „    „     „   mo  „
                       ⌡ you.
                      ⌠ him,
. . . .  „    „    „  ⌡ her,            Caniyàng „    „    „    „     „  na niyà.
                      ⌡ it.
. . . .  „    „    „    „   us.  ⌠ Ating.               ⌠ natin.
                                ⌡ Aming   „    „    „  „  „  ⌡ namin.
. . . .  „    „    „    „   ⌠ ye,         Ynyòng  „    „    „    „   „  „ ninyò.
                           ⌡ you.
. . . .  „    „    „    „   them.         Canilàng „    „    „    „   „  „ nilà.
```

Future indefinite tense.

```
. . shall or will be loved by  me.       Aquing iibiguin, (1). iibiguin (1)  co.
.  „     „    „    „    „  ⌠ thee,        Yyòng    „         „        mo.
                          ⌡ you.
. . „     „    „    „    „ ⌠ him,         Caniyàng „         „        niyà.
                          ⌡ her, it.
. . „     „    „    „    „   us.  ⌠ Ating    „        „  ⌠ natin.
                                 ⌡ Aming              ⌡ namin.
. . „     „    „    „    „ ⌠ ye,          Ynyòng  „         „        ninyò
                          ⌡ you.
. . „     „    „    „    „   them.        Canilàng „         „        nilà.
```

---

(1) *U* is here inserted for prosodical reasons to indicate that *g* has not the guttural sound. It may also be written thus, *iibig-in.*

Future perfect tense.

..shall or will have been loved by me.	Aquing maíbig, iíbiguin na; maíbig co, iibiguin co na.				
.do do do „ { thee, you.	Yyòng „	„	„ „	mo,	„ mo ..
.. „ „ „ „ { him, her, it.	Caniyàng .,	„	„ „	niyà,	„ na niyà.
.. „ .. „ „ { us.	Ating { Aming „	„	„ "	{ natin, namin, "	{ natin. " { namin.
.. „ :. „ „ { ye, you.	Ynyòng ..	„	„ ..	ninyò,	„ .. ninyò.
.. „ „ „ „ them.	Canilàng .,	..	.. ..	nilà.	„ „ nilà.

Imperative.

Let....be loved by thee, you.	Yyòng ibiguin, ibiguin	mo
„ .... „ „ „ him, her, it.	Caniyàng „ „	niyà.
„ .... „ „ „ us.	{ Aming { Ating „ " "	{ namin. { natin.
„ .... „ ,. „ ye, you.	Ynyòng „ ..	ninyò.
„ .... „ „ „ them.	Canilàng ,. :.	nilà.

Verbal.

The state of being loved. the action of loving something.	Ang ibiguin.

ROOT GANTI.

Infinitive.

To be rewarded, to reward some one.	Gantihin.

Present indefinite tense.

..is, are rewarded by me	Aquing guinaganti, guinaganti co.		
.. „ „ „ „ thee, you.	Yyòng „	„	mo.
.. „ .. „ „ him, her, it.	Caniyàng .,	„	niyà.
.. „ .; „ „ us.	{ Ating { Aming „	"	{ natin. { namin
.. „ „ „ „ ye, you.	Ynyòng „	„	ninyò.
.. „ ,. „ „ them.	Canilàng ,.	„	nilà.

Present perfect and past indefinite tenses.

..was, wast, wert, were; has, hast, have been rewarded by me.	Aquing guinanti, guinanti co.		
..do do do do do do „ thee, you.	Yyòng „	„	mo.
.. „ „ „ „ „ „ „ him, her, it	Caniyàng „	„	niyà.
.. „ „ „ „ „ „ „ us.	{ Ating { Aming „	" "	{ natin. { namiu.
.. „ „ „ „ „ „ „ ye, you.	Ynyòng „	„	ninyò.
.. „ „ „ „ „ „ „ them.	Canilàng .,	„	nilà.

Pluperfect tense.

..had. hadst been rewarded by me.	Aquing naganti, guinanti na; naganti co, guinanti co na.	
..do do do do do thee, you.	Yyòng ,, ,, ,, ,, mo, .. mo na.	
.. ,, .. ,, .. her, him. it.	Caniyàng ,, .. ,, ,, niyà, ,, na niyà.	
.. ,, ,, .. ,, us.	Ating .. .. .. { natin. { natin. Aming " ,, " { namin, " " { namin	
.. ,, ,, .. ,, you, ye.	Ynyòng ,, .. ,, ,, ninyò, .. ,, ninyò.	
.. ,, ,, ., ,, them.	Canilàng .. ,, ,, ,, nilà, ... nilà.	

Future indefinite tense.

....shall, shalt, will, wilt be rewarded by me.	Aquing gagantihin, gagantihin co.	
.... ,, ,, ,, ,, ,, ,, thee, you.	Yyòng ,, .. mo.	
.... ,, ,, ,, ., ,, .. him, her, it.	Caniyàng ,, ,, niyà.	
.... ,, ,, ,, ,, ,, ,, us.	Ating .. { natin. Aming ,, ,, { namin.	
.... ,, ,, ,, ,, ,, ,, ye, you.	Ynyòng .. ,, ninyò.	
.... ,, ,, ,, ,, ,, .. them	Canilàng ,, .. nilà.	

Future perfect tense.

..shall, shalt, will, wilt, have been rewarded by me.	Aquing maganti. gagantihin na; maganti co. gagantihin co na	
..do do .. thee, you.	Yyòng ,, ,, .. ,, mo. .. mo na.	
... .. ,, her, him, it.	Caniyàng ,, ... ,, niyà. .. na niyà.	
... ,, ,, .. us.	Ating .. .. .. { natin, { natin Aming ,, .. ,, { namin. " " { nam:	
... ,, ? .. ye, you.	Ynyòng ,, ... ,, ninyò . .. ninyò	
... ,, ,, ,, them.	Canilàng ., ... ,, nilà, .. ,, nilà.	

Imperative.

Let.....be rewarded by thee, you.	Yyòng gantihin, gantihin mo.	
,, ... ,, ,. ,, him, her, it.	Caniyàng, .. ,, niyà	
,, ... ,, .. ,, us.	Ating .. ,, { natin. Aming .. " { namin.	
,, ... ,, ,, ,, ye, you.	Ynyòng ,, ,, ninyò.	
,, ... ,, ,, ,. them.	Canilàng ,, ,, nilà.	

Verbal.

—

The state of being rewarded, the action of rewarding somebody.	} Ang gantihin.

The student should conjugate in the passive voice corresponding to *um,* the following roots:

To ascend, to mount.	Acyat, aquiat.
To look at.	Tiñgin.
To listen to.	Diñgig.
To taste, to relish.	Lasap.
To smell.	Amoy.
To behold, to sight.	Tanáo.
To feel, to touch, to grope.	Hipo.
To call for, to call to.	Táuag.
To answer, to reply.	Sagot.
To ask, to inquire.	Tanong.
To receive, to accept of.	Tangap.

———

What is your servant writing?	¿Anò ang sinusúlat nang iyòng alila?
He is writing the letters you gave him this morning.	{ Sinusúlat niyà ang mañga súlat na ybinigáy mo sa caniyà cañginang omaga.
What is Frederic doing there?	{ ¿Anò ang guinagauá diyán ni Pederico?
Frederic is doing what his master ordered him to do.	{ Guinagauá ni Pederico ang yniutos nang caniyàng pañginoon sa caniyà.
To keep company to.	Sumamà.
To be accompanied, to accompany each other.	} Magsamà.
To join, to be put together.	Pasamahin.
Person standing for father, godfather.	Ynaamá.
,, ,, ,, mother, godmother.	} Yniinà.
,, ,, ,, son, godchild.	Ynaanac.
,, ,, ,, brother.	Quinacapatid.
,, ,, ,, father or mother -in-law.	} Binibianán.
Whom are you calling for?	¿Sino ang tinatáuag mo?
I am calling for my servant, who is never at home.	{ Tinatáuag co ang aquing alila, na parating ualá sa báhay.
Nephew, niece.	Pamangquing lalaqui, babaye.

——— — ———

NINETEENTH EXERCISE.

Is your nephew ascending the mountain? He is ascending the mountain, because he wishes to sight the sea. What is your father's godchild's name? My father's godchild's name is Frank. Whom do you love the most? It is my father whom I love the most. Had you not a father, whom would you love the most? Had I not a father, I should love my husband, wife (spouse) the most. Why did his niece wish to accompany this man to church? Because she is his godchild. Who is her godmother? Her godmother is that woman who was looking at the trees yesterday afternoon. Why did Jesus Christ ascend to Heaven? He ascended to Heaven to receive there all the souls of virtuous people here on Earth. Will my sister-in-law's male godchild listen to the good doctrine which Father Santos will preach to him? He would perhaps listen to it if somebody would lead him to church. Do you like to give a relish to that mango there at your sister's table? I scented it just a while and although it appears a tasteful it is not, so then, I will not taste it. Where is the cat which I bought the day before yesterday? She went out because scented that mouse that got into that hole when we were in the garden and the cat concealed herself in the *tinaja*, How many times did the maid-servant go up into the mirador to look for my sister's spectacles? She went up there three times. Why do you not touch me? Because it is a bad custom to touch persons. What is the servant you called for before, doing? He is always running about the streets and when I call for him he never comes or listens, and although he be asked he never replies at all. Why, then, did you receive him? He seemed to be judicious and honest; but he is, on the contrary, naughty and a thief. What books are those your sister is reading? My sister read your books and she is now reading mine. What other books will she read to-morrow? To-morrow she will go out to buy the birds you told her and she will not arrive here in time. What bread has John's brother eaten? He ate the bread his sister gave him.

TWENTIETH LESSON.
YCADALAUANG POUONG PAGARAL.

PASSIVE VOICE (continued).

Pag, is the proper passive particle for *mag. Pag*, is however dropped in most verbs conjugated actively by *mag*, the *um* passive form of conjugation generally being common to both *um* and *mag* active particles.

When *pag* is retained, in cases and for purposes to be explained in subsequent lessons, *in* is inserted between *p* and *a*, thus forming *pinag* for present and past tenses, and affixed to the root for the imperative and simple future. The first syllable of the root should be repeated in the regular way for present and future tenses.

Two verbs of *mag* conjugation are subjoined as an illustration of both forms of the passive.

ROOT.

Part, share.	Bahagui,

To distribute.	Magbahagui.

Infinitive.

To be distributed, (some thing).	Bahaguinin. (1).

Present indefinite tense.

....is or are distributed by	me.	Binabahagui co. (2).
...„ „ „ „ „	thee, you.	„ mo.
...„ „ „ „ „	him, her, it.	„ niyà.
...„ „ „ „ „	us.	„ { natin. namin.
...„ „ „ „ „	ye, you.	„ ninyò.
...„ „ „ „ „	them.	„ nilà.

Present perfect and past indefinite tenses.

...was, were; has, have been distributed by me.	Binahagui co.
... „ „ „ „ „ „ thee, you.	„ mo.
... „ „ „ „ „ „ him, her, it.	„ niyà.
... „ „ „ „ „ „ us.	„ { natin. namin
... „ „ „ „ „ „ ye, you.	„ ninyò
... „ „ „ „ „ „ them.	„ nilà.

(1). For the sake of euphony, this root inserts *n* before *in*, in all the tenses where is to be affixed.

(2). The prepositive form has been here suppressed; students are already instructed that the one made use of in the example is far more common.

Pluperfect tense.

....had been	distributed by		me.	Nabahagui co,		binahagui co		na.		
.... ,,	,,	,,	,,	thee, you.	,,	mo,	,,	mo	,,	
.... ,,	,,	,,	,,	him, her, it.	,,	niyà,	,,	na	niyà.	
.... ,,	,,	,,	,,	us.	,,	natin, namin,	,,	,,	natin. namin.	
.... ,,	,,	,,	,,	ye, you.	,,	ninyò,	,,	,,	ninyò.	
.... ,,	,,	,,	,,	them.	,,	nilà,	,,	,,	ni'à	

Future indefinite tense.

....shall, will be distributed by				me.	Babahaguinin	co.	
.... ,,	,, ,, ,,	,,	,,	thee, you.	,,	mo.	
.... ,,	,, ,, ,,	,,	,,	him, her, it.	,,	niyà.	
.... ,,	,, ,, ,,	,,	,,	us.	,,	natin. namin.	
.... ,,	,, ,, ,,	,,	,,	ye, you.	,,	ninyò.	
.... ,,	,, ,, ,,	,,	,,	them.	,,	nilà.	

Future perfect tense.

....shall, will have been distribut-ed	by me.		Mabahagui co, babahaguinin co			na.			
....do do do do do	,,	thee, you.	,,	mo,	,,	mo	,,		
.... ,, ,, ,, ,, ,,	,,	him, her, it.	,,	niyà,	,,	na	niyà.		
.... ,, ,, ,, ,, ,,	,,	us.	,,	natin, namin,	,,	,,	natin. namin.		
.... ,, ,, ,, ,, ,,	,,	ye, you.	,,	ninyò,	,,	,,	ninyò.		
.... ,, ,, ,, ,, ,,	,,	them.	,,	nilà,	,,	,,	ni'à		

Imperative.

Let	be distributed by	thee.	Bahaguinin mo.			
,, ... ,,	,,	,,	him, her, it.	,,	niyà	
,, ... ,,	,,	,,	us.	,,	natin. namin.	
,, ... ,,	,,	,,	ye, you.	,,	ninyò.	
,, ... ,,	,,	,,	them.	,,	nilà.	

Verbal.

The state of being distributed.	Bahaguinin.

ROOT.

Stealing, to steal.	Nácao, magnácao.

Infinitive.

To be stolen (something).   Pagnácao, pagnacaoin.

Present indefinite tense.

..... is, are stolen by me.	Pinagnanácao co.
..... „ „ „ „ thee, you.	„ mo.
..... „ „ „ „ him, her, it.	„ niyà.
...... „ „ „ „ us.	„ { natin. / namin.
..... „ „ „ „ ye, you.	„ ninyò.
..... „ „ „ „ them.	„ nila.

Present perfect and past indefinite tenses.

.... was, were; has, have been stolen by me.	Pinagnácao co.
.... do do do do do „ thee, you.	„ mo.
.... „ „ „ „ „ „ him, her, it.	„ niyà.
.... „ „ „ „ „ „ us.	„ { natin. / namin.
.... „ „ „ „ „ „ ye, you.	„ ninyò.
.... „ „ „ „ „ „ them.	„ nilà.

Pluperfect tense.

...had been stolen by me.	Napagnácao co,	pinagnácao co na.	
... „ „ „ „ thee, you.	„ mo,	„ mo „
... „ „ „ „ him, her, it.	„ niyà,	„ na niyà.
... „ „ „ „ us.	„ { natin, / namin,	„ „ { natin. / namin.
... „ „ „ „ ye, you.	„ ninyò,	„ „ ninyò.
... „ „ • „ „ them.	„ nilà,	„ „ nilà.

Future indefinite tense.

.... shall, willl be stolen by me.	Pagnanacaoin co.	
.... „ „ „ „ „ { thee, / you.	„ mo.
.... „ „ „ „ „ { him, / her, it.	„ niyà.
.... „ „ „ „ „ us.	„ { natin. / namin.
.... „ „ „ „ „ ye, you.	„ ninyò.
.... „ „ „ „ „ them.	„ nilà.

Future perfect tense.

..shall, will have been stolen by me.	Napagnácao co,	pagnanacaoin co na.	
..do do do do do „ thee, you.	„ mo,	„ mo „
.. „ „ „ „ „ „ him, her, it.	„ niyà,	„ na niyà.
.. „ „ „ „ „ „ us.	„ { natin, / namin,	„ „ { natin. / namin.
.. „ „ „ „ „ „ ye, you.	„ ninyò,	„ „ ninyò.
.. „ „ „ „ „ „ them.	„ nilà,	„ „ nilà.

Imperative.

Let .... be stolen by thee, you.	Pagnacaoin mo.
„ .... „ „ „ him, her, it.	„ niyà.
„ .... „ „ „ us.	„ { natin.
	„ { namin.
„ .... „ „ „ ye, you.	„ ninyò.
„ .... „ „ „ them.	„ nilà.

Verbal.

The state of being stolen.	Ang pagnacaoin.

The student should conjugate the following verbs in the passive voice corresponding to the particle *mag*. Those not marked with *(pag.)* should be conjugated like *magbahagui*.

To dress, to clothe.	Magdamit.
To tell, to report, to narrate.	Magsalitá.
To tell, to say.	Magsabì.
To carry, to convey.	Magdalà.
To explain.	Magsaysáy, magsalaysáy.
To take away.	Magalís.
To wrap up.	Magbálot.
To lend, to loan.	Magótang, (or magpaótang). (pag).
To accompany.	Magsamà. (pag.).

Vessel or ship of any description.	Sasac-yán.
Bank, border.	Dalampásig.
Beach, shore.	Baybáy.
Long.	Mahaba.
Short.	Maiclí.
Large, broad.	Malápad.
Wide, extensive.	Malouáng.
Straight, narrow.	Maquítid, maquípot.
Tight.	Maquipot.
Fish.	Ysdá.
Right. (place).	Cánan.
Left „	Caliuá.
What shall I say to John?	¿Anó bagú ang sasabihin co cay Juan?
Tell him I am calling for him.	Sabihin mo sa caniyà na tinatáuag co siyá.
Enough.! (interject.).	Siyà.
It is already enough.	Siyà na.
Enough! Don't speak any longer.	Siyà na ang salitá.

TWENTIETH EXERCISE.

Why does not the sailor bring here the vessels I bought at the shore? He is still taking them along the banks of the Pasig, and he will not arrive till the day after to-morrow. How broad is the paper you sent to the carpenter's son? It is as broad as this. Is not that stuff short for one shirt? It is not, for although it seems short, it is long and broad. What is the widest of all things? The widest thing is the sea. Are the shoes you brought, tight? They are very tight indeed. Where did your daughter put the two books I ordered her to take to San Pedro? She put them on the bank. On which border, the right or the left? I believe on the left. Has your tailor already clothed your sister's sons? He has not yet clothed them. What did you pray last Sunday at church? I offered the prayers my mother taught me when I was a child. What is that which is obtained by praying? What is obtained by prayer is Heaven. What did the physician's servant tell your mother? He told her his master will not arrive until the day after to-morrow. What have we taken out from Peter's house? We have taken out the timber we bought from him. What is your wish? My wish is to go presently to Peter's to take to him the money of my purchase of timber. What are you thinking? Nothing. What does the curate send to your son at Manila? He sends him these books.

TWENTY FIRST LESSON.
YCADALAUANG POUO,T, ISANG PAGARAL.

VERBAL INSTRUMENTAL CASE.

The pasive voice may assume in the mayority of cases a verbal instrumental form by prefixing to the root in the *um* conjugation, and to the verbal particle in the others, the particle *i* or *y* in all tenses, the first syllable of the root being repeated in the common way for the present and future tenses. The pluperfect and future perfect tenses may be formed by adding to the respective simple ones the completive adverb *na* or some other importing time; but the suppletory way of respectively prefixing *na* or *ma* is to be preferred. In this latter case *i* or *y* should be inserted between the said particles and the simple or compound root.

With a certain group of verbs, comprising those which require two complements, (such as: to give, to tell, to lend, etc.), and those expressing any expulsive or scattering action (such as, to throw away, to sow, etc.) *y* pasive is used to form a passive nearly analogous to that of English. When used with verbs not included in this group, the *y* pasive forms a voice peculiar to Tagalog, gramatically, but not logically, a passive. In these cases *y* points out the instrument with which, the determinate time in which or the reason or cause by which the action is performed, such instrument, time or reason becoming the grammatical subject of the sentence and is put in the nominative, especially when the sentence includes, besides a direct complement, another indirect expressive of any such instrument etc.

ROOT.

Scissors, to make use of scissors. Gonting or gunting, gumonting.

Imperative.

To make use of (such) scissors. Ygonting.

Present indefinite tense

	scissors are made use of by me.	Yguinogonting	co.
....	" " " " " " thee, you.	"	mo.
....	" " " " " " him, her, it.	"	niyà.
....	" " " " " " us.	"	{ natin. / namin.
....	" " " " " " ye, you.	"	ninyò.
....	" " " " " " them.	"	nilà.

Present perfect and past indefinite tenses.

....scissors were; have been made use of by me.							Yguinonting	co.
.... ,, ,, ,, ,, ,, ,, ,, ,, thee, you.							,,	mo.
.... ,, ,, ,, ,, ,, ,, ,, ,, him, her, it.							,,	niyà.
.... ,, ,, ,, ,, ,, ,, ,, ,, us.							,,	{ natin. { namin.
.... ,, ,, ,, ,, ,, ,, ,, ,, ye, you.							,,	ninyò.
.... ,, ,, ,, ,, ,, ,, ,, ,, them.							,,	nilà.

Pluperfect tense.

....scissors had been made use of by me.	{ Naygonting co, yguinonting co na.						
.... do do do do do ,, thee, you.	,,	mo,	,,	mo	,,		
.... ,, ,, ,, ,, ,, ,, him, her, it.	,,	niyà.	,,	na niyà.			
.... ,, ,, ,, ,, ,, ,, us.	,,	{ natin, { namin,	"	,,	{ natin. { namin		
.... ,, ,, ,, ,, ,, ,, ye. you.	,,	ninyò,	,,	,,	ninyò.		
.... ,, ,, ,, ,, ,, ,, them.	,,	nilà,	,,	,,	nilà.		

Future indefinite tense.

....scissors shall, will be made use of by me.							Ygogonting	co.
.... ,, ,, ,, ,, ,, ,, ,, ,, thee, you.							,,	mo.
.... ,, ,, ,, ,, ,, ,, ,, ,, him, her. it.							,,	niyà
.... ,, ,, ,, ,, ,, ,, ,, ,, us.							,,	{ natin. { namin.
.... ,, ,, ,, ,, ,, ,, ,, ,, ye, you.							,,	ninyò.
.... ,, ,, ,, ,, ,, ,, ,, ,, them.							,,	nilà.

Future perfect tense.

..scissors shall, will have been made use of by me.	{ Maygogonting co, ygogonting co na.						
.. do do do do ,, thee, you.	,,	mo,	,,	mo	,,		
.. ,, ,, ,, ,, ,, him, her, it.	,,	niyà,	,,	na niyà.			
.. ,, ,, ,, ,, ,, us.	,,	{ natin, { namin,	"	,,	{ natin. { namin·		
.. ,, ,, ,, ,, ,, ye, you.	,,	ninyò,	,,	,,	ninyò.		
.. ,, ,, ,, ,, ,, them.	,,	nilà,	,,	,,	nilà.		

Imperative.

Let....scissors be made use of by thee, you.			Ygonting	mo.
,, ...,, ,, ,, ,, ,, him, her, it.			,,	niyà.
,, ...,, ,, ,, ,, ,, us.			,,	{ natin. { namin.
,, ...,, ,, ,, ,, ,, ye, you.			,,	ninyò.
,, ...,, ,, ,, ,, ,, them.			,,	nilà.

ROOT.

Casting, to cast, to throw, to fling. Tapon, tumapon, magtapon.

Infinitive.

To be cast, to be thrown away; to cast, } Ytapon.
to throw away. (some thing)

Present indefinite tense.

.... is, are thrown by	me,	I throw	it.	Ytinatapon co.
.... ,, ,, ,, ,,	thee, you;	thou throwest	,,	,,	mo.
.... ,, ,, ,, ,,	him, her, it;	he, she, it throws	,,	,,	niyà.
.... ,, ,, ,, ,,	us,	we throw	,,	,,	{ natin. { namin.
.... ,, ,, ,, ,,	you, ye;	,,	,,	,,	ninyò.
.... ,, ,, ,, ,,	them,	,,	,,	,,	nilà.

Present perfect and past indefinite tenses.

...	was, were;	has, have been thrown by me.	} Ytinapon co.
I threw,	have thrown	it.		
....	do, do;	do, do do	,,	,, thee, you. }	,,	mo.
Thou threwest, hast	do	do.		
....	do do;	do, do do	,,	,, { him,	,,	niyà.
He, she, threw, has	do	do.		,, { her, it. }	
....	do do;	do, do do	,.	,, us.	,, natin.
We	do have	do	do.		,, namin.
....	do do;	do, do do	,,	,, you, ye,	,, ninyò.
You, ye	do do	do	do.		
....	do do;	do, do do	,,	,, them	,, nilà.
They	do do	do.		

Pluperfect tense.

..had been thrown by me,	I had thrown it.	Naytapon co, ytinapon co	na.
·· ,, ,, ,, ,, { thee, { you;	thou hadst ,, ,,	,,	mo,	,,	mo	,,
·· ,, ,, ,, ,, { him, he, { her, it; she, it } had ,, ,,	,,	niyà,	,,	na niyà.
·· ,, ,, ,, ,, us, we	,, ,, ,,	,,	{ natin, { namin,"	{ natin. { namin
· ,, ,, ,, ,, you, ye; you, ye ,, ,, ,,	,,	ninyò,	,,	,, ninyò.
·· ,, ,· ,, ,, them, they ,, ,, ,,	,,	nilà,	,,	,, nilà.

Future indefinite tense

....shall, will be thrown by	me,	I shall throw it.	Ytatapon	co.
.... ,, ,, ,, ,, ,,	thee, you;	thou, wilt ,,	,,	,,	mo.
.... ,, ,, ,, ,, ,, { him, { her, it;	he, she, } will ,, it	,,	,,	niyà.
.... ,, ,, ,· ,, ,,	us,	we shall ,,	,,	,,	{ natin. { namin.
.... ,, ,, ,, ,, ,,	you, ye;	you, } will ,, ye	,,	,,	ninyò.
.... ,, ,, ,, ,· ,,	them,	they ,, ,,	,,	,,	nilà.

Future perfect tense.

..shall, will have been thrown by me.	}	Maytapon co, ytatapon co na.
I shall have thrown it.		
.. do, do do do do „ (thee,	}	„ mo, „ mo „
Thou wilt do do do. (you.		
.. do, do do do do „ (him,	}	„ niyà, „ na niyà.
He, she, it will do do do. (her,		
(it.		
.. do, do do do do „ us.	}	„ (natin, (natin.
We shall do do do.		„ (namin, „ „ (namin.
.. do, do do do do „ (you,	}	„ ninyò, „ „ ninyò.
You, ye will do do do. (ye.		
.. do, do do do do „ them.	}	„ nilà, „ „ nilà.
·They do do do do.		

Imperative.

Let.....be thrown by thee, throw it (thou).		Ytapon mo.
„ · · · „ „ ., him, her, it; let him, her, it throw it.		„ niyà.
		(natin.
„ · · · „ „ „ us, „ us „ „		„ (namin.
„ · · · „ „ „ you, ye; throw it (ye).		„ ninyò.
„ · · · ·· „ „ them, let them „ „		„ nilà.

Root.

News, tidings; to report, to communi- ⁄	Balita, magbalita.
cate intelligence. (	

Infinitive.

To be reported, to be given notice of.   Ypagbalita.

Present indefinite tense.

..is, are reported by me, I report it.	Ypinagbabalita co.
· · „ „ „ „ thee, you; thou reportest „ „	mo.
· · „ „ „ „ him, her, it; he, she, it reports ., „	niyà.
		(natin.
· · „ „ „ „ us, we report „ „	(namin
· · „ „ „ „ you, ye; you, ye „ „ „	ninyò.·
· · „ „ „ „ them, they „ „ „	nilà.

Present perfect and past indefinite tenses.

..was, were; has, have been reported by me.	}	Ypinagbalita co.
I reported; have reported it.		
.. do, do; do, do do do „ you, thee.	}	„ mo.
Thou reportedst, hast do do.		
.. do, do; do, do do do „ him, her, it.	}	„ niyà.
He, she, it reported, has do do.		
.. do, do; do, do do do „ us.	}	(natin.
We do, have do do.		„ (namin.
.. do, do; do, do do do „ you, ye.	}	„ ninyò.
You, ye do, do do do.		
.. do, do; do, do do do „ them.	}	nilà.
·They do, do do do.		„

Pluperfect tense.

.. had been reported		by me.	I had reported it.	Naypagbalita co, ypinagbalita co na.		

.. do do do „ { thee, you. }
Thou hadst do do.   „ mo, „ mo na.

.. do do do „ { him, her, it. }
He, she, it had do do.   „ niyà, „ na niyà.

.. do do do „ us.
We do do do.   „ { natin, namin, } „ „ { natin. namin. }

.. do do do „ { ye, you. }
You, ye do do do.   „ ninyò, „ ., ninyò.

.. do do do „ them.
They do do do.   „ nilà „ „ nilà.

Future indefinite tense.

..shall, will be reported by me;   I shall report it. Ypagbabalita co.

.. „ „ „ „ „ thee, you; thou wilt „ „ „ mo.

.. „ „ „ „ „ him, her it; he, she will „ „ „ niyà.

.. „ „ „ „ „ us, we shall „ „ „ { natin. namin }

.. „ „ „ „ „ ye, you; you, ye will „ „ „ ninyò.

.. „ „ „ „ „ them, they „ „ „ „ nila.

Future perfect tense.

..shall, will have been reported by me.   Maypagbalita co,
I shall have reported it.   ypagbabalita co na.

. do, do do do do „ { thee, you }   „ mo,
Thou wilt do do do.   „ mo „

.. do, do do do do „ { him, her, it. }
He, she, it will do do do.   „ niyà, „ na niyà.

.. do, do do do do „ us.
We shall do do do.   „ { natin, namin, } „ „ { natin. namin. }

.. do, do do do do „ { you, ye. }
You, ye will do do do.   „ ninyò, „ „ ninyò.

.. do, do do do do „ them.
They do do do do.   „ nilà, „ „ nilà.

Imperative.

Let.... be reported by thee, report it. (thou). Ypagbalita mo.

„ „ „ „ him, her, it; let him, her, it report it. „ niyà.

„ „ „ „ us „ us. „ „ „ { natin. namin. }

„ „ „ „ ye, you; report it. (ye). „ ninyò.

„ „ „ „ them, let them report it. „ nilà.

The student should conjugate the following roots in the verbal instrumental form of passive.

Vomition; to cast up, to vomite.	Sucà, sumucà
To cast up, (some thing), to be cast up or the matter thrown out from the body.	Ysuca.
To sow, to scatter seed.	Sumábog, magsábog.
(Some thing) to be sown.	Ysábog.
To spread about, to propagate.	Cumálat.
(Some thing) to be spread.	Ycálat.
To cause to be spread, to cause propagation.	Magcálat.
(Some thing) to be made spread or propagated.	Ypagcálat.
Incandescent wood.	Gátong.
To throw fuel into the fire, (some thing) to be made burnt.	Gumátong, ygátong.
To stir up the fire.	Mag-gáton.
(Some thing) ordered or made to brisk fire.	Ypag-gátong.
Fishing-hook.	Binuit.
(Some thing) to be got by the hook.	Ybinuit.

OBSERVATION.
—

What has been hitherto explained shows that all forms of Tagalog conjugation are inflective, as no separate sign or auxiliary verb is required. Now, with regard to the *y* and *an* Tagalog passive voices, it would be well if the student should consider them as simple purpose-determining verbal forms and that they would always be translated into English by the active voice. By so doing the important matter of Tagalog construction, which is about to follow, will be better understood.

Every passive sentence in Tagalog requires an element (not always expressed) in the nominative, and another in the possessive case, the latter being always the agent of the verb. The element in the nominative may be the direct object or any of the various divisions of the indirect one. In sentences containing a verb in the *y* passive voice the direct complement should be put in the nominative if the action expressed by such verb is of a kind to require this form of passive. (Verbs requiring two complements, verbs of expulsion, etc.)

I will sow this paddy, this paddy will be sown by me.	Ysasábog co itòng pálay; itòng pálay na itò,i, ysasábog co.
I give this money to the poor, this money is given by me to the poor.	Ybinibigáy co itòng salapí sa mañga duc-há, itòng salapí, ay ibinibigáy co sa mañga duc-há.
I threw away your book, your book was thrown away by me.	Ytinapon co ang iyòng libro, ang libro mo, ay ytinapon co.

The second forms of the above sentences are somewhat emphatic. It may be laid down as a rule that any word which is intented to render emphatic in Tagalog should be put at the beginning of the sentence and in the nominative case, somewhat as to say in English, "money!, I have none", by which arrangement, the word "money" is made more prominent than by saying, "I have no money."

———

TWENTY FIRST EXERCISE.

What did you cut out that shirt with? I have cut it out with scissors. How does the carpenter make tables? He makes them with a hammer. Have you cut that stuff with scissors? Yes, Sir, it is with scissors that I have cut it. What has your sister thrown away before in the morning? She has thrown away her pen. Why has she thrown it away? Because it was already worn out. Would they throw away their money, had they any? No, if they had any money they would not throw it away. What shall I do with this fish? Cast it away. What is the news here in town? They say the Judge will arrive to-day. Who reported that to you? Everybody says so. When will your father-in-law report to his children the death of his servant? He will report it next Sunday. Why do you not wish me to drink wine? I do not wish you to drink wine, because you will perhaps vomit. What did you vomit yesterday? I vomited what I had eaten. What would your father sow in his farm, were the weather fine? If the weather were fine, he would sow rice. What is propagated in a large measure by wicked people? Wicked people spread about vice. What did you do with the wood which your farmer sent you? I cast it into the fire. What are you doing there? I am stirring up the fire.

TWENTY SECOND LESSON.

YCADALAUANG POUO,T, DALAUANG PAGARAL.

THE VERBAL LOCAL CASE.

The passive voice may likewise assume a verbal local case which sometimes corresponds to the dative and sometimes to the local ablative of nouns. This kind of passive, it will be seen, also stands sometimes for the direct object of nouns.

The conjugation is made by suffixing *an* or *han*, as the case may be, to the root or compound in all the tenses. *In*, the true passive particle, is preserved throughout, except where it is a suffix, that is to say, in the infinitive, imperative, and simple future, where *in* or *hin* is dropped and replaced respectively, by *an* or *han*.

Sentences with a verb in the local case are generally constructed by putting the person or place, the English indirect object, in the nominative. In cases where *an* passive stands for the direct complement, the latter should be put in the nominative too.

ROOT

Debt, to borrow.   Otang or útang, umótang.

Infinitive.

To borrow from, to be borrowed from.   Otañgan.

Present indefinite tense.

....is, are borrowed from by   me,   I   borrow from. Ynootañgan co.

.... „ „ „ „ „ { thee, you; } thou borrowest „ „ mo.

.... „ „ „ „ „ { him, her, it; } { he, she, it } borrows „ „ niyà.

.... „ „ „ „ „ us, we borrow „ „ { natin. namin. }

.... „ „ „ „ „ { you, ve; } { you, ye } „ „ „ ninyò.

.... „ „ „ „ them, they „ „ „ nilà.

Present perfect and past indefinite tenses.

```
. . was. were; has, have been borrowed from by me.      }  Ynotañgan co.
I      borrowed, have borrowed from.                     }
   . do, do; do.  do  do   do      „   „, thee, you.      }      „      mo.
Thou borrowedst, hast      do    do.                      }
   . . do, do; do,  do   do   do      ., . . him, her, it. }      „      niyà.
He, she, borrowed, has       do    do.                    }
   . . do, do; do,  do   do   do      ,. „. us.           }          { natin.
We      do,     have      do   do.                        }      „    { namin.
   . do, do; do,  do   do   do      .,  „, you, ye.       }      „      ninyò.
You, ye   do,      do      do   do.                       }
   . do, do; do,  do   do   do      „   „, them.          }      „      nilà.
They      do,      do      do   do.                       }
```

Pluperfect tense.

```
. . had been borrowed from by me   ) Naotañgan   co, inotañgan   co na.
I had   borrowed from               )
 . . do  do  do     do  „  „ { thee,  )
Thou hadst do   do        „  „ { you.  )    „          mo       „    mo na.
 . . do  do  do     do  „  „ { him,  )
He, she, it had    do     „  „ { her,  )    „          niyà.    „    na niyà.
                               { it.   )
 . . do  do  do    do  „  „ { us.    )               { natin,         { natin.
We   do  do      do               )    „            { namin,  ”     ” { namin.
 . do  do  do    do  „  „ { you.   )    „            ninyò,   ,,      „ ninyò.
You, ye  do   do         „  „ { ye.   )
 . . do  do  do    do  „  ,. { them. )    .,          nil ',   „      „ nilà.
They  do  do    do               )    )
```

Future indefinite tense.

```
. . shall. will be borrowed from by  me;  I    shall borrow from. Ootañgan co.
· ·  „     „  „  „     „      „   „ { thee,  thou wilt    „ .   „     „    mo.
                                   { you;
· ·  „     „  „  „     „      „   „ { him,
                                   { her,   he she, it will „   „     „    niyà.
                                   { it;
· ·  „     „  „  „     „      „   „ us;    we shall     „    ·     „  { natin.
                                                                     { namin
· ·  „     „  „  „     „      „   „ { you,  you, ye will „    „     „    ninyò
                                   { ye;
· ·  „     „  „  „     „      „   „ them, they      „      „     „    nilà.
```

Future perfect tense.

```
. . shall, will have been borrowed from by me,  )  Maotañgan co, ootañgan co na.
I          shall have borrowed from.             )
 . do,  do  do do   do      „  „ { thee,  )
                                 { you.    )      .,      mo.   „    mo   „
Thou     wilt   do   do    ·do.           )
 . do,  do  do do   do     ↱  ” { him,    )
                                 { her, it. )      .,      niyà.  „    na niyà.
He, she, it will  do    do   do.          )
 . do,  do  do do   do     .,  ., us.     )             { natin.       natin.
We      shall do    do    do.             )      „      { namin ”     ” nam:
```

Future perfect tense. (continued.)

..will have been borrowed from by ye, you.	Maotañgan ninyò, ootañgan na nin.
You, ye will have borrowed „	
.. do do do do do „ them.	„ nilà, „ „ nilà.
They do do do do.	

Imperative.

Let .. be borrowed from by thee; borrow from. (thou).	Otañgan mo.
„ .. „ „ „ „ { him, her, it; } let { him, her } borrow from.	„ niyà.
„ ... „ „ „ „ us; let us „ „ „	{ natin. namin
„ ... „ „ „ „ { you ye; } borrow from. (ye).	„ ninyò.
„ .. „ „ „ „ them; let them borrow from.	„ nilà.

ROOT.

Suffering, to suffer, to bear with pa- tience, to abide.	Batà, magbatà.

Imfinitive.

To be suffered at. to suffer at, to suffer from.	Pagbatahán.

Present indefinite tense.

---

is, are suffered at by me;	I suffer it	Pinagbabatahán co.
„ „ „ „ „ thee, you;	thou sufferest „	„ mo.
„ „ „ „ „ him, her, it;	he, she, it suffers „	„ niyà.
„ „ „ „ „ us;	we suffer „	„ { natin. namin
„ „ „ „ „ you, ye;	you, ye „	„ ninyò.
„ „ „ „ „ them;	they „ „	„ nilà.

Present perfect and past indefinite tenses.

.... was, were; has, have been suffered at by me. I. sufferred, have suffered at.		Pinagbatahán co.
..... do, do; do, do do do do „ { thee, you } Thou sufferedst, hast do do.		„ mo.
..... do, do; do, do do do do „ { him, her, it } He, she, it suffered, has do.		„ niyá.
..... do, do; do, do do do do „ us. We do, have do do.		„ { natin. namin
..... do, do; do, do do do do „ { ye, you. } Ye, you do, do do do.		„ ninyó.
..... do, do; do, do do do do „ them They do, do do do.		„ nilà.

Pluperfect tense.

. . had been suffered at by me. I had suffered at.	Napagbatahán co, pinagbatahán co na
. . do do do do ,, { thee, Thou hadst do do. (you.	,, mo, ,, mo ,,
. . do do do do ,, { him, He,she, it had do do. { her, { it.	,, niyà ,, na niyà.

. . do   do   do   do ,, } us.
We   do   do   do. }
	,, { natin,
	      (namin, ,, ,, { natin.
	                           (namin.

. . do do do do ,, } you, You, ye do do do. (ye.	,, ninyò, ,, ninyò.
. . do do do do ,, } them. They do do do.	,, nilà, ,, nil .

Future indefinite tense.

. . shall, will be suffered at by me;	I shall suffer at Pagbabatahán co.
,, ,, ,, ,, ,, ,, { thee, (you;	thou wilt ,, ,, ,, mo.

.   ,,   ,, ,,   ,,   ,, ,, { him,
                       { her,
                       (it.
	he, she will ,, ,, ,, niyà.

. ,, ,, ,, ,, ,, ,, us.	we shall ,, ,, ,, { natin. (namin.
. ,, ,, ,, ,, ,, ,, { you, (ye;	you, ye will ,, ,, ,, ninyɔ.
. ,, ,, ,, ,, ,, ,, them,	they ,, ,, ,, nilà.

Future perfect tense.

. . shall, will have been suffered at by me. I shall have suffered at.	{ Mapagbatahán co, pagbabatahán co na
. . . . do, do do do do ., } thee, Thou will do do do } you.	,, mo ,, mo ,,
. . . . do do do do ,, { him, { her, He, she, it will have do (it.	,, niyà ,, na niyɔ.

. . . . do do   do   do } us.
We shall do   do ,,
	,, { natin,
	      { namin, ,, ,, { natin.
	                          (namin.

. . . . do do do } you, You, ye will do do ,, ye.	,, ninyò, ,, ninyò.
. . . . do do do ,, } them. They do do do }	,, nilà, ,, nilà.

Imperative.

Let. . . . be suffered at by thee,	suffer at, (thou).	Pagbatahán co.
,, · · · · ,, ,, ,, ,, him, her, it;	let him, her, suffer at.	,, niyà.
,, · · · · ,, ,, ,, ,, us,	,, us ,, ,,	,, { natin. (namin.
,, · · · · ,, ,, ,, ,, you, ye;	suffer at (ye).	,, ninyò.
,, · · · · ,, ,, ,, ,, them;	let them suffer at.	,, nilà.

The student should conjugate the following roots in the local passive.

Theft, to steal.	Nácao, magnácao.
To be be stolen from, person from whom something is stolen.	Pagnacaoan.
Sentry; watchman; to watch, to look out.	Bantáy, magbantáy.
The thing or person watched.	Bantayán.
The place where watch is kept, sentry-box, beat.	Pabantayan or bantayan.
To experience, to note, to observe.	Magmasid.
What to be experienced.	Pagmasdán. (1).
Wound, to wound (purposely).	Súgat. sumúgat.
To be wounded at, what to be wounded.	Sugatan.
Song, to sing.	Auit, magáuit, magcanta. (2).
To be sung with a specific purpose, person in honor of whom something to be sung, or the place.	Pagauitan, pagcantahan.
Saying, say; to say.	Sabi, magsabi.
To be said at a determined place or to some determined person.	Pagsabihan.
Where is my hat?	¿Sáan naróon ang sambalilo co?
I threw it into the garden.	Ytinapon co sa halamanan, pinagtapunan co ang halamanan, ang halamanan ang pinagtapunan co.
To which child did you give that money?	¿Alíng bata ang biniguián (3), mo niyáng salaping iyán?
I gave it to Peter, the son of our neighbour.	Si Pedro, ang anac nang aming caapirbáhay, ang biniguián co.
Where has your daughter been wounded?	¿Sáan sinogatan bagá ang anac mong babaye?
She has not been wounded, but, on the contrary, she wounded her brother on the head.	Siyá,i, hindí nasugatan, cundí bagcús, sinugatan niyà sa olò ang caniyàng capatid na lalaqui.
Whom are you writing to?	¿Sino bagá ang sinusulatan mo?
I am writing three letters to my mother.	Sinusulatan co si inà nang tatlòng súlat.
To go up stairs.	Pumanhic, manhic.
Grand-father.	Nono or nuno.
Grand-son.	Apó.
Great-grandson.	Apó sa tuhod (literally, grand-son from the knee).
Great-great-grandson.	Apó sa talampacan. (lit. grandson from the foot-plant).
Quill.	Bagüís.
Countryman, fellow-citizen.	Cababayan.
Seed.	Binghí.
Widower, widow.	Báuo or balo { lalaqui. babaye.
Wire.	Cauat.

---

(1). Contraction from *pagmaxiran*.
(2). Corruption from Spanish word *cantar*, "to sing".
(3). *Biniguián*, contraction of *binigayan*.

TWENTY SECOND EXERCISE

From whom does the merchant borrow his goods. He does not borrow any goods from anybody, he buys them from other merchants, but he borrowed some money from one of his countrymen some days ago. Who is he whom the baker will borrow money from? He will borrow some from his uncle's carpenters. Had you already borrowed anything from Peter when I arrived here? No, when you arrived here, I had not yet borrowed anything from Peter. Whom shall I borrow from? Borrow from your aunt. Where did Jesus Christ endure many hardships? It was at Mount Calvary where Our Lord endured many hardships.? Shall you have put up with many grievances when you are old? Yes, I shall have stood many grievances when I am old. Whom have you stolen this book from? I stole this book from nobody, it was given to me by my sister. How often did you steal anything from your parents? Three times. How much at a time? Twice, twenty five cents and once one dollar. What is my sister-in-law watching over? She is watching over her plants. And the soldiers, what do they watch over? They watch over towns and roads. What place is the beat (covers) of John? John's beat is the large bridge. What do you wish me to note? I wish you to note this I am teaching (showing) to you. What is it? That happiness here on Earth soon passes away. What did you wound him with? I wounded him with a knife. Where did you wound him? I wounded him in the arm. Who will sing to-night? Alfred's daughter will sing to-night. In whose honor will she sing? She will sing in honor of her father. What does she say? (what is her saying?) She says, oh mother!. To whom did my female cousin say that? She said that to her aunt. Where did you throw the rotten wood? The sea was the place where I threw the rotten wood. Where did the servant put that cheese? The table was the place where he put it. To whom did their brother write? It was his children to whom he wrote. To which house do you wish to go up? It is to your house that I will go up. What is your father's father? My father's father is my grandfather. And your grandfather's son's son? He is his grandson. And your father's grandson? He is his great-grandson. And your father's great-grandson? He is his great-great-grandson. Is your female-cousin still married? No, she is already a widow.

TWENTY THIRD LESSON.
YCADALAUANG POUO,T, TATLONG PAGARAL.

USE OF THE PARTICLE *UM*.

Um is the chief verbal particle to express the unreciprocated act of the agent, either towards himself or others when the action is not modified in number, manner or time, or otherwise carried away from its simplest sense. In many cases it is difficult to decide upon the choice between *um* and *mag* for conjugating a root, many of the latter admitting of both without any appreciable difference of sense. The fact is, however, that *um* looks forward more to the subject; while *mag*, on the contrary, refers more to the object. The student may however derive useful information from the following remarks:

Roots denoting qualities capable of being assimilated by the agent through a slow process, may be conjugated by *um* to indicate the conversion when still in progress.

The shirt is becoming white. (whitens)	Pungmuputí an baro.
The flower became red. (reddened).	Pungmulá ang bulac-lac.
The water will become cold.	Lalamig ang túbig.
The broth had become hot.	{ Nacainit ang sabáo; (better) ungminit na.
Peter will have grown tall.	{ Lalaqui na Si Pedro. (better) nacalaqui na.
The patient is slowly recovering.	Gungmagaling ang maysaquit.
My niece is becoming lazy.	{ Ang pamangquin cong babaye tungmatamad or naguiguing tamad.
Natives are becoming industrious.	Ang mañga Tagalog ay sungmisípag.
Priests are growing cowards.	Ang mañga pare,i, dungmodóuag.
The women will become wise.	Dudúnong ang mañga babaye.
This string is becoming long.	Ytòng lúbid na itò,i, hungmahaba.
Americans will grow richer.	Yayaman pa ang mañga Americano.

Some adverbs may be likewise conjugated in this sense.

Mary's virtue is surpassing Jane's.	{ Lungmalalo ang cabanalan ni María sa cay Juana.

Actions through which the agent gains control of something.

To buy.	Bumilì.
To overtake. to come at.	Umábut, umabot.
To take.	Cumuha.
To receive, to accept of.	Tumangap.
To borrow.	Umótang.
To come across.	Sumompong.
To go out to meet, to meet some body, to welcome.	{ Sumalóbong.
To catch, to plunder.	Humuli.

| To seize. | Dumaquip. |
| To filch, to purloin. | Umomit. |

Voluntary acts of motion.

To run, to hasten.	Tumacbò.
To leap.	Tumalón.
To jump.	Lumocsò.
To flee.	Tumanan.
To walk.	Lumácad.
To swim.	Lumañgoy.
To stop.	Tumahan.
To cease.	Humimpáy.

Purposely performed acts of posture.

To stand up, to spring to one's feet.	Tumindig.
To lie down.	Humiga.
To lean on.	Humilig.
To crouch, to be with buttoks upwards	Tumouar.
To place one's self face downwards.	Dumapa, tumaob.
To place one's self on one's back.	Tumihaya.
To place one's self with one's face ahead, to place one's self in front of.	Tumapat.
To place one's self on one's side.	Tumaguilid.

The steady progress in self-producing, up-growing processes, if represented as continuous and not intermitent or recurring, when their full development has not yet been accomplished.

To put forth shoots.	Sumibol.
To be growing up. (plants).	Tumubò.
To bud.	Umusbong.
To sprout.	Sumupling.

Atmospheric occurrences, provided the root word does not begin in b.

To be windy, to be blowing.	Humañgin.
To rain, to be raining.	Umulán.
To thunder, to be thundering.	Cumolog.
To lighten, to be lightening.	Cumidlat. (1).
To strike (lightening).	Lumintic.

Astronomical transitions when not otherwise expressed and the change is represented as going on, provided the root does not begin with b.

To be growing light, to be sunny.	Umárao.
To be growing late. (to take an afternoon luncheon).	Humapon.
To be growing dark.	Gumabì.
To rise (the sun or any other luminous body).	Sumicat, sumilang.
To set, to be setting (any luminous heavenly bodies), to launch into, to dive.	Lumobog.
To set, to be setting, to get (some one) drowned.	Lumonod.
To be growing dark.	Sumilim, dumilim.
To eclipse.	Lumimlim, lumaho.

(1). The student will easily understand that the root-word for all these verbs is that part which remains after taking away the particle *um*, and that *Q* is changed into *C* before *a. o, u,* Thus the root for *cumidlat* is *quidlat*.

Destructive intentional actions. (1).

To kill, to extinguish.	Pumatáy.
To destroy.	Sumira.
To set fire to, to commit arson.	Sumónog.
To lay waste, to exterminate.	Lumípol.
To wound.	Sumígat.
To pinch.	Cumorot.
To cudgel.	Pumalo.
To cause to break into pieces.	Bumásag.
To split, to cause to break into splints.	Bumali.

Controllable or uncontrollable, but consciously performed acts of the organic functions, and life-supporting actions.

To make water.	Umihi.
To go to stool.	Tumác.
To weep.	Tumañgis.
To sob.	Humibic.
To laugh.	Tumáua.
To sneeze.	Bumahín.
To blow one's nose.	Sumiñga.
To eat.	Cumáin.
To drink.	Uminom. -
To spit.	Lumura.
To bite.	Cumagat.
To swallow, to glut.	Lumamon, lumagoc.

TWENTY THIRD EXERCISE.

Who is growing rich? The merchant is growing rich. Is the niece of our neighbour growing poor? No, she is not growing poor, she is growing healthy; but her child has been aggravated in her sickness. Did the stuff of my pantaloons become shrunk? No, on the contrary, it has been stretched out. Who is growing old? My father is growing old. Is Anthony's son growing tall? No, he is not growing tall, but he is becoming stronger. Did Tagals become wiser? No, they have not yet become wiser. When will they become industrious? When they will become wealthier. Has your sister received already the letters? She has not yet received the letters. What are Americans buying? They are buying lands. What shall I do? Take some bread and go away. What did your cousin reach? He reached some wine. Who has borrowed money? This man borrowed money. What shall we try to attain? We shall try to obtain riches. What did you find? I found some cheese. Whom are you going to meet? I am going to meet my uncle. Did you catch any mouse? I caught one. Whom do sentries seize? They seize thieves. Why do you purloin money? I do not steal, it is the servant who purloins. Why is your daughter running? She is running because she vishes to catch a bird. What is their brother doing? He is leaping into the sea. Why are the children jumping? They are not jumping, they are only walking? Does the sailor know how to swim? He knows how to swim. Where is the stopping place of your father? My father stops here. Why do you not cease sleeping? Because it is early and I went to bed yesterday at mid-night. What did he say? He said, rise first and then place yourself face downwards. Is it not bet ter that I should place myself on my back? No, face me and then lie on your side. How are already the plants in your garden? They shoot

---

(1). If what causes destruction is an inanimate agent, the verb is conjugated by maca. *Ang lindol ay nacasira sa simbahan.* "the earthquake destroyed the church."

and the trees at the bank of the river are blooming. How was the weather yesterday? Yesterday, it rained, thundered, lightened and flashed, and the sun did not shine. Where are you going at present? I am going home, because it is growing dark and the moon will not shine before mid-night. Why does your brother kill birds, waste the plants, wound swine, break plates and split canes? Because he is cruel, although he is cudgeled by my father. Why is the child crying? He wishes to make water and loose his body, just a moment he was laughing when eating and drinking and swallowing fruits. What is to be done? Let him spit and see that the dog does not bite him.

TWENTY FOURTH LESSON.
YCADALAUANG POUO,T, APAT NA PAGARAL.

THE USE OF *UM* (continued).

In actions implying mutuality, the acts of the agent upon others when such action is not reflected back by the latter, are conjugated by *um*.

To accompany, to lead, to conduct persons.	Sumamà.
To chide.	Umáuay.
To speak to, (but not to converse), to bring up a law-suit.	Umósap.
To withdraw, to separate one person from another.	Humiualáy, yhiualáy.
To unite, to associate.	Pumisan.

The acts of our senses, if they are consciously executed by the agent, provided the first letter of the root be not *B*.

To hear.	Dumiñgig.
To look for, to see.	Cumita.
To look at.	Tumiñgin.
To feel.	Humipo.
To smell.	Umamóy.
To taste.	Lumasap.

Bodily actions when performed upon another person and not upon the subject.

To cure others.	Gumamot.
To shave ,,	Umáhit.
To whip ,,	Humampás.
To comb ,,	Sumucláy.
To cut another's hair.	Gumupit.
To wash another's face.	Humilamos.
To scratch others.	Cumámot.

Roots denoting weapons, tools or instruments if conjugated by *um*, express the handling or playing therewith.

To drum.	Gumimbal.
To shear.	Gumunting.
To spear, to dart.	Sumibat.
To stab.	Umíua.
To handle the adze.	Dumarás.
To plane.	Cumatam.

Finally, by *um* are verbalized the acting of the agent upon others, his own motion in actions which, although intransitive, are consciously or voluntarily executed, and those by which the agent draws something towards himself. So, *gumamot*, means "to cure others"; while *mag-gamot* is "to cure one's self"; *lumabás* from *labás*, "outside"; is "to go out", but *maglabás* is "the drawing out" of something. Though "to go out" is an action intransitive in character, it admits, however of volition and is therefore verbalized by *um; matisor*, "to stumble"; is an act importing motion and of an intransitive kind; but is not a voluntary one and cannot, on this account, be verbalized by *um. Umabot* expresses the reaching of something by the agent for himself; *magabot* is his reaching for others.

Sa, "in", "at", or, better to say, an ablative of place, may be conjugated by *um* to denote permanent, but not transitory stay at a place.

God is everywhere or on everything.	Ang Dios ay sungmasaláñgit.
Jesus Christ is in Heaven.	Si Jesucristo,i, sungmasaláñgit.
Americans settle down in the Philippines.	Ang mañga Americano,i, sungmasa Pilipinas.

For the sake of euphony, roots beginning with *um* or any consonant interchangeable with *m* (I) are not conjugated by *um* in the manner hitherto explained.

The passive of *um* is common to most verbs conjugated by *mag*, since the agent becomes patient in the grammatical sense and the transcendent action cannot go beyond. Only when *mag* intensifies the meaning of the action verbalized by *um* in the way to be explained hereafter, or causative or purposely defined acts are to be expressed, *pag, pinag* should be used. It also serves for some verbs conjugated by *maca*, as, *tacotín mo siyá*, "frighten him".

Bring out some food. (generally boiled rice).	Magalís or maglabás ca nang canin.
Take out this nail.	Alisin mo itòng paco.
Order those pictures to be taken out.	Pagalisín (or, better, ypaalís) mo iyáng mañga laráuan (or *cuadro*, Sp.).

Passional circumstances of the subject expressed by *ma* in the active voice of the verb may be conjugated by the passive of *um* to express the correlative active action.

Jane is afraid.	Natatácot Si Juana, si Juana,i, natatácot.
Frighten her.	Tacotin mo siyá.
The horse is hungry.	Nagogotom ang cabayo, ang cabayo.i, nagogotom.
Starve it, make it feel hungry.	Gotomin mo siyá.
Why did your sister allow the poultry to perish from thirst?	¿Báquit bagá inóhao nang iyòng capatid na babaye ang mañga manoc?

TWENTY FOURTH EXERCISE.

Who accompanies you? Nobody accompanies me now. just a moment I acompanied John who was speaking to his sister, she joined Peter, who was scolding his friend and I took him aside. Does the Frenchman hear something? He hears nothing, but I see birds singing on the branches of trees. Who touches women? Only naughty boys touch women. Is your female-cousin doing something? She smells flowers and tastes fruits. What do physicians do? They cure others, but they neither shave, nor

---

(I) The consonants interchangeable with *m*. in conjugation are *b*. and sometimes *p*.

cut (other people's) hair. Whom is your father whipping? He is whipping his servant, because he did not wash his master's face. Is the servant of Peter doing something? He is combing and scratching his mistress. Who will beat the drum? My son will beat the drum, while his friend shears horses. What will you do with that spear? I will spear boars. Who stabbed Magellan? Natives of Cebú stabbed him. Are the carpenters doing something? Some of them are adzing, some others are planing. Where is Our Lord God? God is everywhere and His precious Son is in Heaven at His right. Why did not your servant take out any seats? He is taking some out, but he has already taken out these tables. Do you want anything else? Yes, order him to take out all the plates that were before on the table. What shall I do to the dogs? Frighten them, for the cats fear them and are hungry. Why does my master chide me? He chides you, because you cause the dogs to suffer thirst and the cats to starve.

TWENTY FIFTH LESSON.
YCADALAUANG POUO,T, LIMANG PAGARAL.

IRREGULARITIES IN THE *UM* CONJUGATION.

Owing to a lack of fixedness throughout in Tagalog, some verbs are conjugated in the active voice either by using *ungm*, in the present tense or by prefixing *na* to the root. Outside Manila it is not uncommon to hear natives say: *nabili, nabasá, nasúlat, naráin*. instead of *bungmibili, bungma, ba á, sungmusúlat, cungmacáin*; but the regular conjugation is also in use.

In the present, past and imperative tenses of the active. most dyssillabic verbs admit of an irregularity analogous to that above-mentioned, if they begin in a vowel or in *b, c, p*, or *t*. In such cases a *n* is prefixed to the vowel; *b, c, p, t*, change into *n* for the present and past tenses: *m*, is prefixed to the vowel, and the afore-said consonants change into *m* for the imperative. as seen in the following tables, but the regular form is likewise in use.

Imfinitive.

To return.   Umouí.

Present indefinite tense.

I, thou, he. *etc*., we, you, they, re-   Nonouí acó. ca, siyá. tayo, camí, cayó.
turn, etc.   silá.

Present perfect and past indefinite tenses.

I, thou, he, etc., we, you, they returned.   Nouí acó. ca. siyá. tayo, camí, cayó.
etc; have, etc. returned.   silá.

Imperative.

Return, let him etc., us, them return.   Mouí ca, siyá. tayo. camí, cayó, silá.

Infinitive.

To go for, to fetch. to call for.   Cumaón.

Present indefinite tense.

I, thou, he, etc., we, you, they fetch etc.   { Nañgaón acó, ca, siyá, tayo, camí,
                                              { silá.

Imperative.

Fetch. let him, etc., us, them fetch.   Maón ca. siyá, tayo, camí, cayó, silá.

Infinitive.

To part a line.   Pumátir.

Present indefinite tense.

I, thou, he, etc., we. you. they, part, etc. } Nanatir acó, ca, siyá, tayo, camí. cay ó, silá.

Present perfect and past indefinite tenses.

I, thou, he, etc., we, you, they parted etc; have etc., parted.   Natir acó, ca, siyá, tayo. camí, cayó silá.

Imperative.

Part, let him etc. us, them, part.   Matir ca, siyá, tayo, camí, cayó, silá

Infinitive.

To tempt.   Tumocsò.

Present indefinite tense

I, thou, he, etc., we, you, they tempt etc.   Nonocsò acó, ca, siyá, tayo. camí, cayó silá.

Present perfect and past indefinite tenses.

I, thou, he, etc. we, you, they tempt-ed, etc., have etc. tempted.   Nocsò acó, ca, siyá, tayo. camí, cayó, silá.

Imperative.

Tempt, let him, etc. us, them tempt.   Mocsó ca, siyá. tayo, camí, cayó, silá.

The student should conjugate the following verbs in the preceding irregular form which they all admit.

To captivate.	Mihag, bumíhag.
To retreat, to go backwards, to fall back.	} Múrong, umúrong.
To go for water.	Miguib, umiguib.
To sting, to peck.	Mucá, tumucá.
To gather flowers.	Mitás, pumitás; cumitil nang bulac-lac
To take the lead, to overrun.	Munà, umunà.

Some trisyllabic and polysyllabic verbs having initial letters as above, are conjugated by the particle *man* and they will be treated of in the proper place.

Verbal roots consisting of more than two syllables and prefixed by the particle *pa* are conjugated in a special manner; *um* disappears completely, *pa* is dropped in all the simple tenses; and replaced by *ma* in the future and imparative, and by *na* in the present and past tenses. Here the second and not the first syllable is repeated in the proper tenses. as shown in the subjoined conjugation:

Infinitive.

To conquer, to overcome to vanquish.   Panalo, manalo,.

Present indefinite tense.

I, thou. he. etc.. we, you, they conquer) Nananalo acó, ca, siyá, tayo, cami, etc.   (cayó, silá.

Present perfect and past indefinite tenses.

I, thou. he, etc., we, you, they con- Nanalo acó, ca, siyá, tayo, camí, cayó, quered; have etc. conquered.   silá.

Pluperfect tense.

I, thou, he, etc., we, you, Nanalo na acó, ca na. na siyá, tayo, camí, cayó, silá, they had etc. conquered.   Nacapanalo , „   „   „   „   „   „

Future indefinite tense.

I, thou, he, etc. we, you, they shall etc. Mananalo acó, ca, siyá, tayo, camí, conquer.   cayó, silá.

Future perfect tense.

I, thou, he etc. we, you, they Mananalo na acó, ca na, na siyá, tayo, cayó, silá. shall etc. have conquered.   Macapanalo „ „   „   „   „   „

Imperative.

Conquer, let him etc., us, them conquer.   Manalo ca, siyá, tayo, camí, cayó, silá.

The following verbs are conjugated like *panalo.*

To listen to.	Paquinyig, paquinig.
To receive Holy Communion, to profit.	Paquinábang.
To serve, to wait upon, to flatter.	Panuyo.
To sight, to look at from afar, to behold.	Panóor.
To lodge.	Panuluyan.
To lead, to guide.	Panógot.
To make water.	Panubig.
To trust, to believe.	Paniuala.
To think, to muse.	Panimdim.
To lean on a staff.	Paniín.
To squat.	Paningcayad.
To kneel down.	Panic-lohor.
.Can, to be able, to be able to do.	Pangyari.

To talk, to reprimand.	Pañgósap.
To precede, to go before, to commence, to start.	Pañgonà
To lose by trade.	Pañgulugui.
To shiver, to cramp, to ague.	Pañgiqui.
To quake, to tremble.	Pañginig.
To drowse, to get drowsy.	Pañgimi.
To be jealous.	Pañgimbolo.
To feel a tingling pain in the teeth.	Pañgiló.
Tr keep holidays.	Pañgilin.
To become disdainful.	Pañgilap.
To warn, to be on one's guard, to sneak away.	Pañgílag.
To shake, to shudder, to be panic-stricken.	Pañgilábot.
To be jealous (the married parties)	Pañgiboghó.
To court, to pay addresses to.	Pañgíbig.
To become humble.	Pañgayompapa.
To dream.	Pañgárap, (aloud); panaguínip.
To hurt, to damage.	Pañganyaya.
To see one's self in a glass.	Pañganinó.
To dread, to fear some imaginary danger.	Pañganib, pañgamba.
To bring forth, to lie in for the first time.	Pañgánay. pañgañgánay.
To bring forth, to lie in.	Pañganac.
To bury one's face in the hands.	Pañgalumbaba.
To place one's self with one's arms folded.	Pañgaloquipquip.
To get tired, to become torpid.	Pañgalo, pañgalós.
To become weak, to become meagre.	Pañgalírang.
To get tired from too much standing.	Pañgálay.
To dare, to venture.	Pañgahás, pañgañgahás.
To promise.	Pañgaco, panata.
To pierce, to pass through, to move, to cause emotion.	Panaimtim.
To persevere, to abide, to persist.	Panatili.
To sit on the ground with one's legs crossed.	Panasilà.
To come, to go down, to go down stairs.	Panaog.
To mourn over.	Panambitan.
To trust, confide.	Panalig.
To put one's self under another's control.	Panaguisuyo.
To sigh, to lament.	Panaghóy.
To envy, to bear an envious feeling.	Panaghili.
To offer, to offer the primices.	Panagano.
To hurry on, to incite, to provoke.	Pamongcahi.
To wave (a dog its tail).	Pamaypóy.
To pray, to crave.	Pamanhic, pamamanhic.
To live in a house.	Pamáhay.
To swell.	Pamagá.
To bathe, to take baths.	Paligo.
To rise early.	Paaga.

Roots beginning with h, if conjugated in the instrumental passive may, for euphony's sake, admit the following irregularity. The particle *in* is inverted or it changes into *na* for present and past tenses, as heraeafter.

Infinitive.

To dash it (some thing) to the ground.   Yhólog.

Present indefinite tense.

I, thou, he etc. we, you, they dash / Ynihohólog or ynahohólog co, mo,
etc. it to the ground.   \ niyà, natin, namin, ninyò, nilà.

Past tenses.

I, thou, he etc. we, you, they dashed) Ynihólog or ynahólog co, mo,   niyà,
etc., have etc. dashed, it to the (natin, namin, ninyô, nilà.
ground.

This irregularity applies also to roots beginning with *l* or with a
vowel, especially to those beginning with *ua, ui, uo*, tho they may also
follow the regular conjugation.   Thus, it may be said with equal propriety
ynilagáy, ynalagáy, or *ylinagáy,* "I put it;" *yninalá,* and *yinualá,* "was
lost"; *yninica* and *yinvica,* "pronounced"; and so forth for the present,
thus avoiding the harsh sound produced by the concurrence of two i's.

TWENTY FIFTH EXERCISE.

When will you return to town?   I wish to return there to-morrow.
Whom did you call for?   I called for the physician.   Can you part this
string?   I can part strings, but I cannot part this.   Why did your
friend tempt Jane?   Because she hurt him.   Did the Americans make
many Tagals, prisioners?   Yes, the Tagals fell back and the Americans
laid hold of many.   Where is your servant going for water?   He goes
for water to that well where birds peck husked rice and your sister gathers
flowers.   Where is the child?   The child is ahead, running to take the
lead of Frank.   Who beat the Spaniards?   The Americans beat the Spaniards..   What does Peter do?   Peter listens to the priest and is going to
receive Holy Communion.   Who serves the man lodging at your father's?
Your sister's servant serves him, but now he is beholding the procession.
Who led the Tagals in their war against the Americans?   The Tagals were
led by Aguinaldo whom they trusted.   Where is the child making water?
He is making water in the garden.   What does the oldman think of?
He thinks of leaning on a staff, as he cannot kneel down.   Whom is the
American talking with?   He is talking with some of his countrymen.
Who takes the lead of Alfred?   Frank took the lead of him.   Do you
gain much by your trade?   I gain nothing by it, I, on the contrary, lose
money.   Is the servant shivering with cold?   No, he is trembling for
fear.   Who is becoming drowsy?   Nobody is getting drowsy, but your
friend's friend is jealous and feels a pain in his teeth.   What do priests
say.   They say to every body to keep holidays, and to take great care of not
becoming disdainful to God.   Why is your wife shuddering?   Because
it is thundering.   Why is Jane's husband jealous?   Because she is being
courted by her neighbour.   Do you become humble before God?   Yes,
and every man should become humble before Him.   What did your cousin
dream last night?   He dreamt that he was hurting his sister, and that
she was seeing herself in the looking-glass.   Why does your sister dread?
She fears because she is going to lie in.   Is she going to lie in for the
first time?   No, it is the second time she brings forth.   Why does his

father bury his face in his hands, and use to stand with his arms folded? He got tired and became weak. Do you dare promise to abide by virtue? I persist in doing that. Why does she not go downstairs and sit there with her legs crossed? She mourns over the death of her husband. Do you trust in the Holy Virgin? Yes, I put my confidence in Her. Why is your sister sighing? Because her friend Mary bears her envy and incites her to take a bath. Do you fear that dog? I don't fear him, because he his waving his tail. Do you live in a house? No, I live in the forests. What do you pray me? I pray you to rise early and to bathe in the sea. What have you on your face? It is swollen. Why did your son throw that dog into the sea? Because it bit him. Why do you not give him a good education? Because I did not put him in a college. Why does not your brother speak English better? Because he does not pronounce well. Did you cause the horse to disappear? It was the servant who made it return to the woods. (who is to be blamed for the loosing of).

TWENTY SIXTH LESSON.
YCADALAUANG POUO,T, ANIM NA PAGARAL.

THE USE OF *MAG*.

Mag, may be used with roots beginning with *m*, which should be conjugated by *um* according to their signification, thus avoiding harshness.

To insult, to dishonor others.	Magmurà.
To start, to commence.	Magmolá.
To experience, to perceive.	Magmasid.
To inherit.	Magmanà.
To perceive.	Magmalas.
To enhance.	Magmahal.

Actions by which the subject loses control of something.

To sell.	Magbili.
To lend.	Magótang. (better) magpaótang.
To take along with, to convey one's self to.	Maghatir.
To give, to deliver.	Magbigáy.
To grant.	Magcalóob.
To present with, to make a gift.	Magbiyaya.
To give back, to restore.	Magsaolí.

Moral or material acts moving from the subject, those meaning scattering included.

To say.	Magsabi.
To give notice.	Magbalita.
To explain.	Magsaysáy, magsalaysáy.
To narrate.	Magsalitá.
To permit, to allow.	Magtúlot.
To grant leave.	Magpahintólot.
To show, to make shown.	Magpaquita.
To throw away.	Magtapon.
To forbid.	Magbáual.
To launch a ship.	Magbonsor.
To throw missiles, to pelt.	Maghaguis.
To fell, to cause to fall to the ground.	Maghólog.
To sow grain, to put seeds into a hole.	Maghasic.
To scatter, to waste.	Magbulagsac.
To diffuse, to spread out.	Magsambúlat.
To sow grain by scattering it about.	Magsábog.

Verbs of remotion in the active sense, that is to say, when the moving affects some outward thing.

To draw something nearer.	Maglápit.
To put in, to put into.	Magsilid.

To lift up, to raise, to heave, to elevate.	Magtáas.
To set up.	Magtayó.
To take down, to lower.	Magpanáog.
To fell. (trees).	Magboual.
To remove to a distance.	Maglayo.
To take away.	Magalís.
To place something upright.	Magtindig.

Bodily actions if performed by the subject upon himself.

To cure one's self.	Mag-gamot.
To shave „ „	Magáhit.
To whip „ „	Maghampás.
To comb „ „	Magsucláy.
To cut one's hair	Mag-gupit.
To wash one's face.	Maghilamos.
To scratch one's self.	Magcamot.
To wound one's self, to become ulcerated.	Magsúgat.
To wet one's self.	Magbasá.
To clean one's self.	Maghugas.

Words, either pure or corrupted, taken from Spanish or other alien languages are generally verbalized by *mag.* Roots of offices may take *mag* to express the discharge of official duties.

Mass, to officiate.	*Misa,* (Sp.), magmisa.
To gamble.	*Jugar,* (Sp.), magsugal, (Tag.).
Tobacco, to smoke, to sell tobacco.	*Tabaco,* (Sp.), magtabaco.
Chocolate, to take, to elaborate, to sell chocolate.	*Chocolate,* (Sp.), magsicolate.
To play base—ball.	Magbesbol.
Mayor, to be a mayor, to act as mayor	*Capitán,* (Sp.), magcápitan, magpresidente.
Father, priest; to be a priest.	*Padre,* (Sp.), magpare.

Roots denoting any piece of wearing apparel, may be verbalized with *mag* to express the wearing thereof.

Trousers, to wear trousers.	Salaual,	magsalaual.
Shoes, „ „ shoes.	Sapin,	magsapín.
Spectacles, „ „ spectacles.	Salamín,	magsalamín.
Hat, „ „ a hat.	Sambalelo,	magsambalelo.
Apron, „ „ an apron.	Tapis,	magtapis.

Mag verbalizes all those personal actions which are dual or collective in character, both sides being meant, as:

To fight, to quarrel.	Magáuay.
To join with, to be associated with.	Magtipon.
To converse.	Magúsap.
To assemble.	Magpólong.
To admit the company of others, to join others in company.	Magsamà.
To dispute, to contend.	Magtalo.

Reciprocal verbs when the action is of such a kind as to admit of rivalry or competition, if no special stress is laid on the contention.

To see each other.	Magquita.
To write to each other.	Magsúlat. (better) magsulatán.
To mix with each other.	Maghâlo.
To reconcile to each other, to greet each other.	Magbati.

Voluntary reciprocal actions, especially those of an affective kind, are likewise conjugated by *mag*; but the root should be affixed with *an*.

To love	. each other.	Magsintahan, mag-ibigan.
To aid	,, ,,	Magtoloñgan.
To bear, to suffer	,, ,,	Magpatauaran.
To curse	,, ,,	Magsumpáan.
To cudgel	,, ,,	Magpaloán.
To obey	,, ,,	Magsunuran.
To bite	,, ,,	Magcagatan.
To laugh at	,, ,,	Magtauanán.
To kick	,, ,,	Magtadyacan, magsicarán.
To mock at	,, ,,	Magbiroán.
To use abusive language, to insult each other.		Magtuñgayauán.

TWENTY SIXTH EXERCISE.

Does your brother insult Peter? He does not insult him, he only reminds him of his duty. What shall I do to make myself respected? If you sell anything, grant reasonable prices, and if the goods are not satisfactory, give back the money. Will your father lend any money to his friend? He did not lend him money, he gave and sent him a present. Have your servants reported the tale to their friends? No, they only explained to them that the children had thrown stones on their roof. Why does your father allow you to go out in the night time? He granted me leave to see the launching of the ship. Where did you throw the rotten fish? I dashed it to the ground. Would you fell many trees if you had an axe? No, I wish to sow grain and to scatter some to the poultry. Did you notice the smell diffused by the flowers? Yes, and I plucked one to put it into the pot. What do you intend to lift? I do not intend to lift anything, but I intend to set up a house and to take down these two pictures. Are you going to take the nails away? No, I am going to place the images upright and to remove them far away. Do physicians cure other people? Yes, but they do not cure themselves. Does your friend shave, comb and whip himself? No, but he cuts his own hair and washes himself? Did Anthony wound himself? Yes, yesterday he wet himself to clean his body and on scratching himself, he wounded his skin. What is the priest doing? He is now gambling but he officiated before. Does your son smoke? He does not smoke, but he takes chocolate every evening. Do priests wear trowsers? No, but they wear shoes, hat and spectacles. Do women in your Province wear aprons? They do not. Did Peter and Mary join? They joined, conversed and quarreled. Why did the principal citizens of the town assemble yesterday? They only kept company to each other and they contended together. Do Jane and Frank see each other? They do not see each other, but they write to each other. Do milkmen mix milk with water? They do. What did you do to the brothers Rosario? I reconciled them to each other. Ought married persons to curse and cudgel each other? No, on the contrary, they ought to love, to help, to bear and to pardon one another. Do the Ruiz couple obey each other? No, they bite, laugh and kick at each other.

TWENTY SEVENTH LESSON.
YCADALAUANG POUO,T, PITONG PAGARAL.

USE OF *MAG* (continued).

In using *mag* to verbalize actions admitting of reciprocity, care should be taken in regard to their nature and to the intension and purpose with which executed; for here, as elsewhere in Tagalog, a great laxity prevails. Properly speaking, *mag*, alone, looks more toward plurality than reciprocity. As *mag*, likewise, intensifies or pluralizes sometimes, and sometimes modifies actions verbalized with *um*, a gradation of methods is established to express reciprocity. Thus, *tumiñgin*, means "to look at", in the positive or simplest degree; but *magtiñgin*, signifies, either the "looking at by many", or "to look at" in some intensive manner. Here, *mag* alone, cannot express true reciprocity, for it makes the superlative degree of *um*. So, *magtiñginan* is necessary to make up the reciprocal sense of looking at each other. Reciprocal verbs must be transitive in so far as they require an object that returns the action. If then, the prefix *mag* and the suffix, *an* combine with a root which has not an active sense, but which admits of competition, the action expressed is one of rivalry. *Lumocsó*, for instance, expresses the simple action of jumping, and *maglocsó*, therefore, the action performed by many or in an intense degree; but *maglocsohan* expresses the action of jumping performed by many in competition as to who will excel or surpass the others. If the action is transitive and this latter sense of rivalry is to be expressed, the single suffix *an* is not sufficient and should be repeated, as in the following illustration.

To push somebody out of his place. (This action is active and may be made reciprocal).   Tumolac.

To push hard, to push by many.   Magtólac.
To push each other.   Magtolacán.

The pushing by many of one another in rivalry as to who will push the most.   Magtolacanan.

Sometimes the discrimination between the pluralizing and reciprocal sense is made by changing the accent, as, for instance, in:

To approach (intransitive.)   Lumápit.
To draw near.   Maglápit.
To approach each other.   Maglapit.
To see many things, or to look at intensively.   Magquitá.
To see each other.   Magquita. **(1)**

---

(1). In this as in everything else, we endeavour to convey to the student's mind some idea of the various modifications of sense which a root may undergo if conjugated by *mag*; but they are so manifold that it would be impossible to exhaust them. Practice alone can be recommended on this point.

Actions conjugated by *um* and which admit of intension may be conjugated by *mag* to denote such intension. or plurality, if the action is not otherwise modified in meaning, as:

To run. (simple action).	Tumacbò.
To run by many, or to run a great deal.	Magtacbò.
To write (simple action).	Sumúlat.
To write a great deal.	Magsulat (The word is made acute).
To drink hard, to drink by many.	Mag-inum.
To eat much, to eat by many.	Magcáin.
To read. (many or a great deal).	Magbasà.
To walk. (simple action).	Lumácad.
To walk quickly.	Maglacad. (1).
To weep. (simple action).	Tumañgis.
To weep. (by many or beyond measure)	Magtañgís.

This manner of intensifying the action or pluralizing the agents is not exclusive and may be considered as of a first degree of intension. *Mag* and the repeating of the first syllable of the root intensifies more, and the repeating of the whole root, even more.

To sell in a wholesale manner.	Magbibili.
The following by many in a rapid order of succession.	Magsonodsonod.
To think deeply.	Mag-isipísip.
To meditate profoundly.	Magnilaynílay.

This latter composition with some verbs of motion denotes sometimes to do what the root means and the contrary.

To pass on and to pass back again and again.	Magdaandáan.
He goes out and in, he goes about going in an coming out.	Naglalabaslabasan siyá.

Verbs denoting an unsteady motion my be formed in the same way.

To oscillate.	Magquilingquíling
To wabble.	Magquindingquinding.
To stagger.	Magsúraysúray.
To change continuously the posture.	Magbilingbiling.
To walk with wavering pace.	Magocorócor.
To flutter.	Magbalingbáling.
To place one's self face downward and then on one's back again.	Magbalibaligtad. (2)

Nag, with these and similar verbs may be dropped in the present. the first syllable being repeated.

He walks on tiptoe.	Titiartiar siyá.
He loafs, wanders about; he walks about purposeless.	Susulingsúling.

---

(1). Here, as in many verbs of motion which are grave in accent, the acceleration is expressed, both by *mag* and by making the word acute. The same is the case for other actions which are intensified as seen above.

(2). The orthography of Tagalog words is yet hardly fixed by any rule. The student may perhaps find these words written *mabaling báling* etc. We write them as in the text, this seeming more in accordance with the inflective character of the language.

If an adjetive of *ma* composition is conjugated by *mag*, the sense resulting is one of boasting, swaggering, if the action admits of boasting: but the word is made acute.

To boast wisdom.	Magmarunong.
To swagger.	Magmatapang.
To boast beauty.	Magmariquit.
To boast prudence.	Magmabait.

If the action does not admit of bragging and the adjective is of double composition, the sense is one of assimilation, growing, becoming.

| To become, to grow forgetful. | Magmalimotín. |
| To grow infirm. | Magmasactín, magmasasactín. |

If *mag* conjugates an abstract noun formed with the prefix *ca* and the suffix *an*, the sense resulting is one of putting into practice the corresponding quality; but such words are only used in the infinitive.

To do justice.	Magcatouiran.
To practice virtue.	Magcabanalan.
To act chastely.	Magcalinisan.
To behave one's self obscenely.	Magcahalayan.

The diminutive sense of verbs is formed in the *um* conjugation by repeating the root, (or the first two syllables thereof if consisting of more than two), as:

To run.	Tumacbò.
To rove, to ramble.	Tumacbò-tacbò.
Peter is gadding.	Tumatacbo-tacbò Si Pedro.
To drizzle.	Umulán-olán.

The same diminutive sense in the *mag* conjugation is likewise generally made by repeating the root and affixing *an* or *han*.

| To write. | Magsúlat. |
| To scrible. | Magsúlatsulatan. |

This manner is common to actions admitting of feigning, gesture, imitation or mockery.

To be a hypocrite, to affect virtue.	Magbanalbanalan, magpapaimbabáo.
To nibble or to feign eating.	Magcaincainan.
To snivel, to make crying grimaces.	Mag-iyac-iyacan.
To affect to be deaf.	Magbiñgi-biñgihan.
To „ „ „ sick.	Magsaquit-saquitan.
To „ „ „ mad.	Magololololan.
The playing of children at making little houses.	Magbahaybahayan.

But attention should be paid to the action, as this same composition forms intensive reciprocal verbs which can only be distinguished by the context.

To embrace each other warmly.	Magyacapyacapan.
To look at each other closely or cross-way.	Magtiñgintiñginan.
To reach many things or to pass them from hand to hand.	Magabot-abotan.

Roots denoting things susceptible of being sold or made, if conjugated by *mag*, express the selling or making thereof.

To sell rice.	Magbigás.
„ „ fish.	Mag-isdá.
„ „ pickled fish or to prepare it.	Magbagóong.
„ „ eggs.	Mag-íitlog.
„ make houses.	Magbáhay.

If nouns denothing correlation or relationship serving as complement to a verb or an adjective are prefixed by *mag*, the action referring to the prefixed noun falls back to its correlative party.

To behave well as a son, to know how to be a son.	Marúnong magamá.
To behave well as a father.	Marúnong maganac.
It is difficult to put up with a mother-in-law.	Mahírap ang magbianán.
It is a sorrowful thing to have sons who do not repay our cares.	Masamá ang maganac na hindí dápat.

Some verbs of the *um* conjugation may admit of the two particles to denote a sense of enterprise, endeavour, earnestness.

To endeavour.	Magpumílit.
To make for, to make the utmost exertions for.	Magsumáquit.
To dispatch one's self, to make haste.	Magdumalí.

A second degree of plurality, besides those hitherto explained, may be made by inserting *ñga*, in the active conjugation of *mag*, the *g* of the particle being transferred to the end, thus, *mañgay* for imperative and future, *nañgag*, for the present tense.

To converse. (two or more persons).	Magósap.
To converse (a multitude)	Mañgagósag.
and so forth for other verbs.	

TWENTY SEVENTH EXERCISE.

Why do the boys run and push my old horse in competition with each other? Because they ate and drank much. Did they write and read a good deal? No, but they walked quickly and wept beyond measure; but let them meditate about their passing to and fro. How do persons walk? Drunkards stagger and oscillate, young girls, wabble; fools, flutter; oldmen, waver; sick persons change posture and children walk on tiptoe. What do persons affect to be? Fools, feign to be wise; cowards, to be gallant; women, to be beautiful; rascals, to be prudent, and hypocrites, to be virtuous. What do other persons become? Love-sick persons become forgetful, and old men, sickly. Does the Judge practice virtue? No, but he does justice. What girls act wisely? The judicious act chastely, but the injudicious act obscenely. Did the children rove in the garden? They did, but they could not go on because it is drizzling. Does the son know already how to write? No, he only scribbles a little. Is Alfred's child judicious? No, he, on the contrary, affects to be virtuous, is always nibbling and sniveling and sometimes he feigns to be mad. Why does my servant affect to be deaf and sick when I call out to him? Because he is naughty and and is always playing at making little houses with other boys. What did the father and the son do? They at first looked at each other closely and then embraced each other effusively. What are those men doing? They are handing over sacks to each other. Do you sell rice and fish? I sell pickled fish and eggs and also make houses. Is your brother a good son and a good father? He is not a good father, but he is a good son. Is he also a good son-in-law? He is, although it is very difficult to be a good son-in-law. What does he say to his son? He says to him, endeavour to learn, make every exertion to be happy and dispatch yourself. What were that multitude doing there? They were conversing.

TWENTY EIGHTH LESSON.
YCADALAUANG POUO,T, UALONG PAGARAL.

THE PASSIVE OF *MAG*

As has been said in lesson twenty fourth, the passive of *um* is common to the *mag* conjugation. Thus, *pag*, the passive particle for *mag*, in the imperative or simple future; *pinag*, in the present or past; and *napag*, *mapag*, in the past perfect and future perfect tenses. should not be used, unless they are required to impart some special sense.

To take away.	Magalís.
Take that away.	Alisín mo iyán.
To give back.	Magsaolí.
Give the money back.	Ysaolí mo ang pílac.
I had already given back the pantaloons, when he arrived.	Naysaolí co na ang salaual, nang siyá.i, dungmating.
Where has he thrown his shirt?	¿Sáan ytinapon niyà ang caniyàng baro?
It was the garden where I threw it.	Ang halamanan, ang tinaponan co.
To attain.	Magcamit.
It is easy to say it, and difficult to attain it.	Maralíng sabihin, maliuag camtán.

Pag should be used in the passive if *mag* is used in the active to intensify the action expressed by the verb or to denote plurality.

To destroy many things	Magsirá.
The swine destroyed these many plants.	Pinagsirá nang mañga bábuy itòng mañga halaman.
There are many plants destroyed.	Maramìng halaman ang pinagsisirá.
To count many things.	Magbilang.
Did Peter count much money?	¿Bungmílang bagá Si Pedro nang maraming salapí?
Oh!, he counted more than ten thousand dollars.!	¡Abáa! mahiguit sa sanglacsáng pisos ang pinagbilang niyà.

When, both actions being transitive, *mag* in the active converts the sense of the root from the subjective, as conjugated with *um*, to the objective sense, *pag* should be used in the passive to make this change of meaning clear.

I borrowed that money I gave him yesterday.	Ynótang co iyáng salapí ybinigáy co sa caniyà cahapon.
I will borrow a hundred dollars from John.	Ootañgan co Si Juan nang sangdáang piso.
I lend this money.	Pinagoótang or pinaoótang co itòng salapí, or ypinagpapaótang or ypinapapaótang co itòng salapí.

I bought this hat.	Binil co itòng sambalilo.
This hat is what I bought, this hat is my purchase.	Ytòng sambalilo ang binili co.
I sell these houses.	Ypinagbibili co itòng mañga báhay.
It is to my neighbour that I have sold this rice.	Ang aquing caapirbáhay, ang pinagbilhan co nitòng bigás.

Reciprocal verbs require *pag* in the passive if the motive or place of the action is expressed.

| Those condemned to eternal punishment in Hell curse each other and help one another in doing evil. | Ang mañga napacasamá sa infierno nagsusumpaan silá at pinagtotoloñgan nilà ang pagauá nang masamá. |
| They abused each other at the market. | Ang tiangui, ang pinagmorahan nilà. |

The same is the case with actions of a dual or collective character.

| Gambling was the reason for them to quarrel. | Ang pagsusugal ay and ypinagáuay nilà. |
| They are assembled in the house of your mother. | Ang báhay nang inà mo,i. ang pinagcatiponan nilà. |

Verbs of fiction require likewise *pag.*

| Menial servants feign to be sick, (so as) not to be whipped. | Ang pinagsaquitsaquitan nang mañga alila,i, ang hindí silá paloin. |
| Fools affect to be wise that they may be praised. | Ang ypinagmamarúnong nang mañga bañgal, ay ang silá,i. purihin. |

Active verbs of *mag* conjugation require *pag* if the place where the action is executed is expressed in the sentence, especially when the verb requires the passive of *an* for the direct object.

I paid my personal tax in Manila when I was still there.	Sa Maynila pinagbayaran co ang aquing bouis, nang doróon pa aeó.
Take care of the horses at the enclosure.	Ang bacoran pagalagaan mo nang mañga cabayo.
Your brother put the plate on this table.	Ytòng lamesang itò,i, pinaglag-ian nang iyòng capatid nang pingán.

Transitive actions of the kind of those which are executed for the benefit of others, require the instrumental conjugation with *pag* if the person for whom performed is expressed, the latter to be put in the nominative case.

For whom are you cooking that fish?	Sino ang ypinagluluto mo niyáng isdá?
I cook this fish for my children.	Ang mañga anac co,i, ang ypinagluluto co nitòng isdá.
For whom did Mary sew the apron?	¿Sino ang ypinagtahi ni Biangui nang tapis?
For Jane.	Si Juana.
Make an omelet for this gentleman.	Ypaggauá mo itòng maguinoò nang isàng *tortila.* (corr. from Sp. word *tortilla*)
I would wash your linen, but I have no soap.	Ypaghohogás sana quitá nang iyòng damit, ñguní,t, ualà acóng sabón.

TWENTY EIGHTH EXERCISE.

Did you do what I told you? No, because I don't know what you ordered me to do. What shall I do? Take away that nail and give back the letter to my brother-in-law. Shall I explain to him the death of the bird? No, don't say to him anything about that. What shall I ask him? Ask him when he will come to visit me. Did you not see each other the other day? Yes, we saw each other on the street. Do you wish me to throw away this pin? No, but throw the wood into the garden. What did you report to your barber? I reported to him the sermon of the priest this morning at church. Where did they launch the ship? The ship was launched at Cebú. Have you sown anything at your farm? Yes, I sowed rice. Where did you sow it? I sowed it at the farm, at the beach. What are you putting into that jar? I am putting some bread into it. Where do you intend to build your house? I intend to build it on that ground bearing trees. Where did they quarrel? They quarreled in the room. Where were the Americans conversing yesterday? They were talking to each other on the Escolta, then they fought each other at the large bridge. Why did you help each other? We helped each other, because we were willing to attain a reward. Why did the countrymen fell so many trees? They felled so many trees, because they wanted wood for their houses. Count them if you did not count them. I have counted already more than three hundred. Whom did you buy these needles from? I bought them from the merchant, but I intend to sell them again to tailors. From whom will you borrow the money you want? I will borrow it from my friends. Did your sister-in-law lend you anything? No, on the contrary, she borrowed from me six reals. Why did you cudgel each other at the wood? Because he insulted me first. And did many people assemble there? Oh! yes, many people gathered on the spot of our quarrelling. Why does your servant feign to be deaf? He feigns to be deaf to avoid coming here. Where did your son put my spectacles? Ho put them on your bed. For whom are you making that chair? For my mother. Is it not for your grandfather that you are sewing those pantaloons? No, it is for the priest. Why does not the carpenter wish to make a table for me? It is because he is a lazy fellow.

TWENTY NINTH LESSON.
YCADALAUANG POUO,T, SIYAM NA PAGARAL.

THE USE OF *MA*.

Students should not lose sight of the fact that no intentional or voluntary act, no state suffered voluntarily by the subject or in any way under his control, nor anything occurring through his consent admits of *ma* conjugation, and that, on the contrary, any action, however transitive in character, may be conjugated by *ma* if it takes place accidentally or beyond the subject's control. Thus, verbs as "to run", "to leap", "to go in", "to go out", etc., though intransitive, are not conjugated by *ma* on account of being voluntary acts. Apparent departures from this rule are found sometimes, but these often arise from a difficulty in classifying a particular verb in Tagalog.

To slip, to slide.	Marulás.
To stumble.	Matísor.
To go astray, to lose one's way.	Malihís, maligáo.
To fall down, to fall to the ground, to lose one's standing.	Mahólog.
To die, to die away.	Mamatáy.
To lose, to miss.	Maualá.

But, to make to disappear, to get rid of somebody or of something, and to flee, which are conscious acts, are expressed by *magualá*.

In the same way acts of the mind which, if consciously or purposely executed, are conjugated by *um* or *mag*, are conjugated by *ma* if unconscious or uncontrollable.

To omit doing something purposely.	Lumisan.
To forget, not to have remembered to do something.	Malisan.
To neglect, to try to forget; not to be willing to recollect, to cast into oblivion.	Lumímot.
To forget. (unconscious atc).	Malímot.

Acts of corporal position may be conjugated by *ma*, if they are involuntary or if status and not the action is meant.

To go to bed. (to place one's self in a lying posture).	Humigá.
To be in bed.	Mahigá, nahigá, nahihigá.
To kneel down (consciously), to bend one's knees.	Lumohod.
To make others kneel down, to kneel down with some thing hanging down.	Maglohod.
To kneel down (unconsciously), to be in a kneeling position.	Malohod, nalolohod

To stand, to be in an upright position.	Matindig natindig, natitindig.
To be a prisoner, to be with one's feet in stocks or bilboes.	Nabibilango, napapañgao.
To be seated.	Naupo, nauupo.
To lie with one's face downwards.	Nataob, natataob.

Sometimes the agent's rationality or irrationality determines whether the action is to be conjugated by *ma* or other verbalizing particles, as shown in the subjoined. illustration.

The pupil stands before his master.	Ang nagaáral tungmatayó sa harap nang caniyàng *maestro*. (Sp).
The pillars of my house are upright.	Ang mañga haligue nang aquing báhay natatayo or matuid.
Place those images upright.	Ytayò mo iyáng mañga laráuan.

Uncontrollable passional states of the subject are generally conjugated by *ma*.

To be sad.	Malumbáy.
" " glad.	Malogod, matouá.
" " angry.	Magálit.
" " ashamed.	Mahiyá.
" " afraid.	Matácot.
" " astonished.	Magúlat.
" " terrified.	Magulangtang
" " hungry.	Magótom.
" " thirsty.	Maóhao.
" " sleepy, to be asleep.	Matólog.

As regards other intransitive actions of the subject which are more or less controllable, as to laugh, to weep, etc., their being consciously or unconsciously performed should be taken into account in applying the proper conjugating particle.

Actions of a destructive character when they are fortuitous or accidental, and not caused by the deliberate act of a conscious agent, or when reference is made to an actual state of destruction, take *ma*.

To become destroyed, to be destroyed.	Masira.
To grow dry, faded; to be dried up out of decay.	Matuyó.
To break off, to be broken.	Mabásag.
To be cleft.	Mabali.
To be parted, to be divided, to be cut off.	Malagot, mapatir.
To rot, to become rotten, to be putrid.	Maboloc.

Here, too, the nature of the destroying agent may determine which conjugating particle ought to be employed. For instance: *sónog*, "burning"; if what causes burning is a person, *sumónog*; if it is some inanimate thing, *masónog*.

Mañga, *nañga*, may likewise be introduced in this conjugation to express multitude.

Many persons are dying or dead.	Marami ang nañganamamatáy.
All of them (a multitude) will be sad.	Siláng lahat ay nañgalulumbáy.

If stress is laid upon the involuntariness of some transition of state going on, the slow process of assimilation by a subject may be expresssed by *ma*, *na*.

Your sister is growing mad.	Nauulol ang capatid mong babaye.
She will become a stutterer.	Magagaril siyá.

Also for the sake of briefness, roots denoting some state of destruction may be used alone, and, generally, any actual state which may be gathered from the context, or from the root, or which is manifest, can be expressed in the same way.

The fish is putrid already.	Boloc na ang isdá.
The dog is dead.	Patáy ang aso.
The work is finished.	Tapus na ang gauá.
The letter is ready.	Yari na ang súlat.

Maca and *naca* are sometimes used for *ma* and *na*, to which particles they are respectively analogous in many respects.

He forgot.	Nacalímot siyá.
He is upright. (standing)	Nacatayó siyá.
He sat.	Nacaupo.

Of course, acts verbalized by *ma* do not admit of passive form, but they may be conjugated in the instrumental or local verbal cases, since any occurrence, however intransitive it may be, can have a reason, an instrument, a time or a place by which or where it takes place. *Ca* is the particle used for those forms of conjugation, what nas been said in the eighteenth lesson about the pluperfect and future perfect tenses in the active voice, holding good for these other forms.

INSTRUMENTAL PASSIVE.

ROOT.

Dying, to die.	Matáy, mamatáy.

Infinitive.

To die from, with, of, or at some specific time.	Ycamatáy.

Present indefinite tense.

I, thou, he etc. we, you, they die etc. from etc.	Yquinamamatáy co, mo, niyà natin, namin, ninyò, nilà.

Present perfect and past indefinite tenses.

I, thou, he etc. we, you, they died etc. from etc.; have died etc. from.	Yquinamatáy co, mo, niyà, natin, namin, ninyò, nilà.

Pluperfect tense.

I, thou, he etc. we, you, they had etc. died from etc.	Yquinamatáy co, mo na; na niyà, natin, namin, ninyò, nilà.

Future indefinite tense.

I, thou, he etc. we, you, they shall etc. will etc die from etc.	Ycamamatáy co, mo, niyà, natin, namin, ninyò, nilà.

Future perfect tense.

I, thou, he etc. we, you, they shall etc. will etc. have died from etc.

Ycamamatáy co, mo na; na niyà natin, namin, ninyò, nilà.

Imperative.

Die (thou), let him etc. us, them die from etc.

Ycamatáy mo, niyà, natin, namin, ninyò, nilà.

The student should conjugate in the instrumental passive the following intransitive verbs.

To be ruined. Maduc-ha, malugui. (by trade).
To be lame. Mapiláy.
To be blind. Mabúlag.
To be deaf. Mabiñgí.

LOCAL PASSIVE.

ROOT.

Drowning. Lonor.

Infinitive.

To be drowned at. Calonoran. (1).

Present indefinite tense.

I, thou, he etc. we, you, they, is etc. are drowned at.

Quinalolonoran co, mo, niyà, natin, namin, ninyò, nilà.

Present perfect and past indefinite tenses.

I, thou, he etc. we, you, they was etc. were; have etc. been drowned at.

Quinalonoran co, mo, niyà, natin, namin, ninyò, nilà.

Pluperfect tense.

I, thou, he etc. we, you, they had etc. been drowned at.

Quinalonoran co, mo na; na niyà, natin, namin, ninyò, nilà.

Future indefinite tense.

I, thou, he etc. we, you, they shall etc. will etc. be drowned at.

Calolonoran co, mo, niyà, natin, namin, ninyò, nilà.

(1). This word also means, "the occident", "the west", for natives say: "the Sun is drowned", instead of saying, "the Sun sets".

Future perfect tense.

I, thou, he etc. we, you, they shall etc. will etc. have been drowned at. Calolonoran co, mo na; na niyà, natin, namin, ninyò, nilà.

Imperative.

Be drowned (thou), let him etc. us, them be drowned at. Calonoran mo, niyà, natin, namin, ninyò, ñilà.

The student should conjugate in the local passive the following verbs:

To be with one's feet in stocks. Mapañgao.
To faint, to swoon. Mahilo.
To be tired out. Mapágod.
To be included in. Masac-láo.
To fall down out of decay, to drop off. Malaglag.
To be extinguished. Maotás.

The prefix *ca* is dropped in the local passive of these verbs when no place or deliberate act, but the person affected by the event or chance is meant, as shown in the following instances.

Let him die in the hospital. Camatayán niyà ang *hospital.* (Sp.).
Let his mother die, let him be deprived of his mother by death, let death deprive him of his mother. } Mamatayán siyá nang inà.
In this house I missed my ring. } Quinaualaan co itòng báhay na itò nang aquing singsing.
The ring was lost (missed) to me. Naualaan acó nang singsing.

Sometimes *ma* combines with *mag* in the local passive to denote the source from which something comes.

The ruin of towns comes from war. { Ang pinagcacasiráan nang mañga baya,i, ang pagbabacà, or, ang yquinasisirá etc.

TWENTY NINTH EXERCISE.

Where did your servant slip and stumble? He, not only slipped and stumbled, but fell down in the forest where he went astray. What have you missed, as you are so sad? Death has deprived me of my son. Where did she die? She died in Manila. Why did your sister omit to confess that sin? Because she forgot to confess it. Why was your mother terrified last night? She was in bed when it was thundering, she became terrified and sprang unconsciously to her feet and we found her knelt down. Did you see the thief? Yes, he was face downwards and with his feet in stocks. Is our neighbour hungry or thirsty? He is neither hungry nor thirsty, he is angry. Who is ashamed? Nobody is ashamed, but Peter is astonished. What is the destruction caused by war? Destruction by war extends itself to many things; buildings, are destroyed; trees, are faded; their branches, cleft, and the wires of the telegraph cut off. Why do they not eat that fish? Because it is already putrid. What did my grandmother die from? She died from age. Where did she die? She died in church. Why is that man staggering? Because he is lame and blind, and he is sad because he is ruined. Why does he feign to be deaf? He does not feign to be deaf, he is certainly deaf. Where did the fugitive fail to be drowned? He failed to be drowned in the river. How is your female-cousin? She is tired out and fainted away. Why did this fruit fall down? Because life in the three is being extinguished.

THIRTIETH LESSON.
YCATLONG POUONG PAGARAL.

THE PARTICIPLE.

True auxiliary verbs not existing in Tagalog, the participle, either present or past, cannot assume an invariable form as in English, where it is complementary to the tense and mood of the auxiliary verb with which it is associated. Admitting however, the existence of such a part of speech in Tagalog, it may be said that there are as many participles as there are tenses of the verb (the imperative excepted) in all its forms of conjugation, and that it suffices to make *ang* or some demonstrative pronoun precede any tense of a verb, to form the proper participle corresponding to such verb and tense, or a participial noun or adjective expressive of the same action and tense. Hence, adjectival or subordinate English clauses containing a relative pronoun may be expressed in Tagalog by these participial or adjectival forms of the verb. The tenses of the active voice serve to form the active or present participles, and those of the passive voice, the passive or past participles in all the forms.

To fall down.	Mahólog.
The place of falling (without any reference to time); the meaning, (the range within which any expression comes to an end).	Ang cahologan; ang cahologán.
The place where some thing will fall.	Ang cahohologan.
The place where some thing has fallen.	Ang quinahologan.
The person on whom some thing fell accidentally.	Ang nahologan.
To dash to the ground.	Maghólog.
The thing dashed to the ground (infinitive or indefinite).	Ang yhólog.
The thing to be dashed to the ground.	Ang yhohólog.
What was dashed to the ground.	Ang yhinólog, or, ynahólog.
To befall, to descend upon.	Humólog.
Wisdom descended upon the Apostles.	Hungmólog ang carunuñgan sa mañga alagad (1). ni *Jesucristo*, or, sa mañga *apóstoles*. (Sp.).
Disease befalls our body.	Hungmohólog and saquit sa ating cataouán.
Remainder, surplus.	Tirá.
To leave off (something), to leave something behind.	Magtirá.
To remain somewhere letting others proceed, to separate one's self from the company.	Tumirá.

---

(1) *Alagad or alagar*, "disciple".

To be left behind, to be left remaining at some place.	Matirá.
What has been left behind as a remainder.	Ang ytinirá.
To write, to make readable characters.	Tumític, magtític.
To write, to inform by writing.	Sumúlat.
To believe in, to profess, to vow.	Sumampalataya.
To obey.	Sumunod.
To suck, to draw milk from the breast.	Sumosò.
To nurse, to feed the suckling.	Magpasosò.
The wet nurse, the teat or dug, considered as the feeding place.	Ang sisíua, ang susuhán.
The milk, the feeding substance; the dug or teat considered as to the food drawn from it.	Ang susuhín.
To report, to tell.	Magsalitá.
Reported, told. (without any reference to time).	Salitín.
The reporting person, reporter.	Ang nagsasalitá.
The person who reported.	Ang nagsalitá.
„ „ „ will report.	Ang magsasalitá.
„ „ „ would „	Ang magsasalitá disín.
What was reported.	Ang sinalitá, ang ysinalitá.
The tale to be reported.	Ang sasalitín, ang ysasalitá.
The tale that is reported.	Ang sinasalitá, ang ysinasalitá.
The person reported to. (infinitive or no specific time).	Ang pagsalitaún.
The person to whom something has been reported.	Ang pinagsalitaán.
The person to whom something will be reported.	Ang pagsasalitaún.
To wrap up.	Magbálot.
Wrapped up. (without reference to time, manner or place).	Balotin.
The thing which is being wrapped up.	Ang binabálot.
That which has been wrapped up.	Ang binúlot.
The instrument by which something will be wrapped up.	Ang ybabálot.
The bundle or the thing to be wrapped in, the covering. (indeterminate).	Ang balotan.
The covering which served for something which was wrapped up.	Ang pinagbalutan.
The destruction of Sodom is written in the Holy Scripture.	Ang pagcasira nang Sodoma,i, natítictic sa Santong Súlat.
The coming of Jésus Christ was written in the Holy Scripture.	Ang pagdating ni Jesucristo,i, nacasúlat sa Santong Súlat.
Write on that paper.	Sulatan mo iyáng papel.
This is the paper for him to write upon.	Ytòng papel na itó, ang siyáng susulatan niyà.
On what paper did you write the verses?	¿Anò bagá áng sinulatan mo nang mañga tulá?
What will be written by your father to your brother?	¿Anò ang susulatin nang amá mo sa iyòng capatid na lalaqui?
He has already written to him to come here inmediately.	Ysinúlat na niyà sa caniyà na paritò siyá pagdaca.
Let them write with this pen.	Ysúlat nilà itòng pluma.
Let this be the pen with which the prayer be written by them.	Ytòng plumang itò ang ysúlat nilà nang panalañgin.

Let this be the pen with which you shall write to your school-master.	Ytòng plumang itò, ang ypagsusúlat mo sa iyòng maestro.
He who believes in Christ and obeys (follows) his doctrine will be saved.	Ang sungmasampalataya cay Jesucristo at sungmosonod sa caniyàng áral, siyá, ang mapapacagaling.
That obeying (obedient) boy will be obeyed when a man.	Yyáng batang sungn osonod, sunorin siyá namán cun lumaqui.
A judicious girl is praised by everybody.	Ang mahinhing dalaga,i, pinupuri nang lahat.
The virtuous man was esteemed.	Ang banal na tauò, ay minahal.
This present is for my sweetheart.	Ytòng biyayang itò,i, sa aquing sinisintà.
The person who is loved and reciprocates.	Ang yniíbig, ang sinisintà.
The person who is loved without being aware of it.	Ang naíbig, ang nasintà.
Creed, the Apostles' creed, the believer.	Sumasampalataya.
To kill.	Pumatáy.
The killing poison. (the poison that kills).	Ang pungmapatáy, or, nacamamatáy na lason.
Killed. (without reference to the action or time).	Patáy, patayin.
The man killed. (he who was killed).	Ang pinatáy na tauò.
The deer that is being killed.	Ang usáng pinapatáy.
The dove that will be killed.	Ang calapating papatayin.
The instrument of killing. (indefinite).	Ang ypatáy.
The sword which was used in killing.	Ang ypinatáy na sandatà.
The one which will be used for killing.	Ang sandatàng ypapatáy.
The person whom the death of the victim affects.	Ang patayán.
The place where the murder is to be committed.	Ang patayan. (the word is made grave)
Do do do has been committed.	Ang pinagpatayan.
The place of a wholesale massacre.	Ang pagpatayanan.

THIRTIETH EXERCISE.

What is the cause for many persons to fall down? The cause for many to fall is their stumbling. Is fever a cause of many persons dying in the Philippines? Not only fever, but also other complaints are the cause of many Europeans dying in the Philippines. Where did the servant fall? He fell on the road. Why did he fall down? He fell down on account of his being drunk. By whom has this been dashed? It has been dashed by our friend. What shall we dart to him? Let us throw an orange to him. For whom did the godfather throw the money on coming out from church? He threw it for the boys. How much is the remnant of the money I sent you last week? The surplus is thirty three dollars. How much of it will be left after paying the tailor? There will remain only sixteen reals. Where did my cousin wish to stay the other day? He remained (willingly) at Cavite. And where was their son left behind by his companions? He was left behind in the woods. Did the pupil dictate well? No, but his handwriting is very good. What did he write with? With a quill. On which paper shall I write? Don't write on any paper, you shall write on a board. Do you believe in God? Yes, Sir, I believe in God and obey Him, because God deserves to be obeyed and loved. Does your baby suck still? It is still sucking, as it is only six months old. Who nurses it? It is fostered by a nurse who came from the country. Has she good milk? She has very good milk and her nursering is very good. What news from abroad? Peace has not yet been made. Who reported that to you? The papers say so. Do you trust what papers say? What the papers say is not always true. What will you tell your grandson? I will tell him nothing To whom did the blacksmith report that news? He reported it to my brother's countrymen. What is the woman wrapping in that paper. It is some stuff she is wrapping up. What thing is to be used by her to wrap the stuff up? She uses paper to wrap it up. What do you say? Do not kill mice with a gun, kill them all with poison. How many wild boars will the native kill? He will kill many, for he is clever. What does he kill them with? He kills them with a spear. Where did he kill those seven he brought the other day? He killed them in the forest. What shall you do with that sword? I shall kill my enemy with it.

THIRTY FIRST LESSON.
YCATLONG POUO,T, ISANG PAGARAL.

THE PASSIVE PARTICIPLE.

The studying of the passive particle in all its forms and the special meaning imparted to it by the particle with which it is composed is of great importance in order to understand the most difficult thing in the Tagalog language, that of determining which of the various passive forms of the verb should be used, and for what purpose.

The participles, as has been previously said, taking, by the article which precedes them, the character of verbal nouns expressive of all the tenses of the verb, it follows that there must be a passive participle or participal noun indeterminate in time corresponding to the infinitive in the passive. Now, in primitive verbs, the root without any particle is sometimes used to express tense, when the latter is otherwise determined by some adverb of time or can be easily gathered from the context.

What do you say?	¿Anò ang sabi mo?.
What is being said by you?	¿Anò ang sinasabì mo?. ¿anò ang sab mo ñgayón?.
What did he say yesterday?	¿Anò ang sabi niyà cahapon?.
What will they say to-morrow?	¿Anò ang sabi nilà bucas?. (better) sasabihin.

The same may be said with regard the passive participle; it is better however to use it in the proper tense, if not otherwise determined. or, if stress is laid on the time.

What is the child doing?	¿Anò ang guinagauá nang bata?
What did he do?, what is the work done by him?	¿Anò ang guinauá niyà?.
What will they do?	¿Anò ang gagaoin nilà?
This is what I did.	Ytò ang guinauá co.

If the action is one of acquisition or assimilation on the part of the agent, the *in* passive participle generally denotes the acquisition; that in *y*, the instrument, if the action admits of one, or the reason for the execution; and that in *an*, the person from whom something is got, or the place.

To seek, to look for.	Humánap, cumita.
The thing to be sought, the thing which has been sought.	Ang hanapin, ang hinánap.
The instrument for some thing to be sought.	Ang yhánap.
Do do with which has been sought.	Ang yhinánap.
The place of seeking.	Ang paghanapan.
To take, to obtain, to get.	Cumoha.

Thing to be taken, thing which has been got.	Ang cunin (contraction), ang quinoha.
The instrument.	Ang ycoha, ang iquinoha.
The person from whom or the place wherefrom.	Ang conan (contraction).
To eat.	Cumáin.
Eating, the food which has been eaten.	Ang canin (contraction), ang quináin.
The place, dining-room.	Ang can-àn, cacanán, (contractions).
To drink.	Uminom.
The drink, what has been drunk.	Ang inomin, ang ininom.
The vessel, the tumbler.	Ang inoman.
To buy.	Bumili.
The purchase, the thing which has been bought.	Ang bilhin (contraction), ang binili.
The money with which to buy something.	Ang ybili.
The money with which some thing has been bought or the person for whom.	Ang ybinili.
The person from whom.	Ang bilhán, ang binilhán (contractions)
To reach for the subject.	Umabot. ⎰ Note the difference in ac-
To overrun, to overtake.	Umábot. ⎱ centuation.
Thing to be reached, and which has been reached.	Ang abutin, ang inabot.
The person overtaken.	Ang abotan.
To grasp.	Cumimquim.
Thing grasped, that which was grasped	Ang quimquimin, ang quinimquim.
To ask for.	Humiñgi.
What asked for, what was asked for.	Ang hiñgín (contraction), ang hiniñgí.
The person from whom.	Ang hiñgán. ,.
To snatch, to pray on.	Cumamcam.
Snatched, been snatched.	Ang camcamín, ang quinamcam.
Person from whom.	Ang camcamán.
With what.	Ang ycamcam, ang yquinamcam.

In verbs which govern two objects as those of giving, saying, etc., *in* is generally replaced by *y*, the latter expressing the direct complement or accusative: *an*, the indirect or dative.

		WHAT IS OR WAS DONE.		PERSON TO WHOM.	
To give.	Magbigáy.	Ang ybinigáy.	Ang	big-ián.	
			,,	biniguián.	
To advise.	Maghátol.	Ang yhinátol.	,,	hatolan.	
			,,	hinatolan.	
To say,	Magsabi.	,, ysinab'.	,,	pinagsabihan.	
		,, ypinagsabi.			
To tell.	Magsalitá.	,, ysinalitá.	,,	pinagsalitaan.	
		,, ypinagsalita.			
To give back.	Magsaolí.	,, ysinaolí.	,,	sinaolían.	
To present with, to make a gift.	Magbiyaya	,, ypinagbiyaya	,,	pinagbiyayaán.	
To report, to announce.	Magbalita.	,, ypinagbalita.	,,	pinagbalitaán.	
To teach.	Umáral.	,, yáral.	,,	aralan.	
		,, yniáral.			
To sell.	Magbili.	,, ypinagbili.	,,	pinagbilhan.	
To show, to point out.	Magtoro.	,, ytinoro.	,,	tinoroan.	
To recommend	Magbilin.	,, ypinagbilin.	,,	pinagbilinan.	

In actions which may be considered as performed for the benefit of others, the passive participle with *y*, in the passive voice of *um*, may likewise be made to express the direct complement, although the one in *in* is also admissible; *an*, generally, denotes the place, and *y*, in the passive of *mag*, the person in benefit of whom something is done.

To cook.	Magloto.
Thing cooked.	{ Ang ylinoto, yniloto, ynaloto, lotoin niloto.
The cooking-pan.	Ang lotoán.
The person for whom something has been cooked.	} Ang ypinagloto.
Place.	Ang paglotoán.
To fry, to roast.	Mag-íhao.
Fried, roasted. (present)	Ang yniíhao.
Frying-pan.	Ang ihaoan.
The person for whom.	Ang ypinag-íhao.
To cook in water, to boil.	Maglaga.
The thing cooked, boiled.	Ang ynilaga.
The boiling-pot.	Ang lagaán.
The person for whom.	Ang ypinaglaga.
To reach for others, to pass over, to hand over.	} Magabot.

Sometimes the thing got at as the result of an intransitive action is expressed by the *in* passive participle, if this is not otherwise expressed.

To run.	Tumacbó.
The thing run for.	Ang tacbohin.
To alight.	Lumósong.
The thing alighted for.	Ang losonguin.
To jump, thing jumped for.	Lumocsó, locsohin.
To go out.	Lumabás.
What to be sought in going out.	Ang lalabasin.
To go upstairs.	Pumanhic.
The person found upstairs.	Ang panhiquin.
The staircase, the ladder. (considered as to the action of going up).	} Ang panhican.
To go, to come downstairs.	Panáog, manáog.
What is being sought in going or coming downstairs.	} Ang pananaoguin.
The staircase (considered as to the action of coming down).	} Ang panaogán.

Involuntary intransitive actions do not, of course, admit of *in* passive participle, unless they are made active by their being recombined with some other verbal particle imparting an active sense.

To be afraid.	Matácot.
Being afraid.	Ang natatácot.
Been afraid.	Ang natácot.
The person feared.	Ang catacotan.
To frighten.	Tumácot.
The person that is being or has been frightened.	} Ang tacotín, tinácot.

In fortuitous occurrences by which somebody is affected, the passive participle indicative of the person affected by the event is made, with *an* suffixed; the place, with *ca* prefixed and *an* suffixed: *yca* indicates the cause or time.

To die.	Mamatáy.
The person affected by the event.	Ang matayán, ang namatayán.
The place.	Ang camatayán.
The cause of death or the time.	Ang ycamatáy, ang yquinamatáy.

But if the action is not fortuitous, *ca* should be used.

To be glad.	Matóua.
The person or thing over whom or which one is glad.	Ang catouaan, ang quinatouaan.
The reason.	Ang ycatóua, ang yquinatóua.

Forwards and towards verbs of motion, take *y*, *yca* for the reason, and *an* for the person.

To come. (here).	Paritò.
The person object of the visit.	Ang paritohan, ang pinaritohan.
The reason or time.	Ang ypinaritò.
To go there. (distant place)	Paróon.
The person whom to see or the place.	Ang paroonan.
The reason.	Ang yquinaparóon, ang ypinaparóon.

Y or *yca* with intransitive verbs also indicates time.

To repent.	Magsisi.
The time or the reason.	Ang ypinagsisi.
To sleep.	Matólog.
The time or cause.	Ang iquinatólog.

THIRTY FIRST EXERCISE.

Where shall I look for the shirt? Look for it in the room. With what is it to be sought? Seek it with this light. What have you taken? I took the book from John. Why does the child refuse to eat and drink? He has nothing to eat or drink and besides he has no plate or tumbler. What has he bought? He has bought a flower from Jane. Have you the wherewithal to buy a house? No, I have not the wherewithal to buy it. Why do you not ask from your uncle? I cannot, I snatched from him this money. What is the advice given by you to your son? I advised him (to him) to give back the money to his uncle. What did your father present you with? He presented me with a watch. What has been announced by you to your friend? I reported to him the death of his sister. What is pointed out by that boy? He points out that tree. To whom has he recommended the commission of his servant? He has recommended it to the priest. What are you cooking? It is some fish that is being cooked by me. For whom do you cook it? I cook it for my brother. Will you also fry some bananas for her? I have no time, for she is washing my linen. What does that sailor intend to reach running so much? He intends to reach that dog. Why does Peter jump so much? He jumps to reach some fruit. For whom did you go upstairs? It was my brother for whom I went upstairs. By which staircase did you came down? By that which leads to the front door. Whom are your sisters afraid of? They fear the dead. Let them fear God and let them not allow themselves to be frightened by ghosts. Whom has the neighbour been deprived of by death? His mother has died (to him) (He mourns the death of his mother). When did she die? She died the first day of March. What did she die from? She was drowned. Over whom do you rejoice? I rejoice over my children. Whom will your relation come for? He will come for my sister to behold the procession. Why did my cousin come here? He came here to pay his debts. Whom are you going to visit? I am going to visit the priest.

THIRTY SECOND LESSON.
YCATLONG POUO,T, DALAUANG PAGARAL.

THE MEANING AND USE OF THE VARIOUS KINDS OF PASSIVE

IN PASSIVE.

The meaning and the proper use of the different passive forms of the verb is of the greatest importance in order to master and thorougly understand the language.

In, is the true passive, to be used with most active verbs when the direct object or necessary complement is specifically expressed in the sentence, and no indirect object or circumstance of place, instrument, reason or time as to the action is added.

As there are some active verbs which, for various reasons, do not admit of *in* passive and, on the other hand, some intransitive ones which admit of it, the following general rules are given as to this important matter.

In passive is used in verbs denoting acts of appropriation, either moral or material, on the part of the subject.

VERBS.		PASSIVE PARTICIPLES
To carry away by birds of prey.	Dumáguit.	Daguitin, dináguit.
To despoil, to pillage.	Sumamsan.	Samsamin, sinamsam.
To choose, to select.	Pumili, mamili.	Piliin, pinili.
To scoop, to take out something from a hole.	Dumócot.	Docotín, dinócot.
To borrow some thing. (not money).	Humiram.	Hiramín, hirmín, (cont.). hiniram.
To pray for, to crave.	Dumalañgin.	Dinalañgin.
To implore.	Dumaying.	Dinaying.
To swallow, to devour.	Lumamon.	Lamonin, linamon.
To suck.	Pumang–ós.	Pinang–ós.
To absorb.	Humithit.	Hithitin, hinithit.
To sip.	Humígop.	Hinígop, higopin.
To call for.	Tumáuag.	Tauaguin, tináuag.
To nod for.	Cumauáy.	Cauayín.
To go for, to send for somebody.	Sumongdó.	Songdoin, sinongdó.
To look after, to search for, to search about.	Humalíhao.	Haliháoin, hinalíhao.
To look about for.	Sumalicsic.	Salicsiquin, sinalicsic.
To grope for.	Umapóhap.	Ynapóhap.
To receive, to accept of.	Tumangap.	Tangapin, tinangap.
To go forth to meet somebody.	Sumalóbong.	Saloboñgin, sinalóbong.

The different manners of getting at something, or the instrument or tool serving to take hold of something, generally admit of *in* passive to indicate the thing got at thereby.

Meshed trap to catch boars or wild beasts.	Bating.
What has been caught by a snare of this kind.	Ang binating.
To hawk.	Pañgatí.
The fowl hawked.	Ang pinañgatí, nacatí.
To hunt by a dog.	Pañgaso, mañgaso.
The game taken.	Ang inaso, pinañgaso.
Fishing-rod.	Siic.
What has been caught thereby.	Ang siniic.
Fishing-net.	Lambat.
Fished with a net.	Linambat.
Fishing-hook.	Binuit.
Fish that has been hooked.	Ang bininuit.
Broom.	Ualís, pañgualís.
Sweepings.	Ang iniualís, niualís.

The acts of the five senses in the general or modified sense admit of *in* passive to express the definite result of such acts. Only *tumiñgin*, "to see", "to look at" in a general sense; *timtim*, "to taste a liquor"; are, on account of euphony, conjugated in the *an* passive for the direct object.

VERBS.		WHAT HAS BEEN DONE.
To sight, to see from afar.	Tumanáo.	Ang tinanáo.
To look askew.	Sumuliap.	„ sinuliap.
To behold.	Panóor.	„ pinanóor.
To look backwards.	Lumiñgon.	„ liniñgón.
To hear.	Dumiñgig.	„ diniñgig.
To listen.	Matyag.	„ minatyag.
To relish.	Lumásap.	„ linásap.
To savor.	Numamnán.	„ ninamnán.
To feel, to touch.	Humipo.	„ hinipo.
To smell.	Umamóy.	„ inamóy.
To scent.	Sumanhor.	„ Sinanhor.

Acts of the mind or will, also admit of *in* passive.

VERBS.		
To think of.	Mag-ísip.	Ang inísip.
To remember of.	Mag-alaala.	„ inaalaala.
To wish.	Umíbig.	„ iníbig
To verify.	Umolotsiha.	„ inolotsiha.
To explain.	Magsalaysáy.	„ sinalaysáy.
To consider, to calculate.	Magbúlay.	„ pinagbúlay.
To love.	Suminta.	„ sininta.
To esteem.	Lumíyag.	„ liníyag.
To caress.	Umírog.	„ inírog.

In verbs the action of which necessarily falls upon a person, the *in* passive generally denotes the person.

VERBS.		PERSON WHO IS OR HAS BEEN.
To invite.	Umáquit.	Ang ináquit.
To wait for.	Humintáy.	„ hintín (contraction).
To ask.	Magtanong.	„ tanoñgin. (to whom)
To prevail on.	Magarogá.	„ inarogá.
To reprimand.	Sumala.	„ salahin.
To succor, to carry an infant in arms.	Sumaclolò.	„ sinaclolò.

Verbs of destruction and those implying change or transformation in the object, generally admit of the *in* passive to indicate the result of such change, if no reference as to the instrument or cause is meant.

VERBS.		THING, EFFECT OF THE ACTION.
To do away with.	Gumibá.	Ang guinibá.
To kill.	Pumatáy.	,, pinatáy.
To set fire to.	Sumónog.	,, sinónog.
To unseam.	Tumastás.	,, tastasin.
To change, to exchange.	Pumalit.	,, pinalit.
To blacken.	Umitim.	,, initim.
To set in order, to disentangle.	Humúsay.	,, hinúsay.

The effect of some destructive animate agent is expressed by putting the root indicative of such agent, in the passive of *in*.

Locustus, destroyed by locustus.	Bálang, binálang.
Rat, ,, ,, rats.	Dagá, dinagá.
Crow, ,, ,, crows.	Ouac, inouac.
Ant, ,, ,, ants.	Langam, linamgam.
Kite, eagle; preyed on ,, kites.	Bánoy, binánoy.

In the same manner, verbs of carrying, cutting, weighing, measuring or moving take the *in* passive for what is the result of any such actions, when considered on the agent's side or terminated therein. Thus, "brought," *dinalà*: "sent, *ypinadalà*.

VERBS.		WHAT DONE.
To carry on one's shoulders.	Pumasán, masán, mag-pas-án	Ang pasanin, ang pinas-án.
To drag along.	Humilà	,, hilahin, ,, hinila.
To carry along with, to carry along some thing hanging down.	Magtagláy.	,, taglayin ,, tinag-láy.
To carry along below the armpit.	Magquílic.	,, quiliquin, ,, quinílic.
To carry in one's arms.	Magcalón.	,, caloñgin, ,, quinálon.
To cut. (generic).	Magpotol, mamótol, pag-pótol.	,, potlín, (cont.) pinótol
To tear.	Gumisi.	,, guisiquin, ,, guinisi
To cut out.	Tumabas.	,, tinabas.
To hew.	Tumagá.	,, Tag-ín, (cont.) tinagá.
To fell, to cut down.	Sumapol, magsapol.	,, sapolín, ang sinapol.
To weigh. (generic).	Tumimbang	,, tinimbang.
To measure grain or liquids.	Tumácal.	,, tinácal.
To measure, to ascertain the quantity of a liquid by sounding it with a rod.	Tumárol, magtarol.	,, tinarol.
To move. (one's body)	Cumibo.	,, quinibo.

The prepositive possessive pronouns are conjugated by this passive to assert the property of, or the holding out of something as appertaining to the persons expressed by the pronoun.

MEANING.	PRONOUNS	CONSTRUCTION.
I repute it to be mine.	Aquin.	Ynaaquin co.
I reputed it ., „ thine.	Yyò.	Yniyohin co.
Hold it as thine.	„	Yyohin mo.
I will hold it to be his or hers.	Caniyà	Cacaniyahin co.
Let him hold it as ours.	Amin.	Aminin niyà.
We repute it as ours.	Atin.	Ynaatin natin.
I will hold it as yours. (plur.)	Ynyò.	Yinyohin co.
Make it theirs.	Canilà.	Canilahin mo.

Adjectives formed with *ma* and having an attributive sense may be construed in the same manner.

Just, fair, upright.	Marápat.
I hold it to be just.	Minamarápat co.
Bad.	Masamá.
He will repute that as bad.	Mamasamáin niyà iyán.

The thing made or to be made, or into which is to be transformed some raw or preparatory material may be conjugated by *in*, the matter acted upon being put in the nominative case, if it is not circumscribed in meaning.

I will make shoes out of this leather.	Ytòng balat na itò,i, sasapinin co.
Make pants and aprons out of that stuff.	Yyáng cayong iyá,i, salaualín at tapisin mo.
What is your father going to make out of that lumber?	¿Anòng gagaoin nang amá mo niyáng cáhoy na iyán?
He is going to make a house out of it.	Ysàng báhay ang gagaoin niyà niyáng cáhoy na iyán.
I made a walking–stick out of that log.	Yaóng cáhoy na yaó,i, tinongcor co.

If a noun expressing a condition capable of being assimilated by, or extended to, others, is conjugated in this kind of passive, the subject's design of acquiring such condition, is expressed.

Make him your friend.	Catotohin mo siyá.
I consider you as my father, you are my godfather. (stand as father to me).	Ynaamá quitá.
Consider me as a son, stand a godfather to me.	Anaquín mo acó.

Some intransitive actions which admit of a definite purpose for their performance may be conjugated passively to express the object toward which the action is directed.

To fly, the object of pursuit.	Lumipad, ang liparin.
To run, the thing run for.	Tumacbò, ang tachohin.
To swim, the thing taking hold of by swimming.	Lumañgóy, ang lañgoyin.
To dive, thing dived for.	Sumísid, ang sisirin,
To peep out, what or who was perceived in peeping out.	Dumoñgao, ang dinuñgao.

The sentences with this king of passive are construed by putting the agent in the possessive case and the object in the nominative. If the sentence includes some indirect complement, the case of the latter remains unchanged and the proper preposition should be used, or the verb is put in the other corresponding passive required by the nature of the indirect complement with the latter in the nominative and the direct one in the accusative,

I bought this house.	Binili co itòng báhay, aquing binili itòng báhay.
Your (thy) brother eats the banana.	Quinacáin nang capatid mo ang ságuing.
He killed him.	Pinatáy niyà siyá.
He killed him with the sword.	Pinatáy niyà siyá nang sandatà, ang sandatà ang ypinatáy, niyà sa canivà.
I sought the chicken in the room.	Hinánap co ang sísiu sa silid, pinaghanapan co ang silid nang sísiu,

THIRTY SECOND EXERCISE.

Why do you pillage the fruits, and the clothes which your father wore? These fruits have been selected by me in the garden, and as to the clothes I borrowed them. What is your sister scooping? She is taking out the needle from a hole. What did you crave of your mother? I craved of her to give me the money. What is that child sucking? He is sucking his brother's sugar-cane. Have you called the servant? I did not call him, I nodded for him. Whom are you going for? I am going for the barber. Did he search about for the hammer? He looked about for it. Have you received the letter? I received the letter and now I am going out to meet my friend. Have the Americans trapped these boars? These boars have been trapped by them. How did this man get at these birds and that fish? He hawked the birds and hooked the fish. Has the sailor sighted the ship? He did not sight the ship. At what is the girl looking askew? She is not looking askew at anything, she is beholding the procession. What did they taste? They tasted the wine. What shall we scent? We shall scent those flowers. Do you remember what your father told you? I remember it because I love him. Do you love too your mother? Yes, indeed, I love her. Did she caress her child? She did not. Whom do you invite? I invite my friend. For whom is she waiting? She is waiting for her husband. Whom do you ask? I ask the neighbour. Whom have you reprimanded the other day? I reprimanded my son, because he did not carry his brother in arms. Who has destroyed (done away with) this house? It was set fire to. Why did they not set their books in order? Because they were unseamed. Can you carry this log on your shoulders? No, but I can drag it along. Whose is that rosary you carry along hanging down? It is my mother's. What do you carry below your armpit? It is a prayer-book, for my child cannot walk and I carry him in my arms. Why did you cut the bread and tear my stuff already cut out? I did not do that, I did hew the log and I felled the trunks of banana-trees. Have you weighed the iron and measured the paddy? I only sounded the wine. Why! do you consider this book as mine? I hold it to be theirs. Do you believe it to be yours? No, I repute it to be ours. Do you hold as just what was done by your son? No, I repute it to be wrong. What is he going to do with that stone? He is going to make a church. Why does your friend consider Peter as his father? Because Peter considers him as his son. What is that kite flying for? It is flying for a chicken. Will you overtake your enemy? I shall overtake him in swimming. What does he dive for? He dives for a ring.

THIRTY THIRD LESSON.
YCATLONG POUO,T, TATLONG PAGARAL.

THE MEANING AND USE OF THE VARIOUS KINDS OF PASSIVE.

(continued)

Y PASSIVE.

Generally, the employing of the verbal case passives is decided by the special modification imparted to the action by some indirect complement existing in the sentence. Y passive is, however, essential to those expulsive acts whereby the subject loses control of something by his own will, and to those acts importing throwing, sowing, scattering, spilling, commixing, adding and placing, which do not generally admit of the *in* passive. So, this is the true passive for the verbs which, on no other account than the nature of the action in its simple sense, are conjugated by *mag*, differently from those conjugated by *um*, which latter generally take the *in* passive.

	VERBS.	PASSIVE PARTICIPLES.	
		What to be (indef.)	*What has been.*
To sell.	Magbili.	Ang ypagbili.	Ang ypinag bili.
To give, to hand over.	Mag–gauar.	„ ygauar,	„ yguinauar.
To sell by retail, to do something little by little.	Magotáy.	„ ypagotáy.	„ ypinagotáy.
To throw away.	Magtapon.	„ ytapon.	„ ytinapon.
To sow.	Magsábog.	„ ysábog.	„ ysinábog.
To scatter.	Magbulagsac.	„ ybulagsac.	„ ybinulagsac.
To propagate, to spread about.	Magcálat.	„ ycálat.	„ yquinálat.
To emit, to send forth.	Magsambólat.	„ ysambólat.	„ ysinambólat.
To spill.	Magbohos.	„ ybohos.	„ ybinohos.
To mix, to add some different substance to.	Maghalo.	„ yhalo.	„ yhinalo.
To add.	Magdagdag.	„ ydagdag.	„ ydinagdag.
To unite.	Maglangcap.	„ ylangcap.	„ ylinangcap.
To place.	Maglagáy.	„ ylagáy.	„ ylinagáy.
To heap, to put things in layers.	Magpátong.	„ ypátong.	„ ypinátong.
To sun, to expose something to sunshine.	Magbilad.	„ ybilad.	„ ybinilar.

In actions capable of being executed for and against the subject or in a manual way, distinction should be drawn as to the performance by the subject or by others for him, and as to the manual act considered objectively, or the objetive effect of such act upon other things. Thus:

To stretch out one's arm to reach some thing, is.	Gumauar.
Ang the thing which the subject reaches at or which is handed over to him by others, is.	Ang gauarin.
To stretch out the arm to pass some thing to others, is.	Mag-gauar.
And the thing thus handed over.	Ang ygauar.
To mix in the sense of shaking, is.	Humalo.
The thing shaken.	Ang hinalo.
To mix, to add some thing by mixing it with.	Maghalo.
And the substance thus added to some other.	Ang yhalo.

Y passive is generally used in sentences with verbs the action of which necessarily requires two complements, (although *in* is sometimes used with some of them), when the direct one is discriminately expressed.

VERBS.		Passive participles indicative of the thing done.
To give.	Magbigáy.	Ang ybinigáy.
To present with.	Magbiyaya.	„ ypinagbiyaya.
To tell.	Magsalitá.	„ ysinalitá.
To ask to.	Magtanong.	„ ytinanong.
To teach.	Umáral.	„ yniáral.
To show.	Magtoro.	„ ytinuro.

The ideas of conforming, adjusting a thing to, of transferring translating or copying into, admit of *y* passive to indicate the thing thus adjusted, etc.

VERBS.		The object of the action.
To conform, to render suitable.	Magbágay.	Ang ybinágay.
To compare.	Maghalimbáua.	Ang ypinaghalimbáua.
To equalize.	Magparà.	Ang ypinaià.
To translate, transfer, copy out.	Magsalin.	Ang ysinalin.

Out of the foregoing cases in which the passive of *y* is used in reference to the especially determined direct object of a sentence, *y*, indicates the instrument or cause by which the action is executed, or the specific time in which executed. It is enough to name any such circumstance with the verb in the proper tense of this passive and the direct object (if there is any,) in the accusative, to make up an *y* passive sentence.

What has he made this ganta with?	¿Anòng yguinauá niyà nitòng salop?
He made it with the knife.	Ang itac, ang yguinauá niyà, yguinauá niyà ang itac.
Why do you bear those grievances?	¿Anò,t, ypinagbabatà mo iyáng mañga cahirapan?
I bear them for God's sake.	Dios ang ypinagbabatà co niyán.
At what time did they arrive?	¿Anòng oras ang ydinating nilà?
They arrived at day-break.	Ydinating nilà ang pagbubucang liuánag or liuayuáy.

Y, meaning the instrument.

If an action of those requiring the *y* passive admits of instrument and the latter is expressed in the sentence, this is generally done in the regular way through the proper preposition.

He threw away this sand with a hoe.	Ytinapon niyà itòng buhañgin nang panhócay.
I sow my rice with the hand.	Ysinasábog co ang aquing pálay nang camáy.

If the root denotes an instrument and is conjugable, the root alone in the proper tense of this passive may stand for the whole indirect object if no direct object represented by a noun is stated in the sentence.

What did they kill it with?	¿Anò ang ypinatáy nilà?
They killed it with a gun.	Ybinaril nilà or binaril nilà, pinatáy nilà nang baril.

What is required to accomplish some action and the means of accomplishing it may likewise be considered as an instrument for the using of *y*.

The priest does not officiate to-day, because he has no garments to say mass.	Hindí nagmimisà ang pare ñgayón, sa pagca,t, ualá siyáng damit na ypagmimisà.
He has not the wherewithal to buy this farm.	Ualá siyáng ybili nitòng búquid.
I have the wherewithal to pay you.	Mayróon acóng ybabáyar sa iyò.

Y, meaning the cause.

Y, generally means the cause with intransitive actions.

The reason for my having wept, was my father's death.	Ang ytinañgís co,i, áng camatayan ni amá.
Thou art the cause of my remaining here, I stay here for your sake.	Icáo, ang ytinira co ditò.
I will go upstairs for his sake.	Siyá,i, ang ypapanhic co.
They follow me for my money's sake.	Ang ari co, ang ysinusonod (or yquinasusonod) nilà sa aquin.

The reason or cause for *ma* intransitive actions or in causative verbs, is made by *yca*, which also serves to indicate time with the same verbs.

The ruin of his estate came from gambling.	Ang yquinasira nang caniyáng ari, ay ang pagsusugal.
It is solitude which makes me sad.	Yquinahahapis co,i, ang pañgoñgolila.

The difference between *y* and *yca* as to the cause of an action, is, that *yca* designates thoroughly perfected acts, in verbs the action of which admits of a slow development.

The weather is the cause of his improvement.	Ang panahó,i, ang yguinagaling niyà.
The taking of this medecine was what made his recovery complete.	Ang pag-inom nitòng gamot, ang yquinagaling niyà.

Y, expressive of time.

The sense of time with *y* differs from that of cause, only in that the causative thing is replaced by some word importing time, in the nominative, *yca* being used with the same verbs and for the same purposes as above explained. *Y* expresses time generally with intransitive verbs.

The day my wife will arrive.	Ang árao na ydarating nang aquing asáua.
The hour at which she died.	Ang oras na yquinamatáy niyà.

If the expression of time is a determinate one, it may be put before or after the verb; if it is indeterminate, it should be put before.

On Lent-Fridays, meat should not be eaten.	Ang viernes nang cuaresma di yquinacáin nang carne, or, di yquinacáin nang carne ang viernes nang cuaresma.
The year in which I embarked for the Philippines.	Ang taóng ysinacáy co sa Pilipinas.

CONSTRUCTION.

Sentences which include a verb requiring this passive are construed by putting the agent in the possesive case and the direct object in the nominative.

I threw away the book.	Ytinapon co ang libro.
He cast up (vomited) the milk.	Ysinucà niyà ang gatas.
Peter gave this money.	Ybinigáy ni Pedro itòng salapí.

Sentences in which *y* passive is used to express instrument, cause or time are construed by putting the word indicative of any such circumstance in the nominative, and the direct complement (if there is one), in the accusative, whith the agent always in the possessive case.

With this string you will fasten the prisoner's hands to his back.	Ytòng pantali ygagapós mo sa bilangoin; ygagapús mo sa bilangoin itòng pantali.
It was on account of her that I came here.	Siyá, ang yquinaparitò or ypinaritò co.
We went away yesterday.	Cahapon, ang ynialís natin.

The putting of the nominative before the verb and the using of the latter in the participial sense, makes the expression somewhat emphatic.

The indirect object of an action performed for the benefit of others, or the person for whom some act is executed, may be put in the nominative with the verb in the proper tense of the *y* passive.

Buy me (for me) this gun.	Ybili mo acó nitòng baril.
Make chocolate for Father Charles.	Ypagloto mo si Pare Carlos nang sicolate.
Have a house made for me.	Ypagbáhay mo acó.
Roaring, bustle, hum.	Ugong.

THIRTY THIRD EXERCISE.

What did the merchant sell by retail? He sold my sister's needles and pins. What do you throw into the fire? I wish to throw my father's wood into the fire. Why does your cousin sow rice on his farm? Because it sends forth a good smell. What did the native mix (add to) with the wine? Water. What did the merchant add to the butter? He added my father's tallow to it. What did your cousin put on that table? He put there my sister's prayer-book. Why do you expose that linen to the sun? Because it was wet. What do you present your mother with? I presented her with a pair of spectacles yesterday. What did he say to your sister-in-law? He asked her about the state of her aunt. What hast thou taught this child? I taught him the doctrine. Which did they show your female-cousin? They showed her my fan. What does the pupil copy? He copies the verses. What have you cut my bread with? I cut it with your knife. What have you written his letter with? I wrote it with a pencil. What has he wounded our friend with? With a stick. Why do you not pay me? Because I have no money to pay with. With what money will Peter buy the bed? He will buy it with the money he received from me. Why does that woman weep so much? Because death deprived her of her child. Why had he remained here? He had remained here for Ann's sake. Why do soldiers obey their chiefs? They obey them through fear. What made him completely wealthy? The sale of hides rounded out his fortune. When would he arrive at the sea had he departed in time? He would have arrived there to-morrow by ten o'clock. Whom are you going to visit here? I came to visit you.

THIRTY FOURTH LESSON.
YCATLONG POUO,T, APAT NA PAGARAL.

THE MEANING AND USE OF THE VARIOUS KINDS OF PASSIVE.
(continued.)

AN PASSIVE.

An passive is but rarely employed in reference to the direct object. There are, however, some verbs which, although requiring the *in* passive if looked upon in regard to the nature of the action, are, for the sake of euphony or the contractions they undergo, conjugated by *an* for the direct complement.

To see,	what seen.	Tumiñgin,	ang tingnán *(*cont.)
To experience,	,, experienced.	Magmasid,	,, pagmasdán. (cont.)
To salt,	,, salted.	Magasín,	,, asnán. (,,)
To pierce,	,, pierced.	Tumalab,	,, tablán. (,,)
To hold, to grasp;	,, held, etc.	Tumañgán. / Magtañgan;	,, tañgán. (,,)
To taste,	,, tasted.	Tumiquim,	,, ticman. (,,)
To pay for	,, paid for.	Magbayad	,, bayaran (,,)

Magáral, "to learn"; admits of *pagaralan* for what is learnt.

Verbs, the action of which properly requires a person as their direct complement, generally take *an* passive to indicate whom the acction falls upon.

VERBS.		PERSON, OBJECT OF THE ACTION.
To threaten.	Magbala.	Ang pagbaláan.
To cohabitate with.	Magapir.	,, apdán. (cont.) (the female party)
To frighten by suddenly rushing out.	Bumalacá.	,, balacaán.
To clothe.	Dumamit.	,, damtán. (cont.)
To deceive.	Magdaya.	,, pagdayáan.
To kiss.	Humalic.	,, hagcán. (cont.)
To smack.	Maghalic.	,, pinaghagcán, (cont.)
To clean of lice.	Humiñgoto.	.. hiñgotán. (cont.)

Sometimes *an* indicates the person, *in*, the thing.

To unfasten, to absolve.	Cumalag.
The person absolved.	Ang calgán. (cont.)
The thing unfastened.	Ang calguín. (cont.)
To hear.	Dumiñgig.
The person listened to.	Ang dingán. (cont.)
What head.	Ang dinguín. (cont.)

If the action is such as to admit a place for its direct object, the latter is generally expressed by the *an* passive.

To open, to lay open.	Magbucás.	Ang bucasan, bucsán. (cont.)
To sprinkle with water from the mouth.	Bumuga. Magbuga.	„ Bughán. (cont.)
To plant.	Magtanim.	„ tamnán. (cont.)
To fill.	Mamonó, magpono.	„ ponan. (cont.)
To line.	Magsapin.	„ sapnán. (cont.)
To cover.	Tumaquip.	„ tacpán. (cont.)

Open the door.	Bucsán mo ang pinto.
John planted his farm.	Tinamnán ni Juan ang caniyàng búquid.
Will they fill the vat?	¿Poponán bagá nilà ang tapayan?
He had already covered the table when I arrived.	Natacpán na niyà ang lamesa nang acó,i, dungmating.

But, most commonly, *an* stands for the local ablative and replaces the adverb of place or the proposition which otherwise should have been, and is to be employed, if the verb obtains in any other form of conjugation. Thus, if a sentence with a verb other than those of the class above-stated includes an indirect complement of place relating to the action, it is enough to name such place with the verb in this passive to express the relation of case which is in English made up by means of a preposition.

Jane is gathering flowers in the garden.	Ang halamana,i, ang lugar na pinipitasan ni Juana nang mañga bulac-lac.
In this house my father died.	Ytòng báhay na itò, ang quinamatayán ni amá.

It may be said that *an* replaces *sa*, a preposition which governs the ablative and sometimes the accusative cases, but which is more adapted to the dative. Hence, if in a sentence, there enters in English a dative of person governed by the preposition "to", (1). the person may be named in the nominative with the verb in the pasive of *an*.

He gave me this nail.	Biniguián niyà acó nitòng paco. Acó, ang binig-ián niyà nitòng paco.
Whom have they sold my shirt to?	¿Sino bagá ang pinagbilhan nilà nang aquing baro.
They sold it to their friends.	Pinagbilhan nilà ang canilàng mañga caibigan, or, ang mañga caibigan nilà ang pinagbilhan nilà.
Are you admonishing Alfred?	¿Pinañguñgusapan bagá ninyò si Alpredo?.
It is not Alfred, but his sister that we are admonishing.	Hindí Si Alpredo, cundí ang caniyàng capatid na babaye ang pinañguñgusapan namin.

An, also stands for the person from whom something comes, in actions by which the subject tries to draw something to himself.

---

(1). "To", governs the dative case when the action is of such a kind as to make the subject part with something. If it is of a mercenary or associative kind and performed for the benefit, or in behalf of others, or if the dative is of *acquisition*, "for" should then be used. We have seen that "for" in this case is translated by the *y* passive. "She sews these pantaloons for me". *Ypinagtatahi niyà acó nitòng salaual.*

VERBS.		PERSON FROM WHOM.
To buy.	Bumilí.	Ang bilhan.
To take.	Cumuha, muha.	„ conan. (cont. and inversion.)
To seek, to claim.	Humánap.	„ hanapan.
To receive, to accept.	Tumangap.	„ tangapán.
To ask for, to require of.	Humiñgi.	„ hiñgán.
To entreat, to pray.	Dumaing.	„ daiñgan.

Sometimes the discrimination between place and person is made by *pag* when the action admits of a place.

VERBS.		PLACE WHERE.
To seek.	Humánap.	Ang paghanapan.
To claim payment, to get one's self paid.	Sumiñgil.	„ pagsiñgilán.

CONSTRUCTION.

When the verb is such as to require the *an* passive in reference to the direct object, the sentence is construed by putting the agent in the possessive case and the direct object in the nominative.

Hold this candle.	Tangnán mo itòng candila.
The son kisses his mother.	Hinahagcán nang anac ang caniyàng irà.
Prop the tree.	Tucoran mo ang cáhoy.

If the sentence includes, besides a direct complement, an indirect one of place, the latter is put in the nominative and the direct one in the accusative.

My grandfather plants a variety of trees in the garden.	Tinatamnán ni nono nang sarisaring cáhoy ang halamanan.
Have you looked for the servant in this road?	¿Pinaghanapan mo bagá sa alila itòng daáng itò?

If *an* stands for a place or a person in the ablative or dative cases, the place or person should be named (that is to say, put in the nominative) and the remainder as above; the agent, in the possessive, and the direct complement, in the accusative. The indirect complement may be put before or after the verb, unless an interrogative pronoun or adverb of place be used in its stead in interrogative sentences, in which case, the adverb or the pronoun precedes the verb. As a rule, the naming of the place or person before the verb is a means of rendering it prominent in the sentence.

I write on this paper.	Sinusulatan co itòng papel.
He wrote my verses.	Ysinúlat niyà ang aquing mañga tulá.
We shall write on that table.	Pagsusulatán namin iyáng lamesang iyán.
He put the book on the floor.	Ang sahig ang linaguián niyà nang libro.
I will give my money to Mr Such a one.	Bibiguián co nang aquing pílac Si Couán.
To whom have you sold this cake?	¿Sinong pinagbilhan mo nitòng matamís?
To my neighbour's son.	Aug anac nang caapirbáhay co.

Whom are you paying for this bed?	¿Sinong binabayaran mo nitòng hihigan?
I am paying the merchant for this bed.	Binabayaran co nitòng hihigan ang comerciante.
I will buy the high house from the owner.	Bibilhan co nang matáas na báhay ang may ari.

THIRTY FOURTH EXERCISE.

What do you see yonder on the top of that mountain? I see trees which bear large branches. Does he notice the roaring of the wind? He does not notice the roaring of the wind, for he is deaf. Has the servant salted the fish? He has not yet salted the fish. Has your brother pierced this buffalo with the spear? He has pierced this buffalo with a spear and tasted its blood. What do you hold in your hand? It is a spear that I hold in my hand. What did you learn? I learned the English language. Whom is the thief threatening? He is threatening that boy; he frightened him at first by rushing out and he is now deceiving him. Did you advise and clothe the child? I clothed him and advised him to kiss his sister. From whom did you hear what you told me about the unfastening of the prisoner? I heard it from a friend of mine. What is his grand-daughter opening? She is opening the garden gate. What are you doing there? I am filling and covering the vat. What will they buy from the American? They will buy my butter from him. From whom have you taken that cane? I received it from my uncle. Of whom have we asked this paper? We craved it of the priest. Where has the servant looked for the hen that disappeared? He searched for it in the garden. From whom have you received this money in payment? I received this money from my debtor. Why does he not give me his bird? Because he has already given it to his sister. Is it this house where they assembled? No, they met together at Mary's house. What did they assemble for? They assembled to speak about the tax. Where shall you go? I shall go nowhere. Have you anything to tell me? I have to tell you something. Where have you put my spectacles? I put them into the room. Whom do you cut down that tree for? I cut it down for my master. Did I not say to you not to cut down any trees? Well, I obey my master.

THIRTY FIFTH LESSON.
YCATLONG POUO,T, LIMANG PAGARAL.

THE PROPER USE OF ANY VOICE OF THE VERB.

The use of the passive is far more common in Tagalog than in Western languages; in fact it is the most common form in narration.

An English transitive verb has two voices which may be made use of in a complete sentence; but the change from the active to the passive is not marked by an inflexion and hence the active voice predominates throughout in English. In Tagalog, where the passive shortens the sentence and concretes the sense in a way requiring some completive words in other languages, the contrary takes place, and it may be said that the proper use of either voice and either kind of passive constitutes the greatest difficulty in the language.

Speaking generally, the active voice looks forward more to the subject which it makes prominent, and the passive, to the object. Thus, if the subject is made emphatic by whatever means of expression fit for the purpose, the active voice is generally employed in Tagalog, even, when looking to the determination of the object, the passive should have been employed; the verb taking the active participial form.

It is I who killed him.	Acó, ang pungmatáy sa caniyà
It is you who shall say that.	Cayó, ang magsasabi niyán.
He himself did it.	Siyá rin, ang gungmauá.
It is they who stole my money.	Silá, ang nagnácao nang salapí co.

The active should likewise be used in incomplete sentences when no reference is made to an especially determined object either mentioned or understood.

I read. (pres.)	Bungmabasà acó.
Thou atest.	Cungmáin ca.
He sees.	Nacaquiquita siyá.
We write.	Sungmusúlat camí.
They will grant pardon.	Magpapatáuar silá.
You begged pardon, you asked for a reduction in price.	Tungmáuar cayó.

But, if we say: *basahin mo, canin niyà, ysinusúlat namin, papatauarin nilà*, it may be assumed that "read it, them"; "let him eat it, them"; "we write it, them, this" or "they will grant pardon to him, her, them", is meant, such English words as "some", "one", "it", "him", "her", "this", etc., being frequently understood and included in the passive particle.

The active is generally made use of in complete sentences when the object thereof is in the partitive or indeterminate sense, if no circumstance of instrument, place or time directly connected with the action is mentioned.

Bring in some cigars.	Magdalà ca ditò nang tabaco.
My brother ate fruit.	Ang capatir co,i, cungmáin nang boñga.

The merchant sells pins.	Nagbibilì nang aspiler ang comerciante
Call for a servant.	Tumáuag cayó nang isàng alila. (bata)
Don't drink any liquor.	Houag ca uminom nang álac.

The same is the case with sentences having an object determinate in quantity or kind, if a portion and not the whole of such determinate substance is meant.

Make use of this money.	Gumámit ca niyáng salapí.
I buy some of these bottles.	Bungmibilì acó nitòng mañga bote.
He will send some of our furniture.	Magpapadalà siyá nang aming casang-capan.
He would take four of my trunks.	Cocoha disin siyá nang ápat sa aquing mañga cabán.

To say, *gamitin mo iyáng salapí, binibilì co itóng mañga bote, etc.*, would indicate the whole.

The active is used with intransitive actions, unless reference is made to instrument, cause, time, place or purpose.

They laugh.	Tungmatáua silá.
We die.	Namamatáy camí.
You walk.	Lungmalácad cayó.

In interrogative sentences when an agent and not an object is inquired after, the active in likewise used.

Who calls them?	¿Sinong tungmatáuag sa canilà?
Which of them loves you?	¿Alín or sino sa canilà ang sungmisintà sa iyò?
What hurt me?	¿Anòng nagpasaquit sa aquin?

In complex sentences in which the subject is enlarged by an adjective clause.

The man who loves God, will attain Glory.	Ang tauòng sungmisintà sa Dios ay magcacamit nang caloualhatían.
The knavish boy who dissipates his fortune deserves to be chastised.	Ang hunghang na bagòng tauòng nag-aacsayá nang caniyàng ari ay dápat siyáng hampasín.

The passive should be used in sentences the object of which is individualized, or is circumscribed and fixed by some attribute or attributive word.

Call for Mary.	Tauaguin mo Si María.
He will bring my book.	Dadalhín niyà ritò ang aquing libro.
Don't whip that cat.	Houag mong hampasín iyáng pusa.
Bring in the shoes I ordinarily wear	Dalhín mo ritó ang mañga sapín na guinagámit cong madalás. (caraníuan).

In interrogative sentences when a determinate object is inquired after.

What do you want?	¿Anóng íbig mo?
Which dog did he kill?	¿Alíng aso ang pinatáy niyà?
Whom do you hate?	¿Sino ang quinapopootan mo?

When *may, mayrón, ualá* or any other verbs are used as determining ones, the verbs determined by them are used in the passive.

I have to say.	Mayróon acóng sasabihin.
You will not have to ask.	Ualá cayóng ytatanong.

He deserved to be punished.	Súcat siyáng hinampás or hampasín.
They deserve to be rewarded.	Dápat siláng gantihín.

INTERCHANGEABILITY OF THE PASSIVES.

The use of the various passives is somewhat arbitrary as there exists a kind of interchangeability with each other which is difficult to fix by any rule. In sentences with a definitely circumscribed object not including any other circumstantial element, the passive to be used is that which the nature of the action requires in regard to the direct object, according to the rules previously laid down for the purpose.

Accept of my good will.	Tangapín mo ang lóob cong magandà.
He will throw away these slippers.	Ytatapon niya itòng mañga *sinelas* (corr. from Sp. word, *chinelas*).
Have you advised him?	¿Hinatolan mo siyá?

In sentences containing one indirect complement directly connected with the action, the discriminating choice between *y* and *an* passives, is made in accordance with the indirect object meaning instrument, place, time or cause.

Search for my needle with this light.	Ytòng ílao yhalíhao mo nang aquing caráyom.
Did you search about the room for his letter?	¿Sinaliesieán mo bagá nang caniyàng súlat ang silid?
On our embarking the hurricane occurred.	Ang pagsasacáy natin yquinataón nang báguio, or, onós.
What does your uncle die from?	¿Anòng yquinamamatáy nang iyòng amaín.

In sentences having more than one indirect complement, the choice of passive is decided by the speaker's desire to lay more stress upon either of them.

Kill this cat in the street with your gun.	Ypatáy mo nitòng pusa ang iyòng baril sa lansañgan.

Stress is hereby laid on the instrument, and the same is made emphatic by saying:

With your very gun, kill this cat in the street.	Ang baril mo rin, ang ypatáy mo nitòng pusa sa lansañgan.
Kill this cat with your gun in the street.	Ang lansañgan, ang patayàn mo nitòng pusa nang iyòng baril.

The place is hereby made prominent. The same is emphasized by saying:

In the street itself kill this cat with your gun.	Ang lansañgan, ang patayán mo nitòng pusa nang iyòng baril.

If stress is laid on the object, the sentence may be construed in the regular way, saying:

Kill this cat in the street with your gun. or made it more emphatic by saying:	Patayín mo itòng pusa sa lansañgan nang baril mo,
This cat, let it be killed by you in the street with your gun.	Ytòng pusang itò,i, ang patayín mo sa lansañgan nang iyòng baril.

Students should take care to distinguish circumstantial members connected with the action from adverbs or adverbial expressions, on using the passive forms.

He did this purposely.	Sadiyang guinauá niyà i'ò.
He assaulted him furiously (with great fury.)	Dinalohong niyà siyá nang bóong bagsic.

Attention should be paid to the following illustrations.

Bring me these books upstairs.	Panhicán mo acó nitòng mañga libro.
He took the child upstairs.	Ypinanhic niyà ang bata sa báhay.
I will meet you upstairs.	Papanhiquín quitá sa báhay.
Will he look for the book which was missed?	¿Hahanapin niyà ang librong naualá?
Overtake my brother.	Habulín mo ang aquing capatir
Run after him and deliver this letter to him.	Habulan mo siyá nitòng súlat.
Whom did you inquire after?	¿Sinong ytinanong mo?
Whom do you inquire from?	¿Sino ang tinatanong mo?
I asked him whether he was her brother.	Ytinanong co sa caniyà cung bagá siyá,i, capatid niyà, or, tinanong co siyá etc.
To discover, to detect.	Tumoclás.

THIRTY FIFTH EXERCISE.

Was it your nephew that cut off the branch? It was not he who cut it off. Is it they who said I was imprisoned? It was my niece who said it. Was it the Italians who discovered America? No, it was not the Italians, it was the Spaniards that discovered it. Who ordered the criminal to be put to death? It was the king that ordered it. Was it not the judge who ordered your cousin to be released? It was not the judge, it was the captain. What are you reading? I am reading the book my friend lent me. Whom do you ask for pardon? I ask pardon from my teacher. Why do you not wish to eat? I don't eat because I cannot. What do you bring? I bring some fruit. Where have you taken it? I took it in the forest. Does the priest take chocolate every morning? He takes chocolate every norning after mass. What will Mary buy? She will buy bread and wine. Would it not be better if she would buy needles and stuff? She has no longer the money you gave her the other day. Why! is it so? Yes, indeed, I thought she had not yet made use of it. Which water shall I drink of? Drink of this water, for it is cool and clear. May I take some of this money? Take only twenty three dollars out of it. Whom are the children laughing at? They are laughing at that drunkard. Why do they laugh? They laugh because he staggers. Why do you walk so much? Because we are in a great hurry. Why did your son wound this dog? He wounded him because he bit him. Who loves your sister? Peter loves her. Who did this? The man that came last Sunday did it. Who is running? The girl that tore your stocking is running. Shall I call for her? Yes, call for her. What has the merchant to tell me? He has to tell you to pay your debt. How much do I owe him? You owe him thirty-six dollars. Who else came to inquire after me? The Chinese tradesman came to claim payment for the shoes. What did you say to him? I told him you had no money to pay with. Why does he whip his servant? Because he stole a ring from him. Did he not reward him some days ago? Yes, he rewarded him for his honesty. Why does not your friend come for you at home? He fears the dog. Why are you not willing to receive this money? Because it is not good.

THIRTY SIXTH LESSON.
YCATLONG POUO,T, ANIM NA PAGARAL.

MODIFICATIVE VERBALIZING PARTICLES.

MAN=PAN.

The Tagalog language abounds in verbal prefixed particles modifying the original range of signification of the root as to the manner, intension and purpose of the action, in a way generally requiring long round-about forms of expression in other languages. These particles are sometimes essential to the verb, that is to say, express the primary action, but, most commonly, they stand for verb attributes, which should otherwise have been employed, thus imparting a wonderful conciseness to the speech.

Man, (active) *pan*, (passive) is one of the principal. It is generally applied to habitual actions and to those which, although may be indifferently or occasionally performed, have acquired a character of fixedness by habit, trade or exercise.

That this sense of habitude may be imparted, it is, however, necessary that the original signification of the verb with *um* or *mag*, be not changed by *man*. Thus, *umasáua*, means "to enter into marriage" (referring to the bridegroom); *magasáua*, "to marry" (both parties); but *mañgasáua*, "to pay addresses" in the simplest sense this can be done. The same may be said of actions not admitting of habit or instrument for their performance, and thus, *mañganac*, "to lie in," "to bring forth"; does not express frequency.

Verbal roots the first letter of which is *b* or *p* and which, according to their signification, should have been conjugated by *um*, are pluralized or intensified by *man*. *Bumili*, "to buy"; *mamili*, "to buy many things"; *pumuti*, "to whiten"; *mamuti*, "to grow rapidly or very white".

The interchangeability of letters which in other conjugations is somewhat vague and sometimes optional, has in this of *man* more consistency. The *n* of *man* or *pan* is dropped before roots beginning with *b*, *p*, *s*, *t*; and replaced by *ñg* in those beginning with a vowel. In roots beginning by *c-q*, both the latter and the *n* of the particle are dropped and replaced by *ñg*. B and *p* are changed into *m*; *s*, *t* and sometimes *d*, into *n*.

The manner of conjugating roots with this particle does not deviate from the regular one in other respects.

ROOTS.

Scoff.	Libac.
Habit, custom.	Bihasà.
Fault, censure.	Pintás.
Curse.	Sumpá.
Temptation.	Tocsò.

Wish, desire, love.	Ybig.
Taking.	Cuha.

PARADIGMS.

To scoff.	Manlibac.
Person or thing.	Libaquín.
Mocker.	Mapaglibac.
To habituate.	Mamihasà.
Habit, custom.	Pinamisanhán. (1).
To train others, to cause others to get accustomed to.	Magpamihasà.
The cause of being accustomed, what causes habit.	Ang nacapamihasà.
To train one's self to.	Magbibihasà.
To what.	Pinagbibihasanan. (1),
To what has been accustomed.	Quinamisanhán. (1).
To find faults with.	Mamintás.
Action censured.	Ang pamintasán.
Censurer, critic.	Mapamintás.
To curse others.	Sumumpá.
To curse many.	Magsumpá.
To be cursed by others.	Sumpáin, pagsumpáin.
Reason or the nature of the curse.	Ang ysumpá, ypagsumpá.
To curse each other.	Magsumpáan.
To curse customarily.	Manumpá.
Nature of the curse or thing cursed over customarily.	Ang ypanumpá.
Person before whom an oath is taken.	Ang panumpáan.
Habitual cursing.	Ang panunumpá.
Habitual curser.	Palasumpá.
To tempt other.	Tumocsò.
Do others. (many or many times)	Magtocsò.
To be tempted by.	Tocsohín.
Do hard or frequently.	Pagtotocsohín.
Do, with or on account of.	Ytocsò.
Do do, hard.	Ypagtotocsò.
Place.	Pagtocsohán.
To go about tempting.	Manocsò.
Do, a great deal.	Magpanocs`.
Do, with.	Ypanocsò.
Place.	Panocsohan.
Tempter.	Manonocsò.
To wish, to want, to desire.	Umíbig.
Do, do (by many); to go about flirting.	Mañgíbig.
To be loved. (without one's being known).	Macaíbig.
Loved. (*ex intentione*).	Ybiguin.
Loved. (*casualiter*).	Naíbig.
Whom one loves.	Caibigan.
To long for.	Mag–íbig.
Thing longed for.	Pinag-ibigan.
Love of something.	Caibigán. (2).
Thing loved.	Quinaibigan.
Loving, lovely, lovable, aimable.	Caibig-íbig.
To love this and that over again.	Mañgíbig.
Flirting, amorous.	Maibiguín. (2).

(1) For the sake of euphony, this root inserts *n* in this composition.
(2) Notice the accentuation,

To have a leaning for.	Maíbig.
Covetousness.	Pagcaíbig.
To pay addresses to.	Mañgibig.
To love each other.	Mag-iíbig, magcacaibigan.
To like.	Macaíbig.
To take. (for one's self).	Cumoha, moha.
Thing taken.	Conin.
Person from whom.	Conan.
Taking.	Pagcoha.
To go about taking.	Mañgoha.
Thing.	Pañgonin.
Taker.	Mapagcoha.
Thing taken. (*casualiter*).	Nacoha.
What can be taken.	Macocoha.

CONJUGATION.

ACTIVE.

Infinitive.

To scoff.	Manlibac.

Present indefinite tense.

I, thou, he, etc. we, you, they scoff, etc.	Nanlilibac acó, ca, siyá, tayo, camí, cayó, silá.

Present perfect and past indefinite tenses.

I, thou, he, etc. we, you, they scoffed etc.; have, etc. scoffed.	Nanlibac acó, ca, siyá, tayo, camí, cayó, silá.

Pluperfect tense.

I, thou, he, etc. we, you, they had etc. scoffed.	Nacapanlibac acó, ca, siyá, tayo, camí, cayó, silá. Nanlibac na acó, ca na; na siyá, tayo, camí, cayó, silá.

Future indefinite tense.

I, thou, he, etc. we, you, they shall, etc. will, etc. scoff.	Manlilibac acó, ca, siyá, tayo, camí, cayó, silá.

Future perfect tense.

I, thou, he, etc. we, you, they shall, etc. will, etc. have scoffed.	Macapanlibac acó, ca, siyá, tayo, camí, cayó, silá. Manlilibac na acó, ca na; na siyá, tayo, camí, cayó, silá.

Imperative.

Scoff (thou, ye.) let him, etc. us, them scoff.	Manlibac ca, siyá, tayo, camí, cayó, silá.

Verbal.

—

The actiong of scoffing.   Ang panlilibac.

IN PASSIVE.

—

Infinitive.

—

To be scoffed at or of.   Panlibaquin.

Present indefinite tense.

—

...... am, etc. are scoffed at by me,   Pinanlilibac co. mo, niyà, natin na-
thee, him, etc. us, ye, them.   min, ninyò, nilà.

Present perfect and past indefinite tenses.

—

...... was. etc. were; have, etc. been } Pinanlibac co. mo, niyà, natin. namin,
scoffed at by me, thee, him, etc. us, } ninyò, nilà.
ye, them.

Pluperfect tense.

—

...... had, etc. been, scoffed at by me, ⎰ Napanlibac co, mo, niyà, natin, namin,
thee, him; etc.. us, ye, them.   ⎪ ninyò, nilà.
                                        ⎪ Pinanlibac co na, mo na; na niyà
                                        ⎱ natin, namin, ninyò, nila.

Future   indefinite   tense.

—

...... shall, etc.; will, etc. be scoffed   Panlilibaquin co. mo, niyà, natin, na-
at by me, thee, him, etc. us, ye, them.   min, ninyò, nilà.

Future perfect tense.

—

...... shall, etc.; will, etc. have been ⎰ Mapanlibac co, mo, niyà, natin, na-
scoffed at by me. thee, him, etc. us, ye, ⎪ min, ninyò, nilà.
them.   ⎪ Panlilibaquin co na, mo na; na niyà,
                                          ⎱ natin, namin, ninyò, nilà.

Imperative.

—

Be scoffed at, let...... be scoffed at   Panlibaquin mo, niyà, natin, namin,
by thee, him, etc. us. ye, them.   ninyò, nilà

Verbal.

—

The state of being scoffed at.   Ang panlibaquin.

Y PASSIVE.

Infinitive.

To scoff on account of.   Ypanlibac.

Present indefinite tense

I, thou, he, etc. we, you, they scoff etc. on account of.   Ypinanlilibac co, mo, niyà, natin, namin, ninyò, nila.

Present perfect and past indefinite tenses.

I, thou, he, etc. we, you, they scoffed etc.; have etc. scoffed on account of.   Ypinanlibac co, mo, mo, niyà, natin, namin, ninyò, nilà.

Pluperfect tense.

I, thou, he, etc. we, you, they had etc. scoffed on account of.   { Napanlibac co, mo, niyà, natin, namin, ninyò, nilà.
Pinanlibac co na, mo na; na niyà, natin, namin, ninyò, nilà

Future indefinite tense.

I, thou, he, etc. we, you, they shall etc. will, etc. scoff on account of.   Ypanlilibac co, mo, niyà, natin, namin, ninyò, nilà.

Future perfect tense.

I, thou, he, etc. we, you, they shall etc., will etc. have scoffed on account of.   { Maypanlibac co, mo, niyà, natin, namin, ninyò, nilà.
Ypanlilibac co na, mo na; na niyà, natin, namin, ninyò, nilà.

Imperative.

Scoff (thou, ye); let him, etc., us, them scoff on account of.   Ypanlibac mo, niyà, natin, namin, ninyò, nilà.

Verbal.

The action of scoffing on account of.   Ang ypanlilibac.

AN PASSIVE.

Infinitive.

To scoff in. (place)   Panlibacán,

Present indefinite tense.

I, thou, he, etc. we, you, they scoff etc. in.

Pinanlilibacán co, mo, niyà, natin, namin, ninyò, nilà.

Present perfect and past indefinite tenses.

I, thou, he, etc, we, you, they scoffed etc.; have, etc. scoffed in.

Pinanlibacán co, mo, niyà, natin, namin, ninyò, nilà.

Pluperfect tense.

I, thou, he, etc. we, you, they had, etc. scoffed in.

{ Napanlibacán co, mo, niyà, natin, namin, ninyò, nilà.
Pinanlibacán co na, mo na; na niyà, natin, namin, ninyò, nilà.

Future indefinite tense.

I, thou, he, etc. we, you, they shall, etc., will. etc. scoff in.

Panlilibacán co, mo, niyà, natin, namin, ninyò, nilà.

Future perfect tense.

I, thou, he, etc. we, you, they shall, etc., will, etc. have scoffed in.

{ Mapanlibacán co, mo, niy', natin, namin, ninyò, nilà.
Panlilibacán co na, mo na; na niyà, natin, namin, ninyò, nilà.

Imperative.

Scoff (thou, ye), let him, etc. us. them scoff in.

Panlibacán mo, niyà, natin, namin, ninyò, nilà.

Verbal.

The action of scoffing in.

Ang panlilibacán.

The student should conjugate in the active and in the various passives, the following verbs.

To arise, to proceed from, to take rise or origin from.	Mangáling.
To cure habitually or professionally.	Mangamot.
To imitate, to mimic, to mock.	Mangagar.
To mix. (by trade or customarily).	Mangamáo.
To reprimand, to criticise loudly.	Mangasá.
To milk.	Mangatas.
To exercise, to practice.	Mangauá.
To lay waste, to cause havoc, or to gain a living by drawing products from the forest.	Mangúbat,
To scout.	Manhánap.
To wash one's face.	Manhilamos.

To take away the nits.	Manlisá.
To soothsay.	Manghola. (1).
To live by rapine.	Manghuli.
To put forth shoots the bamboo trees, or, to gather in the same shoots.	Manlabong.
To cast the net for fish.	Manlambang.
To fish with a net.	Manlambat.
To sail or walk along the banks of a river for.	Manlambáy.
To hover about one place, to haunt.	Manlígao.
To stare, to look crossly al some one.	Mamlísic.
To gather fruit by shaking the tree.	Manloglog.

The following roots are given to illustrate the change of letters they undergo conjugated by *man*.

Habit, custom, cunning, craft; to use, to be accustomed.	Bihasà, mamihasà.
Censure, fault; to censure, to find faults with.	Pintás, mamintás.
Curse, to curse.	Sumpá, manumpá.
Temptation, to tempt.	Tucsò, manucsò.
Love, desire; to flirt, to be of an amorous disposition.	Ybig. (nasa, náis); mañgíbig.
Taking, to take continually, to be engaged in taking.	Coha, mañgoha.

ACTIVE.

Infinitive.

To habituate.	Mamihasà.
To find fault with.	Mamintás.
To curse, to swear.	Manumpá.
To tempt.	Manucsò.
To flirt.	Mañgíbig.
To take.	Mañgoha.

Present indefinite tense.

Use, –st, –s.	Namimihasà.
Censure, –st, –s.	Namimintás.
Swear, –est, –s.	Nanunumpá.
Tempt, –est, –s.	Nanunucsò.
Flirt, –est, –s.	Nañgiñgíbig.
Take, –st, –s.	Nañgoñgoha.

Present perfect and past indefinite tenses.

Used, -dst; have, hast, has used.	Namihasà.
Censured, do do do do do censured.	Namintás.
Swore, „ „ „ „ „ sworn.	Nanumpá.
Tempted, „ „ „ „ „ tempted.	Nanucsò.
Flirted, „ „ „ „ „ flirted.	Nañgíbig.
Took, „ „ „ „ „ taken.	Nañguha.

(1). If the root begins with *h*, may receive *g* before.

Pluperfect tense.

Had, dst used.		Nacapamihasà, namihasà na.
„	„ censured.	Nacapamintás, namintás na.
„	„ sworn.	Nacapanumpá, nanumpá na.
„	„ tempted.	Nacapanucsò, nanucsò na.
„	„ flirted.	Nacapañgíbig, nañgíbig na.
„	„ taken.	Nacapañgoha, nañgoha na.

Future indefinite tense.

Shall, -lt,	will, -lt	use.		Mamimihasà.
„	„	„	„ censure.	Mamimintás.
„	„	„	„ swear.	Manunumpá.
„	„	„	„ tempt.	Manunucsò.
„	„	„	„ flirt.	Mañgiñgíbig.
„	„	„	„ take.	Mañgoñgoha.

Future perfect tense.

Shall, -lt,	will, -lt,	have used.			Macapamihàsà, mamimihasà na.
„	„	„	„	„ censured.	Macapamintás, mamimintás na.
„	„	„	„	„ sworn.	Macapanumpá, manunumpá na.
„	„	„	„	„ tempted.	Macapanucsò, manunucsò na.
„	„	„	„	„ flirted.	Macapañgíbig, mañgiñgíbig na.
„	„	„	„	„ taken.	Macapañgoha, mañgogñoha na.

Imperative.

Use,	let............use.	Mamihasà.
Censure,	„ ....censure.	Mamintás.
Swear,	„ ....swear.	Manumpá.
Tempt,	„ ....tempt.	Manucsò.
Flirt,	„ ....flirt.	Mañgíbig.
Take.	„ ....take.	Mañgoha.

Verbals.

The action of using.			Ang pamimihasà.
„	„	„ censuring.	„ pamimintás.
„	„	„ swearing.	„ panunumpá.
„	„	„ tempting.	„ panunucsò.
„	„	„ flirting.	„ pañgiñgíbig.
„	„	„ taking.	„ pañgoñgoha.

IN PASSIVE.

Infinitive.

To be accustomed.		Pamihasanhin.
„	„ censured.	Pamintasin.
„	„ cursed.	Panunpáin.
„	„ tempted.	Panucsohin.
„	„ flirted.	Pañgibiguin.
„	„ taken.	Pañgonin.

Present indefinite tense.

Are, rt, is accustomed.	Pinamimihasà.
,, ,, ,, censured.	Pinamimintás.
,, ,, ,, cursed.	Pinanunumpá.
,, ,, ,, tempted.	Pinanunucsò.
,, ,, ,, flirted.	Pinañgiñgíbig.
,, ,. ,, taken.	Pinañgoñgoha.

Present perfect and past indefinite tenses.

Was, -st, were; have, hast, has been accustomed.	Pinamihasà.
,: ,, ,, ,, ,, ,, censured.	Pinamintás.
,, ,, ,, ,, ,, ,. cursed.	Pinanumpá.
,, ,, ,, ,, ,, ,, tempted.	Pinanucsò.
,, ,, ,, ,, ,, ,, flirted.	Pinañgíbig.
,, ,, ,, ,, ,, ,, taken.	Pinañgoha.

Pluperfect tense.

Had, –dst been	accustomed.	Napamihasà, pinamihasà na.
,, ,, ,,	censured.	Napamintás, pinamintás na.
., .. .,	cursed.	Napanumpá, pinanumpá na.
,, ,, ,,	tempted.	Napanucsò, pinanucsò na.
,, ,, ,,	flirted.	Napañgíbig, pinañgíbig na.
,, ,. ,,	taken.	Napañgoha, pinañgoha na.

Future indefinite tense.

Shall, -lt, will, -lt be	accustomed.	Pamimihasanhin. (epenthesis.)
,, ,, ,, ,, ,,	censured.	Pamimintasin.
., ,, ,, ,, ,,	cursed.	Panunumpáin.
,, ,, ,, ,, .,	tempted.	Panunucsohin.
,, ,, ,, ,, ,,	flirted.	Pañgiñgibiguin.
, ,, ,, ,. ,,	taken.	Pañgoñgonin.

Future perfect tense.

Shall -lt, will, -lt, have been accustomed.	Mapamihasà, pamimihasanhin na.
,, ,, ,, ,, ,, ,, censured,	Mapamintás, pamimintasin na.
,, ,, ,, ,, ,, ,, cursed.	Mapanumpá, panunumpáin na.
,, ,, ,, ,, ,, ,, tempted.	Mapanucsò, panunucsohin na.
,, ,, ,, ,, ,, ,, flirted.	Mapañgíbig, pañgiñgibiguin na.
,, ,, ,, ,, ,, ,, taken.	Mapañgoha, pañgoñgonin na,

Imperative.

Be, let........ be accustomed.	Pamisanhín.
,, ,, ... ,, censured.	Pamintasín.
,, ,, ... ,, cursed.	Panumpaín.
,, ,, ... ,, tempted.	Panucsohín.
,, ,, ... ,, flirted.	Pañgibiguín.
,, ,, ... ,, taken. .	Pañgonin,

Verbal.

—

The state of being accustomed.	Ang pamihasanhin.
„ „ „ „ censured.	„ pamintasin.
„ „ „ „ cursed.	„ panumpáin.
„ „ „ „ tempted.	„ panucsohin.
„ „ „ „ flirted.	„ pañgibiguin.
„ „ „ „ taken.	„ pañgonin.

Y PASSIVE.

Infinitive.

—

To accustom because of.	Ypamihasà.
„ censure. „ „	Ypamintás.
„ curse at.	Ypanumpá.
„ tempt with.	Ypanucsò.
„ flirt on account of.	Ypañgíbig.
„ take with.	Ypañguha.

Present indefinite tense.

Accustom, –est, –s because of.	Ypinamimihasà.
Censure, –st, „ „ „	Ypinamimintás.
Curse, „ „ at.	Ypinanunumpá.
Tempt, –est, „ with.	Ypinanunucsò.
Flirt, „ „ on account of.	Ypinañgiñgíbig.
Take, –st, „ with.	Ypinañgoñgoha.

Present perfect and past indefinite tenses.

Accustomed, -dst; have, hast, has accustomed because of.	Ipinamihasà.
Censured, do do do do censured „ „	Ipinamintás,
Cursed, „ „ „ „ cursed at.	Ipinanumpá.
Tempted, „ „ „ „ tempted with.	Ipinanucsò.
Flirted, „ „ „ „ flirted on account of.	Ipinañgíbig.
Took, „ „ „ „ taken with.	Ipinañgoha.

Pluperfect tense.

Had, –dst, accustomed because of.	Naypamihasè, ypinamihasì na.
„ „ censured „ „	Naypamintás, ypinamintás na.
„ „ cursed at.	Naypanumpá, ypinanumpá na.
„ „ tempted with.	Naypanucsò, ypinanucsò na.
„ „ flirted on account of.	Naypañgíbig, ypinañgíbig na.
„ „ taken with.	Naypañgoha, ypinañgoha na.

Future indefinite tense.

Shall, –lt, will, –lt accustom because of.	Ipamimihasà.
„ „ „ „ censure „ „	Ipamimintás.
„ „ „ „ curse at.	Ipanunumpá.
„ „ „ „ tempt with.	Ipanunucsò.
„ „ „ „ flirt on account of.	Ipañgiñgíbig.
„ „ „ „ take with.	Ipañgoñgoha.

Future perfect tense.

Shall, –lt, will, –lt	} have accustomed because of.	}	Maypamihasà,	ypamimihasà na.
,, ,, ,, ,,	do censured do do.		Maypamintás,	ypamimintás na.
,, ,, ,, ,,	,, cursed at.		Maypanumpá,	ypanunumpá na.
,, ,, ,, ,,	,, tempted with.		Maypanucsò,	ypanunucso na.
,, ,, ,, ,,	{ ,, flirted on account of.	}	Maypañgíbig,	ypañgiñgíbig na.
,, ,, ,, ,,	,, taken with.		Maypañguha,	ypañguñgúha na.

Imperative.

Accustom, let	accustom because of.	Ypamihasà.
Censure, ,, ...	censure ,, ,,	Ypamintás.
Curse, ,, ...	curse at.	Ypanumpá.
Tempt, ,, ...	tempt with.	Ypanucsò.
Flirt, ,, ...	flirt on account of.	Ypañgíbig.
Take, ,, ...	take with.	Ypañgoha.

Verbal.

The action of accustoming because of.	Ang	ypamihasà.
,, ,, ,, censuring ,, ,, ,,		ypamintás.
,, ,, ,, cursing at.	,,	ypanumpá.
,, ,, ,, tempting with.	,,	ypanucsò.
,, ,, ,, flirting on account of.	,,	ypañgíbig.
,, ,, ,, taking with.	,,	ypañgoha.

AN PASSIVE.

Infinitive.

To be accustomed to.	Pamihasanhan. (epenthesis).
To animadvert on.	Pamintasan.
To curse before.	Panumpáan.
To tempt at or in.	Panucsohan.
To flirt with.	Pañgibigan.
To take from.	Pañgonan. (contraction).

Present indefinite tense.

Am, art, are accustomed to.	Pinamimisanhán.
Animadvert, –est, –s, on.	Pinamimintasán.
Curse, –st, ,, before.	Pinanunumpaán.
Tempt, –est, ,, at or in.	Pinanunucsohán.
Flirt, ,, ,, with.	Pinañgiñgibigan.
Take, –st, ,, from.	Pinañgoñgonan.

Present perfect and past indefinite tenses.

Was, –st, were; have, hast,	has been accustomed to.	Pinamisanhán.
Animadverted, –dst; have, hast,	,, animadverted on.	Pinamintasán.
Cursed, ,, ,, ,,	,, cursed before.	Pinanumpaán.
Tempted ,, ,, ,,	,, tempted at or in.	Pinanucsohán.
Flirted, ,, ,, ,,	,, flirted with.	Pinañgibigan.
Took, ,, ,, ,,	,, taken from.	Pinañgonan.

Pluperfect tense.

Had –dst –been accustomed to.	Napamisanhán,	pinamisanhán na.
,, ,, animadverted on.	Napamintasán,	pinamintasán na.
,, ,, cursed before.	Napanumpaán,	pinanumpaán na.
,, ,, tempted at or in.	Napanucsohán,	pinanucsohán na.
,, ,, flirted with.	Napañgibigan,	pinañgibigan na.
,, ,, taken from.	Napañgonan,	pinañgonan na.

Future indefinite tense.

Shall, –lt, will, –lt be accustomed to.	Pamimihasanán. (1).
,, ,, ,, ,, animadvert on.	Paminintasán.
,, ,, ,, ,, curse before.	Panunumpaán.
,, ,, ,, ,, tempt in or at.	Panunucsohán.
,, ,, ,, ,, flirt with.	Pañgiñgibigan.
,, ,, ,, ,, take from.	Pañguñgunan.

Future perfect tense.

Shall, -lt, wilt -lt have been accustomed to.	Mapamisanhán, pamimisanhán na
,, ,, ,, ,, ,, animadverted on.	Mapamintasán. pamimintasán na
,, ,, ,, ,, ,, cursed before.	Mapanumpaán, panunumpaán na
,, ,, ,, ,, ,, tempted in or at.	Mapanucsohán, panunucsohán na
,, ,, ,, ,, ,, flirted with.	Mapañgibigan, pañgiñgibigan na.
,, ,, ,, ,, ,, taken from.	Mapañgonan, pañgoñgonan na.

Imperative.

Be,	let . . be accustomed to.	Pamisanhán.
Animadvert,	,, ... animadvert on.	Pamintasán.
Curse,	,, ... curse before.	Panumpaán.
Tempt,	,, ... tempt at or in.	Panucsohán.
Flirt,	.. . . . . flirt with.	Pañgibigan.
Take,	,, . . take from.	pañgonan.

Verbals.

The state of being accustomed to.		Ang pamisanhán.
The action ,, animadverting on.		,, pamintasán.
,, ,, ,, cursing before.		,, panumpaán.
,, ,, ,, tempting at or in.		,, panucsohan.
,, ,, ,, flirting with.		,, pañgibigan.
,, ,, ,, taking from.		,, pañgonan.

The student should conjugate by *man* the following roots:

Share,	to distribute.	Bahagui,	mamahagui.
Care,	to care for.	Bahala,	mamahala.
House,	to live in a house.	Búhay,	mamúhay.
	(as opposed to live in the woods.)		
Town,	to live in town.	Bayan,	mamayan.
Pale,	to grow pale.	Putlá.	mamutlá.

(1). The root, in this tense, inserts *n* for the sake of euphony.

Eel,	to fish eels.	Palós,	mamalós.
Frog,	to fish frogs.	Palacá,	mamalacá.
Cut,	to cut up.	Pútul,	mamótol.
Letter,	to write professionally.	Súlat.	manúlat.
Snare,	to lay snares for.	Silo,	manilo.
Destroyed,	to go about destroying.	Sira,	manira.
Claim for payment,	to collect money.	Siñgil,	maniñgil.
Winning, conquering;	to win, to overpower.	Panalo,	manalo.
Blasphemy,	to blaspheme.	Tuñgáyao,	manuñgáyao.
Apron,	to wear an apron.	Tapis,	manapis.
Prayer,	to pray for.	Dalañgin,	manalañgin.
Teaching,	to preach.	Aral,	mañgáral.
Light,	to fish with a torch.	Ylao,	mañgílao.
First, prior;	to precede, to go before.	Oná,	mañgoná.
Shunning,	to flee.	Ylag,	mañgilag.
Biting,	to go round biting.	Cagat,	mañgagat.
Clinging,	to cling to here and there.	Cápit,	mañgápit.
Eating,	to devour.	Cáin,	mañgáin.

Man is fit to express the seasonable production of plants.

To blossom, to bloom.	Mamulac-lac. (from *bulac-lac*).
To fructify, to beat fruit.	Mamuñga. (from *boñga*).
To put forth or gather in the shoots of bamboo-trees.	Manlabong.

It expresses habit, frequence of acts or multitude of agents in some actions, the first degree of which is expressed by *um* or *mag*.

To cut off with the hand.	Pumuti, cumitil.
To gather flowers.	Mamuti, mañgitil.
To spin.	Sumúlid.
To spin, to be spinner.	Manúlid.
To give, to lavish.	Magbigáy, mamigáy.

But the sense with those actions which may be mercenary is one of engagement or trade. Thus, for instance.

To sew.	Tumahí.
To sew a great deal.	Magtahí.
But, to engage in tailoring, to earn a living by sewing.	Manahí.
To write, (the action looked upon as to the agent)	Sumúlat.
To write something.	Magsúlat.
But to earn one's livelihood by writing.	Manúlat.

Roots of instruments, tools or arms are conjugated by *man* to indicate that they are worn or made use of to some purpose.

Sword.	Sandatà.
To wear side-arms.	Manandatà.
Axe, to wear an axe.	Palacol, mamalacol.
Chopping knife, to wield it.	Tabac, manabac.
Dagger, to wear a dagger.	Yua, mañgíua.
Life, to live.	Búhay, mamúhay.

Common nouns of places are conjugated by *man* to indicate habitation or residence therein.

Mount, hill; to settle on a mountain.	Bondoc, mamondoc.
Town, to live in town.	Bayan, mamayan.
Sea, to lead a sea-faring life.	Dágat, manágat.

Roots of wearing garments if conjugated by *man*, indicate the wearing thereof. The difference in sense between the conjugating of the same by *mag* and *man*, is that the former expresses the occasional and the latter the customary wearing.

Shirt, to wear a shirt.	Baro, mamaro.
Apron, to wear an apron.	Tapis, manapis.
Hat, to wear a hat.	Sambalilo, manambalilo.

The extractive industry of forestry and fishing products being so widely spread throughout the Islands, roots indicative of any such products may be conjugated by *man* to denote the engaging in the working as a business.

Wood, to excercise the wood–monger's trade.	Cáhoy, mañgáhoy.
Rattan, to gather rattans.	Ouáy, mañgouáy.
Deer, to chase deer.	Usá, mañgusá.
Fish, to be a fisherman.	Ysdá, mañgisdá.
Oyster, to gather oysters.	Talabá, manalabá.
Shell, mother of pearl shell; to pick up, to gather shells.	Capis, mañgapis.

The instrument made use of in fishing, chasing or getting at such products may likewise be conjugated by *man*.

Fishing-rod, to be a rod fisherman.	Bíuas, mamíuas.
Hook, to use hooks in fishing.	Binuit, maminuit.
Net, to fish with a net.	Lambat, manlambat.
Gun, fowling-piece; to hunt with a gun.	Baril, mamaril.

But distinction should be drawn between these instruments conjugated by *man*, and the same conjugated by *um*. *Um*, looks forward to the action or use, *man*, to the work or effect. Thus, *ilao*, "light;" *umílao*, "to make use of a light;" that is, to say, "to light;" *mañgílao*, "to get a living by employing a light". (To fish, using a torch).

Man, conjugation is a very important one and the pupil is recommended to acquaint himself with it as thoroughly as possible. Into it, many a root of *um* and *mag* conjugations, if beginning with *b, p, t, s, c,* or a vowel, come to be resolved. *Bigáy, mamiyáy; pásoc, mamásoc; tocop, manócop; sola, manola; calácal, mañaglácal* etc.

THIRTY SIXTH EXERCISE.

Whom does my son scoff at? He scoffs at you. Why does he scoff at me. Because you are curing my dog. Where do they come from? (take origin of) They come from the first settlers. Does he know how to mimic cats? No, but he know how to milk cows. Whom are Americans scouting for? They scout for rebels. Did John practice medicine? No, but he practises soothsaying. What do rebels live by? They live by rapine. Where do children lay snares for birds? They do not lay snares for birds, they earn their living by netting and by fishing with a hook. What are you accustomed to? I am accustomed to censuring and cursing. Whom is the youngman always tempting? He is tempting his female–cousin. When did you flirt? I used to flirt with girls when a lad. What was your father engaged in taking? He was engaged in taking thieves. Among whom do you distribute that money? I distribute it among my relations. Does your servant take care of the garden? He takes care of his farm, for he does not live in town, but in the country. What kind of fishing is our neighbour engaged in? He is engaged in fishing eels and frogs. What is your trade? My trade is that of a writer. What do insurgents go about destroying? They go about destroying farms and villages, and collecting money, and they blaspheme because they do not conquer. Whom do you pray customarily? I pray God and the Holy Virgin. Is the priest preaching to those women wearing aprons? Yes. What is her husband engaged in? He is engaged in fishing with a torch. Is that dog used to bite and devour boars? It is not used to bite, but the boars are used to flee and do not allow themselves to be overrun (preceded). What is the condition of the trees in your garden? They do not yet bear fruit; but they are already in bloom. What was Jane engaged in when still alive? She was engaged in spinning and gathering flowers. How does he earn his living (provide for)? He sews and writes. Do officers wear side-arms? They wear a sword, but they do not wear axes. Does your grandfather lead a sea-faring life? No, he was a woodman and a chaser of deer. Was not your father engaged in fishing? He has engaged in gathering oysters and shells. Did they fish with a hook or a rod? He fished with a torch and sometimes with a net. Does his friend hunt boars with a gun? No, he used to hunt boars with dogs.

THIRTY SEVENTH LESSON.
YCATLONG POUO,T, PITONG PAGARAL.

MODIFICATIVE VERBALIZING PARTICLES.

$$MACA\frac{CA.}{MA.}$$

On encountering dissyllabic and trisyllabic verbal particles, the student should be reminded of the general rule regarding the repeating of the second or third syllable of the particle instead of the first of the root, for the present and future tenses. In applying this rule to *maca*, we must say that here, as elsewhere, the rule is somewhat arbitrary, and that the custom prevails in some parts of the Islands of repeating *ca*, while the first syllable of the root is repeated in others. The latter form is to be preferred, especially in those roots which admit of *ca* in the passive.

Maca, applied to roots admitting of *um* or *mag* conjugations verbalizes in a potential sense, and in a causative one, if applied to those involuntary actions that are conjugated by *ma*, that is to say, according to *maca* being made use of for actions or affections. The pluperfect and perfect future tenses of *maca* have very little use and cannot, of course, be formed in the suppletory way of respectively prefixing *naca* and *maca*, without entailing confusion with the past indefinite tense and the imperative. Thus, these latter with the completive particle *na* after them are used to express the respective perfect tenses.

ROOTS.

Pace.	Lácad.
Sadness.	Hapis.

PARADIGMS.

To walk.	Lumácad.
Thing walked for.	Lacarin.
Place whereto. or person to whom somebody takes anything, by walking.	Lacaran.
To walk a great deal, or to carry some thing along with one while walking.	Maglacad.
Thing thus carried along, or the foot.	Ilácad.
Person to whom.	Lacaran.
Route whereby.	Paglacarán.
To walk merely as a pastime.	Maglacarlacar.
Place whereon.	Paglacarlacaran.
To be able to walk.	Macalácad.

To be sad.	Mahapis.
Cause.	Icahapis.
The object causing sadness.	Cahapisan.
How sad!	Cahapis-hapis.

CONJUGATION.

ACTIVE

Infinitive.

To be able to walk.	Macalácad.
To sadden.	Macahapis.

Present indefinite tense.

Can, –st walk. Sadden, -est, -s.	Nacacalácad- (1). Nacahahapis. (1).

Present perfect and past indefinite tenses.

Could. -dst; have, hast, has been able to walk. Saddened, -dst; have, hast, has saddened.	Nacalácad. Nacahapis.

Pluperfect tense.

Had, -dst been able to walk. Had, -dst saddened.	Nacalácad na. Nacahapis na.

Future indefinite tense.

Shall, -lt, will, -lt be able to walk. „ „ „ „ sadden.	Macalalácad. (1). Macahahapis. (1).

Future perfect tense.

Shall, -lt. will, -lt have been able to walk. „ „ „ „ „ saddened.	Macalácad na. Macahapis na.

Imperative.

Be able, let....be able to walk. Sadden, let....sadden.	Macalácad. (2). Macahapis.

Verbals.

The action of being able to walk. „ „ „ saddening.	Ang pagcalácad. Ang pagcahapis.

THE PASSIVE.

The potencial sense of *maca*, admits of the three passives; the causetive sense only admits of *y* passive. The passive particle correspond-

---

(1) *Nacacalácad, nacacahapis; macacalácad, macacahapis* are also in use.
(2) Speaking properly, *lócad*, in ·the potential sense, lacks imperative.

ing to the potential sense is *ma*, the one corresponding to the causative sense, is *ca*; (*yca*, since such verbs admit but of *y* passive). In the passive of *in*, this particle is dropped in all the tenses, which is a peculiarity of *maca* conjugation, only *ma* or *na* remaining as seen hereafter.

IN PASSIVE.

Infinitive.

To be run over. (*to be able to be run over*).   Malácad.

Present indefinite tense.

Am. art, is, are run over.   Nalalácad.

Present perfect and past indefinite tenses.

Was, -st, were; have, hast, has been run over.   Nalácad.

Pluperfect tense.

Had, -dst been run over.   Nalácad na.

Future indefinite tense.

Shall, -lt, will, -lt be run over.   Malalácad.

Future perfect tense.

Shall, -lt, will, -lt have been run over.   Malalácad na.

Imperative.

Be, let. . . . be run over.   Malácad.

Y PASSIVE.

Infinitive.

To be able to walk with. (a staff.)   Maylácad.
To sadden by.   Ycahápis.

Present indefinite tense.

Can, -st, walk with.   Naylalácad.
Sadden, -est, -s.   Yquinahahapis.

Present perfect and past indefinite tenses.

Could, -dst walk; have, hast, has been
able to walk with. Saddened, -dst; } Naylácad, Yquinahapis.
have, hast, has saddened by.

Pluperfect tense.

Had, -dst been able to walk with.   }   Naylácad na. Yquinahapis na.
    „   „   saddened by.   }

Future indefinite tense.

Shall, -lt. will, -lt be able to walk with. }   Maylalácad. Ycahahapis.
   „   „   „   „   sadden by.   }

Future perfect tense.

Shall, -lt. will, -lt have been able to }   Maylalácad na. Ycahahapis na.
            walk with.   }
   „   „   „   „   do do saddened by. }

Imperative.

Let. . . . . . be able to walk with.   Maylácad.
Sadden, let. . . . . . sadden by.   Ycahapis.

Verbals.

The action of being able to walk with. }   Ang maylácad.   Ang ycahapis.
  „   „   „   saddening by.   }

AN PASSIVE.

Infinitive.

To be able to walk at.   Malacaran.

Present indefinite tense.

Can, -st walk; am, art. is able to walk }   Nalalacaran.
at.   }

Present perfect and past indefinite tenses.

Could, -dst walk; was, -st, were; have, }   Nalacaran.
hast, has been able to walk at.   }

Pluperfect tense.

Had, -dst been able to walk at.   Nalacaran na.

Future indefinite tense.

Shall, -lt, will, -lt be able to walk at.   Malalacaran.

Future perfect tense.

Shall, -lt, will, -lt have been able to }   Malalacaran na.
walk at.   }

Imperative.

Let........... be able to walk at.   Malacaran.

Verbal.

The action of being able to walk at.   Ang malacaran.

The student should conjugate the following verbs by *maca*, both in the active and in the various forms of passive.

To make merry, to gladden, to cheer.	Macatóua.
To make melancholy.	Macalumbáy.
To frighten, to intimidate.	Macatácot.
To harm, to do ill.	Macasamá.
To cause pain, to grieve.	Macapañganyaya.
To strengthen, to cause health.	Macagaling, macalacás.
To be able to do or to make.	Macagauá.
To terrify.	Macapañgilabot.
To beautify.	Macagandà.
To cause the disgust of satiety.	Macabusog.
To hinder, to cumber.	Macagambala.
To mitigate grief.	Macaguinhaua.

Maca may be recombined with any other conjugation admitting of potentiality by being prefixed to the passive particle of any such conjugation. Care should be taken in employing the proper particle required by the kind of action, so as to make the proper discrimination of sense.

To be able to go out.	Macalabás.
,, ,, ,, ,, take out.	Macapaglabás.
,, ,, ,, ,, go away.	Macaalís.
,, ,, ,, ,, take away.	Macapagalís.
,, ,, ,, ,, teach.	Macaáral.
,, ,, ,, ,, study.	Macapagáral.
,, ,, ,, ,, preach.	Macapañgáral.

Any such particle indicative of the primary sense should be preserved in the passive.

I could get out from Manila.	Ang Maynila, ang nalabasan co.
I could take out from the church.	Napaglabasan co ang simbahan.

In actions, *maca*, refers more to a material or physical than to a moral capability or permissive power. The latter is better expressed by *mangyari* or *súcat*, although *maca* is also sometimes used.

Meat may not be eaten on fast-days.	{ Sa mañga viernes nang cuaresma,i, di súcat cumáin nang lamangcati.
It may be given to him, he may be trusted with it.	{ Súcat siyáng big-ián.
Might it be?	¿Mangyayari bagá?.

The potential active and passives of *maca* may be used indiscriminately without paying any attention as to whether there are objects or not in the sentence, or whether they are or are not circumscribed in sense.

I can write this book.	{ Nacacasúlat acó nitóng libro. Ytóng libro,i, nasusúlat co.
I could.	Nacacaya acó, nacaya co.

Maca is fit to express such actions as are inherent in the powers of mind or the corporal senses, to indicate the capability they are endowed with to perform such acts as are peculiar to them, without the will taking any part therein. Thus.

To understand, that is to say, to apply the power of will to understanding.	Tumalastás.
To comprehend.	Magtalastás.
But, to understand, to have the understanding free.	Macatalastás.
To hear purposely, to listen.	Dumiñgig.
To hear a good deal or many things.	Magdiñgig.
But to hear, to have the hearing free.	Macariñgig.

In the same sense:

To think.	Macaísip.
To remember.	Macaalaalà.
To make out.	Macatanto.
To feel.	Macaramdam.
To see.	Macaquita.
To smell.	Macaamóy.
To taste.	Macalásap.
To touch.	Macaramà. or, macadamà.
To say. to pronounce.	Macauica.
To divert.	Macalibang.
To learn.	Macapagáral.
To explain.	Macasaysáy, macasalaysáy.
To show, to declare.	Macaháyag.
To perceive, to know how, to know as a fact.	Macaálay.
To conceive.	Macamálay.

If an act admitting of volition is conjugated by *maca*, the same sense of involuntariness is imparted as if *ma* were used.

On my loitering about, I got into my uncle's inclosure. (without my being aware of it)	Acó,i, nalilígao ay nacapásoc acó sa bacoran nang aquing amaín.
I was reading when I fell asleep.	Sa aquing pagbasà,i, nacatólog acó.

In verbs denoting the initiative on the part of the subject towards some end, the tendency is expressed in the regular way; but the attainment is expressed by *maca*.

To look for. To find.	Humánap. Macahánap.
	Cumita. Macaquita.
To ask for. To obtain.	Humiñgi. Macahiñgi.
To run for. To overtake.	Humábol. Macahábol.

The passive of *an* serves to denote the same sense of being overtaken by unconscious agents.

Night came down upon us before we arrived at Manila.	Nagabihan camí bagó dumating sa Maynila.
The army were surprised on their way by the rain.	Naolanán ang hocbó sa dáan.

Maca is very much made use of by natives in a potential elusive sense to indicate something which they are ashamed to declare or vouch for.

In confessing what may bring punishment upon them or what my hurt the feelings of the person they are speaking to, they, generally, employ *maca* as an insinuation for any such acts as they are, however, well assured of.

Have you ever purloined anything?	¿Ungmomit ca bagá nang anomán.?
I have sometimes purloined. (I may have purloined.)	Marahil nacaomit acó.
Did you see me kill him?	¿Naquita mo acóng pumatáy sa caniyà?,
I saw.	Nacaquita acó, naquita co.

CONSTRUCTION.

Active sentences the verb of which obtains in *maca* conjugation are constructed in the regular way, with the agent in the nominative case and the object in the accusatiwe, in whatever sense the verb may be used; but the object of a verb in the causative sense should always be preceded by *sa* and not by *nang*. Passive sentences in which *maca* is used in the potential sense also follow the general rule of construction; the agent in the possessive case, and the patient in the nominative; but the agent should be put in the nominative and the patient or object, in the possessive. for passive sentences where *maca* is used in the causative sense.

He can write the letters.	Nacacasúlat siyá nang mañga súlat.
	Nasusúlat niyà ang mañga súlat.
Chastity imparts health to (strengthens) the body.	Ang calinisa,i, nacagagaling sa cataouán. Yquinagagaling nang cataouán ang calinisan.

THIRTY SEVENTH EXERCISE.

Why can you not walk? I cannot walk, because I am lame. What saddens her? Her mother's death saddened her. With whom will he be glad? He will be glad with his children. What caused your father's melancholy? Sea-faring life frightens him. What made you sick last week? Fruit injured me. And what made you recover? Some medicines cured me. Can he do that? He cannot do that. What terrifies children? Thunder terrifies children. What beautifies girls? Modesty beautifies girls. What causes satiety? Sweet patatoes cause satiety. What would hinder him? His office hinders him. Who mitigated your grief? My wife mitigated my grief. Will he be able to go out now? He cannot go out now, but he will go away to-morrow. Have you been able to take out the stone? I could not take out the stone. Can you not teach Tagalog? No, I cannot, but I can learn it. Can he preach to the people? He is not a priest, so he cannot preach. May I (am I permitted) take the book? You may take it. Do you understand me? I don't understand you. Do you comprehend what I say? I do. Does he hear the roaring of the wind? He does not. he is deaf. Can you think upon it? I cannot think, but I can remember. Can he make out the meaning of this word? He can feel and see; but he cannot make out the meaning. Could he smell the fragance of flowers? He could before, but he cannot now even perceive objects by touching nor liquors by taste. Will he be able to pronounce? He will not be able to pronounce, for he stutters somewhat. Can they explain the case? They can lay it before the Judge. Do they know how to read? They do. What do you do here on the beach? I arrived here without my being aware of it. Has the servant looked for the key? Yes, but he could not come across with it. Has your sister asked our neighbour for flowers? No, because she knows she will not be given them. What did the boy do? He ran for Frank and he overtook him. When shall we depart? Start early in the morning that you may not be harmed by sunshine. And if night come upon us in the way? Go on, for you will have the benefit of enjoying moonlight; but take care not to be surprised by the rain.

THIRTY EIGHTH LESSON.
YCATLONG POUO,T, UALONG PAGARAL.

MODIFÍCATIVE VERBALIZING PARTICLES.

MAGPA=PA.

Magpa, commonly verbalizes chiefly in a factitive sense. It being dis-syllabic in structure, *pa*, the last syllable of it, is repeated to form the simple present and future tenses. The passive particle for *magpa* is *pa* (sometimes *pagpa*, *papag*, according to the verb requiring *um* or *mag* in its primary or secondary sense.). *Pa*, being monosyllabic, the first syllable of the root and not that of the particle should be repeated in the proper tenses of the passive. Care should be taken to introduce the passive particle required by the verb in its primary sense, by inserting it before or after(gen-erally after) *pa*, the passive particle of this conjugation, in the pluperfect and future perfect tenses of the active and passives, and the other tenses of the latter requiring it for distinguishing the sense.

The two following examples of conjugation have been selected to make this discrimination more noticeable.

ACTIVE.

Infinitive.

To order to teach, to cause to teach.
To order to learn, to cause to learn. } Magpaáral. Magpapagáral.

Present indefinite tense.

Order, -st, -s to teach; to learn.   Nagpapaáral; nagpapapagáral.

Present perfect and past indefinite tenses.

Ordered, -dst; have, hast, has ordered
to teach; to learn. } Nagpaáral; nagpapagáral

Pluperfect tense.

Had -dst ordered to teach; to learn. { Nacapagpaáral, nagpaáral na.
Nagpapagpapagáral, nagpapagáral na.

Future indefinite tense.

Shall, -lt, will, -lt order to teach;
to learn. } Magpapaáral; magpapapagáral.

Future perfect tense.

Shall, -lt, will, -lt have ordered to teach; to learn. { Macapagpaáral, magpapaáral na.
/ Macapagpapagáral, magpapapagáral na.

Imperative.

Order, let....order to teach; to learn. Magpaáral; magpapagáral.

Verbals.

The action of ordering to teach; to learn. Ang pagpaáral; ang pagpapagáral.

IN PASSIVE.
—

Infinitive.

To be ordered to teach; to learn. Paáral; papagáral.

Present indefinite tense.

Am, art, is, are ordered to teach; to learn. } Pinaaáral; pinapagaáral.

Present perfect and past indefinite tenses.

Was, -st, were; have, hast, has been ordered to teach; to learn. } Pinaáral; pinapagáral.

Pluperfect tense.

Had, -dst, been ordered to teach; to learn. { Napaáral, pinaáral na.
/ Napagpaáral, pinapagáral na.

Future indefinite tense.

Shall, -lt, will. -lt be ordered to teach; to learn. } Paaaralin; papagaaralin.

Future perfect tense.

Shall, -lt, will, -lt have been ordered to teach; to learn. Mapaáral, paaaralin na.
Mapagpaáral, papagaaralin na.

Imperative.

Be ordered, let......be ordered to teach; to learn. { Paaralin; papagaralin.

Verbals.

The state of being ordered to teach; to learn } Ang paáral; ang pagpaáral.

Infinitive.

To order to teach; (something) to learn. (something). } Ypinaáral; ypagpaáral.

Present indefinite tense.

Order, -est, -s to teach; to learn.   Ypinaaáral; ypinapagaáral.

Present perfect and past indefinite tenses.

Ordered, -dst; have, hast, has ordered to teach; to learn. } Ypinaáral; ypinapagáral.

Pluperfect tense.

Had, -dst, ordered to teach; to learn. { Naypaáral, ypinaáral na.
 Naypagpaáral, ypinapagáral na.

Future indefinite tense.

Shall, -lt, will, -lt order to teach; to learn. } Ypaaáral; ypapagaáral.

Future perfect tense.

Shall, -lt, will, -lt have ordered to teach; to learn. { Maypaáral, ypaaáral na.
 Maypagpaáral, ypapagaáral na.

Imperative.

Order, let... order to teach; to learn.   Ypaáral; ypapagáral.

Verbals.

The action of ordering to teach; to learn. } Ang ypaáral; ang ypapagáral.

AN PASSIVE.

Infinitive.

To order to teach to; to learn from.   Paaralan; papagaralan.

Present indefinite tense.

Order, -est, -s to teach to; to learn from. } Pinaaaralan; pinapagaaralan.

Present perfect and past indefinite tenses.

Ordered, -dst; have, hast, has ordered to teach to; to learn from. } Pinaaralan; pinapagaralan.

Pluperfect tense.

Had, dst ordered to teach to; to learn from.

Napaaralan, pinaaralan na.
Napagaralan, pinapagaralan na.

Future indefinite tense.

Shall, -lt, will, -lt order to teach to; to learn from. } Paaaralan; papagaaralan.

Future perfect tense.

Shall, -lt will, -lt have ordered to teach to; to learn from.

Mapaaralan, paaaralan na.
Mapapagaralan, papagaaralan na.

Imperative.

Order, let....order to teach to; to learn from. } Paaralan; papagaralan.

Verbals.

The action of ordering to teach to; to learn from. } Ang paaralan; ang papagaralan.

The student should conjugate the following verbs by *magpa* in the active and in all the forms of the passive.

To enact, to order to institute.	Magpahalal.
To create, to order to bring forward.	Magpalalang.
To order to do or make.	Magpagauá.
To order to go or come upstairs.	Magpapanhic.
To order to have something upstairs.	Magpapagpanhic.
To order to go or come downstairs.	Magpapanáog.
To order to get something downstairs.	Magpapagpanáog.
To be able to order to get into.	Macapagpapásoc. (1).
To order to plant.	Magpatanim.
„ „ „ write.	Magpasúlat.
„ „ „ bolt.	Magpasusi.
„ „ „ sew.	Magpatahi.

Magpa in the foregoing instances refers to actions to be executed by a person other than the subject. If the action is active and such as to be suffered by the subject, *magpa*, means to allow one's self to suffer willingly, or to let one's self be acted upon by the acts of others.

---

(1) Potential and factitive senses combined: *maca* is conjugated, and *pa* is repeated in the present and simple future tenses.

To allow one's self to be cheated.						Magparaya.
,,	,,	,,	,,	,,	,, touched.	Magpahipo.
,,	,,	,,	,,	,,	,, whipped.	Magpahampás.
,,	,,	,,	,,	,,	,, slapped.	Magpatampal.
,,	,,	,,	,,	,,	,, crucified.	Magpaparipà.
,,	,,	,,	,,	,,	,, punished.	Magpaparusà.
,,	,,	,,	,,	,,	,, combed.	Magpasucláy.
,,	,,	,,	,,	,,	,, belied.	Magpasoat.

If *magpa* is applied to a root denoting a physical state got at from another contrary previous one by a slow self-working process, the action of the subject either to promote or not to interfere with the transition is meant.

To allow to become cool, to make cool by exposure.	Magpalamig.
To allow to grow rotten, te allow rottenness to go on.	Magpaboloc.
To allow to get dried. to put to dry.	Magpatuyó.
To allow to fall into decay.	Magpaguibá.

Attention should be paid to what is said either previously or subsequently to discriminate the sense of, "to order to demolish" from that of "to allow to fall into decay".

When the same effect is to be got at through the influence of an external agent, the latter may be conjugated by *magpa* and the purposed act of the subject to profit by such influence is indicated.

To expose to sunshine.	Magpaarúo. (1)
,, ,, ,, the wind.	Magpahañgin.
,, ,, ,, rainfall.	Magpaolán.

This is only with regard to the effect sought for in the performance of such actions by an agent incapable or producing the working power; but if the same are looked upon with regard to the causer, as God or any Power to which they may be attributed, the sense is of causality.

To cause the Sun to shine.	Magpaárao.
To cause the billows to rise.	Magpaalon.
To thunder. (looked upon as to the power which produces it).	Magpacolog.
To lighten. (do do).	Magpaquidlat.
It is God who causes thunderbolts to fall down, and the trees to bloom and bear fruit.	Ang Dios, ang nagpapalintic, nagpapabulac-lac at ang nagpapahoñga namán sa mañga cáhoy.

If not the effect, but the time of such atmospherical events is considered, *magpa* indicates refraining on the part of the subject until such emergencies are over. Care should be taken to make the sense clear by some other completive or discriminative word with those verbs to which *magpa* imparts different significations.

To wait until rain is over, to wait for the rain to cease.	Magpatila.
To wait until dawn breaks.	Magpaomaga.
,, ,, ,, the day or sun grows less hot.	Magpalamig nang árao.
To wait until the sun rises.	Magpasíïang.
To allow the water to be cooled.	Magpalamig nang túbig.

---

(1) The word is made grave to distinguish this sense of that of "to wait until the sun rises."

Magpa is fit to express such acts on the part of the subject as may redound to the benefit of others and which can be resolved into the different ways of giving with roots having an active sense in what regards the agent.

To impart sight, to cure blindness.	Magpaquita.
To feed.	Magpacáin.
To quench, to provide drinks.	Magpainom.
To shelter, to afford a shelter.	Magpatulóy.
To lend money (without reference to reluctance or readiness).	Magótang.
To lend money. (willingly).	Magpaótang.
To clothe, to provide clothing for somebody.	Magparamit.
To invest money on interest.	Magpatubò. (from *tubò*, "to grow").
To send, to forward.	Magpadalà.

But if the root has a passive force, the sense is one of exaction or asking for.

Alms.	*Limós.* (corr. from Sp. word *limosna*).
Pledge.	Sanlá.
Tribute. (capitation tax).	Bouís.
To give alms.	Maglimos.
To ask for alms, to beg.	Magpalimós.
To ask for pledge.	Magpasanlá.
To pay tribute.	Bumouís.
To collect, to exact tribute.	Magpabouís.

It should also be noticed that if *magpa* is made use of by a person inferior in rank to that addressed, the sense is reversed. Thus, *magpagauá ca niyán sa iyòng amá, magpaulán ca sa Dios*, do not mean respectively, "order your father to do that", "make God to send down some rain", but, "crave your father to do that"; "pray God for rain", and so forth in similar cases.

Every student will easily make out the difference in meaning between "to confess to the priest" and "to confess by the priest". Any such actions having a passive sense as to the performer, are conjugated by *magpa*.

To hear confessions.	Magpacumpisal.
To confess to the priest.	Magcumpisal.
To ask for pardon, to haggle, to ask for a reduction of price.	Tumáuar.
To grant a reduction of price.	Magtáuad.
To grant pardon, to pardon.	Magpatáuar.

Magpa is therefore a particle forming a certain kind of deponent verbs. (1).

To get shaved.	Magpaahit.
To have one's shoes shined.	Magpalinis nang sapin.
To get one's hair cut.	Magpagupit.

To say, to recite something by many or many times as in prayers, may be expressed by *magpa*.

Say (plural) amen and amen.	Magpaamén cayó.

Through a looseness of rules which prevails everywhere in Tagalog, *magpa* may be made to mean conscious acting of the subject upon himself.

---

(1). We preserve to the word *deponent* the sense it has in Latin, where it means a verb having an active meaning with a passive form or vice--versa.

To embellish one's self.	Magpagandà.
To deck one's self.	Magpabut`.
To elate, to draw credit or praise upon one's self. }	Magpapurì.

A sense of involuntariness or the natural effect of inanimate agents, is expressed, in this conjugation, by dropping the *g* of *magpa.*

Smoke sweeps upwards.	Napapaitáas ang asò.
Water flows downwards.	Napapaibabá ang túbig.
Vapors of the soil rise in the atmosphere.	Ang mañga siñgáo nang lupa napapasaimpapauid.
Rivers flow into the sea.	} Napapasadágat ang agus nang mañga ílog.
My heart throbs unto (is drawn towards) Thee my Lord.	Ang aquin puso, napapasainyò, Pañginòon cong Dios.

Verbs to which *magpa* does not impart an ordering sense may be made to express it by repeating *pa.*

God commands to give alms to the poor.	Ang Dios ay nagpapalimos sa mañga duchá.

But it is clearer to say: *Ang Dios ay nagoótos maglimos sa mañga duc-há.*

THIRTY EIGHTH EXERCISE.

Did you order the children upstairs? I did. Do you order the servants to bring up some firewood? I do. What does George's father order him to do? He orders him to continue studing. Why do you not order your son to learn? I don't order him to learn, because he is sick. Does your brother-in-law order his servants to attend mass every holy-day? He does. Why did you not wait till the rain ceased? I waited till the sun rose and did not start till the sun grew less hot. Why do you allow the plants to grow rotten? I don't allow them to become rotten, but, on the contrary, I expose them to the wind and sunshine. Is he waiting till the rain ceases? Yes. Why does he not wait until the sun rises? Because he is in a hurry. What did Peter order his servant to do? He said to him, don't let the flowers fade. (get dry). Why doest nót thou allow the water to cool? Because it is already cooled. Why does your sister allow herself to be cheated? Because she is very shy. Who causes the sun and the moon to shine? God. What else does He cause to happen? He causes the rain to fall down, the lightening to flash, the thunder to crack, and the billows to rise. Does He cause too the trees to bloom and to bear fruit? He does. From whom did that beggar ask for alms? He begs from my aunt. Why did not the rich man feed those people? He said to his servant, feed them. Shall I quench their thirst? Yes, give them wine to drink. Who is that man over there asking for alms? He is a beggar whom I sheltered last night. Does he collect plenty of alms? No, Sir, it is not sufficient for his living. Why do you not lend him money? Because I have none, as I invested my money at interest (loaned). Why did not Anthony provide clothing for his children? Because he has nothing to buy clothes with. Where shall I put water to cool? Put water to cool in this shed. Which priest received your confession? Father Jonh heard my confession. Why does that girl embellish herself? Because she wishes to be praised. In what direction does water flow? Water flows downwards. What penance did the priest impose you? The penance he inflicted me was to fast. Did you provide the poultry with water? I did. What did you feed them with? I fed them with husk-rice. Did he order his son to rise? He did. Why do you not allow me to pass farther? I will not allow you to pass farther until you give me water to drink.

THIRTY NINTH LESSON.
YCATLONG POUO,T, SIYAM NA PAGARAL.

MODIFICATIVE VERBALIZING PARTICLES.

MAQUI=PAQUI.

Maqui, for the active; *paqui*, for the passive, is a less important verbal particle, which, if applied to a root capable of being converted into an action of companionhip, imparts a sense of intermeddling or joining on the part of the subject. In only admits of *y* and *an* passives. *In* passive finds no place with this particle (*paqui* indicating an act *ad extra* on the part of the agent), unless, however, it be combined with *magpa. Papaquipagaralin mo ang anac mo sa mañga batang iyán,* "order your son to join those children in learning". *Y*, which is the proper passive, stands for the thing, object of joining or association; *an*, for the person whom one meddles with in anything. This particle being dissyllabic, repeats *qui* for present and future tenses. The pluperfect and futuro perfect tenses have very little use and cannot be formed with *naca. maca; na* and *ma.*

ROOT.

Knowing. (as a fact)	Alam.

PARADIGM.

To be growing wise.	Umálam.
To know something.	Macaálam.
What known.	Naalaman.
Kindness.	Caalaman. (obsolete)
Reason of being kind.	Yalam.
Person enjoying a benefit.	Pinagmamaálam.
To feign to know.	Magmaálam.
Bulletin-board, posting place.	Pinagcaalaman.
To report, to warn.	Umalam. (1)
Person warned.	Alamín.
To make one's self acquainted with a thing.	Maquialam.
Thing acquainted with.	Ypaquialam.
Person from whom.	Paquialamán.

---

(1). Notice the accentuation.

CONJUGATION.

ACTIVE.

Infinitive.

To investigate, to set about to in-
quire, to make one's self thoroughly } Maquialam.
acquainted with, to sift into.

Present indefinite tense.

Investigate, -st, -s.   Naquiquialam.

Present perfect and past indefinite tense:

Investigated, -dst; have, hast, has) Naquialam.
investigated.   }

Pluperfect tense.

Had, -dst, investigated.   Naquialam na.

Future indefinite tense.

Shall, -lt, will, -lt investigate.   Maquiquialam.

Future perfect tense.

Shall, -lt, will, -lt have investigated. Maquiquialam na.

Imperative.

Investigate, let......investigate.   Maquialam.

Verbal.

The action of investigating.   Ang paquiquialam.

Y PASIVE.

Infinitive.

To be investigated, sifted into.   Ypaquialam.

Present indefinite tense.

Is, are sifted into.   Ypinaquiquialam.

Present perfect and past indefinite tenses.

Was, were; has, have been sifted into.   Ypinaquialam.

Pluperfect tense.

Had been sifted into.   Ypinaquialam na.

Future indefinite tense.

Shall, will be sifted into.   Ypaquiquialam.

Future perfect tense.

Shall, will have been sifted into.   Ypaquiquialam na.

Imperative.

Let......be sifted into.   Ypaquialam.

Verbal.

The state of being sifted into.   Ang ypaquiquialam.

AN PASSIVE.

Infinitive.

To inquire from.   Paquialamán.

Present indefinite tense.

Inquire, -st, -s from.   Pinaquiquialamán.

Present perfect and past indefinite tenses.

Inquired, -dst; have, hast, has inquired from.   Pinaquialamán.

Pluperfect tense.

Had, -dst inquired from.   Pinaquialamán na.

Future indefinite tense.

Shall, -lt, will, -lt inquire from. Paquiquialamán.

Future perfect tense.

Shall, -lt, will, -lt have inquired from.   Paquiquialamán na.

Imperative.

Inquire, let.... inquire from.   Paquialamán.

Verbal.

The action of inquiring from.   Ang paquialamán.

The student should conjugate by *maqui* actively and passively the following verbs:

To join officiouly in the teaching of others.	Maquiáral.
Do do do do do do the studying do do	Maquipagáral.
„ „ „ „ „ „ playing „ „	Maquipaglaró.
To embark sneakingly, to sneak into a ship, to embark with others.	Maquisacáy.
To meddle in conversation.	Maquipagósap.
To join in weeping.	Maquitañgís.
To join in rejoicing.	Maquitóua, maquipagcatóua.
To pick a quarrel.	Maquipagáuay.
To meddle in contention.	Maquipagtalo.
To sneak into company.	Maquisamà.
To participate, to claim a share in.	Maquirámay.

Maqui may be made to mean sharing, resemblance in or to have a leaning for customs or manners, if applied to roots denoting qualities capable of being imitated.

To conform one's self to, to comply with customs.	Maquiogali.
To adopt natives' manners.	Maquitagálog.
To behave in a manlike way, to use to flirt or mix with male-people.	Maquilalaqui.
To assume Spanish manners.	Maquicastila.
To be a partisan of the American polity.	Maquiamericano.
To resemble a beast.	Maquiháyop.
To resemble a human being, to be (an animal) tamed as not to be afraid of persons.	Maquitauò.
To be effeminate, to be of a lecherous disposition	Maquibabaye.

The asking for small portions of victuals and cooking necessaries, such as are commonly exchanged freely in rural or village-life among neighbours, may de made by conjugating by *maqui* the root indicative of any such commodities.

To ask for a little cocoa-nut oil.	Maquilañgís.
„ „ „ „ „ vinegar.	Maquisuca.
„ „ „ „ grain of salt.	Maquiasín.
„ „ „ „ small drink.	Maquiálac.
„ „ „ „ handful of rice.	Maquibigás.
„ „ „ „ particle of fire.	Maquiapúy.

A sense of intension is made in the conjugation of *maqui* by affixing *an* or *han* to the verb.

To hate bitterly, to detest.	Maquipagtaniman.
To meddle with others to jeer contentiously.	Maquipagbiróan.
To meddle in the romping of others.	Maquipaglaróan.
To interfere officiously in the conversation.	Maquipagsalitáan.
To launch one's self into controversy, to dispute obstinately.	Maquipagsagutan.

From whom has he asked a grain of salt.	¿Sino bagá ang pinaquiasinan niyà?
What have you thanked for?	¿Anóng ypinaquihiñgi mo?
I have thanked for a red-hot coal.	Naquiapúy acó.
Do not detest thus your neighbour.	Houag cang maquipagtaniman sa cápoua mo tauò.
Why does your nephew meddle in controversy with John?	¿Báquit naquiquipagsagutan ang iyóng pamangquing lalaqui cay Juan?.
Mary is a girl who behaves in a man-like way.	Naquiquilalaqui si María.

PARTICLES AND WORDS USED AS DIFFERENT PARTS OF SPEECH.

Reference has already been made to the pliable character of Tagalog words and how they may stand for different parts of speech. The independent particles too, have, most of them, an enlarged range of meaning and may sometimes stand for parts of speech other than those which they most commonly stand for. In this and other lessons to follow, the various meanings of those words most usual in common topics will be considered.

ANG.
—

The article and relative pronoun *ang* may stand, besides, for a sub-ordinate causative conjunction.

You did not pay any attention to (looked at) me, because I am poor.	Di mo acò liniñgon, ang acó,i, duc-há.
I cannot rise, for I am sick.	Hindí acó nacacabañgon or macabañgon, ang acó,i, may saquit.

AT.
—

At, the copulative conjunction may likewise stand in the same way for a causative one.

He could not come, because he had work.	Di siyá nacaparitó, at may abala siyá.

At=t comes after a causative or adversative conjunction as a completive ligament.

I cannot pay, because I have no money.	Hindí acó nacababáyad or macabáyad, sa pagca,t, ualá acóng salapí.
She is ugly, but she is judicious.	Siyá,i, páñgit, ñgoní,t, siyá,i, mabait.
All of them sang, but him.	Siláng lahat ay nagáuit, alintana,t, siyá,i, hindí.

THIRTY NINTH EXERCISE.

Why do you meddle to converse with old people? I meddle in their conversation because I am anxious to become wise. Why do you enjoin me not to meddle with women in jeering? I enjoined you that, because it is indecorous to meddle with women in romping. Why did he meddle in disputing with his neighbour? Because his neighbour meddles to inspect impertinently. Does your brother assume Spanish manners? No, he does not assume Spanish manners. What are you going to thank the neighbour for? I am going to thank him for a handful of rice. Whom do you ask it for? I ask it for my friend that is sick, and has nothing to eat. What did they thank for? I asked for a little wine. Whom have you thanked for it? I asked it from the sailor. Did I not say to you not to ask it from such a niggardly fellow? I asked some from him as there was no other. Is he esteemed? He was esteemed by his master when still young. How old is your son? He is hardly three years old; but my brother is about sixteen years and the infant one is already eight months. What did you give to those children? I gave them nothing yesterday, but I had already given them what you told me when you arrived. Will he give me that walking-stick? No, but he will give you the book you charged him with. Do you wish to sell that horse? Why!, are you willing to buy it? If it is cheap I will buy it. On which paper is he writing? He is writing on this paper. Is he going to call for the priest? No, he is going to call for the physician. What are those children doing there on the beach? They are playing. What will you ask for from your father when he arrives? That I be given money. Where are those women going? They are going to a very distant place. Did he pour wine into my cup? He did not pour wine, but he poured water into it. What are you doing? I am putting water into your tumbler that is very large. What are those men looking at? They examine the image of the Virgin. What is your friend studying? He is studying Latin. Where is he studying? In Manila. Is it difficult to learn Latin? It is. Why does not Peter salute you? As I am poor, nobody looks at me, were I rich I should be esteemed by everybody.

FORTIETH LESSON.
YCAAPAT NA POUONG PAGARAL.

MODIFICATIVE VERBALIZING PARTICLES.

PA=PA.

As a verbal particle *pa*, for active and passive, differs from *magpa* mainly in its being applied to form the verbs of motion. In other minor respects both particles differ in that *pa* refers more to the subject while *magpa* looks forward to the object. This similarity extends itself to the conjugation, for *pa* is prefixed by *na* in the present and past tenses.

The five adverbs of place, *dini, ditó, diyán, dóon, saán* are conjugated by *pa* to mean "to come". "to go"; *dini*, indicating a place more determinate than *ditó*; *diyán*, the place where the person addressed stands, and *dóon*. a place far away from both interlocutors, *Saán*, indicates motion to an unknown place and means "to move towards". Any other root indicative of place or resort my be conjugated by *pa* if motion thereunto is to be meant; but *sa*, although not absolutely necessary, should be inserted between the particle and the root.

Pa, being a monosyllabic particle, the first syllable of the root is to be repeated in the proper tenses of the conjugation. If, however. *sa* is inserted to conjugate a nominal root of place, *sa* and not the first syllable of the root should be repeated, *pasa* being then considered as a true independent particle. As to the conjugation of the above four adverbs of place, the use has been to some extent established of repeating either the particle or the first syllable of the adverb, it being indifferent to say, *paparitó, pariritó*, etc., although the latter form is more to be recommended.

ROOTS.

House. Báhay.
Aid. Tólong.

PARADIGMS.

To live in a house. Mamáhay.
To build houses. Magbáhay.
To be an inmate. Maquipabáhay, maquipamáhay.
To beg for a parcel of ground to build a house upon. Maquibáhay.
To aid, to assist other persons. Tomólong.
To render effective aid to others. Magtólong.
Person to whom. Toloñgan.
Do do (intensive). Pagtoloñgan.
Reason or instrument. Ytólong, ypagtólong.
Assistant. (one of the aiding parties). Católong.
To aid customarily. Manólong.
To aid each other. Magpanoloñgan.

CONJUGATIONS.

ACTIVE.

Infinitive.

To come here.	Paritò.
To go home.	Pasabáhay.
To crave help.	Patólong.

Present indefinite tense.

Come, –st, –s.	Napariritò. (napaparitò).
Go, –est, –es home.	Napasasabáhay.
Crave, –st, –s help.	Napatotólong.

Present perfect and past indefinite tenses.

Came, –st; have, hast, has come.	Naparito.
Went, –est; have, hast, has gone home.	Napasabáhay.
Craved, –dst; have, hast, has craved help.	Napatólong.

Pluperfect tense.

Had, –dst come.	Nacaparitò, naparitò na.
„ „ gone home,	Nacapasabáhay, napasabáhay na.
„ „ craved help.	Nacapatólong, napatólong na.

Future indefinite tense.

Shall, –lt, will, –lt come.	Pariritò. (paparitò)
„ „ „ „ go home.	Pasasabáhay.
„ „ „ „ crave help.	Patotólong.

Future perfect tense.

Shall, –lt, will, –lt have come.	Macaparitò, pariritò na. (paparitò na).
„ „ „ „ „ gone home.	Macapasabáhay, pasasabáhay na.
„ „ „ „ „ craved help.	Macapatólong, patotólong na.

Imperative.

Come, let . . . . . come.	Parit`.
Go home, „ . . . . . . go home.	Pasabáhay.
Crave, „ . . . . . crave help.	Patólong.

Verbals.

The action of coming.	Ang pagparitò.
„ „ „ going home.	„ pagpasabáhay.
„ „ „ craving help.	„ pagpatólong.

THE PASSIVE.

Verbs of motion being intransitive do not admit of *in* passive, unless they be recompounded with some other particle imparting an active sense. Thus, that they may be conjugated in such passive, they must be combined with *magpa* in the ordering or bespeaking sense; as, *paparitohin mo siyá*, "order him to come here". In the instrumental or causal passive, *ca*, the proper particle for neuter verbs or involuntary actions in said passive, should be inserted between the sign and the verb, thus making *yca, yquina*, etc.

IN PASSIVE.

Infinitive.

To be ordered here.	Paparitohin.
„ „ „ home.	Papasabahayin. (1).
„ crave to be helped.	Patoloñgin.

Present indefinite tense.

Am, art, is, are ordered here.	Pinariritò. (pinapaparitò).
„ „ „ „ „ home.	Pinapasasabáhay.
Crave, st, -s to be helped.	Pinatotólong.

Present perfect and past indefinite tenses.

Was, -st, were; have, hast, has been ordered here.	Pinaparitò.
„ „ „ „ „ „ „ „ home.	Pinapasabáhay.
Craved, -dst; have, hast, has craved to be helped.	Pinatolóng.

Pluperfect tense.

Had, -dst been ordered here.	Pinaparitò na. (2).
„ „ „ „ home.	Pinapasabáhay na.
„ „ „ craved to be helped.	Pinatólong na.

Future indefinite tense.

Shall, -lt, will, -lt be ordered here.	Papariritohin. (papaparitohin).
„ „ „ „ „ „ home.	Papasasabahayin.
„ „ „ „ crave to be helped.	Patotoloñgin.

Future perfect tense.

Shall -lt, will, -lt have been ordered here.	Papariritohin (papaparitohin na.)
„ „ „ „ „ „ „ home.	Papasasabahayin na.
„ „ „ „ „ craved to be helped.	Patotoloñgin na.

(1) The form in the example is merely illustrative, as the passives of this root are very little made use of.

(2) This, and the future perfect tense are but rarely used. The form *naparitó*, is not admissible, as it will entail confusion with the active.

Imperative.

Be ordered, let .... be ordered here. Paparitohin.

„ „ „ .... „ „ home. Papasabahayin.

Crave, let .... crave to be helped. Patoñigin.

Verbals.

The state of being ordered here. Ang pagpaparitò.

„ „ „ „ „ home „ pagpapasabaháy.

The action of craving to be helped. „ pagpapatólong.

Y PASSIVE.

Infinitive.

To come on account of. Ycaparitò.

To go home on account of. Ycapasabáhay.

To crave assistance on account of. Ycapatólong.

Present indefinite tense.

Come, -st, -s here on account of. Yquinaparirító. (yquinapaparitò.)

Go, -est, -es home „ „ Yquinapasasabáhay.

Crave, -st, -s assistance „ „ „ Ypinatotólong, yquinapatotólong (1).

Present perfect and past indefinite tenses.

Came, st; have, hast, has come here on account of. Yquinaparitò.

Went, -est; „ „ „ gone home „ „ Yquinapasabáhay.

Craved, dst; „ „ „ craved assistance „ „ { Ypinatólong, yquinapa- túlong.

Pluperfect tense.

Had, -dst, come here on account of. Nayparitò, yquinaparitò na.

„ „ gone home „ „ „ { Naypasabáhay, yquinapasabáhay na.

„ „ craved assistance „ „ „ { Naypatólong, ypinatólong na, yqui- napatólong na.

Future indefinite tense.

Shall, -lt, will, -lt come here on account of. Ycapariritò, (ycapaparitò).

„ „ „ „ go home „ „ „ Ycapasasabáhay.

„ „ „ „ crave assistance „ „ „ Ypatotólong, ycapatotólong.

Future perfect tense.

Shall, -lt, will, lt have come here on account of. { Mayparitò, ycapari- ritò na.

„ „ „ „ „ gone home „ „ „ { Maypasabáhay, yca- pasasabáhay na.

„ „ „ „ „ craved assistance „ „ „ { Maypatólong, ypato- tólong or ycapatotó- long na.

---

(1) Both forms are used in this and the other tenses.

Imperative.

Come here, let ....come here	on account of.	Ycaparitò.
Go home, ,, ...go home	,, ,, .,	Ycapasabáhay.
Crave, ,, ...crave for assistance ,,	,, ,,	{ Ypatólong or ycapató- { long.

Verbals.

The action of coming here	on account of.	Ang ycapaparitò.
,, ,, ,, going home	,, ,, ,,	,, ycapapasabáhay.
,, ,, ,, craving assistance	,, ,, ,,	{ ,, ypapatólong or ycapa- { patólong.

AN PASSIVE.

Infinitive.

To come here for, to come here to pay a visit to (a person).	Paritohan.
To go home for.	Pasabahayan.
To provide help to be rendered by.	Patoloñgan.

Present indefinite tense.

Come, –st, -s here for.	Pinariritohan. (pinapaparitohan).
Go, –est, -es home for.	Pinasasabahayan.
Provide, st, -s help to be rendered by.	Pinatotoloñgan.

Present perfect and past indefinite tenses.

Came, -st; have, hast, has come here for.	Pinaritohan.
Went, -est; ,, ,, ,, gone home for.	Pinasabahayan.
Provided, -dst; have, hast, has provided help to be rendere 1 by.	Pinatoloñgan.

Pluperfect tense.

Had, -dst come here for.	Naparitohan, pinaritohan na.
,, ,, gone home for.	Napasabahayan, pinasabahayan na.
,, ,, provided help to be render-ed by.	{ Napatoloñgan, pinatoloñgan na.

Future indefinite tense.

Shall, -lt, will, -lt come here for.	Pariritohan. (paparitohan).
,, ,, ,, ,, go home ,,	Pasasabahayan.
,, ,, ,, ,, provide help to be rendered by.	{ Patotoloñgan.

Future perfect tense.

Shall, -lt, will, -lt have come here for.	Maparitohan, pariritohan na.
,, ,, ,, ,, ,, gone home ,.	Mapasabahayan, pasasabahayan na.
,, ,, ,, ,, provided help to be rendered by.	{ Mapatoloñgan, patotoloñgan na.

Imperative.

Come, let.... come here for.	Paritohan.
Go, „ ......go home for.	Pasabahayan.
Provide, „ ......provide help to be rendered by.	Patoloñgan.

Verbal.

The action of coming here for.	Ang paritohan or paparitohan.
„ „ „ going home „	„ pasabahayan or papasabahayan.
„ „ „ providing help to be rendered by.	„ patoloñgan or papatoloñgan.

Y passive stands for the cause or reason; *an*, for the place or person in verbs of motion, and for the person to whom a service is rendered, in the others.

Why does he go to Manila?	¿Anóng yquinaparoróon niyá sa Maynila?
The paying of my tax is the reason of my going there.	Ang pagbáyad nang aquing bouís, siyá ang yquinaparoróon co.
Where is he going?	¿Saán ang paroroonan niyà?
He is going to Cebú.	Ang Cebú ang paroroonan niyà.
Whom did you come to see here?	¿Sino bagá ang pinaritohan mo?
I came here to pay you a visit.	Pinaritohan quitá. (catá)
Whom does he order to render assistance to him?	¿Sino ang pinatotoloñgan niyà?

The student should conjugate in the active and passives of *pa*, the following verbs:

To go there.	Pariyán.
To go yonder.	Paroón.
To come here.	Parini.
(Where?). to go.	¿Pasaán?
To repair to, to go towards.	Patoñgò.
To go to church.	Pasasimbahan.
To go into the country, to go to the farm.	Pasabúquid.
To go to market.	Pasatianggui.
To go to the sea-shore.	Pasadágat.
To go to the mount.	Pasabundoc.
To ask for mercy.	Paáua.
„ „ „ protection.	Paampón.
„ „ „ support.	Pacopcop.
„ „ „ aid, succour.	Pasangalang.
„ „ „ defence.	Patangol.

The above-mentioned adverbs of place prefixed with *pa* may be considered as simple roots and conjugated by *um*.

To come here.	Pumaritò, pumarini.
To go there.	Pumariyán, pumaróon.
(Saán?) to go.	¿Pumasaán?.

In passive in verbs of motion stands for the person ordered to repair to (some place).

Order my servant to come here.	Paparitohin mo ang aquing bata.
Did you say to him to repair there?	¿Pinaparóon mo siyá?.

I did already.	Pinaparóon co na siyá.
Order him to go there.	Papariyanín mo siyá.

Pa coincides with *magpa* in the acquiescing sense, but *pa* denotes more readiness on the part of the patient.

To ask to be kissed.	Pahalic.
„ „ „ „ touched.	Pahipo.
To consent to be beaten.	Patalo.
„ „ „ „ deceived.	Parayá.

"To say", in any specific manner denoted by the root is conjugated by *pa*, but it does not indicate plurality as *magpa* does.

To say yes, to affirm, to consent in anything.	Paóo.
To say, no, to deny.	Padili, pahindí.
To say not to be willing, to say refusal.	Paayáo.
To say, Jesus.	Pajesús.
To say, the deuce!	Padiablo.

PARTICLES AND WORDS USED AS DIFFERENT PARTS OF SPEECH.

ANO.

The interrogative pronoun *anó* is used is several ways:
As an interrogative conjunction of cause, followed by *at.*

Why did you not come in time?	¿Anò,t, di ca naparitó sa capanahonan?
And why do you eat fruit?	¿At anó,t, cungmacáin ca nang bonga?

Anó, stands for the admirative interjection "why"!, "what"!.

What!, are you per chance a king?	Anò,! ¿hari ca cayá?

The reply to the same when the tone of the question is one of surprise, may be made by *anó* preceded by *ay.*

Of course. (I am).	Ay anò.

Anó is conjugable by *um, mag, ma,* etc., as, more or less, every word in Tagalog can be, the sense being that which the verbal particle with which conjugated imparts to the action that is inquired after.

What is your business here?	¿Nagaanò ca ditó?.
Well now, and what of that?, what is to be done?	¿Anhin bagá?.
What is he going to do there?	Magaanó siyá dòon.?.
What are you being done upon?	¿Ynaaanò ca?.
Nothing can be done to you.	Hindí ca maaanó.

Anó, repeated means "at random" "unaccounted for" and is used in the negative.

This work is not accounted for.	Ualáng anò anò ang gauáng itó.
He slapped me without the least reason.	Tinampal acó niyá ualáng anò anò.

Idioms and phrases.

Well then..........	¿Anò bagá?.
What else?	¿Anò pa?.
How can it be?	¿Di anò pa?.
What matters?	¿Di anhin?.
For he says that.....	Di anhin dáo na...........
They say. it is said;	Di umanò.

FORTIETH EXERCISE.

Where are your parents going? They are going to church. Do your brothers go to school? They go to the sea. What port is the ship bound for? She is bound for Manila. Does she not make for Cavite? No, she makes for the Pasig river. Have you to go anywhere? Yes, I have to go somewhere. Which town is your destination? The city of Manila is my destination. What do you go to Manila for? I am going there on account of my brother. Hast thou ordered my servant to come here? I have already ordered him to come here. If my friend comes, what shall I thell him? Tell him to go there. Has he craved assistance of me? He craved that you would assist him. What did you say to John? I said to John to assist me. When will you say to him to assist you? I will tell him to-morrow to assist me. Why do you not allow me to kiss your hand? I shall not allow you to kiss it, for it is unclean. Why does she consent to be touched? She does not consent to it, she does not allow any man to touch her. What did the priest say in his sermon? He said, do not allow yourselves to be overcome by temptation, ask the Holy Virgin for mercy. Did he not ask you for mercy? Yes, he asked me to take mercy on him. What did Peter ask you? He asked me to go with him, and I told him I was not willing. Why did you say you were not willing? Because he says I am a rogue. Did you consent to marry your lover? I said to him, no. Why did you say the deuce? I did not say the deuce!, I said my Jesus!. Is it just to respect old age? We ought to respect old people. Where are you making for? I am making for Manila. What does your father plant? He plants this rice. What did he show to his son? He shows him this book. Is she alone at home? Yes, she is alone at home. Did you see my brother? I did not. Has the master already arrived? He has not yet arrived. Did he take my shirt? He did not. What is his tale? It is said there wás a king who was rebellious to God. Will you not go to meet your father? I will. When will you come back? Next week. Do you not wish to present yourself to the priest? No, for I am ashamed. What are you smelling? I am smelling these flowers. What is my uncle gathering there? He is gathering flowers. Why did she weep? Because her mother went away. When does she come back (return)? I don't now. Did the peppers your servant planted in the garden put forth? Not yet. Who will remain at home? Our father will stay. Did you leave him any food? I did not leave him anything. Have you put on (made use of) the dress yours mistress gave you? I have not yet worn it. What are you chewing? I chew betel.

FORTY FIRST LESSON.
YCAAPAT NA POUO,T, ISANG PAGARAL.

MODIFICATIVE VERBALIZING PARTICLES.

MAGCA=PAGCA.

Magca, in the active; *pagca*, in the passive, as a verbal particle, verbalizes intransitively, imparting a sense of plenty in what generally comes out or is produced naturally and drops off of itself without the designed interference of any active or conscious agent. It points out a previous condition of lack or scarcity which is resolved into the opposite denoted by *magca*. It differs from *man* in that the letter lays stress on the action, while *magca* denotes state, without reference to how it has been brought about, this being the reason for its intransitiveness and for its not admitting of *in* passive. Thus, *mamoñga*, means the action of fructifying; while *magcaboñga*, means to be laden with fruit. Speaking properly, *magca* is but *mag* and the passive particle of *ma, ca. Ca*, the last syllable of the particle, should be repeated in the proper tenses of the conjugation.

ROOT.

There, then, at that time (future, tense);)
there is. (*there to be, there to have*).) Dóon.

PARADIGM.

To have property, to possess, to own.	Magcaróon.
Cause.	Ypagcaróon.
If it is so ......how much...... will be	Dóon pa.
If he does that, he being only a child, how much he will do when a man.	Bata pa,i, gungmagauá nang ganitò, dóon pa cun lumaquí.

CONJUGATION.

ACTIVE.

Infinitive.

To have, to possess, to abound with.   Magcaróon.

Present indefinite tense.

Abound, est, –s with.   Nagcacaróon.

Present perfect and past indefinite tenses.

Abounded, –dst; have, hast, has abounded with.   Nagcaróon.

Pluperfect tense.

Had, –dst abounded with.   Nagcaróon na. (1).

Future indefinite tense.

Shall. -lt, will, -lt abound with.   Magcacaróon.

Future perfect tense.

Shall, -lt, will, -lt have abounded with.   Magcacaróon na. (1).

Imperative.

Abound, let......abound with.   Magcaróon.

Verbal.

The state of abounding with.   Ang pagcacaróon.

Y PASSIVE.

Infinitive.

To abound with, on account of.   Ypagcaróon.

Present indefinite tense.

Abound, -est, -s with, on account of   Ypinagcacaróon.

Present perfect and past indefinite tenses.

Abounded, -dst; have, hast, has abound- ⎱ Ypinagcaróon.
ed with, on account of.   ⎰

Pluperfect tense.

Had. -dst abounded with, on account of.   Naypagcaróon. ypinagcaróon.

Future indefinite tense.

Shall, -lt, will, -lt abound with, on account of.   Ypagcacaróon.

Future perfect tense.

Shall, -lt, will, -lt have abounded ⎱ Maypagcaróon, ypagcacaróon na.
with, on account of.   ⎰

---

(1). The pluperfect with *naca* cannot be used; the same is the case with *maca* in the future perfect tense.

Imperative.

Abound, let ...abound with, on account of.   Ypagcaróon.

Verbal.

The state of abounding with, on account of.   Ang ypagcacaróon.

AN PASSIVE.

Infinitive.

To abound with, at.   Pagcaróonan.

Present indefinite tense.

Abound, -est, -s with, at.   Pinagcaróonan.

Present perfect and past indefinite tenses.

Abounded, -dst; have, hast, has abounded with, at.   Pinagcaróonan.

Pluperfect tense.

Had, -dst abounded with, at.   Napagcaróonan, pinagcaróonan na.

Future indefinite tense.

Shall, -lt, will, -lt abound with, at.   Pagcacaroonan.

Future perfect tense.

Shall, -lt, will, -lt have abounded with, at. Napagcaroonan, pagcacaroonan na.

Imperative.

Abound, let ... abound with, at   Pagcaroonan.

Verbal.

The state of abounding with, at.   Ang pagcacaroonan.

Y passive, in this conjugation, stands for the reason or cause; *an*, for the place or person, according to the nature of the action.

What he inherited from his uncle is the reason of his being wealthy.	Ang ypinagcacaróon niyà ay ang pamana sa caniyá nang amaín niyà.
I own a great deal of property in Cavite.	Ang Cavite, ang pinagcacaróonan co.
He owes a great deal to his father-in-low.	Pinagcacautañgan niyà ang caniyàng bianáng lalaqui.

The student should conjugate by *magca* in the active and passives the following verbs:

To be of judgment, to arrive at the age of reason.	Magcaísip, magcabait.
To bear fruit.	Magcabuñga.
To carry illness about one's self.	Magcasaquit.
To be lucky.	Magcapálad.
To abound in issue, offspring.	Magcaanac.
To be gray headed.	Magcauban. (1).
To rage. (a plague.)	Magcasálot.
To rage (small-pox)	Magcabolótong.
To forbid.	Magcacasala.
To sin.	Magcasasala.

Magca, also means plurality or universality in the working of emergencies by which many are affected, although this universal sense is better made by repeating *ca* and rendering the root acute in accentuation.

To prevail, to spread about. (famine)	Magcacagotom.
To spread about. (fire)	Magcacasonog.
To be blowing a hurricane.	Magcacabaguió.
To be engaged in public rejoicings.	Magcacatouá, magcacapiesta.
To be engaged in revolution.	Magcacagoló.

Fortuitous meeting or assemblage of many may be expressed by *magca*.

To meet (many, accidentally).	Magcasalubong.
To assemble, to gather together.	Magcatipon.
To assemble in company.	Magcasamá.
To coincide.	Magcaaayon.
To be many engaged in quarrelling.	Magcaáuay.

Sometimes *magca* and the repetition of the root imparts a sense o completeness in intransitive actions.

To break off into very small bits.	Magcalansag-lansag.
To be torn away in rags.	Magcauindang-uindang.
To be in state of complete destruction.	Magcasirasirá.
My son has already entered the age of reason.	Nagcacaísip na ang anac co.
Had I money, I should not be in such condition as I am.	Cun magcaróon sana acó nang pílac, ay hindí acó nagcacaganitò.
Many people gathered together.	Nagcatipon ang mañga tauò.
Resort. (place of resort)	Pinagcatiponan.
Assembly.	Pinagcapisanan.
University. academy.	Pinagcapisanan nang mañga marurúnong.

PARTICLES AND WORDS USED AS DIFFERENT PARTS OF SPEECH.

BAGAY.

—

Bágay, as a noun, means "thing", "matter", "subject", "gait".

Sometthing, some object.	Yáang bágay.
What is the matter, subject?	¿Anò bagá ang bágay?
What is his appearance, American or native?	¿Anòng bágay or anyó niyâ, americano ó tagalog?.

---

(1) The pupil should not lose sight of the fact that the root is that part of the word which remains after taking away the particle or particles entering to compose it. Thus, *uban* means "gray-hair."

Bágay, as a verb, means "to equal", "to suit", "to make ready".

The penalty will be proportioned to the offence.	Pagbabagayan nang hírap or parusá ang casalanan.
Is it becoming for a girl to walk about the streets?	¿Nababágay bagá sa isàng dalaga ang paglácad (pagligáo) sa mañga lansañgan?
Make the children ready for the ball.	Magbágay nang mañga batang magsasayáo.

Bágay, as an adverb, is followed by *sa* and means "as to", "as for", and governs the dative case.

As for me, him.	Bágay sa aquin, sa caniyà.
As for my child.	Bágay sa anac co.
As to the death.	Bágay sa camatayan.
Different things.	Bágay bágay.

BAGO.

Bagò, as an adjective, means "new".

New clothes.	Bagòng damit.
New lord, new custom.	Bagòng pañginóon, bagòng ugali.

Bagò, as a verb. means "to renew", "to renovate", "to handsel".

I renew the payment.	Namamagò acó nang báyad.
I will renovate my house.	Pagbabagohin co ang aquing báhay.
These trowsers will be handseled on me.	Acó ang pamamagohan nitòng salaual.

Bagò, as an adverb of time, means "before".

Before you eat, wash your hands.	Bagò ca cumáin, manhináo ca mona.

Bagò, may be used as a conjunction, having the meaning of "nevertheless", "still", "yet".

It is he who is the culprit and nevertheless I am punished.	Siyá, ang may sala, bagò acó ang pinarusahan.
It is already twelve o'clock and still he is not here.	Tanghali na, bagò,i, ualá pa siyá.

FORTY FIRST EXERCISE.

Do those trees already bear fruit? Yes, they already bear fruit. Was there fire in this town? No, there was not fire in this town. Was there plague about these houses? Yes, there was plague about them. Are people flocked in the church? There is a crowd in the church. Was there war in these countries? Yes, war raged here. Are your friends well off? Yes, they are well off. Do their sons abound in offspring? No, but they are lucky. Does malady spread about among the inhabitants? Yes, they are afflicted with small-pox. Is famine raging in The Philippines? No. but they are afflicted with storms and conflagrations. Are natives engaged in Revolution Yes, and they are engaged in fighting and the farms are altogether in destruction. Where is their place of meeting? They gather together in the recesses of forests. Does it become a man to about naked? No, it does not become a man to go about naked. Why do you not equalize those two shirts? I have no scissors to equalize them. Did you make ready the tools for the making of the table? Not yet. Where are the new silk handkerchiefs? They are in the chest. Have you a new master? No, we have a new priest. Have you handseled the suit of clothes? I have. Are you not willing to appear before the priest? No, for I am afraid. Why does your cousin spit at his brother? Because he was first spitten upon. Who will remember me? Your mother will remember you. What has your father planted there? He has planted banana-trees. What is he going to put into the room? He is putting nothing into the room, he is putting water into my glass. Why do they not draw nearer that candle burning away? Because they have no stools to sit upon. Do you consider the practice of virtue a heavy thing? I don't consider it heavy, I remember the eternal fire. What will he do to me? He will do nothing to you. What was done to you? Nothing was done to me. Who is saying mass? Our priest. Why does your femae-cousin put on an upper petticoat? She does not put on an upper petticoat, she wears an apron. Will you smoke? Thanks, I don't smoke. Why does your servant feign to be sick? He feigns to be ill to avoid punishment. What was the reason for your neighbours quarreling? Gambling. Where did they quarrel? This house was their quarreling place.

FORTY SECOND LESSON.

YCAPAT NA POUO,T, DALAUANG PAGARAL.

MODIFICATIVE VERBALIZING PARTICLES.

MAGUIN=PAGUIN.

Maguin or *maguing*, active; *paguin* or *paguing*, passive, as a verbal particle means conversion into the thing or quality denoted by the root it is applied to. The transformation of one quality into another by slow gradual process of assimilation is expressed by *um*; but *maguin* denotes conversion off hand of one thing or quality into another, thus differring from *um* and *ma* or *na*. The last syllable, that is to say, *gui* (since *guin* is three-lettered) (1) should be repeated in present and future tenses.

ROOT.

Fair, just, deserving.   Dápat.

PARADÍGM.

To become worthy.   Maguindápat.
With what.   Ycapaguindápat.
Merits, desert.   Carapatán.

CONJUGATION.

ACTIVE.

Infinitive.

To become worthy.   Maguindápat.

Present indefinite tense.

Become, −st, −s worthy.   Naguiguindápat.

Present perfect and past indefinite tenses.

Became, -st; have, hast, has become worthy. Naguindápat.

---

(1). *U*, in this case, is not reckoned as a letter.

Pluperfect tense.

Had, -dst become worthy.　　　　　Nacapaguindápat, naguindápat na.

Future indefinite tense.

Shall, -lt, will, -lt become worthy.　　Maguiguindápat.

Future perfect tense.

Shall, -lt, will, -lt have become worthy.　Macapaguindápat, maguiguindápat na.

Imperative.

Become, let.... become worthy.　　　Maguindápat.

Verbal.

The action of becoming worthy.　　Ang paguiguindápat.

IN PASSIVE.

That verbs with *maguin* may admit of *in* passive, they should be recompounded with *magpa* which makes them active. The object being verbalized which is justly what would require it, is the reason for this particle lacking this passive.

Infinitive.

To be enabled to become worthy.　　Papaguindapatin.

Present indefinite tense.

Am, art, is, are enabled to become worthy.　Pinapaguiguindápat.

Present perfect and past indefinite tenses.

Was, -st, were; have, hast, has been enabled to become worthy. Pinapaguindápat.

Pluperfect tense.

Had, dst been enabled to become worthy.　Pinapaguindápat na.

Future indefinite tense.

Shall, -lt, will, -lt be enabled to become worthy.　Papaguiguindapatin.

Future perfect tense.

Shall -lt will, -lt have been enabled to become worthy　Papaguiguindapatin na.

Imperative.

Be enabled, let.... be enabled to become worthy.　Papaguindapatin.

Verbal.

The state of being enabled to become worthy.   Ang papaguindapatin.

Infinitive.

To become worthy on account of.   Ypaguindápat.

Present indefinite tense.

Become, -st, -s worthy on account of.   Ypinaguiguindápat.

Present perfect and past indefinite tenses.

Became. -st; have, hast. has become worthy on account of.   Ypinaguindápat.

Pluperfect tense.

Had. -dst become worthy on account of.   Ypinaguindápat na.

Future indefinite tense.

Shall, -lt, will, -lt become worthy on account of.   Ypaguiguindápat.

Future perfect tense.

Shall, -lt, will, -lt have become worthy on account of.   Ypaguiguindápat na.

Imperative.

Become, let....become worthy on account of.   Ypaguindápat.

Verbal.

The action of becoming worthy on account of.   Ang ypaguiguindápat.

As *maguin* denotes a state, it admits of *ca* in the passive of *y:* thus, it may be said: *yquinapaguiguindápat, yquinapaguindápat, ycapaguiguindápat, ycapaguindápat,* which emphasizes more the causative sense.

Infinitive.

To become worthy at or in.   Paguindapatan.

Present indefinite tense.

Become, -st, -s worthy at or in.   Pinaguiguindapatan.

Present perfect and past indefinite tenses.

Became. -st; have, hast, has become worthy at or in. Pinaguindapatan.

Pluperfect tense.

Had, -dst become worthy at or in. Pinaguindapatan na.

Future indefinite tense.

Shall, -lt, will, -lt become worthy at or in. Paguiguindapatan.

Future perfect tense.

Shall, -lt, will, -lt have become worthy at or in. Paguiguindapatan na.

Imperative.

Become, let . . . . . . become worthy at or in. Paguindapatan.

Verbal.

The action of becoming worthy at or in. Ang paguiguindapatan.

The student should conjugate by *maguin* in the active and passives, the following verbs.

To be converted into wine, to convert into wine.	Maguingálac.
Do do do do vinegar.	Maguingsuca.
„ „ „ „ gall.	Maguingapdo.
„ „ „ „ a beast.	Maguingháyop.
To turn out a virtuous fellow.	Maguingbanal.
„ „ „ „ miser.	Maguingmarámot.
To become deaf.	Maguingbiñgì.
„ „ mute.	Maguingpipi.
„ „ blind.	Maguingbulag.
To be converted to manhood, to take corporeal form or human attributes.	Maguingtauò.

Y passive stands in this conjugation for the reason or cause; *an*, for the place; although they are little in use. Attention should be paid to the following illustrations showing the use of these passives.

His wisdom and judgment made him worthy to fill the office.	Ang carunuñgan,t, ang cabaitan niyà,i, siyáng ypinaguindápat niyáng magcaróon nang catungculan.
My God, enable me to become worthy of attaining eternal life.	Papaguingdapatin mo acó, Pañginóong cong Dios na magcamit nang búhay na ualáng hangán.
The Son of God assumed human attributes for the sake of redeeming mankind.	Ang pagsácop sa tauo, ang siyáng yquinapaguintauò nang anac nang Dios.
Nazareth was the place where Jesus Christ grew into a man.	Ang bayang Nazaret, ang siyáng pinaguintauohan ni Jesucristo.
It was in Manila where he was ordained a priest,	Ang Maynila ang pinaguinparían niyà.

The sense of conversion denoted by *maguin* may entail volition on the part of the subject with the possessive pronouns.

I will be yours, I will become your slave.	Maguiguing-iyò acó.
You will be mine.	Maguiguingaquin ca.

Maguin, imparts sometimes a sense of doubt, especially with numeral adjectives.

What will my fate be?	¿Anò cayá ang maguiguinpálad co?
Will it be true?	¿Maguiguingtotoò bagá?.
After about six months.	Cun maguing ánim na bouan.
To be owing to.	Maguindahilán.
About how many will they be?	¿Maguiguing-ilán silá?.
They may be about ten.	Maguiguinsampóuo.

Maguin is also apt to express the copula on account of the close relation in signification existing between "to be" and "to become". Thus, it may properly be said; *?Naguiguinalila ca sa Pare?*. "Are you the priest's servant?".

It was Abraham's son, Isaac; and it was Isaac's son, Jacob; and it was Jacob's son, Juda and his brothers.	Naguing anac ni Abrabam, si Isaac; at naguing anac ni Isaac, si Jacob; at naguing anac ni Jacob, si Judá at ang caniyàng mañga capatid.

PARTICLES AND WORDS USED AS DIFFERENT PARTS OF SPEECH.

CAYA.

—

Cayá, as noun, means any instrument used for hunting or fishing, and also stands for the game or for what has been caught, but in this sense it is becoming obsolete.

Bows, muskets, and night strollers are laid hands upon by constables.	Ang bósog, ang pana pati nang mañga manlilígao ay quinacaya nang mañga alguacil. (*alguacil*, Sp. word for a "bumbailiff).

Cayá, as a verb, means "can", "tó be able" in a material sense, but it is however conjugated by *maca*.

Has he strength enough for that?	¿Macacaya bagá niyà iyán?
I cannot bring it here.	Dili co macayanan dalhín ritò.

Cayá, as an adverb, is used postponed in interrogations, having, as *bagá*, an expletive sense and means "how"?, "how now"?, "by chance".

Are you, by chance, the son of Peter?	¿Ycáo cayá bagá ang anac ni Pedro?
How!, is he the murderer?.	¿Siyá cayá ang nacamatáy?.

Cayá, as a conjunction, is used before the verb and means "since", "therefore".

You have been called for, and since you are well go there.	Tináuag ca, cayá yámang magaling ca na, paróon ca.
He is sick, therefore I will pay him a visit.	Siyá,i, may saquit, cayá dadalauin co siyá.

Cayá, is followed by the affirmative and completive particles. *Cayá ñga*, means "wherefore", "just that", in the second sentence.

Just because she is a woman she endeavours to be chaste. — Cayá ñga, siyá.i, babaye magpacahinhin siyá.

Just for that reason I will not give you any money. — Cayá ñga,i, di bibiguián catá nang salapí.

Cayá ñgani is more emphatic than *cayá ñga* and is used in the negative.

Since you have no farm, lease one. — { Cayá ñgani ualá cang búquid mamouís ca.

Cayá ñga yata is also used for "therefore"; *caya ñganit*, for the adverbial phrase "no sooner," as soon as".

I no sooner arrived than I arrested him. — Cayá ñganit pagdating co,i, dinaquip co siyá.

Notice must by taken of the common native habit (not one to be imitated by Europeans learning the language) of inserting in a sentence words which have no meaning to fill a temporary hiatus while the speaker is thinking of his next word. These prop—words are numerous in Tagalog and vary in different localities; but the most usual one is:

COAN.

perhaps the word most in use by natives. It stands for what one does not remember or serves as a periphrasis or euphemism for anything which is already understood between the interlocutors, for what will be shameful to express or may hurt the feelings of others.

Mr. Such a one. — Si Coán, or, couán.
What (is understood). — Ang coán.
The privy parts. — Ang coán.

Coán, in the same sense, can be made into a verb and be conjugated by all the verbal particles which the nature of the action it stands for may admit.

She is growing so and so. — Cungmocoán siyá.
She might. (consent). — Macacoán siyá.
Order her so and so. — Magpacoán ca sa caniyà.
She meddles in doing this and that. — Naquiquicoán siyá.

FORTY SECOND EXERCISE.

Who took man's attributes? The Son of God took man's attributes. Why did He take man's attributes? He took man's attributes for the sake of our redemption. Did your son become worthy to be ordained a priest? No, but he became worthy of obtaining an office. Did what I told you turn out true? Yes, it turned out true. Shall I be yours and you mine? No, thou shalt neither be mine nor I thine. What has been the reason? This has been the reason. What will become of me (will be my fate)? What your fate will be, nobody knows. What shall I do to become worthy of others' consideration? Pay what you owe. Shall the servant do anything? Let him put water into this vat. Where has your wife been buried? Here in this spot she was buried. Why does not your tailor put down that clothing? He has no place to put it on. Why did he get in without bowing? Because he is an uneducated man. Did she consent? She did without reluctance. What does he puff up for? He does not remember his origin. Why do you use to find fault with everybody? I did not get accustomed to that. Will you accompany me? I will keep you company. Where are you going? I am going to fish with a rod. What is your father distributing? What he is distributing is known by my brothers to whom he is distributing it. Who converted water into wine? Jesus Christ converted water into wine. Who was converted into a beast? Luthbel was converted into a beast. Did the wine convert itself into vinegar? It did. What was your friend converted into? He was converted into a miser. What has your aunt become? She became deaf, mute and blind. Can you lift that? I cannot lift that. What have you laid hands upon? I laid hands upon the thief. Do you chance to be Mary's brother? I am. What do you intend to do? Whereas (since) he has not come, I will go for him.

FORTY THIRD LESSON.
YCAAPAT NA POUO,T, TATLONG PAGARAL.

MODIFICATIVE VERBALIZING PARTICLES.

MAGSI=PAGSI.

Magsi, active; *pagsi,* passive, does not impart any peculiar modifying sense to the root it conjugates. It is but one of the manifold ways of expressing plurality in Tagalog and means that many or the whole people alluded to, do perform the action denoted by the root. Thus, *magsi* is used but in the plural and may be conjugated in the passives the nature of the action may admit of. It being dissyllabic, repeats *si* in present and future tenses.

ROOT.

To behold, to gaze.   Panóor, manóor.

PARADIGM.

To behold, to gaze. (intensive).	Magpanóor.
Thing beheld at.	Panoorin, pagpanoorin.
Place.	Panooran.
Spectacle, show, a pageant.	Panoorin or capapanooran.
To behold, to gaze by many people.	Magsipanóor.
Thing.	Pagsipanoorin.
Place.	Magsipanooran.

CONJUGATION.

ACTIVE.

—

Infinitive.

To behold. (by many).   Magsipanóor.

Present indefinite tense.

Behold. (by many).   Nagsisipanóor.

Present perfect and past indefinite tenses.

Beheld, have beheld. (by many).   Nagsipanóor.

Pluperfect tense.

Had beheld. (by many). Nacapagsipanóor, nagsipanóor na.

Future indefinite tense.

Shall, will behold. (by many) Magsisipanóor.

Future perfect tense.

Shall, will have beheld. (by many.) Macapagsipanóor magsipanóor na.

Imperative.

Behold (ye), let (us, them) behold. Magsipanóor.

Verbal.

The action of beholding. (by many). Ang pagsisipanóor.

IN PASSIVE.

Infinitive.

To be beheld. (by many.) Pagsipanoorin.

Present indefinite tense.

Am, art, is, are beheld. (by many.) Pinagsisipanóor.

Present perfect and past indefinite tenses.

Was, –st, were; have, hast, has been beheld. (by many). Pinagsipanóor.

Pluperfect tense.

Had, –dst been beheld. (by many.) Napagsipanóor, pinagsipanóor na.

Future indefinite tense.

Shall, -lt, will, -lt be beheld. (by many.) Pagsisipanoorin.

Future perfect tense.

Shall, –lt, will, –lt have been beheld. (by many) } Mapagsipanóor, pagsisipanoorin na.

Imperative.

Be beheld, let.... be beheld. (by many.) Pagsipanoorin.

Verbal.

The state of being beheld. (by many.) Ang pagsipanóorin.

Y PASSIVE.

Infinitive.

To behold (by many) on account of.   Ypagsipanóor.

Present indefinite tense.

Behold (we, ye, they) on acccount of.   Ypinagsisipanóor.

Present perfect and past indefinite tenses.

Beheld, have beheld (we, ye, they) on account of.   Ypinagsipanóor.

Pluperfect tense.

Had beheld (by many) on account of.   Naypagsipanóor, ypinagsipanóor na.

Future indefinite tense.

Shall, will behold (by many) on account of.   Ypagsisipanóor.

Future perfect tense.

Shall, will have beheld (by many) on account of.   Maypagsipanóor, ypagsisipanóor na.

Imperative.

Behold (ye). let (us, them) behold on account of.   Ypagsipanóor.

Verbal.

The action of beholding (by many) on account of.   Ang ypagsipanóor.

AN PASSIVE.

Infinitive.

To behold (by many) in.   Pagsipanooran.

Present indefinite tense.

Behold (we, ye, they) in.   Pinagsisipanooran.

Present perfect and past indefinite tenses.

Beheld, have beheld (by many) in.   Pinagsipanooran.

Pluperfect tense.

Had beheld (by many) in.   Napagsipanooran, pinagsipanóoran na.

Future indefinite tense.

Shall, will behold (by many) in.   Pagsisipanooran.

Future perfect tense.

Shall, will have beheld (by many) in.   Mapagsipanooran, pagsisipanooran na.

Imperative.

Behold (ye), let (us, them) behold in.   Pagsipanooran.

Verbal.

The action of beholding (by many) in.   Ang pagsipanooran.

The student should conjugate actively and passively the following verbs, some of which include combination with other verbalizing particles.

To teach. (many).	Magsiáral.
To learn. (").	Magsipagáral.
To preach. (").	Magsipañgáral.
To confess. (by many penitents).	Magsipagcumpisal.
To confess (by many priests).	Magsipagpacumpisal.
To enter, to go in. (many).	Magsipásoc.
To get (something) into. (by many).	Magsipagpásoc.
To go out. (many).	Magsilabás.
To draw (something) out. (by many).	Magsipalabás.
To weep. (many).	Magsitañgis.
To laugh. (many).	Magsitauá.

Still the sense of plurality may be carried to a higher degree of numerousness by inserting in this, as in other conjugations, *ñga*, between the changeable and changeless portion of the particle.

All the children of this school learn.	Ang mañga bata nitòng escuelahan nañgagsisipagáral.
All of you there outside come in.	Mañgagsipásoc cayóng naririyán sa labás.
Honor the masters who teach you.	Pagpitaganan mo ang mañga umaáral or maestro nañgagsisiáral sa iyo.
All this crowd made a confession this morning and they all will behold the procession to-morrow.	Ytòng maraming mañga tauó nañgagsipagcumpisal cañginang umaga at mañgagsisipannóor nang procesión bucas.

Corner.	Súloc.
Log, lumber.	Cálap.
The inside.	Ang lóob.
Within.	Sa lóob.
Within the church.	Sa lóob nang simbahan.
The outside.	Ang labás.
Outside, outwards.	Sa labás.
Outside the town.	Sa labás nang bayan.
To commemorate.	Magdiuang.
Highwayman.	Tulisán.
Foot-pad.	Manghahárang.
Where is her house?	?Nasaán ang caniyàng báhay?

It is within the town.	Na sa lóob nang báyan.
And yours?	¿At ang iyò?
It is outside the wood.	Na sa labás nang gúbat.
Just what.	Ganán.
Take just what you wish.	Muha ca nang ganán íbig mo.
Take just what suffices for a shirt.	Muha ca nang ganán súcat baróin,
That is only for me.	Ganán aquin iyán.
You (plur.) take for yourselves what is for me.	Naggaganán inyò cayó nang ganán sa aquin.
As for my part.	Sa ganán aquin.
As for him.	Sa ganán caniyà.
As for my part, I abandon her.	Sa ganán aquin, pinababayáan co siyá.

PARTICLES AND WORDS USED AS DIFFERENT PARTS OF SPEECH.

CASI.
—

Casì, as a noun, means, as already said, "intimate friend".

They are intimate friends.	Magcasì, magcacasì silá,

and conjugated by *mag* means to engage in close familiarity.

He engages in intimacy.	Nagcacasi siyá.

Casì, as a verb, also means "to pervade", if conjugated by *um*.

The Holy Ghost pervaded the souls of the Apostles.	Ang Dios *Espíritu Santo*, ang cungmasí sa calóloua nang mañga *Apóstoles*. (Sp.)

Still *casì* conjugated by *um* means "to accept of a secret or clandestine gift". as to be bribed, and by *mag*, "to bribe".

The judge accepted of my gift.	Ang hócom ay ang quinasihan co.

Casì may be used as an impersonal verb meaning "it seems".

It seems that he went there.	Naparóon casì siyá.
It seems he does not know her.	Di niyà naquiquilala casi.

DI.
—

Di, the contraction of *dili* an *hindi*, is always a prepositive particle meaning "not", "in", (Latin prefix), "un".

Insufferable.	Di mabatà.
Unspeakable.	Di mauica.

Di cannot be conjugated by *pa* on account of its monosyllabic structure, thus, to "say no," is expressed by the full word *hindí* or *dili*, saying *pahindí*, *padili*.

Di serves to affirm in an alternative or contrasting sense.

Whom but Our Lord God, should I pray?.	¿Di sino ang dadaiñgan co cundí ang Dios ating pañginóon?.

Di joins to adverbs, imparting a negative sense.

Not yet.	Di pa.
Although, although not.	Di man.
Not only ...but even.	Di man nauá.
Greatly, exceedingly.	Di hamac.
Why not?.	¿Sáan di ganóon?.
Does he not wish to eat yet?	¿Di pa íbig niyàng cumáin?
Although you don't weep I will whip you.	Di ca man tumañgis hahampasín quitá.
Exceedingly wealthy.	Mayaman di hamac.
Why not so?	¿Sáan di ganóon?.

DILI.

Dili, besides its proper signification as a negative adverb, is used at the end for an alternative negative conjunction.

Will he pay or not?	¿Babáyad siyá, dili?.

DIUA.

Díua is another impersonal verb having a dubitative sense as *casi*, *tila*, *yata*. It likewise stands or "it seems", "it appears".

It seems to be he.	Díua,i, siyá.
It appears as if you would despise me.	Díua,i, pinauauaʰan mo na acóng halagá.

Díua, as a noun, means "spirit", "genius", "vapor", although in this sense is very little used.

The spirit of martyrs.	Ang díua nang mañga *mártir*. (Sp.)

Díua, has also an adjectival force meaning "fresh thing"; but it is better to say *saríua*.

The fresh leaves of trees.	⟨ Ang saríuang dahon nang mañga cáhoy.

DOON.

Dóon, is, as the student knows, the adverb indicative of place far away from the interlocutors. It may also be used as an adverb of time meaning "then". "at that time", "in those days."

When you eat, you shall know then what kind of food is in store for you.	Cun cumáin ca, dóon maaalaman mo cun anò ang háin.
In those days the Patron Saint's feast was celebrated.	Dóon sa mañga árao na yaón ypinadidiuang ang Pintacasing Santo.

Dóon, if associated with *pa* has an admirative conjunctional sense as indicated by the following illustration.

He, being so young, does that, what shall he do when a man?.	Bata pa,i, gungmagauá nang ganitò. ¿dóon pa cun lumaqui?.

We have seen that *dóon* may be made a verb with *magca*; *magca-*

33

róon, "to have", "to own", "to be worth"; still it may be conjugated by *man*: *mandóon*, *manróon*, "to take something out of a heap".

Give them some fruit out of the basket.	Biguián mo silá nang nandoróon.

FORTY THIRD EXERCISE.

What do those people do there? They are beholding the image of the Holy Virgin. Was it beheld by many people? Yes, it was largely beheld. Where is it beheld? It is beheld at the church. Do all the teachers teach? They all teach. Whom do they teach? They teach all the children in the town. Were all the priests preaching? They were all preaching. What did they preach? They all preached the observance of holy commandments. Where did they all preach? They all preached at the door of the church. Do all these children study? All of them study. What do they study? They all study grammar. Are there many who are making confession? Yes, indeed, they are very many who make a confession. Are there many priests receiving confessions? All the priests are receiving confesssions. Are there many people going into church? No, the mass is over, and many people come out of church at present. What are that crowd taking out from my uncle's? They all are taking out the household furniture, as fire is spreading. Are all those boys laughing or weeping? They all are laughing at a drunkard who staggers about. Who is at the corner? Peter is at the corner. Where does your house stand? It stands within town at the corner of the market. Are there many highwaymen about your city? Yes, indeed, there are a great many. Where is he going to? He is going outside the road. How much shall I spend? Spend just what you need. All that money is only for me? As for me, take it all. Are they intimate friends? They are intimate friends. Why does the American abandon that woman? It is because he is going to embark for his country. Are pious people pervaded by the spirit of God? Pious people are pervaded by the Holy Ghost. Do you know that person coming here? It seems I don't know him. Have you not eaten the meat? I did not eat the meat but the boiled rice. Do you intend to engage in trade? What shall I do but to engage in trade? Why do you ask me that? Because I want to know whether you go there or not. Where do you go? I go to church. What are you going to do there? I am going there to attend mass. Had the letter been already read when you were at home? The letter had already been read. Had the hen been looked for? It had not yet been looked for. Were our ancestors stronger than we? Our forefathers from whom we descend, were stronger.

FORTY FOURTH LESSON.
YCAAPAT NA POUO,T, APAT NA PAGARAL.

MODIFICATIVE VERBALIZING PARTICLES.

MAGSA=PAGSA.

Magsa, active; *pagsa*. passive; is another verbal particle which if applied to the root of a national adjective denotes imitation, following of the manners or customs of that nation. This particle is little in fashion, as the same sense may be conveyed by *maqui* and other means of expression. We give, however, an example of it in the subjoined conjugation and it will be seen that *sa*, the last syllable of the particle, is repeated in the proper tenses.

ROOT.

Spaniard. Castila.

PARADIGM.

To speak, to translate into Spanish; to dress like Spaniard.	Magcastila.
Thing.	Castiláin.
Person with whom one converses in Spanish.	Ang pagcacastiláan.
Cause, or the subject of a conversation in Spanish.	Ypagcastila.
Place where or meeting of many Spaniards.	Cacastiláan.
To adopt Spanish manners.	Magsacastila.
In what Spanish manners or customs are followed.	Ang sinasacastila.
Cause or reason whereby adopted.	Ang ypagsacastila.

CONJUGATION.

ACTIVE.

Infinitive.

To behave as a Spaniard, to follow Spanish customs.	Magsacastila.

Present indefinite tense.

Follow, est, s Spanish customs.	Nagsasacastila.

Present perfect and past indefinite tenses.

Followed, -dst; have, hast, has followed Spanish customs.   Nagsacastila.

Pluperfect tense.

Had, -dst followed Spanish customs.   Nacapagsacastila, nagsacastila na.

Future indefinite tense.

Shall, -lt, will, -lt follow Spanish customs.   Magsasacastila.

Future perfect tense.

Shall, -lt, will, -lt have followed Span- } Macapagsacastila, magsasacastila na.
ish customs.

Imperative.

Follow, let... follow Spanish customs.   Magsacastila.

Verbal.

The action of following Spanish customs.   Ang pagsasasacastila.

IN PASSIVE.

In passive in this particle drops *pag* and is conjugated after the same passive of *um* conjugation, only *sa* persisting.

Infinitive.

(What) to be adopted of the Spanish)
customs, in what Spanish customs to } Sacastiláin....ang.
be adopted, by.

Present indefinite tense.

(What) is adopted of the Spanish)
customs, by. } Sinasacastila....ang.

Present perfect and past indefinite tenses.

(What) was, has been adopted of)
Spanish customs, by. } Sinacastila ...ang.

Pluperfect tense.

(What) had been adopted of the Spanish customs, by.   Sinacastila na....ang.

Future indefinite tense.

(What) shall, will be adopted of the Spanish customs, by.   Sasacastiláin. .ang.

Future perfect tense.

(What) shall, will have been adopted of the Spanish customs, by. } Sasacastilain na....ang.

Imperative.

Let (what) be adopted of the Spanish customs, by. Sacastiláin ang.

Verbal.

The state of (what) being adopted of the Spanish customs. Ang sacastiláin...nang.

Y PASSIVE.

Infinitive.

To follow Spanish customs on account of. Ypagsacastila.

Present indefinite tense.

Follow, –est, –s Spanish customs on account of. Ypinagsasacastila.

Present perfect and past indefinite tenses.

Followed, -dst; have, hast, has followed Spanish customs on account of. } Ypinagsacastila.

Pluperfect tense.

Had, –dst followed Spanish customs on account of. } Naypagsacastila, ypinagsacastila na.

Future indefinite tense.

Shall, –lt, will, –lt follow Spanish customs on account of. Ypagsasacastila.

Future perfect tense.

Shall, –lt, will, –lt have followed Spanish customs on account of. } Maypagsacastila, ypagsasacastila na.

Imperative.

Follow, let ... follow Spanish customs on account of. } Ypagsacastila.

Verbal.

The action of following Spanish customs on account of. } Ang ypagsacastila.

Infinitive.

To follow the Spanish customs at.   Pagsacastiláan.

Present indefinite tense.

Follow, -est, -s the Spanish customs at.   Pinagsasacastiláan.

Present perfect and past indefinite tenses.

Followed, -dst; have, hast, has fol- } Pinagsacastiláan.
lowed the Spanish customs at.

Pluperfect tense.

Had -dst followed the Spanish cus- } Nagpasacastiláan, pinagsacastiláan na.
toms at.

Future indefinite tense.

Shall, -lt, will, -lt follow the Spanish customs at.   Pagsasacastiláan.

Future perfect tense.

Shall -lt, will, -lt have followed the } Magpasacastiláan, pagsasacastiláan na.
Spanish customs at.

Imperative.

Follow, let. . . follow the Spanish customs at.   Pagsacastiláan.

Verbal.

The action of following the spanish customs at.   Ang pagsacastiláan.

The student should conjugate actively and passively the following imitative actions.

To follow Chinese customs.			Magsainsic.
,,	,,	native ,,	Magsatagúlog.
,,	,,	American ,,	Magsaamericano.
,,	,,	Bisayan ,,	Magsabisayá.
,,	,,	English ,,	Magsainglés.
,,	,,	Moorish ,,	Magsamoros.

Magsa, is fit to express the purposely-made exposure to the action of an atmospherical agent, the working on of which is expressed by *magpa. Magsa,* in this sense, is but the adverb of place *sa,* conjugated by *mag.*

Sun yourself.	Magsaárao ca.
Put linen to sunshine.	Magsaárao ca nang damit.
Put that shirt to the wind.	Ysahañgin mo iyáng baro.

Keller's wife adopts German customs.	Ang asáua ni Keller ay nagsasaalemán.
Americans customs are adopted by *Filipinos*.	Nagsasaamericano na ang mañga Tagálog.
They adopt American customs in dressing.	Ang pagbibihís ang sinasaamericano nilà.
Mr. Singer while in the Philippines follows native customs.	Ang Pilipinas ang pinagsasatagalogan ni señor Singer.

PARTICLES AND WORDS USED AS DIFFERENT PARTS OF SPEECH.

YBA.

—

Ybà is the indefinite adjective pronoun for "other", "another".

Other man.	Yl à ng tauò.
Another pen.	Ybàng panúlat.

As a verb, *ibà* has different meanings according to the particle with which conjugated.

To change.	Mag-ibà.
To be influenced by, to feel the changing of.	Mañgibà.
To be different from what it was before.	Magcaibà.
To singularize, to be peculiar, to have a leaning for aliens.	Maquiibá.

Ybà, as an adjective of quality, means "different".

This is different from that.	Ytò,i, ibà diyán.
Uncommon, unsatisfactory.	Caibà.

Ybà has an adverbial sense, as in:

Jests aside, apart.	Ybà sa biro.

Ybà is used as a noun in the sense of "stranger", "not akin".

He is not my relation.	Ybà sa aquin siyá.
Do you know that his wife chances to be my kinswoman?.	¿Naaalaman mo na ang caniyàng asáua ay hindí ibà sa aquin?.

YCAO.

—

Ycáo is the well known prepositive form of the second person pronoun. It may be made a verb and conjugated by *um* or *pa*.

To thou.	Umicáo.
Who thous you?	¿Sinong ungmiicáo sa iyo?
Ask him to thou you.	-Paicáo ca sa caniyà.

YLAN.

—

Ilán is the indefinite pronoun for "some".

Some days.	Ilán aráo.
Some, á few.	Mañga ilán.

It is used in interrogations for "how many"?. It is plural. but it may come before a singular noun of a numerable thing.

How much money?.	¿Iláng salapí?.
How many men?	¿Iláng tauò?, ¿ilán catauò?.

INDI.

Indí is another form of the negative adverb *di*, *dilí*, *hindí*, meaning "no", "never", "not yet" and is somewhat emphatic. It is joined to the other particles its synonyms.

Neither, nor either.	Indí man, indí rin.
Not only, solely.	Indí lámang.

Indí pa, denotes continuance; *indí na*, discontinuance; with the peculiarity as to the former that it causes the first syllable of the root to be repeated.

He has not yet finished.	Indí pa niyà natatapus.
He stays no longer there.	Indí na siyá dóon tungmitirá.

LABI.

Labì, is the comparative adverb "more".

More than I, me.	Labì sa aquin.
More than a hundred men.	Labì sa sangdáang tauò.

Labì may likewise stand for the adverb of excess "too", "too much".

He is too cruel, stern.	Labìng mabagsic siyá.
How much is the price of this trunk?	¿Magcanò ang halagá nitóng cabán?.
Twenty dollars.	Dalauàng póuong píso.
That is too much.	Labì iyán.

Labì, as a verb, means "to exceed", "to add", if conjugated by *um*.

He exceeds two inches.	{ Lungmalabì siyá sa dalauàng *pulgada*. (Sp.)
The water overflows.	Lungmalabì ang túbig.
Add water to the broth.	Labihan mo nang túbig ang sábao.

Labì, if conjugated by *mag*, means "to leave behind as surplus".

They left behind one bushel of rice. Linabì nilà isàng cabán na bigás.

Labì, as a noun, means "excess", "surplus".

The excess is three reals. Ang labì, tatlóng sicápat.

Slowly, carefully, understandingly.	Marahan.
Quickly, briefly.	Madalí.
Often, hurriedly, repeatedly.	Madalás.
Rarely, slowly.	Madálang.
Would to God, may God permit.	Loobin nauá nang Dios.
Would to God they would die.	Maanòng mamatáy silá.
Cloud.	Pañganurin, alapáap.
Mist.	Olap.

Atmosphere, thick cloud.	Impapauid.
Thick, dense.	Macapal.
Thick, dense mist.	Macapal na ólap.
Modesty, civility.	Cahinhinan, hinhín.
Chastity, honor.	Calinisan.
Bearing, port, carriage, demeanor.	Cabinían, bini.
Honorable lady, gentlewoman.	Binibini.
Circumspection, prudence.	Catimtiman.

FORTY FOURTH EXERCISE.

Why do you wonder at that woman following Chinese customs.? I wonder at it, because it is not customary for natives of this country to adopt Chinese fashions and manners. But do you know who she is.? I don't. Do you not know that she is the wife of a wealthy Chinese merchant.? I did not; but, if so, I no longer wonder at her having adopted Chinese customs. Would you adopt English customs if I should adopt native ones? I should adopt English customs even if you would not adopt native ones. Whom are Moorish customs adopted by.? Moorish customs are adopted by some natives living round the shores of Mindanao Island. Do ever Moors adopt Bisayan customs.? They adopt Bisayan customs partly. Is there no other cotton than this.? There is other cotton and other iron. Has he another hammer.? He has another hammer and another plane. Does my aunt change hats.? She changes hats. Are you influenced by this climate.? Yes, I am hard influenced by this climate. Did your son change to a different man than before.? He did. Is iron different from steel? Iron is different from steel. What are they different in.? They are different in hardness. What is done to you.? They do nothing to me, cheer up. Is your neighbor a relation of yours.? He is not my relation. Do you know that her husband is my relation.? I don't know. Why does that man thou your daughter.? He thous her, because he is going to marry her. Why do you say thou to your father.? Because it is a native custom to do so. How many weeks will you be absent.? Some weeks only. Have you my book? I have it not. How many men came.? A few only came. Why do you not reduce your expenses.? Because my money is not growing less. Has he not received his trunk yet.? He has not received it yet. Why do you write so carefully.? Because I am not in a hurry. Are there any thick clouds in the atmosphere.? The atmosphere is fraught with thick clouds. Who is that boy.? He is a modest fellow. What did the villagers meet together for.? They met to speak about the visit of the general. Whom did you bow to.? To Gardiner, he is a nobleman. Why is he ashamed of his parents.? He is ashamed of his parents, because they are poor.

FORTY FIFTH LESSON.
YCAAPAT NA POUO,T, LIMANG PAGARAL.

MODIFICATIVE VERBALIZING PARTICLES.

MANHI=PANHI.

Manhi, active; *panhi*, passive; is a compound of *man=pan* and the adverbial particle *hi*, the latter having an ironical adversative sense, somewhat after the one denoted by the English prefix "for" in "forswear". "forbear". Thus, *ganti*, "reward"; *gumanti*, "to reward"; *manhiganti*, "to revenge"; *pilay*, "husk-rice"; *mamálay*, "to gather in paddy"; *manhimálay*, "to glean"; *pálad*, "good luck", "fortune"; *magcapálad*, "to be lucky"; *manhimálad*, "to predict by fortune-tellers". *Man* is in this conjugation the verbal particle. *hi* being only complementary of the sense. Hence the roots conjugated by *manhi* undergo the same change of the initial letters which they would undergo if conjugated by *man*.

The form of conjugation, in other respects, follows the general rules; *hi*, the last syllable, being repeated in the proper tenses.

ROOT.

Reward, prize.	Ganti.

PARADIGM.

To reward.	Gumanti.
Person.	Gantihin.
With what.	Yganti.
The rewarding.	Ang pag-ganti.
To correspond one another.	Mag-gantihan.
The action of rewarding each other.	Ang pag-gagantihan.
To revenge, to avenge.	Manhiganti.
Person who avenged an offence.	Pinanhiganti.
Person wronged, or the instrument or means which served to inflict revenge.	Ypanhiganti, ypinanhiganti.
To revenge upon, to requite, to retaliate.	Manhiganti.
Person on whom revenge is to be taken.	Panhigantihin.

CONJUGATION.

ACTIVE.

Infinitive.

To revenge.	Manhiganti.

Present indefinite tense.

Revenge, –st, –s.   Nanhihiganti.

Present perfect and past indefinite tenses.

Revenged, –dst; have, hast, has revenged.   Nanhiganti.

Pluperfect tense.

Had, –dst revenged.   Nacapanhiganti, nanhiganti na.

Future indefinite tense.

Shall, –lt, will, –lt revenge.   Manhihiganti.

Future perfect tense.

Shall, –lt, will, –lt have revenged.   Macapanhiganti, manhihiganti na.

Imperative.

Revenge, let.... revenge.   Manhiganti.

Verbal.

The action of revenging.   Ang panhihiganti.

IN PASSIVE.

Infinitive.

To be avenged of.   Panhigantihin.

Present indefinite tense.

Am, art, is, are avenged of.   Pinanhihiganti.

Present perfect and past indefinite tenses.

Was, –st, were; have, hast, has been avenged of.   Pinanhiganti.

Pluperfect tense.

Had, –dst been revenged of.   Napanhiganti, pinanhiganti na.

Future indefinite tense.

Shall, –lt, will, –lt be avenged of.   Panhihigantihin.

Future perfect tense.

Shall, –lt, will, –lt have been avenged of.   } Mapanhiganti, panhihigantihin na.

Imperative.

Be avenged, let....be avenged of.　　Panhigantihin.

Verbal.

The state of being avenged of.　　　Ang panhigantihin.

Y PASSIVE.

Infinitive.

To revenge with or by.　　　　Ypanhiganti.

Present indefinite tense.

Revenge, –st, –s with or by.　　　Ypinanhihiganti.

Present perfect and past indefinite tenses.

Revenged, –dst; have, hast, has revenged with or by.　Ypinanhiganti.

Pluperfect tense.

Had, –dst revenged with or by.　　Naypanhiganti, ypinanhiganti na.

Future indefinite tense.

Shall, –lt, will, –lt revenge with or by.　Ypanhihiganti.

Future perfect tense.

Shall, –lt, will, –lt have revenged with or by.　} Maypanhiganti, ypanhihiganti na.

Imperative.

Revenge, let.... revenge with or by.　　Ypanhiganti.

Verbal.

The action of revenging with or by.　　Ang ypanhiganti.

AN PASSIVE.

Infinitive.

To take revenge upon.　　　　Panhigantihán.

Present indefinite tense.

Take, –st, –s revenge upon.　　　Pinanhihigantihán.

Present perfect and past indefinite tenses.

Took, –est; have, hast, has taken revenge upon.   Pinanhigantihán.

Pluperfect tense.

Had, –dst taken revenge upon.   Napanhigantihán, pinanhigantihán na.

Future indefinite tense.

Shall, –lt, will, –lt take revenge upon.   Panhihigantihán.

Future perfect tense.

Shall, –lt, will, –lt have taken re-venge upon. } Mapanhigantihán, panhihigantihan na.

Imperative.

Take, let, ..take revenge upon,   Panhigantihán.

Verbal.

The action of taking revenge upon. Ang panhihigantihán

The student should conjugate by *manhi* actively and passively the following roots.

Husk-rice.	To glean.	Pálay.	Manhimálay.
Stain.	To wash one's face.	Lamos.	Manhilamos.
Spoiled child.	To act fickly.	Mosmós.	Manhimosmós.
Trifle, small commodity.	To sell by retail or about the streets. / To sell bad, but apparently good things.	Laco.	Manhilaco.
Cruel.	To rebel.	Bagsic.	Manhimagsic.
Workman.	To affect doing something, to fidget about for no purpose.	Pandáy.	Manhimandáy.
Scarf, skin.	To flay.	Pánit.	Mahimánit
Bereavement.	To be stricken with bereavement.	Panglaó.	Manhimangláo.
Dying.	To swoon away.	Matáy.	Manhimátay.
Mustache.	To comb the mustache smooth and even.	Mísay.	Manhimísay.
Swelling of the eyelids or the eyes.	To wash the sore eyes with lukewarm water.	Poctò.	Manhimoctò.

They avenged me.   Pinanhiganti acó nilà.
He avenged himself by not paying him.   Ypinanhiganti niyà ang di maghá-yad sa caniyà.
I will take revenge on him.   Siyá ang panhihigantihán co.

Manhi is proper to express acts of corporal cleansing of filth or parasitary expurgation.

Wax of the ear.	To clean the ear from wax.	Tutulí.	Manhinulí.
Foulness of the teeth.	To clean one's teeth from foulness.	Tiñgà.	Manhiniñgà.
Crab-louse.	To clean one's self from lice.	Tumà.	Manhinomà.
Nail of the fingers or toes.	To clean one's nails.	Cocó.	Manhiñgocó.
Lippitude.	To clear out one's lippitudes.	Motà.	Manhimoʻà.
Nit.	To clean one's self from nits.	Lisá.	Manhilisà.

PARTICLES AND WORDS USED AS DIFFERENT PARTS OF SPEECH.

LOOB.

Lóob, as a noun, means "the inside", "the inner part of some closed space", not the contents, which is expressed by *lamán*. Metaphorically, *lóob* means "will", "good-will", "heart".

The inside of the room.	Ang lóob nang silid.
Mercy, grant.	Caloob.
Gratitude.	Utang na lóob.
Coward, spiritless, ungrateful fellow.	Tauòng ualáng lóob.

As a verb, *lóob* means "to enter", "to allow", "to permit", "to do something willingly", according to the particle.

To enter, to fall upon, to break open.	Lumóob, manlóob.
To allow something in, to give admitance, to allow pillage going on.	Magpalóob.
To bestow graces, mercies.	Magcalóob.
To allow, to do something willingly.	Maglóob.
Do it heartily.	Maglóob cang gumauá.
What do you desire?	¿Anòng lóob mo?.
If you are not willing, don't go there.	Cundí mo lóob, di cang paróon.

Loób, as an adverb, stands for "inside", "in", "within", and must be complemented by the proposition *sa*.

| Within, in, inside. | Sa lóob. |
| Heartily, willingly. | Sa lóob, nang lóob, sa bóong lóob, nang bóong lóob. |

OCOL.

Ocol, as a noun, is fit to express "good fortune", "fitness".

| I lack good luck. | Tauò acóng ualáng ócol. |
| You are both of the same temper. | Magcaócol cayóng dalauà. |

Ocol, as a verb, is used in several ways.

| Soul is for (belongs to) God. | Ang calolóua ay naoócol sa Dios. |
| Measure on him this stuff to see whether if is enough for his shirt. | Yócol mo sa caniyà itòng cayo na babaroin niyà. |

It suits Peter to be judge.
Ocol cay Pedro ang maghocom.

I yield to the will of God.
Ynoocolan or inaayonan co ang lóob nang Dios.

PONO.

Pono, as a noun, means "source", "origin", "trunk of a tree", "foreman", "leader".

God is the source of truth.
Ang Dios ay ang pono nang catotohanan.

How many banana-trees are there in your farm?
¿Ylán bagá ang mañga pono nang ságuing na nasa iyòng búquid?

He is the chief of the fleet.
Siyá,i, ang pono nang hocbó sa dágat.

Generative organs.
Ponong cataouán.

Head place or town, president of the town, mayor.
Ponong bayan.

Pono, as a verb, means "to fill", "and also "to make up".

Fill the vat.
Ponán mo ang tapayan.

Make up one hundred.
Magponó ca nang sangdáan.

QUITA—CATA.

These two pronouns when used in the nominative express the plural in a way even more restricted than *camí,* as they mean "thou and I alone", but they have a somewhat interjectional exhortative sense.

Well then, let us go to mass.
Quitá,i, magsimbá.

Well, let us set about it.
Catá, quitá na.

Let us eat.
Quitá,i, cumáin.

But, most commonly, *quitá-catá,* stand for the possessive case with regard to the speaker or agent, and for the nominative of the patient, both of them being used in the passive as a contraction of *co icáo,* "thou by me".

I will keep you company, you shall be accompanied by me.
Sasamahan quitá or catá.

I will wake thee.
Guiguisiñgin catá or quitá.

You are whipped by me.
Hinahampás quitá or catá.

Allways, constantly.
Touí, touí nang touí, touí-touí na.

Whenever.
Touíng......

Whenever you read a book (something)
Touí cang masá nang súlat.

Whenever you write.
Touíng susúlat ca.

Whenever I study he plays.
Touíng acó,i, nagaáral, siyá,i, naglalaró.

Brightness, luminousness, blaze.
Cabanaagan, bandag.

Illustrious man.
Tauòng mabunyí.

Famous   „
„   mabantog.

Conspicuous man.
„   marañgal.

Crippled, maimed man.
„   lumpò.

Mute   „
„   pipí.

Deaf   „
„   biñgí.

Stutterer   „
„   otal.

Lame man.	Tauòng pílay.
Cross-eyed „	„ duling
One handed, awkward handed man.	„ quimáo.
Blind. „	„ bulag.
To swell, to expand.	Bumintog.

FORTY FIFTH EXERCISE.

Why does the soldier take revenge on that dog.? He takes revenge on it, because it bit him. Will the blind man be avenged of the offence.? He will be avenged by his son. On whom will he take revenge. He will take revenge on the boy who led him astray. Why does that poor man glean.? He gleans because he is hungry. Do you wash your face every morning.? I always wash my face after rising from bed. Why does he think so childishly.? He thinks childishly, for he is still a spoiled child. Did Chinese undersell merchants.? They undersell them, because they sell bad things for good ones. Against whom did natives rebel.? They rebelled against Spaniards and Americans. What does the carpenter do.? He does nothing, he affects doing something (fidgets). Why does your brother flay the deer.? He flays it to sell the meat. What is the matter with the crippled man.? He swooned away yesterday. Is your male--cousin combing his mustache smooth.? No, he is washing his swollen eye--lids with lukewarm water. Does the beggar clean himself from lice? No he is cleaning his ear from wax and his teeth from foulness. Does he use to clean his nails.? He, not only cleans his nails, but also he clears out his lippitudes and his nits. Where is his grandson.? He is within the room. Why do you compare those two gantas.? I compare them to see whether they are equal. Will they conform to the will of their father.? They will. Who is the leader of the army.? The leader of the army is the king. What is the servant filling up.? He is filling your glass. Will you keep me company.? I will keep you company if you go to Manila. Will you punish me whenever I don't obey you.? I will punish you whenever you don't obey me. Who is the most famous, most celebrated and illustrious man of North America.? Washington is the most famous. What are you eating,? I eat the fruit sought by my mother. Why do you not drink that wine.? Because I never drink.

FORTY SIXTH LESSON.

YCAATAT NA POUO,T, ANIM NA PAGARAL.

MODIFICATIVE VERBALIZING PARTICLES.

$$MAGPACA = \frac{PAGPACA.}{PACA.}$$

Magpaca, active; *pagpaca=paca*, passive; may be considered as an enlargement of *magpa*, (which it somewhat resembles in sense in some respects) with the intransitive particle suffixed thereto. Hence it does not generally admit of the *in* passive and *pa* and not *ca* is repeated in the present and future tenses. Its principal signification is, like *magpa*, to allow, to suffer willingly what the root it joins to means. The discrimination between the passive and the self-acting upon sense should be made by adequate expressions for verbs admitting of both. *Nagpacamatáy si Jesucrisso cusa niyà*, "Jesus Christ gave up His life"; *nagpacamatáy Si Caton sa caniyàig sarili*, "Cato committed suicide".

ROOT.

Dead.   Patáy

PARADIGM.

To kill.	Patáy, pumatáy.
To sentence to death or to have somebody killed by other's hands.	Magpatáy, magpapatáy.
To kill one by one, by many blows, or by one who kills many.	Magpapátay. (1).
To kill many by many, or one by many.	Mañgagpapatáy, magsipatáy.
Killed person or animal.	Patayin.
Instrument, weapon.	Ypatáy.
Mourning person, the relatives of the victim.	Patayún. (1).
Place.	Patayan, pagpatayan. (1).
To go about killing.	Mamátay. (1).
To swoon away, to become drowsy.	Manhimatáy.
To allow one's self to be killed, to commit suicide.	Magpacamatáy.

---

(1) Notice the accentuation.

CONJUGATION.

ACTIVE.

Infinitive.

To give up one's life, to commit suicide.   Magpacamatáy.

Present indefinite tense.

Commit, –est, –s suicide.   Nagpapacamatáy.

Present perfect and past indefinite tenses.

Committed, -dst; have, hast, has committed suicide.   Nagpacamatáy.

Pluperfect tense.

Had, –dst committed suicide.   Nacapagcamatáy, nagpacamatáy na.

Future indefinite tense.

Shall. –lt, will, –lt commit suicide.   Magpapacamatáy.

Future perfect tense.

Shall, -lt, will -lt have committed   Macapagpacamatáy magpapacamatáy
suicide.   na.

Imperative.

Commit, let . . . , commit suicide.   Magpacamatáy.

Verbal.

The action of committing suicide.   Ang pagpapacamatáy

Y PASIVE.

Infinitive.

To commit suicide with or on account of.   Ypagpacamatáy.

Present indefinite tense.

Commit, -est, -s suicide with or on account of.   Ypinagpapacamatáy.

Present perfect and past indefinite tenses.

Commited,-dst; have, hast, has commit- ⎰ Ypinagpacamatáy.
ted suicide with or on account of.   ⎱

Pluperfect tense.

Had, -dst, committed suicide with or on account of. { Naypagpacamatáy, ypinagpacamatáy na.

Future indefinite tense.

Shall, -lt, will, -lt commit suicide with or on account of. } Ypagpapacamatáy.

Future perfect tense.

Shall, -lt, will, -lt have committed suicide with or on account of. Maypagpacamatáy. ypagpapacamatáy na.

Imperative.

Commit, let... commit suicide with or on account of. } Ypagpacamatáy.

Verbal.

The action of committing suicide with or on account of. Ang ypagpacamatáy.

AN PASSIVE.

Infinitive.

To commit suicide in or at. Pagpacamatayán.

Present indefinite tense.

Commit, –est, –s suicide in or at. Pinagpapacamatayán.

Present perfect and past indefinite tenses.

Committed, –dst; have, hast, has committed suicide in or at. } Pinagpacamatayán.

Pluperfect tense.

Had, -dst committed suicide in or at. Napagpacamatayán, pinagpacamatayán na.

Future indefinite tense.

Shall, -lt, will, -lt commit suicide in or at. } Pagpapacamatayán.

Future perfect tense.

Shall, -lt will, -lt have committed suicide in or at. Mapagpacamatayán, pagpapacamatayán na.

Imperative.

Commit, let....commit suicide in or at.   Pagpacamatayán.

Verbal.

—

The action of committing suicide in }
or at.   } Ang pagpacamatayán.

———

The student should conjugate actively and passively by *magpaca,* the following verbs:

To humble one's self.	Magpacababa.
To give up fortune.	Magpacaduc–há.
To become mean spirited.	Magpacaliit.
To embellish one's self, to allow one's } self to be led into the right path. }	Magpacabutì.
To allow one's self to be insulted.	Magpacaapí.
To repent.	Magpacasisi.
To value one's self highly.	Magpacamahal.

Y passive stands generally in this conjugation for the instrument or cause of the action; that of *an,* for the place or the object, according to whether the verb admits or not *an* passive for the direct object.

Jesus Christ gave up His life for the redemption of mankind.	Ang ypinagpacamatáy ni Jesucristo,i, ang pagsacop sa catauohan.
It was on the cross that Jesus Christ gave up His life.	Ang *crus* ay ang pinagpacamatayán ni Jesucristo.
Notice carefully what I tell you.	{ Pacatandaán mo ang sinasabi co sa { iyò.

It should be taken into account that *pagpaca* in the passive is for those actions which require to be conjugated by *mag* in some special discriminative sense; *paca,* for the others.

Endeavour to teach your children good habits.	Pacaaralan mo ang iyòng mañga anac nang mabuting ásal.
Endeavour to learn the English language.	Pagpacapagaralán mo ang inglés na uica.

Hitherto *magpaca* has been applied either to intransitive actions or to those which do not go beyond the subject. When *magpaca* conjugates verbs the action of which is voluntary or capable of admitting a direct complement other than the subject, it indicates a purposed earnest desire, a special care of executing the action in the highest possible degree of efficiency, and in this sense it admits of the *in* passive.

To do something carefully.	Magpacarahan.
To think deeply.	Magpacaísip.
To observe carefully.	Magpacatandá.
To be upon one's guard.	Magpacaiñgat.
To behave one's self very mindfully.	Magpacabaet.
To put in order, to settle things } heedfully. }	Magpacahúsay.
To study in earnest.	Magpacapagáral.
To esteem highly.	Magpacamahal.
Modesty enhances woman's beauty.	} **Ang** cahinhina,i, nagpapabuti sa ba- } baye.

The reason for my female–cousin embellishing herself is that she may be praised.	Ang ypinagpapacabuti nang aquing pinsáng babaye,i, ang nang siyá,i, mapuri.
Meek people allow themselves to be abused to acquire merits towards God.	Ang ypinagpapacaapí nang mañga banal na tauo, ang nang magcaroón nang carapatan sa harap nang Dios.
Repent earnestly of all your wrongs.	Pacapagsisihan mo ang lahat mong masamáng gauá.
Think carefully of that.	Pacaisipin mo iyán.
I do esteem you.	Pinagpapacamahal quitá or pinaca-mamahal.

Reciprocal actions with *mag* and *an* are greatly intensified by *magpaca*.

| They harm each other bitterly. | Nagpapacasamáian silá. |
| You aided each other earnestly. | Nagpacatoloñgan cayó. |

Magpaca drops the *g* and remains *mapaca* when a fortuitous and not a purposely executed action is meant.

To allow one's self to be led into the right path.	Magpacagaling.
To be saved, to attain salvation.	Mapacagaling.
To be condemned, to incur eternal punishment.	Mapacasamá.

In the passive, when *paca* is used, the first syllable of the root should be repeated.

He endeavours to purify his habits.	Pinacalilinís niyá ang caniyàng mañga ásal.
He will be purified of all his sins.	Pacalilinisan niyà ang lahat niyàng mañga casalanan.
Thou shalt be saved if thou keepest my holy commandments.	Mapapacagaling ca cun sinusunod mo ang aquing mañga santong utos.

--- --- ---

PARTICLES AND WORDS USED AS DIFFERENT PARTS OF SPEECH.

SAAN.

—

Sáan, as its structure, *sa-an* indicates, is, most commonly, the adverb of place "where", "whereto".

| Where is the quilt? | ¿Sáan naróon ang cómot?. |
| Whereto do you go? | ¿Sáan ca paroróon.? |

Sáan may be made a verb if conjugated by *pa*, in which case it stands for the verb of motion which it replaces, meaning, "to make for, or, towards".

| Where is she going to? | ¿Napasasáan bagá siyá?. |

Sáan is joined to other particles imparting various senses thereto.

Anywhere, wherever, everywhere.	Sáan man.
Everywhere, anywhere in the Earth.	Sáan man sa lupa.
Anywhere you go.	Sáan man pumaróon ca.

Sáan, sáan pa is negative in regard to the action, but affirmative in regard to the reason.

You shall be punished.	Hahampasin ca.
Of course, it is obvious that I shall not be punished.	Sáan acó hahampasin.
You shall go there.	Paroróon ca.
Where else shall I go?	¿Sáan pa acó paroróon?

Saan di pa is affirmative in a contrary sense to that of *sáan, sáan pa.*

How can it be true?	¿Sáan pa di totoó?
How can he be whipped?	¿Sáan pa di siyá hahampasin?

We know already that *sáan, haan* preceded by *ma* or *na*, expresses "to be" as a neuter and not as a copulative verb.

Where Frank will be?	¿Masasáan bagá si Isco?
Where is the book?	¿Nasáan ang libro?

SANA.

—

Sana, as has been said, is a particle fit to express the conditional or future consequent tense.

John would have arrived had he not been sick.	Si Juan sana,i, dungmating dañga,t. nagcasaquit.
Had they cured him he would not have died.	Cun guinamot siyá nilá ay hindí sana namatáy.

Sana preceded by *cun* has a peculiar sense better to be learned by the following illustrations.

It is harder than stone, and let pass stone as a term of comparison.	Matigás pa sa batò, cun sana sa batò.
The spoliation, the theft as it were.	Ang pagágao, ang pagnanúcao cun sana pananúcao.

Sana is sometimes contracted into *sa.*

I should go.	Naparóon sa acó.

Young cock.	Tandang.
Fighting cock.	Sasabuñigin.
I will allow this rooster to grow into a fighting cock.	Sasabuñiginin co itóng tandang.
Blast of wind.	Hihip nang hañgin.
Zephyir.	Símoy.
To embrace.	Yumácap.
To shine, to glow.	Magningning.
To wait for.	Maghintáy.
Wait a moment.	Hintáy ca mona.
In the allurements of this woman, modesty shines.	Nagniningning ang cahinhinan sa quilos nitóng binibini.
To spring, to flow from.	Bumucal.
To put into.	Magsilir.
Where does this river flow from?.	¿Alíng ang binubucalán nitòng ílog na itò?.
The butterfly.	Ang paroparó.
Gnat.	Lamoc.
Ant.	Langam.
Cock-roach.	Ipis.
Glow-worm.	Alitaptap.

FORTY SIXTH EXERCISE.

Who will be saved.? Only the virtuous will be saved. What saves man.? It is fair works that save man. What did the priest say in his sermon.? He said, shun wickedness lest you be damned. What did Jesus Christ give up His life for.? He gave up His life for the redemption of man. Where did He give up His life.? He gave up His life on Mount Calvary. What does the pious man do.? He humbles himsef before God and he rises before men. What did the Son of God do.? He made himself poor and meek, and allowed himself to be insulted, lashed and crowned with thorns. Why did that girl embellish herself.? She embellished herself that she may be praised. Do you repent of all your sins.? Yes, I do repent of all **my** sins. Why does your sister value herself so highly.? She values herself so highly because she is proud. Why does the servant do that carefully.? Because he is afraid of punishment. Did you meditate on what I told you.? I did. What do you order me.? Observe carefully the dog and take great care not to be bitten by it, act very judiciously and keep your accounts accurately. Does that youngman study earnestly.? He studies earnestly that he may be esteemed highly. What shall I do to be saved.? Endeavour to correct your habits, if you desire to be saved, for only those keeping the Holy Commandments of God will be saved. Where are you going.? I am going to school. Where is your father.? My father is at home. Where shall I go.? Wherever you go you must work and suffer. What did the father and his son do.? As soon as they met they embraced each other. Is your cock a fighting cock already? No, it is still a young cock. What winds prevail outside at sea.? Mild breezes, the zephyirs swelled the sails of our ship. Do gnats hurt you by night.? Yes, gnats and cock-roaches hurt me. Are there many butterflies in your garden.? There are many of them, and also ants and glow-worms.

FORTY SEVENTH LESSON
YCAAPAT NA POUO,T, PITONG PAGARAL.

MODIFICATIVE VERBALIZING PARTICLES.

MAGPATI=PAGPATI.

Magpati, active; *pagpati*, passive; is a very little used verbal particle. It may be considered as a compound of *mag* or *magpa* and *ti*, contraction of *tig*; *tigtig* meaning "to shudder with sudden terror". It is only applied to those roots which if conjugated by *um* or *ma* express motion or corporal position, to which *magpati* adds a sense of voluntary suddenness, or, if the *g* is dropped, of unconscious hurry. In *magpati=pagpati*, pa is repeated in present and future tenses, and admits only of *y* (*yca*) and *an* passives.

ROOT.

Knee.   Lohor.

PARADIGM.

To kneel.	Lumohod.
To crouch, to kneel down before.	Maniclohod.
To remain in a kneeling posture out of stumbling.	Napaluhod, napatilohod.
Place, person or thing in honor of whom, or the cushion for kneeling upon.	Linolohorán, lohorán.
To kneel down having something with or hanging as a rosary.	Maglohod.
Thing held during kneeling.	Ylohod.
To fall on one's knees.	Magpatilohod.
Cause.	Ypagpatilohod.
Place, or person before whom.	Pagpatilohorán.

CONJUGATION.

ACTIVE.

Infinitive.

To fall on one's knees.   Magpatilohod.

Present indefinite tense.

Fall, –est, –s on....knees.   Nagpapatilohod.

Present perfect and past indefinite tenses.

Fell, –est; have, hast, has fallen on'....knees.   Nagpatilohod.

Pluperfect tense.

Had, –dst fallen on....knees.   Nacapagpatilohod, nagpatilohod na.

Future indefinite tense.

Shall, -lt, will, -lt fall on....knees.   Magpapatilohod.

Future perfect tense.

Shall, –lt, will. -lt have fallen on } Macapagpatilohod, magpapatilohod na.
....knees.

Imperative.

Fall, let....fall on....knees.   Magpatilohod.

Verbal.

The action of falling on....knees.   Ang pagpapatilohod.

Y PASSIVE.

Infinitive.

To fall on one's knees on account of.   Ycapagpatilohod.

Present indefinite tense.

Fall, -est, -s on....knees on account of.   Yquinapagpapatilohod.

Present perfect and past indefinite tenses.

Fell, -est; have, hast, has fallen on...knees on account of.   Yquinapagpatilohod.

Pluperfect tense.

Had, -dst fallen on ...knees on } Naypagpatilohod, yquinapagpatilohod na.
account of.

Future indefinite tense.

Shall, -lt, will, -lt fall on....knees on account of.   Ycapagpapatilohod.

Future perfect tense.

Shall, -lt, will, -lt have fallen on } Maypagpatilohod, ycapagpapatilohod na.
....knees on account of.

36

Imperative.

Fall, let....fall on....knees on account of. Ycapagpatilohod.

Verbal.

The action of falling on ..knees on account of. Ang ycapagpatilohod.

AN PASSIVE.

Infinitive.

To fall on one's knees at or before. Pagpatilohorán.

Present indefinite tense.

Fall, –st. –s on....knees at or before. Pinagpapatilohorán.

Present perfect and past indefinite tenses.

Fell, –est; have, hast, has fallen on....knees at or before. Pinagpatilohorán.

Pluperfect tense.

Had, -dst fallen on....knees at or before. { Napagpatilohorán, pinagpatilohorán na.

Future indefinite tense.

Shall, –lt, will, –lt fall on....knees at or before. Pagpapatilohorán.

Future perfect tense.

Shall, –lt, will, –lt have fallen on....knees at or before. { Mapagpatilohorán, pagpapatilohorán na.

Imperative.

Fall, let....fall on....knees at or before. Pagpatilohorán.

Verbal.

The action of falling on ..knees at or before. Ang pagpatilohorán.

The student should conjugate actively and passively by *magpati*, the following verbs:

To spring to one's feet.	Magpatitindig.
To prostrate one's self.	Magpatirapá.
To throw one's self down. to stretch one's self at full length.	{ Magpatihigá.
To sit down of a sudden.	Magpatiopó.
To turn one's back suddenly.	Magpatitalicod.
To place one's self quickly side on.	Magpataguilid.

Y passive, in this conjugation, stands generally for the cause, *an* passive, for the place or person.

His distracted love made him bend his knee.	Ang calacasan nang caniyàng sintà,i, ang ypinagpatiluhod niyá.
He prostrated himself before the altar.	Ang *altar* (Sp.) ang pinagpatirapaan niyá.
I prostrate myself before my king.	Ang pinagpapatirapáan co,i, ang a-quing Hari.

The *g* of *magpati*=*pagpati* is dropped according as the action is voluntary or involuntary, the latter also being expressed by *mapa.*

To spring into.	Magpatiholog.
To tumble downwards.	Mapatiholog, mapatihápay, mapatibouang.
To toss.	Magpatihapáy, magpatibouang.
To totter down subitaneously.	Mapatihapáy, mapatibouang.
To remain involuntary in a lying down posture.	Mapatihigá.
Spring into the sea.	Magpatihólog ca sa dágat.
I rose unconsciously to my feet.	Napatitindig acó.

PARTICLES AND WORDS USED AS DIFFERENT PARTS OF SPEECH.

SILA.

Silá is the well known third person pronoun in the plural, meaning "they".

They, always they, are given.	Silá nang silá ang binibiguián.

Silá, and *silá po* are used in addressing a single person and by so doing the sense is carried to the utmost degree of respect.

You, thou. (simplest sense.)	Ycáo, ca.
You. (sing.) (polite)	Ycáo po, cayó, cayó po.
You, thou. (Your Excellency, Your Majesty, Your Highness).	Silá, silá po.

This, however, does not exclude the use of the address in the proper way.

Your Excellency.	Yyò, inyò pong camahalan.

Silá is made a verb in the ways already explained for the other personal pronouns.

The child says silá.	Napapasilá ang bata.

Silà, thus accented, as a verb, means "to eat meat or fish".

The servant is eating the meat or fish.	Sinisilahin nang alila ang cati.

SIYA.

Siyá, besides standing for "he", "she", "it", also stands for the compound relative pronoun, "what", or "that which", or better to say, it is a kind of demonstrative pronoun or a somewhat emphatic means of recalling to memory the subject of a sentence.

Joseph, it is he who stole.	Si José, siyá ang nagnácao.
My mother, it is she who wept.	Ang aquing inà, siyá ang nagtañgis.
Drunknness is what killed him.	{ Ang calañgohan siyá ang ypinatáy sa caniyà.
You yourself!, is what I said.	Ycáo ñga, siyú ang ysinabí co.

It may be said that in this sense *siyá* stands for every gender of the reflective pronoun in reference to a noun.

The blacksmith himself made it.	Ang pandáy bácal, siyá ang gungmauá.
The aunt herself returned it back.	Ang alí siyáng nagsaolí.
Wealth itself caused his ruin.	{ Ang cayamana,i, siyá ang yquinasamá niyà.

Siyà, conjugated by *pa*, means "to assent", "to abide by other's opinion".

He assents.	Napasisiyà.
Do not agree to that, don't assent to.	Houag mo ypasiyà.

Siyà, conjugated by *magca*, means "to suit", "to become", "and also" to be enough, sufficient".

That dress suits her.	Yyáng damit nagcasisiyà sa caniyà.
That stick is not enough for a pillar.	Hindí nagcacasiyà iyáng cáhoy sa isàng haligue.

Conjugated by *um*, *siyì* means to reach the point of full development.

Her body has already reached its full development.	} Sungmiyà na ang catouáng niyà.

Siyà, if conjugated by *man*, means "to fill up the whole room", "to go on growing".

His sore is coming up in flesh. (is healing.)	} Naniniyà na ang caniyàng súgat.
Adjustment, agreement, suitableness.	Casiyahán. (notice the accentuation.)
Enough, average, common, ordinary thing.	} Casiyahan.

Siyá may also stand for the person addressed in a politely respectful sense.

Your mercy.	Siyá po.

Siyà may be used as an adverb or interjection.

So, just so, just it.	Siyà.
Bravo!.	Siyà.

But, most generally, it is associated with some other particle.

Enough!.	Siyà na.
It is he himself!, it is just that, just it.	Siyá ñga.
Although he be.	Siyá man.
Would to God, amen, happiness to you.	Siyà nauá.
It is he then....	Siyá palá.....

SUCAT.
—

Súcat, as a noun, means "measure", that is to say, some standard apparatus proper to ascertain quantity. As a verb, it has the following significations:

To measure. (simple sense.)	Sumúcat, manúcat.
To measure a great deal.	Magsucat. (notice the accentuation.)

The meaning of pattern, standard, which, *súcat* has is applied in many ways. It is used in a potential sense as *mangyari*, *maca*.

She can work.	Súcat siváng gumauá.
They may be given it.	Súcat siláng biguián.

But if the sense is a passive one or the action does not admit of potentiality, it means "duty or moral obligation," the same as *dápat*.

You deserve to be punished.	Súcat cang hampasín.
He is worthy to be appointed captain.	Súcat siyá maguingcapitan.
It is beneath their nobleness.	Dili súcat sa caniláng camahalan.

Súcat na means the same as *siyá na*, "enough". *Súcat na*, followed by an infinitive means the hourly occasion of doing something.

It	is	time	to	eat.	Súcat	nang	cumáin.
"	"	"	"	go out.	"	"	lumabás.
"	"	"	"	study.	"	"	magáral.
"	"	"	"	walk.	"	"	lumácad.
"	"	"	"	sleep.	"	"	matólog.

To pray, to say prayers.	Manalañgin.
To attend church service, to worship.	Magsimbà, magsambà.
In my opinion.	Sa aquing acala, sa ísip co.
Till, until, as far as.	Hangán.
Till evening.	Hangáng gabí, hangán sa gabí.
Till to-morrow.	Hangáng bucas.
As far as the bridge.	Hangán sa tuláy.
Till I die.	Hangán sa camatayan co.
To, towards.	Daco, sa daco, dápit.
Towards the forest.	Sa dacong gúbat.
„ „ sea.	„ „ dágat.
„ „ land.	„ „ lupa.
Upwards.	Dacong itáas.
Downwards.	Dápit ibabá.
Eastwards.	Dacong silañganan.
Westwards,	„ calunuran.
On, upon.	Sa ibábao.
Above, over.	Sa itáas.
Under, underneath.	Sa ilálim.

FORTY SEVENTH EXERCISE.

Where did I fall on my knees.? You fell on your knees before the Archbishop. Did you not prostrate yourself before the image of the Holy Virgin?. I prostrated myself before the altar. What caused your grandfather to throw himself down.? Old age and weakness caused him to throw himself down. What are the children doing.? They are always sitting down and rising up. What did the patient do when he saw the physician.? He placed himself side on of a sudden. Why did the sailor spring into the water.? He did not spring into the water, the mast tumbled down suddenly and he fell downwards. Did the wind toss down the tree.? It was not the wind, it was a thunderbolt that tossed it down. Why does he call out for them constantly.? He has no others to call out for. What are the dog and the cat eating.? The dog eats meat, the cat is eating fish. Does money suffice to bring about happiness.? Money does not suffice to bring about happiness. Did he drink too much.? He drank only in the ordinary way. Do I go on speaking.? Enough!, don't speak any more about that. Was it he who said it.? He himself said it. Do you fear him.? Although he be a leader I don't fear him. Did your measure the stuff I sent you.? I did not measure it, the Chinese merchant did it. Did you yourself take the measure for the trousers.? I took the measure myself. Can he pay.? He cannot pay. Why do you not go on working.? It is already time to sleep. Till when will Mary be in town.? She will be here until to-morrow. How far did you accompany him.? I accompanied him as far as the river. Where does this river flow towards.? This river flows towards the North. Where is the ship bound for.? She steers towards the land. Where did you put the pin.? I put it on the table. Is your sister above.? She is below.

FORTY EIGHTH LESSON.
YCAAPAT NA POUO,T, UALONG PAGARAL.

MODIFICATIVE VERBALIZING PARTICLES.

MAGCAPA=PAGCAPA.

Magcapa, active; *pagcapa*, passive; is a verbal particle used only with roots of suh corporal motions as may be affected by terror or sudden fright to indicate the involuntary panic-stricken posture, effect of any such cause. *Pa* is repeated in the proper tenses and, on account of the involuntariness of the action, this conjugation lacks the imperative and only admits of *y* and *an* passives.

ROOT.

Gesture grimace, showing of the teeth at.	Ñgisi.

PARADIGM.

To gesticulate.	Ñgumisi.
Do, a great deal.	Mañgisi.
Cause and also the mouth or the teeth.	Yñgisi, ypañgisi.
To go about gesticulating that way.	Mañisi.
Person, place at.	Pañgisihan.
To remain beating one's teeth out of terror.	Magcapañgisi.
Cause.	Ycapagcapañisi.
Place.	Pagcapañgisihan.

CONJUGATION.

ACTIVE.

Infinitive.

To remain showing one's teeth out of terror.	Magcapañgisi.

Present indefinite tense.

Remain, –est, –s etc.	Nagcapapapañgisi.

Present perfect and past indefinite tenses.

Remained, –dst; have, hast, has remained etc.	Nacapañgisi.

Pluperfect tense.

Had, –dst remained etc.   Nacapagcapañgisî, nagcapañgisî na.

Future indefinite tense.

Shall, –lt, will, –lt remain etc.   Magcapapapañgisî.

Future perfect tense.

Shall, –lt, will, –lt have remained etc.   Macapagcapañgisî, magcapapañgisî na.

Verbal.

The state of remaining etc.   Ang pagcapapañgisî.

Y PASSIVE.

Infinitive.

To remain showing one's teeth out of terror on account of.   Ypagcapañgisî.

Present indefinite tense.

Remain, –est, –s, etc. on account of.   Ypinagcapapañgisî.

Present perfect and past indefinite tenses.

Remained, -dst; have, hast, has remained etc on account of.   Ypinagcapañgisî.

Pluperfect tense.

Had, –dst; remained etc. on account of. { Naypagcapapañgisî, ypinagcapañgisî na.

Future indefinite tense.

Shall, –lt, will, –lt remain etc. on account of.   Ypagcapapañgisî.

Future perfect tense.

Shall, -lt, will, -lt have remained etc. on account of. { Maypagcapapañgisî, ypagcapapañgisî na.

Verbal.

The state of remaining etc. on account of.   Ang ypagcapañgisî.

AN PASSIVE.

Infinitive.

To remain showing one's teeth out of terror, in or at.   Pagcapapañgisihan.

Present indefinite tense.

Remain, -est, -s, etc. in or at.   Pinagcapapañgisihan.

Present perfect and past indefinite tenses.

Remained, -dst; have, hast, has remained etc. in or at.   Pinagcapañgisihan.

Pluperfect tense.

Had, dst, remained etc. in or at.   Napagcapañgisihan, pinagcapañgisihan na.

Future indefinite tense.

Shall, -lt, will. -lt remain etc. in or at.   Pagcapapañgisihan.

Future perfect tense.

Shall, -lt, will,- lt have remained etc. in or at.   Mapagcapañgisihan, pagcapapañgisihan na.

Verbal.

The state of remaining etc. in or at.   Ang pagcapañgisihan.

The student should conjugate actively and passively the following roots to which almost exclusively the particle *magcapa* is applied.

Opening of the eyes. To open one's eyes.	Dílat, múlat. Dumílat, mamúlat.	
To remain with one's eyes open out of panic.	Magcapadílat, magcapamúlat.	
Opening of the mouth. To open one's mouth.	Ñgañgà.	Ñgumañgà.
To remain with one's mouth open etc.	Magcapañgañgà.	
Placing of one's legs wide, to place one's self with the legs wide.	Magbisaclat.	
To remain with one's legs wide etc.	Magcapabisaclat.	

PARTICLES AND WORDS USED AS DIFFERENT PARTS OF SPEECH.

TABI.

Tabi, as a noun, means "border", "bank", "shore", "extremity".

The river bank.	Ang tabi nang ílog.
The sea–shore.	Ang tabi nang dágat.

As a verb or a verbal noun, *tabi* has the following significations:

To be on the border.	Matabi.
To go about bordering.	Mapatabi.
To place one's self at the border, edge.	Tumabi.
Let him not place himself at the edge.	Houag siyá tumabi.
Place that at the extremity.	Ytabi mo iyán.

Place yourself at the very edge.	Patatabì ca.
The extremity, the foremost point of something.	Ang catabihan.
Laystall, the dirtiest place.	Tabihan.

Tabì is very much made use of as a polite warning for somebody to get out of the way when persons, generally inferiors, want room for themselves to pass on, by or through.

By your leave.	Tabì po.
Please, make room for me to pass.	¡Tabì! acó daráan.

It is also a respectful expression to ask permission for something to be done.

Pardon, Sir, I am going to make water.	Tabì po, acó,i, iihí.

TAGA.

Taga, as has been said, denotes nativity, pertaining to the place of birth.

Where are you from?, what country are you from?	¿Taga sáan ca?
I am a Tondoman.	Taga Tondo acó.

Taga, as a noun, also means "fishing-hook" of any size, *binuit* being a small one.

Bait your hook.	Painan mo ang iyòng taga.

Taga, as a verb, signifies "to hew" in a longitudinal way.

To hew downwards.	Tumaga.
To hew a great deal.	Magtaga.
To go about hewing.	Managa.

Tumaga means also to lay hold of, some holdfast thing, as the anchor.

The anchor laid hold on land.	Tungmaga sa lupa ang sinípit.

Metaphorically it may be said:

His words pierce deeply into my heart.	Tungmataga mandin sa lóob co ang caniyàng uica.

Taga, as a prepositive particle of frequentative nouns, will be treated of in proper place.

TALAGA.

Talagá, is, like *ócol*, either a telling or an attributive word denoting an idea of bias, predestination, fitness, better to be known by the following examples.

Naturally, in a natural, innate way.	Talagá
The lemon is sour by nature.	Talagàng maasim ang dáyap.
This misfortune was destined to me by God.	Talagá nang Dios sa aquin itòng aquing cahirapan.
To keep something to be devoted to.	Magtalagà.
I keep this candle to be offered to the Most Holy Virgin.	Pinagtatalagahan co ang casantosan Virgen nitòng candila.

To yield, to be resolved.	Tumalagà.
I yield to anything you may order me.	Tungmatalagà acó sa anomán yo-otos mo sa aquin.
He is resolved to do that.	Tungmatalaga siyá gaoin iyán.

TAMBING.

Tambing, adverb of time, means "inmediately," "forthwith".

Do it immediately.	Tambing mong gaoin.

Tambing, as a verb, is conjugated by *may* and means "to do something quickly," "to dispatch," "to prepare."

Make haste.	Magtambing ca.

In the passive, it follows that required by the verb it is joined to.

Take it forthwith.	Tambiñgin mo cunin.
Give it at once.	Ytambing mo ybigáy.

If used independently, it follows the general rules of the passive: *y,* for the thing; *an,* for the person or place.

Make haste as to the money for Peter.	Tambiñgan mo si Pedro nang salapí.
The money for Peter, made haste with it.	Ang salapí ytambing mo cay Pedro.

To betray.	Maglilo.
To get rid of.	Lumigtás.
To be in flames.	Magniñgas.
Were it not for.	Dañgan, cundañgan.
Were it not for me he would have fallen.	Cundañgan acó ay nahúlog siyá.

It is to be noticed that *dañgan* and *cundañgan* govern the nominative case.

Draw nigh.	Hali ca.
Come on, please.	Hali na.
Come over here.	Hali ca na, hali na cayó.
Are you acquainted with it?, do you understand?	Ha, haní, haniá.
To wonder at, to be astonished.	Manguilalás, magtacà.
Wonderful, admirable.	Caguilaguilalás.
It is not to be wondered at.	Di ñga súcat pagtac-han.
Big words, abusive language.	Mañga uicang hindí dápat.
Regarding ...with regard to as to.	Tungcol sa, bágay sa.
With regard to his behaviour, I have to say to you......	Bágay sa caniyàng paglácad may sasa-bihin acó sa iyò.....
Formerly, anciently.	Sa onàng panahón, sa ónang arao.
On that day.	Niyóng onàng árao.
At, by those times.	Sa daco róong árao.
To hit the mark, to conjecture rightly.	Matoto.
To praise.	Magpuri.
To steer, to be bound for, to make for.	Tumoñgò, mapatoñgò,
Where are you going towards.?	¿Sáan ang patotoñgohan mo.?
Occupation, business.	Abala.
I have business now.	Acó,i, may abala ñgayón.

FORTY EIGHTH EXERCISE.

Whom is that child showing his teeth at.? He makes gestures at that old man that is drunk. What does he show his teeth for.? He makes grimaces at his being inebriated. Had he already remained beating his teeth when yow went home.? Yes, he had. Why did he remain showing his teeth.? He remained showing his teeth on account of fright. Where did he remain shivering his teeth in convulsion.? He remained beating his teeth on the ground of the church. Why did your sister remain with her eyes open.? She remained with her eyes open at the news of her mother's death. Why is that man's mouth kept open.? He remained with his mouth open on account of a fit. Did the thief remain with his legs wide apart on leaping over the fence.? He remained with his legs wide apart when he leapt over the fence. Does the fisher walk along the river bank.? He walks along the river bank to catch fish. Would it not be better for him to sail along the sea shore.? It would be easier for him; but he would not catch so much, for fish is to be found at the bank of the river. Why do you place yourself at the border of the sea.? It is to see the ships. Do you not remember your father said to you, don't place yourself at the very edge.? Well, I remember that. Where did Saint Job pass the greater part of his life? At a laystall. Why did you not say *tabi* on your passing on.? I said Sir, by your leave!. What is your country.? My country is North America. Whom do you hold that flower for.? I hold it for my sweetheart. Did you bait your fishing-hook.? It has been baited with worms. What are you doing.? I am hewing this log lengthwise. What is your uncle's trade.? He earns his living by hewing wood. What is the Americans, innate disposition.? They are industrious by temperament, but natives, on the contrary, are inclined to laziness. Are you resolved to keep the commandments of God.? I am resolved to it. What do you say.? Sew my shirt immediately. Who betrayed Jesus:? One of His disciples betrayed Him. What produces that blaze.? It is a wood which is in flames. Was Peter saved.? Were it not for me, he would have perished. What did the priest say to the child and to the servant.? He said to the child, come on my child, and to the servant, come over here. What do you wonder at.? I wonder at the great works of God. Why did you use big vords towards Ann.? I used big words towards her on account of her behaviour.

FORTY NINTH LESSON.
YCAAPAT NA POUO,T, SIYAM NA PAGARAL.

MODIFICATIVE VERBALIZING PARTICLES.

MAGCAN=PAGCAN.

Magcan, active; *pagcan*, passive; is the last verbal particle we shall treat of, although perhaps some others of a narrow local range may be in use. It is an intransitive particle rarely used, and generally applied to roots of such fluids as flow or are expelled form the human body, to indicate that the shedding or flowing is involuntary and out of some cause which renders the excretion either unconscious or uncontrollable. *Magcan* is dissyllabic; *ca*, the last syllable, consists of three letters of which only the two first, *ca*, are taken for repetition according to the general rule. Now, if this is done, confusedness might arise with the particle *magca*, to avoid which both *ca* and the first syllable of the root are repeated, the latter in all and *can* in the present and future tenses. On account of the involuntariness of the action this particle only admits of *y* and *an* passives, and cannot be used in the imperative.

ROOT.

Tear. Luha.

PARADIGM.

To weep.	Lumoha.
To shed tears.	Magloha.
Cause, reason.	Yloha.
Person over whom tears are shed.	Linoháan, quinalolohaan.

CONJUGATION.

ACTIVE.

Infinitive.

To shed tears without one's being conscious thereof. } Magcanluluha.

Present indefinite tense.

Shed, -st, -s tears etc. Nagcacanluluha

Present perfect and past indefinite tenses.

Shed, -est; have, hast, has shed tears etc.   Nagcanluluha.

Pluperfect tense.

Had, –dst shed tears etc.   Nacapagcanluluha, nagcanluluha na.

Future indefinite tense.

Shall, –lt, will, –lt shed tears etc.   Magcacanluluha.

Future perfect tense.

Shall, -lt, will, -lt have shed tears etc.   Macapagcanluluha, magcacanluluha na.

Verbal.

The shedding of tears etc.   Ang pagcacanluluha.

Y PASSIVE.

Infinitive.

To shed tears etc. on account of.   Ypagcanluluha.

Present indefinite tense.

Shed, –est –s tears etc. on account of.   Ypinagcacanluluha.

Present perfect and past indefinite tenses.

Shed, –dst; have, hast, has shed tears etc. on account of.   Ypinagcanluluha.

Pluperfect tense.

Had, –dst shed tears etc. on account of.   Naypagcanluluha, ypinagcanluluha na.

Future indefinite tense.

Shall, –lt, will, –lt shed tears etc. on account of.   Ypagcacanluluha.

Future perfect tense.

Shall, -lt, will, -lt have shed tears etc. on account of.   } Maypagcanluluha, ypagcacanluluha na.

Verbal.

The shedding of tears etc. on account of.   Ang ypagcanluluha.

AN PASSIVE.

Infinitive.

To shed tears etc. at.   Pagcanluluháan.

Present indefinite tense.

Shed, –st, –s tears etc. at.   Pinagcacanluluháan.

Present perfect and past indefinite tenses.

Shed, -dst; have, hast, has shed tears etc. at.   Pinagcanluluháan.

Pluperfect tense.

Had, –dst shed tears etc. at.   Napagcanluluháan, pinagcanluluháan na.

Future indefinite tense.

Shall, –lt, will, –lt shed tears etc. at.   Pagcacanluluháan.

Future perfect tense.

Shall, –lt, will, –lt have shed tears etc. at.   Mapagcanluluháan, pagcacanluluháan na.

Verbal.

The shedding of tears etc. at.   Ang pagcanluluháan.

The student should conjugate actively and passively by *magcan* the following roots.

Urine.	To suffer from incontinence of urine.	Yhi.	Magcaniihi.
Blood.	To bleed. (unconsciously)	Dugó.	Magcandudugó.
Perspiration.	To sweat out of fright, ague, etc.	Páuis.	Magcanpapáuis.
Saliva.	To slaver.	Láuay.	Magcanlaláuay.

Figuratively the sense of *magcan* is extended to other roots of phisical or moral acts performed by the rational being and even to those outside the conscious subject.

To burst out laughing, to culminate in laughter.	Magcantatauà.
To blush.	Magcanhihiya.
To pour over, to overflow.	Magcanlalabis.
To drop off.	Magcanlalaglag.
My heart overflows with joy.	Ang touà,i, nagcacanlalabis sa aquing pusò.
I cannot refrain from laughing.	Nagcacanlalabis ang táuа sa cataouán co.

PARTICLES AND WORDS USED AS DIFFERENT PARTS OF SPEECH.

TAPAT.

Tapat, as an adjective, means "just", "right", "upright".

Right action.	Tapat or matatapat na gauá.
To give alms to the poor is a right action.	Ang paglilimós sa mañga duc-hà,i, tapat na gauá.

Tapat, as a verb, has several meanings according to the particle with which it is conjugated.

To stand opposite, to place one's self in front.	Tumapat.
Two things placed opposite each other.	Pinagtapat.
More than two things placed in front of each other.	Pagtatapatapatín.
To go directly to, to go the shortest way, to act rightfully.	Magtapat.
Cut by which a road or path is shortened.	Tapatan.
To lie. (two things opposite one another).	Matapat, nagtatapat.
To belong to, to be incumbent on.	Matapat.
Mass is only incumbent on priests.	Sa mañga pare lámang natatapat ang misa.

TILA.

Tila is, as *diua*, *casi* and other expressions, a kind of impersonal verb standing for "it seems", "it appears".

It seems to be a person.	Tila tauò.
It appears that he went there.	Tila naparóon.

Tila, as a verb, is conjugated by *um*, *magpa* or *pa* and means "to cease raining", "to wait till rain is over."

Rain is subsiding.	Tungmitila na.
Let us wait until rain is over.	Patiláin ta mona ang ulán.

TOLOY.

Tolóy, adverb, means "as well as", "at the same time", "jointly", conjointly".

Give my son this and fetch my book on the way.	Ybigáy mo itò sa anac co, tolóy acó,i, ycoha mo nang aquing libro.
Let him sell the bushel of rice along with the bag. (cover).	Ypagbilí niyà ang cabán na bigás, tolóy nang bayong.

Tolóy in the past tense of the passive still retains its adverbial sense, meaning "wholly", "completely", or the perfective sense imparted to some verbs by the English particle "up".

It was killed at once, upright.	Pinatáy din tinolóy.

I made it up.	Yinari cong tinolóy.
I bought up his pledge.	Tinolóy cong tubusín ang sanlá niyà.

Tóloy is made a verb with various significations.

To make up, to conclude.	Tumóloy, magtóloy.
To go on with, to go further, to proceed.	Magtolóy. (notice the accentuation).
Go on with punishing.	Ypatolóy ang parusà.
To lodge at, to take shelter in.	Tumolóy. (not. the acc.)
To afford shelter.	Magpatolóy.
Inn, lodging house.	Toloyan.
He affords shelter to by-passers, palmers.	Nagpapatolóy siyà sa taga ibàng bayan.

TONGCOL.

—

Tongcol is, like *ócol* and *talagá*, a word having attributive sense. Used as a noun it means "propriety", "adequateness".

Whom does this correspond to?	¿Sinong may tungcol nitò?
It corresponds to me.	Natotongcol sa aquin.
Duty, obligation, authority, office.	Catongcolan.
This is my duty.	Catongcolan co itò.

Use of *tongcol* as a verb:

To distribute to each party what is due to him.	Magtongcol, magpatongcol.
God designed this for me.	Acó,i, pinatotongcolan nang Dios nitò.
To apportion one's task, to take one's part of the task.	Tumongcol.

Tongcol may be used as an adverb in the sense of *gánang, ganán sa*.

As for me.	Tongcol sa aquin.

To be alone.	Mag-isà.
She is there all by herself.	Nag-iisà siyá dóon.
Do it all by yourself.	Gaoin mong mag-isà.
It is not proper, just.	Hindí carampatan, catampatan.
Nor it is just to insult other people. (our fellow beings.)	Hindí namán catampatan ang pagmomorà sa cápoua tauó.
Pity, tenderness.	Aua, caauáan.
Tender, merciful.	Maauain, mahabaguin.
Meek.	Maamó, maamóng lóob.
Humble.	Mababang lóob.
To desire, to be fond of.	Mauili.
Amateur, fond.	Mauilihín, maibiguín, matoaín.

FORTY NINTH EXERCISE.

Why do you not mind that baby over there weeping? I don't mind him, for babies weep without being conscious thereof. Why does that girl show tears in her eyes? It is on account of sickness that she sheds tears unconsciously. Does the curate of your parish preach well? He preaches effectively and he sheds tears in the pulpit. How is your husband? My husband is aggravated in his complaint, he suffers from incontinence of urine and he bleeds unconsciously; he covers himself with perspiration and slavers; sometimes he swoons away and bursts out into laughter. Did the maid blush? She blushed at the sight of her lover. Why is there so much fruit strewn on the ground? Because it is too ripe and drops off from the trees. Do the children romp? Thy are overjoyed with their toys. What do you laugh at? Laughter tickles all over me. Is to afford shelter to people, good? To afford shelter to other people is an upright action. Why did you not shun him? He placed himself right in front of me. How are the trees in your garden, arranged? They are placed opposite each other. Did you go the shortest way to Mariquina? I lelf the high road and ventured on the cross–path. Do I release the prisoner? That is not incumbent on you. Is not that sail on the sea, white? It seems to be yellow. Does it not appear to be a steamer? No, it seems to be a sailing vessel. Are you going out at once? No, I shall wait until the rain is over. What? Fetch my spectacles and at the same time take away this chair. Did the servant drink any milk? He drank up the whole. What shall I then do? Go on with whipping him. Where does your friend lodge? He lodges at my house. What is your duty? My duty is to judge. What office does he fill? His office is that of a collector. Did you distribute the salary to the journeymen? I did. What part of the task did the soldier take for himself? He took upon himself to keep guard at the outpost. Why are the couple alone? They are all by themselves, because they are married to each other. Do you wish me to accompany you? No, I will go alone. Is it proper to owe and not to pay? No, it is not proper to owe and not to pay, nor it is just to run into debt. Is his master cruel or merciful? He is meek and merciful. Are you fond of riding? I am not fond of riding.

FIFTIETH LESSON.
YCALIMANG POUONG PAGARAL.

THE GERUND.

The gerund is, in English, a verbal noun preserving the same government as the verb it is derived from, as in "I like eating apples". The termination "ing" of the English verbs is, outside of the above mentioned case, parsed properly or improperly, as verbal noun, present or predicative participle, participial adjective, etc., according to its being used in one way or another. It is also a peculiarity of the English language to use the gerund, instead of the infinitive which most other languages require, after some preposition either expressed or understood, as in, "after playing", "he continues growing up". But in other languages the gerund is also that form of the verb expressing the action in an adverbial manner, as illustrated by the following expressions: "He reads standing", "he learns by teaching". Tagalog has no proper inflexion for the English verbal forms of "ing" termination, thus, all of them will be included in the explanations hereafter.

The present participle, as has been said in a foregoing chapter, is expressed by the active form of the verb, preceded by the article, and adapts itself to every tense and case.

The loving girl. (maid).	Ang sungmisintàng dalaga.
Of the obeying child.	Nang sungmusunod na bata.
To, for the working man.	Sa gungmagauàng tauò.
I gave a dollar for the fighting (he who fought) soldier.	Ybinigáy co sa naquipagbacang sundalo ang piso.
I will buy a book for the studying pupil. (he who will study)	Ybibilì co ang magaáral na alagad nang isàng libro.

When the "ing" termination makes a verbal noun, this, is expressed by the Tagalog verbal noun.

Reading is very amusing.	Ang pagbasà,i, nagbibigáy aliu
Preaching well is very difficult.	Ang pañgañgáral na mabuti ay maliuag na totoò.
Eating too much is dangerous	Ang pagcacàii,i, nacapañgañganib.

When the termination "ing" makes the gerund, as considered in English. it is translated by the infinitive.

I like shooting fowl.	Nauiuilì acóng mamaril nang ibon.
I would like eating fish.	Ybig co sana cumáin nang isdá.
He tries buying this house.	Nagbabantà siyá bilhín itòng báhay.

If the English present participle is used attributively, that is to say, adjectivally, connected with a noun or pronoun, it is generally translated in Tagalóg by the infinitive.

I saw her playing the harp.	Naquita co siyá tumogtog nang *arpa.* (Sp.)

I heard my father whipping him.	Nariñgig co ang amá cong humampás sa caniyà.

The present tense may also be used if the determining verb obtains in the present or the action is considered as going on.

I behold my herd pasturing.	Nanonóor acó sa aquing caban na nananabsab. (from *sabsab*, "pasture").
I notice my servant rowing. (oaring.)	Pinagmamasiran co ang aquing alilang gungmagaor.

The English present participle used predicatively to form a compound tense is generally translated in Tagalog by the corresponding tense.

He is mustering people for the cockpit.	Pinagtatáuag niyà ang mañga tauò sa saboñgan.
I was writing when he called me.	Sungmusúlat acó nang acó,i, tináuag niyà
They will be gambling when you arrive there.	Magsusugal silá cun dumating ca dóon.

There is in Tagalog no proper progressive conjugation; if, however stress is laid on the going on of an action, *sa* and the root with its first syllable and then the whole root repeated, is sometimes used in the present tense in á sense of displeasure or reprimand.

He is looking at there as a fool.	Sa titiñgintiñgin siyá.
He is standing purposeless.	Sa tatayotayó siyá.
They are present without saying a word.	Sa haharapharap silá.

The present participle used adverbially is generally translated by the Tagalog verbal noun preceded by *sa*.

Bottles are made by blowing.	Ang mañga bote,i, guinagauá sa paghihihip.
Cold is expelled by walking.	Ang guínao ay napalalabás sa paglalacad.
Teachers learn by teaching.	Ang mañga ungmaáral ay nagaáral sa pagáral.
By practicing virtue, Glory is attained.	Sa pag-gauá nang cabanala,i, quinacamtam ang caloualhatían.

But if condition is implied, the imperative or infinitive preceded by *cun* is used.

He will arrange the matter by paying the debt.	Maghuhúsay siyá nang bágay cun bayaran niyà ang ótang.
Mary singing, he refuses to play.	Nanayáo siyáng tumogtog cun nagaáuit Si María.

If an idea of time is prominent in the expression, *cun*, before the present or future tenses is used.

Old people speaking, children should be silent.	Cun nagsasalitá ang matatandá, dápat tumahimic ang mañga bata.
The sermon commencing. I will go away.	Cun pinupunuan ang pañgáral, ay aalís acó.

The idea of a past time with the gerund is generally expressed by the past tense preceded by *nang*.

He dying. the doctor arrived. | Nang siyá,i, namatáy na, dungmating ang médico.

They sailing, their mother went back. | Nang naglalayag na silá,i, nouí ang canilàng inà.

The English gerund coming· after some preposition or adverb and replacing the infinitive is translated in several ways according to the sense imparted to the action by the adverb or preposition.

"On" with the gerund, denoting simultaneity or continuance is translated by *pag* prefixed to the root, with the possessive case of the agent and the accusative of the object (if any) following.

On my finishing this work I shall read. | Pagtapus co nitòng gauá, acó,i, babasà.
On striking twelve o'clock we shall go to rest. | Pagtogtog nang á lasdoce (Sp.), magpapahiñgá tayo.
On my father going upstairs. he fell down. | Pagpanhic nang amá co,i, naholog siyá.
On his preaching, rain came down. | Pagpañgúral niyà nagmulá ang ulán.

If the action is past or complete, *pagca*, instead of *pag*, is prefixed to the root, with the same construction.

After having finished my breakfast I shall go church. | Pagcatapus nang aquing pamáhao, magsisimbà acó.
On having paid for the shoes, I bought a bed. | Capagcabáyad co nang sapin, bungmili acó nang isàng hihigáan.

"After" with the gerund is translated by *pagca*.

After dining. | Pagcapananhali.
After saying this. he embraced his uncle. | Pagcasabi niyà nitò yungmácap siyá sa caniyàng amaín.
The mass over, the priest took choco-late. | Pagcamisa, nagsicolate ang pare.

If other prepositions are used before the gerund, the infinitive or verbal noun may be used in Tagalog with the proper particle preceding.

In making use of gunpowder great care should be taken. | Sa pag-gamit nang pólvora (Sp.) .i, magpapacaiñgat ang tauò.
This (kind of) herb is good for curing toothache. | Ytòng camantigui ay mabuti sa pag-gamot sa saquit nang ñgipin.

PARTICLES AND WORDS USED AS DIFFERENT PARTS OF SPEECH.

TOUI.

—

Touí is an adverb meaning "always" and has sometimes the conjunctional sense of "whenever".

Always, constantly. | Touíng tóuí. touí nang touí.
You are constantly busy. | Touíng touí mayróon cang abala.
Whenever you read something. | Touíng bumasà ca nang anomán.
Whenever he writes. | Touíng siyá,i, sumúlat or sungmusúlat.

Toui may also stand for an adjective.

Every day, every year. | Touíng árao, touíng taón.

It may also be used as a conjunction for "while", "as far as". "as long as"

| While, as far as, as long as manhood is not erased from the world. | Touíng di mapauí ang pagcatauò sa sanglibutan. |

UALA.

Ualá, is sometimes used as a substantive for "gulf", "sea", "main", and may also be made a verb in this signification.

| Put to the open sea. | Maualá ca. |
| He carried his rapine into the sea. | Nagpaualá siyá nang caniyàng samsamin. |

Ualá besides the well known signification of "lack", "want", has many others as a verb.

To flee, to pardon, to exonerate.	Magualá.
To disappear.	Maualá.
It is not possible to flee now.	Hindí macauaualá ñgayón.
It disappeared from my hands.	Naualá sa camáy co.
Absolutely nothing.	Ualáng ualá.
I have absolutely everything.	Ualáng di ualá sa aquin.
He did not put in an appearance yesterday.	Ualá siyá cahapon.
Free me from my debt.	Ualín mo na ang ótang co sa iyò.
God pardons our sins.	Nagpapaualá ang Dios nang mañga casalanan natin.

Ualá is joined to many words forming adversative or negative expressions better to be learned by practice.

Endless, eternal.	Ualáng hangán.
Easy, possible.	Ualáng líuag.
Innocent, blameless.	Ualáng sala.
Sound, healthy.	Ualáng saquit.
Ungrateful. (there are no words to express his wickedness)	Ualáng turíng (siyá).

YARI.

Yari is one of the forms of the demonstrative pronoun, "this", "this here", which is more commonly expressed by *itò*.

| This heart of mine. | Yaríng aquing puso. |

Yari is used as an absolute verb for bringing to an end some business or talk.

Finished!.	Yarí na.
Conclusion.	Cayarían.
What did your business come to?	¿Anòng pagcayayarí nang osap ninyò?

To be on the lookout for.	Sumoboc.
It would be better, rather.	Mahañga.
It would be better not to have been born a man.	Mahañga,i, houag naguinglalaqui.
And thanks be given.	Salámat at.
Ang thanks be given he did not fall.	Salámat at di siyá naholog.
Scale... (horny plate).	Calisquis.
Fins of fishes.	Palicpic.
Wing.	Pacpac.

Frying pan.	Cauali.
Earthen cooking-pot.	Palayoc.
Beans.	Patani.
Any thing to be eaten with the bread or boiled rice.	Ulam.
To hiss; to whistle.	Sumotsot; magpasouit.
To bet.	Pumusta, magposta (from Sp. word apuesta, "bet".)

FIFTIETH EXERCISE.

Do you like to hear the singing birds in the morning.? I like to see the singing birds and the fighting cocks in the pit. Whose book is that.? It is the learning boy's. Does the Chinaman lend any money to the gambling parties.? He lends a hundred dollars to the gambling parties. Is that needle for my sister.? No, it is for the reading girl. Is fishing an art.? No, fishing is a pastime, but writing is an art. Is shooting toilsome in the Philippines.? It is toilsome on account of the bushes; but it is easy on account of the plenty of game. Is yachting dangerous.? Yatching is sometimes dangerous. What did you catch the servant doing.? I caught him stealing my watch and putting on my shirt. What did she try playing.? She tried to play the piano, but she did not succeed. Is he betting on your cock.? He is betting on my cock. What was the priest doing when you entered church.? He was preaching and crying. Will they be supping if we go now.? No, they will not be supping, they will be playing at cards. How do tailors sew.? They sew while hissing. How are monkeys caught.? They are sometimes caught (while) eating bivalves at the beach. How is your father being cured.? He is being cured by bathing him in ice water. Do servants sleep, their masters working.? Servants do not sleep their masters working. Was he planting the trees while he was digging the earth.? He was planting the trees while he was staying in the farm. When did he go to the farm.? He went there on your going out. What did he eat after having learnt his lesson.? After having learnt his lesson he ate some bananas. When did the stranger intend to start.? He will start the supper being over. Is he engaged in handling the plough.? No, he is engaged in driving carts. What is that fish good for.? It is good for bait. Should I wear spectacles when I write.? You should wear spectacles for reading and writing. Shall I visit him every day.? No, you should visit him every week. Where is the chicken that disappeared.? It did not disappear, here it is. Is God eternal.? He is eternal and Almighty. May we attain the eternal life.? We may attain eternal life by keeping the commandments. Is he blameless.? He is culpable and wicked beyond measure. What shall we do after having finished this work.? After having finished it, we shall go for a walk. Is his body covered with scales.? His body is covered with scales. Did the cook take away the fins of the fish.? He did. Where is he going to fry it.? He is going to fry it in the frying pan. What is he going to fry it with.? He is going to fry it in the frying pan. What is he going to fry it with.? He is going to fry it with beans and that will be our course.

FIFTY FIRST LESSON.
YCALIMANG POUO,T, YSANG PAGARAL.

USE AND INTERCHANGE OF TENSES.

The Tagalog language is in the use of tenses, as in everything else, very lax. It has already been said that the root alone may be used with some adverb or word importing time to express every tense. The following directions about the use of tenses are however given to assist the learner to some understanding of the subject.

The present indefinite is used for any actual action whether it is represented as habitual, true, or as going on at the time it is being spoken of.

He visits her every other day.	Dinadálao niyá siyá sa touíng dalauàng árao.
Her niece goes to mass every holyday.	Ang caniyàng pamangquing babaye nagsisimbà touíng árao nang *piesta*. (corr. from Sp. word *fiesta*, "feast")
He bows to, salutes her.	Bungmabati siyá sa caniyà.
The bird is pecking.	Nanunuca ang ibon.
The leader is writing.	Sungmusúlat, nasúlat ang pono.

This same tense serves for the past indefinite of the progressive conjugation with some adverb denoting past time, or without it if the epoch is otherwise expressed or understood.

The children were yesterday playing in the garden.	Naglalaró cahapon ang mañga bata sa halamanan.
I was dressing myself when she entered my room.	Nagdadamit acó nang pungmásoc siyá sa aquing silid.
You were running.	Tungmatacbò cayó cañgina.

The same sense of continuance may be expressed by the adverb *pa*, "still".

Stars are shining.	Nagniningning pa ang mañga bituin.

The past indefinite (when the action is not simultaneous with any other) and present perfect tenses are expressed alike.

Jesus Christ resuscitated on the third day after his death.	Nabúhay olí si Jesucristo sa ycatlòng árao nang caniyàng pagcamatáy.
I have finished the work.	Nagtapus acó nang gauá.
I gave them yesterday your books.	Ybinigáy co na sa canilà cahapon ang mañga libro mo.

The pluperfect exists in Tagalog only as a remote degree of the past and hence the completive particle *na*, "already"; after the simple past serves as a means of expressing what is called the past perfect tense, especially when two past actions, one of which is anterior to the other, are compared. The form of the pluperfect with *naca* and *na* is merely supplemental.

I had already eaten yesterday when you arrived.	Nacacáin na acó cahapon nang dungmating ca.
The servant had already looked for the cat that disappeared when Frank found her. (it)	Pinaghánap na nang alila ang pusang naualá, nang naquita ni Quicoy.

The future indefinite is used in the proper way for any action to be executed at some future time.

The Son of God will come down again on Earth to judge the living and the dead.	Ang Anac nang Dios ay mananáog olí sa lupa, hohocoman niyà ang nagñgagbubúhay pa at ang nañgamatáy na.

But it is also employed to express the English infinitive which comes after a verb importing initiative, start.

I am going to study.	Acó,i, magaáral.
The priest is going to read.	Ang pare ay babasà.
He is going to eat.	Siyá,i, cacáin.
We are going to get out.	Camí, aalís na.
You are going to write.	Cayó,i, susúlat.
They are going to sleep.	Matutúlog na silá.
My mother is going to say her prayers.	Magdarasal si inà.

What has been said above about the past perfect applies also to the future perfect; *na*, for the same reason, postponed to the simple future, forms the perfect.

I shall have cooked the fish you charged me with when you come back.	Lolotoin co na ang isdá na iyòng ypinagbilin sa aquin cun icáo,i, bumalic.
The house will have been destroyed by moths when you are ready to tenant it.	Sisirain na nang anáy ang báhay cun matolóy cang mamáhay.

The imperative, besides its own proper use, also serves for the present subjunctive with some conjunction of doubt or purpose.

If I write.	Cun sumúlat acó.
Although he go there.	Paróon man siyá.
Endeavour to be virtuous that you may attain eternal life.	Magpacabanal ca nang icáo,i, macapageamit nang búhay ualáng hangán.

We know already that the tenses of the subjunctive mood are expressed by the corresponding ones of the indicative with the proper particles either preceding or following.

I should pay fot it if I had any money.	Babayaran co sana cun acó,i, may caroonan.
Provided you do not do it.	Houag mo lamáng gaoin.
Would to God he would come.	Pumaritò nauá siyá.
Should that be true I would kill him.	Cun iyán sana,i, totoò papatayin co siyá.
Obey your father, lest you be punished.	Sumónod ca sa iyòng amá maca parusahan ca.

INTERCHANGE.

It is very frequent in Tagalog to use one tense for another, the idea of tense being but somewhat accesory.

Present indefinite is sometimes used for the past tense.

Has the carpenter arrived.	¿Dungmating na ang anlouague.?
He has not yet arrived.	Hindí pa dungmarating. (for dung-mating.)

Future indefinite may be used:
For the present indefinite.

Does he laugh still.?	¿Tatáua pa siyá.? (for tungmatáua.)
I am going away.	Acó,i, aalís. (for nanalís).

For the imperative.

Before you eat wash your teeth clean.	Bagò ca cumáin, manhihiniñga (for manhiniñga) ca mona.
Bring me a book to read.	Dadalhán (for dalhán) mo acó nang isàng librong babasahin.
Don't forget your parents.	Houag mong calilimotan (for calimo-tan) ang iyòng mañga magúlang.

Future perfect may be used for pluperfect.

When I had already gone out my enemy appeared.	Nang macaalís (for nacaalís) na acó, hungmárap ang aquing caáuay.
I received the money when I had already paid.	Tinangap co ang salapí, nang acó,i, macabáyad (for nacabáyad) na.

The imperative may be used:
For present indefinite.

He sends the letter.	Magpadalà (for nagpapadalà) siyá nang súlat.

In potential negative sentences.

Can you not speak.?	¿Hindí ca macapañgósap. (for naca-capañgósap).
I cannot declare it.	Hindí co maypaháyag. (for naypa-paháyag).

For the past.

He saw the dog and killed it.	Maquita (for naquita) niyà ang aso,i, pinatáy niyà
When I heard thundering I was frightened.	Nang mariñgig (for nariñgig) cong cungmucúlog ay natácot acó.

The imperative may also be used for the complete present participle.

He, having said this, died.	Nang sabihin (for pagcasabí) niyà itò, siyá,i, namatáy.
Having finished the work, they went to the theatre.	Nang matapus (for pagcatapus) nilà ang gauá, napasateatro silá.

The infinitive may stand for all the tenses, as already said.

When the master gets angry, he punishes all the scholars.	Cun nagagálit ang maestro, caniyàng parusahan (for pinarurusahan) ang lahat na alagad.
When I bought the house, I did not say anything to them.	Nang bilhin (for binili) co ang báhay, ualá acóng sinabing anomán sa canilà.
Who shall not laugh.?	¿Sinong di tumáua? (for tatatáua.)

Don't carry about your infant broth- Houag mo calunñgin and capatid
er in your arms. mong bungsó.

To declare, to lay before.	Magpaháyag.
To cloak, to connive at.	Maglíhim.
Hiddenly, deceitfully.	Sa líhim.
Here, here it is.	Naitò.
There it is.	Nandiyán, nandóon.
Before doing, before being done.	Bagò gumauá, bagò gaoin.
Before doing this.	Bagò gaoin itò.
Before your writing this letter.	Bagò mo sulatin itò.
Beginning, commencement.	Pono, mola.
Edge, point, extremity.	Dolò.
End.	Catapusan, hangán, cahanganan.
God is increate.	Ang Dios ay ualáng puno,t, dulò.
He is eternal.	Ualá Siyáng hangán.
Even so, even being so.	Gayón man.
Even your sin being so.	Gayón man ang casalanan mo.
Besides. (preposition).	Bucod pa, bucod namán.
Besides this.	Bucod pa ritò, bucod pa sa rit .
Besides that.	Bucod namán sa róon.
Wherever. (conjunction).	Sáan man.
Wherever you go.	Sáan man paróon ca.
However, whatever. (conjunctions)	Matáy man.
However, whatever you think of it.	Matáy mong isipin.
Whereas, wherefore, therefore, since, for that reason, that is the reason why.	Cayá, cayá ñga.
That is the reason why he is here.	Cayá ñga niniritò siyá.
To prepare one's self.	Gumayac.

FIFTY FIRST EXERCISE.

Have you seen my brother.? I have not seen him. Has the servant already arrived.? He has not yet arrived. Have you taken my
book.? I have not taken it. Has he met his sister-in-law.? Yes,
when he was going out she arrived. Who gave you that ring.? My
aunt gave it me when my father was still here at home. Did your
daughter catch the butterfly.? No, when she was about to catch it, it
disappeared from her sight. Did her mother call her.? Yes, when she
was about to come downstairs, her mother called her. Do you forget
me.? I don't forget you. Do you pay attention to what I am saying
to you.? I pay close attention to what you say. What do you order
me to do.? Don't abandon your friends. What did he enjoin me before.? Before you go to bed, pray. (first) What did you say to me.?
Before you write, think of what you are going to say. Why does she
not eat.? She does not eat, because she is not hungry. Why do you
make the sign of the cross.? Because my mother told me, before your
doing something, make the sign of the cross. Why does [not your father
allow Mary to read this book.? Because before she reads it he wants
to examine it. Where shall we go after dining.? We shall go to the
beach after dinner. What shall I do after reading. After you read,
write (also). What shall I do after reading the letter.? After your
reading the letter, give it to me. When did you receive my letter.?
I received your letter after I had already written. What did his brother do.? When he saw his master he concealed himself. What has
happened.? On my doing what you ordered me, he forbade me to do

it. What did you say to him.? On my trying to speak to him he refused to listen and went away; but when the mass was over he called out to me. Why do you not study.? I cannot study. Can your son not write.? He can write, but he cannot speak. Can he pronounce.? He cannot pronounce. Can they not declare it.? They cannot declare it. Can they not fail to go.? They cannot fail to go. How can that be.? It is ordered so by law. Was not that made publicly.? No, it was made secretly. Where is my watch.? Here it is. Where is your father.? There he is. Where does this road begin.? It begins at the beach. How was your female-cousin wounded.? She was wounded with the point of a pin. Who created God.? God is increate and eternal. Is He merciful.? His mercy is endless, however great your sins may be He will pardon them; besides that, He helps man through virtue. Where is He.? He is everywhere, wherever you may go there He is and whatever you do, He sees it. Since it is so , prepare yourself to be one day in His presence.

FIFTY SECOND LESSON.
YCALIMANG POUO,T, DALAUANG PAGARAL.

PECULIARITIES.

Proper auxiliary verbs, as they are conceived in other languages, do no exist in Tagalog; but, in a certain sense, it may be said that *uala.* in the negative, *mayróon* and *may*, but especially the latter, in the affirmative, are used somewhat after the manner in which "not to have", "have not", etc.; "to have", "have", etc., are used in English, only that they adapt themselves to every tense. The English impersonals "there to have", "there not to have"; "there not to be", "there to be", "there is", "there is not", etc., followed by a noun in a partitive sense or a past·participle, may be translated, respectively, by *may* and *uala*, with the proper tense in Tagalog after them.

Has he not eaten any bread.?	¿Ualá siyáng bagá quináing tinápay.?
He has eaten some bread.	Siyá,i, may quináing tinápay.
Is there no one eating.?	¿Ualá bagáng cungmacáin.?
There is nobody eating.	Ualáng cungmacáin.
Was there no one who told it to him.?	¿Ualáng nacapagsabi or macapagsabi sa caniyà.?
Nobody told it to him.	Ualáng nagsabi diyán sa caniyà.
Will there not be anybody who will go there.?	¿Ualá bagáng paroróon.?
There will not be anybody to go there.	Ualáng paroróon.
Will there not be any one whom to give their quilt.?	¿Ualá bagáng mabiguián nang cúmot nilà.?
There will be nobody whom to give their quilt to.	Ualáng mabiguián nang canilàng cúmot.
Does he buy?, is he buying.?	¿May binibili bagá siyá.?
He buys, he is buying.	May binibili siyá.
Have you drunk any wine.?	¿May ininom ca bagáng álac.?
I have drunk some wine.	May ininom acóng álac.?
Will your sister cull out of these flowers.?	¿May pipiliin bagá ang iyòng capatid na babaye dità sa mañga bulac-lac.?
She will cull some of these flowers.	May pipiliin siyá dità sa mañga bulac-lac.
It is agreed between them not to pay it.	May pinagcaisahan siláng hindí nilà bayaran.
It was enacted to serve in the army.	May ypinagotos na maglingcod sa hocbó.
It will be resolved to proceed up to the end.	May ypasisiyàng ytóloy.

Mayróon is used for "to have to" with the agent in the nominative case and the verb which stands for its direct complement following in the corresponding tense or that peculiar to Tagalog, in the passive.

What have they to say.?	¿Mayróon bagá siláng sasabihin.?
They have to say that....	Mayróon siláng sinasabi na....
Had you to buy something.?	¿Mayróon bagá cayóng binibiling ano-mán.?
We had to pay the debt.	Mayróon camíng binayarang ótang.
Shall I have anything to do.?	¿Mayróon bagá acóng gaguoin.?
You shall have to sweep the door-sill.	Ycaó ay mayróong naualisang pintoan.

May is also used before a common noun in a sense of ownership, parentage or appertenance.

The owner, the proprietor.	Ang may ari.
the father, one of the parents.	Ang may anac.
The maker.	Ang may gauá.
Author, inventor, fabricator, designer.	May cathá.
Who composed these verses.?	¿Sino ang may cathá nitòng tula.?
The Creator.	Ang may lalang, may capal.
The powerful man.	Ang may capangyarihang tauò.
The Almighty.	Ang may capangyarihan sa lahat.
The lover.	Ang may sintà.
Who is the owner of this farm.?	¿Sino ang may ari nitòng búquid.?
Our neighbour is the owner.	Ang aming caapirbáhay ang may ari.
Who is the father of this maid.?	¿Sinong may anac ditò sa dalaga.?
The Chinaman at the corner is the father.	Ang insic sa suloc ang may anac.
Who are the inventors of this kind of pillow.?	¿Sino sino ang mañga may cathá nitòng ganitòng olonan.?
The Japanese are the inventors.	Ang mañga taga Japon ang may cathá.
Who is the Creator of everything.?	¿Sino ang may capal sa lahat ?
God, our Lord is the Creator and the Almighty.	Ang Dios. Pañginóon natin, siyá ang may lalang at ang may capang-yarihan sa lahat.

May=mey is put before substantive roots having a passive force, and converts them into adjectives.

Sick.	May saquit.
Guilty, culprit.	,, sala.
Wise, learned.	,, dónong.
Denticulated, toothed.	,, ñgipin.
Golden, gold-yielding.	,, guintò.

May=mey is still used preceded by *sa* for the preposition "near".

Near the tree.	Sa may cáhoy.
,, ,, house.	,, ,, báhay.
,, ,, church.	,, ,, simbahan.
What is that near the border of the sea.?	¿Anò cayá yaóng na sa may tabi nang dágat.
That near the sea is a pirogue.	Yaóng na sa may dágat ay isàng bangca.

Another peculiarity of Tagalog is the using of some roots in an absolute impersonal verbal manner for every tense. The roots most commonly made use of in such way, are:

Coming from, deriving.	Gáling.
Concluded, made up.	Yari.
Finished, ended.	Tapús.
Condign. (punishment)	Súcat.
Deserving, worthy, just, right, proper.	Dápat.
Wishing, willing.	Ybig.

Not knowing.	Ayauán.
Refusing, not willing.	Ayáo.
It is, was, will be said; he, she, they, says, say, said; will be said.	Dáo, conó.

Dáo and *conó* are always postponed to the verb, *dáo* being far more in use.

It is said you are very rich.	Mayamang mayaman ca dáo.
It was said you were dead.	Namatáy ca dáo.
It will be said he will become mad.	Maoolol siyá dáo.
He says let him go out.	Lumabús siyá dáo.
They say they are not willing.	Nanáyao conó silá.
He says he will study.	Magaáral dáo siyá.

Ayáo governs the noun or pronoun in the nominative or possessive case, according to whether the sentence is active or passive.

Are you not willing to enter.?	¿Ayáo cang pumásoc.?
I refused to marry.	Nayáo acóng magasáua, or, ayáo acóng nagasáua.
Will you refuse to give my money back.?	¿Ayáo mong ysaolí ang salapí co.?

Ayauán = auán is used absolutely in a grudging manner for "I don't know", "I don't-care".

Do you know what your master said.?	¿Naaalaman mo cun anó ang sali nang iyòng pañginóon.?
I don't know, I don't care.	Ayauán, auán.

Although *ibig* is sometimes used actively, it adapts itself better to the passive.

Do you wish to read.?	¿Ybig mong (ca) humasà.?
I wish to read the book.	Ybig cong basahin ang libro.
Did he wish to work.?	¿Yníbig niyàng magtrabajo? (1).
He wished to pay his debt.	Yníbig niyàng bayaran ang caniyàng ótang.
Will your friend be willing to come here.?	¿Yibiguin bagá nang caibigan mo paritò.?
He will be willing to come here to see you.	Yibiguin niyàng paritohan ca niyà.

Dápat and *súcat*, as absolute impersonal verbs, are used in passive sentences; *dápat*, generally for reward, and *súcat* for penalty.

It is just to punish him.	Súcat siyáng hampasín or parusahan.
It will be right to hang them.	Súcat siláng bitayin.
He deserves to be granted the prize.	Dápat siyáng pagcalooban nang ganti.
They deserved to obtain the office.	Dápat niláng camtán ang catongcolan.

Tapus and *yari* are used with the particle *na* after them; *tapus*, may indifferently refer to time or work, *yari*, only to the work.

The rain is over.	Tapús na ang olán.
In the month of November southern winds will cease.	Sa bouán nang Noviembre tapús na or matatapus ang taghabagat.
Have you completed your work.?	¿Yarí na ang gauá mo.?
It is already completed. (finished).	Yarí na.

---

(1) The letter *j*, which is exotic, is still retained in some Sp. words as *trabajo*, etc.

Gáling, as many other roots, may be used without the proper composition for the sake of briefness when stress on the action can be dispensed with and the tense is determined otherwise or is tacitly understood.

Where do you come from.?	¿Súan ca gáling.?
I come from Tayabas.	Gáling acó sa Tayabas.
Yesterday, when we met your servant, where was he coming from.?	Cahapon, nang nasalobong namin ang alila mo, ¿súan siyá gáling.?
He was coming from the well.	Gáling siyá sa bucal.

In the same way, many other verbal roots can be used absolutely in the imperative for briefness' sake, especially when the verb is used without any direct or indirect complement. This manner of using the verb is greatly in use among natives and is somewhat interjectional.

Walk.!	Lácad.
Take!.	Cuha.
Run!.	Tacbò.
Run for it!, overtake!.	Tacbohin.
Drag along.	Hila.
Eat!.	Cáin.
Come on.	Hali ca, tóloy.

Sometimes the imperative is used with the verbal ligament for a greater emphasis if the verb ends in a consonant.

Kill it.	Patayi.
Receive it.	Tangapi.
Wrap it.	Baloti.
Drink.	Ynomi.

It is not only in the imperative that the root alone, can be used without the verbal particle. Some verbal roots when they are not carried away from their original sense by some modifying verbal particle, are used for every tense if the latter is otherwise determined by some other words. (1).

What do you bring.?	¿Anò ang dalà mo.?
I bring nothing to-day.	Ualá acóng dalà ñgayón,
Yesterday I brought some fruit.	Ang dalà co cahapo,i, buñga.
What will he be willing to have to-morrow.?	¿Anòng íbig niyà búcas.?
What does he say.?	¿Anòng sabì niyà.?
He says that......	Sabì niyà,i,......

Some compound words either nouns or adjectives, are fit to be used absolutely as verbs.

Wise, learned.	Marúnong.
Does he know.?	¿Marúnong siyá.?
Do you know how to read.?	¿Marúnong cang bumasà ?
No, sir, I cannot read.	Hindí po, di acó marúnong bumasà.
Do they know how to speak English.?	¿Marúnong siláng magüicang inglés.?
They do not know how to speak English; but they know how to speak Tagalog.	Hindí silá marúnong magüicang inglés; ñguni,t, marúnong silá magüicang tagálog.

Need, want; it is necessary.	Cailañgan.
What do I need.?	¿Anòng cailañgan co.?

---

(1) We insist that this important point be not lost sight of by the student.

You need to be cured.	Cailañgan cang gamotín.
They need to work.	Cailañgan siláng magtrabajo.
The orphan.	Ang olilá.
To leave off.	Juan.
Leave off reading.	Juan mo ang pagbasá.
The poor follow, the unfortunate.	Ang mahírap.
Have you no parents.?	¿Ualá cayóng magugúlang.?
No, Sir, we are parentless.	Hindí po, camí, po, mañga olilá.
Pure, genuine.	Taganás, pulós.
This ring is of genuine gold.	} Ytóng singsing na itô,i, taganás na guintô.
That image is pure ivory.	Yyáng laráuang iyá,i, polós na garing.
Customary, habitual.	Caraníuang, caratihan.
Customary dress.	Caraníuang damtín.
Inveterate habit.	Caratihan ásal.
Enough, sufficient.	Casiyahan, caiguihan.
That is sufficient.	Yyá.i, caiguihan na.
To pass, to elapse.	Lumipas.
The time has passed when....	Lungmipas na ang panahón na....
To exceed, to excel, to overdo.	Lumalo.
He excels in wisdom.	Lungmalalo ang pagcarúnong niyá.

FIFTY SECOND EXERCISE.

Had you anything to eat.? I had nothing to eat. Has he not seen my brother? He has not yet seen him. Has he not slept yet.? He has not yet slept. What was there included in the business.? There was included in the business the paying of his salary. What will there be looked upon.? There will be her marriage considered. Have you anything to tell me.? Yes, I have something to tell you. Have you anything to do.? Yes, I have something to do. Has he anything to desire.? He has nothing to desire. Have you said anything.? I have said nothing. Has he killed a man.? He has killed a man. Who is the father of this child.? Peter is the father of this child. Who is the maker of the world.? God, our Lord, is the maker. Are you perchance the owner of this land.? I am not the owner, but my brother-in-law. Who are the owners of this forest.? The landlords of the town are the owners of the forest. What is that near the church.? That near the church is a very beautiful tree. Who is sick.? My father is sick. Are they the culprits.? No, they are not the culprits. Is the master learned.? He is very learned. Where is your servant coming from.? He is coming from the river. Is this book concluded.? It is not yet concluded. Is the month ended.? It is ended. Ought he to be punished.? He ought not to be punished. Are your cousins worthy of reward.? They deserve a reward. Is he willing to write.? He is willing to write. What does he say.? He says he is a stranger. Ask him whether he knows how to play the harp.? He says he knows. Do you want this flower.? Yes, Sir, if you want it, take it. Do you know my friend loves you.? I don't care. Don't they wish to go to school.? They don't wish to. Why.? Because they say they are not willing. What do you say.? I say it is not possible. Does he know how to sew.? He does not know how to sew. Can you speak Tagalog.? I can speak Tagalog. Are you a judge of writing.? I am not a judge of writing. Are you acquainted with cooking.? I am not acquainted with it. Is it necessary to take a bath.? It is not necessary to take a bath. Is it necessary.? It is necessary. Is it necessary to say it.? It is necessary that I should declare it. Where is your father.? Our father is dead, we are orphans. Did John leave off gambling.? He has not yet left it off. Who is that man.? He is an unfortunate. What is that crown of.? It is of pure silver. Is it his

customary manner of speaking.? It is his inveterate habit. Is that sufficient.? It is not sufficient, Why do you not dance.? When the age
of forty years is reached youth has already passed. What does your
father excel in.? He excels in preaching.

FIFTY THIRD LESSON.
YCALIMANG POUO,T, TATLONG PAGARAL.

USE OF *NANG* and *SA* IN THE OBJECTIVE CASE.

The use of *nang* or *sa* before a common noun, direct object of an active sentence, is generally decided by the nature of the action. *Nang*, which is, by far, better adapted to the direct object, if it is represented by a common noun, is used:

With verbs denoting assimilation on the part of the agent.

To obtain glory.	Magcamit nang calualhatían.
To eat cherries.	Cumáin nang lombóy.
I found money.	Nacapólot or nacaquita acó nang salapí.
He borrowed ten dollars.	Ungmótang siyá nang sangpóuong piso.
We take the book.	Cungmocoha camí nang libro.
They will receive fifteen dollars.	Tatangap silá nang labing limàng piso.
Buy a farm.	Bumili ca nang búquid.

With verbs the action of which necessarily requires two complements (accusative and dative) either expressed or understood, although they may mean expulsive acts on the part of the subject. In such cases the direct object (generally a thing) goes with *nang* and the indirect (generally a person), with *sa*.

He writes two letters to your father.	Nagsusúlat siyá nang dalauàng súlat sa amá mo.
I sold my estate to the natives.	Nagbili acó nang ari co sa mañga tagálog.
We shall give the eggs to the baker.	Magbibigáy tayo nang mañga itlog sa magtitinápay.
Send the trunk to the carpenter.	Magpadalâ ca nang cabán sa anloague.
The uncle lent the money.	Ang amaí,i, nagpaótang nang salapí.
They had said everything to the master.	Nacapagsabi na silá nang lahat sa pañginóon.
You will have returned the book to the priest.	Nacapagsaolí na marahil cayó nang libro sa pare.
I granted him permission.	Nagcalóob acó sa caniyà nang pahintólot. (1).

Before any common noun, the direct object of the sentence, if it is used in a partitive or indefinite sense.

Put some rice (the boiled rice which constitutes natives' principal food), on the fire.	Magsaapúy ca nang canin or morisqueta.

---

(1). The student should not lose sight of the fact that these sentences are better constructed in the passive. If they are here expressed actively, it is only to make more noticeable the use of *nang* and *sa*.

He counts money. — Bungmibílang siyá nang salapí.

We ask for something. — Hungmihiñgi camí nang anomán.

Ask some vinegar on passing by. — Maquiráan ca nang suca.

They have sown paddy. — Naghasic silá nang pálay.

They shall gather (cut off with the fingers) some betel leaves. — Mañgiñgitil silá nang mamin.

Gather some flowers. — Mitás or mamitás ca nang bulac-lac.

Don't pick up any quarrels. — Houag cang humánap nang ósap.

Will you have some bread.? — ¿Ybig mo nang tinápay.?

I want a little. — Ybig co nang cauntí.

Nang is generally used in all cases not otherwise specified in the subjoined paragraphs for the use of *sa*.

He cannot lift the vat. — Hindí siyá macabuhat nang tapayan.

We build our house of stone. — Nagbabatò camí nang báhay namin.

Peter reduced the price. — Nagbabá Si Pedro nang halagá.

Drive away the poultry. — Bumúgao cayó nang manoc.

They will undo (untie) the agreement. — Cacalag silá nang tipán or pinagcaisahan.

It is a sin to listen to (hearing) obscenities. — Sala ang dumiñgig nang uicang mahálay.

Paint the board. — Humibo ca nang *tabla*. (Sp.).

Why did not the servant transfuse the water into the wat. — ¿Báquit hindí nagsalin ang alila nang túbig sa tapayan.

Snuff the candle. — Pumótol ca nang *pabilo* (Sp., "wick") nang candila.

Correct (rectify) your bad habits. — Tumóuir ca nang masamáng úsal mo.

Sa is used before the direct object in the active:
In sentences the verb of which obtains in the causative sense of *maca* conjugation.

Modesty enhances woman's beauty. — Ang cahinhinan ay nacagagandà sa mañga babaye.

His arrival caused pleasure to his mother. — Ang pagdating niyà,i, nacatóua sa caniyàng inà.

Why does war cause sorrow to your sister.? — ¿Báquit cayá ang pagbabacà,i, nacalu!umbáy sa capatid mong babaye.?

This fruit is green and will harm my children. — Ytòng boñgang itò,i, hiláo pa,t, macasasamá sa mañga anac co.

It is the remedies that cure the sick. — Ang mañga gamot ay siyáng nacacagaling sa mañga may saquit.

His brags cause fright to the boys. — Ang mañga cayabañgan niyà,i, nacatatacot sa mañga bata.

The tears of David washed his couch. — Ang mañga luha ni David nacadilig se caniyàng hihigaan.

With verbs which more or less require a person for their direct object.

To salute, to bow at, to greet. — Magbati, bumati.

Salute the priest. — Bumati ca sa pare.

To betray. — Magcanuló.

Saint Peter betrayed his master. — Si San Pedro.i, nagcanoló sa caniyàng maestro.

To cure. — Gumamot.

Jesus Christ cured the sick. — Si Jesucristo,i, gungmamot sa mañga may saquit.

To whip, to cudgel. — Humampás.

Shall we whip our servant.? — ¿Hahampás tayo sa alila natin?

To incite, to cajole, to spur on.	Pamongcahi.
She cajoles the man. (male).	Namomoncahi siyá sa lalaqui.
To slap.	Tumampal, magtampal.
I will slap the scoundrel.	Tatampal acó sa tampalasan or tacsil.

In certain verbs which may take a thing or a person for their direct complement, *nang*, comes before the thing; *sa*, before the person.

To pay the (for the) maintenance.	Magbáyad nang yquinabubúhay.
He paid the physician.	Nagbáyad siyá sa médico or mangagamot.
To obey (to keep) the commandments of God.	Sumonod nang mañga otos nang Dios.
Your friend does not obey his mother.	Ang caibigan mo,i, hindí sungmosonod sa inà niyà.
Ask (inquire) the reason of that.	Magtanong ca nang cadahilanang niyán.
Ask the servant whether he swept the bath-room.	Tumanong ca sa alila cun niualisan na niyà ang paligóan.

Sa is also generally used with indicative verbs, that is to say, those signifying pointing or aiming at, if the action, not the effect, is meant.

To look at the sky.	Tumiñgin sa láñgit.
I aimed at the general.	Tumurlá acó sa *general.* (Sp.)
They point to the thief.	Tungmotoro silá sa magnanácao.
We will shoot (fire) at the birds.	Babaril camí sa mañga ibon.
To throw arrows at.	Magpana sa . . . . .

To wring, to twist.	Míhit, magpíhit.
To turn, to retract, to fall back.	Magbalic, bumalic, malic.
Turn your heart to God.	Magbalic cang lóob sa Dios.
To join, to approach.	Umagápay.
To turn one's back to.	Tumalicod.
To carry about along with, to bea	Dalà.
To be in a family way.	Dalàng bata, tauò.
To bear anger, envy.	Dalàng póot.
To have fear.	Dalàng tácot.
To carry shame along.	Dalàng hiya.

Dalá is used in the sense of having over one, with words similar to those in the examples and it may be conjugated by *mag.*

This boy carries shame about him.	Nagdadalàng hiya itòng batang itò.
To swoon away, to be giddy.	Mahilo.
I swooned away at the shock, stroke.	Yquinahilo co ang pocpoc.
To stop.	Humintó, maghintó.
To calm, to compose one's self, to grow calm.	Tumíguil, magtíguil, magtíguil.
The wind grows calm.	Titiguiltíguil ang hañgin.
Noise, clamor, bustle.	Yñgay.
Be silent.	Houag mag-iñgáy.
To go to Manila, to go down the river.	Lumouás.
I shall go to Manila.	Lulouás acó.
I hold it to be good.	Ynaari cong mabut'.
At times, sometimes.	Cun minsán.
Other times, at other times.	Cun minsán namán.
Sometimes above, sometimes below.	Cun minsán sa itáas, cun minsán namá,i, sa ibabá.
To chew.	Ñgumoya.

To chew betel nut.	Ñgumañga.
To nibble.	Ñgumalot, ñgumatá.
To gnaw.	Ñgumatñgat.
To gesticulate, to make grimaces.	Ñgumisi.
To smile bashfully.	Ñgumiti.
To go beyond, to transpierce.	Tumalab.
Miracle.	Himalá.
To be overcome, afflicted with.	Tablán. (contraction.)
I am overawed.	Tinatablán acó nang tácot.
To be present.	Maharap.
The present time.	Ang panahóng hinaharap.
Nowadays.	Sa panahóng hinaharap.
The past time.	Ang panahóng tinalicdán.
Formerly.	Sa panahóng tinalicdán.
Futurity, the time to come.	Ang panahóng haharapín.
In the future.	(Sa panahóng haharapín, sa panahóng (daratíng.
Finally, in a word.	Sa catagáng uica.
In a few words.	Sa madalíng sabi.
According. according to.	Ayon sa. alinsúnod sa.
According to the census.	Ayon sa bílang nang mañga tauò.
According to this.	Sa bágay na itò.

FIFTY THIRD EXERCISE.

What must I do to obtain the pardon of my trespasses.? If you want to obtain the pardon of your sins, make a good confession. Do you write when you study? When I study I do not write. What does Joseph's father say to him.? He is saying to him, don't eat when writing. Did you enjoin the children not to sleep when in prayer.? I did. Why do they stop there.? They stop there to see a ship under sail. Do you hold it to be bad to listen to obscenities.? I do hold it to be very bad. Does your master repute it as a good thing to serve God.? Yes, indeed. Where do you go.? I go to Manila. When will you come back.? I shall come back in the evening. Does your son refuse to appear before his master.? He refused to present himself, for he fears punishment. When will he read the book I gave him.? He will read it next Sunday. Do Americans think of going away.? They don't think going away. Why did you not reply to the priest.? I was overcome with shame. Will he make a retraction of his insults.? He will retract his foul words. Why do you not turn the back to your wrongs.? Because I still bear anger towards my enemies. Whom does that school–boy fear.? He fears his master. Did the old woman swoon away.? She swooned away, but she soon recovered from her fit and now is growing calmer. What bustle is that.? It is the children that are romping about in the street. Did you tell them to be silent.? I told them to be silent. Do natives plot.? They plot sometimes openly (publicly) sometimes hiddenly. Who use to chew tobacco.? Americans use to chew tobacco. Do natives chew betel nut.? The majority do. Do mice nibble at the cheese.? Mice nibbled at the cheese. What is the dog gnawing.? It is gnawing a bone. At whom does that boy make grimaces.? He does not make grimaces at any body, he smiles. Did the sailor go beyond The Cape.? He did not go beyond, as he was overawed. What miracles did Jesus Christ work in former times.? He wrought many miracles. Are miracles wrought at present.? No, there are no miracles wrought nowadays nor probably will there be any in the future. What did he say.? I will tell you in a few words what he said. How many inhabitants are there in this town.? According to the census taken last year, there are about seven thousand inhabitants.

.

FIFTY FOURTH LESSON.
YCALIMANG POUO,T, APAT NA PAGARAL.

THE ADVERB.

Adverbs in Tagalog are not distinguished by any prevailing termination corresponding to the English "ly", Those expressed by a single root are few when compared with those including composition with a prefix or some other separate self-signifying particle or word. Many of them have the adjectival composition of *ma*, others have the particle *sa* before them, there being also a number of adverbial clauses consisting of roots with particles or words either preceding or following them. The majority of adverbs if not all (monosyllables excepted) admit of declension and conjugation as is the case in Tagalog with most roots and even particles. Many adjectives and some prepositions and conjunctions are used adverbially.

ADVERBS OF MANNER.

Of these, the following are simple:

As, so, like.	Gaya, ga, para. paris.
Purposely, knowingly, intentionally, designedly.	Tiquis, pacsá.
Willingly.	Cusa.
Hardly, scarcely.	Bahaguiá.
Especially.	Bucod, tañgi.
Conjointly, as well as.	Sabáy.
According.	Ayon, alinsonod.
As if selling.	Ganagbibili.
This lizard is like a caiman (is caimanlike.)	Gaboaya itòng tocong itò.
He did it on purpose.	Tiniquís niyà, pinagsá niyà.
You are like me.	Ycáo,i, paris co.
It is hardly sufficient.	Bahaguiá na magcasiyà.
He has been especially summoned.	Bucor siyáng natáuag.
Man as well as woman, the man and the woman too.	Ang lalaqui casabáy nang babaye.

The following are compound adverbs of manner.

So, thus, that way.	Ganóon, gayón.
So, thus, in this manner.	Ganitò.
So, thus, as that.	Ganiyán.
Finally, at last.	Catapustapusan, cauacasuacasan.

English adverbs of manner ending in "*ly*" are generally expressed by the corresponding adjectives.

Swiftly.	Matulín.
Quickly.	Madalí.

Slowly, understandingly.	Marahan.
Well, goodly.	Mabutì, magaling.
Badly.	Masamá.
Clearly.	Malínao.
Carefully.	Mahúsay.
Strongly.	Malacás.
Do it quickly.	Gaoin mong madalí.
Wrap it up carefully.	Balotin mong mahúsay.
He pushed the boat strongly.	Ytinolac niyà nang malacás ang bangca.

It is well to say, however, that not all the adjectives can be used as adverbs. In the latter, those, for instance, which are simple as *lupit*, *olol*, etc., are included. Of the ones formed with *ma*, those only denoting manner or degree are used adverbially; but not the others as *marúnong*, *mabaet*, etc..

Some substantive roots are made adverbs of manner by preceding them with the particle *sa*.

Openly, publicly.	Sa háyag.
Hiddenly, secretly.	Sa líhim.
Commonly, customarily.	Sa ogali, sa caogalían.
Judiciously.	Sa bait.

Adverbs admit of a superlative degree in the same way as adjectives.

Very carefully.	Mahúsay na mahúsay.
Very well.	Mabuting mabutì.
Very badly.	Masamáng masamá.
Very slowly.	Ynot inot, marahan dahan.

ADVERBS OF PLACE.

Many of these are verbal roots preceded by *sa*.

Where.?	¿Sáan.?
Here, hither.	Ditò, dinì.
There. (near you)	Diyán.
There. (at that place)	Dóon.
Near, close.	Malápit, sa may, sa síping, sa tabi.
Far, far off, away.	Malayo, sa malayo.
Within, inside.	Sa lóob.
Out, outside.	Sa labás.
Before, opposite.	Sa hárap, sa tapat.
Behind.	Sa licod.
Above.	Sa itáas.
Below.	Sa ibabá.
On, upon.	Sa ibábao.
Under.	Sa ilálim.
In the middle, midway.	Sa guitná.
In the middle, halfway.	Sa paguitan.
By, by the side of.	Sa píling.
Sideways, on that side.	Sa cabilá.
Both sides.	Sa magcabilá.
On all sides.	Sa magcabicabilá.
Anywhere, everywhere.	Sáan man.
At midnight.	Sa hating gabì.
We are halfway in the journey.	Na sa paguitan tayo sa paglácar.
My mother was close by me.	Napasasíping co si inà.
He went abroad, on the other side of the sea.	Naparóon siyá sa cabilá nang dágat.
On both sides of the ship.	Sa magcabilà nang sasaquián.

The demonstrative adverbs of place may be made verbs also by *um*, to indicate the voluntary standing of the agent at the place expressed by the adverb. *Dungmidini acó.* "I place myself here". The active sense is made by *mag*, *magdiyán ca nang tinapáy*, "put some bread there".

ADVERBS OF TIME.

When?.	¿Cailán.?
Now.	Ñgayón.
To-day.	Ñgayón árao na itò.
To-morrow.	Bucas.
Ago.	{ Ca, camaca. (particles indicating past time.)
Yesterday.	Cahapon.
Last night.	Cagabì.
The day before yesterday.	Camacalauá.
Some days ago.	Camacailáng árao.
Five days ago.	Camacalimàng árao.
Before, a while ago, just now.	Cañgina, cañgina pa, bago pa.
By and by, presently.	Maméa, mamayá, mameameá.
Early.	Maaga.
Already.	Na.
Still, yet.	Pa.
Not yet.	Di pa.
Always.	Touí, touitouí, cailán man.
Constantly, continually.	Palagui, parati.
Suddenly, off hand.	Caalam-alam, caracaraca.
Instantly.	Biglá, sa biglá.
Immediately.	Agad, tambing.
For ever, everlastingly.	{ Magparati man sáan, hangán cailán man.
Never, no more, no longer.	Cailán pa man, caicailá,i, hindí.
Often, frequently.	Malímit, di mamacailán.
From.	Mula, mula sa, búhat.
Till, until.	Hangán.
Formerly, anciently.	Sa unà, sa dati, sa unàng árao.
Sometime, sometimes.	Cun minsan.
Now and then, occasionally.	Manacanaca, maminsán-minsún.
Rarely.	Bihira, madálang.
Late.	Tanghali na, gabì na, huli.
Daily.	Arao-árao.
Hourly.	Oras-oras.
Weekly.	Lingo-lingo.
Monthly.	Bóuan-bóuan.
Yearly.	Taón-taón.

CONJUNCTIVE ADVERBS OF TIME.

As soon as, no sooner than, on.	Sa pagca, pag.
Then, at the end, afterwards.	Sacá.
Then. (at that past time).	Nóon, niyón.
When, at the time of. (future).	Cun.
Whenever.	Cun touí.
When, at the time of. (past).	Nang.
When, at that past time.	Nóon.
After.	Pagca, capag.
After having.	Pagca, capagca.

41

First, firstly. — Mona.
Before, previous to, previously. — Bagò.

Cailán is mainly interrogative.

When did he come? — ¿Cailán siyá napari ò.?
Before, in the morning. — Cañginang omaga.
Before, in the afternoon. — Cañginang tanghali.
He was here just a while ago. — Canicañgina,i, nariritò siyá.

Maméa=mamayá, is middle between *tambing* and *sacá*.

I shall write by and by. — Susúlat acó maméa.

We shall always love each other. — { Magsisintahan catáng dalauà cailán man.

He died instantly. — Namatáy siyáng biglá.
He prostrated himself immediately. — Nagpatirapá siyáng agad.

Eat immediately. — { Cumáin cang tambing, tambiñgin mo cumáin.

God exists *ab æterno*. — { Ang Dios, ay Dios din magpaparating man saán.

I never drink liquors. — { Cailán man acó.i, hindí ungmiinom nang álac.

I often take baths. — Malimit acóng naliligo.
They frequently committed sin against God. — Di mamacailán nagcasala silá laban sa Dios.
From this day on. — Mula ñgayón, búhat ñgayón.
From Thursday till Saturday. — Mula sa Jueves hangán sa Sábado.
In former times. — Sa onáng panahón.

This child cries but rarely. — { Bihirang tungmatañgis itòng batang itò.

My sister arrived late at mass. — { Ang aquing capatid na babaye nahuli sa misa.

It is late. (in the morning). — Tanghali na.
It is late. (in the evening). — Gabì na.

For the proper use of the conjunctive adverbs the following rules should be taken into account.

Sa refers to a principal action immediately following the secondary one to which it is applied. It indicates rather punctuality than simultaneity.

On his saying these words, he died. — { Sa pagsabi niyà nitòng mañga uica ay namatáy.

On their noticing the earthquake, they ran away. — Sa pagcamálay ni à nang lindol, silá,i, tungmacbò.

Pag refers to the subordinate action which it represents as accomplished or in progress with some other simultaneous action. It goes with the possessive case of the agent and the accusative of the object.

As soon as I told it to him. — Pagsabi co sa caniyà.
No sooner he went in. — Pagpásoc niyá.
As soon as you greet him, come back. — Pagbatí mo sa caniyà mouí ca.
As my father went away, he arrived. — Pagalís nang amá co, dungmating siyá.
On my arriving at the house, I saw an innumerable crowd. — Pagdating co sa báhay naquita co ang isàng catiponan di mabílang na tauò.

Pagca is used if the same sense and with the same construction. It points out the action as past and does not indicate simultaneity.

No sooner he had finished the work than he came to pay me a visit. — Pagcatapus niyà nang ganá, dinálao acó niyà capagdaca.

After studying we shall go for a walk.	Pagcapagaáral namin, magpapasial camí.
After striking nine o'clock, we shall go for rest.	Pagcatugtog nang á las nueve, magpapahiñga tayo.

Pagca is sometimes used for "from", "since".

From my infancy down.	Pagcabata co.

Capag, capagca refer to an action altogether past and perfect.

After his having finished speaking, they embraced each other.	Capagcapañgósap niyà, nagyacapan silá.
The function being over, I went home.	Capagcatapus nang piesta, napasabáhay acó.
After having concluded that, they began to dance.	Capagyari nilà niyón nagmula siláng magsayáo.

Capag and *capagca* are very important particles both of them referring to an action altogether past; *capag*, represents the action at the start; *capagca*, as aoomplished and perfected, and they may be rendered, respectively, "on starting", "on having finished"...; but if the action is such as not to admit of duration, both particles may be used in the perfective sense.

They should be considered in two ways: as present participles and as adverbs. As participles, they adhere to the verbal particle which the nature of the action requires, with the possessive case of the agent following.

After his commencing to teach.	Capagáral niyà.
After I began to study.	Capagpagáral co.
After the priest starting to preach.	Capagpañgáral nang pare.
After your having finished saying that.	Capagcasabihin mo iyán.
After my having finished learning.	Capagcapagáral co.
After his having finished preaching.	Capagcapañgáral niyà.
After his arriving.	Capagcadating or capagdating niyà.
After my having thrown away my ring.	Capagcaytapon or capagytapon co ang aquing singsing.

Capag, capagca and even *pagca* and *pag*, as adverbs, are written separately in the sense of "when", "on," and may govern the nominative case of the agent, with the verb in the active, if the action is represented as present, simultaneous or probable.

As soon as I receive a letter, I give an answer.	Capag acó,i, tungmatangap nang súlat, acó,i, sungmasagot.
No sooner do I get up than I take a bath.	Pagca acó,i, nabañgon ay naliligo acó.
As soon as my son is twelve years old, I shall make him work.	Pag ang aquing anac ay may labing dalauà ig taón, papilitin co siyáng magtrabajo.

Pag is used with the negative in a a sense of menace.

You shall see how I beat you.	Pag hindí quitá paloin.
If he does not come I shall not pay him.	Pag hindí siyá pumarini ay hindí co siyá babayaran.

Pag is used for active verbal nouns; *pagca* for intransitive ones.

The throwing down of bombs.	Ang paghólog nang *bomba*. (Sp.)
The falling down of the fruit.	Ang pagcahólog nang boñga.

Pag, applied to actions admitting of time for their development, expresses the action as going on; *pagca*, as completed.

| The growing light. | Ang pagliuánag. |
| The clearness of day. | Ang pagcaliuánag. |

With regard to the government of *pag* and *pagca* in verbal nouns, great care should be taken in distinguishing whether the person is active or passive as to the action. Any disregard of this rule may lead to many striking mistakes.

The beheading of Saint John. (that is to say, inflicted on him)	Ang pagpógot cay San Juan.
The beheading by the executioner of Mary Stuart.	Ang pagpógot nang mamumúgot cay María Estuardo
The birth of The Holy Virgin.	Ang pañgañganac cay María Santísima
The bringing forth of The Holy Virgin.	Ang pañgañganac nang Santísima Virgen.

Sacá, as an adverb, indicates more futurity than *mamayá*.

| God made the skies first, and man long afterwards. | Guinauá nang Dios ang lañgit, sacá ang tauò. |
| He laughed, and then? | Natauá siyá ¿at sacá? |

Cun, nang; nóon, niyón or *niyáon*, as adverbs, cannot be used indiscriminately. *Cun* should be used in reference to the present or future tense.

| When I go to Manila I shall buy a hat for you. | Cun pumaróon acó sa Maynila ybibili quitá nang sambalelo. |
| When Peter comes let me know of it. | Cun darating Si Pedro alamín mo acó. |

Cun may be used with the past indefinite tense if the action appears as performed customarily.

| When I was in London, I went frequently to play. | Cun acó,i, naroróon sa Londres, napasasateatro acóng malímit. |

Nang is used with all degrees of the past tense.

| When he came yesterday to visit me I was sick. | Nang acó,i, dinálao niyà cahapon, nagcacasaquit acò. |
| When my sister arrived we had already eaten. | Nang dumating ang capatid cong babaye nacacáin na camí. |

Nóon, niyón, niyáon, come at the beginning of a past narration. They lay stress on the epoch and not on the action.

| On that day the battle was fought. | Nóon isàng árao ay nangyari ang pagbabacà. |
| In those times when Jesus Christ was still on Earth. | Nóon, nariritò pa sa lupa si Jesucristo. |

Bagò, as an adverb, always comes before the verb.

| Before you marry think on it carefully. | Bagò ca magasáua pacaisipisipin mo mona. |
| Before you read, sweep the room. | Bagò cang bumasà ualisan mo ang silid. |

Mona always comes after the verb and is largely used expletively.

| Do it first. | Gaoin mo mona. |
| Wait. | Hintáy ca mona. |

| Endlessly, incessantly, without intermission. | Ualáng humpáy, ualáng tahán, ualán lícat. |

Firstly, in first place.	Ona-onà, caonaonahan.
Forthwith, in the twinkling of an eye.	Sa sandalí, sumandalí, sa isang quisap matá.
While, in the mean time.	Sa mantala, hangán.
While he is still alive.	Hangán nabubúhay siyá.
At nightfall.	Taquip silim.

FIFTY FOURTH EXERCISE.

How far is Manila.? From here to Manila there is six miles' distance. Did she do it voluntarily.? She did. What shall I do.? Do as if you were angry. Who made the table.? The table as well as the chair were made by the carpenter. Will he do it in this manner.? He must do it in that manner. Which runs more swiftly; a sailing vessel or a steamer.? A steamer runs more swiftly. Do I write well.? You write badly. Why do you whip your servant so hard.? Because he purposely broke the pot. Are there any people within.? There are no people within, all of them are outside. Is his house opposite the church.? No, it is behind the church. Is my brother above or below.? He is under the bed. Where do I put the trunk.? Put it in the middle of the road. Where are we in our journey.? We are halfway in our journey. Where is the child.? The child is by his mother's side. Where is his farm.? It is at the other side of the road. Where is yours.? On both sides of the river. When do you intend to pay the tailor.? I intend to pay him to-morrow. Did you not see the ship the day before yesterday.? No, I saw her some days ago. Were you last night at the theatre.? I was there a week ago. Are my friends here.? Just now they were here, but I think they will come back by and by. At what time shall I get up to-morrow.? Rise early. Have the servants already come.? Not yet. Are you always reading.? I have not the time, I am constantly working. When shall I send for the physician.? Send for him immediately. Do you intend to remain here for ever.? I do. What did the priest say in his sermon.? He said, sin no more. How many days are there from to-day till the end of the year.? There are sixty five days till the end of the year. Did this tree bear fruit formerly.? It did and even now it fructifies occasionally. Does he often go to school.? He goes to school rarely. How often does my sister go to Manila.? She goes there yearly. When will he write.? After having read this letter he will write. When did they become frightened.? They became frightened when they saw the snake. When will you go to bed.? I will go to sleep after supping. When will your son study his lesson.? After hearing mass he will go to study. Did you see the cathedral.? Whenever I go to Manila I visit (see) the cathedral. When does your mother drink.? When she eats she drinks. Why do you not read.? When I write I don't read. When did your brother-in-law arrive.? When I was writing he arrived. Why did not my cousin write.? Because your uncle had already written when your brother arrived. When did he go away.? As soon as his father went away, he also went away. What did the count do when he approached the king.? On the count's arriving before the king, he prostrated himself immediately. What did the king do after the count spoke.? No sooner the count had finished speaking, he was embraced by the king. When did my brother arrive.? He arrived after you went away. Where shall I go.? Go to your uncle's and after your greeting him come back. When shall we take a bath.? The mass over we shall take a bath. How did that come off.? On my friend's beguinning to speak, I swooned away. What will the servant do before eating.? Before he eats he must go for water. Which of this books shall I read first.? Read that first.

FIFTY FIFTH LESSON.
YCALABING POUO,T, LIMANG PAGARAL.

THE ADVERB. (continued).

Notice should be taken of the adverbial verbs, that is to say, of adverbs which are made verbs and conjugated in various ways. The adverbs most commonly used for this purpose are those of manner, time, and degree.

To act thus. (in that way).	Gumaniyán, gumayaón or gumayón.
Make it in this way.	Gaitohin mo.
Let us profit of this opportunity.	Samantalahin natin.
I composed this book by working at short intervals.	Ytòng libro,i, minamayá mayá co.
Throw it away at once.	Tangbiñgin mo ytapon.
His fever increases.	Lungmalalo ang caniyàng lagnat.
„ money is running short.	Cungmuculang ang caniyáng salapí.

ADVERBS OF DEGREE.

Much.	Marami, lubhá.
Little, somewhat.	Cauntî.
More.	Lalo, higuit, mahiguit.
Less.	Cúlang.
Too, too much.	Labis.
Enough.	Casiyahan, caiguihan.
Only.	Lámang.
Sufficiently.	Catatagan, siya na, súcat na.
Almost, nearly.	Halos.
Except, but.	Liban.
Exceedingly, very.	Lubhá. di sapala.
Greatly.	Masáquit, maínam.
Do you write much.?	¿Sungmusúlat ca bagá nang marami.?
I write but little.	Sungmusúlat acó nang cauntí lámang.
This is more than that.	Mahiguit itò dóon.
It rained too much.	Ungmolán nang labis.
That is sufficient.	Caiguihan na yaón.
He nearly died.	Halos siyá namatáy.
He is almost in destitution.	Halos na sa cahirapan siyá.
Very rich, exceedingly rich.	Mayamang lubhá, mayaman di sapala.

ADVERBS OF AFFIRMATION.

Yes.	Oo.
Yes indeed.	Oo ñga, nañga, ñgani.
Of course, no doubt.	Siyá ñga, mandin, ñgani, mangyari.
Certainly.	Totoò:

Most certainly.	Totoòng tot ò
Also.	Namán.
Will you go to the theatre.?	¿Paroroón ca bagá sa teatro.?
Of course, why should I not go.?	¿Mangyari, anò,t. di acó paroróon?

ADVERBS OF NEGATION.

No.	Hindí, di. dili, ualá.
Neither.	Hindí rin.
No, don,t.	Houag.
Not even one.	Di isà man.
Neither he not I.	Siyá,i, hindí. acó man, ay hindí rin.

DUBITATIVE ADVERBS.

Lest.	Maca, baca, maca sacali.
Perhaps.	Maráhil.
Perchance.	Cun sacali, cun bagá sacali.
Then, perchance.	Bagá, cayá, sana, disin, diuá.
Don't run lest you fall.	Houàg cang tumacbò, macá mahólog ca.
Perhaps to-morrow.	Maráhil bucas.
Perhaps he will arrive.	Maráhil darating siyá.
Perhaps it may be so.	Maráhil ganóon.
If you, perchance, see him.	Sacaling maquita mo siyá.
If, perchance, he comes.	Cun bagá sacali pumaritò siyá.
If, then, he finds money.	(Cun siyá sana,i, macaquita nang sa- lapí.

Say, –est, –s; said. –dst.	Ang uica.
Says, said he.	Ang uica ˆ niyà.
Says, said Jesus Christ.	Ang uica ni Jesucristo.
You say, said.	Ang uica mo, ninyò.
Saint Peter says, said.	Ang uica ni San Pedro.

Uica, "word;" is another root proper to be used verbally in an impersonal and absolute manner, It is generally applied to quotations and requires the postpositive forms of the personal pronouns in the possessive case after it.

Money, old people say, is the best friend.	Ang salapí, ang uica nang matatandá, siyáng lalong mabuting caibigan.
The debt, he says, is small.	\ Ang ótang, ang uica niyà i, muntí- / lámang.

Truly.	Tantó mandín.
At some time, day.	Sa bálang árao.
I truly saw it.	Tantó mandíng naquita co.
Some day I will do it.	Sa bálang árao gagaoin co.
In that very manner, way.	Casing gayón, casing ganiyán.
Anyhow.	Paanò man.
Some way or other.	Sáan mang paráan.
Care, attention.	Bahala.
Do as you like.	Ycáo na ang bahala.
Leave that to my care.	Acó na ang bahala niyán.
To care for, to look after.	Mamahala, magcaliñga.
To tend, to care for animate beings.	Magalaga.
To live, to possess means of living.	Mamúhay.
To instil life.	Magbúhay, magpabúhay, bumúhay.
To pull off.	Múnot, mamúnot. (from búnot.)

To commence. to start.	Mamuno. (from *pono*, "commence-ment.")
Then, therefore.	Diyata, caya ñga.
You alone were here, then you are the thief.	Ycáo lámang ang niritò, caya ñga icáo ang magnanácao.
Is it possible.?	¿Diyata.?
Is it possible he died.?	¿Diyata bagá,i, namatáy siyá.?
Some way or other.	Sa higpit at sa louag.
Either for being tight or for being loose the dress was thrown away.	Sa higpit at sa louag ang damit ay ytinapon.
Accomplished, perfect.	Sacdal.
The pith of wisdom.	Sacdal carunuñgan.
Most learned.	Sacdal nang dúnong.
The pith of purity.	Sacdal calinisan.
The purest.	Ang sacdal nang linis.
The hardest.	Ang sacdal nang tigás.
Outshining.	Sacdal dilag.
Little by little.	Ontí ontí, inot inot.
To stop, to halt.	Maghintó, humintó.
To halt here and there.	Maghintóhintó.
Don't stop there.	Houág cang humintó diyán.
Thanks.	Salámat.
Well and good.	Di siyáng salámat.
Welcome!, welcome to you.	Salámat at dumating ca.
Lucky, to be lucky.	Palarin.
Unfortunate, to be unlucky.	Sam-íng palad(from *samá*)
If I have good luck.	Cun acó, i, pinapalad.
He was unlucky.	Siyá, i, sinamá.
To think it just.	Matapatín marapatín.
„ „ „ hard.	Mahirapín mabigatín.
„ „ „ obvious.	Magaanín.
„ „ „ sweet.	Matamisín.
Does she think the practice of virtue hard.	¿Minamahírap bagá niyà ang paggauá nang cabanalan.?
She thinks it sweet to bear grievances for the sake of Jesus Christ.	Minamatamís niyá ang pagtitíis nang hirap álang-álang cay Jesucristo.
The north.	Ang hilagáan.
The south.	Ang timugan.
The east.	Ang silañganan. silañgan.
The west.	Ang calonoran.
The wind blows from the north.	Hungmihilaga ang hañgin.
The wind blows from the south.	Tungmitímog ang hañgin.
North-east wind.	Sabalás, *nordeste*. (Sp.)
North-west wind.	Habágat.
This road leads to the west.	Ytóng dáan itò,i, tungmutuñgò sa dacong calonoran.
To take off one's hat in reverence.	Magpúgay.
Why do you not take off your hat in reverence to the priest.?	¿Báquit hindí mo pinagpugayan ang pare.?
To invite, entertain.	Mamiguing, magpiguing, magyápac.
To take leave of.	Magpaálam.
To dress, to put on clothes.	Magsóot.
To change clothes.	Magbihis.

FIFTY FIFTH EXERCISE.

Has the tailor much money.? He has but little. Why do you not go to-night to the meeting.? I cannot go, I am somewhat ill.? Has the carpenter more nails than hammers.? He has less hammers than nails. Have you too much butter.? I have not enough. What time is it.? It is nearly noon. Did they all go.? All of them went, but him. Does it thunder hard.? It does not thunder, but it rains hard. Are you the friend of my friend.? Yes. Is it true he paid.? It is, indeed. Are you a merchant.? No. Shall we go mass.? Neither you nor your brother must go. Why should I not do this.? Don't do that, lest you hurt yourself. Will he come.? Let him come. Do you chance to have some money about you.? I don't know, if, perchance, I have some I will give it you. What is Faith.? Faith, say the holy fathers, is to believe what we have not seen. What is the amount of Peter's debt.? Peter's debt, says my son, amount to thirty dollars. Did you speak with the soldier about that business.? An agreement, he says, has been arrived at. Did you, then, speak to him.? Truly, I did speak to him. When will he write to us.? He will write to you, said he, some day. Will you marry her.? I will marry her anyhow. But have you money enough to do that.? No, but some way or other I will do it. How.? Leave that to me. What does the servant do.? He looks after swine. Is your grandfather still alive.? No, he is dead. What miracles did Jesus Christ work.? He gave life to many. Does your sister pull off her hair.? She does. Is it possible.? She is mad, so she does many foolish things. Is his mother virtuous.? She is the very pith of virtue. Is your servant dirty.? He is the dirtiest. How shall I write the letter.? Write it little by little. Does their servant walk quickly.? He walks very slowly, he halts here and there at every shop. Did you thank Mary for her present.? I thanked her. Who is there.? Our friend is here, welcome Frank!. Where do you go now.? I am going to the gambling room to see whether I am lucky. How did you come out in gambling? I was unlucky, I lost all my money. Don't you think it hard to lose money in that way.? I don't think it sweet. What quarter does the wind blow from.? It blows from the north. Where does this path lead to.? It leads to the southern shore. Whom does that child take off his hat to.? He takes off his hat to his master. Did your father invite him.? He did. Have you anything else to say.? No, I now take leave of you. What are you doing there in the room.? I am dressing myself. How often do you change clothes.? I change to clean clothes every week.

FIFTY SIXTH LESSON.
YCALIMANG POUO,T, ANIM NA PAGARAL.

THE PREPOSITION.

The pliable condition of Tagalog words to perform the functions of different parts of speech applies largely to adverbs, prepositions and conjunctions. The mutual relations of words are expressed in Tagalog in several ways, only the purpose for which the words establishing the relations are made use of, according to the systematic division established by grammar, serve to clasify them as adverbs or prepositions. Some of these aptly illustrate the difficulty of classifying Tagalog words according to the parts of speech usually recognised by grammarians. The nominal ligaments too, sometimes stand in Tagalog for prepositions.

To, at.	Sa, cay, caná.
Before, facing.	Sa harap, sa tapat.
Under.	Sa ilálim.
Near, by.	Sa mey, sa píling, sa síping.
With, along with.	Sa, nang, cay, caná, sabáy, acbáy.
With, by, through.	Nang, dahilan sá.
Against.	Laban sa.
Of.	Nang, sa, ni, cay, niná, caná, na, ng, g.
From.	Sa, nang, gáling sa, mula, mula sa.
In, at.	Sa.
Among.	Sa.
Between.	Sa, sa guitná, na sa guitná.
Towards, to.	Dapit, daco, sa daco.
Till, until.	Hangán.
To, as far as.	Hangán.
For.	Sa, cay, caná.
Without.	Ualá, cúlang.
On, upon, about.	Sa, nang, bágay sa, tongcol sa.
Behind.	Sa licod.

Sa, as a preposition, is for every case of a common noun, except the nominative, and the vocative (nominative of address). It should be put before the object of possession and not before the possessor when used in relation to the possessive case. *Sa* is exclusive for the dative.

The depth of the river.	Ang sa ílog na calaliman. or, ang calaliman nang ílog.
I wrote to the priest.	Sungmúlat acó sa pare.
This plant is for the garden.	Ytòng pananim itò,i, sa halamanan.
He is shooting (aiming at) wild boars.	Nagtuturlá siyá sa bábuy damó.
We shoot (arrows) at birds.	Pungmapana camí sa mañga ibon.
They look at the stars.	Tungmitiñgin silá sa mañga bituín.

Sa governs the local ablative mainly indicating place, no matter whether the verb denotes rest, motion or direction.

I pray at home.	Nagdadasal acó sa báhay.
This child cries greatly at school.	Nagtatañgis itòng bata sa escuelahan.
He sleeps in bed.	Natotólog siyá sa hihigaan.
We shall play in the garden.	Maglalaró tayo sa halamanan.
They walked in the road.	Naglácad silá sa dáan.
You go to Cebú.	Napaparóon cayó sa Cebú.
The ship is bound for Manila.	Tungmotoñgò ang sasaquián (or ang dáuong) sa Maynila.
This road leads to the beach.	Tungmotoñgò sa dalampásig itòng dáan itô.

Cay is for proper nouns of persons what *sa* is for common ones. What has been said of *sa* in the possessive case holds good also for *cay*. Due allowance should be made for the local ablative, as persons are not places.

John's house.	Ang cay Juang báhay, ang báhay ni Juan.
Mary's needle.	Ang cay Maríang caráyom, ang caráyom ni María.
I gave flowers to Jane.	Nagbigáy acó nang bulac-lac cay Juana.
That shirt is for Anthony.	Cay Antonio yaóng baro yaón.
I don't buy from Diana. (Chinese name).	Hindí acó bungmibili cay Diana. (better). Hindí si Diana ang binibilhan co.
He received the money from Robinson.	Tungmangap siyá nang pílac cay Robinson. Tinangapan niyà Si Robinson nang salapí.

Caná is *cay* for the plural of companionship.

The estate of the Wallaces.	Ang caná Wallace na búquid, ang búquid niná Wallace.
Smith, Bell & Co's werehouses.	Ang caná Smith Bell na mañga camàlig, ang mañga camàlig niná Smith Bell.
The book is for Arthur and his family	Ang libro,i, caná Arturo.
He visited the García family.	Dungmálao siyá caná García.
He ran for the Wheatleys.	Sungmondó siyá caná Wheatley. (better). Sinondó niyá siná Wheatley.
Your sister went out with her aunt.	Ang inyòng capatid na babaye ungmalís casabáy nang caniyàng alí.
I walked along with my friend, with George, and with the La Rosa family.	Naglácad acó casamà nang aquing caibigan, ni Jorge, niná La Rosa.
He was by the tree.	Nariyán siyá sa may cáhoy.
I did it through charity.	Guinauá co dahilan sa áua.
Blasphemy is a sin against God.	Ang pagtotoñgáyao ay casalanang laban sa Dios.

Nang, as a preposition governing the possessive and objective (direct object) case, has been so fully treated of in foregoing chapters as to dispense with the need of further explanations. *Nang* (preposition,) governing the ablative case denotes the instrument when the latter has not been expressed in the proper passive form of the verb.

Cover that with a mat.	Tacpán mo iyán nang banig.
He whipped his servant with a string.	Hinampás niyà ang caniyàng alila nang lúbir.

Why did my mother do this with a needle.?	¿Báquit guinauá ní inà ito nang caráyom.?, or, ¿báquit ang yguinauá ni inà nitò ay ang caráyom.?
He is praised by every body.	Pinupurì siyá nang lahat.
They killed the cock-roach by stamping it.	Pinatáy nila ang ipis nang yápac.
He obtained the office through the influence of his father.	Nang mamaguitan nang caniyáng ama ay quinamtán niyà ang catungcolan.

The English preposition "of" is translated into Tagalog several ways. When denoting possession it is always translated by *nang, ni, niná*, placed before the possessor (but after the thing of possession) or by *sa, cay, caná*, in the manner above explained, according to the former being represented by á common, a personal or a companionship noun.

The ear of the dog.	Ang taiñga nang aso.
Joseph's book.	Ang libro ni José.
The house of the Makays.	Ang báhay niná Mackay.

The same is the case if the relation is merely adjectival.

The bank of the river.	Ang tabì nang ílog.
The glory of Heaven.	Ang caloualhatían nang lañgit.

For translating English compound nouns having the preposition "of" understood between their members, the following directions are given.

If the relation is one of matter, the two members are tied together by the nominal ligaments, the matter coming after the thing.

Stone house.	Báhay na batò.
Gold ring.	Singsing na guintó.
Silver looking-glass.	Salamíng pílac.
Steel pen.	Plumang patalim.

If the relation is one of origin, the placing of the two words in the same order may be sufficient, the ligament should be used if the word ends in a vowel, although *sa* is generally introduced without any ligament.

Berlin flowers.	Bulac-lac Berlin, bulaclac sa Berlin.
Ilocos man.	Taòng Iloco, tauò sa Iloco.
Calamianes wax.	Pacquit Calamianes, pacquit sa Calamianes.

The ligaments stand for "of" in the relation of contents.

Two pecks of rice.	Dalauàng salop na bigás.
A glass of water.	Isàng vasong túbig.
A pitcher of cocoa-nut oil.	Ysàng tapayang lañgís.

Sa, also expresses application or the use a thing is intended for.

Prayer-book, book for praying.	Libro sa dasal.
Water-glass.	Vaso sa túbig. inomán.
Mass garments.	Damit sa pagmimisa.

Hangan is used both for time and place.

From to-day until to-morrow.	Búhat ñgayón hangáng búcas.
From here to Cavite.	Mula ditò hangán sa Cavite.

Other prepositions are translated according to their sense in the way already explained.

He forced a passage among the crowd.	Sungmagasa, siyá sa caramihan.

Between the house and the garden.	Sa guitná (paguitan) nang báhay at nang halamanan.
The path towards the forest.	Ang landás sa dacong gúbat.
The dog without a tail.	Ang asong ualáng (ór cúlang) bontot.
He speaks about the marriage.	Nañgoñgosap siyá tongcol sa pagaasáua.
The house behind the church.	Ang báhay sa licod nang simbahan.

Amiable.	Caibig-íbig.
Delightful.	Catouatóua, caligaligaya.
How delightful to listen to the singing of birds.	Caligaligaya paquiñgan ang huni nang mañga ibon.
Terrible, ghastly.	Catacottácot.
Horrible.	Casindacsindac.
Gloomy, sorrowful.	Calumbáylumbáy, calunoslunos.
Painful.	Cahapishapis.
Gallant, courageous, victorious.	Bayani.
To tear down, to cleave.	Lumápac.
Her house is a place of resort for many people.	Ang báhay niyà,i, báhay na pinapapanhican nang maraming tauò.
Hell is a place of torment for sinners.	Ang impierno, ang pinaghihirapan nang mañga macasalanan.
Why do you not place those chairs facing each other.?	¿Báquit hindí mo pinagtatapat iyáng mañga upóan?
Put also the two beds facing each other.	Pagtapatín mo namán ang dalauàng hihigàan.
Why had you this child chastised.?	¿Anò,t, pinahampás mo itòng bata.?
Because he made light of me.	Sa pagca,t, acó,i, pinañgisihan niyà.
Don't laugh at the poor.	Houag mong paglibaquin ang mañga duc-há.

--- -- --- ----

FIFTY SIXTH EXERCISE.

Why is Ann always at the window.? She is always at the window. because she likes to see passers-by. Why do you change to new clothes.? I change to new clothes, because I must go to church. How many times does he undress himself every day.? He only undress himself on going to bed. Is he empowered to imprison me.? He has no power (authority) to do that, don't fear, he can do nothing to you. How can that be.? It cannot be. Why cannot it be.? Because it cannot happen. Am I very sick.? No, you can still recover. Is he wise.? No, but he can still become wise. How will you reward me.? I have nothing with which to reward you. What has happened.? There was an earthquake yesterday and our house tumbled down. Where is God.? God is everywhere. Where is Jesus Christ now.? Jesus Christ is now in Heaven at the right of the Father. Who is happy.? The man who is in the grace of God is happy. Where is Peter's house.? It is at the middle of the cocoa-plantation. With what did he sew his trowsers.? He sewed them with a needle and some thread. With what shall I make this.? Make it with an auger. Whose ships are these.? They are Wise & Company's. Shall I write the letter in pencil.? Yes, write it in pencil. How did he kill the wild boar.? He killed it with a spear. How are the houses in your town.? All of them but three are nipa houses. Have you bought any gold ear-rings.? No, I have bought three wooden images. From where are those pieces of furniture.? They are Vienna furniture. What kind of shell is that.? It is Cavite shell. How many pecks of rice did you sell.? I sold three pecks of rice and two bottles of wine. Where is the rice-pot.? The rice-pot is at the corner of the table. Which cat is your friend looking for.? The three-legged one. Which is the most courageous among you.? The most courageous is Henry's friend. Do you wish to go by this pirogue.? I don't wish to, it is a pirogue where many embark. Is there anything more horrible than an earthquake.? An earthquake is, indeed, a horrible thing. Is John's house high.? It is very high. How many houses has your father built.? He has built three. Are they nipa or stone-houses.? Two of them are stone, the other is wood. Do you like to live in a nipa-house.? Yes, indeed, how delightful it is to live in a nipa-house. When do you go to your friend.? I will go to him next Sunday.

FIFTY SEVENTH LESSON.
YCALIMANG POUO,T, PITONG PAGARAL.

THE CONJUNCTION.

Many words and particles which we are already acquainted with as adverbs or prepositions are likewise used as conjunctions for connecting two sentences or words in different ways, only their function in the sentence or clause serving to distinguish which part of speech they are.

The following may be classed as.

COPULATIVE CONJUNCTIONS.

And.	At, ay, ni, nang, sacá.
As well as, both, likewise, even.	Patí, sampón, sacá, sabáy, casan à
Also, even, likewise, besides, moreover, further, furthermore.	Namán, pa.
Not only..... but.	Hindí lámang...... cundí bagcús.

At is well known as a copulative conjunction serving to link two nouns or independent sentences to each other.

Heaven and Earth.	Ang láñgit at lupa.
Angels, men, and animals, all of them were created by God.	Ang mañga *ángeles* (Sp.), ang mañga tauò, at ang mañga háyop ay paraparang quinapal nang Dios.
She plays and sings	Tungmotogtog at nagaauit siyá.

Ay, the verbal ligament, may be used as a copulative conjunction at the beginning of an interrogative sentence, as connecting the sense to a mental reflection or to something previously said or understood.

Well now, why does he refuse.?	¿Ay báquit nanayáo siyá.?
And then.? what.?	¿Ay sacá, anò.?

As has been already said in foregoing lessons it is a peculiarity of the Tagalog language that two nouns, two pronouns, or a personal noun and a pronoun may be linked by the particle of the possessive case. In the latter case the pronoun, if in the singular, should be put in the plural. In the case of two pronouns joining, the order of first, second and third person should be kept, by naming first (in the plural) that which stands first in rank although they be differently constructed in English. These forms are however becoming obsolete and replaced by the more natural ones used in Spanish.

Henry and Mary.	Enrique ni María.
I, John and even my father.	Camí ni Juan at ang amá co pa.
You and George.	Cayó ni Jorge.
He and I.	Camí niyà. (not silá co)

Ye and they.	Cayó nilà. (not silà niny..)
Mary and I.	Camí ni María.
He and his father.	Silá nang caniyàng amá.

Sacá is used at the end of a third noun or sentence when stress is laid on the time elapsed.

At six o'clock my father and I arrived, and at nine, the judge.	Camí nang amá co,i, dungmating nang a las seis, sacá nang a las nueve ay dungmating ang bocom.
She bore a child on 1885, another on 1886, and the last in 1900.	Nañganac siyá nóong 1885, nañganac nóong 1886, sacá nang cahulihulí ay 1900.

Patí, sampón, casabáy, as copulative conjunctions, are more emphatic than *at* and denote an idea of a closer connection of the words or sentences they serve as a link to. They are sometimes used to avoid repeating *at* and for the sake of euphony. They govern the nominative case unless the noun they link is preceded by the article, in which case, they generally govern the possessive. The *n* of *sampón* may be dropped before a word beginning with the same letter. *(n)*

Soul as well as body.	Calolóua patí cataouán.
	Calolóua sampó nang cataouán.
Both the gold in the church and the silver in the house.	Ang guintó sa simbahan patí nang pílac sa báhay. Ang guintó sa simbahan sampó nang pílac sa báhay.
Even what he eats, he borrows.	Patí nang quinacáin ay inoótang niyà.
The coward and even the brave a'l of them fled.	Patí nang mañga matápang sampó nang mañga dóuag ay nagtacbohan.
The night is still, and the sea is calm, and the breeze is mild.	Tahímic and gabì, ang dágat ay payapa, sampó nang hañgi,i, amihan.

Namán and *pa* are postpositive conjunctions, and *pa* is sometimes used for expressing surprise, or reluctance to do something.

Also you shall be punished.	Ycáo namá,i, parurusahan.
And still I am to go there.?	¿Acó pa ang paroróon.?
I could not do it, and you can.?	Di co nagauá, ¿icáo pa.?

ALTERNATIVE CONJUNCTIONS.

Or.	*O,* (Sp.) cayá. dili.
Whether.	Man.
Either......or.	Maguin,........o.
To-morrow or the day after to-morrow I will pay.	Bucas o sa macalauà ay magbabáyad acó.
You or I.	Ycáo o acó.

Cayá should be used at the end in alternative sentences. It denotes doubt.

This month or perhaps in June.	Ñgayóng bóuan, sa Junio cayá.

Dili, as an alternative conjunction is also placed at the end. It includes the conjunction and the negative adverb and is generally employed in interrogative sentences putting forth a dilemma.

Do you wish or not.?	¿Ybig mo, dili.?
Shall I accompany you or not.?	¿Sasamahan quitá, dili.?

Man is always a postpositive particle which only differs from *dili* in the latter having an interrogative use.

Whether he goes or not.	Paróon man siyá di man siyá paróon.
Whether he says it or not what is that to you.?	Sabihin man di man niyá sabihin ¿ay anhin mo.?

Maguin is used in the manner already explained, for the correlative conjunction "either....or".

Either at my house or at yours we shall speak about the matter.	Maguing sa aquing báhay maguing sa iyó, magoósap tayo tongcol sa bágay na iyán.
Either at Manila or New-York, I shall print this work.	Maguing sa Maynila maguing sa Nueva-York ypalilimbag co itóng librong ito.

ADVERSATIVE CONJUNCTIONS.

But.	Ñguní,t, cundí, datapóua, subali, alintana.
Neither, nor.	Man, hindí, rin, at hindí rin.
Rather........than.	Cundí, bagcús, mona, bago.
Though, although.	Man, bagamán, bistá, matáy man, cahit, cahiman.
In spite of, with all that.	Man, ganóon man, gayón man, ganiyán man.
Whereas.	Palibhasa,i,.
Nevertheless, however, notwithstanding, yet, still.	Subali, datapóua.
Although if.	Sucdán, mayápat, matáy.
Or else, otherwise.	Cundí.

All the adversative conjunctions ending in a vowel, *cundí* and *palibhasa* excepted, take the contracted form of *at* after them. *Palibhasa* is followed by *y=i*, the contraction of the verbal ligament *ay*.

Ñguní, cundí, datapóua, subali, alintana are all used for every sense of the English adversative conjunction "but". *Ñguní* is used in the subordinate sentence, generally in answers, and is not proper to start a sentence.

I should like to eat, but I cannot.	Ybig co sanang cumáin ñguní,t, hindí acó mangyayari.
I saw him, but I did not speak to him.	Naquita co siyá, ñguní,t, hindí co siyá inósap.

Cundí is also for the subordinate sentence and generally requires the pricipal one to be negative.

It is not a male, but a female child.	Hindí lalaqui, cundí babaye ang bata.
This is not a fib, but the very truth.	Yto,i, hindí casinoñgaliñgan, cundí catotohanang ganap.

Datapóua is somewhat emphatic and is used to make the contrast more noticeable.

He is rich, but unhappy.	Mayaman siyá, datapóua,t, cúlang pálad.
Don't scorn old people. but honor them.	Houág ca magpaualáng halagá sa mañga magúlang, datapóua,t, purihin mo silá.

Subali and *alintana* have a somewhat conditional import as "but for," except," in English.

I would buy some clothing, but for my not having any money.	Ybig co sanang bumili nang damit, subali,t, ualá acóng salapí.

43

He was cured, but with all that he died.   Guinamot siyá, alintana,t, namatáy.

Man and *hindí rin* are correlative conjunctions used postpositively: *man*, generally, in the first member, and *hindí rin*, in the last, when the latter is employed for the sake of a greater emphasis.

Neither I nor yet he.	Acó man, siyá man hindí rin.
We have neither betel not even tobacco.	Ualá camí, tabaco man, mamin man.

Hindí rin may come at the beginning of a sentence when used as an emphatic negative adverb.

However wise we may be, we cannot conceive (sound) the essence of God.	Cahit anòng marúnong camí ay hindí rin natin mataroc ang pagcadios nang Dios.

Cundí, bagcús, the latter especially, are used in the sense of "rather," and both of them may join in the same sentence.

Whatever your condition may be, do not give yourself up to despair, but rather trust in God.	Cahit anò ang pagcalagáy mo, hindí mo pagpatiuacal, cundí bagcús maniuala ca sa Dios.
Not only he does not gain (earn), but rather he loses by the trade.	Hindí iámang di siyá naquiquinábang, cundí nañguñgulugui pa siyá.
Not only not sound, but rather, ill.	Dili gumaling, bagcús sumamá.

Bagamán, bistá, matáy man, cahit=cahit, and the compound *cahiman* or *cahimat* come before; *man*, after, the word they refer to.

John, though poor in money is rich in honesty.	Bagamán si Juan, ay duc-há, sa purî namán, ay mayaman siyá.

Bistá, bista,t, bistat is more formal and its use is rapidly dying away.

Though he is angry with me, he will give me the money.	Bistá,t, siyá,i, nagdadalàng póot sa aquin, ay bibiguián din niyà acó nang salapí.

Matáy man is emphatic and may stand for "ever so much", with a verb.

Think I ever so much about it, I cannot understand it.	Matáy co man isipin, hindí acó nacatatalastás.
Though my earnest desire was to come here, my strength failed.	Matáy man acó nacaíbig paritò, ay di co macayanan.

Cahit and its compounds are used in the same way as *matáy man*.

Although I be cudgeled, I will say nothing.	Cahit acó,i, hahampasin, ualá acóng sasabihin.
I will go though he may not consent to it.	Cahima,t, di máyag siyá, paroróon din acó.
Though he is rich, he is a miser nevertheless.	Mayamán man siyá, siyá,i, maramot namán.
I will not pay you in spite of that.	Hindí acó maghabáyad sa iyò ganóon man.

Palibhasa is used for "since," "whereas;" it is followed by *y=i* and shares somewhat of the nature of causative conjunction.

Whereas my neighbour trespassed, I may also sin, since I am as frail as he.	Cun ang cápoua co tauò ay nacasasala, macasasala namán acó, palibasa,i, acó,i, tauòng mahina para rin niyá.

Whereas He is God He can do everything.	Nacapangyayari sa lahat, palibhasa,i, Siyá,i, Dios.

Sucdán=socdán is used in the sense of "no matter that," "be that as it may."

Be I first satiated no matter if I get ill.	Nagpapacabúsog mona acó, sucdán acó,i, magcasaquit.
I fire, be that as it may.	Babaril acó sucdán anòng manyayari.

Mayapa=mayapal is very little used in a sense of surprise and reluctance.

What, because I drank I must pay.?	¿Mayapa,t, acó,i, ungminom, ¿cailañgang na acóng magbáyad.?
Go, or else I will say it.	Paróon ca, cundí sasabihin co.

CAUSATIVE CONJUNCTIONS.

Why.?, what for.?	¿Báquit.? ¿baquin,? ¿anò,t,.?
Therefore, as, so.	Palibhasa, baquin, di baquin.
Since, whereas.	Yáman, hámang, yayámang, at.
Why not.	Báquit hindí, di.
Because, for, as.	Sa pagca,t, at, ang, dahil sa, báquit.
Hence, whence.	Manáa. (lit., behold!)

The interrogative adverbial conjunction "why" is expressed either by *báquit = baquin* or by *anò* followed by the contraction of the copulative conjunction.

Why did he send so many books.?	¿Baquin nagpadalà siyá nang gayón maraming libro.?
Why do you look for the black hen.?	¿Anò,t, hinahánap mo ang inahíng maitim.?

If the sentence is both interrogative and negative and the form with *anò* is employed, the latter may be suppressed.

Why did he not come.?	¿At di siyá naparitò.?

At anò, ay at, ay anò are inquisitive expressions for "what of,?" "what about,?" "how is it about.?"

What about your law-suit.?	¿At anò ang ósap mo.?
And the marriage, what.?	Ay at ang tungcol sa pagcasal ¿ay anò.?
How is it about the money.?	¿Ày anò ang salapí.?

Báquit also denotes "as," "how".

As you are also a rogue.	Báquit icáo ay tampalasan namán.
And so, how do you not do it.?	¿Ay baquin di guinagauá mo.?
Now, do you not see it is nonsense.?	¿Ay baquin di mo naquitang iyá,i, buhag-hag.?
Since (whereas) you broke the plate. pay for it.	Yaman or yayaman binásag mo ang pingán, iyòng bayaran.
Because I laughed, he became angry.	Sa pagca,t, acó,i, napataua, nagalit siyá.
I cannot go, because I am sick.	Hindí acó nacapaparóon, at acó,i, may saquit.
She refuses, because he is old.	Nanayáo siyá, ang siyá,i, matandá na.
He does not pay, for he is poor.	Di siyá nagbabáyad at siyá,i, mahirap
You did not believe me, hence your disgrace	Di mo acó pinaniualáan, manáa ang cahirapan mo.

Sa may also be a causative conjunction.

As he did not come, I went there.   Sa di siyá naparito, naparóon aoó.

CONDITIONAL CONJUNCTIONS.

If.	Cun.
Provided.	Cun lámang, houag lámang.
Unless.	Cundí lámang, liban na, cun diri lá-- mang.
Lest.	Macá, baca.
Were it not for.	Dañgan, cundañgan.

Cun and *cundañgan* etc. generally come before the nominative case.

If he scolds you, do not become angry.	Cun icáo ay auayan niyà, houag cang magálit.
If he looks for you.	Cun hanapin ca niyà.
Were it not for him I should have beat you.	Cundañgan siyá hinampás catá.
Were it not for Our Lord Jesus Christ having redeemed us, all of us should have certainly been damned.	Cundañgan ang ating Pañginóon Si Jesucristo ay sungmacop sa atin, ta- yong lahat ay napacasamá rin.

The following illustrations will show the use of the other conjunctions of this group.

I shall give it you, provided you do not say it.	Bibiguián catá, houag lámang sabihin mo.
He will not go unless I order him so.	Hindí siyá paroróon, liban na sa siyá,i, otosan co.
Don't run lest you fall down.	Houag cang tumacbò, maca mahólog ca, or, macá icáo ay mahólog.
Go quickly, lest dark surprise you on the road.	Paróon cang madalí maca magabihan ca sa dáan.

ILLATIVE CONJUNCTIONS.

Well then, that is the reason why.	Cayá cayá ñga, yayamang.
Consequently.	Diyata, sa macatouir.
Inasmuch, in so fas as.	Yayamang.
That, in order that.	Nang, upang.
That.	Na.
You have been called, since you are well, go.	Tináuag ca, yamang icáo ay magaling paróon ca.
As he has no farm, he leases one.	Palibhasa,i, ualá siyáng búquid, ung- mupà siyá.
I saw him yesterday, consequently (therefore) he did not embark.	Naquita co siyá cahapon, sa maca- tour hindí siyá sungmacáy.
He can do it inasmuch as he is king.	Mangyayaring gaoin niyà yayamang siyá,,i, hari.

The most important conjunctions of this group, are *nang* and *na*.

He says that I slept.	Nagsasabi siyá na acó,i, natólog.
Be virtuous that you may be happy here and in the life to come.	Magpacabanal cayó nang magcapálad cayó, ditò sa lupa at sacá sa cabi- ling búhay.
Allow yourself to be cured in order that you may recover.	Magpagamòt ca, nang icáo ay guma- ling.

A, the contracted form of the article *ang*, is prefixed to the possessive case of nouns or of the personal pronouns, in a verbal sense, the same as *uica*, when quotation of or reference to the words or sayings of such persons or texts are to be expressed, somewhat after the defective "quoth" in English.

God says, or said.	Anang Dios.
Peter says, or said.	Ani Pedro.
The Holy Scripture says.	Anang Santong Súlat.
Says, or said he.	Aniyà.
Jesus Christ says, said.	Ani Jesucristo.
Says, said the Apostle.	Anang apóstol.
I say, said.	Anaquin.
They say, said.	Anilà.
We say, said.	Anamin, anatin.

N is inserted for euphony's sake when the possessive begins with a vowel, as seen in *anaquin*, etc.

Scoundrel; vile, mean fellow.	Bulisic.
Issue, result, consequence.	Casapitan.

FIFTY SEVENTH EXERCISE.

Who went to school.? Clara and Matilde went to school. Did you taste the wine I sent you.? Yes, I have already tasted it. And what, do you think it good.? No, I think it bad. Where do you go.? I am going down to the garden if you permit me. Do you permit me to go.? Yes, but don't gather any fruit, because it is still green; lest you feel pain in your teeth. Where shall I sit.? Don't be seated on that chair, for it is broken. How did Lincoln die.? He died assassinated by a fanatic a sad and terrible thing the death of so great a man was.! Did he commit sin.? He will rather die than sin. What do you want that chair ·for.? I take it for my friend to sit on. Why does he affect to practice virtue.? He affects to be virtuous that he may be praised. Why do you not wash your face every day.? Because the water is cold. What did you order me to do just now.? Run for the priest and in case you should meet any acquaintance on the street don't stop to converse with him. Why shall I not talk with him.? Because it is a very pressing business. But I have to go to Henry's. Well then, if you go to him don't tarry there. Do the trees you planted, already fructify.? They do not yet fructify; but they already blossom. What does your father say to you.? He says do not go to the forest lest you be assaulted by highwaymen.? What.? Do not go up into that house, lest there are some people above. What.? Do not run lest your mother beat you. Why was he afraid.? He feared, lest he should be heard. Will she write to me every month.? She will write to you provided she is not busy. Who is mad.? Either her father is mad or she is a fool. Will he come or not. Whether he comes or not, is nothing to me. Did they both go.? Neither the one nor the other went. Will you also go.? I would rather pay a fine. Did you not hear your brother is a scoundrel.? Although he may be a scoundrel, he is not a rebel. Did you learn your lesson by heart.? Though I study much I cannot learn it. Would they come if I offer them some money.? They would not come even in spite of that. Are you resolved to fight him.? I will fight him though I be killed. Do you know that I have been beaten at play.? You did not mind me, behold the issue now. Will you visit my mother, since you are here.? Since I am here I will visit her. Why did not the servant bring my horse.? Because you said nothing to him about it.

FIFTY EIGHTH LESSON.
YCALIMANG POUO,T, UALONG PAGARAL.

THE INTERJECTION.

Among the Tagalog words serving as interjections. *abá, aróy* and *inà
co* (the latter contracted into *nacó=nacú*), which natives profusely employ,
are the most important. *Abá* is used for wonder, surprise, cheer, pain,
warning etc., and it would be difficult to exhaust its meanings.

O dear me.!	¡Abá.!
Alas.!	¡Abá.!
Alas, poor me.!	¡Abá co.!
Alas, poor thee,¡ warn thee.!	¡Abá mo.!
Let us go.!	¡Abá tayo!, ¡abá tayo na.!
Well!, did I not say to you not to go there.?	¡Abá! ¿di co uica sa iyò na houag cang paróon.?
How!, did I not say so to you.?	¡Abál ¿dili gayón ñga ang uinica co sa iyò.?
What!, what is the matter.?	¡Abá!, ¿anò.?

Aróy or *aráy* is exclusively for sudden or intense. pain.

Oh,! woe.!	¡Aróy!, ¡aráy!.
Oh,! this pain.!	¡Aróy!, ¡masaquit.!

Ynà co is an exclamation importing surprise or wonder.

Oh mother!.	¡Ynù co!.
Oh mother!, the rain. (how hard it rains!)	¡Ynà co!, ang olán.

Among many other exclamations. the following are frequently in use.

Oh how. .....!	¡Ayáa!. (always postponed)
Oh, how pretty!.	¡Butì ayáa!.
It is a pity!.	¡Sáyang!.
What a pity, so much money lost!.	¡Sáyang ang salapí gayóng marami!.
Would to God!.	¡Cahimanuari!, ¡nauá!, ¡maanong!.

Cahimanauari and *maanong* are used before; *nauá*, after the verb.

Would to God you might attain Heaven	Cahimanauari macamtán mo ang ıañgit
Would to God he would die.	Maanong siyá,i, mamatáy.
Would to God he may come.	Dumating siyá nauá.
Be quick.!	¡Dalí.!
Away,!	¡Sulong.!
Back.!	¡Orong.!
Beware.	¡Tabi!
Hush.! silence.!	¡Houag maguiñgáy.!
Be silent.!	¡Houag cang mag-iñgáy.!

Bravo.!	¡Buti ñga.!
Poor thing.!	¡Caáua áua.!
Oh God.!	¡Ay Dios co!.
Fury.!	¡Lintic.!

Ayáa, bapáa are little in use nowadays and are postpositive interjections proper to express wonder. *Ayáa.* is more in use by women; *bapáa,* by men. Both of them may concur in the phrase, *bapáa* preceding, to render the expression more emphatic.

How pretty.!	¡Diquit ayáa.!
How great.!	¡Laqui bapáa,! ¡laqui bapáa ayáa.!
How beautiful to see.!	¡Gandà bapáa panoorin.!

When the thing object of wonder is expressed, the second *a* of *bapá, ayá* is transferred to the end of the admirative clause.

Oh how good this is.!	¡Galing bapá nitò a.!
Oh how sweet that is.!	¡Tamís ayá niyáng a.!

Hyperbolical expressions can be made with *pagca, anò, ca,* put before the root in the possessive case. *Ca* and *pagca* are used prefixedly. The root may be repeated for the sake of greater exaggerative sense.

How immense the sea is.!	¡Pagcalaqui nang dágat.!
How pretty these flowers are.!	¡Pagcadiquitdiquit nitòng mañga bulaclac.!
How the stars glare in a still night.!	¡Anòng pagcaningning nang mañga bituín sa isàng gabíng tahímic.!
What a crowd.!	¡Caraming tauò.!

As exclamative expressions may also be considered those formed with the prefix *ca* and the repetition of an adjective or affective verbal root in the way to be explained in subsequent lessons.

How tall.!	¡Catáastáas.!
How long.!	¡Cahabahaba.!
How pitiful.	¡Caauaáua.
How gloomy.	¡Calunoslunos.!
How amiable Jane is.	Caibigíbig si Juana.
How horrible is death.	Caquilaquilábot ang camatayan.

Imprecations are greatly in fashion among natives. Every tense, but especially the past or the imperative, is maid use of for the purpose.

May a caiman swallow thee.!	¡Canin ca nang boaya.!
May the sea glut him.!	¡Lamonin siyá nang dágat.!
May a flash (thunderbolt) strike you.!	!Tinamáan ca nang lintic.!
Would to God they would die.!	¡Maanong mamatáy silá.!
May a snake sting you.	¡Tuquín ca nang ahas.!

To bury.	Maglibing, magbaón.
Burying place.	Papagbaonan.
Coffin.	Cabáong.
To thrust in, to drive into.	Tumíric, magtolos.
To carry on one's back.	Mamas-án, mapas-án.
To endeavor, to force.	Pumílit, magpílit.
To melt away, to melt.	Matónao, tumónao.
Melted lead.	Tónao na tíñgá.
Decrease of the moon.	Tonáo na bouán.
To open, to lay open, to uncover.	Mamucás, magbucás.

Order that I be admitted in. — Pabucasan mo ac i.

Order them to uncover the image. — Pabucsán mo ang laráuan sa canilá.

To join, to collect, to put together. — Magtipon, mag-ipon.

To amass, to put on over again. — Magsosóni.

To mix, (certain substances to make up a beverage called salabat). — Magsalabat.

An amassment of misfortunes. — Susonsusong cahirapan.

A medley of curses and foul words. — Salasalabat na sumpá,t, tuñgáyao.

To bend, to bend back. — Mamaloctot.

Twisted horns. — Balobaloctot na suñgay.

To twine, to twist, to curl un. — Maglicao.

Winding way or passage. — Licolicong dáan.

Twisted thorns. — Licaolícao na tinic.

Miscelaneous things. — Sarisaring bágay.

Variety of colors. — Sarisaring cúlay.

Trap, snare, slipknot. — Silo.

To lay traps for. — Manilo.

Bait. — Pain.

To walk for amusement. — Magpasial. (corr. from Sp. word pasear. "to take a walk").

The public place for walking. — Pasialan.

Substitute, delegate, successor, succeeder. — Cahalili.

The priest is the delegate of God. — Ang pare,i, ang cahalili nang Dios.

To substitute, to act in behalf of other. — Humalili.

To plead for. — Magpintacasi.

Intercessor, mediator. — Pintacasi.

The patron saint. — Ang pintacasi.

To feign, to personate others. — Magpangap.

To dissemble, to counterfeit. — Magbalintona.

To please. — Magbigáy lóob.

To despise, to scorn. — Magpaualáng halagá, magalipostá.

To augment. — Magdagdag.

To elate, to become proud. — Magpalalo.

To exalt one's self. — Magmalaqui, magmatáas.

He who wishes to please God must endeavour to shun sin. — Ang tauòng ungmiíbig magbigáy lóob sa Dios dápat magpumilit umílag sa pageacasala.

To inspire compassion. — Macaáua.

To cling to. — Cumuyápit, mañguyàpit.

To cling to, to grasp at. — Cumápit, mañgápit.

To be downcast. — Mañgolilà.

To transpire. — Mañganínag.

Bush. — Síit.

Sickle. — Lílic, pangapas.

To mow. — Gumapas.

To mow rice. — Mag-ani.

To clear a wood. — Magcaíñgin.

To transport, to carry. — Humácot.

To bite, to sting, to peck. — Tumucá, manucá.

To sting by gnats. — Sumiguid, maniguid.

To nibble. (by fish at the bait.) — Cumibit.

A snake stung me. — Acó,i, tinucá nang ahas.

Gnats are stinging about. — Naniniguid ang mañga lamoc.

Do mosquitoes sting you.? — ¿Sinisiguid ca nang mañga lamoc?

Yes, and they bother me. — Oo, at acó.i, sinasactán.

Tortoise shell. — Cala.

Sea tortoise. — Pauican.

To tuck up the sleeves or petticoats. — Maglilís.

Why do you tuck up your pantaloons.? — ¿Báquit ca naglililís nang salaual.?

To break through, to run over, down.	Sumagasa.
To hold, to wield, to handle.	Humauac.
To trample, to tread on.	Tumongtóng.

FIFTY EIGHTH EXERCISE.

Who are there.? The children of our neighbour. Why did you admit them.? Away.!, my master is angry, back!, be quick.! How.! Beware,! the buffaloes come on. Have they already finished the work.? They have. Bravo.! Do you know what has happened.? No, what.? The Chinaman's horse ran over your friend's child and he is dead. Poor thing,! what a pity not to have my gun on hand.! Where are the children roaming about.? In the corral. You, naughty people, be silent.! Drive them out, fury;! they are stamping on my plants. Did you notice how beautiful his female—cousin is.? Yes, and how modest she is too. Have the labourers already planted the stakes for the enclosure.? They are still carrying them. Where did you bury your child.? This is the place where we buried him. Who bore the coffing? His schoolmates bore it. What is that the Chinaman is melting there.? He is melting wax. Have you already laid your chest open.? Not yet. Order it to be laid open immediately. Why are so many people gathering together.? They assemble to welcome the Judge. Why does the blacksmith bend down the point of that spear? He bends it down to make a sickle out of it. Where did they buy the thimbles.? They bought them at a shop of miscelaneous things. What have you in your garden.? I have a variety of trees and flowers of various colours. What do you set traps for.? I set traps for the monkeys. What bait do you employ to catch them? I employ cocoa-nuts as bait. For whom is your son a substitute.? He is a substitute for his cousin. What saint do you plead before as an intercessor to God.? Saint Patrick is my intercessor. When is the feast of the patron saint of this village.? Saint John is the patron saint and the feast is on fhe 24th of June. Whom did the thief impersonate.? He impersonated an officer. Whom did he deceive by artful contrivances.? He deceived many people. Is riding pleasant to you.? Riding and swimming are very pleasant to me. Does he despise her.? He does not despise her. Are priests despised by everybody.? They are honored by worthy people and despised by the wicked. Why did that man become so proud.? Because his fortune has been augmented by an inheritance. Is it on account of that that he exalts himself.? It is on that account, but he inspires compassion and his action inspires shame. What is the matter.? There is a man being drowned in the river. What shall we do to save him.? Throw that log out to him for him to cling to. Has he grasped it already.? No, but he is going to grasp it, he looks downcast. Did the business transpire.? It does not transpire. Where is the deer.? It got into the bush. What is that sickle for.? It is for mowing rice. Is it not to mow grass or to clear woods.? No. Where does he carry that straw. (chaff)? He carts it to the enclosure. Have you been stung by a snake.? No, but I was stung by gnats. Are there any tortoises in this river.? There are a great many. Are their shells good for anything.? They are good for many things. Why did Ann tuck up her petticoat on crossing the road.? Because there is a great deal of mud.

FIFTY NINTH LESSON.
YCALIMANG POUO,T, SIYAM NA PAGARAL.

PARTICLES FORMING SUBSTANTIVES AND ADJECTIVES

Most of the particles have been noticed in speaking of the verb, but there are some that have likewise a nominal or adjectival use. Some others, which are not verbal, enter into composition for various purposes forming idioms and other peculiar ways of expression. Although explanations and hints about some of them have already been given occasionally in foregoing lessons, a separate study of all is now subjoined, anything relating to particles being very important in Tagalog.

AN. CA.

An, (*han*, when the last vowel bears the sharp accent) is always a suffix and the most important one. It is applied conjointly with the prefix *ca* to adjectival roots purporting a quality, to form the abstract noun for such quality.

ADJECTIVE.	ABSTRACT.	QUALITY ROOT.	ABSTRACT NOUN.
Quiet.	Quietness.	Tahímic.	Catahimican.
Noble, dear.	Nobleness.	Mahal.	Camahalan.
Liar.	Lie.	Buláan.	Cabulaanan.
Mad.	Madness.	Olol.	Caololan.
Bad, naughty, cruel.	Naughtyness, cruelty.	Tampalasan.	Catampalasanan.
Foolish.	Foolishness.	Hung-hang.	Cahung-hañgan.
Industrious.	Industry.	Sípag.	Casipagan.
Firm.	Firmness.	Tíbay.	Catibayan.
Strong.	Strength.	Lacás.	Calacasan.
Deep.	Depth.	Lalim.	Calaliman.
Broad.	Breadth.	Lápad.	Calaparan.
Heavy.	Heaviness.	Bigat.	Cabigatan.
Light.	Lightness.	Gáan.	Cagaanan.
Meek.	Meekness.	Amo.	Caamoan.
Round.	Roundness.	Bílog.	Cabilogan.
Beautiful.	Beauty.	Gandà.	Cagandahan.
Large, long, great.	Length, greatness.	Laqui.	Calaquihan.
Lordly.	Nobility.	Guinoò.	Caguinoohan.
Young.	Youth.	Bata.	Cabatáan.

This composition is likewise used to form collective nouns.

Boy.	Young people.	Bata.	Cabatáan.
Christian.	Christendom.	*Cristiano* (Sp.)	Cacristianohan.
Island.	Archipelago.	Polo.	Capoloan.
Earth. (material).	Earth, world.	Lupa.	Calupáan.

An=han, without *ca*, is appended to a root having a nominal or verbal force to form the place or the instrument on which, not by which, the work is accomplished, using the future tense for those roots admitting of contraction, or beginning with *l*.

To bathe.	Bath-room.	Paligo.	Paligoan.
To put into a harbour.	Wharf.	Dóong.	Dooñgan.
To spit.	Spitting-box.	Lura.	Lulurán.
To eat.	Dining-room.	Cáin.	Cacanán.
To drink.	Vessel.	Ynom.	Ynoman.
To strike fire by percussion or rubbing.	Steel or instrument for striking fire.	Pinquí.	Pinquían.
To lie down.	Bed, couch.	Higa.	Hihigáan.
To put into.	Storing place.	Silid.	Sisidlan.
To worship.	Temple.	Simbà.	Simbahan.
To make cocks fight.	Cock-pit.	Sábong.	Saboñgán.
To pasture.	Meadow.	Sabsab.	Sabsaban.
Mud, dirtiness.	Quagmire.	Pusalí.	Pusalían.
Sugar-cane.	Sugar plantation.	Tubò.	Tubohan.
Bamboo.	Bamboo-grove.	Cauayan.	Cauayanán.
Cocoa-nut.	Cocoa-nut plantation.	Niog.	Niogan.
Banana.	Banana plantation.	Ságuing.	Saguiñgan.
Head.	Pillow, bolster.	Olo.	Olonán.
Foot.	Pedestal, foot-stand.	Paà	Paahán.
First, anterior.	Fore-front.	Unà.	Unahán.
Last, posterior.	Back, hindermost place.	Huli.	Hulihán.
To wrap up.	Bundle.	Bálot.	Balotan.

The future tense of the *an* passive should also be used in other conjugations with such nouns as indicate places which carry along with them an idea of futurity or potentiality for the actions performed thereon.

To baptise.	Baptistery.	Binyag.	Pagbibinyagán.
To preach.	Pulpit.	Pañgáral.	Pañgañgaralán.
To sentence, to pass judgment.	Hall where a court or a judge sits.	Maghocom.	Paghohocomán.
To kill.	Slaughtering-place.	Magpatáy.	Pagpapatayán.
To hang.	Gibbet.	Magbítay.	Pagbibitayán.

But if the verbal root is intransitive in character, *ca* should be used and the first syllable of the root repeated.

To stumble.	Stumbling-place or place or thing serving as an obstacle.	Matísod.	Catitisoran.
To fall.	Place where many fall down.	Mahólog.	Cahologan.
To slide, to slip down.	Slippery place.	Marulás.	Carorolasan.

The student should notice that in most nouns thus formed from a verbal root, the stress of the accent is on the last vowel. This is, in many cases to draw a distinction between the person or the place. Thus *pañgañgara-lan* means the person to whom something is to be preached, while *pañga-ñgaralán*, is the place, to say, "the pulpit."

An comes at the end of a diminutive noun or of those things being not real, but represented by any graphic means or of which one speaks in contempt.

Little bird or the figure of a bird painted or drawn.	Ybonibonan.
Human figure painted or despicable person.	Tauotauohan.
Petty king or person who plays the role of a king.	Hariharían.
Canopy, ceiling.	Lañgitlañgitan.
Quack, empiric in physic.	Medimedicohan.
God, idol.	Diosdiosan.

Sometimes, *an* applied to a noun root converts it into an adjective of a characteristic quality in a somewhat augmentative sense.

Head.	Club–headed.	Olò.	Olohan.
Nose.	Large–nosed person.	Ylong.	Ylongan.
Snout.	Long-snouted.	Ñgoso.	Ñgosoán.
Shoulder.	Broad shouldered.	Balicat.	Balicatán.
Mouth.	Large – mouthed, charlatan.	Bibig.	Bibigán.

Ca, is another important prefix word-building particle.

Ca, as has been said, comes before roots importing companionship, likeness, reciprocalness or conformity, to indicate one of the corresponding parties.

Companion.	Casamà.
Commensal.	Casalo.
Fellow-passenger.	Casacáy.
Inmate, one of the persons living at the same house.	Casangbaháy.
Contrary, foe, one of the quarelling parties.	Caáuay.
Assistant, aiding party.	Católong.
Competitor.	Catalo.
Playing-fellow.	Calaró.
Equal, fellow officer, officer of the same rank.	Capara.
To scorn, scorning–party.	Tumuyá, catuyá.
Namesake.	Cañgalán, casañgáy.
Face-resembling.	Caniuc-há.
Equal, similar.	Capantáy, cahalimbáua.
Resembling thing or party.	Catúlad, cahalintúlar, cahambing, cauañgis.
Journey-fellow-passenger.	Calacbáy.
Contemporary, of the same age.	Capanahón.
Drinking party.	Cainom.

The first syllable of the root is sometimes repeated.

Fellow-villager, compatriot.	Cababayan.
Scorning party.	Cabibiro, cabiro.

Ca comes before the quality root, object of comparison, if it is put at the end in comparative sentences with *ga*.

As hard as stone.	Gabatò catigás.
As long as this.	Ganitò cahaba.
As tall as that.	Ganiyán catáas.
As sweet as sugar.	Gaasúcal catamís.
How old is he.?	¿Gaanò siyá catandá.?

Ca is also used as a particle expressing past time with some roots importing time.

Yesterday.	Cahapon.
Last night.	Cagabi.
The day before yesterday.	Camacalauà.

Ca has a limitative force when applied to roots of numerable things.

One handful.	Caracot.
One piece, only one piece.	Capótol.
Only one palm. (length measure)	Carangcal.
One drop only.	Capatac.
One person only.	Catanò.
In a word.	Sa catagang uica.
One load only.	Cadalhán, cadalahan.
Only two persons.	Dalauà catanò.

Ca may be repeated to express a greater degree of limitation.

Absolutely one piece.	Cacapótol.
Absolutely one person.	Cacatanò.

This limitative force of *ca* is also applied to actions which require time for their accomplishment. The sense imparted by the English verb "to have just" may be expressed this way in Tagalog. The first syllable of the root should be repeated in this kind of expressions, with the subject in the possessive case, for these are passive clauses.

He has just come down.	Capapanáog pa niyà.
I have just arrived.	Cararating co pa.
They are just gone out.	Caalís lámang nilà.
We have but come upstairs.	Capapanhic lámang namin.

This same construction may also be made to mean "no sooner than," "as soon as," "immediately," etc.

No sooner did he start speaking than he was miscarried.	Cauinica niyà,i, nagcamalí na.
As soon as I arrived there, I was given food.	Casasápit co dóon ay pinacáin acó.
Immediately that he left, he saw you.	Capanáo niyà ditò ay naquita ca niyà.

The same construction (that of *ca* and the repetition of the first syllable) with the subject in the nominatve case, serves, in actions admitting degrees of intension, to exhort, to excite to do the work in the manner most energetic possible.

Pray most devoutly to the Holy Virgin	Cahihiñgi cayó sa mahal na Virgen.
Beware,! be careful. be cautious.	Caiiñgat cayó.
Behave most judiciously.	Cababaet cayó.

It has been seen in the preceding lesson that if *ca* is prefixed to an adjectival root and the latter is repeated, exclamative adjectival expressions are formed.

How amiable.!	Caibigíbig.
How pitiful.!	Cababaghabag.

How disgusting.!	Cadumaldumal.
How admirable, wonderful.	Catac-hatac-há, catacatacá.
How prodigious.	Caguilaguilalás.

This same arrangement forms some adverbs or adverbial expressions of time.

Suddenly.	Caalamalam.
All at once.	Caguinsaguinsa.
Off hand.	Caracaraca.

Ca, in this construction, it should be noticed, carries the sense to the highest degree of intension and it is even applied to some roots of things as in *cataloctaloctocan* which means the very summit of the mountain, the peak.

| Is there any spring yonder at the summit of that mountain.? | Dóon sa cataloctaloctocan nang bondoc na yaón, ¿may batis bagá.? |

Ca with the suffix *an=han* forms the superlative degree of adjectives, the root being repeated as already explained.

This is very precious.	Camahalmahalan itó.
Very savory.	Casarapsarapan.
Very obscene.	Cahalayhalayan.
Very good.	Cabutibutihan.

Some adverbs of time are formed in the same manner.

| Lastly. | Catapustapusan. |
| Finally. | Cauacasuacasan. |

The repetition of the root may be dispensed with if some adverb or word importing time comes in the expression.

To leave for, to go away.	Pánao, mamánao.
To carry away.	Magpúnao.
To exile.	Magpapánao.
This very week I shall leave.	Capanaoan co itóng lingo.
When he was on the point of dying.	Niyóng camatayan na niyà.
When he was about to kill them.	Niyóng capatayan na sa canilà.

FIFTY NINTH EXERCISE.

Do you wish to accompany me.? Yes, I will accompany you, where do you go.? I am going to fish whith a rod. Why do you scorn your fellow-citizens.? I don't scorn them. But you find faults with them, do you not know it is improper to find faults whith others.? What do you admire most.? I admire the marvelous things made by God and especially I admire the beauty of the stars on the skies. Can they be trusted.? They cannot be trusted. May not they then be intrusted with that business. I don't know. May I still become healthy.? You may still get healthy. Can you go to Manila.? I cannot go to Manila, for I am ill. Can your brother go to Manila.? He cannot go to Manila, because he is very busy. May this medicine alleviate the suffering of the patient.? It may alleviate it. Where is the nobility (aristocracy) of this town.? They are at church. Has this house any bathroom.? There is here a bath-room for grown up people: young people bathe at the river. What do natives use for drinking.? Natives use cocoa-nuts as drinking vessels. Where is the pedestal of this image.? It is in the cell. Where do the native people assemble.? They assemble at the cock-pit.

Does your friend own any sugar plantations.? He does not own any sugar plantation, but he owns two cocoa-nut farms. When did you arrive.? I have just arrived. Where is your master.? My master is just gone out. Did you see her husband.? He had just got into the house when I saw him. Do you wish to dine with us.? No, I have just dined. What shall we do.? Think on it carefully and be on your guard. What has happened to you.? No sooner did I start walking than I stumbled. Where did you slip down.? There, there is a slippery place and I came across a place full of stones. Did you find the book.? As soon as I started looking for it, I found it out. How long is it.? It is as long as this. Is that wood hard.? It is as hard as stone. What a bat is it like.? It is as a bird when flying. Whom are you conversing with.? I converse with my fellow inmates. Whom are you going to take as a companion for the journey.? Your enemy. Are they orphans.? They are, how sad it is to be an orphan. Did you taste pineapples.? Yes, how sweet they are.! What do those people do at the beach.? They are bathing, how indecorous to see male and female people bathing together. Did you swim.? Yes, I did, how amusing swimming is.

SIXTIETH LESSON.

YCAANIM NA POUONG PAGARAL.

PARTICLES FORMING SUBSTANTIVES AND ADJECTIVES (continued)

IN. MA. MACA.

In is a prefix, a suffix or an insertable particle; *hin*, its more sonorous form, is always a suffix.

In is prefixed to or inserted in nominal roots to form derivatives denoting resemblance or sharing of the properties possessed by the root.

A berry, octogonal in shape.	Anything cut up in an eight-sided shape.	Balingbing.	Binalingbing.
Night scenting flower.	Anything resembling such flower.	Sampaga	Sinampaga.
Verdure, culinary vegetables, garden stuff.	Anything sharing in the green colour.	Gúlay.	Guinúlay.
Needle.	Needle pointed rice.	Caráyom.	Quinaráyom.
To boil rice.	Boiled rice food.	Sáing.	Sináing.
To spin.	Spinning thread.	Súlid.	Sinúlid.
To boil meal, flour.	A sort of fritters. any soft pap.	Lógao.	Linógao.
To knead.	Bread.	Tápay.	Tinápay.

The first syllable of the root (as for the present tense) should be repeated for anything which is permanent in kind, as these are but participial nouns.

Father.	Godfather.	Amá.	Inaamá.
Mother.	Godmother.	Ynà.	Iniinà.
Son or daughter.	Stepson or step-daughter	Anac.	Inaanac.
Brother or sister.	Half brother or sister.	Capatid.	Quinacapatid.
Aunt.	Some woman who stands for an aunt.	Alí.	Inaalí.
Sister-in-law.	One's brother's mistress.	Hípag.	Hinihípag.

In, either prefixed or inserted, is the well known form of the past participle which, generally, stands for the direct object.

The sweetheart or the beloved person.	Ang sinisintà.
The esteemed person.	Ang minamahal.
The already known person.	Ang quinocoan.

My property, what is held as mine.	Ang inaaquin.
Others' property, their property.	Ang quinacanilà.
What is yours. (plur.).	Ang iniinyö.

The same composition is likewise used to mean the passive effect of some destructive agent.

What is destroyed by mice.	Ang dinadagá.
„ „ „ „ ants.	Ang linalangam.
Bananas are done away with by crows, ravens.	Ynoouac ang ságuing.

Every present or past stage of a bodily complaint is expressed by the root of the latter with *in* either prefixed or inserted.

Itch. mange.	Person suffering from itch	Galís.	Ang guinagalís.
Small-pox.	Person who has suffered from small-pox.	Bolótong.	„ binolótong.

The same is the case with the root of any limb or part of the body capable of being affected by pain.

Stomach.	Siemura.
John suffers from the stomach.	Sinisiemura si Juan.
Breast.	Dibdib.
I suffered from breastache.	Dinibdib acó.

In or *hin*, is suffixed to roots of the above said complaints to express their suffering either at some future time or if they appear as chronic or habitual, forming, in the latter case, nouns expressive of the patient.

Gout.	Person who will be afflicted with gout.	Piyó.	Pipiyohin.
Itch.	Itchy, scab.	Galís.	Galisin.
Asthma.	Asthmatic.	Hica.	Hicáin.

The same may denote a defect.

Small-pox.	Pitted by the small-pox.	Bolótong.	Bolotoñgín.
Lippitude.	Person bearing lippitudes.	Mota.	Motáin.
Belly.	Big-bellied.	Tiyán.	Tiyanin.

In or *hin*, suffixed to verbal transitive roots stands for the thing or work which is the result of the accomplished action, if the verb admits of the *in* passive for the direct object.

To sew.	Needle work.	Tahí.	Tahíin.
To eat.	Food.	Cáin.	Canin.
To drink.	Drink.	Ynom.	Ynomin.

But if the thing on which the work remains patent is meant, the *an* passive particle is used.

To embroider mats	Mat with twisted drawings on.	Sabat.	Sinabatán.
Honey.	Cake made with honey.	Polot.	Pinolotán.
Egg.	Pie with eggs in.	Itlog.	Initlogán.

The same composition is employed for what is left behind as offal by the effect of some actions.

To mow, to reap.	Stubble.	Gapas.	Guinapasan.
To cull, to choose.	Refuse, offal, dregs	Pili.	Pinilían, pinag-pilían.
To cut out stuffs.	Cuttings, clippings	Tabás.	Pinagtabasan.
To pick rattans quite clean.	Peelings, parings.	Cayás.	Quinayasan, pinagcayasan.

If the root denotes a passion, an act of the mind or an involuntary action, the root should be prefixed by *ma*, the particle for adjectives, with the same composition of *in-hin* suffixed, thus forming frequentative adjectival nouns which are, for the most, acute in accent to distinguish them from the corresponding tenses of the verb.

Compassion.	Tender hearted humane.	Aua.	Maauaín.
Love.	Loving, affectionate.	Sintà. Irog.	Masintahin. Mairoguin.
Bias, liking.	Amateur.	Uili.	Mauilihín.
Desire.	Longing, capricious.	Ybig.	Maibiguín.
Wrath.	Irascible.	Gálit.	Magalitín.
Laugh, smile.	Smiling, pleasing, agreeable.	Táua.	Matauanín.
Weeping.	Mourner.	Tañgis.	Matañgisín.
Obedience.	Obedient.	Sonor.	Masunorin.
Sleep.	A dull sleepy person.	Tólog.	Matologuín.

If the root admits of being contracted, begins with *l* or an intensive degree is meant, the first syllable of the root may be repeated.

Forgetfulness.	Short of memory, forgetful.	Límot.	Malilimotín.
Joy.	Joyful.	Logod.	Malologdín.
Fear.	Faint-hearted.	Tácot.	Matatacotín.
Sickness.	Infirm, sickly.	Saquit.	Masasactín.
Fever.	Person subject to fever.	Lagnat.	Malalagaatin.
Bashfulness.	Bashful, diffident.	Hiya.	Mahihiyín.

Ma is the well known prefix particle to form adjectives of those roots that are not adjectives by themselves.

Bravery.	Brave.	Tápang.	Matápang.
Wisdom.	Wise.	Dúnong.	Marúnong.
Soundness.	Sound.	Galing.	Magaling.

The adjectives thus formed may be conjugated by *mag* in the sense of affecting or boasting of the quality they denote.

Anthony affects to be brave.	Nagmamatapang si Antonio.
John boasts of wisdom.	Nagmamarunong si Juan.

If they are conjugated in the *in* passive of the *um* conjugation, the sense is that of holding or reputing the object as possessing the quality expressed by the adjective.

I consider that good.	Minamabuti co iyán.

| I hold vice to be a bad thing. | } Minamasamaí co ang masamáng qui- / naogalían. |
| He reputes as judicious what Peter says. | Minamagaling niyà ang sinasabi ni Pedro. |

Ma, is also joined to a substantive root indicative of a thing capable of being possessed of, imparting a sense of the subject abounding in such commodity as is denoted by the root. *Ma*, in this case, is but the contraction of *may*.

There is plenty of rice in this town.	Mapálay itòng bayan itó.
Henry possesses a great deal of gold.	Maguintó si Enrique.
This house is provided with many rooms.	} Masilid itòng báhay.

Ma, as a potential particle, comes before a verbal root, forming adjectives indicative of the possibility or capability of the action being performed. English adjectives ending in "able", "ible", or any other termination denoting potentiality may be expressed in this way.

Sufferable.	Matiís, mabatà.
Pronounceable.	Mauica.
Feasible, practicable.	Magauá.
Easy.	Madalí, magaán.
Eatable.	Macáin.

The repetition of the first syllable of the root (as for the future passive tense of *maca* conjugation) may be used, especially if an idea of futurity is meant, either form being used almost indifferently.

Feasible.	Magagauà, mangyayaring gaoin.
Eatable.	Macacáin.
Potable, drinkable.	Maiinom.
Possible.	Mangyayari.
Visible, perceptible at sight.	Maquiquita.
Speakable.	Masasabi.

But if negation or inversion of the meaning of the root is to be expressed as when the Latin prefixes "in", "dis", or the Saxon "un" are used in English, the sense is made by the simple root (as for the imperative) prefixed by *ma* and preceded by the negative adverb.

Insufferable.	Di matíis.
Untolerable.	Di mabata.
Incomprehensible.	Di matingcala, di maalut mang ísip.
Indissoluble.	Di macalag.
Inaccessible, unapproachable.	Di malapitan.
Interminable.	Di matapus.
Unserviceable.	Di magamit.
Uneatable.	Di macáin.
Impossible.	Dili mangyayari.
Inexplicable, unexplainable.	Di masaysáy.

If the capability is expressed by an adjective or an adjectival clause, the verb should be put in the proper passive.

Easy to be done.	Madalíng gaoin
Difficult to say.	Malíuag sabihin.
Troublesome to be attained.	Mahírap camtán.
Unapproachable.	Di malapitan.
Easily pronounceable.	Madalíng uicáin.

Susceptible, punctillious.	Di mauicáan.
It is easier to say it than do it.	Madaling sabihín mahírap gaoín.

Maca, may be assimilated to *ma* as a particle forming adjectives, if prefixed to verbal roots. What *ma* is for the potential sense, *maca* is for the causative one.

Agreable, what causes pleasure.	Macatotóua.
Causative of shame.	Macahihiya.
Mortal, destructive of life.	Macamamatáy.
Laughable, causing laughter.	Macatatáua.

Maca is also prefixed to the cardinal numbers to form the adverbial numerals of time, the first being wholly, and the second and third, partly irregular, as has been explained.

Once.	Minsán.
Twice.	Macalauà.
Thrice, three times.	Macaitlò, macatatlò.
Five times.	Macalimà.
A hundred times.	Macasangdáan.

Spark.	Quislap, alipato, pilantic.
To cause weariness.	Macayamot.
To disgust, to cause disgust.	Macasáua.
To inflame, to cause to be inflamed.	Macasonog.
To produce anxiety.	Macabalisa.
To produce nausea.	Macasuclam, macarimarim.
To cause the disgust of satiety.	Macasuya.
It cannot be.	Hindí mangyayari.
Can but.....	Hindí mangyayari di......
I can but go.	Hindí mangyayari di acó pumaróon.
It may be.	Mangyayari din.
It may not be.	Hindi mangyayari.
It may be, it may happen.	Súcat mangyari.
It can hardly be, happen.	Di súcat mangyari.
To examine, to look into into the qualifications of some candidate.	Sumúlit.
My brother passed examination before the master and came out qualified.	Sinúlid and capatid co nang maestro at siyá,i, nacasúlit.
Nobody knows it.	Ualáng nacacaálam.
Nobody understand it.	Ualáng nacatatalastás.
Do you understand it.?	¿Natatalastás mo bagá.?
He feels warm.	Siyá,i, naiinitan.
He was swayed (blind) with wrath.	Nabulagan siyá nang gálit.
Lest.	Macá, sacali.

SIXTIETH EXERCISE.

Shall I do it.? Don't do that lest you be damned. Do I go out then.? Go out and beware; don't fail to do what I told you. Shall I go upstairs.? Don't go up, lest there may be some people over there. What are you going to do.? I am going fishing to see whether I can hook some fish. Why did he not lift the bag.? He is going to try whether he can lift it up. Did they shoot arrows at the birds.? Yes, they did and they shot down some. Did you run after him.? I ran for him, but I could not overtake him. Do you wish me to go out now.?

Don't go away at present, for you will be affected by sunshine and you will feel warm. Shall I stay here any longer.? No, begone, lest you may be overtaken by dark in the wood. What happened to them.? They were sailing and they were overtaken by a storm at sea. What has happened to you.? Our house was burnt down. What has happened.? The thread parted. What has happened to your brother-in-law.? His strength failed, his senses vanished and his mind gloomed, his breath was cut short and he breathed the last. How was it.? His walking-stick split and his ankle was sprained. Why do you laugh.? I laugh because that fellow stumbled and fell down. Do I assist him.? No, make him walk slowly, lest he may slip. Do you fear.? Yes, I do. What are you afraid of.? I am afraid of the souls of the dead. Why do you fear the ghosts,? fear God and do not fear ghosts, as they will do nothing to you. Where did you stumble.? I stumbled against this stone. What house did your mother die in.? In our grandfather's house. What did she die of.? She died of fever. Why does that woman weep.? Because death deprived her of her infant child. I don't see your sister, where is she.? She is there knelt down near the altar. And your brother, where is he.? There he is standing near the pillar. Is he not that one who is seated on the bench.? No, he is that one who is by him. Who is your godfather.? My godfather is my friend Charles' father, and my godmother, his sister. Do you take that as yours.? No, I take it as theirs. How is your rice field.? It has been eaten up by locusts. Is your servant afflicted with itch.? No, he is afflicted with asthma. Does his stomach pain him.? No, he has a handache. Is his father a big bellied man.? No, he is big headed. Where did you put the thrashings.? I put them by the side of the sweepings. Is your servant obedient.? No, he is, on the contrary, obstinate. Is there any money in the safe.? There is plenty of money in the safe. Is this letter pronounceable.? Yes, it is easy to pronounce. Is sea-water drinkable.? It is not drinkable. Is poison destructive of life.? Poison is destructive of life. Is the priest an asthmatic.? No, he is a gouty man. Are sparks dangerous.? They are, a spark can set a town in flames. Is sweet potato eatable.? Yes, but it sometimes causes satiety. Did you come out well from the examination.? No, I was disqualified.

SIXTY FIRST LESSON.

YCAANIM NA POUO,T, ISANG PAGARAL.

PARTICLES FORMING SUBSTANTIVES AND ADJECTIVES. (continued)

MAG. MAN. MAPAG.

Mag, as a particle forming nouns, is the contrary of *ca*. *Ca*, contracts the sense to one party; *mag*, indicates two at least.

Mag comes before those nouns which are conceived only in couples to indicate both parties, and denotes plurality without the employment of the pluralizing particle being necessary.

The two sisters-in-law.	Ang maghípag.
The married couple.	Ang magasáua.
Both quarrelling parties.	Ang magáuay.
The engaged parties.	Ang mag-ibigan.
The parents.	Ang magúlang.
The two brothers–in–law.	Ang magbayáo.

If the parties are of such a kind as to be conceived in a number greater than two, *ca* should be used after *mag*.

The two brothers.	Ang magcapatid.
The two companions.	Ang magcasamà.
The two friends.	Ang magcaibigan.

If the parties are more than two, *ca* should be repeated.

More than two brothers.	Magcacapatid.
,, ,, ,, companions.	Magcacasamà.
.. .. .. friends.	Magcacaibigan.

Correlative nouns are expressed by *mag* prefixed to the principal correlative.

Father and child.	Magamá.
Mother and child.	Mag-inà.
Father or mother and son or daughter-in-law.	Magbianán.
Master and servant.	Magpañginóon.

Hence these compound nouns may be verbalized in reference to the secondary party.

Paul is a devoted son. (that is to say, he knows how to honor his parents)	Si Pablo,i, marúnong magamá.
Patrick is not a devoted son to his mother.	Hindí marúnong mag-inà Si Patricio.
To keep a mother-in law is a disagreeable thing.	Mahírap ang magbianán.

If t e second correlative is named conjointly with the principal one, the latter is prefixed by *mag* and the former put in the possessive case.

Jesus and His Mother.	Mag-inà ni Jesus.
Flora and her father-in-law.	Magbianán ni Flora.
Peter and his father.	Mag-amá ni Pedro.

Mag denotes totality with some roots importing time.

The whole day, throughout the day, all the day long.	Maghapon.
All the night long, the whole night.	Magdamag.

Mag is prefixed to verbal roots of the first and second conjugations to form the verbal noun signifying the agent or doer. The first syllable of the root should be repeated as if to form the future tense.

Farmer, laborer, husbandman.	Magsasacà
Robber.	Magnanácao.

Man, is another important prefix. *Man*, drops the *n* ang causes the same changes in the first letter of the root it joins to, as have been explained for it as a verbal conjugating particle.

Man, as has been said, if joined to a root denoting a unity of measure, forms distributive numeral expressions of the standard unity.

Twenty five cents' money piece.	Cahati.
Twenty five cents each, at twenty five cents each.	Mañgahati.

Dollar.	Piso.
One dollar each.	Mamiso.
Real.	Sicápat.
One real each, at one real each.	Manicápat.
Half real.	Sicolò, sicaualò.
Half real each.	Manicolo.
Yard, ell.	*Bara.* (corr. from Sp. word *vara.*)
One yard each.	Mamara.
Peck, ganta.	Salop.
One peck each.	Manalop.
Bushel.	Cabán.
One bushel each.	Mañgabán.
Palm. (a measure of length from the thumb to the little finger extended).	Dangcal.
One palm each.	Manangcal.
Fathom.	Dipà.
One fathom each.	Mandipà.
Inch.	Sandali.
One inch each.	Manandáli.
Hundred.	Daán.
One hundred each.	Manaán.

Man is more proper and ussual than *mag* to express with a verbal root the agent or doer, especially if trade or habitual engaging in the action is meant.

To sew.	Tailor.	Tahi.	Mananahi.
To write.	Writer.	Súlat.	Manunúlat.
To weave.	Weaver.	Habi.	Manhahabi.
To redeem.	Redeemer.	Tubós.	Manonobos.

To spin.	Spinner.	Súlid.	Manunúlid.
To solder.	Solderer, gold-beater.	Hínang.	Manhihínang.
To foresay, to foretell.	Sooth-sayer.	Hola.	Manhohola.
To reap, to mow.	Reaper.	Gapas.	Mangagapas.
To tempt.	Tempter.	Tucsò.	Manunucsò
To conquer.	Conquerer.	Talo.	Mananalo

Man also comes before a root denoting the instrument through which something is got at, or. before that of a thing to be got at in a customary or mercenary way, forming the verbal noun or the agent engaged in the trade.

Saw.	Sawer, sawyer.	Lagari,	Manlalagarí.
Goods, merchandise.	Tradesman.	Calácal.	Mañgañgalácal.
Sea.	Seaman.	Dágat.	Mananágat.
Fish.	Fisherman.	Isdá.	Mañgiñgisdá.
Dog.	Hunter with a dog.	Aso.	Mañgañgaso.
Medicine, root, radix.	Quack, physician.	Gamot.	Mangagámot.

Mapag adheres to a verbal root to form, like *man*, the verbal noun for the agent or doer, if the action is represented as occasional or it is of such a nature as not to appear as a mercenary or life-supporting one.

To draw interest from, to invest money on interest.	Usurer, griper.	Pagtubò.	Mapagpatubò.
To grant, granting	Bountiful, liberal, frank.	Biyaya.	Mapagbiyaya.
Respecting, honoring.	Obedient.	Pitagan.	Mapagpitagan.
To elate.	Overbearing.	Palalo.	Mapagpalalo.
Destroying.	Destructor.	Sira.	Mapagsira.
Scoffing.	Scoffer, jeerer.	Libac.	Mapaglibac.
Jesting.	Jester.	Biro.	Mapagbiró.
Lavishing.	Squanderer.	Acsayá.	Mapagacsayá.
Observing.	Observer.	Masid.	Mapagmasid.
Grudging.	Detractor.	Bolong.	Mapagbolong.

To get a morsel stopped in the throat.	Mahirin.
He had a fin (thorn) stuck in his throat.	Mahirinan siyá nang tinic.
To become, to be proper.	Mabágay.
Do you think is it proper for a girl to go alone about the streets?	¿Ang ísip mo bagá ay nababágay sa isàng dalaga, ang paglácad na mag-isà sa mañga lansañgan.?
To hold, to be sufficient.	Magcasiya.
To mistake, to err, to make a mistake.	Magcamalí.

Maguin, may be made to denote doubt or chance.

Will it be perchance true.?	¿Maguiguing totoò cayá iyáng.?
Why might not that be true.?	¿Sáan di maguiguintotoò ñga iyán.?
After a certain number of days.	Nang maguing-iláng árao.
When one month may be elapsed.	Cun maguing-isàng bouan na.
To meddle with.	Manhimasoc. (from pásoc).
Why do you meddle to look into other people's business.?	¿Baquin mo pinanhihimasocan ang búhay nang ibàng tauò.?

To laugh more and more.	Táua nang táua.
He prays more and more.	Dasal nang dasal siyá.
To walk and ever to walk.	Lalácad nang lalácad.
Read without rest.	Bumasà ca nang bumasà.
Repeat constantly the name of God.	Ang Dios nang Dios ang uicáin mo.
They constantly call me, as if there were no other but me.	Acó nang acó ang tinatáuag nilà, díua,i, ualáng ibà cundí acó.
I mean, I say.	Sa macatouir.
The Almighty, that is to say, God.	Ang Macapangyarihan sa lahat, sa macatouir, ang Dios.
So to say, as it were.	Alaláong, alaláong bagá, cun bagá sa.
The soul, the vital principle as it were.	Ang calolóua, alaláong, ang dili baga nang búhay.

The diversity of meanings which the pronoun *anó* may embody are very important and we subjoin some illustrations thereof.

What.?	¿Anò? ¿anò bagá?
What is your business here.?	¿Aanò ca ritò? ¿ungmaanò ca ritò?
What is his business there.?	¿Aanò siyá róon?
What is the matter with Peter that he cries so much.?	¿Inaanò bagá si Pedro, nag–iiyac siyá paganóon?
They do nothing to him.	Hindí siyá inaano.
And what does that matter to you.?	¿Anhín mo bagá iyán? ¿anóng masaquit sa iyò?
What do I need that book for.? what is that book to me.?	¿Anhin co iyáng libro?
How.?	¿Paanò?
What will become of me when I have no money.?	¿Mapapaanò bagá acó cun acó,i, ualáng salapí?
What has happened to him on his falling down, what was the issue of his fall.?	¿Napaanò bagá siyá sa caniy.ng pagcahólog?
See whether he was hurt, inquire whether anything has been the matter with him.	Alamín mo cun napaanò siyá.
Do you know how his handwriting is.?	¿Naalaman mo bagá cun papaanò ang caniyàng pagtític?
To what purpose more comment.?	¿Paganhín saysayin?
Well then, as I was saying	Ay anò,i, ...
What else.? what more.?	¿Anò pa ñga?

SIXTY FIRST EXERCISE.

Who are those two women.? They are sisters-in-law. Who are those people.? They are the parents of this child. Who is that couple sitting there.? They are wife and husband. Are those two persons brothers.? They are brothers. Are those three boys companions.? They are companions. And these two, are friends.? They are friends. Did the father and the son go to church.? The father and the son, the master as well as the servant went to church this morning. Are John and his mother here.? It is Mary and her father that are here. Did you take a walk yesterday.? I was walking all the day long. Were you at the neighbour's last night.? I was there the whole night. Has the husbandman come.? He has. Has the robber been found out.? No. How much shall I pay these weavers.? Pay them at one dollar each. How much cloth did he give them.? He gave one yard each. How much rice did every one of them receive.? They received a bushel each. How many pecks of rice did he sell to every reaper.? He sold them one peck each. Is your friend a tailor.? No, he is a writer. Who was the redeemer of mankind.? Jesus Christ was the redeemer of mankind. Did you see the spinner.? No. I saw the solderer. Where is the sawyer.? The sawyer is at the tradesman's. Is he a fisherman.? No, he is a hunter with dogs. What has the physician said.? He ordered the sailor to take a hot bath. Is this man a griper.? He is a squanderer. Is our neighbour's son obedient.? He is not obedient, but rather overbearing, and a detractor. Are you then a scoffer.? I am not a mocker, but an observer. Can that bottle hold one pint.? It cannot hold one pint. What has happened to the priest.? He made a mistake. Will what the American said to us prove true.? It may perhaps be true. Why do you meddle to converse with my neighbour's servants.? Because they do nothing but call ever for me. Why does the tradesman do nothing but walking.? Because he is a wanderer. What do you order me to do.? Read and read again. Why do you not pray.? Because my master is ever calling me. What is done to you.? I am always laughed at by these bakers. What do you want that pin for.? I want it to clean my teeth. How is the daughter of the writer.? She is already well.

SIXTY SECOND LESSON.
YCAANIM NA POUO,T, DALAUANG PAGARAL.

PARTICLES FORMING SUBSTANTIVES AND ADJECTIVES. (continued)

PA. PAG. PAGCA. PALA. PAN.

Pa is prefixed to a noun or verbal root indicative of such thing or action as can be assigned to a person, to form verbal nouns denoting contents or the portion thus assigned to or handed over by an agent. The change or dropping of the first letters of the root also takes place sometimes in this kind of composition.

Punishment, pe-nance.	Penalty inflicted.	Dusâ.	Parusà.
Inheritance.	Legacy.	Mana.	Pamana.
Marrow. flesh, contents.	The contents, what is written on a paper.	Lamán.	Palamán.
Tumor, abscess.	Swelling.	Bagá.	Pamagá.
New.	Offering of the first fruits, tithe.	Bagó.	Pamagò.
Food kept from the previous night for the morning.	Breakfast.	Báhao.	Pamáhao.
House.	Household furniture, chattels.	Báhay.	Pamáhay.
Note, registry.	Poll, a record of inhabitants.	Tandá.	Pamandá.
To carry.	Load, remittance, sending.	Dalà.	Padalá.
To conceal.	Thing concealed.	Tago.	Patago.
To borrow things.	Thing borrowed.	Hiram.	Pahiram.

As for the government of sentences in which a noun of this kind enters, the agent should be put in the possessive case, the thing object of the action, if it is expressed, in the nominative, and the person to whom it is apportioned, in the dative. The following examples will illustrate the rule.

I bequeath this to my nephew.	Pamana co itò sa aquing pamangquín.
This was bequeathed to me by my father.	Ytò,i, pamana sa aquin nang amá co
What I do is a penance inflicted on me by the priest.	Ang guinagauá co,i, parusà sa aquin nang parè.
This book I borrowed from my mother..	Ytóng libro i, pahiram sa aquin ni inà.
That is what I made him carry.	Yaò,i, ang padalà co sa caniyà.

If *pa* is prefixed to a root expressive of a certain manner of placing, the posture, without any reference whatever to the cause, is expressed.

Seated. (status)	Paupó.
Standing.	Patindig.
Laid down.	Pahigá.
Lengthwise.	Pahaba.
Sidewise, incidentally.	Pataguilid.
Side–across.	Pahalang.
Knelt down.	Palobod.
Face downwards.	Pataob.
Face upwards.	Patihaya.

But if such posture is represented as the effect of some cause and stress is laid on the latter, *pa* should be prefixed by *na*.

He fell face–downwards.	Naparapá siyá.
I fell down and remained seated.	Napaupó acó.

Pag has already been fully treated of as the proper prefix to form the verbal nouns expressive of the action in *um* and *mag* conjugations, the first syllable of the root, for the latter. being repeated as has been explained.

The eating, the action of eating.	Ang pagcáin.
The killing.	Ang pagpatáy.
The weeping.	Ang pagtañgis.
The weeping much, the action of weeping hard.	Ang pagtatañgis.
The giving.	Ang pagbibigáy.
The throwing away.	Ang pagtatapon.

Pag, as a particle forming. either alone or with *sa* preceding. adverbial expressions of time, has also been so fully explained in foregoing lessons as to dispense with further explanations.

On his writing.	Sa pagsúlat niyà.
After my reading the book.	Pagbasà co nang libro. or, pagcabasà, etc.
On my finishing the work.	Pagtapus co nang trabajo.

By the *an* passive with *na* prefixed to a root of a thing or action of anything capable of being exchanged for or of bringing about profit in return, expressions indicative of the way by which the gain has been come at. are formed.

This money I came at by serving. (rendering menial services).	Napaglicoran co itòng salapí.
This money he got at by his selling rice.	Napagbigasan niyà itòng salapí.

Pagca, is for intransitive involuntary actions, what *pag* is for transitive or for intransitive, but voluntary ones.

The dying.	Ang pagcamatáy.
The falling.	Ang pagcahólog.
The stumbling.	Ang pagcatísod.
The slipping down.	Ang pagcadulás.
The sleeping.	Ang pagcatúlog.

When *pagca* is prefixed to an active verbal root or to a voluntary action, it expresses manner. mode, fashion.

Your fashion of walking.			Ang pagcalacad mo.
Your manner of pronouncing.			Ang pagcanica mo.
Their manner of expression.			Ang pagcasabi nila.
Her handwriting, penmanship.			Ang pagcasúlat or pagcatític niyà.

Pagca builds up abstract nouns expressive of what constitutes the essence, the innermost nature constitutive of a quality.

Divinity.			Ang pagcadios.
The attributes of God.			Ang pagcadios nang Dios.
What is inherent in mankind.			Ang pagcatauò.
Manhood.			Ang pagcalalaqui.
Womanhood.			Ang pagcababaye.
Philosophy.			Ang pagcadúnong.

Pala is prefixed to a verbal or nominal root denoting an action or thing capable of being converted into, or of being object of, a vice, to form adjectival nouns expressive of the habitual indulgence in such vice.

Idol.	Heathen.	Anito.	Palaanito.
Curse.	Curser, mordacious.	Sumpá.	Palasumpá.
Litigation, law-suit.	Barrator.	Osap.	Palaosap.
Drinking.	Drunkard.	Inom.	Palainom nang álac.
Eating.	Glutton.	Cáin.	Palacáin.
Love.	Wooer.	Sintà.	Palasintà.
Chat, speaking.	Chatterer.	Osap.	Palaósap.
Quarrelling.	Peevish, quarelsome.	Auay.	Palaáuay.

Pan, prefixed to a verbal root capable of admitting of an instrument for the action or for the thing to be made by, expresses the instrument, when the latter is not indicated by *y* in the manner already explained.

Pan, being the passive particle for *man,* drops *n* and causes the first letter of the root to undergo the same changes which have been spoken of in *man* conjugation. It is by paying attention to the signification and character of the root, that *pan* derivatives can, in some cases, be distinguished from those formed with *pa*.

To seal.	Seal.	Tatac.	Panatac.
Hole.	Auger.	Butas.	Pamutas.
To mow.	Sickle.	Gapas.	Pangapas.
To shave.	Razor.	Ahit.	Pañgahit.
To dig.	Pickax, hoe.	Húcay.	Panhúcay.
To cart.	Pannier, basket.	Hácot.	Panhácot.
Stick, club.	Cudgeling-stick.	Palo.	Pamalo.
To rub.	Dishclout.	Pahir.	Pamahir.
To cling.	Hook.	Cáuit.	Pañgáuit.
To pinch.	Pincers.	Sípit.	Panípit.
To sprinkle, to make aspersion.	Water-sprinkler.	Uisic.	Pañguísic.
To sound.	Sounding lead.	Taroc.	Panaroc.
To scratch.	Scratcher.	Cámot.	Pañgámot.
To strike.	Hammer.	Pocpoc.	Pamocpoc.
To write.	Pen.	Súlat.	Panúlat.
To tie.	Tying rope.	Tali.	Panali or pantali.
Dash, line drawn with a pen.	Ruler for drawing a straight line.	Guhit.	Pangúhit.

If *pan* is prefixed to a root itself an instrument. *pan*, then, has the same import as *pinaca*, that is to say, what substitutes for that instrument, is formed.

| Auger. | What serves as an auger. | Licop. | Panlicop. |
| Saw. | What substitutes for a saw. | Lagarí. | Panlagarí |

Prime, the most excellent or valuable part of a thing; intensity, the culminating point of an action.	Salocoy.
Do do do. (abstract)	Casalocoyan.
In the prime of.	Sa casalocoyan.
To be in the prime of youth.	Masacasalocoyan nang cabatáan.
The time in which the sowing is in full swing.	Casalocoyan nang patatanim.

The same for thrashing.	Casalocoyan nang pagguiic.
Your child is now at the point of growth.	Ang anac mo,i, nasacasalocoyan ñgayón nang paglaqui.
His sister is now in the prime of life.	Ang caniyáng capatid na babaye ay nasacasalocoyan ñgayón nang cabatáan.

SIXTY SECOND EXERCISE.

What penalty did the judge inflict upon you.? I have been fined twenty dollars. What legacy did you receive from your uncle.? He bequeathed me a thousand dollars. Is that true.? These words were the contents of his letter. What kind of food is that.? This food is for my breakfast. What has Mr. Such-a-one sent.? This is what he sent. Is that auger yours.? No, it has been borrowed from the carpenter. How shall I do the work.? You shall do it sitting. (seated) How should this be cut.? Cut it lengthwise. How shall I pray.? You should pray knelt down. Is he up or lain down.? He is lain down. How is his manner of speaking.? His manner of speaking is by stuttering. How is the essence of God.? The essence of God is incomprehensible to man. Is he a believer.? No, he is an idolater. Is your friend a drunkard.? He is not a drunkard, but he is a glutton. Is your cousin a wooer.? He is a wooer and a chatterer. Is he also peevish.? He is peevish and a barrater. What is that your writer has in his hand.? It is a seal. Is it not an auger.? No, it is a razor. Where did the servant put the dishclout.? He put it together with the pincers. What are you going to do with this sickle.? I am going to mow grass. Who has found the carpenter's hammer.? Peter found it in the pannier. Who has the sounding lead.? The sailor has it and the scratcher as well. Where is my pen.? Your pen and the hook have been carried away. Have you no ruler for ruling this paper.? I have one. Where is the tying rope for these logs of wood.? The tying rope is in the house.

PARTICLES FORMING SUBSTANTIVES AND ADJECTIVES. (continued)

PINACA. SANG. TAG. TAGA. TIG. YCA.

Pinaca is prefixed to nominal or adjectival roots, forming compounds expressive of what serves as a substitute or is reputed to stand for the thing or quality signified by the root. The following instances will better illustrate the matter.

Boiled rice stand for bread with natives.	Ang canin ang siyáng pinacatinápay nang mañga tagalog.
We consider you our leader.	Ycáo ang pinacapono namin.
The lion is considered the king of animals.	Pinacahari ang *leon* (Sp.) nang mañga háyop.
Sin is reputed to be the greatest evil.	Ang pinacamalaquì sa lahat, na casamáa,i, ang casalanan.
What accidentally serves as a broom.	Pinacaualís.
He who stands for a parent.	Ang pinacamagúlang.
He whom somebody reputes as his lord.	Pinacapañginóon.
What serves as a pen in case of need.	Pinacapanúlat.
Anybody acting for a servant.	Ang pinacaalila.
The mistress, the minion, anybody whom one reputes as husband or wife.	Ang pinacaasáua.

Sang is but a determinated form of *isà*; the latter may stand alone; *sang*, is always joined to the thing or unity determined or counted.

It precedes the first unities of the decimal system of numeration.

A denary.	Sang pouò.
A hundred.	Sang dáan.
A thousand.	Sang libò.
A ten thousand.	Sang lacsà.
A hundred thousand.	Sang yota.
A million.	Sang pouong yota, sang áñgao-áñgao.

It expresses totality, length of time.

He came one day.	Naparitò siyá isàng árao.
All the day long.	Sang árao.
For a whole hour.	Sang oras.
Throughout the week.	Sang lingo.
All the month round.	Sang bóuan.
The length of the year.	Sang taón.

It denotes the contents of some thing, not the vessel or continent.

A *tinaja* (large earthen pot) of, or, for water.	Y-àng tapayang túbig or sa túbig.
One tinajaful of cocoa–nut, oil.	Sang tapayang lañgís.
One bottle of wine.	Sang boteng álac.
One spoonful of honey.	Sang *cucharang* (Sp.) polot.

Sang precedes nouns of towns, meeting–places or resorts to indicate the whole population or attendance.

All the inhabitants of Manila.	Sang Maynila.
The whole population of Cebú.	Saug Sebú.
The full attendance at church.	Sang simbahan.
The spectators of a play.	Sang teatro.
The whole offspring.	Sang anacan.
The litter, the number of pigs farow-ed at once.	Sang anacan bábuy.
Brood of a she-dog.	Sang anacan aso.
The whole crew of a ship.	Sang dáuong.
The people sailing on a pirogue.	Sang bangca.

Collective nouns formed with *ca* prefixed and *an* or *han* suffixed admit of *sang* before to indicate totality.

The full house, all the tenants.	Sang bahayan.
The whole town, all the villagers.	Sang bayanan.
All the heavenly legions.	Sang calañgitan.
The whole of mankind.	Sang catauohan.
All the world. (people).	Sang calibotan.
The whole of Christendom.	Sang cacristianohan.
The whole Archipelago.	Sang capoloan.
All the Saints in Heaven.	Sang calañgitan Santos.

———

Tag is but a contracted form of *taga*. It serves to form the seasons, monsoons or the prevalent time of any atmospherical occurrences.

Spring.	Tagárao.
Summer.	Tagbisi, tagárao, tag-init.
Autumn.	Tagolán, (rainy season)
Winter.	Tagguínao, taglamig. (cold season).
Prevailing time of the south–west wind monsoon.	Taghabágat.
The portion of the year during which north-east winds prevail.	Tagamihan.
Space of time during which typhoons are most frequent.	Tagbaguió.

———

Taga, besides the sense of origin and the others which have been already treated of, forms, like *man*, frequentative verbal nouns, generally indicating the trade the person is engaged in for a salary, and is put before verbs.

To tend, to watch.	Watchman, tend-er.	Tanod.	Tagatanod.
To boil rice for food.	Cook, man charg-ed with boiling the rice.	Sáing.	Tagapagsáing.
To watch over, to be on the lookout for.	Sentry.	Bantáy.	Tagapagbantáy.
To look out, to be careful.	Overseer.	Iñgat.	Tagapag-íñgat.
To haunt.	Haunter.	Ligáo.	Tagaligáo.

| Herdsman, swine keeper. (for other people's herd). | Tagatanor nang bábuy. |

Tig forms, with the cardinal numerals, the distribute numerals, the first syllable of the cardinal being repeated from five upwards in the way already explained. It differs from man in the latter being only applied to unities of measure, while tig is but for numbers.

One each.	Tig-isà.
Two each.	Tigdalauà, tigalauà.
Five to every one.	Tiglilimà.
Ten to each.	Tigsangpouò, tigsasangpouò.

Yca=ica, prefixed to numeral cardinals converts them into ordinals, the first three being irregular.

The first.		Ang onà, ang naonà
The second.		Ang ycalauà.
The third.		Ang ycatlò.
Four.	Fourth.	Apat.	Ycaápat, ycápat.
Five.	Fifth.	Limà.	Ycalimà.
Ten.	Tenth.	Sang póuo.	Ycapóuò, ycasangpouò.
Twenty three.	Twenty third.	Dalauàng póuo,t, tatlò.	Ycadalauàng pouò,t, tatlò.

Man, my friend. (used to attract attention).	Mama. (colloquial name given to any male person, generally older than the speaker).
Woman, madam. (do do do).	Alí (do do do for female persons).
Good fellow, come here, please.	Mama, halí ñga cayó.
Good woman, madam, stop, please.	Alí, hintáy po cayó.
My boy, my child.	Bungsò. Ytóy. Otóy. colloquial names for male children.
My girl, my child.	Yning. Ytáy. (do do for female ones).
Colloquial term, pretty name.	Paláyao.
Linage, race.	Angcán.
Nobility, race.	Lahi.
Come here, my girl.	Yning, hali ca ñga.
Uncle Tom.	Si mamang Tomás.
Aunt Emma.	Si alíng Iláy.
In or at the Autumn, in or at the rainy season.	Sa tagolán.
When do you sow your rice fields.?	¿Cailán ytinatanim ninyò ang inyòng pálay.?
At the rainy season, we are now still in the dry season.	Sa tagolán, ñgayón tayo,i, na sa tagárao pa.
Where are you from.?	¿Taga sáan ca.?
I am from Malabon.	Taga Malabón acó.
Where are these men from.?	Taga sáan bagá itòng mañga tauo.?
They are highlanders.	Taga bondoc silá.
Is your servant from Ilocos.?	¿Taga Iloco bagá ang iyòng alila.?
No, my servant is from here, from Manila.	Hindí, ang aquing alila,i, taga ritò, taga Maynila.

DIMINUTIVE VERBS.

If an action capable of a scurrilous performance is carried away from its natural sense so as to be made denote fiction, slowness, mockery or awkward execution, the verb, in Tagalog, is said to be in a diminutive form. This manner of representing the action, which is very common among natives, is generally made by repeating the entire verbal root, whatever else refers to the mechanism of the conjugation being preserved.

To walk.	Lumácad.
To walk in a scurrilous manner.	Lumacadlácad.
To say, to speak.	Magüica.
To speak and pronounce indistinctly like little children.	Magüicauica.
To sleep.	Matólog.
To slumber, or, to feign sleeping.	Matologtólog.
Carried, taken.	Dinalà.
Carried and brought in again and over again.	Dinaladalà.
To write.	Sumúlat, magsúlat.
To scribble.	Sumúlatsúlat, magsúlatsúlat.
Te eat.	Cumáin, magcáin.
To eat very little as sick persons do; to eat and slaver as babies.	Cumaincáin, magcaincáin.
To weep.	Tumañgis, magtañgis.
To whine.	Tumañgistañgis, magtañgistañgis.
To rain.	Umolán.
To drizzle.	Umolanolán.
To build houses.	Magbáhay.
To raise little houses as children do.	Magbaybahayan.

To carry off a prey.	Dumaguit.
The sick person can already walk a little, can make some steps.	Ang mey saquit nacacalacadlácad na.
The child begins to mutter some words.	Ang bata,i, naguiuicauica na.
Do not trust him, he only feigns to sleep.	Houag mo siyáng paniualáan, nagtotologtologán siyá lámang.
Why are you always taking the book in and out.?	¿Báquit mo dinadaladalà ang libro.?
The male and the female child write each other little love-letters.	Ang dalauàng bata nagsusúlatsulatan nang palasintahan.
My child begins to eat, to swallow some food.	Ang bata co.i, cungmacaincáin na.
Her baby is always whining.	Ang caniyàng bungsò.i, palaguing nagtatañgistañgis.
The children are making little houses out of earth in the garden.	Ang mañga bata,i, nagbabahaybahayan nang lupa sa halamanan.

SIXTY THIRD EXERCISE.

What stands for bread in the meals of natives.? Boiled rice is for them what bread is for us. Who will stand for your leader now.? We shall take the priest as our leader. What should be reputed as the greatest of evils.? Sin is to be reputed as the greatest evil. What did your servant make use of as a broom to sweep the door-sill.? He made a cane serve as a broom to sweep it. Why do you respect your uncle so much.? I respect him so much, for he stands as a father to me. What stands for fork in the manner natives swallow food. Their fingers stand for forks. How did you write the letter.? I had no steel-pen at hand and made this quill serve as a pen. In what condition did he hold his nephew.? He considered him as a menial servant. How long were you at Manila.? I was there a whole day. Have you waited for me a long time.? I waited for you a full hour. How long is he going to stay with us.? He is going to be here one entire week. How many years' rent is our farmer going to pay.? He is going to pay one year's. What did the Manila population do many years ago when they were visited with an earthquake.? The whole Manila population went away to the open country. How many puppies does the brood consist of.? It consists of seven dogs. Where is the ship.? The ship sank, all the crew were drowned. How many passengers of the pirogue came on shore.? All the people came on shore. Are there no inhabitans in this town.? All the villagers are now attending mass. Has this house no tenants.? All the tenants died. Who redeemed mankind.? Jesus Christ redeemed all mankind and he is revered by all christians. Did the plague spread largely.? Plague spread about the whole Archipelago... What season are we now in.? We are now in summer time. Do you like winter.? I don't like winter, it is a very cold season. In what months of the year do the north-east monsoon winds prevail.? North-east winds prevail in the Philippines from November to June. In what part of the year do typhoons occur most frequently in Manila.? From the middle of October until the end of December. How much salary does he pay to the herder of his cattle.? He pays his herder ten dollars monthly. How did he distribute the candles.? He gave one to every man; two, to every woman; and three, to every child. Who was the first man.? Adan was the first man and Eve the first woman. What book is that.? It is the third volume.

SIXTY FOURTH LESSON.
YCAANIM NA POUO,T, APAT NA PAGARAL.

THE COLLOQUIAL LANGUAGE.

To the many rules of syntax and illustrations of Tagalog construction hitherto given, it will be well to append a few notes on colloquial Tagalog which are suggested by a consciousness of some of the common errors into which Europeans are apt to fall.

FIRST. Get rid of the notion that it is necessary in Tagalog to express invariably by nouns or pronouns the agents and objects of the actions spoken of. Sentences in Tagalog are arranged in a more impersonal and elliptical manner than in the civilised languages of Europe.

Give me.	Big–ián acó.
Tell him.	Sabihin sa caniyà.
Read it.	Basahin.
Don't say it.	Houag sabihin.
Give it back.	Ysaolí mo.
Let us give them back to him.	Saolían natin.
I think, I believe.	Acala co,i,..... (my guess is).
He wishes, he is willing.	Ibig niyà,i,..... (his desire is).
It seems.	Díua,i,..... (the appearance is).
They say.	Ang sabí, ang balita,i,.... (the report is).
I am told, people tell me.....	Ang sabi nang mañga tauò sa aquin ay....
I hear that she is going to be married.	Ang sabi,i, na siyá,i, magaasáua.
I like walking better than driving.	Mabutì pa ang paglácad sa *pagcacarruage* (Sp.) (Walking is better than driving).

Even in scolding others, natives, sometimes, adopt such an indirect mode of address as to dispense with the Tagalog equivalent for "you", that should be used in similar English sentences.

Are you mute,? why don't you answer.?	¿Pipi bagá itòng bata,? ¿at di siyá sungmasagot.? (Lit. is this boy mute?; why does he not answer.?
How stupid you are.! can't you see the cats eating the cheese.?	¡Abáa!, itòng tauòng itò. ¿Di niyá namamasdán na ang quiso,i, pinupusa.? (Lit. Oh!, this boy!. Does he not give heed to the cheese being nibbled at by cats.?
What a lazy fellow you are.!	!Ayáa, !matamad na matamad itòng tauó.

SECOND, Learn to employ the various passive forms of the verb and try to overcome the difficulties of construction peculiar to these forms.

The rats ate up the candles.	Ang mañga candila,i, dinagá.
Wild boars use to uproot hemp-producing trees.	Ang mañga ponong abacá,i, inoongcal nang bábuy damó.
To officers of the Board of Health set fire to the nipa houses and prevented the plague from spreading.	Pinasonog nang mañga *sanitario* (Sp.) ang mañga báhay na páuid at hinahárang ang sálot na cumúlat.

THIRD. Bear in mind the distinction between the sense given to an intransitive verb by the particle *um* and that which is imparted by prefixing *mag*. *Um*, expresses a state; *mag*, an action. Such verb, for instance, as "to swim" may be considered either as descriptive of the condition of the person who swims or as of some circumstance of the action of swimming. Hence. *lumañgóy*, "to swim"; *maglañgóy*. "to take along something in swimming". On the other hand, to say, *tumañgis* is to put more stress on the person who weeps, while *magtañgis*, is more in reference to the cause of weeping; *sungmusúlat siyá*, refers more to the manual action of his penmanship; *nagsusúlat siyá*, lays stress on the thought he conveys to other people in writing; *bumauas* or *mauas*, "to waste, to lessen by taking out a portion out of a heap for the subject"; *magbauas* "to diminish by giving a portion to others, but practically, the difference here is not great.

To following verbs will add to the illustrations given above.

To walk.	Lumácad.
To carry along something in walking.	Maglácad.
To fly.	Lumipad.
To fly to and fro.	Maglipad.
To leap.	Lumocsò.
To rush on, to leap along with.	Maglocsò.
To fall back.	Umòrong.
To withdraw, to take back.	Magòrong.
To dive.	Sumísid.
To dive for.	Magsísid.
To sit down.	Umupó.
To sit down. (many)	Magopó.

FOURTH. Try to employ the specific instead of the generic word for the action to be described, when, as is generally the case in Tagalog, there is a verb for that particular manner of action. It may be possible to make one's self understood by using *gauá* and adding the complementary term for every kind of work, but it is much better to employ the appropriate term for the particular manner or object of working, as seen in the following illustrations.

Working, doing.	Gauá. (root-word) (generic).
To make (something) speedily.	Magmadalí.
To make, to do something superficially.	Humapáo.
To do carefully.	Lumánay.
To make carefully.	Maglánay.
To do, to practice, to train, to exercise.	Magsánay.
To make something slowly or little by little.	Maghinay-hínay, mag-inot-inot, magotay-otày
To work by night, to wake.	Lumámay.
To make something by night.	Maglámay.
To do at random.	Magpasumala.
To do something willingly.	Magcusa.
To make something. (many at the same time)	Mañgagsabáy.
To make something again.	Bumagò.
To work manually.	Cumimot.

To make a retraction.	Tumaliuacás.
To do harm.	Magpañganyaya.
To work earnestly.	Magsáquit, magsumáquit.
To work by the job.	Magpaquiáo.
To make salt.	Magtásic, magasín.

This, besides the common way of prefixing *mag* to a root expressing any thing that can be made, as explained in *mag* conjugation.

To break, to fracture, to smash.	Bumásag, másag, magbásag.
To destroy.	Sumira. (generic)
To split ,to cleave.	Mali, magbali.
To rip, to unseam.	Tumastás, magtastás.
To rend, to tear.	Gumisí.
To break, to divide, to separate by using one's teeth.	Ñgumalot.
To break some metallic object.	Bumigtal.
To break asunder.	Bumiac.
To break asunder rattans.	Manhimatir.
To crush, to break by collision.	Magpoçol.
To crack. (as a nut or an egg-shell)	Magpisá.
To pound husk rice.	Bumayò.
To part, (a line), to disunite. (trans)	Pumatid, matir, magpatid; lumagot, maglagot.
To part (intrans.) to be disunited.	Mapatid, malagot.

To strike.	Pumocpoc, mocpoc, magpocpoc (generic).
To strike, to beat, to cudgel.	Pumalo, humampás.
To knock about, to deal out blows with a stick.	Humanbalos.
To strike with the open hand, to slap.	Tumampal.
To strike with the fist, to box.	Sumuntoc.
To strike, to beat (as wool, cotton etc.) for cleansing or fulling; to shake clothes clean.	Pumagpag; magpagpag. (intensive)
To flap, to applaud, to clap.	Pumacpac, magpacpac.
To strike, to pound.	Pumitpit, magpitpit.

To throw away, to cast off.	Magtapon. (generic)
To throw someting to the ground, to dash.	Maghólog.
To throw up into the air.	Magtálang.
To thrust, to dart a spear.	Magborlong, sumibat.
To pelt, to throw stones at, to hurl.	Humaguís, maghaguís.
To throw about, to scatter.	Magbulagsac.
To cast up, to vomit, to emit.	Sumucá, magsucà.
To throw splints at.	Magbalibang, magbahbat.
To shoot at, to aim at.	Tumurlá.

To look at.	Tumiñgin. (generic.)
To look at for.	Cumita.
To look back.	Lumiñgon.
To look at something in astonishment, to behold, to gaze at.	Panóor.
To look sideways at.	Sumuliap.
To look upwards.	Tumiñgalá.

To look at from afar, to sight.	Tumanáo.
To stare. to look at fixedly.	Tumítig.

FIFTH. Try to get accustomed to the use of the radical alone, or the radical with the passive particle in the second persons of the imperative, leaving tone or gesture to complement the meaning.

Run.	Tacb'.
Finish.	Tapús.
Take. (it, them, some.) } (what is at hand, sight.) }	Cunin.
Kill. (it, them.) do	Patayí.
Cast. (it, them.) do	Ytapon.
Look at. (it, them, him, her.)	Tingní, tingnán.
Buy. (it, them.)	Bilhín.
Seize.	Daquip.

SIXTY FOURTH EXERCISE.

What shall I buy for his children.? Buy some toys for them. Shall I send the servant for bread.? Send him. Shall I kill the big cock.? Kill it. What should he do with that money.? Let him return it to him. Do you believe there will be money enough.? I think there will not be sufficient. What does he wish to have.? He wishes to have something to drink. How does he feel.? He seems to be very ill. What did your sisters tell him.? They told him that they will come by six o'clock. What about Mr. Reynolds.? I hear that he is going to start a rice-husking business. Why do you go on foot.? I like better to walk than (to) ride. What do you bring me there.? I bring you some oil. What an idiot you are.! I tell you to bring water, and you bring oil, you are behaving badly and it will serve you right if you got a drubbing. Why are these clothes thus destroyed.? Because they were eaten up by moths. Where is the fruit destroyed by ravens.? I threw it to the swine. What has been spoiled by ants.? The plants of my garden, have been all of them spoiled by ants. and the trees dug up by swine. What does he carry along in walking.? He carries along some food to eat on his way. (journey). What do kites carry off.? Kites carry off chickens. Why is the food so badly cooked.? Because the cook has cooked it in a hurry. Did you read the paper I lent you yesterday.? I did superficially (perused, looked over). How shall I make this translation.? Make it slowly. Do you engage in prayer the whole night.? I pray the whole night. Did she do it willingly.? She did. Is this letter well written.? No, write it again. Did he use a tool to make that.? No, he made it with his hands. Does the carpenter work on wages or by the job.? He works by the job. Did you rip your shirt.? No, I have not yet ripped it. Did Peter tear the book-leaves.? He did. How does your grandmother break the betel nut.? She uses to crack it with her teeth. Will your sister break the ring.? She will. Is the rope parted. It is. Whom did he slap.? He slapped his servant. Why did not my brother shake (flap) his clothes clean.? He had to pound the rice. Why does your child throw away fruits.? He is amusing himself by throwing some in the air. What are those boys doing.? They are hurling stones at your horse. May I take that book.? Take it. Where shall I put these papers.? Throw them away. Where are the birds.? Over there, look at them. Do you wish your friend to buy the horse.? Let him buy it. What are you looking at.? I am looking at the stars on the sky, they shine very brightly. Whom are you looking to see on that window.? I am looking to see my child who was just a while playing with his schoolmates, but I no longer see him. Whom is Pete looking back for.? He is looking back for Mary who remained at the well. What did you see at the theatre.? I beheld there the killing of king Richard the Third. What vere the love—engaged parties doing.? They were looking sideways at each other. Why do you not climb up that tree.? Because I am afraid of your looking upwards at me. From where did you sight the ship.? I sighted her from the summit of that mountain. Why does his sister look fixedly at me.? Because she likes you.

SIXTY FIFTH LESSON.
YCAANIM NA POUO,T, LIMANG PAGARAL.

MANNER OF SUBSTITUTING WORDS FOR THOSE WANTING
IN TAGALOG.

The student will probably be much surprised when at this stage of the work he has not found such abstract terms as are common in modern languages. This lack of specific terms is only natural to every language or dialect in its primitive state. The ancient condition of Tagals and their present comparatively backward state of culture account for such deficiency Every abstract idea of a thing, action or event not occurring to their minds or being presented to their senses, such as they could not be acquainted with in their isolated condition of life before the conquest, has to be conveyed to them by having recourse to Spanish words or through parables or metaphors, while, on the other hand, they have a profusion of words, either of a general or local use, for every shade of meaning of such things and actions as represent their customary dealings and transactions. A fair opportunity offers itself to the learner for exercising his mind by availing himself of the words he is already acquainted with, to convey the notion of such things and acts as have not proper terms of expression in Tagalog. If the speaker is conversant with Spanish and considers that the native whom he is addressing has been initiated in the language or that he has held some intercourse with Spaniards, the former will do well in trying first if by Tagalizing the proper Spanish term for the abstract notion he wants to convey, he succeeds to make himself understood. If he fails, he must then have recourse to such Tagalog words as may best serve his purpose, by using them in the way of parable or definition.

We subjoin sets of words and expressions showing the copiousness of terms for certain things and the scantiness for others, and how the latter may be replaced. In the latter case an English translation, as literal as it can be, of the allegorical Tagalog phrase is added on a third column; little care having been paid to the sense that the student may thus receive more valuable information.

DIFFUSIVENESS.

Rice.	(generical term).	Bigús.
Do.	(containing a great deal of starch).	Malagquit.
Do.	(coming early in the season).	Paunà, paaga.
Do.	(when it has not yet attained a state of maturity).	Malagatas.
Do.	(coming last in the season.)	Pahulì.
Do.	(coming from or resembling that of Camarines.)	Quinamálig.

Rice.	(having agglutinant proper-ties.)	Pirorotong.
Do.	(resembling in shape certain little fish called *dolong*.)	Dinolong.
Do.	(black in colour.)	Tinintá.
Do.	(the ear of which somewhat resembles a flower named *candá*.)	Quinandá.
Do.	(very pointed in shape.)	Quinaráyom. (from *caráyom*, "needle").
Do.	(bearing a downy matter enveloping it.)	Bolohan.
Do.	(a kind of rice, the ear of which abounds with grain.)	Calibo.
Do.	(a kind of rice which seed came from Macan.)	Macán.
Do.	(a kind of rice very white and savory.)	Quinastila.
Do.	(a kind of odoriferous rice, the grain of which resembles anis seeds.)	Sinanquí.
Do.	(a kind of rice resembling in shape a fish named *sombilang*.)	Sinumbilang.
Do.	(a kind of rice flavoring of musk.)	Quinastoli.
Do.	(the grain of which is licelike.)	Tinoma.
Do.	(the plant of which bears resemblance to common reed grass).	Tinalahib.
Do.	(big-eared rice.)	Binatad.
Do.	(a kind of rice of a metallic glitter).	Tinumbaga.
Do.	(a kind of rice, the shoot of which resembles an herb called *bambang*).	Binambang.
Do.	(a king of rice bearing gossamer all over).	Bontot pusa. (cat-tail.) Bontot cabayo. (horse-tail.)
Do.	(roasted rice.)	Sañgag, sinañgag.
Do.	(unclean rice for pigs.)	Pináua.
Do.	(food, boiled rice.)	Cánin, sináing, morisqueta.
Do.	(void rice, empty husk of rice.)	Ipa.
Do.	(roasted green pounded rice.)	Pinípig.

To give, (generical term.)	Bigáy, magbigáy.
To give, to grant permission.	Pahintólot, magpahintólot.
To give the first fruits.	Pamagò.
To give an account, lesson.	Súlit, magpasúlit.
To give money on interest.	Magpatubò.
To give a pledge.	Sanlá, magsanlá.
To give a salary.	Opà, umupà.
To give warning.	Alam, umalam.
To give satisfaction.	Hinauad, manhinauad; magbigáy loób.
To give earnest money in token that a bargain is ratified.	Tampá, tumampá; patiñga, magpatiñga.
To give word, promise.	Pañgaco.
To give on credit.	Magótang, magpaútang.
To give bountifully.	Biyaya, magbiyaya.
To give freely, willingly.	Calóob, magcalóob.
To give, to present with.	Handog, maghandog.

SCANTINESS.

ENGLISH.	TAGALOG.	LITERAL TRANSLATION.
Accident, fit.	Bigláng. saquit.	Sudden evil.
In future.	Sa panahóng haharapin. or darating.	At a time which will be present, at a time to come.
Isolated.	Napaisà.	Left alone.
Common sewer, gutter. gully.	Bangbang na inaagosan nang mañga dumi, at pinaghugasán.	Trench, the place which serves for the filth and the rest of mud flowing.
Mason.	Pandáy batò, mangaga-uá nang báhay na batò.	Stone -artist. maker. of stone houses.
The Koran.	Ang inaaring santong súlat nang mañga turco, o, librong quinapapalam-nán nang mañga cautu-san ni Mahoma.	What is considered as the Holy Scripture of the Turks, or, book in which the commandments of Mohammed are contained. (printed)
Knocking, rap given with the knocker.	Pagtogtog sa pinto.	Sonorous striking at the door.
Reservoir for rain-water.	Pinagtitiponan nang túbig sa olán.	Place where rain water is gathered.
Warehouse.	Báhay o camálig na pinagtatagoan nang sari-sari.	House or construction. the place where several things are concealed.
Auction, judicial sale of property by public auction.	Pagbibilì sa cahayagan nang pagaari na católong at caálam ang Justicia. (Sp.)	Sale in public of property with the assistance and knowledge of justice.
Allocution, address, harangue.	Pananaisay o paháyag, na di malauig, nang pono sa caniyàng mañga sacop.	Account or explanation, not long, from the chief to his subordinates.
Highness. (kink of address.)	Gálang at pagbati sa mañga dugong hari.	Respect and salutation to those of royal blood.
Alveolus or socket of the teeth.	Butas na quinatatamnán nang ñgipin.	Hole which holds the teeth.
Ambidextrous.	Caliuá at canan; tauòng ang caliuá,i, para rin canan.	Left and right; person. the left equally right.
Amnesty.	Patáuad o paglímot nang hari nang caniyàng gálit sa isàng bayan o sa maram ng tauò.	Pardon or forgetting of the King's wrath towards a town or towards many people.
Anathema.	Patatacuil sa Yglesia sa tauòng souail na hung-mahámac nang Caniyàng cautosan.	Expulsion from the Church of (to) the person who is rebellious or who scorns Her commandments.
Anatomy.	Pagbabahagui nang isàng bangcáy nang maquilala ang casangcapan nang catauoán upang tamán ang paggamot.	Division of a cadaver, that the parts of the body may be known and the remedy may be discovered.
Amphibious.	Háyop na nabubúhay sa túbig at sa cati.	Animal that lives in water and on land.

ENGLISH.	TAGALOG.	LITERAL TRANSLATION.
Antediluvian.	Nang di pa nagcacagónao	When there was not yet inundation.
Atheist.	Tauòng aáyao maniuala na may Dios.	Person who refuses to own (trust) there is (one) God.
Bastard.	Anac sa calupáan, anac sa lígao.	Son from lecherousness, adventitious son.
To baptize.	Magbinyag.	To throw water from above.
Bible.	Santong Súlat.	Holy writing.
Library.	Lalaguián nang maraming libro.	Place for many books to be placed.
Bigamy.	Pag-aasáua nang may asáua na.	Marriage of a person being married already.
Biography.	Salitá nang búhay nang iisàng tauò.	Account of the life of only one person.
Vault.	Lañgit-lañgitan.	Little sky.
Botany.	Caronoñgang naoócol sa pagquilala nang pananim.	Knowledge that looks forward to the acquaintance with plants.
Breviary.	Librong dasalan nang mañga Pare.	Book containing the prayers for clergy.
Bull. (an instrument dispatched from the papal chancery.)	Bula. (Sp.) Súlat na gáling sa Papa na quinalalamnán nang caniyàng caloób o hatol.	Writ arising from the Pope in which his mercies or advices are written. (printed).
Letter-box.	Butas na pinaghohologang súlat sa correo.	Hole through which letters are dropped into the post-office.
Cavalry.	Hocbòng sacáy.	Mounted army.
Compositor. (in printing.)	Tauòng nañgañgasíua sa pagsasamà, t, paghahánay nang mañga letra (Sp.) sa limbagan.	Person charged with the joining and combining of the letters in the printing-plant. (place).
Calendar, almanac.	Munting librong quinapapalamnán nang mañga Santo na may capistahan árao-árao at nang pagsícat, pagbilog at pagcatúnao nang bóuan.	Small book where the daily commemoration of the Saints and the rising, full, (rounding) and waning moon are printed.
Chalice.	Copang (Sp.) guintó o pílac na guinagámit sa cagalang-gálang na sacrificio (Sp.) nang misa ó pagaálay sa Dios.	Cup (glass) of gold or silver, used in the sublime sacrifice of mass or offering to God.
Antipope.	Ang ungmañgao sa catongcólang pagcápapa. Catalo o caágao nang Papa. (Sp.)	He who assumes the dignity constitutive of Papacy. Competitor or rival of the Pope.
Antipode.	Tauò patiuaric sa atin ó tungmatahan sa cabilá nang lupang ating catapat.	Person lying in an inverse position to ours, or, living at the other side of the Earth facing ours.
Cannibal, anthropophagi.	Ang cungmacáin nang cápoua tauò.	He who eats his fellow-creatures.
Wardrobe.	Tagoan nang damit.	Concealing place for garments.

ENGLISH.	TAGALOG.	LITERAL TRANSLATION.
Surname.	Ycalauàng pañgalan.	Second name.
Appendix.	Dagdag sa libro.	Addition to a book.
Apoplexy.	Himatáy.	Fit, resemblance of death.
Apostasy.	Pagtalicod sa ating Pañginóon Jesucristo.	Turning the back on Our Lord, Jesus Christ.
Apostle.	*Apostol* (Sp.) Alagad ni Jesucristo.	Disciple of Jesus Christ.
Tariff.	Talaán nang opà, báyad o halagáng táning o tadhaná nang mañga puno.	Advertisement of salary, pay or price fixed or enacted by the rulers.
Archipelago.	Capisanan nang maraming polo.	Gathering of many islands.
Archives.	Tagoan nang mañga mahalagáng casulatan.	Hiding-place for valuable writings.
Rain-bow.	Bahag-hari.	King-hood. (muffle, king loing-cloth.)
Armory.	Báhay o camálig na pinagiiñgatan nang sarisaring sandatà.	House or construction, the place where diversity of weapons are kept.
Harmony.	Cariquitan nang togtog; pagcacaayonayon nang togtog o tinig.	Beautifulnes of sound; conformity of sound.
Architect.	Maestrong marúnong gumauá nang mañga simbahan at báhay na batò.	Master who knows how to make churches and stone-houses.
Promotion.	Pagcataás, pagcasúlong nang catongcolan.	Rising, forwarding in office.
Astronomy.	Caronoñgang ócol sa mañga bitoín.	Knowledge about the stars.
Canon.	Pasiá nang Santa Yglesia ócol sa pagsampalataya,t, magaling na ogali.	Decision from the Holy Church relative to Faith (the believing) or fair customs.
Chaos.	Ang pagcacahalohalo nang lahat na bágay bagò linalang at pinagbobocodbocod. nang Dios.	The confusion (medley) of all things when not yet created and separated by God.
Cardinal.	Matáas na pareng casangoni nang Papa.	Conspicuous (high) priest counsellor of the Pope.
Charity.	Pag-íbig sa Dios at sa cápoua tauó.	Love unto God and unto our neighbour.
Chastity.	Pag-iiñgat sa cahalayan.	Caution against obscenity.
Catechism.	Librong quinasusulatan nang dasal.	Book on which doctrine is written.
Catechumen.	Tauòng nagaáral nang dasalan.	Person who learns doctrine.
Christendom.	Catiponan ó capisanan sang sangcacristianohan.	Gathering or assemblage of the whole christendom.
Onion.	Sibuyas.	(Corr. from Sp. word *cebollas*)
Zenith.	Daco nang láñgit natatapat sa ating olò	Point of the sky right opposite our head.
Rye.	Ysáng bágag na pananim ó binhí.	A sort of plant or seed.

ENGLISH.	TAGALOG.	LITERAL TRANSLATION.
Ceremony.	Caasalan, s e r e m o n i a. (corr. from Sp, word *ce-remonia*).	Custom.
Beer.	Ysàng álac na ganitò ang ñgalan; serbesa. (c o r r. from Sp. word *cerreza.*)	A liquor thus called.
Science.	Dúnong.	Learning.
Circulation.	P a g c a c a b a g o b a g ò sa ibà,t, ibàng camáy.	The state of passing continually from one hand to another.
Civilization.	Pagcasúlong nang mañga baya,t, mañga tauò sa ca-ronoñgan.	Advancement of towns and people in wisdom.
Chimney, funnel.	Ang p i n a g d a d a a n a n nang asò.	The passing-through way for smoke.
Code.	Catiponan nang mañga caotosan at pasiá nang hari.	Collection of laws and regulations from the king.
Cabbage.	Ysàng bágay na gulayín, *coles* (Sp.)	A sort of vegetable.
College.	Capisanan nang mañga tauòng tungmatahan sa isàng báhay na natatala-gá sa pagtuturo,t, pag-aáral nang carunuñgan.	Assembly of persons lodging at the same house and who are devoted to the teaching or learn-ing of knowledge.
Colony.	Capisanan nang mañga tauòng ypinadadala sa ibàng lupaín nang maca-pamayan dóon. ó, ang *lugar* (Sp.) namáng pina-mamayanan.	Congregation of persons who are taken to other land, there to settle in towns, or, also the place where they gather in towns.
To communicate, to re-ceive Holy Communion.	Maquinábang.	To receive benefit.
Conscience.	Pagquilala nang maga-ling na dápat sundín at nang masamáng súcat pañgilagan.	Knowing of the good which should be follow-ed, and of the evil deserv-ing to be shunned.
Concordat.	Pinagcasondoan n a n g Papa at nang Hari.	Covenant made by the Pope and the King.
Conclave.	Capolofigan nang mañga *cardenales* (Sp.) sa pag-halal nang Papa.	Meeting of cardinals to elect the Pope.
Earl, count.	Tauòng may carañgalàn na gavón ang táuag, *con-de* (Sp.)	Person possessing the dig-nity thus called.
Confectionery.	Tindahan nang sarisa-ring matamís.	Shop of various sweet meats.

SIXTY FIFTH EXERCISE.

What does fit mean.? A sudden ill. What does isolated mean.? Left alone. What is a mason.? A maker of stone houses. What is the Koran.? The Koran is what is considered as the Holy Scripture for the Turks, a book containing the doctrine and laws of Mohammed. What is a warehouse.? A house or construction for several things to be concealed in. What is a public auction.? The sale in public of property with the assistance and knowledge (advice) of Justice. What is a harangue.? A short address from a chief to his subordinates. What is an amnesty.? A pardon or forgetting on the part of the king towards rebellious people. What is anathema.? The expulsion from the Church of the person who scorns her commandments. What is Anatomy.? A science treating of the different parts of the body. What does amphibious mean.? Amphibious means an animal that can live both in water and on land. What does antediluvian mean.? Antediluvian means what existed before the deluge. What is an Antipope.? He who assumes unlawfully the dignity of Pope. What is an antipode.? The inhabitant living at a point of the Earth opposite ours. Who is a cannibal.? He who eats his fellow creatures. What is a wardrobe. It is the concealing place for clothes. What is an appendix.? An addition to a book. What is apoplexy.? The resemblance of death. What is apostasy.? The turning of the back on our Lord Jesus Christ. What is an apostle.? An apostle is a disciple of Jesus Christ. What is a tariff.? Salary, pay or price fixed by the Authorities. What is an Archipelago.? Sea containing many islands. What kind of things are Archives.? The concealing place for papers and valuable writings. What is an armory.? House or construction, the place where a diversity of weapons is kept. What is Harmony.? Beautifulness or conformity of sounds. What is an architect.? An artist knowing how to make churches and houses. What is Astronomy.? Knowledge about the stars. What is an atheist.? Person who refuses to acknowledge the existence of God. What is a bastard.? A child not born from marriage. What is the Bible.? A book containing the Holy Scripture. What is a library.? The place where many books are collected. What is bigamy.? A second unlawful marriage. What is a biography.? An account of the life of one person. What is a vault.? A little sky. What is Botany.? The science of plants, What is a breviary.? A book containing prayers for clergy. What is a bull.? A writ dispatched from the Pope to make his mercies or advices known. What is a letter–box.? A hole through which letters are dropped into the post office. What is Cavalry.? A mounted army. What is a compositor.? Person who joins and combines letters in a printing house. What is an almanac.? A small book containing the feats of every saint. What is a chalice.? A gold or silver cup used in the mass. What is a canon.? A decision from the Holy Church, relative to Faith. What is chaos.? The confusion of all things before their being created by God. What is a cardinal.? A conspicuous priest counsellor of the Pope. What is charity.? Love unto God and unto our neighbour. What is Chastity.? Caution against obscenity. Who is a catechumen.? A person who learns doctrine. What does zenith mean.? The point of the sky right opposite our heads. What is beer.? A sort of liquor. What is Science.? Science is wisdom. What is Civilization.? Advancement of nations or people in science.? What is a chimney.? A conduit for the smoke. What is a Code.? A collection of laws and regulations from the king. What is a cabbage.? A sort of vegetable. What is a college.? An assembly of persons living at the same house and who devote themselves to the teaching or acquiring of knowledge. What is a colony.? A congregation of persons who are taken to another land, there to settle in towns. What is conscience.? Knowing of the good to be followed and of the evil to be avoided. What is conclave.? The meeting of cardinals to elect a Pope. What is a count.? A person bearing the dignity thus called. What is a confectionery.? shop of various sweet meats.

SIXTY SIXTH LESSON.
YCAANIM NA POUO,T, ANIM NA PAGARAL.

MANNER OF SUBSTITUTING WORDS FOR THOSE WANTING IN
TAGALOG. (continued).

ENGLISH.	TAGALOG.	LITERAL TRANSLATION.
To confess.	*Compisal.*	(Corr. from Sp. word *confesar.*)
Conspiracy.	Pageacatipong lihin sa paglaban sa pono.	Secret meeting to oppose a ruler.
Commemoration.	Pagaalaalà.	Action of remembering.
Constellation.	Catiponan nang mañga bitoin na hindí pabago-bagò.	Cluster of stars not changing place.
Smuggling.	Calácal na báual.	Prohibited commodity.
Convent.	Tahanan nang mañga *fraile* o *monja.* (Sp.)	Lodging-place of friars or nuns.
Choir.	Lugar na pinagtitiponan nan mañga pare sa pagdadasal.	Place where priests assemble for prayers.
Chorus.	Catiponan nang mañga tauòng nagaauit.	Meeting of persons who sing.
Colonel.	Ysàng pono nang mañga sondalo.	A chief of soldiers.
Cosmogony.	Caronoñgang naoócol sa pagquilala nang lagáy at pageayari nitong *mun lo.* (Sp.)	Knowledge referring to the aquaintance with the position and shape of this world.
Cosmography.	Pagcasalaysúy nang calagayan nitong mundo.	Explanation of the location of the parts of this world.
Crater.	Bibig o butas nang mañga *volcán.* (Sp.)	Mouth or hole of volcanoes.
Creation.	Paglalang. Pageoha sa ualá nang Pañginóon Dios nang mañga bágay.	Act of creating. Snatching of the things from Chaos by Our Lord God.
Creed (the Apostles').	Sungmasampalataya.	(I) believe.
Creature.	Ang lahat na linalang nang Dios.	Every thing created by God.
Crucifix.	Ang laráuan ni Cristong nápapapaco sa *cruz.* (Sp.)	The image of Christ in a posture nailed to the cross.
Crusade.	Pageacatipon at pagsusúlong nang hocbóng laban sa mañga di binyagan.	Meeting and march of the army against heathens. (those not baptized.)

ENGLISH.	TAGALOG.	LITERAL TRANSLATION.
Pocket-book, pamphlet.	Soson-sosong papel na ticlop at tinahing anaquing libro.	Parcel of papers folded and stitched together as a book.
Quadrant.	Ycaápat na bahagui nang mabílog.	Fourth part of what is circular. (round)
Lent.	Cuaresma. (Sp.) Ang panahóng nauuná sa Pascó (corr. from Sp. word Pascua) nang pagcabúhay, na ypinagotos nang Santa Iglesiang houag cumáin nang lamángcati.	Easter. The time (space) preceding the feast of Resurrection, during which the Holy Church orders to refrain from eating meat.
Birth-day.	Arao na caganapan nang taón capañganacan sa i-àng tanò.	Day of the year in which the one of the birth of a person is accomplished.
To tan leather.	Pagloloto nang mañga balat na guinaganáng sapin.	Cooking of hides out of which shoes are made.
Decalogue.	Ang sangpóuong otos nang Dios.	The ten commandments of God.
Deicide.	Casalanang pagpatáy sa Dios na para nang guinauá nang mañga Judío (Sp.) sa Ating Pañginóon Jesucristo.	Sin, the act of killing God as it was done by Jews to Our Lord Jesus Christ.
Dentist.	Mangagámot, manlilinis at manhuhusáy nang ñgipin.	Curer, cleaner and arranger of teeth.
To thaw.	Magtónao.	To melt, to dissolve.
Pantry.	Tagoán nang mañga pagcáin.	Concealing place for victuals.
Dictionary.	Librong parang tandáan na quinasusulatan nang lahat na uica.	Book like a registry where all the words are written.
December.	Diciembre. (Sp.) Pañgalan nang bóuang catapusan nang taón.	Name of the month at the end of the year.
Deluge.	Gónao.	Inundation . (occurring once only.)
Divinity.	Pagcadios.	Essence of God.
Dynasty.	Pagcacasonodsónod nang mañga hari na iisang lahi.	Orderly succession (concatenation) of kings of the same (only one) stock.
Diocese.	Lupang nasasacopan at pinagpoponoan nang isàng obispo.	Land belonging to, and within the jurisdiction of a bishop.
Divorce.	Paghihiualáy nang magasáua.	Separation of both married parties.
Selfishness.	Labis na pag-íbig sa caniyà lámang.	Excess of love for himself. (only.)
Elasticity.	Urong-sólong. Umicsí,t, humaba.	Backwards and forward. To stretch in and to stretch out.
Emigration.	Pagalís nang tau sa caniyàng bayan.	Going away (exit) of people from their town.
To pave.	Maglátag nang batò.	To outspread stones.

49

ENGLISH.	TAGALOG.	LITERAL TRANSLATION.
Incarnation.	Cagalang-gálang at matáas na *misterio* (Sp.) na pagcacataouan tauò nang *Verbong* (Sp.) daquila.	Most venerable and lofty mystery of the Incarnation (the act of assuming a body) of the Word. (second person of Holy Trinity).
Encyclopædia.	Catiponan nang lahat na carunuñgan.	Collection of all the sciences.
To book-bind.	Balatán ang libro.	To skin books.
January.	*Enero.* (Sp.) Pañgalan nang unâng bóuan nang taón.	Name of the first month of the year.
Epiphany.	Piesta nang tatlòng hari.	Feast of the three kings.
Epoch.	Panahón.	Time, weather.
To ride.	Sumacáy sa cabayò.	To embark on horse.
Foreigner, stranger.	Taga ibâng lupaín.	From other land.
Gospel.	Casulatan quinasasaysayan nang caguilaguilalás at cagalang-gálang na búhay ni Cristo.	Writing in which the admirable and venerable life of Christ is exposed.
Extreme unction.	Santong lana.	Holy oil.
Faith.	Pananampalataya.	Belief.
February.	Pañgalan nang isáng bóuan. *Febrero.* (Sp.)	Name of a month.
Parishioners.	Mañga tauòng nasasacop nang isàng cura tongcol sa caloloua.	Persons dependent of a curate in what refers to the soul.
Feminine.	Naoócol sa babaye.	Relative to woman.
Fermentation.	Paghílab.	Swelling.
Fervidness.	Caniñgasang nang lóob.	Inward blaze.
Fœtus.	Anac na nasatián pa.	Son still in the womb (belly)
Philantropy.	Pag-íbig sa cápoua tauò.	Loving our neighbour. (fellow creature)
Frenzy, distraction.	Caololan mabañgis na may halong lagnat.	Furious madness with a mixture of fever.
Frontier.	Hanganan nang isàng caharían.	Boundary of a kingdom.
To smoke.	Manabaco. (Sp. word *tabaco* conjugated by *man*). Manigarrillo. (Sp. word *cigarrillo* conjugated by *man*).	To use tobacco, To use cigarettes.
General.	Pono sa hocbó.	Army-chief.
Giant.	Tauòng sacdal nang laqui	Person, the pith of tallness.
Glory, bliss.	Loualhati.	Rest.
Gratefulness.	Pagquilalà pagpahalagá nang ótang na lóob.	Acknowledgment of the value of a debt from the heart.
Grammar.	Ang capisanan nang mañga panotong casangcapan sa mahúsay na pagsasalitá,t, pagsúlat.	The collection of rules necessary to speak and to write in an orderly manner.
Infantry.	Hocbóng lácad.	Walking army.
Improbable.	Malayo sa catunayan.	Far from being real.
Irremediable.	Ualáng dáan ycahúsay.	Lacking the way to be arranged.

ENGLISH.	TAGALOG.	LITERAL TRANSLATION.
Pony.	Cabayong muntí.	Small horse.
July.	Pañgalan nang bóuang ycapitò sa lácad nang taón. *Julio*. (Sp.)	Name of the seventh month in the way (course) of the year.
June.	*Junio*. (Sp.). Ycaánim na bóuan sa lácad nang taón.	Sixth month in the way of the year.
New moon.	Bagòng bóuan.	New moon.
Full moon.	Cabilogan nang bóuan.	Roundness of the moon.
Waning moon.	Túnao. Ycaápat sa pagliit.	Melting. Fourth part towards the growing less.
Crescent.	Ycaápat sa paglaqui.	Fourth part towards the growing up.
March.	*Marzo*. (Sp.) Pañgalan nang bóuan ycatlò sa lácad nang taón.	Name of the month, third in the way (course) of the year.
Masculine.	Naoócol sa lalaqui.	Relative to male.
Maternity.	Pagcainà.	Essence of motherhood.
May.	*Mayo*. (Sp.) Pañgalan nang bóuan ycalimà sa lácad nang taón.	Name of the month, fifth in the way (course) of the year.
Metaphor.	Talinghaga.	Mystery.
Metamorphosis.	Pagbabagò, pag-iibà.	Renewal, changing.
World.	Sanglibotan, sangtinacpan.	The whole around, everything covered.
October.	*Octubre*. (Sp.) Pañgalan nang bouan ycasangpouò sa lácad nang taón.	Name of the month, tenth in the way (course) of the year.
Pigeon-hole.	Báhay lapati.	Pigeon house.
Womb.	Báhay bata.	House of the child.
Bread.	Tinápay.	Kneaded.
Pope.	Papa. Cataastaasan *Pontífice* (Sp.) sa Roma cahalili nang ating Pañgiñoón Jesucristo sa lupa.	Highest Pontiff in Rome, substitute for our Lord Jesus Christ, on Earth.
Parable.	Talinghaga.	Mystery.
Paradise.	Caguinhauahan, caloualhatían.	Resting-place.
Mother–country, fatherland.	Lupang tinoboan.	Soil where (one) has grown up.
Patriotism.	Pag-íbig sa caniyàng bayan.	Love for his town.
Pedestal.	Tontoñgan, paahan.	Foot-standing place.
To petrify.	Maguingbatò.	To convert into stone.
Pillar.	Haliguing batò.	Stone column.
Silver–smith.	Pandáy pílac.	Silver-worker.
Door–keeper.	Bantáy pinto.	Door-guard.
Profane.	Bágay na di naoócol sa Dios ó sa simbáhan.	Matter which does not belong to God or to the Church.
To profane.	Paggamit sa dili dápat nang mañga bágay na naoócol sa Dios.	The using to some undue purpose of the things corresponding to God.
Prophet.	Manhohola.	Diviner.
To progress.	Magsólong.	To get (push) forward.
Inch.	Sangdali, sangdaliri.	The whole space (contents) of a finger.

ENGLISH.	TAGALOG.	LITERAL TRANSLATION.
Hostage.	Sanláng mahal na tauò.	Pledge of a conspicuous person.
Queen.	Haring babaye.	Female–king.
Watch, clock.	Orasan.	Place of the hours.
To tow.	Hilà.	Dragging.
To apostatize.	Tumalicor sa ating Pañginóon Jesucristo.	To turn the back on our Lord Jesus Christ.
Repudiation.	Pagtatacuil sa asáua.	Dismissal of (to) a the spouse.
To resuscitate. (trans.)	Buhaying olí, buhayin panibagò.	To make live again, to make live anew.
Priest.	Cahalili nang Dios, amá nang cololoua.	Substitute for God, father of souls.
Sacrilege.	Calapastañganan sa mañga bágay na naoócol sa Dios.	Audacity in the things which belong to God.
Sacrilegious.	Tauòng lapastañgan sa Dios ó sa mañga naoócol sa Dios.	Bold person towards God or towards things belonging to God.
Sacrament.	Gamot sa caloloua.	Medecine for the soul.
Sacred.	Naoócol sa Dios.	Relative to God.
Psalm.	Auit sa pagpupuri sa Dios.	Song for praising God.
Psalmody.	Catiponan nang isàng dáa,t, limàng pouòng salmo (Sp) quinatha ni David.	Collection of the hundred and fifty psalms composed by David.
Salvation.	Pagcacamit nang cagaliñgan.	Attainment of the good.
Saviour.	Manonobos, mananacop.	Redeemer, redempter.
September.	Septiembre. (Sp.) Pañgalan nang bóuan icasiyam sa lácad nang taón.	Name of the month, ninth in the order (course) of the year.
Century.	Sangdáang taón.	Space of one hundred years.
Simony.	Pagbibili nang mañga biyaya ó bágay na naoócol sa calolóua.	Selling of the gifts or things appertaining to the soul.
Synagogue.	Simbahan nang mañga Judío.	Temple of the Jews.
Syntax.	Hánay nang pañgoñgósap.	Twisting of the speech.
Dream.	Boñgang tólog.	Fruit from sleep.
Subsistence. livelihood.	Pagcabúhay.	The essence of life.
Suicide, self-murder.	Pagpapacamatáy.	Act of allowing one's self to be killed.
Substance.	Lamán.	Contents, inside.
Maintenance.	Iquinabubúhay.	What causes life.
Tactics.	Caronoñgan magtalatag nang hocbó.	Science for the placing of an Army in order.
Short-handwriting.	Paraán nang pagsúlat na casingtulin nang pañguñgúsap.	Art of writing as swiftly as speaking.
Telescope.	Panifiging totòong malavò ang abot	Looking instrument very far-reaching.
Drop curtain.	Tabíng nang comediahan.	Curtain of the playhouse.

ENGLISH.	TAGALOG.	LITERAL TRANSLATION.
Theology, Divinity.	Caronoñgang naoócol sa pagquilalà sa Dios.	Science looking forward to the knowing of God.
Theory.	Pagcaquilalà nang mañga bágay sa pag-iisip lámang.	Knowledge of things by the understanding only.
Tiara.	Potong nang Papa.	Crown of the Pope.
Translation.	Pagsasalin sa ibàng uica.	Copying into other language.
Trinity.	Catatlohan. Ang cagalan-gálang na tatlòng persona. (Sp)	Joining of three. The venerable three Persons.
Table service, crockery.	Mañga babasaguín.	Things which will be broken.
Virginity.	Cabooang cataouán.	Entirety of the body.
Mare.	Cabayong babaye.	Female horse.

SIXTY SIXTH EXERCISE.

What is a conspiracy.? A meeting to oppose a ruler. What is a commemoration.? An action of remembrance. What is a constellation.? A cluster of stars not changing place. What is smuggling.? A prohibited commodity. What is a convent.? A lodging-house for friars or nuns. What is a choir? The place where priests assemble to say prayers. What is a chorus.? A number of persons singing together. What is a colonel.? A chief of soldiers. What is Cosmogony.? The science acquainting us with the position and shape of this world. What is Cosmography.? An account of the formation of the different parts of this world. What is a crater.? The mouth of volcanoes. What is a creature.? Any thing created by God. What is a crucifix.? The image of Christ nailed to the Cross. What is a quadrant.? The fourth part of a circumference. What is Lent,? The space of time preceding the Resurrection feast-day and during which Roman Church forbids to eat meat food. What is a birth-day.? The day anniversary of the birth of a person. What is the Decalogue.? The ten commandments of God. What is a dentist.? A curer, cleaner and arranger of teeth. What is a pantry.? Concealing-place for victuals. What is a dictionary.? Book in the way of registry, where all the words are written. What is a dynasty.? The orderly succesion of kings of the same lineage. What is a Diocese.? Land within the jurisdiction of a bishop. What is Divinity. The attributes of God. What is selfishness? Excess of love for the self. (one's body). What is emigration.? Exit of people to another land. What is to pave.? To stretch out stones. What is a foreigner.? A person from another land. What is Gospel.? Book in which the life of Christ is exposed. What is feminine.? What refers to woman. What is a fœtus.? Creature still in the womb. What is Philanthropy.? Love for our fellow creatures. What is to smoke.? To use tobacco or cigarettes. What is a general.? An army-chief. What is bliss.? Rest. What is gratefulness.? Acknowledgment of a debt from the heart. What is grammar.? The collection of rules to speak and write properly. What is Infantry.? Army marching on foot. What is a pony.? Small horse. What is masculine.? What refers to male. What is a pigeon-hole.º A lodging for pigeons. What is the womb.? The fœtus' lodging-place. Who is the Pope.? The highest Pontiff at Rome. What is a parable.? A mystery. What is Paradise.? A resting-place. What is Patriotism.? Love for one's country. What is a pedestal.? A foot-standing place. What is a pillar.? A stone pole. What is an inch.? The length-space of a finger.

What is a queen.? A female–king. What is a sacrament.? A medecine for the soul. What is sacred.? What relates to God. What is a century.? A hundred years' space of time. What is Syntax.? Twisting of words. What is a tiara.? The Pope's crown.

SIXTY SEVENTH LESSON.
YCAANIM NA POUO,T, PITONG PAGARAL.

SYNCOPES AND EPENNHESES.

As indicated elsewhere in this work we now subjoin a list of the most usual contractions and other peculiar ways os forming Tagalog compounds, especially those in which the suffixes *in* and *an* enter.

The majority of these figures of diction are syncopes or contractions affecting the last vowel of the root, or the latter and the final consonant or consonants thereof, which are dropped before receiving the aforesaid suffixes. There are, however, some which are epentheses, that is to say, some, in which some letter or letters are replaced, inverted or inserted in the middle of the root, the structure of which is, in the latter case, expanded for the sake of euphony.

The following compounds may be considered as examples of

EPENTHESES.

ENGLISH.	TAGALOG ROOTS.	COMPOUNDS.	INSTEAD OF.
Uneasiness.	Balisa.	Cabalisanhan.	Cabalisahan.
Certain.	Totoò.	Catotoohanan.	Catotoohan.
To roof.	Atip.	Aptán aptín.	Atipan, atipin.
Commission, charge.	Bilin.	Binlán.	Bilinan.
Pinch. pinching.	Corot.	Cotdán, cotdín or regular.	Corotan, corotin.
Deposit.	Habilin.	Habinlán.	Habilinan.
Cell, apartment.	Silir.	Sidlán.	Siliran.
To pass through, to pierce.	Talab.	Tablán.	Talaban.
To plant.	Tanim.	Tamnán.	Taniman.
To shift, to put on clean clothes.	Bihís.	Bisán, bisín.	Bihisan, bihisin.
To spill.	Bohos.	Bosán.	Bohosan.
To blow.	Hihip.	Hipán.	Hihipan.
To deviate, to turn away.	Lihis.	Lisán.	Lihisan.
To fail, to err, not to hit the mark.	Sala.	Sanlán.	Saláan.
To accustom.	Bihasa.	Bihasnán, bihasnín.	Bihasáan, bihasáin.
To kiss.	Halic.	Hagcán, hagquín.	Halican, haliquin.
To substitute, to act for.	Halili.	Halinhán, halinhín.	Halilíhan, halilihin.
To take.	Coha.	Conan, cunin.	Coháan, coháin.

ENGLISH.	TAGALOG ROOTs.	COMPOUNDS.	INSTEAD OF.
To arrive.	Dating.	Datnán, datnín.	Datiñgan, datiñgin.
To repair to, to hurry to.	Agad.	Agdán, agdín.	Agaran, agarin.
Slave.	Alipin.	Caalipnán, alipnán, alipnín.	Caalipinan, alipinan, alipinin.
Chilblain.	Alipoñga.	Aliponghán.	Alipoñgáan.

SYNCOPES.

Disciple.	Alagad.	Alagdán, alagdín.	Alagaran alagarin.
What.	Anò.	Anhín.	Anohin.
To cohabitate.	Apid.	Apdán, apdín.	Apiran, apirin.
To pound in company.	Asod.	Asdán, asdín.	Asoran, asorin.
Salt, to salt.	Asín.	Asnán, asnín.	Asinan, asinin.
Spouse.	Asáua.	Asaoín.	Asauáin.
Low, meek.	Babá.	Babán.	Babáan.
To bear on one's shoulder.	Babà.	Babhín.	Babahin.
Tumor.	Baga.	Bagán.	Bagáan.
To wet.	Basa.	Basán, basín.	Basáan, basáin.
To suffer, to bear.	Batà.	Bathán, bathín.	Batahan, batahin.
To pound rice.	Bayó.	Bayán, bayín.	Bayóan, bayóin.
To give.	Bigáy.	Big-ián.	Bigayan.
To buy.	Bilì.	Bilhán, bilhín.	Bilihan, bilihin.
To except.	Bocod.	Bocdán, bocdín.	Bocoran, bocorin.
To lay open, to uncover.	Bucà.	Buc-hín.	Bucáhin.
To open.	Bucás.	Bocsán.	Bucasin.
The other side.	Cabilá.	Cabilán, cabilín.	Cabiláan, cabiláin.
To itch.	Cati.	Cathán.	Catihan.
To cloak, to deny.	Cailá.	Cailán.	Cailáan.
To bite.	Cagat.	Cagtán, cagtín.	Cagatan, cagatin.
Left.	Caliuá.	Caliuán, caliuín.	Caliuáan, caliuáin.
To loose, to untie.	Calag.	Calgán, calguín.	Calagan, calaguin.
To attain, to obtain.	Camit.	Camtán.	Camitan.
To eat.	Cáin.	Canán, canín.	Cainan, cainin.
To grope for.	Capá.	Capán, capín.	Capáan, capáin.
To grasp, to embrace.	Capit.	Captán, captín.	Capitan, capitin.
To apprehend, to seize.	Daquip.	Dacpín.	Daquipin.
To clothe.	Damit.	Damtán, damtín.	Damitan, damitin.
To bring, to carry.	Dalà.	Dalhán, dalhín.	Dalahan, dalahin.
To touch.	Damà.	Damhán, damhín.	Damahan, damahin.
Road, to pass.	Dáan.	Danán, danín.	Daanan, danin.
To prostrate.	Dapá.	Dapán.	Dapáan.
To stick, to adhere.	Dicquit.	Dictán, dictín.	Dicquitan, dicquitin.
To hear.	Diñgig.	Dinggán, dingguín	Diñgigan, diñgiguin.

ENGLISH.	TAGALOG ROOTS.	COMPOUNDS.	INSTEAD OF.
To stretch out one's arms.	Dipà.	Diphán, diphín.	Dipahan, dipahin
Blood.	Dugó.	Dugán, duguín.	Dugóan, dugóin.
To do one's duty, to fulfill.	Ganap.	Gampán.	Ganapan.
Work, to do, to work.	Gauá.	Gaoán, gaoin.	Gauáan, gauáin.
To awake.	Guising.	Guisnán.	Guisiñgan.
To pull down, to destroy.	Guiba.	Guibán, guibín.	Guibáan, guibá-in.
To repair to, to run to the assistance of somebody.	Guibic.	Guibán.	Guibican.
To conjecture, to note, to guess.	Halata.	Halatán, halatín.	Halatáan, halatáin.
To send, to remit, to take along, to accompany.	Hatir.	Hatdán.	Hatiran.
Ribbon, band, chord.	Hapin.	Hapnán.	Hapinan.
To sow, to scatter seed.	Hasic.	Hascán.	Hasican.
To borrow, to lend things.	Hiram.	Hirmán, hirmin.	Hiraman, hiramin.
To lie down.	Higa.	Higán.	Higáan.
Shame, bashfulness.	Hiya.	Hiyín.	Hiyáin.
To complain.	Hinanaquit.	Hinanactán.	Hinanaquitan.
To ask for.	Hiñgi.	Hiñgán, hiñgín.	Hiñgían, hiñgíin.
To wait.	Hintáy.	Hintín.	Hintayin.
To clean from lice.	Hiñgoto.	Hiñgotán, hiñgotín.	Hiñgotóan, hiñgotóin.
Other, to change.	Ybà.	Ybhán, ibhín.	Ybahan, ibahin.
To go for water.	Yguib.	Ygbán, igbín.	Yguiban, iguibin.
To make water.	Yhi.	Yhán.	Yhían.
To unload, to alight, to light from.	Ybis.	Ybsán, ibsín.	Ybisan, ibisin.
Large, great, to grow.	Laquì.	Lac-hán, lac-hín.	Laquihan, laquihin.
Strength.	Lacás.	Lacsán.	Lacasan.
Inside, inward contents.	Lamán.	Lamnán.	Lamanan.
To soften.	Latá.	Latán, latín.	Latáan, latáin.
Far, distance.	Layo.	Layán.	Layóan.
Five.	Limá.	Limhán.	Limahan.
To put, to place, to range.	Lagáy.	Lag-ián, lag-ín.	Lagayan, lagayin
To make merry.	Logod.	Logdán, logdín.	Logoran, logorin.
To spit.	Lura.	Lorán.	Loráan.
Nit.	Lisá.	Lis-án, lis-ín.	Lisáan, lisáin.
By and by.	Mamayá.	Mamayín.	Mamayáin.
To mistake.	Malí.	Malán, malín.	Malían, malíin.
To observe, to experience.	Masid.	Masdán.	Masiran.
To begin, to commence.	Molá.	Molán.	Moláan.

50

ENGLISH.	TAGALOG ROOTS.	COMPOUNDS.	INSTEAD OF.
To open one's mouth.	Ñgañgà.	Ñganhán, ñgan-hín.	Ñgañgahan, ñga-ñgahin.
To make thin.	Nipís.	Nipsán.	Nipisan.
To chew.	Ñguya.	Ñguyín.	Ñguyáin.
To return, to repeat.	Olí.	Olán, ol-ín,	Olían, olíin.
To settle. to appease.	Palagáy.	Palag–ián.	Palagayan.
To contain, to include, to print, to lie manifest.	Palamán.	Palamnán.	Palamanan.
To dream.	Panaguínip.	Panaguimpán.	Panaguinipan.
Name.	Pañgalan.	Pañganlán.	Pañgalanan.
To itch.	Pañgatí.	Pañgathín.	Pañgatihin.
To listen.	Paquinig.	Paquingan.	Paquinigan.
To part. to split, to break.	Patid.	Patdán, patdín.	Patiran, patirin.
To squeeze.	Pigá.	Pigán, piguín.	Pigáan, pigáin.
To throw a kerchief round one's head.	Piñgì.	Pinghán.	Piñgihan.
To crush, to crack.	Pisá.	Pisán, pisín.	Pisáan. pisáin.
To press into the hands.	Pisil.	Pislín.	Pisilin.
To fill.	Ponó.	Ponán, ponín.	Ponóan, ponóin.
To cut.	Pótol.	Potlán, potlín.	Potolan, potolin.
To sweat, to perspire, perpiration.	Páuis.	Pausán.	Pauisan.
White, to whiten.	Putí.	Putín.	Putíin.
To nibble.	Quibit.	Quibtán, quibtín.	Quibitan, quibit-in.
To cut off with the fingers.	Quitil.	Quitlán, quitlín.	Quitilan, quitilin.
To embark, to mount.	Sacáy.	Sac-yán.	Sacayan.
Pain, to rack.	Saquit.	Sactán, sactín.	Saquitan. saqui-tin.
Tale, to narrate.	Salitá.	Salitán, salitín.	Salitáan, salitáin.
Fault, harm.	Samá.	Samán, samín.	Samáan, samáin.
Branch.	Sañgà.	Sanghán, sang-hín.	Sañgahan, sañga-hin.
To come back, to give back.	Saolí.	Saolán, saolín.	Saolían, saolíin.
To render narower.	Siquip.	Sicpán, sicpín.	Siquipan.
To set fire to sweepings.	Sigá.	Sigán.	Sigáan.
To eat, to devour.	Sila.	Silán, silín.	Siláan, siláin.
To follow, to obey.	Sonod.	Sondín.	Sonorin.
To wonder.	Tacà.	Tac-hán.	Tacahan.
To cover.	Taquip.	Tacpán.	Taquipan.
To hew, to cut sharply.	Tagá.	Tag-ín.	Tagáin.
To turn one's back on.	Talicod.	Talicdán.	Talicoran.
To hold, to grasp.	Tañgan.	Tañgnán.	Tañganan.
To stand.	Tayó.	Tayán.	Tayóan.
To taste, to test.	Tiquim.	Ticmán.	Tiquiman.

ENGLISH.	TAGALOG ROOTS.	COMPOUNDS.	INSTEAD OF.
Purposely.	Tiquís.	Ticsín.	Tiquisin.
To look.	Tiñgin.	Tiñgnán.	Tiñginan.
To save, to be frugal.	Tipid.	Tipdán, tipdín.	Tipiran, tipirin.
To redeem.	Tubos.	Tubsán. tubsín.	Tubosan, tubosin.
To leave behind as a surplus.	Tirá.	Tirán.	Tiráan.
To crush lice with the nails.	Tirís.	Tisdán.	Tirisan.
To peck, to sting.	Tocá.	Tocán, toquín.	Tocáan, tocáin.
Dry.	Toyo.	Toyán, toyín.	Toyóan, toyóin.
Nothing, to lack.	Ualá.	Ual-án, ual-ín.	Ualáan, ualáin.

SIXTY SEVENTH EXERCISE.

Truth. Pinch that child. Slavery. Salt the fish. Bear the log. Suffer the punishment. Pound that rice. Give me bread. Buy the oil. Lay aside two for me. Lay open the chest. I cannot attain it. This is boiled rice. Grasp that knife. Seize the thief. Put on this shirt. Clothe that child. Bring that. Take it to your father. Lie down on your face upon this mat. Stick this paper to the wall. Whom have you heard it from.? Kneel down and stretch out your arms before this image. Do it. John perceived that I was angry. Chord that harp. Sow this rice in the garden. Borrow this. Lie down on the floor. Complain of your friend. Ask ("for") a dollar from John. Wait for your mother. Clean that poor man from lice. Change the word. Go for water to the well. Make water into this pot. Lighten the servant of the load. Raise my wages to five dollars. Place that on the table. Amuse this child. Spit on him. Clean him from nits. Leave that off for a little while. Mistake in writing. Watch closely whether the dog is rabid. Commence the work. Make this stick thinner. Repeat the word. Pour beer into the glass. Write a good advice in the contents of the letter. Impose a name on your godchild. Listen to me. Part with that bad habit. Squeeze that lemon. Tie the kerchief round your head. Crack that egg. Press my hand. Fill up that vat. He is in perspiration. Cut out one yard of that stuff. Whiten those pantaloons. Nibble at the sugar. Cut off that flower with your fingers. Mount on that horse. Tell what he said. Cut off some branches of the mango-tree that there may be plenty of fruit. Restore back to Frank the money. Do not make your heart narrow. Set that filth on fire. Eat that meat. Follow your father. Admire the greatness of God. Cover that plate. Hew that tree. Turn your back on him. Hold the candle. Stand on the border. Taste this banana. Do it on purpose. Look at it. Save your money. Leave him some food. Crush that louse on the comb. Redeem your pledge. Put those clothes to dry. Blot out (cancel) what I owe you.

SIXTY EIGHTH LESSON.
YCAANIM NA POUO,T, UALONG PAGARAL.

PROVERBS.

In no better way is the natives' fancy displayed than in proverbs, adages, riddles and paradoxes, which, one might say, constitute the very pith of their speech and are considered by them the highest form of wit.

We give hereafter some Tagalog proverbs which have fairly exact counterparts in English. A translation, as literal as it can be, of the Tagalog words is offered opposite in a third column. This translation will be found in many cases to trample upon English syntax and accurateness. It is needless to say that this has been done on purpose and with a view to help the learner to a better understanding of the matter.

ENGLISH.	TAGALOG.	LITERAL TRANSLATION.
The thread will break where it is weakest.	Anò mang tíbay nang torseng abacá, capagnagsosolo (1). ualá din puersa (2).	However strong the hemp fiber may be, if left alone lacks strength.
A man's word should be as good as his bond.	Cun sinong umaco, siyáng napapaco.	Whoever promises, he becomes nailed.
We see the mote in our neigbour's eye, and not the beam in our own.	Marúnong cumita nang sa ibàng úling, bagò,i, sa muc-há niyà,i, naglauit ang aguiu.	One knows how to see other's coal stain, while his face hangs with soot.
A word is enough to the wise.	Súcat ang catagáng sabi sa marúnong umintindî (3).	A single word suffices to a wise understander.
Paper speaks when men are silent.	Ualáng mabuting sacsi para nang sa papel sabi.	There is not so good witness as what is said in a paper.
Money makes the mare go.	Pag may salaping titic, pusa ma,i, tatalic.	There being ready money, even the cat will dance.

(1) Spanish word *solo*, "alone",
(2) Corr. from Sp. word *fuerza*, "strength".
(3) *Umintidi* is the Spanish verb *entender*, "to understand"; tagalized and conjugated by *um*.

ENGLISH.	TAGALOG.	LITERAL TRANSLATION.
Opportunity lost is seldom regained.	Ang hindí magsamantalà, magcamit ma,i. mahírap na.	He who does not avail himself of an opportunity though he may succeed, gets into trouble.
Nothing venture, nothing have.	Ang di magsapalaran, hindí macatatauir nang caragatan.	He who does not risk anything will not cross the seas.
The scalded cat dreads cold water.	Pag ang tauò nasosocò tinatandàan ang pagtoñgò.	When a man has butted his head he takes care to bend it.
No one can tell what is to happen to him.	Ang nagùiuica nang tapús ay siyáng nacacapús.	He who speaks of success, is just he who fails.
He that flatters you more than he was wont to do, either intends to deceive you or needs your assistance.	Ang mapanuyo,t, magálang may masamáng tinatacpán.	He who is officious and flattering conceals evil.
The master's eye fattens the horse.	Ang sa cabayo pagtabá sa matá nang may alaga.	What makes a horse grow fat is (through) the attendant's eye.
ss brings no—	Ang naghahañgad nang caguiná, sangsalop ang nauaualá.	He who longs for half a peck, a whole one is missing.
your company ill tell you what re.	Ang calabáo na di manguiguiba, cung sumamà sa manguiguiba,i, manguiguiba na pati.	The buffalo that is not destructive, if it joins to the destructive will also become so.
ell me your company nd I will tell you what ou are.	Pagsumonod sa calabáo na may pútic, magcacapútic na pati.	In following a buffalo besmeared with mud one will be filled with mud as well.
As you live you shall die.	Cun anò ang búhay siyáng camatayan.	As the life so the death.
There is many a slip betwixt cup and lip.	Cun ang caning ysinusubo ay nalalaglag pa, ¿di lalo pa cayá ang ualá sa camáy.?	If boiled rice when taken to the mouth crumbles, how more will be with that which is not yet on hand.?
Look before you leap.	Ang ísip ni Capaho (1), ang magaasáua,i, biro, mamin bagá,t, ysubo,i, lua cun mapaso.	Jack thinks that to marry is a matter for fun, somewhat as to chew betel that when taken to the mouth is cast out if it burns.

(1) *Capaho*, is an imaginary name used to avoid any possibility of a real person being alluded to.

ENGLISH.	TAGALOG.	LITERAL TRANSLATION.
He who gets under a good tree has a good shelter.	Ang lumápit sa batis na-quiquinábang nang la-mig.	He who approaches a stream shares its cool-ness.
Perseverance overcomes every difficulty.	Ang batò,i, naoóquit sa pinatac-patac nang tú-big.	The stone becomes pierc-ed by the continual drop-ping (drop by drop) of the water.
At night all cats are grey.	Pagcamatáy nang sínag, ualáng pintarong (1) ba-yauac.	The sun-beams being ex-tinguished, there is no colored *iguana.* (a lizard.)
A closed mouth catches no flies.	Ang bibig na ualáng imic, sino ma,i, ualáng babañgit.	Speechless mouth hurts nobody's feelings.
Cheap things are dear-est.	Ang bumili nang murà, siyáng namamahalan.	Buying cheaply just turns out the dearest.
The more we have, the more we want.	Ang bolsa (2) nang ma-yaman parating cólang.	The wealthy person's purse always is in need.
It will happen when two Sundays come together.	Bucas cun macalipás, sa lingo cun macalampás.	To-morrow if yet to e-lapse, yesterday, (on Sun-day) if elapsed.
It is not for asses to lick honey.	Ang cabayò big-ián man nang asúcal at tinápay, hindí cacanin, ang *gusto* (Sp.) ay ang compáy.	You may give a horse sugar and bread, he will not eat any, for he only likes grass.
No smoke without fire.	Di man maquita ang ni-figas, asò ang magpapa-háyag.	Although the flames may not be seen, the smoke will disclose them.
To jump out of the fry-ing pan into the fire.	Ang umílag sa baga, sa nifigas nasusugba.	He who shuns live coal falls into the fire.
A rolling stone gathers no moss.	Mahírap ang magbagò, sangtaóng paróo,t, pari-tò.	It is troublesome to change, for one year (pas-ses in going) here and there.
Walls have ears.	May taiñga ang lupa, may pacpac ang balita.	The soil has ears, news has wings.
He who sows winds will reap storms.	Ang magpaótang nang hañgin, búguio ang aani-hin.	He who lends winds will reap in storms.

(1) *Pintarong*, corr. from Sp. word *pintado,* "colored".
(2) *Bolsa,* (Sp.) "purse."

ENGLISH.	TAGALOG.	LITERAL TRANSLATION.
He who is not accustomed to shoes will have corns if he wears them.	Ang dati sa bahag, magsalaual ma.i, alisuag.	He who is accustomed to a loin-cloth, although he may put on trousers (will feel) uneasy.
Half a loaf is better than no bread. Something is better than nothing.	Ang bigás na basá, ¿báquit di ysáing sa panahóng ualá.?	Moist rice, why not to be fried in time of scarcity.?
A man is not wise at all times.	Ualáng marúnong at batid sa gauá,i, hindí nalihís.	There is no wise and expert man who never failed.
Still waters run the deepest, or, save me from a snake in the grass.	Ang caualing lupa, malamig ma,i, pag–init ay daig ang caualing bácal.	The earthen pot though it may be slender (cold). if warmed. preserves the heat longer than the kettle. (more literally) The earthen vessel overcomes the iron vessel if warmed.
Short reckonings and long friends.	Ang malinis na *cuenta* (Sp.) mahaba ang pagsasamà.	Clear accounts, long company.
Misfortune never comes alone.	Pag ang tauò ay naghihírap, casabáy and pagdadalita.	On a man being in distress, suffering joins to it.
Birds of a feather flock together.	Mahírap sa mayaman ang duc-há,i, paquisamahan; mahírap sa duc-há namán sa mayaman maquipisan.	It is hard to the wealthy to join the poor; it is also hard for the poor to join the wealthy.
Covetousness brings nothing home.	Ang tauòng gahamgahaman ninanasa,t, di macamtán, lungmalayo and capalaran.	The covetous man desires and cannot obtain, (his) happiness gets away.
All is not gold that glitters.	Hindí ang lahat nang cungmiquinang ay guintó.	Not all that glitters is gold.
No one is so deaf as he that will not hear.	Madalí pang guisiñgin ang natotológ nang mahimbing, sa nagtotolog–tologan naguiguísing.	Sooner arouses he who is deeply slept than he who, being awake, feigns to sleep.
Spare the rod and you will spoil the child.	Ang totoòng minamahal siyáng pinaghihirapan.	He whom one esteems truly is just whom one causes pain.

ENGLISH.	TAGALOG.	LITERAL TRANSLATION.
Vicious habits are seldom thrown off.	Ang visio (1) at natural (1) sisiñgao maminsan-minsán.	Vice and temper will transpire now and then.
He measures every man's corn by his own bushel.	Ang ísip nang magnanácao, magnanácao ang lahat.	A thief's thought, everybody is a thief.
A bad agreement is better than a law suit.	Ang macocoha sa opó houag nang ytindig.	What can be reached from the seat, do not (reach it) standing.
Save a thief from the gallows and he will cut your throat.	Ang magalilà nang ouac matá ang binubulag.	He who takes care of crows will become blind.
No one goes worse shod than the shoemaker's wife.	Ang pandáy-búcal, siyáng ualáng sundang.	Just the blacksmith has no knife. (cutlass)
All keys hang not at the same girdle.	Ang isàng pintong masarhan sangpouò ang mabubucsán.	One door closed, ten will be open.
Many brooks make a river.	Capag nagpoldopoldo nagboboòng sigaro. (2)	After wrapping and wrapping the cigar is completed.
Knowledge is preferable to riches.	Daig ang may tinongcós nang mabutìng hinocod.	He who has money-bags is surpassed by a smart.
Look before you leap.	Ang di tumiñgin sa onà, sa huli mapag-iisà.	He who does not look forward will be left alone behind.
In for a penny, in for a pound.	Cun mahólog ca,i, dóon sa layogan, houag sa mababa nang di ca tauanan.	If you fall down, let it be from a high place, never from a low one, that you may not be laughed at.
A bird in the hand is worth two in the bush.	Ybà ang pogon huli na sa sunñgayang dadacpín pa.	A quail already caught is different from a horned head of cattle (a stag) to be taken hold of yet.
A hog in armour is still but a hog.	Cahima,t, paramtán ang háyop na machín magpacailán ma,i, machín cun tauaguin.	Though the monkey be clothed he will always be called a monkey.
To see the mote in our neighbour's eye and not the beam in our own.	Ang machín ay tungmatáua sa haba nang buntot nang baca, bagò,i, hindí naquiquita ang haba nang bontot niyà.	The monkey laughs at the length of the cow's tail, and he does not see the lenght of his own.

(1) *Visio*, corr. from Sp. word *vicio*, "vice". *Natural*, (Sp.) "natural disposition".
(2) *Sigaro*, corr. from Sp. word *cigarro*, "cigar".

ENGLISH.	TAGALOG.	LITERAL TRANSLATION.
Better alone than in bad company.	Marami man at di tono, mahañga,i, nagsosolo.	Tho' many (and) if at odds, better to be alone.
Hunger is the best sauce.	Pag ualáng túbig na línao iinumin labo man.	There not being any limpid water even the turbid will be drunk.
First come, first served.	Ang licsi ay daig nang agap.	Caution overcomes swiftness.
One scabby sheep spoils the whole flock.	Ang isàng masamáng topa, sa ibà,i, nacahihila.	A bad sheep can drag the others along.
There is a great difference between saying and doing.	Na sa uica,i, ualá sa gauá.	In speech not in work.
Tell me what you are worth and I will tell you what you are.	Pag ualá cang cayamanán, cúlang ca na camahalan.	On your lacking wealth, you lack worthiness.
You must never look a gift horse in the mouth.	Ang cabayòng bigáy ang ñgipin ay houag mong titingnán.	Don't look at the teeth of a gift horse.
Idleness in youth brings sorrow in old age.	Ang sa cabatáa,i, ualáng gauá, mahihirapan cun tumandá.	He who does not work in youth will be in distress when (becomes) old.
Out of sight, out of mind.	Ang malayo,t, patáy ay ualá nang caibigan,	The absent and the dead persons have no friends.
Better to be the head of a mouse than the tail of a lion.	Mabuti pa ang munting aquing sa malaquíng habilin.	Better the little mine than the much that is taken charge of.
Silence gives consent.	Ang hindí ungmiimic ay ungmaaco.	He who is silent, admits of (accepts).
Cocks crow well upon their own dunghills.	Ang sa sarili matápang, maamó sa ibàng bayan.	He who in his own (land), is brave, meek in alien town.
He that does his best should not be censured.	Ang gungmagauá nang macacayanan ay ualá nang casalanan.	He who does what he can is not to be blamed. (has no blame).
Bought wit is the best.	Sa mañga nadadalá nanggagáling ang nañgagtatandá.	From those tutored by experience the cautions come out.
A foolish question requires no answer.	Ang mañga uica nang hunghang di dápat paquingán.	The fools' words should not be listened to.
Beggars must not be choosers.	Ang manhihiñgí di dápat mamili.	Those who use to beg should not go about choosing.

51

ENGLISH.	TAGALOG.	LITERAL TRANSLATION.
Help yourself, and God will help you.	Cun íbig mong guminhauà ay magpacapágod ca.	If you are willing to become well off, try earnestly to toil.
A liar should have a good memory.	Ang tauòng sinoñgaling, cailañgan maguing matandáin.	A (the) liar needs to be keen.
Passed waters grind no mill.	Ang patáy ay pátay na; ang búhay ay ypagadyà.	The dead, dead already; the living, are (is) to be cared for. (defended.)
When the cat is away the mice will play.	Pagualá ang pusa, piesta nang mañga dagá.	On the cat going away, a holiday for the mice.
A good shop wants no sign.	Ang cayo cun maínam nagbibili na sa cabán.	The stuff, if good, is sold in the case. (chest).
To close the stable door when the horse is run away.	Cun ang cabayò,i, patáy na, ang cúmpay ay ¿aanhín pa.?	If the horse is already dead, to what purpose the forage.?
Sloth breeds poverty.	Ang tauòng matámad cailán ma,i, salat.	The lazy fellow is always in lack. (destitution.)
The rich and the poor are alike in the grave.	Ang duc-há,t, cardenal magcaparis cun mamatáy.	The poor man and the cardinal (are) alike when they die.
Between honest friends compliments are useless.	Sa túnay na magcaibigan ualá nang maraming cabulaanan.	Among true friends there is no simulation.
Great talkers are little doers.	Capag ang túbig ay maíñgay asahan mong mabábao.	If (on) the water being noisy be sure it is shallow.
Cut your coat according to your cloth.	Houag cang mañgahás lumipad cun cúlang ca pa sa pacpac.	Don't dear fly if you lack wings.
Beware of the silent man, and of the dog that does not bark.	Pag-iñgatan mo ang tauong ang bibig ay hicom at ang asong di tungmatahol.	Beware of the man whose mouth is closed and of the dog that does not bark.
A fault once denied, is twice committed.	Cun ang isàng sala,i, tinatanguihan dalauà ang quinacamtán.	If a fault is denied, two (faults) are caught in.
He that does evil must expect the same in return.	Cun anò ang iyòng ytanim siyá mong aanihin.	As you sow (plant), just you will reap.
Spare the rod and you will spoil the child.	Ang laquì sa láyao caraníua,i, hubad.	He who has grown up in indulgence, generally is naked.

ENGLISH.	TAGALOG.	LITERAL TRANSLATION.
Give a dog an ill name and he will soon be hanged.	Cun magaling ang isàng súgat, ang masamáng uica,i, di cungmucupas.	A wound heals; a foul word does not fade away.
He deserves not the sweet who will not taste the sour.	Ang pulot ay lalong matamís, cun macatiquim nang mapait.	Honey is (the) more sweet if the sourness has been tasted.
Opportunity makes the chief.	Ang bucás na caban nacatotocsò sa banal.	An (the) open safe can tempt the honest.
A wise man will change his mind; a fool, never.	Ang catigasa,i, sarili nang hunghang.	Obstination is the property of the fool.
Time brings truth to light.	Ang gauáng lihim sa calauna,i. napapansin.	What done secretly, in the long is discovered.
Skill is better than strength.	Ang calacasa.i, daig nang paráan.	Strength is overcome by skill.
One gift is better than two promises.	Mabutì ang isàng ybinibigáy na sa dalauàng ybibigáy pa	Better one "gives" than two "will be given."
The foolish and head-strong make lawyers rich.	Hunghang at cariloso (Sp) nagpapayaman sa abogado. (Sp.)	Foolish and frivolous people enrich lawyers.
All truths are not to be told at all times.	Hindí lahat nang totoò ay masabi.	Not all that is true may be said.
A pound of care will not pay an ounce of debt.	Bayaran mo ang ótang mo at iyòng maalaman ang ganáng iyò.	Pay your debts and you will know what belongs to you.
Whatever one loves, appears handsome to him.	Ualàng páñgit sa isàng ungmiíbig.	There is nothing ugly for one who loves.
Who speaks much, often blunders.	Pagmarami ang salitá, marami ang sala.	On the speech being long the mistakes (will be) many.
Lend to your friend, and you will make him your enemy.	Ang nagpapaótang sa caibigan ay cungmiquita nang caáuay.	He who lends to a friend finds an enemy.
He that has time and waits for more, loses both.	Cun magagauá at di gaoin, dì na magagauá cun ibiguin.	When something can be done and it is not done. it will not be possible to do it when one is willing.

SIXTY EIGHTH EXERCISE.

THE LORD'S PRAYER.

Our Father who art in heaven, hallowed be Thy name; Thy kingdom come; Thy will be done on earth as it is in heaven; give us this day our daily bread. and forgive us our trespasses as we forgive them who trespass against us; and lead us not into temptation; but deliver us from evil. Amen.

THE ANGELICAL SALUTATION.

Hail Mary, full of grace, the Lord is with Thee, blessed art thou among women, and blessed is the fruit of thy womb, Jesus.

Holy Mary, Mother of God, pray for us sinners, now and at the hour of our death. Amen.

THE APOSTLES' CREED.

I believe in God the Father Almighty, creator of heaven and earth; and in Jesus Christ, His Only Son, our Lord, who was conceived of the Holy Ghost, born of the Virgin Mary, sufferred under Pontius Pilate. was crucified. dead and buried; He descended into hell; the third day He rose again from the dead; He ascended into heaven, sitteth at the right hand of God the Father Almighty; from thence He shall come to judge the living and the dead. I believe in the Holy Ghost; the Holy Catholic Church, the communion of Saints; the forgiveness of sins; the resurrection of the body; and life everlasting. Amen.

THE GLORIA PATRI.

Glory be to the Father, and to the Son, and to the Holy Ghost! As it was in the beginning. is now, and ever shall be. world without end. Amen.

THE SALVE REGINA.

Hail holy Queen. Mother of Mercy, our Life, our Sweetness, and our Hope; to thee do we cry, poor banished sons of Eve; to thee do we send up our Sighs, mourning and weeping in this valley of tears. Turn, then. most gracious Advocate, thine eyes of mercy towards us, and after this our exile, show unto us the blessed fruit of thy womb, Jesus, O clement, O loving, O sweet Virgin Mary.

SIXTY NINTH LESSON.

YCAANIM NA POUO,T, SIYAM NA PAGARAL.

ON THE LIGAMENTS.

To what has been said in the part devoted to Prosody and in the fourth lesson about the ligaments we now append some additional remarks on the subject, one likely to tax the learner's patience.

G, ng and na, as ligaments, require two different terms to be linked. Thus, nouns referring to the very same person or entity are not linked together.

Father Charles.	Si Pare Carlos.
Saint John Chrysostomus.	Ang póon Si San Juan Crisóstomo.
The Rodriguez family.	Siná Rodriguez.

In the same way and for the same reason, nouns in the vocative case are not linked either.

You, Americans.	Cayó, mañga Americano.
You, natives.	Cayó, mañga Tagálog.
Listen, my brethren.	Paquingán, aquin mañga capatid.
Ye, sinners, beware!.	Mag-íñgat cayó, mañga macasalanan.

If, however, a characteristic predicate is added to an historical name, or an adjective or numeral is used as an epithet to a noun, the ligament or the article should be employed, as it is also the case with the latter in English.

King Ferdinand the Saint.	{ Ang Hari Si Pernandong Santo. or. Pernando ang Santo.
Peter, the learned.	{ Si Pedrong marúnung. or. Si Pedro ang marúnong.
Lesson the second.	{ Pagaáral na ycalauá. or, ycalauáng pagaáral.

The same takes place with any adjectival clause.

Jane, the daughter of our servant.	{ Si Juanang anac nang aming alila. or, Si Juana, ang anac nang aming alila.

As for the use of na after words ending in two different vowels, it may be said that this is generally done with such vocables as are accented on the antepenultimate syllable, and that, if the vocable is otherwise accented, ng is to be preferred.

Limpid water.	Malínao na túbig.
Clear day.	Arao na maliuanag.
Plundering fellow.	Magnanácao na tauo.

| Good fellow. | Tauòng mabutì. |
| Tenth exercise. | Ycasangpouóng pagsasánay. |

Copulative and alternative conjunctions, whether polysyllabic or not, cause the preceding word to drop the ligament. Thus, nouns or sentences put in relation by means of any such conjunctions either expressed or understood, are not linked.

Life and death.	Ang búhay at camatayan.
John, Peter and Frank.	Si Juan, Si Pedro,t. Si Quícoy.
Water and liquors.	Ang túbig patí álac.
Body and soul.	Ang catauoán sampong calolóua.
The Cruz family and Jane.	Siná Cruz ni Juana!
Little birds feed on worms and the former are eaten (devoured) by kites.	Ang óor, ay quinacáin nang mumuntíng ibon at ang muntíng ibon ay linalamon nang láuin.
This or that.	Ytò ó (cun) iyán.
Whether long or short.	Mahaba man, maiclí man.
Be it true or false.	Maguing totoò, maguing cabulaanan.
Shall you come or not?	¿Pariritò ca, dili.?

Any pause in the speech, generally indicated in English by the comma or a similar sign of punctuation, is, in Tagalog, tantamount to the dropping of the ligament.

You, Sir, are vealthy; I, a poor man.	Cayó po,i, mayaman; acó,i, mahírap na tauò.
Don't say that, you will be punished.	Houag sabihin íyán, icáo ay hahampasín.
The articles of Faith are fourteen, seven of which refer to the divinity of Jesus Christ.	Ang mañga punong sinasampalatayanan ay labìng ápat, pitò sa canilà,i, naoócol sa pagcadios ni Jesucristo.

In the same way and for the same reason, explanatory phrases introduced in the sentence by way of parenthesis, and words of a digressive character are not linked to either the word preceding or following them.

Soul,i, e., the vital principle.	Ang calolóua, díua bagá nang catauoán.
Religion, I say, not only is the word of God; but also . .	Ang Religión, anaquin, hindí lámang uica nang Dios; cundí namán........
Pay forthwith the debt, he says.	Bayaran mo dáo capagdaca ang útang.
The servant, it seems, lacks prudence.	Ang alila, anaqui, ualáng cabaitan.
The priest, he says, is dead.	Ang Pare, uica niyà,i, namatáy.
Faith, the Holy Fathers say, is like a torch that . . .	Ang pananampalataya, sabi nang mañga Santong Pare ay parang isàng tangláo . . . . .

If between a noun and its qualifying word or vice-versa, some particle adding to the sense is inserted, the ligament incumbent on the first of the two, passes over to the particle.

Tall person.	Tauòng matáas, or, matáas na tauo.
Person already tall.	Tauò nang matáas, or, matáas nang tauò.
She is likewise a wealthy woman.	Siyá,i, babaye namáng mayaman.
Old person still strong.	Malacás pang matandá, or, matandá pang malacás.
Much money indeed.	Maramì ñgang salapí.

If two or more of such particles are inserted the ligament adheres to the last article.

| A girl who is already also a school-mistress. | Dalaga na namáng maestra. |
| Saint John the disciple always most beloved by Jesus Christ. | Si San Juan, ang alagad na parati at lalo pang iniíbig ni Jesucristo. |

This rule holds good also for the monosyllabic pronoun *ca*.

| You are a good boy. | Bata cang mabait. |
| You are, certainly, a scoundrel. | Tauò ca ñganing tacsil. |

As indicated elsewhere the rule is not applicable to negative adverbs.

You did not write.	Hindí ca sungmúlat.
I will not say it.	Di co sasabihin.
You did not stop, that is the reason why you did not see it.	Di ca tungmahán, cayá di mo naquita.

Houag is, however, an exception, as it causes the pronoun or the particle to be linked to the verb if the former is inserted, but not otherwise.

Let Peter be cudgeled no longer.	Houag nang hampasín Si Fedro, or. houag hampasín na Si Pedro.
Do not run. (plural).	Houag cayóng tumacbò, òr, houag tumacbò cayó.
Don't buy it. (sing).	Houag mong bilhin.
Let them not come here.	Houag siláng pumaritò.
Let him not kill the pig.	Houag niyàng patayín ang bábuy.

Two verbs, one of which is as a direct complement to the other, are linked together if the first of them ends in vowel; but not if it ends in consonant. (*n* excepted).

| We desire to learn. | Tayo,i, nagnanasang magáral. |
| They endeavour to learn. | Silá,i, nagsusumaquit magáral. |

The same is the case with phrases where an adjective governs the infinitive with the verb "to be" understood.

Beautiful to see.	Magandàng tingnán.
Easy to be made.	Magáang gaoin.
Hard to be broken.	Matigás biaquin.
Light for running.	Malicsìng tumacbò.

or, if the past participle is governed by an adverb.

| Newly made. | Bagòng guinauá. |
| Written on purpose. | Tiquis sinúlat. |

Neither adverbs of place and negation nor the words following them take the ligament.

Write here.	Ditò ca sumúlat.
He ate there.	Diyán siyá cungmáin, or, cungmáin siyá diyán.
There my father died.	Dóon si amá namatáy, or, namatáy dóon si amá.
I don't wish to go out.	Di co íbig umalís.
He is not willing to drink any liquor.	Hindí siyá íbig uminom nang álac.

Of the causative and adversative conjunctions, *sa pagca, ñguni, datapóua,* are linked by means of *t; palibhasa,* by means of *i,* as explained in foregoing lessons; the other are used without any ligament at or before them.

Man should be honest although he be poor.	Ang tauô,i, dápat magmabuting ásal bagamán siyá,i, duc-há.
This is not yours, but mine.	Ytô,i, hindí iyò, cundí aquin.
Buy it, since you have money.	Yyòng bilhin, yámang icâo,i. may salapí.
Not a scoundrel, but rather a saint.	Hindí tacsil, cundí bagcús santo.

Interjections drop the ligament, unless they are made substantives.

Would to God he would come.!	¡Cahimanauari pumaritò siyá.!
What a pity, so much money.!	¡Sáyang,! ganiyán caraming pílac.
What does this (word) *abá* mean.?	Ytông *abáng* itò, ¿anò ang cahulogán.?

The interrogative pronouns excepted, any other interrogative word drops the ligament.

How many days.?	¿Ylán árao.?
Where are they going towards.?	¿Sáan silá napatotoñgò.?
Why did you read it.?	¿Baquin mo binasà.?
When will you (plur.) pay.?	¿Cailán cayó magbabayad.?

Ay—i, is employed when the verb is used in merely the verbal sense or stress is laid on the action; *ang*, when it is used in the participial sense or stress is laid on the agent.

He stole.	Siyá,i, nagnácao.
It is he who stole.	Siyá ang nagnácao.

Notwithstanding all that has hereinbefore been said on the ligaments the student should remember that Tagalog is hardly yet fixed on this and other points, nor is it likely to be so for years to come, and that, as a consequence thereof, he will probably find these rules disregarded in practice. The fact is that the language has not yet been developed to a point where theory and practice can be made to coincide with any great degree of accuracy, and thus, the rules laid down should be considered as being only approximative.

SIXTY NINTH EXERCISE.

THE CONFITEOR.

I confess to Almighty. God, to blessed Mary ever Virgin, to blessed Michael the Archangel, to blessed John the Baptist, to the holy Apostles, Peter ang Paul, and to all the Saints, that I have sinned exceedingly, in thought, word, and deed, through my fault, through my fault, through my most grievous fault. Therefore, I beseech the blessed Mary, ever Virgin, blessed Michael the Archangel, blessed John the Baptist, the holy Apostles Peter and Paul, and all the Saints, to pray to the Lord our God for me.

May the Almighty God have mercy upon me, forgive me my sins, and bring me to ever-lasting life. Amen.

May the Almighty and most merciful Lord grant me pardon, absolution and full remission of all my sins. Amen.

FIRST VISIT TO THE MOST HOLY SACRAMENT.

Behold Jesus in the Holy Sacrament, the source of every good, inviting all to visit Him. "Let him that thirsts come to me"–Saint John VII– Oh! what waters of grace have the Saints continually drawn from this fountain, where, according to the prediction of Isaias, Jesus dispenses all the merits of His passion! "You shall draw waters of joy from the fountains of your Saviour" –Isaias XII.– From her long and frequent visits to Jesus Crist in the Holy Eucharist, the Countess of Feria, that illustrious disciple of the venerable Father M. Avila, was called the Spouse of the Sacrament. Being asked how she was employed during the hours which she spent at the foot of the altar, she replied: "I would remain there for all eternity; for the Holy Sacrament contains the essence of God, who will be the food of the blessed. Good God! I am asked what I do in the presence of my Saviour. Why am I not rather asked, what do I not do.? I love Him, I praise Him, I thank Him for His favours. I supplicate His mercy; I do what a beggar does in the presence of a rich man, what a sick man does in the presence of his physician, what a person parched with thirst does before a clear fountain, or what a man fainting from hunger does before a splendid table".

O my most amiable, sweet, and beloved Jesus, my life, my hope, my treasure, and the only love of my soul. How dearly has it cost Thee to remain with us in this Sacrament!. To dwell on our altars, and to assist us by Thy presence, Thou hadst first to die on a cross, and afterwards to submit to numberless injuries in the Holy Sacrament. Thy love and Thy desire to be loved by us, have conquered all difficulties.

Come, then, O Lord!. Come and take possession of my heart. Lock the door of it for ever, that no creature may ever enter, to share in that love which is due to Thee, and which I desire to give entirely to Thee. O my dear Redeemer, mayest Thou alone possess my whole being, and, should I ever be wanting in perfect obedience to Thee, chastise me with severity, that, for the future, I may be more careful to please Thee in all things. Grant that I may never more desire or seek any other pleasure than that of pleasing Thee, of visiting Thee, and of receiving Thee in the Holy Sacrament. Let others seek Earthly goods, I love and desire only the treasure of Thy love. This gift only do I ask of Thee at the foot of Thy altar. Grant that I may forget myself to remember only Thy goodness. Ye, blessed seraphin, I do not envy your glory, but your love for your and my God. Teach me what I must do to love and please Him.

SEVENTIETH LESSON.
YCAPITONG POUONG PAGARAL.

READING AND TRANSLATING EXERCISES.

Books in Tagalog being very scanty, we have had recourse to a collection of sermons and selected the one which is given hereafter for practice in reading and translating. We can hardly commend it as a good morsel of Tagalog literature; it may serve however as an illustration of the manner in which religious truths are served to native people by clergymen.

The arrangement is so devised as to give the student a gradual assistance in his endeavours to translate. In the first part, every Tagalog word or phrase is marked by a number placed above it, and so also is marked the corresponding one of the English text over against it in the second column. In the case of phrases, whenever two or more words in Tagalog have a meaning to be expressed by a single word in English, the former have been enclosed in a parenthesis, the same having been done for English words and phrases in a similar case. When this could not be done, as when a Tagalog word or phrase is to be rendered by two or more English terms requiring the insertion of a third word between, the words bear separately the same number on the English side.

In the second part, both texts are brought face to face and compared without any numbers or parentheses; in the third and last one, the Tagalog text stands alone for the student to do the work and consult the key, if necessary, for what he may not understand; while, on the other hand, the whole exercise is supplemented with foot-notes.

The rendering in the first part is as literal as it can be, the proper rules of English syntax being sometimes disregarded for the purpose: the second part is somewhat less literal, but not so idiomatic and free as the closing one which will he found in the key.

1 2 3 4
Touíng iníisip co, (ang uica ni) (Pó-
5 6 7 8
on Santo) Tomás de (1) Villanueva,
9 10 11 12
touing iníisip co (sa aquing lóob na
13 14
mag–isà) ang (mañga hamac na tóua)
15 16 17 18
nang (mañga tauò) sa mundo (2) (ang
19 20 21
canilàng mañga) panimdín (na ualáng
22
cabuluhan), (ang canilàng mañga)

1 3 2 4 5 6
Whenever I think, (says) (Saint) Tho-
7 8 9 11 10
mas of Villanueva, whenever I consider,
12 13 14
(all alone by myself) the (frivolity) (1)
15 16 17 18 19
of (men) (here in the) world, (their)
21 20 22
(futile) (2) designs, (their)

---

(1) *De*, Spanish preposition for "of". The saint's name is also in Spanish.
(2) *Mundo*, Spanish, "world".

(1) Literally in Tagalog, the worthless rejoicings.
(2) Literally in Tagalog, "not worth a down hair."

23   24   25   26

masasamáng pagnanasa at (ang cani-
     27   28   29   30

làng) capañgahasan na (anaqui), (di
 31   32   33   34   35

mahiyang) ibiguin nilà ang (mañga
 36   37   38

gauá) nang Dios (1) (lalo pa sa) yni-
39 40   41   42 43   44

íbig nilà (sa Dios) din, na (may gauá)
 45 . 46 47   48   49

(sa canilà), acó,i, pinapapasocan nang
50   51   52   53 54

isàng malaquing calumbayan at (ang
      55   56 57 58

luha), (i, tungmutulo) sa aquing matá
    59   60   61

(sa pagca,t.) ¿(sino cayá) (anang San-
 62   63   64

to) (2) ang (di malulumbáy) cun ma-
65 66   67   68   69

quita niyà (ang ganóong) damìng tauò
70 71   72

na bagamán (silá rin ang yguinauá
                     73

nang Pañginóon Dios) (nang lángit),
 - 74   75   76   77

(nang lupa) at (ang lahat) na na-
78   79 80   81

quiquita nati,t, (di naquiquita) (ay
 82   83   84   85

nacalilimot) silá (sa diláng) (magaga-
   86   87   88

ling) at (hindí nilà naalaalà) (ang ygui-
            89

nauá nang Pang-inóon Dios sa canilà)?

---

23   24   25 26   27

wicked desires and their impudence,
28   29   30—31

that (I say), (they are not ashamed)
     32—33   34   35   36

(of their loving) the (works) (1) of
37   38   40   39   41

God (better than) they love (God)
   42   43   44   45   44 46

himself, who is their Creator, I
 47   48   49 50 51   52

become pervaded with a great afflict-
   53   54   55   56 57 58 59

ion and tears (flow) from my eyes; for
60   61   62

who, (says the Saint), (is he who) (will
     63   64 66 65 67

not be saddened) if he sees (such)
     68   69   70

(a great number) (of people) who,
71   72

although (it was for their sake that
           73   74   .75

God created) (Heaven), (Earth) and
     76   77 79 78 80

(everything) that we see and (we do
81   83   82   84

do not see), they forget (all that) (is
85   86   87

good) and (they do not remember)
     88   89

(what God made them for).

---

(1) *Dios*, Spanish, "God".
(2) *Santo*, (Spanish) "Saint."

(1) That is to say: "the creatures, the things made by God."

At houag ninyòng acaláin na ang mañga moros, judíos, herejes (1) cayá ó mañga hindí binyagan (2) ay silá lámang ang pinañguñgusapa,t, pinañgañgáral ni Póong Santo Tomás; hindí, mañga capatid co, cundí ang pinañguñgusapa,t, pinatatamáan niyà,i, ang lahat na nasasacopan nang Santa Yglesia, (3) ang mañga cristianos (4) bagá, na sungmasampalataya sa isàng Dios na totoò; ang mañga cristianos na hindí dápat turang cristiano, cundí sa pañgalan lámang, at ang maramìng tauò na ang

And do not think that it was the Moors, the Jews or Gentiles, to them only (to) whom Saint Thomas addressed (himself) and preached; no, my brethren, it was rather all who were subjects of Holy Church that he addressed, and aimed at; the very Christians who believe in one true God; those Christians who deserve to be called so but in name, and the many people

---

(1) *Moros, judíos herejes*, (Sp), "moors," "jews," "heretics."
(2) Root. *binyag*, "to baptize"; *binyagan*, "baptized."
(3) *Santa Yglesia*, (Sp., "Holy Church."
(4) *Cristianos*, (Sp.) "Christians."

canilàng hinahabol ditò sa mundo, ay ang mañga cayamanan; ang canilàng ninanasa ay, ang mañga pinipita nang canilàng catauoáng lupa; at ang canilàng hinahañgad, ay ang matatáas na catongcula,t, carañgalan (1). Itòng lahat na itò at ang ibà pa ganitò rin ay siláng pinañguñgusapa,t, pinangañgaralan niyóng mahal na Santo at tinatañgisan paniyà ang canilàng búhay at caogalían (2) na ualáng cauculan (3) muntí man sa mahal at matáas na caloualhatíang (4) ynilaláan (5) nang Pañginóon Dios sa mañga mamimintuho (6) sa Caniyà.

¿Anò pa ang súcat cong ydugtong sa mañga sinasabì ni Póon Santo Tomás de Villanueva.?

¿Di ñga cahabag-habag tiñgnán ang masamáng asal nang mañga bata, ang di pagaalumana nang mañga matatandà sa canilàng calolóua, ganóong calapit na silá sa húcay.? (7)

¿Di calumbay-lumbày tiñgnán ang pagmamalibog (8) nang mañga babaye sa pananamit (9), sa mañga quilos nang cataouán at sa il`à pa, at ang paglililuhan nang mañga may asáua.?

¿Di cahabag-habag tiñgnán ang gayòng caraming tauóng nabubúhay sa canilàng pagnanácao at ang hindí mabílang na mañga cristiano na ang pinagcacasipagan (10) nilà gabì,t, árao ay ang paguusapusap (11) nang búhay nang il`à at ang pagsira nang purì nang cápoua tauò.?

Itòng lahat na itò,i, siyáng tinatañgisan (12) ni Póon Santo Tomás nang siyá,i, nabubúhay pa,t, nañgañgáral sa mañga tauò, at siyá ñga namán ang súcat ycatañgis nang mañga may tacot sa Dios at ypag-uicang casamà ni David: "Notum fac mihi, Domine, finem meum". Sa macatouid, "ypatalastás mo sa aquin, Pañgi-nóon rong Dios, ang

whose sole pursuits here in the world are riches; their only desires, the brute appetites of their earthly bodies; and their longings, high offices and vanity. All this and other things of the same kind were just those which that great Saint was treating and preaching about, and he even wept over their behavior (lives) and propensities that paid no regard, however little, to the great and lofty glory that our Lord has prearranged for those who profess to obey Him.

What else should I add to what Saint Thomas of Villanueva says.?

Is it not a pitiable thing to witness (see) the children's ill demeanor and old people's disregard for their souls, the latter being already so near the grave.?

Is it not sorrowful to witness (to see) the impudence of women in dressing, in waddling, and in other ways, and the infidelity (treachery) of married people.?

Is it not a sad thing to witness (to see) so many people who live upon their robberies and the numberless Christians whose most eager pursuits, day and night, are back-biting at others' lives and destroying the characters of their fellow-creatures.?

All this was what Saint Thomas wept over when he was still alive and was preaching to men, and just this, too, is what men fearing God ought to mourn over, and also what (ought) to make them exclaim with David: "Notum fac mihi, Domine, finem meum"; that is to say; "make known to me my Lord God,

(1) From dañgal, "fame", "dignity," carañgalan, abst.
(2) From ogali, "custom", "habit," abst. caogalían, "propensity of mind", "bías.'
(3) From ucol, "to suit", cauculan, "conformity'.
(4) Root, loualhati, "glory", "rest"; caloualhatían, "bliss".
(5) Root, láan, "to make ready"; ynilaláan instead of ylinaláan.
(6) Root, pintoho or mintoho, "to obey".
(7) Húcay, "grave".
(8) From libog, "lecherous", pagmamalibog, "growing lecherous".
(9) From damit pananamit, "manner of dressing".
(10) Root, sipag, "care", "watchfulness"; hence, pinagcacasipagan, "what one is eagerly undertaking".
(11) Diminutive verb meaning "to speak idly".
(12) Tinatañgisan, present tense for tinañgisan, past tense.

maquiquing cararatnán (1) *nang búhay co,* sa pagca,t, gayóng carami ang mañga casalanang naquiquita nang matá co ditò sa mundo at gayóng carami ang mañga escándalong (2) nacacálat (3) sa mañga ciudad (4) at sa mañga bayan, na halos di co naalaman cun anò,t, vpinañganac (5) ni inà sa aquin, halos di co naalaman ang yguinauá Mo sa aquin.

Cayá, mañga capatid co, ang punong (6) pácay (7) at sadiyang (8) yguinauá nang Dios sa tauò ay siyá binabantá (9) cong saysayi,t, ypagsermón (10) sa inyò ñgayón. Paquingán ninyò: Sa lahat na quinapal nang Panginóon Dios, ang tauò lámang ang pinacamasouáin. At totoò ñga, mañga capatid co, sa pagca,t, ang ibàng guinauá nang Panguinóon Dios ay parapararang sungmosonod at tungmutupad (11) nang mañga ytinúcoy (12) nang Dios sa canila, at ang tauò,i, hindí.

Ang árao, and bóuan, at ang ibà mañga astro (13) nagsisipihit (14) at nacaliliuánag (15) árao,t, gabi ditò sa sanglupáan.

Ang lupa, namá,i, tinutubúan nang pálay, maís, (16) at nang sarisaring guguláin at nang mañga cáhoy na parapara,i, namumulac-lac at namumuñga sa canicanilàng (17) tacdáng panahón, at ualá isà man mañgañgahas sumuáy sa ypinatutungcol (18) nang Pang-inóon Dios sa canilà.

Ang mañga háyop ay gungmaganap (19) din nang mañga yniotos nang Pang-inóon Dios sa canilà at namamang-inóon (20) pa sa tauò.

what the end of my life will be"; for so many are the sins my eyes (eye) see here on Earth and so many the scandals spreading over cities and towns that I can hardly understand what my mother brought me forth (into the world) for, and scarcely know what Thou createdst me for.

Therefore, my brethren, the main purpose and final destiny God made man for, will be the topic I intend to develop, and the reason of my preaching to you to-day. Listen: Of all things that have been created by God, man only is indeed disobedient. Yes, indeed, my brethren, for the other things created by God, our Lord, all of them obey and fulfill the task assigned by God to them, but man does not.

The sun, the moon and the other stars turn around and impart brightness, day and night, here to the (whole) Earth.

The soil, too, produces rice, maize and a variety of vegetables, and trees as well, all of which alternately blossom and bear fruit in their respectively appointed seasons and not even one (of these things) dares revolt against the task imposed by God on them.

Animals do carry out the commands of God to them and they besides acknowledge man as (their) master.

---

(1) Root *dating*, "to reach"; *cararatnán*, contracted future verbal noun meaning "halting place", "goal", "end". *Maquiquing* imparts a sense of doubt and conversion.

(2) *Escándalong*, (Sp. w.) *escándalo*, "scandal".

(3) Root, *cálat*, "to spread", "to propagate".

(4) *Ciudad*, (Sp. w.) "city".

(5) From *anac*, "son or daughter"; *mañganac*, "to bring forth".

(6) *Pono*, "main", "principal", "trunk of a tree", "stock".

(7) *Pácay*; "purpose", "aim".

(8) *Sadiya*, "object", "goal".

(9) *Bantá*, "to intend", "to propose".

(10) Root *sermón*, (Sp. w.) for "sermon".

(11) Root-word *tupad=tupar* or *topad=topar*, "to discharge one's duty," "to fulfill one's promise."

(12) Root, *tótoy*, "prearranged thing," *ytinícoy*, "what a thing or an action is intended for."

(13) *Astro*, (Sp. w.) "star," "any luminous body."

(14) Root, *pihit*, "to turn around," "to rotate;" *magsi* is in reference to the great number of stars.

(15) Root, *liuánag*, "clearness."

(16) *Mais*, (corr. from Sp. w.) *maíz*, 'maize'.

(17) *Canicanila*, is an instance of a double plural; it refers both to the trees and to the different seasons.

(18) Root-word, *tongcol*", "to impose a task."

(19) *Ganap*, "to fulfill."

(20) From *Pang-inóon*, "lord;" *mamang-inóon*, "to acknowledge as a master", "to serve as a slave."

Ang calábao, sa halimbáua, ay, gungmagauá sa lupa, hungmahacot nang bató, lupa,t, buhañgin; hungmihilà nang mañga cáhoy at cauayan, at dinadalà niyà sa mañga parián ang inyòng pálay, maís at bálang nang ynilalaco ninyò.

The buffalo, for instance, works the soil, carts stone, earth and sand; drags along timber (lumber) and reed-cane, and carries to market-places your husked-rice, maize and anything you deal in.

Ang cabayo,i, nagpasasacáy sa tauò at ynihahatid niyà ang caniyàng pang-inóon sa bálang paroroonan (1).

The horse allows himself to be mounted (ridden) by man and he carries his master to any place whatever.

Ang aso,i, nagbabantáy sa báhay, sungmasamà sa caniyàng pang-inóon sa bundoc, sa búquid, sa pañgáñgaso, (2) at nag-aalaga (3) pa nang catauoán at mañga pag-aari nang pinacapanginóon niyà.

The dog keeps watch at home, accompanies his master to the woods, to the cornfields, to hunting (with a dog) and takes care of the person (body) and property of him whom he considers as his master.

Ang topa,i, nagpaparamit sa tauò at nagpacáin pa sa caniyàng masarap na carne (4) o lamán (5).

The sheep yields clothing to man and feeds him too with its tasteful meat.

Ang manoc, ay, ungmiitlog sa báhay at nag-aanac nang maraming sísiu na siyáng yquinahahánap (6) nang tauò nang caniyàng pagcabúhay.

The hen lays eggs at home and brings forth many ckickens, the same serving man as a means to earn his livelihood.

At ang lahat na háyop ay paraparang sungmosonod sa catongcolan ynihalal (7) nang Pang-inóon Dios sa canilà.

And all animals conjointly fulfill the ends which were prearranged for them by God.

Ang tauò lámang, ay siyáng masouáil (8) sa lahat, sa pagca,t, siyá ñga lámang ang nañgañgahás lumabán at sumuáy sa may gauá sa caniyá. Anaqui, hindí niyà naalaman ang yquinapal nang Pang-inóon Dios sa caniyà, na ualáng dahilang ibà cundí ang quilalanin niyà ang Dios din, alaalahanin, ibiguin,t, sundín ditò sa búhay na itò nang mapanóod niyà,t, calugdán (9) sa caloualhatían sa Láñgit.

Man, only, is the most rebellious creature of the whole, for it is only he who dares face (stand) and disobey his Creator. It seems as if he did not know the end for which he was created by God, which was for (no) other purpose but that he might know the true God, remember, love and obey Him here in this life that he may behold and enjoy Glory in Heaven.

¿Di ñga bagá itò ang yguinauá nang Pang-inóon Dios sa inyò? ¿At di itò rin ang hindí iníisip at inaalalà nang caramihang tauò na nagbabansag (10) anac nang Dios?

Is it not this very object (end) God created you for? And is it not just this that most men who boast to be the sons of God do not think upon and remember of?

!Ang di pagsisimbà bagá cun Domingo at piestang (11) pañgilin!

Not to hear mass, therefore, on Sundays and holidays! (feast-keeping days.)

!Ang di pagcocolasión (12) sa mañga

Failing to fast on the

---

(1) *Paroroonan*, reaching-place and also the thing or reason gone for; from *paróon*, "to go there".

(2). From *aso*, "dog;" *pañgañgaso*, "the hunting with a dog."

(3) *Alaga*, "to take care of", "to look after" generally living things.

(4) *Carne* (Sp. w.) "meat", "flesh".

(5) *Lamán*, "the inside", "the pith of anything." Here it is used redundantly, so as to avoid misunderstanding on the part of those who might not be acquainted with the Spanish-word *carne*.

(6) *Yquinahahánap*, "what serves as an instrument in seeking.

(7) Root, *halal*, "to prepare" (beforehand), *ynihalal* for *ylinalal*.

(8) *Masouáil*, grudging-fellow".

(9) From *lojod*, "gayety", "rejoicing", *calugdán*, contracted second derivative abstract noun.

(10) *Bansag*, "to boast".

(11) Corr. from Sp. w. *fiesta*, "feast", "holiday".

(12) Corr. from Sp. w. *colación*, "diet to be kept in fast days".

árao na ypinag-uutos!. ¡Ang pagco-compisal at pagcocomulgar na hindí tapat at mahúsay!. ¡Ang madláng (1) inaacala.t, pinapacsá (2) nang tauò na may cahalong hañgin (3) nang capalalóan!. ¡Ang malaquing capanaghilíang nacadadalamhati (4) sa maraming tauò na ualáng bait. Ang pagsisilve (5) nang manga mañgañgasauá (6) nang isà, dalauà ó tatlong taón sa canilàng bibiyananin (7) na laban sa catouiran, palibhasa,i, itòng ogali ninyò itò,i, báual nang Pang-inóon Dios at báual namán nang mañga pono natin. Ytòng lahat na itò, anaquin, at ibàng ganganitò,i, ¿mañga gauá cayá nang mañga tauòng nacaiibig mamintuho sa Pang-inóon Dios ditò sa búhay na itò, nang macamtán nilà bálang árao ang caloual-hatían sa Láñgit?.

appointed days! The confessing and receiving of Holy Communion unscrupulously and undeservedly! The numberless thoughts and forethought contrivances (designs) of the man who is moved through the vain wind of pride: The great envy (that) many fickle men (lacking wisdom) brood; the serving of the male-betrothed parties for one, two, or three years (to) their future fathers and mothers-in-law, which is contrary to right, (because) this custom of yours is forbidden by the Lord, God, and is also prohibited by our authorities. All of this, I say, and other similar things, are they, then, the actions (acts) of men professing to obey God, the Lord, here in this life, that they may some day attain Glory in Heaven?.

---

(1) *Madlá* or *marlá*, indeterminate or spread about multitude of things in contradistinction to *marami*, which denotes things capable of being counted.

(2) *Pacsó* and *pácay* express what is done consciously and purposely.

(3) *Cahalong hañgin*, "wind triffles", "vain frivolities".

(4) *Dalamhati*, "to fret", "to take pains for", "to brood."

(5) *Silve* or *silvi*, corr. from Sp. w. *servir*, "to serve," "to wait upon."

(6) From *asáua*, "either of the married parties", *pañgañgasauá*, (note the accentuation) "to pay addresses with a view to marry."

(7) From *bianán* or *biyanán*, "father or mother-in-law"; *bibiyananin*, future father or mother-in-law. This refers to a widely-spread native custom of bride-parents exacting personal services from their future sons-in-law, before the former give up their daughters in marriage.

¡Ay mañga capatid co!. ¡Páuang ualáng capapacanan iyán mañga gauá ninyòng iyán!. ¡Cundí ninyò ytuñgò sa Pang-inóon Dios ang inyòng mañga gauá!. ¡Cundí ang Pang-inóon Dios ang tuñgò ninyò, ang carongsolan (1) nang inyong lóob, at ang cararatnán (2) hinahañgad ninyò,t, pinapacsá!. ¡Cundí iuán ninyò ang alín man ibàng sadyá at ang alín man ibàng pagnanasa!. ¡Cundí, anaquin. lisan (3) ninyò,t, talicoran (4) ang anò anò (5) man quinacapalaran (6) ninyò ditò sa lupa, liban sa Dios!. ¡Ay páuang ualáng cabolohan ang inyòng mañga gauá at hindí mandin mangyayaring maguing dáang ycapapasaláñgit (7) ninyò!.

Napaáral cay Moisés ang iilán mañga tauò na lubháng ninanasa nilàng maalaman ang magaling na áral na ycapapasaláñgit nilà. ¡Manáa! ang sagot sa canilà niyóng banal at santong Si Moisés; naalaman ninyò na ang lahat na gauá nang mañga tauò ditò sa mundo, ay mayróon din quinapapatuñguhan.

Maram'ng hírap ang tinitiis nang isàng sondalo sa panahón nang pagbabacà: tinitiis niyà ang gútum, ang ohío, ang pagod, at lumulusob (8) pa siyá sa mañga caáuay, marami man silá at malaqui man ang pañgánib na ycamamatáy niyà, at cayá gayón, sa pagca,t, siyáng ynihihintáy niyà nang malaquìng gantì nang caniyàng Hari.

Hindí ynaalumana (9) nang magsasacá ang cainitan nang árao, ang casamíían nang panahón, ang capagalan, ang páuis at ang ibàng dahilang, súcat ycaliuag nang caniyàng gauá; sa pagca,t, ang gayóng pagsasaquit niyàng gumauá,i, siyáng ynihihintáy niyà nang magaling na pagaani (10).

Ang magcacalácal ay hindí natatacot tumauir (11) nang dágat, malacás man ang hañgin, malaqui man ang daluyon (12) at ang pañgánib ay malaqui rin, cun inaacala niyà na ang gayóng pagtauir ay siyáng ycasusúlong (13) niyà nang caniyàng laco sa mabuti at matáas na halagá.

Ang may saquit ay hindí naáua sa caniyàng cataouán, cundí bagcús tinitiis niyà nang magandàng lóob ang pait nang purga (14), ang hapdí nang parapit, (15) ang antac (16) nang súgat at ang búlang mamatapating (17) gaoin nang médico sa caniyàng cataouán, cun itò mañga gauáng ṭitò,i, siyáng ycagagaling at ycababañgon (18) niyàng maloualhati (19) sa caniyàng saquit.

---

(1) Root, *dongsol*, "to level at", hence, *carongsolan*, "the place looked at", "the thing leveled at".

(2) Root, *dating*, "to arrive", "to reach"; *cararatnán*, contracted abstract noun, for the place to be reached at. the thing aimed at.

(3) *Lisan*, "to give up".

(4) *Talicod*, "back", "to turn one's back on", "to renounce".

(5) *Anò anò*, plural.

(6) Root, *pálad*, "happiness"; *quinacapalaran*, "what causes happiness".

(7) *Ycapapasaláñgit*, what "will lead (cause to go) into Heaven.

(8) *Lumusob*, "to break through".

(9) *Alumana*, "to be of moment", "to matter".

(10) *Ani*, "rice harvest"; *pagaani*, "the gathering in of it".

(11) *Tumauir=d*, "to ford", "to cross".

(12) *Daluyon*, "wave", "billows".

(13) From *súlong*, "forward"; *ycasusúlong*, "what will cause promotion, advancement."

(14) *Purga*, (Sp. w.) "purge", "medecine".

(15) *Parapit*, "caustic-plaster".

(16) *Antac*, "rack", "anguish", "ache".

(17) From *matapat*, "just", "fair"; *matapatin*, "something fit, adequate".

(18) From *bañgon*, "to lift", "to rise".

(19) *Maloualhati*, "rest", "alleviation", "recovery".

Cayá, ytinatanong co sa inyo: ¿Sáan cayá ypinatutuñgò ninyò ang in
yòng mañga gauá?. ¿Sáan di po, (1) ang ysasagot ninyò, seguro, (2) sa aquin
¿sáan di po cundì sa pagcapacagaling (3) namin sa Láñgit, sa pagcacamit
namin bagá nang mapálad cararatná,t, caloualhatíang ynilaláan nang
Pañg-inóon Dios sa atin.? Cun gayón, ang uica co sa inyò, cun gayón, ay ga-
yahan ninyò ang sondalo, ang magsasacà, ang magcacalácal at ang may
saquit. Sa macatouid, magcasipag (4) cayóng humánap nang ycagagaling
nang inyòng calolóua para nang pagpapacasipag nang mañga naturan (5)
cong tauò sa paghánap nang ycalalaqui nang canilàng cayamana,t, ycagagaling nang canilàng catauoán.

Tungmatamá dito sa lugar na itò ang mañga tanong nang Santong Hari
Si David, na ang uica: ¿Quis ascendet in montem Domini? ¿Aut quis stabit
in loco sancto ejus.? Sa macatouir, ani David. "¿Sino cayá ang mapálad
na tauòng macaaquiat at macarating sa matáas at mahal na calalaguían (6)
nang ating Pang-inóon Dios? ¿Sino cayá ang mamalagui (7) sa caniyàng
Santa Gloria?. ¿Sino bagá ang mapálad na tauòng macapagcamit nang
magaling na cararatnáng ynilaláan nang Dios sa atin?. At dito sa mañga
tanong na itò,i, siyá rin ang sungmasagot na ang uica: Innocens manibus
et mundo corde, qui non accepit in vano animam suam. Sa macatouid;
Ang mañga tauòng malilinis na camáy at malilinis na lóob, at ang maru-
rúnong na magmahal sa canilàng calolóua; na, cun sa bágay, (8) ay itò
ang cahologán: ang mañga tauòng ualáng casalanan ay silá lámang ang
mapapacagaling sa Láñgit.

Diyata, (9) ang tanong co ñgayón: ¿Mayróon bagá mañga tauòng hindí
marúnong magmahal sa canilàng calolóua o inaari (10) cayá nilàng hámac
ang canilàng calolóua.? Mayróon din ang sagot co namán.

Ang ating calolóua,i, súcat ninyò ypara sa mañga casangcapang (11)
guinagámit nang tauò sa caniyàng pamamúhay (12) cun sa paghánap nang
caniyàng pagcabúhay. Ay anò, ang araróng (13) hindí guinagámit sa pagaararo (13) ¿di parang inaaring hámac nang nagpagauá niyón?

Ang saya (14), ang tapis, (15) ang baro, ang salaual at ibá pa ganitò na
binibilì ninyò,t, ypinatatabás (16) at ypinatatahi sa marúnong. ay, ¿di parang
inaari ninyò hámac cun pagcayari, (17),t, sacá ytatago ninyò sa cabán at hindí
ysusuot (18) sa catauoán.?

Ang itac na ypinagauá ninyò sa pandáy at talagang gagamitin sa
báhay cun sa pagtagá nang caouayan o sa ibàng cailañgan, ay, ¿di parang
inaari ninyò hámac cun sacali,t, yniiñgatan ninyò sa caloban (19) ó ysi-
nusucsoc (20) ninyò sa dingding.?

---

(1) *Sáan* has here the sense of "of course;" *sáan di po*, "where, of course, but to?."
(2) *Seguro*, (Sp. w.) for "sure", tagalized into "perhaps," "no doubt."
(3) *Pagcapagaling*, "salvation."
(4) *Magcasipag*, "try," "endeavour," "toil". (imp).
(5) *Naturan*, "named," "said," "above mentioned," "aforesaid."
(6) From the root *lagiy*, "putting", placing, &; *calalaguian*, contracted abstract
noun, meaning "place," "position."
(7) From *palagui*, always," "constantly;" *mamalagui*, "to stay, to be forever
at a place."
(8) *Na*, *cun sa bágay*, "which means," "that is to say."
(9) *Diyata*, "wherefore."
(10) *Inaari*, "estimates," "values," (pres. ind. 3rd. pers. pass.)
(11) From *sangcap*, "tool," "piece of furniture;" *casangcapan*, "fixtures," "utens-
ils," "furniture."
(12) From *báhay*, "house," "nest;" *pamamáhay*, "dwelling."
(13) *Araro*, corr. from (Sp. w.) *arado*, "plough;" *pagaararo*, "the ploughing."
(14) *Saya* (Sp. w.) "upper petticoat."
(15) *Tapis*, "apron worn by native women."
(16) From the root *tabás*, "to cut out stuffs with scissors"; *ypatabás*, "to have
stuffs cut out."
(17) *Pagcayari*, "finished," "already made."
(18) From *suot*=*soot*, "to put on clothes."
(19) *Caloban*, "sheath," "scabbard."
(20) From *sucsoc*, "to enchase," "to infix."

¿Di parang inaari cong hámac itòng lámpara (1) nang simbahan cun sacali,t, di co paiilauang sa mañga sacristán? (2) ¡Ay! gayón din, mañga capatid co, ang aquing masasabi tongcol sa ating calolóua.

¿Di cayá parang inaari hámac nang tauò ang caniyáng calolóua cundí gamitin niyà ang mañga pinañgañgalan potencias, (3) ang alaalà bagá, ang bait at ang lóob sa mañga bágay na ytinúcoy nang Pang-inóon Dios sa canilà?

¿Di hámac anaquin, ang alaalà cundí gamitin nang tauò sa pag-alaalà niyà sa Dios, sa caniyàng mañga biyaya, sa macatouid, sa pag-alaalà nang tauò na siyá,i, guinauá nang Pang-inóon Dios calarauan (4) niyà,t, tinobós ni Jesucristo nang caniyàng mahal na dugó at pagcamatáy sa Crus, áua niyà lámang sa caniyà. (5)?

¿Di hámac, anaquin, ang bait cundí gamitin nang tauò sa pagquilala sa Dios at sa pag-iisip na ang carunuñgan, catouira,t, capangyarihan nang Dios din ay ualáng hangán at ang Siyá ñga namá,i, punong pinangaliñga,t, quinaouian nang lahat. (6)?

¿Di hámac ang lóob cundí gamitin nang tauò sa pag-iibig niyà sa Dios na parang amá,t, macapangyayari sa lahat; sa pag-iibig namán sa cápouang tauò at sa pag-íbig at pagsunod nang diláng cabanalang ásal na ycapapasaláñgit nang caniyàng calolóua at sa pandidiri (7) nang diláng casalanan ycapapacasamá (8) niyà sa infierno.?

Cayá, mañga capatid co, ypalaman ninyò sa lóob it ng áral na ypi-nañg-áral co sa inyò. Ynyòng pacatantóin (9) na ang yguinauá nang Pang-inóon Dios sa inyò ay ang siyá,i, alaalahanin, quilalanin, ibigui,t, sundín ninyò ditò sa lupa, nang macamtán ninyò dóon sa búhay na ualáng hangán.

Ang pananampalataya (10) ninyò,t, pagcatalastás (11) nitòng áral na itò,i, siyáng ycapag-iiguì (12) ninyò nang inyòng masasamáng gauá, at siyá rin namáng ycapagbabagò ninyò nang dating ásal na masasamá.

Ang pananampalataya ninyò,t, pagcatalastás nitòng áral na itò,i, si-yáng ycasusúlong nang inyòng lóob sa pagtitiis nang mañga cahirapan ala ng-álang (13) sa Dios para nang pagtitiis nang sondalo nang di masa-bing (14) hírap alang-álang sa caniyàng Hari.

Ang pananampalataya ninyò,t. pagcatalastás nitòng áral na itò,i, siyáng ypagsasaquit (15) manalo sa mañga caáuay nang inyòng calolóua, para nang pagsasaquit nang mañga magsasacà sa paggauá sa canilàng búquid, maga-ling man di man (16) ang panahón, nang macamtán nilà ang mabuting pag—ani.

Ang pananampalataya ninyò,t. pagcatalastás nitòng áral na itò,i, siyáng ycapag-aalís (17) ninyò sa inyòng cataouán nang catamaran (18) sa pagsimbà at sa pagcocompisal at nang lahat na dinadahilan ninyò sa di pagsunod nang otos nang Dios at nang Santa Yglesia.

(1) Lámpara, (Sp. w.) "lamp," "lustre," "cresset."
(2) Sacristán, (Sp. w.) "sexton," "church clerk."
(3) Potencias, (Sp. w.) "the powers of soul;" memory, understanding and will.

(4) From laráuan, "image", "pattern"; calaráuan, "one pattern. model" &.
(5) Aua niyà lámang sa caniyà, "only for his sake." (man's).
(6) Punong pinangaliñga,t, quinaouian nang lahat, "the source which everything flows from and comes again back into".
(7) Diri, "to loathe", "to abhor".
(8) From samá. "idea of wickedness"; magcapapasamá. "to incur eternal punish-ment".
(9) Pacatantóin, "endeavour to understand." (imp.)
(10) From sampalataya, "to believe", "to give credit to".
(11) From tálastás, "to comprehend."
(12) Root, iguì, "idea of goodness"; ycapag-iguì, "what causes improvement".
(13) Alang-álang sa, for the sake of".
(14) Di masabì, "unutterable".
(15) From saquit, "pain", "toil", "hardship"; magsaquit, "to endeavour"; ypagsa-saquit ninyò, "will assist you in".
(16) Magaling man, di man; (magaling), understood.
(17) From pag-aalís, "taking away".
(18) Root, támad or támar, "lazy"; catamaran, "laziness".

At, sa catagáng uica, ang pananampalataya ninyò,t, pagcatalastás na maigui nang ponong pácay at sadiyang yguinauá nang Pang-inóon Dios sa inyò ay siyáng icapagsisípag gamitin sa magaling ang mañga potencias o cabagsican (1) nang calolóua; ang alaalà bagá,i, gamitin sa pag-aalaalà sa Dios at sa mañga biyayang ypinagcacalóob niyà sa inyò; ang bait ay, sa pagquilala sa Dios at nang caniyáng capangyariban. at ang lóob ay sa paguíbig sa Dios nang lubós na pag-íbig ditò sa búhay na itò nang macamtán ninyò dóon sa búhay na ualáng hangán. Siyá nauá (2).

END OF THE GRAMMAR.

———

(1) From *bagsic*, a root meaning "power", "tyranny", "swell"; *cabagsican*, abstract noun.

(2) *Siyá nauá*, amen.

THE TAGALOG LANGUAGE.

TAGALOG KEY

TO

THE ENGLISH EXERCISES.

—◦•◦—

In going over the Tagalog exercises the student must endeavor to guard himself against writing *ñg.* as printed therein, instead of *ng̃* as it should be, that is to say, the tittle should be written in the middle over the two letters and not above the *n*.

KEY TO THE EXERCISES.

UNANG PAGSASANAY.

¿Mayróon cang tinápay?. Oo, po, mayróon acóng tinápay. ¿Na sa iyò bagá ang tinápay co?. Na sa aquin ang tinápay mo. ¿Na sa iyò bagá ang carne o lamán?. Na sa aquin ang lamán. ¿Na sa iyò bagá ang iyòng carne?. Na sa aquin ang carne co. ¿Na sa iyò baga ang asín?. Na sa aquin ang asín. ¿Na sa iyò cayú ang asín co?. Na sa aquin ang iyòng asín. ¿Na sa iyò bagá ang asúcal?. Na sa aquin ang asúcal. ¿Na sa iyò bagá ang túbig?. Na sa aquin ang túbig. ¿Na sa iyò bagá ang túbig mo?. Na sa aquin ang túbig co. ¿Anóng papel ang na sa iyò?. Ang papel co ang na sa aquin.

YCALAUANG PAGSASANAY.

¿Ang amá co,i, mayróon asín.? Siyá,i, ualá. ¿May inà ca bagá.? Acó,i, mayróon. ¿Mayróon bagáng capatid na babaye ang hari.? Ualá. ¿May capatid na lalaqui ang obispo.? Mayróon. ¿May túbig bagá si Juan.? Si Juan ay mayróon túbig. ¿Mayróon bagá siyáng báhay.? May báhay ñga siyá. ¿May capangyarihan bagá ang Dios.? Oo, ñga, Siyá,i, may capangyarihan. ¿May cabagsican bagá ang iyòng sintà.? Oo, ang sintà co,i, may cabagsican. ¿Ang Dios, ay, may sintà bagá sa tauò.? Oo. ang Dios ay may sintà sa tauò. ¿Mayróon bagáng libro sa báhay mo? Oo, sa báhay co,i, may libro. ¿May cabagsican bagá ang sintà nang inà mo? Oo, ñga. ¿Alíng libro ang na sa iyò?. Ang libro ni Pedro ang na sa aquin. ¿Anòng búquid ang na sa amá mo?. Ang búquid nang hari ang na sa caniyà (his, her, of her, of him.)

YCATATLONG PAGSASANAY.

¿Mayróon bagá tayong baet?. Oo, tayo,i, mayróon. ¿Mayróon bagá siláng mabubutèng damit?. Hindí, silá,i, ualá. ¿Mayróon bagá cayóng mañga salamíng masasamá?. Mayróon caming masasamá. ¿Na sa aquin bagá ang iyòng maririquit na cabayo.? Oo, (ang mañga cabayo),i, na sa iyò ñga. ¿Na sa batang mababaet ang mañga aso cong maririquit?. Oo, na sa canilà (1)

_____

(1) *Canilà*, "their, of them".

ang mañga aso mong maririquit. ¿Na sa canilà bagá ang aquin mañga librong maririquit?. Ualá. ¿Alíng sambalelo ang na sa amin. (1)? Ang mañga sambalilo ni Pedro ang na sa inyò. (2). ¿Na cay Juan bagá ang mañga mabutìng cabayo nang aquing mañga capatid na matandá?. Ualá sa canilà. ¿Na sa amá ni Pedro baga ang mañga cabayong matandá nang aquing mañga bata?. Ualá sa caniyà. ¿Ang mañga matandá.i, mayróon bagáng sintá sa mañga bata? Oo, po, silá,i, may sintá sa mañga bata. ¿Mayróon bagá Siná Juan mañga mabuting báhay?. Hindí, silá,i, ualáng mabubuting báhay, cundí silá,i, mayróon mañga búquid na magagandà. ¿Anò ang mañga búquid niná Pedro?. Siná Pedro,i, mayróon mañga búquid na magagandà. ¿Na sa canilà bagá ang caná Juang mañga páñgit na báhay?. Ualá sa canilà ang caná Juang mañga páñgit na báhay. ¿Mayróon bagá mañga libro sa mañga lamesa?. Ualá mañga libro sa mañga lamesa. ¿Ang mañga capatid mong babaye, mayróon bagáng mañga asong matatandá?. Hindí, ualá siláng asong matatandá.

---

(1) *Amin*, "our, of us".
(2) *Inyo*, "your, of you". (plur.)

YCAAPAT NA PAGSASANAY.

¿Nasáan ang amá mo?. Na sa báhay ang amá co. ¿Sáan naróon ang anac nang capatid co?. Siyá,i, nasasimbahan. ¿Sáan naróon ang canilàng anac na babaye?. Na sa simbahan ang canilàng anac na babaye. ¿Nasáan bagá ang aming anac na lalaqui?. Ang anac naming lalaqui na sa escuela. ¿Naritò cayá ang bata.? Ualá, siyá,i, ualá ditò, na sa búquid siyá. ¿Nariyán bagá ang mañga bata nang capatid mong babaye.? Ang mañga bata nang aquiñg capatid na babaye,i, ualá diyán. (ditò). ¿Nasáan cayá silá.? Silá,i, na sa báhay. ¿Siyá (ñga) bagá.? Abáa, siyá ñga. ¿Cayó ñga bagá.? Hindí ñga camí. ¿Nariyán bagá ang mañga capatid na lalaqui ni inà? Ang mañga capatid na lalaqui ni inà,i, ualá diyán, silá,i, na cay Juang báhay. ¿Naróon bagá ang bundoc.? Oo, naróon ñga ang bundoc. ¿Ang singsing mo,i, guintó bagá.? Hindí, ang singsing co,i, pílac. ¿Ang iyòng lamesa, cáhoy bagá.? Hindí, ang lamesa co,i, búbog. ¿Ang mañga obispo ninyò,i, mayróon bagáng mañga singsing na bácal.? Ualá, ualá siláng mañga singsing na bácal; silà,i, mayróon mañga singsing na guintó. ¿Ang mañga salamín namin, pílac bagá.? Hindí po, ang mañga salamín namin, ay búbog. ¿Mayróon ca bagáng mañga librong patalim.? Ualá, acó,i, mayróon mañga librong papel. ¿Ang mañga capatid mong babaye, mayróon bagá siláng plumang cáhoy.? Ualá, ualá siláng mañga plumang cáhoy; silà,i, mayróon mañga plumang patalim. ¿Mayróon bagá acóng sambalelong cáhoy.? Ualá, ualá acóng sambalelong cáhoy, mayróon acóng dalauàng sambalelong búlac.

YCALIMANG PAGSASANAY.

¿Na sa iyò bagá ang aquing sintas na guintó.? Ualá, ualá sa aquin. ¿Mayróon ca bagáng anomán.? Ualá. ¿Na sa iyò bagá ang aquing plumang patalim.? Ualá, ualá sa aquin. ¿Aling panúlat ang na sa iyò.? Ang aquing mabuting panúlat na pílac ang na sa aquin. ¿Anò mayróon ca.? Ualá. ¿Na sa iyò bagá ang aquing plumang patalim ó ang pílac cayá.? Ang iyòng panúlat na patalim, ang sa na aquin. ¿Na sa iyò bagá ang sabón co?. Ualá sa aquin. ¿Na sa iyò bagá ang candelero co? Ualá sa aquin. ¿Aling candelero ang na sa iyò.? Ang candelero cong guintó ang na sa aquin. ¿Na sa iyò bagá ang lúbid co.? Ualá sa aquin. ¿Na sa iyò bagá ang álac cong mabutì.? Ualá sa aquin. ¿Na sa iyò bagá iyáng librong iyán.? Ualá sa aquin. Na sa iyò bagá iyáng lamáng iyán.? Na sa aquin ñga. ¿Mayróon ca bagáng anománg mabutì.? Ualá acóng anománg mabutì. ¿Anòng mariquit na bágay (1) ang na sa iyò? Ang mariquit na sintas na guintó ang na sa aquin. ¿Mayróon ca bagáng anománg páñgit.? Ualá acóng anománg páñgit. mayróon acóng anománg mariquit. ¿Anòng mariquit na bágay ang na sa iyò.? Ang mariquit na aso, ang na sa aquin. ¿Na sa iyò bagá ang iyòng panúlat na búbog.? Ang tenedor mo, ang na sa aquin. ¿Na sa caniyà bagá itò ó (cun) iyáng pótong.? Ytò,i, na sa caniyà, iyá,i, ualá. ¿Na sa aquing mañga capatid na babaye bagá ang damit niyáng mañga batang iyán.? Ualá sa canilá ang diyán sa mañga batang damit na iyán; ang sa canilàng mañga capatid na lalaqui, ang na sa canilà. ¿Yaóng panúlat na yaón, dóon sa tauòng yaón bagá.? Yaóng panúlat ay hindí dóon sa tauòng yaón, at yo,i, dóon sa mañga babaye.

_____

(1) Bágay, "thing", "matter". "subject".

YCAANIM NA PAGSASANAY.

¿Na sa hari bagá ang panúlat na búbog ó ang patalim.? Ang hari, ay ualáng panúlat na búbog man, ó patalim man. ¿Aling panúlat bagá ang na sa obispo.? Ang mariquit na panúlat ang na sa obispo. ¿Ang medias ay na sa aquin cayá.? Ualá sa iyò ang medias man, ang aspiler man. ¿Na sa inglés bagá ang pambucás nang prongo.? Ualá sa inglés ang pambucás man, ang caráyom man. ¿Naritò cayá ang mapagcalácal.? Ualá, ualá siyá dìtò. ¿Na sa pransés bagá ang páyong co.? Ualá sa caniyá ang iyòng páyong. ¿Na sa lamesa bagá ang pambucás nang prongo.? Na sa anlouague. ¿Na sa canino bagá ang canilàng pamocpoc.? Ualá sa anlouague ang pamocpoc man, ang paco man. ¿Aling mañgañgalácal ang mayróon serbesa.? Ang comersiante sa bayan co mayróon dalauàng basong serbesa. ¿Canino bagá iyáng tintang iyán.? Sa aquing capatid na lalaqui. ¿Anòng polot bagá ang na sa mañga inglés.? Ang mañga inglés ay mayróon polot, na mabutì. ¿Aling tungcod ang na sa anac na babaye nang iyòng inà.? Ualá ñga (or ualáng ualá) tungcod ang anac na babaye nang inà co, ang dedal niyà, ang caniyàng caráyom, ang caniyàng aspiler, at ang aquing orasán ang na sa caniyà. ¿Mayróon bagá mañga tupa sa España.? Oo, mayróon ¿Ang lamán nang topa,i, mabuti bagá.? Mabutì ñga. ¿Na ca canino baga ang mañga cómot ni inà.? Na cay Pedro. ¿Ang aquing itac ay bácal baṭà.? Hindí, ang itac mo,i, patalim. ¿Sa aling (or sa canino) tauò iyáng sópot na iyán.? Yyáng sópot na iyá,i, sa mañga capatid cong babaye. ¿Cayó po,i, mañga castila bagá.? Oo, mañga castila camí. ¿Na sa canicanino ang aquing bigás.? Na sa mañga inglés. ¿Yaóng salop na yaón, iyò bagá. o sa anac cong lalaqui.? Yaóng salop, hindí man iyò, hindí namán caniyà. ¿Sáan naróon si Juan.? Si Juan ualá dìtò, siyá,i, ualá maguing na sa simbahan ó na sa escuelahan. ¿Ualá siyá sa báhay.?. Na sa báhay siyá. ¿Taga sáan cayó.? Taga Prancia camí. Taga sáan yaóng mañga tauòng yaón.? Silá,i, taga ritò. Yaóng mañga tauòng yaó,i, insic bagá.? Silá,i, hindí insic.

Ytòng báhay na itò,i, hindí cáhoy. Yyán mañga salamí,i, hindí pílac. Ytòng mañga singsing ay hindí guintó. ¿Anò bagá po cayó.? Mañga anlouague camí.

YCAPITONG PAGSASANAY

¿Naritò sa tau'ng itò ang lapis.? Ualá sa caniyà. ¿Na sa aquin bagá ang sicolate.? Ualá sa iyò ang sicolate man, ang asúcal man. ¿Na sa aquing caibigan bagá ang iyòng tungcod.? Ualá sa caniyà ang aquing tungcod, ang aquing páyong ang na sa caniyà. Ang aming báhay ¿mariquit bagá.? Ang báhay nami,i, hindí mariquit, cundí mabuti. ¿Anò bagá iyán na sa mañg, camáy mo.? Ang na sa aquin mañga camáy, isàng lapis. ¿Anò bagá iyán na sa canilàng mañga daliri.? Ang na sa canilàng mañga daliri, mañga singsing. ¿Anò cayá ang na sa mañga matá co.? Ang na sa iyòng mañga matá, ay mañga salamín. ¿Mayróon bagá tayong mañga ñgipin.? Tayo,i, may mañga ñgipin. ¿Tayong mañga tauò may dila bagá.? Oo, tayong mañga tauò,i, may dila. ¿Ang ilong nang mañga taga Pilipinas ay magandà bagá.? Hindí, hindí magandà. ¿Maririquit cayá ang canilàng mañga quílay.? Ang canilàng mañga quílay, maririquit. ¿Sáan naróon ang dalaga.? Ang dalaga,i, na sa báhay. ¿Sino bagá ang amá nitòng binata.? Ang amá nitòng binata,i, ang mananahi. ¿Na sa canino ang sa panaderong sutlá,i, na sa aquing mañga anac na lalaqui. ¿Naháan ang caniyàng mañga sísiu.? Ang mañga sísiu niyà,i, na sa búquid. ¿Na sa canino ang mañga lapis nang mañga caibigan namin.? Ualá. ¿Mañga caibigan namin bagá silá.? Silá,i, aming mañga casi. ¿Na sa canino bagá ang sicolate nang aquing camagánac.? Na sa cabán nang caniyàng caibigan. ¿Sáan naróon ang bayong nang maguinóong babaye.? Ualá ditò ang bayong nang maguinóo. ¿Sáan naróon bagá ang susi nang cabán.? Na sa magsasacà. ¿Anò bagá ang yaóng mañga bote.? Yaóng mañga bote,i, búbog. ¿Mayróon ca bagáng alilang lalaqui.? Ualá acóng alilang lalaqui, ang na sa aqui.i, dalauàng alilang babaye. ¿Na sa simbahan bagá ang iyòng mañga camagánac.? Ualá, ang aquing mañga camagánac ay ualá sa simbahan; silá,i, na sa bayan. ¿Sáan naróon ang simbahan.? Ang simbahan,i, na sa bundoc. ¿Yaóng maguinóong babaye, inà niyà bagá.? Siyá,i, hindí niyà inà. ¿Mabubuting caibigan bagá tayo.? Tayo,i, mabubuting caibigan. ¿Sino sino bagá ang mañga caibigan mo? Ualá acóng mañga caibigan. ¿Ang camagánac ni Jua,i, caibigan mo bagá.? Silá,i, mañga caibigan co.

YCAUALONG PAGSASANAY.

¿Naparóon bagá ang amaín mo.? Hindí naparóon ang amaín co, ang naparóo,i, ang aquing ali. ¿Ang caibigan nang asáua mo,i, naparitò bagá.? Siyá,i, hindí naparitò, siyá,i, napasabáhay. ¿Naparóon bagá sa inyò ang magpañginòong ni Alpredo.? Naparóon silá sa amin. ¿Sáan naróon ang magcasamà ni Juan? Silá,i, napasabayan. ¿Naparíyán bagá silá.? Oo, silá,i, napariyán; ñguni,t, Siná Cruz na magcacapatid ay napaparitò. ¿Ang magamá ni Pedro,i, hindí silá napasabúquid? Ang magamá ni Pedro,i, hindí napasabúquid; napasimbahan silá. ¿Naparoróon bagá sa gúbat ang magasáua.? Napasasabayan silá. ¿Ang iyòng damit ay bagò ó luma bagá.? Ang damit co,i, luma na. ¿Ang mañga salamín nilá,i, boò bagá o basag.? Hindí basag, cundí luma. ¿Ang mañga pusa mang mañga capatid na babaye ni inà mapuputí bagá o maiitim? Ang mañga pusa nang mañga capatid na babaye ni inà,i, hindí mapuputí, at hindí namán maiitim. ¿Malaqui bagá ang cabanalan nang iyòng capatid na babaye.? Ang cabanalan nang capatid cong babaye,i, malaqui. ¿Malaqui bagá ang carunoñgan nang Dios.? Ang carunoñgan nang Dios ay ualáng capara. ¿Sino sino bagá ang marorónong.? Ang mañga marónong ay ang magagaling. ¿Magandà bagá ang caputían nang ating calolóua.? Ang caputían nang calolóua nati.i, magandà. ¿Ylán magcasacáy silá? Si Pedro, pati ni Juan at ni María ay magcacasacáy. ¿Ylán cayóng magcacasamà.? Camí ni Jorge,i, magcasamà ¿Ylán mañga caáuay ang naparitò.? Ualáng caáuay na naparitò. ¿Cayó ni María, nagcamuc-há bagá.? Oo, camí ni María ay mag camuc-há. ¿Ylán siláng magcacapatid? Siláng magcapatid ay dalanà. ¿Magpañginóon bagá cayó.? Oo, magpañginóon camí. ¿Magamà bagá cayó.? Hindí, hindí camí magamà.? ¿Maghípag bagá silá? Oo, silá, maghípag. ¿Magcaibigan bagá silá.? Hindí, hindí silá magcaibigan. ¿Ang magcapatid ni Juan ay napasagúbat bagá.? Ang magcapatid ni Jua,i, hindí napasagúbat. at na sa escuela silá. ¿Ang magaamá bagá. ay naparitò.? Ang magaamá,i, hindí naparitò. ¿Ang mag-inà ni Juana napasasimbahan bagá.? Hindí, ang mag-inà ni Juana napasa Cavite. ¿Sino bagá ang na sa báhay.? Ualá. ¿Sáan naparóon ang calabáo nang amaín co? Ang calabáo nang amaín mo,i, napasabúquid. ¿Ang caniyàng ibon ay naparóon bagá sa báhay nang iyàn bianàn.? Hindí, naparóon sa báhay nang manúgang cong lalaqui. ¿Anò bagá ang guinagauáng salapí.? Ang guinagauáng salapí ay guintó, pílac at tangsó. ¿Anóng ñgalan mo.? Ang aquing ñgala,i. Antonio. ¿Sáan naróon ang ualís nang alila co.? Ualá rito ang pañgualís nang iyòng alila. ¿Magaling bagá an iyòng paà.? Hindí magaling. ¿Sáan naróon ang mañga ñgipin.? Ang mañga ñgipin ay na sa bibig. ¿May napasa Iloilo bagá.? Ualá sino man napasa Iloilo. ¿Ylán tinápay mayróon ang aquing capatid na babaye.? Anò man tinápay ang na sa caniyà ay cacaontí. ¿Sa alíng (or sa caninong) tauò cayá iyàng mañga ibong iyán.? Sa alin man (or sa canino man)

YCASIYAM NA PAGSASANAY.

¿Canino bagá itòng mañga cáhoy na itò.? Sa aquing amá. ¿Nino.? Sa aquing amá. ¿Canino bagá iyán mañga batang iyán? Sa aquin. ¿Alíng baril ang na sa caniyà? Ang baril niyà ang na sa caniyà. Naróon bagá cahapon sa langsañgan ang asáua mo? Nariyán siyá camacalauà ¿May tauò bagá nóon sa dáan.? Ysà man tauo ay ualá sa dáan. ¿Ang tauò ay may caloobang magaling sa Dios.? Oo, ang tauò ay may lóob sa Dios. ¿Anò bagá ang alaalà.? Ang alaalà,i, isàng capangyarihan nang ating calolóua. ¿Mayróon tayo bagàng ótang na lóob sa ating magugúlang.? Oo, tayo,i, may ótang na lóob sa mañga magúlang natin. ¿Ang mañga mahal na tauò,i, mañga tampalasan bagá.? Ang mañga mahal na tauò ay hindí silá mañga tampalasan. ¿Anò bagá iyán na sa olò mo.? Ang na sa olò co,i, ang sambalilo. ¿Ang pinsán co, cosinero bagá siyá maméa.? Ang iyòng pinsá,i, hindí cosinero agad-agad, cundí sastre. ¿Ang bianán cong babaye may isàng batà bagá.? Siyá,i, may dalauang batà. ¿Ang taga ibàng lúpaín (bayan) niàyróon bagá nitòng halaman sa caniyàng halamanan.? Ualá, ualá siyá nitò siyá,i, mayróon mañga ilà. ¿Malaquì bagá ang dágat.? Ang dágat ay malaqui. ¿Sáan naróon ang mañga taga-

rágat.? Ang mañga tagarágat ay na sa halamanan nang aming caapidbáhay. ¿Mayróon bagá siláng butil sa caniláng mañga cartera.? Ualá
siláng butil. ¿Sáan naróon ang inyòng mañga tambóbong.? Ang mañga
tambóbong co.i, na sa búquid. ¿Sáan naróon ang caguinoohan nitòng báyan.?
Ang caguinoohan nitòng baya,i, na sa simbahan. ¿Ylán mañga halaman
mo ang na sa halamanan niyà.? Ualá acóng halaman sa caniyàng halamanan. ¿Ang bohoc niyà,i, maitim bagá nóon.? Ang bohoc niyà,i, maitim
nóon. ¿Sáan cayá naróon ang noò. ang mañga labi at ang liig.? Na sa
olò. ¿Na sa olò bagá ang mañga balícat.? Ualá. ualáng balícat ang olò.
¿Ang olilang lalaqui malacás bagá o mahina.? Siyá,i. mahina. Yáong
tauòng naparitò, capatid mo bagá.? Ang capatid co,i, ang naparoróon. ¿Yyán
mañga súlat na iyán, sa amá mo bagá.? Ang mañga súlat sa aquing amá,i.
ang na sa lamesa. ¿Yyáng babayeng iyán bagá ang sinisintà mo?? Ang
babayeng sinisintà co,i, ang aquing inà. ¿Anòng sasabihin co sa aquing
capatid na babaye.? Sabihin mo sa iyòng capatid na babaye na houag
siyàng pasa Iloilo. ¿Sasabihin co bagá sa canilà na pasabúquid silá.?
Houag mong sabihin iyán. ¿Alín ditò sa dalauàng libro ang sa pinsán
co.? Ang librong bagò ang sa iyòng pinsán, itòng i-à, sa iyòng anac na
lalaqui. ¿Yyáng boteng iyán, ditò sa batang itò cayá.? Hindí, iya,i, diyàn
sa isà. ¿Naparóon ca bagá cañgina sa halamanan.? Hindí acó naparóon.
(acó,i, hindí naparóon.) ¿Cailán naparitò si Juan.? Camacailán árao naparitò si Juan. ¿Napasabayan bagá cahapon ang inà nang hípag co.?
Naparóon siyá camacalauá.

YCASANGPOUONG PAGSASANAY.

¿Anòng cáhoy iyán.? Ytòng cáhoy na itò,i, moláuin. ¿Ang caniyang
mañga daho,i, malalaqui at magagandà bagá.? Oo, ñga. ¿Caninong anac
itòng mañga batang itò.? Ytò,i, mañga anac co. ¿At yaóng isà, caninong
anac.? Sa aquing caibigan. ¿Ang isang taón, may ilán bóuan cayá.? May
labìng dalauàng bóuan ang isàng taón. Pañgalanan mo.—Enero at ibà pa.
¿Ilán árao ang isàng lingo.? Ang isàng lingo,i, may pitòng árao. Pañgalanan mo.—Lingo at ibà pa. ¿Anòng bóuang itò.? Bóuang Abril. ¿Naritò ca
bagá sa bóuang Abril.? Ualá acó ritò sa bóuang Abril, acó,i, naritò sa bóuang
Julio. ¿Cailán ca mapasabúquid.? Mapapasabúquid acó sa Jueves. ¿Di
na sa bayan ca palá cun Martes.? Na sa bayan acó cun Lingo. ¿Cailán
ca napasa Maynila.? Acó.i. napasa Maynila sa Sábado. ¿Napasasasimba-
han siyá cun Lunes.? Siyá,i. napapasasimbahan cun Lingo. ¿Anò itòng
árao na itò.? Viernes. ¿Cailán silá napasasahalamanan.? Silá,i, napasasahalamanan sa mulang árao nang Lingo. ¿Anò cayá ang árao na sa catapusan nang bóuan.? Ang catapusan nang bóuan ay Miércoles. ¿Anòng
bóuan ang na sa catapusan nang taón.? Ang bóuan na sa catapusan nang
taón ay Diciembre. ¿Anò bagáng cúlay nang pono niyàng cáhoy.? Ang
cúlay nang pono nitòng cáhoy ay mapulà. ¿Hindí bagá madiláo.? Hindí,t.
maitim itim. ¿Madilim bagá ang árao.? Hindí, hindí madilim. ¿Anò caya
ang árao sa paguitan nang sang Lingo.? Ang Jueves ay ang na sa paguitan nang sang Lingo. ¿Ay anò.? Ualá ñga. ¿Ay anò, ualá bagáng Dios
ditò sa lupa.? Abáa, sáan ma,i, may isàng Dios. ¿Ay anò. ang capatid
ni Pedro bagá ang naparóon.? Siyá rin ñga ang naparóon. ¿Ay anò naritò ca palá.? Mangyari, naritò ñga acó. ¿Ay anò, malaqui bagá ang
Dios.? Abáa, malaqui ñga siyá. ¿Ay anò, icáo palá ang nariyán.? Mangyari, acó ñgani. ¿Icáo rin bagá ang naparóon sa Maynila nóon Octubre.?
Acó rin ang naparóon. ¿Sino sino bagá ang nagnácao nang libro.? Ang
mañga babaye, ang nagnácao nang libro. ¿Ang mañga taga Europa, ma-

puputí caya silá.? Abáa mapuputí ñga silá. ¿Sáan naróon ang Dios.? Saan man icáo ay pumaróon, naróon ang Dios. ¿Sino ang may sabi niyán.? Sino ma,i, nagsasabi. ¿Na sa simbahan bagá si Juan.? Naritò man siyá sa bayan hindí siyá pasasimbahan. ¿Totoò bagá iyán.? Totoò ñga.

.

YCALABING ISANG PAGSASANAY.

Anim na pouo,t, tatlò. Sangdáan dalauàng pouò,t, uolò. Dalauàng dáa,t, labing lim à. Limáng dáa,t, labing siyam. Anim na dáan, tatlòng pouò at isà. Siyam na ráa,t, labing isà. Sanglibò, tatlòng dáan, ápat na pouò,t, dalauà. Tatlòng libò. Pitòng libò, ualòng dáan, siyam na pouò,t ápat. Sanglacsà, ánim na ráa,t, labing ápat. Dalauàng lacsà, limàng libò. ualòng dáa,t, labìng tatlò. Tatlòng lacsà, pitòng libò at labing ualò. Pitong lacsà at ualòng dàin. Sangyota, limàng dáan, dalauàng pouò,t, ánim Tatlòng yota, ánim na lacsà, dalauàng dáan at labing ápat. Ualòng yota, tatlong lacsa, ánim na libò, limàng dáan, ánim na pouò,t limà. Labìng dalauàng yota, tatlòng lacsà,t, dalauàng libò, tatlòng pouò,t, ánim. Tatlòng pouò,t, ápat na yota, tatlòng lacsà, apat na libò, ánim na ráa,t, ualò. ¿Magcanò bagá ang halagá niyáng quiso.? Tatlong piso. ¿Ang amá mo bagá, ilán báhay mayróon.? Ualá siyáng báhay. ¿Ang iyòng capatid na babaye mayróon bagàng maraming salamín.? Mayróon siyáng dalauàng pouò. ¿Na sa mañga magúlang mo bagá ang lahat na singsing.? Ualá sa canilà ang lahat. ¿Ylán ang mañga anac nang capatid ní Antonio.? Mayróon siyáng pitò. ¿Magagandà bagá siláng lahat.? Ang tatlò sa canilà,i, magagandà, ang ibá,i, mañga páñgit. ¿Ang iyòng amaín mayróon siyáng ilán capatid.? Ang amaín co,i, mayróon limang capatid. Ylán bagá sa canilà ang mañga lalaqui.? Ang tatlò sa canilà,i, mañga lalaqui; ang ibá,i, mañga babaye. ¿Ang aquing alí, mayróon bagá maraming cáhoy.? Siyá,i, mayróon mañga ilán. ¿Sáan bagá naróon ang magbayáyo.? Na sa Cebú silá. ¿Ylán cayáng mañga babayeng ang naróon cahapon.? Maraming marami. ¿Ualá bagàng libro sa báhay.? Camí,i, mayróon marami sa báhay. ¿Marami bagá diyán mañga aso.? Mayróon, iilán lámang. ¿Ang pinsán co bagá mayróon ilàng pusa cayá.? Siyá,i, mayróon iisà. ¿Mayróon bagáng dalauàng pouòng ibon sa báhay mo.? Mayróon dóong labis sa dalauàng pouò. ¿Sáan naróon.? Na sa mañga sañgà nang mañga cáhoy. ¿Sino ang nagsabi sa iyò na mayróon maraming simbahan sa Maynila.? Ang aquin mañga caibigan ang nagsabi sa aquin. ¿Tayo,i, mayróon ilàng calolóua.? Tayo,i, mayróon i-à lámang. ¿Ylán cayàng daliri ang na sa camáy mo.? Aápat lámang. ¿Ay anò,i, nasáan bagá ang ibà.? Ay anò, ang ibà,i, tinago. ¿Ylàn bagáng pono mayróon dito sa halamanang it).? Mayróon maraming marami. ¿Ylán cayá sa canila ang may sañgà at ilán namán ang ualá.? Ang mañga ualáng sañgà,i, iilán lámang. ¿Sino ang caona-onahang tauò.? Ang caonaonahan tauò ay Si Adán. ¿At ang caonaona hang babaye cayà.? Si Eva. ¿Ang capatid mong babaye ycailán siyá sa escuelahan.? Siyá,i, ang ycalimà. ¿Ycailán ca bagá.? Ycaáninm na ráan, tatlòng pouó,t, ualò acó. Mahal ca bagá.? Acó,i, ang cahulihulihan nang mañga tauò. ¿Masasamá bagá ang lahat na mañga tauò.? Hindí, iilán lámang sa canilà,i, ang masasamá. ¿Ang lahat na babaye mañga mabait bagá.? Ang caramiha,i, mababait. ¿Mayróon ca pong mahiguit sa tatlòng pluma.? Mayróon acóng higuit sa ánim ña pouò. ¿Ang caibigan mo,i, lalo pang matandá sa caniyáng capatid? Siyá,i, lalong matáas, ñguni,t, hindí siya lalong matanda. ¿Mayróon ca pang mañga anac.? Mayróon pa acóng dalauà. ¿Anong árao caya ngayon sa sanglingo.? Ngayo,i, Martes.

¿At ycailán árao bagá nang bóuan cahapon.? Cahapo.i, ang ycadalauang pouò,t. limá. ¿Mañga ilán cayáng piso mayróon ca.? Acó,i, mayróon mañga tatlòng pouòng piso.

YCALABING DALAUANG PAGSASANAY.

¿Anòng libro ang na sa iyò.? Ang na sa aquin ay ang unàng libro. ¿At nasaan ang ycalauà.? Na sa aquing capatid. ¿Di bagá ycasiyam na bóuan nang taón ang Octubre.? Hindí po. ycasangpuòng bóuan ang Octubre. ¿Macailán bagáng nagnácao ang bata mo.? Miminsán. ¿Macatatlò bagáng napasahalamanan ang amáin mo.? Miminsán lámang napasahalamanan siyá. ¿Paano ang pagbibigáy mo nang iyòng libro.? Ysa isà ang pagbibigáy co, ñguní,t, ang aquing pang-inóon ay tatlò tatlò ang pagbibigáy. ¿Pasasaescuela ca bagá touíng Jueves.? Acó,i, napaparóon árao-árao. ¿Ylán oras naroróon ca sa escuela sa umaga.? Naroróon acóng dalauàng oras. ¿Sa anòng árao nang sauglingo ang mañga anac mo.i, hindí napapasaescuelahan.? Cung lingo,i, hindí silá napapasaescuelahan. ¿Ang mañga pluma,i, tig-ilán cung ybigáy mo.? Nagbigáy acó narg tigpipitò. ¿Tig-ilán ang sabi mo.? Sabi co,i, tigpipitò. ¿Tig-ilán cun pagbibigáy mo nang salapí sa mañga bata mo.? Mamiso ang pagbibigáy co. ¿Gaanòng bigás ang pagbibigáy nang canilàng amá sa canilà.? Manalop ang pagbibigáy nang canilàn amá. ¿At ang canilàng amáin.? Ang canilàng amaí.i, ualáng manbelis mang lámang na ybinibigáy sa canilà; ang canilàng ali mañgaroba ang ibinigáy na minsán. ¿Ang tauò ay may iláng bahagui.? Dadalauàng bahagui ang tauò, ang catauá.t, ang calolóua. ¿Cailán acó paparitò.? Paritò ca sa catapusan nang bouan at naritò ca sa capanahonan. ¿Mabuti bagá ang panahón sa bóuang Octubre.? Ang panahón sa bóuang Octubre.i, masamá. ¿Cailán ca papasahalamanan.? Paparóon acó búcas nang omaga. ¿Sa báhay mo,i, mayróon bagáng maraming bulilit.? Mayróon iilán. ¿Mayróon bagáng dagá sa búquid mo.? Mayróon mañga dagá,t. mañga ibon. ¿Mayróon bagáng cotò ang olò nang anac mo.? Siyá,i, ualá; cundí mayróon siyáng mañga tuma sa caniyàng damit. ¿Maran i bagá ang mañga bábuy mo.? Mayróon acóng lámang isàng bábuy damó,t, isàng anacán.

YCALABING TATLONG PAGSASANAY.

¿Cayó nang anac mo.i, mabuti bagá ang lagáy.? Oo po, caming dalauá,i, mabuti ang lagáy. ¿Ang pinsán mong lalaqui,i, mayróon bagá bulac-lac sa caniyàng halamanan.? Oo po, siyá,i, mayróon maraming bulac-lac. ¿Mayróon bagá siyáng ibàng halaman.? Oo po, siyá,i, mayróon ibàng halaman. ¿Sino sino ang mañga may báhay.? Ang mañga mayayama.i, mayróon báhay. ¿Dóon sa inyòng bayan mayróon bagáng mabubuting báhay.? Oo pò, dóo,i, mayróon mabubuting báhay. ¿Anò pang mayróon cayó.? Camí, mayróon pang baca. ¿Mayróon ca pa bagáng maraming salapí.? Ang panadero co,i, mayróon pang maraming maràmi. ¿Mayróon pa bagá siyáng pápel.? Siyá,i, mayróon pa. ¿Ang capé at ang cha nang tagarágat ay magcasingdan i bagá.? Ang capé at ang cha niyá,i, magcasingdami. ¿Mayróon bagá itong tauong ito mañga caibigan casingdámi nang caniyàng caáuay.? Ang mañga caibigan at ang mañga caáuay niyà,i. magcasingdami. ¿Mayróon cayá siláng saping caparis nang dami nang canilàng medias." Silá,i, ualáng medias. ¿Ang sa aquing capatid na sambalelo singdiquit bagá nang aquin.? Ang sa capatid mo,i. singdiquit nang iyò. ¿Marónong ca bagá para nang amáin co.? Hindí acó marúnong para niyà. ¿Banal bagá Si Juan para nang aquing capatid na babaye.? Siláng dalauà,i, magcasingbanal. ¿Yyáng búhog na iyán matigás bagáng parang batò.? Ang batò,i, hindí matigás para nitòng búhog. ¿Maputí bagá ang bácal para nang pílac.? Ang bácal ay hindí maputí para nang pílac. ¿Ganitò bagá caitim ang tinta.? Ang tinta co,i, ganiyán caitim. ¿Ang sa aquin amáng patalim at ang aming amáin, singbubutí bagá.? Para parang mabu'i ¿Ytòng mañga asong itò, magagandà bagáng ganga nóon.? Ytòng mañga aso,i, hindí ganóon cagandà. ¿Ang paggauá nang tinápay ay ganitò bagá.? Oo, ganiyán ñga. ¿Gaanò catandá ang aquing amá.? Ang iyòng amá,i, singtandá nang aquin. ¿Ang alila nang aquing alí gaano casamá.? Gamagnanácao siyá casamá. ¿Gaanò cariquit ang ibon co.? Gabulac-lac cariquit. ¿Mabait bagá Si Antoniong para co.? Cayóng dalauà,i, para parang mabait. ¿Anòng íbig niyà.? Ang íbig niyà ganagtatañgis. ¿Ganga niyán bagá capulà silá.? Silá,i, ganga nitò capulà. ¿Ang iyòng hiyas mahal bagá para nang sa iyòng capatid cong babaye.? Ang hiyas co,i. hindí mahal para nang sa iyòng capatid na babaye. ¿Ycáo ay mayróon iláng suclày.? Mayróon acóng dalauà. ¿Ang taiñga mo,i, maitim bagá para nang ilong co.? Maitim para nang iyòng galanggalañgan. ¿Sáan naróon ang mañga bóol at ang mañga quiliquili mo.? Ang mañga bóol co,i, na sa aquing mañga paà, ang quiliquili, na sa ilalim nang balícat. ¿Mañga mayaman bagá Siná Cruz.? Silá,i, mayayaman. ¿Gaanò silá cayaman.? Ang cayamanan nilà,i, ga sa isàng Hari. ¿Ang bayào mo,i, mabuti bagá ang lagáy.? Siyà,i, mabuti ang lagáy.

YCALABING APAT NA PAGSASANAY.

¿Mayróon bagá ang alila mong isàng mabuting ualís.? Siyá,i, mayróon isà. ¿Ang mañga magsasacà mayróon bagá nitò ó niyán mañga bayong.? Silá,i, ualá nitò man niyán man. ¿Sino bagá ang mayróong isàng mabuting cabán.? Ang aquing capatid na lalaqui mayróon isà. ¿Mayróon bagá siyáng isàng cabán na balat ó isà cayá na cáhoy.? Mayróon siyáng isà na cáhoy. ¿Ang anlouague, mayróon bagáng maraming pacong bácal.? Mayróon siyáng marami. ¿Sino bagá ang mayróong baril.? Ang mañga Americano,i, mayróon. ¿Na sa iyò bagá ang pamocpoc na cáhoy nang pransés ó nang inglés.? Ualá acó alín man. ¿Anò bagá ang lalo pang mahal sa cayamanan.? Ang cabanalan. ¿Anò bagá ang daquilà sa lahat.? Ang Dios. ¿Sino sino bagá ang lalo pang bata sa aquin mañga capatid.? Ang mañga anac nang amáin mo lalo pang bata. ¿Sino sino bagá ang mayróon lalong cayamanan sa cabanalan.? Ang mañga mayaman. ¿Sino sino ang may lalong cabanalan sa cayamanan.? Ang mañga duc-háng tauò. ¿Acó,i, lalo pa bagáng malíit cay Pedro.? Oo ñga, siyá,i, matáas (malaquì) sa iyò. ¿Alín sa mañga bulac-lac na itò,i, ang lalong mariquit sa lahat.? Ang lalong mariquit sa lahat ay yaón na sa búbong. ¿Sino sino ang malacás sa mañga babaye.? Ang mañga lalaqui ñgani. ¿Ang mañga cabayò,i, malicsí pa bagá sa mañga calabáo.? Silá,i, lalo pang malicsí. ¿Ang mañga Tagalog ay lalo pang siláng marami sa mañga Americano.? Silá,i, alañgan ang dami. ¿Ang capatid nang caapidbáhay, camaganac mo bagá.? Hindí co cadugó siyá, cundí cabalaye. ¿Ylán bagá ang cahinlogan mo. ¿Ang cahinlogan co,i, pitòng lalaqui,t, apat na babaye. ¿Ang mañga ba-

nal na tauò nanásoc bagá sa Lángit." Ang mañga banal na tauò lámang ay
ang nanásoc sa Lángit. ¿Ybá bagá ang óling na bato sa óling na cáhoy.?
Oo, nga, ang carbong batò ay ilá sa óling. ¿Marami bagá ang mañga bi-
tuin sa lángit cung gabi.? Oo maraming marami. ¿Ang pinsán mong lalaqui may mabuting ásal bagá.? Hindi. siyá.i, mabagsic. ¿Ang iná mo bagá,i, may saquit.? Hindí. siyá.i, magaliug; nguni.t, ang mauhihibo,i, may
saquit. ¿Magcanò ang dosena niyáng mañga mansana.? Dalauàng pouòng
séntimos. ¿Ang iyòng alí mayróon bagáng maraming laráuan sa caniyàng
báhay.? Siyá,i, mayróon tatlòng laráuan sa báhay niyà. ¿Ang bóbong
nang báhay nang iyòng caapidbáhay, ano bagá.? Ang bóbong nang báhay
nang caapidbáhay ay páuid. ¿Ang halamang pauid anò bagá.? Sasà.
¿Mayróon bagáng sasahán sa iyòng probinsia.? Oo, mayróon. ¿Nasáan
ang pang-inóon mo.? Siyá,i, na sa simbahan. ¿Mabagsic bagá siyá.?
Hindí, siyá,i, hindí mabagsic, mabuting ásal siyá. ¿Anòng dasal iyán.?
Ang Amá Namin. ¿Ylán bagá ang tauò dóon.? Mayróon tatlò, si Juan, si Alpredo sampong ni Ricardo. ¿Alín bagá ang lalong marúnong sa canila.?
Ang lalong marúnong sa canilà,i, Si Juan. ¿Alín bagá ang lalo pang matandá.? Ang lalo pang matandá,i, Si Alpredo. ¿Alín ang lalong maputí
sa canilà.? Ang lalong maputí, Si Ricardo. ¿Alín sa iyòng mañga capatid na babaye ang lalong magandà.? Si Juana,i, magandà, Si María,i,
lalo pang magandà; datapóua,t, Si Clara ang magandà sa lahat: abáa Si
Clara,i, magandàng magandà. ¿Masípag na masípag bagá ang mañga Americano.? Silá,i, masípag na masípag. ¿Matamís na lubhá bagá ang polot.?
Oo, ñga, ang polot ay matamís di sapala. ¿Mañga pángit bagá ang mañga calabáo.? Oo rin, ang mañga calabáo ay pángit na pángit. ¿Anòng
háyop ang malicsi di hámac.? Calicsilicsihan ang cabayo. ¿Ang mañga
ibon malicsi bagá sa mañga cabayo.? Oo, ang mañga ibo,i, malicsi pa silá
sa mañga cabayo. ¿Ang mañga Tagalog bagá caitimitiman.? Hindí, silá,i,
hindí maiitim na lubhá. ¿Ang pilicmatá mo,i, maiitim na maiitim bagá.?
Mañga maiitim na maiitim. ¿Malalim cayá ang dágat.? Ang dágat ay
calalimlaliman. ¿Ang mañga mansana cayá maguinhauàng maguinhauá.?
Oo, silá,i, caguinhaguinhagualan. Ang ibo,i, ualáng caparis nang licsi.
¿Banal bagá ang amá mo.? Ang amá co,i, ualáng capantáy nang cabanalan.

YCALABING LIMANG PAGSASANAY.

¿Ang asáua mo,i. ilán cayá ang sapín.? Siyá,i. mayróon dalauà lámang.
¿Sino bagá ang matamad.? Ang alilang babaye,i, matamadtamad siyá. ¿Alín
bagá ang boñgang lalong masarap sa lahat na boñga sa Pilipinas.? Ang piña,t,
ang saguing ay masarapsarap. ¿Maasim bagá ang dalandán.? Maasimasim
lámang ang dalandán. ¿Ytòng túbig na itò,i, maalat bagá.? Hindi maalat-
alat lamang. ¿Lalo pang matulin bagá ang mañga sísiu sa manoc.? Ang
mañga sísiu cun silá,i, maliliit pa matulintulin lámang. ¿Masarap bagá
iyáng mansanang iyán.? Masarapsarap. ¿Ibig mo bagá ang tinápay.? Ibig
co nang caontí. ¿Ayáo ca bagáng pasaescuelahan.? Ybig cong pasasimbahan,
nguni.t, ang aquing caibigan Si Quicoy ay aáyao. ¿Mayróon ca bagáng maraming
pilac.? Mayróon acó caontí lámang. ¿Anò bagá ang lagáy niyáng gátas (better)
Maanò bagá iyáng gatas na iyán.? Ytòng gatas na itò,i, maasimasim.
¿Anò iyáng laráuan.? Ytòng laráuang itò iboniboñan. ¿Maraming bagá
tauotauohan diyán sa laráuang iyán.? Mayróon dalauàng pouòng tauotauohan ditò sa laráuang itò. ¿Ang caniyàng capatid ay médico bagá.?
Siyá,i. medimedicohan lámang. ¿Anò iyáng hinihibo diyán sa laráuang iyán.?
Bahaybahayan. ¿Magaling bagá ang panadero mo.? Siyá,i, may saquit.
¿Gaanò calubhá ang saquit niyà.? Siyá,i, magalinggaling na. ¿Napasasim-

bahan cayóng lahat cañginang omaga.? Siláng lahat ay naparóon liban sa aquin. ¿Mayróon cayá ilán Dios.? Ysà ñga lámang ang Dios. ¿Ylán salapí mayróon ang pare.? Ang pare,i, may salapíng labís. ¿Anò bagá iyáng naróon sa bayong na iyán.? Ytò,i, papel. ¿Ybig niyà bagá nang caontíng suca.? Ayúo siyá; sa pagcat,t, ang caniyàng lalamonan ay masaquit. ¿Sáan naróon ang mañga ugat.? Ang mañga ugat nang mañga cáhoy ay na sa lupa; ang sa mañga háyop ay na sa lahat nang cataouán nilà. ¿Anò ang otac.? Ang mañga otac, ay ogat nang mañga iitid. ¿Mayróon bagáng lañgís diyán sa tapayang iyán.? Ualáng ualà, itòng tapayang itò,i, ualáng lamán. ¿Sáan mayróon túbig.? May túbig sa bal—on. ¿Ang iyòng amá,i, patáy na bagá.? Oo, ang amá co,i, namatáy na. ¿Sáan naróon ñgayón ang mañga calolóua nang nañgamatáy na tauò.? Ang sa mañga banal na tauò, ay na sa láñgit; ang sa nang masasamá,i, na sa Impierno. ¿Ang pare,i, anò bagá.? Ang pare,i, ang cahalili nang Dios. ¿Anòng bágay ang mahálay.? May maramìng ganà na mahálay. ¿Naoócol bagá sa isàng lalaqui ang paggauà nang baro.? Yyán ay naoócol sa mañga babaye. ¿Ang mañga háyop at ang mañga tauò ay magcapares bagá.? Hindí, ang mañga háyop ay ibà sa mañga tauò; ang mañga háyop ay naoócol sa lupa, ang mañga tauò ay sa Dios.

YCALABING ANIM NA PAGSASANAY.

¿Ungmaáral ca bagá nang Tagalog.? Oo po, ungmaáral acó nang Tagalog. ¿Anò cayáng yniáral niyà cahapon.? Ang yniáral niyà,i, inglés. ¿Sungmúlat bagá camí nang súlat sa lingong nacaráan.? Camí, sungmúlat nang maran i. ¿Cailán silá,i, sungmúlat nang mañga dasalan.? Silá,i, sungmúlat nang ilán camacailáng árao. ¿Cailán susúlat ang canilàng amá.? Siyá,i, susúlat sa macalauà. ¿Nacabasà ca bagá nang súlat nang dungmating ang aquing capatid na babaye.? Nang ang capatid mong babaye,i, dungmating, acó,i, nacabasà na nang súlat. ¿Anòng sabì nilà sa canilàng mañga anac.? Nagsabì silá sa canilà, bumasà cayó. ¿Iinom sana cayá siyá nang túbig cun mayróon disin.? Cun mayróon disin siyáng álac, hindí siyá iinom nang túbig. ¿Hungmiñgi bagá nang anomán ang mananahi sa caniyàng inà.? Hungmiñgi siyá nang tinápay sa caniyà. ¿Cun mayróon sana acóng libro, iíbig ca cayáng bumasà.? Cun mayróon ca dising libro, marahil acó babasà nang ilán. ¿Cun napasabayan bagá siyá papásoc cayá siyá sa báhay nang caniyàng alí.? Cun paroróon sana siyá sa bayan marahil siyá papásoc sa báhay nang caniyàng alí. ¿Tatachò bagá acó.? Houag cang tumachò nang ganiyán, macá pumaritò ang amá mo. ¿Lalabás ca sana cun bagá ang panahó,i, mabuti.? Cun ang panaho,i, hindí masamá, acó,i, marahil ay lalabás. ¿Bibilì ca bagá sana nang pluma cahit maparitò ang iyòng pañginóon.? Bibilì disin acó nang pluma bagamán ang aquing pañginóo,i, pumaritò. ¿Cacáin ca bagá nang maramìng canin sa lingong papásoc.? Cahima,t, acó,i, mayróon maramì ay hindí acó cacáin nang maramì. ¿Alín bagá ang lalong mabutì, ang pagtachò o ang paglácad.? Ang paglácad ay lalong mabutì sa pagtachò. ¿Cailán darating ang obispo.? Ang pagdating nang obispo,i, minsán lámang sa taón taón. ¿Aalís ca bagá.? Acó,i, aalís bagamá,t, masamá ang panahon. ¿Macabasà na acó cun ang anac co,i, dungmating cayá.? Di man siyá,i, pumaritò, babasà rin acó suedáng anò ang mangyari.

YCALABING PITONG PAGSASANAY.

¿Bungmibili bagá o nagbibili nang tinápay ang iyòng panadero? Nagbibili siyá nang tinápay; ñguní,t, bungmibili siyá nang cáhoy. ¿Gungmagauá bagá nang anomán ang iyòng pañginóon dóon sa Maynila? Siyá,i, nagaáral nang inglés at ungmaáral nang Tagálog. ¿Nag-iísip ca bagáng magbigáy nang anomán sa mañga duc-há? Di acó nagbibigáy nang pílac sa canilá; sa pagca,t, acó,i, mayróon cacaontí lámang; datapóua,t, nagnanasa acóng magcaróon nang maramì at sacá magbibigáy acó sa canilá nang tinapay at nang damit. ¿Báquit ang mañga capatid na lalaqui nang aming manúgang na babaye ay nagnanasang umalís? Ybig niláng umalís; sa pagca,t, silá,i, pasasabáhay nang caniláng amá maglalabás nang pingán. ¿Cailán bagá Sina Docot nag-iísip umalís? Siláng lahat ay aalibucas nang hapon at íbig niláng cumoha nang pílay sa búquid nang caniláng iná. ¿Sáan ca nagdadalá nang salapí? Acó,i, nagdadalá ditò nang caontí; sa pagca,t, acó,i, nagiísip bumili nang báhay na batò. ¿Nagdadalá dóon si Pedro nang ganóong salapí? Ualá, siyá nagdalá ditò nang sanglibòng piso sa camacailan. ¿Nahahatid bagá nang anomán ang caapidbáhay mo sa caniyàng mañga anac? Naghatid siyá sa canilá nang bigás. ¿Báquit ca nagootos cay Juang magsimba lingo-lingo? Sa pagca,t, acó,i, nagaalaala na ang pagsimbá,i, isá sa mañga otos nang Dios. ¿Sáan bagá silá naglagáy nang bandejado co? Ynilagáy nilá ang bandejado sa halamanan. ¿Anò ang sabì mo? Caoin mo iyán pagdaca at sacá pumaróon ca sa halamana,t, magdalá ca ditò narg damó. ¿Nagsasabì bagá nang anomán si Biangui tongcol caná Juan? Nagsasabì siyá nang ganitò: cun gaanò ang magugúlang ay siyá rin ang mañga anac. ¿Nagnanasa ca pang pumaróon sa dágat at magdalá ditò nang tagarágat? Nagnanasa acóng pumaróon at magdalá nang salapí sa aquing mañga caibigan. ¿Mayróon ca pa bagáng maramìng caibigan? Ualá po cacaontí na ang mañga caibigan co; sa pagca,t, ang caramiha,i, patáy na. ¿Ano bagá iyán na sa camáy mo? Gunting. ¿Mayróon ca pang ilàng gunting? Hindí, mayróon lámang acóng isàng lanseta.

YCALABING UALONG PAGSASANAY.

¿Maanò ang caibigan mo? Tila siyá,i, natotólog; datapóua,t, sa acala co,i, siyá,i, namamatáy. ¿Natólog ca na cañginang omaga nang dungmating ang aquing capatid na babaye? Hindí, hindí acó natólog pa. ¿Ano bagá ang catúlad nang isàng tauò na natotólog na malalim? Ang tauòng natotúlog nang malalim ay catulad nang bangcáy. ¿Sino, sino sa inyò ang nagugutom? Ysà man sa ami,i, hindí nagugutom; ñguní,t, caming lahat ay naoóhao. ¿Báquit natatácot ang inyòng mañga caapidbáhay na babaye? Silá,i, natatácot, sapagca,t, ang caniláng amá,i, may saquit na lubhá,t, natatácot silá na siyá,i, mamatáy. ¿Anòng nagauá mo bagá,t, icáo,i, nahihiya nang ganiyán? Acó,i, nahihiya, sa pagca,t, may isàng bóuan na di acó nagsimbá. ¿Naguiguináo bagá Si Juana, ang capatid na babaye nang mananahí? Siyá,i, hindí naguiguináo, anaqui siyá,i, naguiguináo; datapóua,t, siyá,i,

naiinitan. ¿Anò,t. ang canilàng mañga anac ay natotóua.? Silá,i, natotóua; sapagca,t, ang canilàng amá,i, nagaacalang maghatid sa canilàng
lahat sa Maynila. ¿Nahahapis bagá ang inyòng pare.? Nahahapis siyá
sa pagca,t, cacaontí lámang ang mañga tauóng nagsi-simbà lingo-lingo.? ¿Canino bagá yaóng mañga báhay na nasosónog.? Ang mañga báhay na
nasosónog ay sarili nang caibigan mo, ang amaín ni Juan. ¿Sino bagá
ang gungmisi nang iyòng baro.? Ualá gungmisi nang aquing baro; tila
naguisi; datapóua,t. napotol lámang. ¿Ang caniyàng alí, magbabàsag bagá
nang tanán pingán, baso; bote at tapayan.? Di po, ang íbig niyà lámang, magbàsag nang tapayan; ñguni,t, hindí siyà nagbantáng magbàsag
nang diláng ibàng bágay. ¿Baquin bagá hindí nagdadalá dito ang alila
nang cauayan bigáy co sa caniyà cahapon sa gabí.? Siyá,i, natatácot at
nahihiyang parito; sa pagca,t, siyá,i, nagbali nang cauayan. ¿Sino ang
nagpatid nitòng lúbid na itò.? Ang alí nang alila ni Juan ay siyáng
naglalagot niyá,t, maraming ibàng lúbid. ¿Anò nagtatagpi ca bagá diyàn.?
Nagtatagpí acó nang baro,t, sapin. ¿Ano,t. ang anac mo,i, hindí magpú-
púlot nang mañga caráyom.? Hindí niyà íbig magpúlot nang caráyom man,
nang manga man. ¿Nagbabantáng humánap bagá nang anomán ang tauòng
banal.? Ang isàng banal na tauò ay nagbabantáng humánap nang lanchás
patoñgò sa Lañgit. ¿Mainit bagá o malamig ang túbig sa dágat.? Ang túbig
sa dagat ay mainitinit. ¿Ang iyóng alí, ilán na bagá siyáng taón.? Labis
na siyá sa tatlòng pouò,t, ánim na taón. ¿Magcanò ñgayón ang halagá
nang bigás.? Tiglilimàng piso ang cabán. ¿Ano ang sabi mo sa aquin.?
Ang sabi co sa iyò,i, magandàng árao po, sa pagca,t. ñgayó,i, umaga; cun
lipas na ang tanghali, ang sasabihin co sa iyò,i, magandàng hapon at
sacá cun dumating ang gabi ang sasabihin co,i, magandàng gabi hangán sa hating gabi. ¿Alín sa acala mo ang lalong mabuting boñga sa
lahat.? Sa acala co,i, ang ságuing ay ang boñgang lalong mabutì sa lahat,
datapóua,t, may ibàng tauòng nagaacala nang ang manga, ang lalong mabuti
sa lahat. ¿Anò ang halamang pálay.? Ang pálay ay isàng halaman na
may óhay. ¿Anò bagá mayróon ang báua,t. isàng tauò.? Báua,t, isàng
tauò ay mayróon damit na sarili, at yámang silá,i, mayróon damit, natatácot siláng guinisi nang sa ilà. ¿Mamamatáy bagá ang tauò.? Ang
sangcatauoha,i, mamamatáy; ang páuang halama i, matotoyó at ang diláng
bitui,i, magdidilim.

YCALABING SIYAM NA PAGSASANAY.

¿Ungmaacyat (nanacyat) bagá ang iyòng pamangquin sa bundoc.?
Nanacyat siyá sa bondoc, sa pagca,t, íbig niyàng tumanáo sa dágat. ¿Anò
ang ñgalan nang inaanac nang amá mo.? Ang ñgalan nang inaanac ni
amá,i, Si Quico. ¿Sino bagá ang iniíbig mong lalo sa lahat.? Ang iniíbig
cong lalo pa sa lahat, ay ang aquing amá. ¿Cun ualá ca sanang amá sino
bagá ang iibiguin mo disin lalo sa lahat.? Cun ualá acó sanang amá
iibiguin co disin ang asáua co na lalo sa lahat. ¿Báquit íbig nang caniyàng
pamangquing babaye na samahan itòng lalaquing itò sa simbahan.? Sa
pagca,t, siyá,i, inaanac niyá. ¿Sino bagá ang iniinà niyá.? Ang caniyàng
iniinà,i, yaóng babaye tungmitiñging sa mañga cáhoy cahapon nang hapon.
¿Báquit cayá nacyat si Jesucristo sa Lañgit.? Siyá,i, ungmacyat sa Lañgit
nang tangapín niyà dóon ang tanáng calolóua nang mañga tauòng banal ditò
sa lupa. ¿Ang inaanac na lalaqui nang aquing hípag, didiñgiguin bagá niyá
ang mabuting áral na ypañgañgáral ni Pare Santos sa caniyà.? Marahil didiñgiguin niyá cun sasamahan sana siya nang sino man sa simbahan. ¿Ibig mo
cayáng lasapín yaóng mangang nadoróon sa lamesa nang capatid mong

babaye.? Inamóy co cañgina at bagamán tila masarap ay hindí, cay á
ñga hindi co lalasapin. ¿Sáan naróon ang pusang binili co camacalauà.?
Ungmalís, sa pagca,t, inamóy niyá iyáng dagá iyán na pungmásoc dóon
sa butas, nang naróon camí sa halamanan at ñgayó,i, ang pusa,i, nagtago
sa tapayan. ¿Macailán bagá ang alilang babayeng naquiat (ungmacyat)
sa tanauan, nang caniyàng hanapin ang salamín nang capatid co.? Nacyat
(ungmacyat) siyá dóon macatatlò. ¿Báquit di mo acó hinihipo.? Sa pagca,t, masamáng ásal ang paghipo sa mañga tauò. ¿Anò bagá ang guinagauá
nang alilang tináuag mo cañgina.? Tungmatacbò parati (nagtatacbò) siyá
sa mañga lansañgan at cun siyá,i, tinatáuag co,i, cailán man hindí napaparitò
o dungmidiñgig at tinatanong man siyá,i, hindí rin sungmasagot. ¿Báquit
cayá tinangap mo siyá.? Tila, siyá,i, mabait at banal mona, datapóua,t,
siyá,i, malicot at magnanácao. ¿Anò anò yaóng mañga librong binabasà
nang iyòng capatid na babaye.? Binasà na nang capatid co ang mañga
libro mo at ñgayón ay binabasà niyá namán ang aquin. ¿Anò anòng
itàng mañga libro ang babasahin niyà bucas.? Bucas, siyá,i, lalabás na
bibili nang mañga ibon na sinabi mo sa caniyà at hindi siyá darating
sa capanahonan. ¿Anòng tinápay ang quináin nang capatig ni Juan.?
Quináin niyá ang tirápay na ybinigáy nang caniyàng capatid na babaye
sa caniyà.

YCADALAUANG POUONG PAGSASANAY.

¿Báquit caya ang tagarágat ay hindí niya dinadalà ditò ang mañga
sasacquián na binili co sa baybáy.? Dinadalà pa niyà sa mañga dalampásig
nang Pásig at hindí siyá darating hangán macalauà. ¿Gaanò calapad ang papel
na pinadalà mo sa anac nang anlouague.? Ganitó calapad. ¿Hindí bagá
maiclí iyáng cayong iyán, sa isàng baro.? Hindí, sa pagca,t, tila man
maiclí, mahaba,t, malapad. ¿Anò cayá ang bágay na lalong malouang sa
lahat.? Ang bágay na lalong malouang sa lahat ay ang dágat. ¿Maquipot
bagá ang mañga sapín dinalà mo ditò.? Maquipot ñga. Sáan pinaglalagáy
nang anac mong babaye ang dalauàng libro pinagotos co na dalhin niyà
dóon sa San Pedro? Pinaglalagáy niyà sa dalampásig. ¿Alín bagà dalampásig, ang sa canan o ang sa caliuá.? Aquing inaacala, ang sa caliuí.
¿Ang mananahi mo nagdamit na bagá sa mañga anac nang iyòng capatid
na ,babaye.? Hindí pa siyá nagdamit sa canilà. ¿Anò ang dinasal mo
sa lingong nacaráan sa simbahan.? Dinasal co,i, ang dasalan yniáral ni
nanáy sa aquin, nang acó,i, bata pa. ¿Anò ang quinacamtán nang pagdadasal.? Ang quinacamtán sa pagdadasal ay ang Láñgit. ¿Anò ang sabi nang
alila nang médico sa inà mo.? Sinabi niyà sa caniyà na hindí darating ang
caniyàng pañginóon hangán sa macalauà. ¿Anò ang ynilabás namin sa
báhay ni Pedro.? Ynilabás namin ang cáhoy na aming binili sa caniyà.
¿Anong íbig mo.? Ang íbig co,i, ñgayóp din ay paróon acó sa báhay ni
Pedro at dadalhin sa caniyà ang salaping nang bayaran sa cáhoy. ¿Anò
ang iniísip mo.? Ualá. ¿Anè ang pinadadalà nang Pare sa anac mo sa
Maynila.? Pinadadalà niyà itong mañga libro sa caniyà.

YCADALAUANG POUO,T, ISANG PAGSASANAY.

¿Anòng ypinótol mo niyàng baro.? Ang gonting ang ypinótol co. ¿Anò bagá ang yguinauá nang anlouague nang lamesa.? Pamocpoc ang yguinagauá niyà. ¿Guinonting mo bagá iyàng cayong iyán.? Oo po, ang gonting ang ypinótol co nang cayo. ¿Anò ang ytinapon nang iyòng capatid na babaye cañginang umaga.? Ytinapon niyà ang caniyàng pluma. ¿Báquit ytinapon niyà.? Sa pagca,i, luma na. ¿Ytatapon sana nilà ang canilàng salapí, cun mayróon disin silá.? Hindí, cun mayróon sana siláng salapí, hindí nilà ytatapon. ¿Anòng gagaoin co nitòng isdá.? Ytapon mo. ¿Anò cayá ang ñanga balita ditò sa bayan.? Ang sabi nang mañga tauò na ang hocom ay darating ñgayón. ¿Sino bagá ang nagbalita niyán sa iyò.? Yyà,i, ang sabi nang lahat. ¿Caílán ybabalita nang iyòng bianàn sa mañga anac niyà ang pagcamatáy nang caniyàng alila.? Sa lingong darating ay ybabalita niyá. ¿Anò,t, nanayáo ca na acó,i, uminom nang álac.? Acó,i, nanayáo na uminon ca nang álac, sa pagca,t, marahil ay ysusucá mo. ¿Anò ang ysinucá mo cahapon.? Ang quináin co, ang aquing ysinucá. ¿Anò bagá ang ysasábog sana nang amá mo ditò sa búquid na itò cun mabuti ang panahón.? Cun mabuti sana ang panahón ang ysasábog disin niyà,i, pálay. ¿Ano bagá, ang yquinacálat na lubhá nang masasamáng tauò.? Ang masamáng tauò ay cungmacálat nang masamáng ásal ¿Anò ang guinauá mo sa cáhoy na ypinadalà sa iyò nang iyòng magsasacà. Yguinátong co. ¿Anòng guinagauá mo diyán." Acó,i, maggagátong

YCADALAUANG POUO,T, DALAUANG PAGSASANAY.

¿Sino ang inootañgan nang mañgañgalácal nang caniyàng mañga calácal.? Ualá isà man inootañgan niyà nang mañga calácal, ibàng mañgañgalácal ang binibilhan niyà; ñguní,t, isàng cababayan niyà ang inootañgan niyà nang salapí sa macailán. ¿Sino ang ootañgan nang salapí.? Ang sa caniyàng amaín mañga anlouague ang ootañgan niyá. ¿Naotañgan mo bagá na si Pedro nang salapí, nang dungmating acó ditò.? Hindí, nang icáo ay dungmating ditò di pa si Pedro inotañgan co nang anománn. ¿Sino bagá ang ootañgan co nang salapí.? Ang iyòng ali ang ootañgan mo. ¿Alíng lugar ang pinagbatahan ni Jesucristo nang maraming cahirapan.? Ang Bondoc nang Calvario, ang pinagbatahan nang ating Pañginóon nang maraming cahirapan. ¿Macapagbatà ca na cayá nang maraming cahirapan cun icáo ay tumandá.? Oo ñga, magbabatà na acó nang maraming cahirapan cun acó,i, matandá na. ¿Sino cayá pinagnacauan mo nitòng libro. Ysá man tauò ay di co pinagnacauan nitòng libro, ybinigáy sa aquin itò nang aquing capatid na babaye „Macailán cang nagnácao nang anomán sa mañga magúlang mo.? Macatatló. ¿Magcanò sa búua,t, isà. Macadalauà ay cahati, at minsá,i, piso. ¿Anò cayá ang binabantayán nang aquing hípag.? Binabantayán niyà ang caniyàng mañga pananim. ¿At anò ang binabantayán nang mañga sundalo.? Ang mañga báyan at ang mañga dáa,i, binabantayán nilà. ¿Saán ang pinagbabantayán ni Juan.? Ang pinagbabantayan ni Juan ang tuláy

na malaqui. ¿Anòng íbig mong pagmasdáu co.? Ybig co na iyòng pag-
masdán itòng aquing ytuturo sa iyò. ¿Anò bagá iyán.? Na ang capalaran ditò sa lupa,i, lungmilipás na madalí. ¿Anò ang ysinúgat mo sa
caniyà.? Yeàng itac ay ysinúgat co sa caniyà. ¿Sáan bagá siyá sinoga-
tan mo.? Ang camáy niyà ang siñogatan co. ¿Sino bagá ang magaauit
ñgayóng gabì.?. Ang anac na babaye ni Alpredo, ang magaauit. ¿Sino
cayá ang pagaauitan niyà.? Ang amá niyá ang caniyàng pagaauitan.
¿Anò ang sabi niyà.? Ang sabi niyà,i, abúa! inà co, ¿Sino cayá ang
pinagsasabihan nang pinsán cong babaye niyán.? Pinagsabihan niyà ang
caniyáng alí niyán. ¿Alín ang tinaponan mo nang cáhoy na buloc.?
Ang dágat ang tinaponan co nang cáhoy na boloc. ¿Alín ang pinagla-
guiún nang alila niyáng quiso.? Ang lamesa. ang pinaglaguián niyà. ¿Sino
ang sinolatan nang canilàng capatid.? Ang caniyàng mañga anac ang si-
nulatan niyà. ¿Sa alíng búhay íbig mong pumanhíc.? (Alíng búhay ang
íbig mong panhícan.)? Ang búhay mo ang papanhícan co. ¿Anò bagá
ang amá nang amá mo.? Ang amá nang amá co,i, aquing nono. ¿At ang
anac nang anac nang nono mo ¿ay anò bagá.? Siyá,i, apó niyà. ¿At ang
apó nang amá mo.? Siyá,i, apó sa tuhod. At ang apó sa tuhod nang
iyòng amá ¿anò bagá sa caniyà.? Siyá,i, apó sa talampacan sa caniyà.
¿May asáua pa ang pinsán mong babaye.? Hindí, (or ualá) siyá,i, balo na.

YCADALAUANG POUO,I, TATLONG PAGSASANAY.

¿Sino ang yungmayaman.? Ang yungmayama,i, ang mañgañgalácal
¿Ang pamangquing babaye nang ating caapidbáhay dungmuduc-há bagá.?
Hindí, hindí siyá dungmuduc-há; siyá,i, gungmagaling. alintana,t. ang caniyàng bata lungmuhá sa saquít. ¿Ungmiclí bagá ang cayo nang aquing salaual.?
Hindí, cundí bagcús humaba. ¿Sino ang tungmatandá.? Tungmatandá ang
amá co. ¿Ang anac ni Tonio lungmalaqui bagá.? Hindí, hindí siyá lungmalaqui; cundí lungmalacás. ¿Dungmúnong bagá ang mañga Tagálog.? Hindí.
hindí pa silá dungmúnong. ¿Cailán cayá silá sisípag.? Cun silá,i, mayaman na. ¿Tinangap na bagá nang capatid mong babaye ang mañga
súlat.? Hindí pa niyà tinangap ang mañga súlat. ¿Bungmibili ang mañga
Americano nang anomán.? Bungmibili silá nang búquid. ¿Anò bagá ang
gagaoin co.? Cumuha ca nang tinápay at umalis ca na. ¿Anòng inabot
nang iyòng pinsán.? Ungmabot siyá nang álac. ¿Sinong ungmútang nang
pílac.? Ytòng tauòng itò,i, ungmótang nang pílac. ¿Anò ang babantéin
nating camtán.? Magbabantá tayo magcamit nang cayamanan. ¿Anò bagá
ang sinompong mo.? Sumompong acó nang quiso. ¿Sa canino sasalúbong
ca.? Sasalúbong acó sa aquing amaín. ¿Hungmuli ca bagá nang dagá.?
Hungmuli acó nang isà. ¿Sa canino dungmadaquip ang mañga bantáy.?
Dungmaraquip silá sa mañga magnanácao (or tulisán.) ¿Báquit ca ungmuumit nang salapí.? Hindí acó ungmuumit, ang alila ang ungmuumit.
¿Báquit tungmatacbò ang iyòng anac na babaye.? Siyá,i, tungmatacbò,
sa pagca,t, íbig niyàng humuli nang isàng ibon. ¿Anò ang guinagauá
nang canilàng capatid.? Tungmatalon siyá sa dágat. ¿Anò,t, longmolocsò
ang mañga bata.? Hindí silá lumolocsò; silá,i, lungmalácad na lámang.
¿Ang tagarágat ay marúnong lumañgóy.? Marúnong siyá lumañgóy. ¿Sáan
ang tahanang nang amá mo.? Ditò siyá tungmatahan. ¿Baquin hindí
ca hungmahumpáy sa pagtólog.? Sa pagca,t, maaga pa at lungmigá acó
cahapon sa hating gabi. ¿Anò ang sabi niyá.? Nagsabi siyá tumindig ca
mona at dumapá ca. ¿Hindí bagá lalong mabuti ñg acó tumihaya.?
Hindí, tumapat ca sa aquin at sacá tumaguilid ca. ¿Maanò na bagá ang
mañga halaman sa iyòng halamanan.? Sungmisíbol na at ang mañga ca-

hoy na sa dalampasig nang ílog ay ungmunsbong na. ¿Maanó bagá capapon ang panahón? Cahapon ay ungmulán, eungmolog, cungmidlat at lungmintic at di sumícat ang árao. ¿Alín ang paroroonan mo ñgayón? Napapasabáhay acó, sa pagca,t, dungmidilim na at ang bóua,i, hindí sísícat hangán sa hating gabí. ¿Báquit cayá ang iyòng capatid ay pung mapatáy nang ibon, lungmilipol nang halaman, sungmusúgat nang báboy. bungmabásag nang pingán at bungmabalí nang cauayan? Sa pagca,t, siyá,i, mabagsic, pinapalo man siyá ni amá. ¿Báquit tungmatañgis ang bata? Ybig niyàng umihi at tumáe, cañgicañgina lámang siyá,i, tüngmatáua. nang cungmacáin, ungmiinom at lungmalamon nang boñga. ¿Anó ang gagaoin? Lumura siyá at tingnán mo na houag siyáng cacagatín nang aso.

YCADALAUANG POUO,T, APAT NA PAGSASANAY.

¿Sino ang sungmasamà sa iyò? Ualáng sungmasamà sa aquin ñgayón. cañgina lámang ay sungmamà acó cay Juan na ungmoosap sa caniyàng capatid na babaye, siyá,i, sungmasamà cay Pedro, na (Si Pedro) ungmaáuay sa caniyàng caibigan at húngmiualáy acò sa caniyà. ¿Dung midiñgig bagá ang pransés nang anomán? Siyá,i, dungmidiñgig nang anomán, ñguní,t, tungmitiñgin siyá nang mañga ibon sa mañga sañgá nang cáhoy. ¿Sino-sino bagá ang hungmihipo sa mañga babaye? Ang mañga batang tampalasan lámang ang hungmihipo sa mañga babaye. ¿Gungmagauá bagá ang iyòng pinsáng babaye nang anomán? Siyá,i, ungmamóy nang bulac-lac at lungmalasap nang buñga. ¿Anòng guinagauá nang mañga médico? Silá,i, gungmagamot sa ibà ñguní,t, hindí silá ung maáhit at di rin gungmugupit sa ibà. ¿Sa canino bagá hungmahampas ang iyòng amá? Hungmahampas sa caniyáng alila, sa pagca,t, hindî hung milamos sa pañginóon niyà. ¿Gungmagauá bagá nang anomán ang alila ni Pedro? Siyá,i, sungmacamot sa cungmacamot sa caniyáng pañginóong babaye. ¿Sino ang guiguimbal? Ang aquing anac ang guiguimbal, sa mantala ang caibigan niyà,i, gungmugupit sa cabayo. ¿Anòng gagaoin mo niyáng sibat na iyán? Sisibat acó nang bábuy damó. ¿Sino ang ungmíua cay Magallanes? Ang mañga taga Sebú ang ungmíua sa caniyà. ¿Guinagauá bagá nang anomán ang mañga anlouague? Ang ibà sa canilà,i, dungmadarás. ang ibà namán ay cungmacatam. ¿Nasaán ang Dios na ating Pañginóon? Ang Dios ay sungmasalahat at ang Caniyàng mahal na Anac ay sungmasaláñgit sa caniyàng canan. ¿Báquit bagá di naglalabás nang upóan ang inyòng alila? Siyá,i, naglalabás nang ilán. ñguní,t, ynilabás na niyà itòng mañga lamesa. ¿Ibig mo po bagá nang ibàng bágay? Oo, ypacuha mo ang lahat na pingán na sasalamesa cañgina. ¿Anó ang gagaoin co sa mañga aso? Tacutín mo, sa pagca,t, ang mañga pusa nañgagcacatácot sa canilà at nagugútom. ¿Báquit bagá ang pañginóon co,i, ungmaáuay sa aquin? Ungmaáuay siyá sa iyò, dahil sa inóhao mo ang mañga aso at iyòng guinútom ang mañga pusa.

YCADALAUANG POUO,T, LIMANG PAGSASANAY.

¿Cailán ca oouí sa iyóng bayan? Ibig cong umouí doón bucas. ¿Sino bagá ang quinóon mo? Aquing ypinatáuag ay ang médico. ¿Nangyayari

bagáng patirin mo itòng lúbid.? Mangyayaring pumatid acó nang mañga
lúbid. ñguní,t, di co maaring patirin itô. ¿Báquit ang caibigan mo nucsó
cay Juana.? Dahil sa inanyaya ni Juana siyà. ¿Bungmíhag bagá ang mañga
Americano nang maraming prisionerong Tagálog.? Oo, ang mañga Tagálog
ay ungmórong at ang mañga Americano,i, dinaquip silá. ¿Saán ungmiiguib
ang alila mo.? Siyá,i, umiiguib doón sa bal-óng tinutucaan nang mañga
ibon nang pálay at quiniquitilan nang bulac-lac nang iyòng capatid na babaye. ¿Saán naróon ang bata.? Ang bata,i, tungmatactò, upan maonahan
niyà Si Pransisco. ¿Sino sino ang nanalo sa mañga castila.? Ang mañga
Americano ay nanalo sa mañga castila. ¿Anò ang guinagauá ni Pedro.? Si Pedro,i, naquiquinig sa cura at naquiquinábang. ¿Sino ang nanunuyo sa tauòng
nanunuluyan sa búhay nang iyòng amá.? Ang alila nang iyòng capatid na
babaye ang nanunuyo sa caniyà, ñguní,t, ñgayó.l, nanonóod siyá nang procesion. ¿Sino ang namamatnógot sa mañga Tagálog sa paquiquibacà laban
sa mañga Americano.? Ang mañga Tagálog ay pinamamatnogotan ni Aguinaldo na siyà niláng pinanaligan. ¿Saán nanunúbig ang bata.? Ang pi-
nanunubigan niyà,i, ang halamanan. ¿Anòng pinapanimdim nang matandáng lalaqui.? Ang pinanimdim niyà,i, ang paniin sa tongcod, sa pagca,t,
hindí mangyaring siyá,i, lomohod. ¿Sino sino ang quinacausap nang Americano.? Ang quinacausap niyà,i, ang ilán niyáng cababayan. ¿Sino ang
nañguñgunà cay Alfredo.? Siyá,i, niunahan ni Prancisco. ¿Naquiquinábang
ca nang marami sa iyòng caálcal.? Acó,i, hindí naquiquinábang, cundí
bagcús acóng nañguñgulugui. ¿Nañgiñgilig bagá sa lamig ang alila.?
Hindí, siyá,i, nañgiñginig sa tácot. ¿Sino ang nañgiñgimi.? Ualáng nañgiñgimi, datapóua,t, ang caibigan nang caibigan mo,i, nañgiñgimbolo at
nañgiñgilo. ¿Anòng sabi nang mañga cura.? Ang sabi nilá sa lahat ay
mañgilin cun piesta at pag-iñgatan houag mañgílap sa Dios. ¿Anò,t,
nañgiñgilábot ang iyòng asáua.? Nañgiñgilábot siyá dahil sa cungmuculog.
¿Anò,t, naninibughò ang asáua ni Juan.? Sa pagca,t, siyá,i, pinañgiñgi-
bigan nang caniyàng caapidbáhay. ¿Nañgañgayupapa ca bagá sa harap
nang Dios.? Oo, at lahat na tauò,i, dápat mañgayupapa sa harap Niyà.
¿Anò ang pananaguínip nang pinsán mo cagabí.? Siyá,i, nanaguínip na
inaanyaya ang caniyàng capatid na babaye at itò namá,i, nañgañganino
sa salamín. ¿Báquit nañgañgambà ang capatid mong babaye.? Siyá,i,
nañgañgambà dahil sa siyá,i, mañgañganac. ¿Mañgañgánay bagá siyá.?
Hindí, ycaıauà pañgañganac niyà yaón. ¿Anò,t, ang canilàng amá,i,
nañgañgalumbaba at bihasang humaloquipquip? Siyá,i, nañgalo at na-
ñgálay. ¿Nañgañgahás cang mañgaco na mananatili sa cabanalan?. Na-
nanatili acó sa pagauá niyán. ¿Anò,t, hindí siyá nananáog sa hagdán
at di siyá nananasila diyán.? Ypinanambitan niyà ang pagcamatáy nang
caniyàng asáua. ¿Nananalig ca bagá sa mahal na Virgen.? Oo, siyá
ang aquing pinananaligan. ¿Anò,t, nananaghóy diyán ang capatid mong
babaye.? Sapagca,t, ang caibigan niyà Si María,i, nananaghili sa caniyà
at namumungcahi sa caniyà sa pagliligo. ¿Natatácot ca bagá diyán sa aso.?
Hindí acó natatácot, sa pagca,t, namamaypóy. ¿Namamáhay ca bagá.?
Hindí, acó,i, tungmitirá sa gúbat. ¿Anò ang ypinamamañhic mo sa aquin.?
Ang ypinamamanhic co sa iyò na icáo ay bumañgon maaga,t, magligo
sa dágat. ¿Anòng mayróon ca sa muc-há.? Namamaga. ¿Báquit ytinapon
nang iyòng anac sa dágat iyáng asong iyán.? Sa pagca,t, siyá,i, quinágat
¿Báquit hindí mo siyá biniguián nang mabuting áral.? Sa pagca,t, di co
siyá ynilagáy sa isáng colegio. ¿Báquit ang capatid mong lalaqui ay hindí
nagsasalitá nang lalong magaling nang uicang inglés.? Sa pagca,t, di siyá
macapagüicang magaling. ¿Pinaualá mo bagá ang cabayo.? Ang alila ang
siyáng may casalanan sa pagcaalpás nang cabayo.

YCADALAUANG POUO,T, ANIM NA PAGSASANAY.

¿Minomorà bagá Si Pedro nang capatid mong lalaqui? Hindí niya minomorà, ypinaala-alà lámang sa caniyà ang caniyàng catungcolan. ¿Anòng dápat cong gaoin nang acó,i, mahalin? Cun magbibilì ca nang anomán, houag mong mahalín at cun ang calácal mo,i, hindí magaling, iyòng ysaoli ang pílac. ¿Magoótang (better magpapaótang) bagá ang amá mo nang salapí sa caibigan niyà? Hindí siya nag-ótang (nagpaótang) sa caniyà nang salapí, nagbigá lámang at nagcalóob pa nang handog. ¿Ybinalita bagá nang iyòng mañga alila sa canilàng caibigan ang nangyari? Hindí, ysinaysáy lámang sa canilà na ang boboñgan nilà,i, hinagnis nang batò nang mañga bata. ¿Báquit pinahihintolotan ca nang iyòng amá na umalis cun gabi? Pinahintolotan acó niyà upan mapanóod co ang pagbobonsod sa sasac-quián. ¿Sáan mo ytinapon ang isdáng buloc? Yhinagcis co sa lupa. ¿Magbobual mo bagá nang maraming cáhoy cun mayróon cang palacol? Hindí, íbig cong maghasic nang binghi, at ang ilà,i, ysábog sa manoc. ¿Naamóy mo bagá ang samyong ysinasambúlat nang mañga bulaclac? Oo, at acó,i, cungmitil nang isà upang maylagáy sa masetero (Sp. w. "flower-pot"). ¿Anòng inaac la mong ytias? Di acó nagaacalang magtáas nang anomán; cundí ang ninanasa co,i, magtayó nang báhay at ypanáog yaóng dalauàng cuadro. ¿Aalisin mo bagá ang mañga paco? Hindí, aquing ytitindig ang mañga laráuan,t, ylalayo. ¿Gungmagamot bagá ang mañga médico sa ibà? Oo, ñguni,t, silá,i, hindí gungmagamot sa canilàng sarili (or naggagamot). ¿Ang caibigan mo,i, nagaahit bagá, nagsusucláy at naghahampás (sa caniyàng sarili)? Hindí, cundí siyá,i, naggogopit at naghihilamos. ¿Nasugatan bagá Si Antonio? Oo, cahapon siyá,i, nagbasá at sa caniyàng pagcamot nagcasúgat sa balat. ¿Anòng guinagauá nang cura? Siyá,i, nagsusugal ñgayón, ñguni,t, nagmisa cañgina. ¿Nagtatabaco bagá ang anac mo? Hindí siyá nagtatabaco; cundí nagsisicolate touíng hapon. ¿Nagsasalaual bagá ang mañga Pare? Hindí, cundí silá,i, nagsasapin, nagsasambalelo,t, nagsasalamín. ¿Nagtatapis cayá ang mañga babaye sa iyòng Provinsia? Hindí silá nagtatapis. ¿Nagsamà bagá Si Pedro at Si María? Silá,i, nagsamà, nagcalitáan at nagáuay. ¿Báquit nagtipon ang caguinoohan nang bayan cahapon? Silá,i, nagsama-samà lámang at nañgagtalo. ¿Nagquiquita bagá Si Juana at Si Francisco? Silá,i, hindí nagquiquita, cundí nagsusulatanan. ¿Naghahalo bagá ang mañga mag-gagatas nang túbig sa gatas? Oo, naghahalo. ¿Anòng guinauá mo sa magcapatid ni Del Rosario? Pinagbati co silá. ¿Ang mag-asaúa,i, dápat cayáng magtuñgayaui,t, maghampasan? Hindí, cundí bagcús siláng dápat mag-ibigan, magtoloñgan, magtiisan,t, magpatauaran. ¿Ang mag-asáua ni Ruiz, ay nagsosonoran bagá? Hindí, silá i, nagcacagatan,t, nagtatadyacan.

YCADALAUANG POUO,T, PITONG PAGSASANAY.

¿Báquit ang mañga bata nañgagtatachò, at pinagtutulacanan ang aquin cabayong matandá? Sa pagca,t, silá,i, nagcái,t, nag-inom. ¿Nañgagsúlat at nañgagbasá bagá silá? Hindí, cundí silá,i, nañgaglacad at nañgagtañgís.

ñguní,t, pag-isipisipin nilà ang magpadaandáan. ¿Paano-auò bagá ang pag
calácad nang mañga tauo? Ang mañga lasing, ay nagsnsuray-súray at nag-
quiquiling-quíling; ang mañga dalaga,i, nagquiquinding-quinding; ang mañga
mangmang ay nagbabaling-báling (bungmabaling-báling); ang mañga matandá,i, nagocor-ocor; ang mañga may saquit, ay bungmabalibaligtag, at ang
mañga bata,i, nagtitiar-tiar. ¿Anò ang caraníuang ypinaacala nang tauó?
Ang mañga mangmang ay nagmamarúnong; ang mañga dóuag, ay nagta-
tapang-tapañgan; ang mañga babaye,i, nagmamariquit; ang mañga tacsil, ay
nagbabait-baita,t, ang mañga mapagpaimbabáo, ay nagbabanal banalan. ¿Anò
ang nangyayari namán sa ibá.? Ang mañga masintahi,i, nagmamalimoti,t,
ang mañga matandá,i, nagmamasasactín. ¿Gungmagauá bagá nang may cabanalan ang Hocom.? Hindí, cundí siyá,i, gungmagauá nang may cotouiran.?
¿Alín mañga dalaga ang may magaling na ásal.? Ang mababait ay gungmagauá nang calinisan, ñguní,t, ang hindí mababait gungmagauá nang
cahalayan. ¿Tungmacbo-tacbò bagá ang mañga bata sa halamanan.? Tungmacbo-tacbò silá, datapoúa,t, hindi nangyaring matolóy, sa pagca,t,
ungmoolan-olán. ¿Maálam nang sumúlat ang caniyàng anac.? Hindí,
cundí nagsusulat-sulatan pa lámang. ¿Mabait bagá ang ànac ni Alpredo.?
Hindi, subali.t, siya,i, nagbanal-banalan, nagcacain-cainan palagui at
nag-iyac-iyacan, at cun minsá,i, nag-olol-ololan. ¿Báquit biga ang aquing
alila,i, nagbibiñgibiñgiha,t, nagsasaquit-saquitan.? Sa pagca,t, siyá,i, masonín
at palaguing magbabahay-bahayan casamá nang ibàng bata. ¿Anòng gui
nauá nang mag-amá.? Silá,i, mona nagtiñginan, at sacá nagyacapán.
¿Anòng guinauá niyòng mañga tauó.? Nag-aabut-abutan nang mañga
bayong. ¿Nagbibigás at nag-iisdá ca cayá.? Acó,i, nagbibili nang bagóong
at itlog at nagtatayó namán nang búhay. ¿Ang iyòng capatid na lalaqui,i,
marúnong bagá mag-amá at mag-anac.? Hindí siyá marúnong mag-anac,
cundí marúnong mag-amá. ¿Marúnong namán bagá siyá magbianán.? Oo,
bagamán mahírap ang magbianán. ¿Anòng sinasabi niyà sa caniyàng anac.?
Sinabi niyàng, magpumílit cang magáral, magsumáquit cang maguing ma-
púlad, at magdumalí ca. ¿Anòng guinagauá cañgina dóon niyóng caramihan.?
Nañgag-oósap.

YCADALAUANG POUO.T. UALONG PAGSASANAY.

¿Guinauá mo ang sinabi co sa iyo.? Hindí, sa pagca,t, di co nalalaman
ang ypinagotos mo sa aquin. ¿Anò ang aquing gagaóin.? Alisín mo iyáng paco
at iyòng ysaolí ang súlat sa aquing bayáo. ¿Ysasaysáy co sa caniyà ang
pagcamatáy nang ibon?. Hindí, houag cang magsabi sa caniyà nang anomán
tungcol sa bágay na iyán. ¿Anòng aquing ytatanong sa caniyà? Ytanong
mo cung cailán niyà acó dadalauin. ¿Nagquita bagá cayó nóong isàng árao?
Oo, nagquita cami sa langsañgan. ¿Ybig mo bagá ytapou co itòng aspiler? Hindí, ñguní,t, ang halamanan ay pagtaponan mo nang cahóy.
¿Anòng ybinalita mo sa iyòng balbero" Aquing ybinalita co sa caniyà
ang sermón nang Pare cañginang omaga sa simbahan. ‘Sáan nilà ybi-
nonsod ang sasac-yán? Ang pinagbonsoran nang sasac-yá.i, ang Sebú.
¿Pinagtaniman mo bagá nang anomán ang iyòng búquid.? Oo, naghasic
acó nang pálay. ¿Sáan mo yhinasic? Yhinasic co sa búquid na dacong
dágat. ¿Anòng ysinisilid mo diyán sa tapayan? Sinisidlán co nang tinápay. ¿Sáan mo ytatayó ang iyòng búhay? Ang pagtatayóan co,i, yong lupang may mañga cáhoy. ¿Sáan silá nagáuay? Ang pinagauayan nilá,i,
ang silid. ¿Sáan bagá nagoósap ang mañga Americano cahapon.? Ang
Escolta, ay ang pinagosapan mona nilà, sacá sa tuláy na malaquì, silá
nagáuay. ¿Báquit nagtoloñganan cayó.? Camí,i, nagtoloñganan, dahil sa

nasang aming magcamtán ang ganti. ¿Anò,t, ang mañga magsasacà, ay bungmóual nang ganóong caraming cáhoy.? Silá,i, nagboual nang ganóong caraming cáhoy, sa pagca,t, cailañgan nilà sa pag-gauá nang báhay. Yvòng bilañgin cundí mo pa nabibílang. Ang nabílang co na, ay mahíguit na tatlóng daán. ¿Sino ang binilhán mo niyáng mañga caráyom.? Ang binilhan co nitò,i, ang magcacalácal, ñguni,t, íbig cong ypagbilì olí sa mañga mananahi. ¿Sino ang ootañgan mo nang salapíng iyòng cailañgan.? Ang mañga caibigan co ang aquing ootañgan. ¿Nagpaótang bagá sa iyò ang iyòng hípag.? Hindí. subali,t, acó ang inotañgan niyà nang únim na sicápat. ¿Báquit nag-hampasan cayó sa búquid.? Dahil sa acó mona ang minorà niyà. ¿At nagtipon bagá dóon ang maraming tauò.? Abàa;! oo, maramìng nagtipon sa pinagaauayan namin. ¿Báquit ang alila mo,i, nagbibiñgi-biñgihan.? Ang ypinagbibiñgi-biñgihan niyà,i, ang houag pumaritò. ¿Sáan ynilagáy nang iyòng anac ang mañga salamín co.? Ang hihigan mo ang pinaglag-ián niyà. ¿Sino ang ypinag-gagauá mo niyáng upóan.? Ang aquing inà. ¿Di bagá ang iyòng nono ang ypinagtatahi mo niyáng mañga salaual.? Hindí, ang Pare, ang aquing ypinagtatahi. ¿Báquit ang anglouague, ay aayáo acóng ypapaggauá nang isàng lamesa?. Sa pagca,t, siyá,i, matamad na tauò.

YCADALAUANG POUO,T, SIYAM NA PAGSASANAY.

¿Saán narulás at natísod ang iyòng alila.? Hindí lámang siyá nadulás at natísod, cundí nahólog pa sa gúbat na caniyàng quinaligaoan. ¿Anò ang naualá sa iyò, at icáo, ay ganiyán nalulumbáy.? Acó,i, namatayán nang anac. ¿Saán namatáy siyà.? Ang Maynila ang bayang quinamatayan niyà. ¿Báquit nilisan nang capatid mong babaye na ycompisal niyóng casalanan.? Sa pagca,t, nacalisanan niyà. ¿Anò,t, nagulantang ang inà mo cagabi.? Nahihigá siyá nang cungmocolog, nagulantang siyá, at bigláng napatindig, at nang siyá,i, naquita namin, ay nacalohod. ¿Naquita mo ang magnanácao? Oo, siyá,i, nacataob at napapañgáo. ¿Nagogótom bagá o naoóhao ang ating caapidbáhay.? Siyá,i, hindí nagogótom at hindí rin naoóhao, cundí nagagálit. ¿Sino ang nahihiya.? Ualáng nahihiya, ñguni,t, Si Pedro, ay nagugúlat. ¿Alin-alín ang mañga casiráang gáling sa pagbabacà.? Ang casiráang gáling sa pagbabacà ay sungmasacláo sa maraming bágay; ang cabahaya,i, nañgasísira; ang mañga cáhoy ay nañgatutuyó, at caniyàng mañga sañgà, ay nañgagcacabali at ang mañga cáuat nang telégrapo, ay napapatid. ¿Báquit hindí nilá quinacáin iyáng isdá? Dahil sa buloc na. ¿Anò ang yquinamatáy nang aquing nonong babaye? Ang catandáa,i, ang yquinamatáy niyà. ¿Sáan siyá namatáy.? Ang simbahan ang quinamatayan niyà. ¿Báquit yaóng tauò,i, nagsusuling súling.? Dahil sa siyá i, piláy at bulag, at nalulumbáy, sa pagca,t, siyá,i, naduduc-há. ¿Báquit siyá nagbibiñgi-biñgihan? Hindí siyá nagbibiñgibiñgihan, cundí tunáy na biñgì. ¿Sáan muntí (or halos) na malónod ang tungmatanan? Halos malolónod na sa ilog. ¿Anòng lagáy nang pinsán mong babaye? Siyá,i, napapágod at nahilo. ¿Báquit nalaglag itòng boñga nang cáhoy.? Sa pagca,t, ang búhay nang cáhoy, ay unti-unting naootás.

YCATLONG POUONG PAGSASANAY.

¿Ano ang yquinahohólog nang maraming tauò.? Ang yquinahohólog nang maramì, ay ang pageatísod. ¿Ang lagnat bagá ang yquinamamatáy. nang maraming tauò sa Pilipinas.? Di lámang ang lagnat, cundí ang ibà,t, ibà pang saquit ang yquinamamatáy nang maraming taga Europa sa Pilipinas. ¿Saán nahólog ang alila.? Ang dáan. ang quinahologan niyà. ¿Anò,t, nahólog siyá.? Nahólog dahil sa siyá.i, lasing. ¿Yhinólog bagá nino itò.? Yhinólog nang ating caibigan. ¿Anòng yhohólog natin sa caniyà? Hulugan nating siyá nang isàng dalandán. ¿Sino-sino ang hinologan nang inaamá sa binyag nang salapí, sa paglabás niyà sa simbahan.? Ang mañga bata. ¿Magcanò ang natirá sa salapíng ypinadalà co sa iyo noóng lingong nacaráan.? Ang natirá.i, tatlòng póuo,t, tatlòng piso. ¿Magcanò ang matitirá cun mabayaran na ang mananahi.? Labíng ánim na sicápat lámang ang matitirá. ¿Saán iníbig nang pinsán cong matirá nóong isàng árao.? Tungmirá siyá (cusa) sa Cavite. ¿At sáan bagá ang canilàng anac ytinirá nang caniyàng mañga casamà.? Sa gúbat. siyá.i, ytinirá. ¿Sungmúlat bagáng mabuti ang nagaáral.? Hindí. cundí ang pageatítie niyà,i, mahúsay. ¿Anò ang ysinúlat niyà.? Ysàng bagüís ang caniyàng guinamit. ¿Aling papel ang susulatan co.? Houag mong sulatan ang alín man papel, cundí isàng lamesa ang iyòng sulatan. ¿Sungmasampalataya ca bagá sa Dios.? Oo, po, ang Dios, ay aquing sinasampalatayana,t, sinosonod. ¿Sungmososó pa bagá ang iyòng sangol.? Sungmososò pa, dahil sa aánim na bóuan pa lámang. ¿Sino ang nagpapasosò sa caniyà.? Ysàng sisíuang galing sa búquid, ang siyá niyàng sinosohan. ¿Ang gatas niyáng sosohín. ay mabuti bagá.? Siyá,i, mayróon mabuting gatas na susuhín at ang caniyàng, pagpapasosò.i, magaling na magaling. ¿Anòng salisalitá sa labás.? Ang capayapáa,i, di pa nayayari ¿Sino ang nagsalitá niyán sa iyò.? Ang mañga periódico (Sp. w.) (panulatan, Tagalog w.) ang may sabì. ¿Ang mañga periódico,i, pinaniniualáan mo bagá.? Hindí lahat nang sinasali nang mañga periódico, ay totoò. ¿Anò ang sasabihin mo sa iyòng apóng lalaqui.? Ualá acóng sasabihin anomán sa caniyà. ¿Caninong ysinasalitá nang pandáy bácal ang balitang iyán.? Ang mañga cababayan nang aquing capatid na lalaqui, ang siyáng pinagsalitáan niyà. ¿Anò ang binabálot nang babaye diyán sa papel.? Cayo ang binabálot niyá. ¿Anòng ybinabálot niyá sa cayo.? Ang binabálot niyà,i, papel, ¿Anòng sabì mo.? Houag ang baril ang ypatáy mo sa mañga dagà. ang ypatáy mo,i, lason. ¿Ylán bábuy damó ang papatayín nang tagálog.? Mapapatáy niyà,i, marami. dahil sa siyá,i, bihasa. ¿Anong ypinapatáy niyà.? Sibat ang ypinapatáy niyà. ¿Sáan pinatáy vaóng pitòng dinalà niyà dito noóng isàng árao.. Ang pinagpatayan niyà noón mañga yaón ay ang gúbat. ¿Anòng gagaóin mo iyáng sandatà.? Siyá, (ang sandatà) ang yparatay co sa aquing caáuay.

YCATATLONG POUO.T. ISANG PAGSASANAY.

¿Ang baro, ay sáan co hahanapin.? Ang silid ang paghanapan mo. ¿Anòng yhahánap.? Ytòng ílao ang yhánap mo. ¿Anò ang iyòng quinoha.?

Quinoha co cay Juan ang libro. ¿Báquit ang bata,i, ayáo cumáin at uminom." Ualá siyá macáin at mainom, bocod sa ualá pang pingán at inuman. ¿Anó ang binili niyà.? Si Juana ay binilhán niyá nang isàng bulaclac. ¿May ybibili ca bagá nang báhay.? Hindí, acó,i, ualáng maybili. ¿Báquit di ca humiñgi sa iyòng amaín.? Hindí mangyari, siyá,i, quinancaman co nitòng salapí. ¿Anò ang hátol na ybinigáy mo sa iyòng anac na lalaqui.? Aquin siyáng hinatulan na ysaolí ang salapí sa caniyàng amaín. ¿Anò ang ybiniyaya sa iyò nang amá mo.? Ang ybiniyaya niyà sa aquin ay isàng orasán. ¿Anong ybinalita mo sa iyòng caibigan.? Ybinalita co sa caniyà ang pagcamatáy nang capatid niyàng babaye. ¿Alín ang ytinotoro niyaóng bata.? Yaóng cáhoy ang caniyàng ytinotoro. ¿Sino ang pinagbilinan niyà nang bilin nang caniyàng alila.? Ang Pare ang caniyàng pinagbilinan. ¿Anò ang niloloto mo.? Ysdá ang aquing niloloto. ¿Sino ang ypinagloloto mo.? Ang aquing inà ang siyá cong ypinagloloto. ¿Ypagpipritos mo namán siyá nang ságuing." Ualá acóng panahón, sa pagca,t, linalabahan nivà ang aquing damit. ¿Anòng ninanasang abotan niyàng mandarágat sa ganiyàng pagtac-bò.? Ang ninanasa niyò,i, abotan yaòng aso ¿Anò,t, Si Pedro,i, lungmolocsò nang paganiyán.? Ang mañga boñga, ang linolocsò niyà. ¿Sino ang pinanhic mo? Ang capatid cong lalaqui ang aquing pinanhic. ¿Alín ang pinanaogan mo.? Ang patoñgò sa pintong harapan ang pinanaogan co. ¿Sino ang quinatatacotan nang mañga capatid mong babaye.? Ang mañga patáy ang siyá nilàng quinatatacotan. Catacutan nilà ang Dios at houag nilàng cagulatan ang mañga calolóua nang mañga patáy na. ¿Sino ang namatáy sa caapidbáhay.? Siyá,i, namatayán nang inà. ¿Cailán siyá namatáy.? Namatáy siyá nang onàng árao. nang Marzo. ¿Anò ang yquinamatáy niyà.? Nalonod. ¿Sino ang quinatotouáan mo.? Ang quinatotouáan co,i, ang aquing mañga anac. ¿Sino ang paparitohan nang camaganac mo.? Ang paparitohan niyà,i, ang aquing capatid na babaye, nang manóod sa procesión. ¿Anò ang ypinaritò nang aquing pinsán? Ang ypinaritò niyà,i, ang pagbáyad nang caniyàng útang. ¿Sino ang paroróonan mo.? (or dadalaoin.)Ang Pare ang paroroonan co (or dadalaoin).

YCATATLONG POUO,T. DALAUANG PAGSASANAY.

¿Báquit sinasamsam mo ang boñga,t, ang damit na guinamit nang iyong amá? Ytòng mañga boñgang itò,i, pinili co sa halamanan, at tungcol sa damit, ay aquing hiniram. ¿Anò ang dinodócot nang capatid mong babaye.? Dinodócot niya ang caráyom sa butas. ¿Anò ang dinaying mo sa iyòng inà.? Ang dinaying co sa caniya,i, big-yán acó nang salapí ¿Ano ang pinapang-ós niyáng bata.? Ang pinapang-ós niyà,i, ang tubò nang caniyàng capatid. ¿Tináuag mo bagá ang alila." Di co siyá tináuag, cundí siyá,i, aquing quinauayan. ¿Sino ang iyòng sosondoin.? Sinosongdò co ang balbero. ¿Hinalíhao niyà cayá ang pamocpoc.? Sinalicsic na niyà. ¿Tinangap mo bagá ang súlat.? Tinangap co na ang súlat at ñgayó,i, sasaluboñgin co ang aquing caibigan. ¿Binating bagá nang mañga americano itòng mañga bábuy damó.? Binating nilà (nahuli). ¿Pinaanò ang paghuli nitòng tauò, ditò sa mañga ibo,t, isdá.? Nacatí niyà ang mañga ibon at bininuit (nabanuit) ang mañga isdá. ¿Tinanáo bagá nang mandarágat ang sasaquián.? Hindí niyà tinanáo (natanáo) ang sasaquián. ¿Anòng inusuliap nang dalaga.? Ualá siyáng sinusuliap, ang pinanóod niyà,i, ang procesion. ¿Anòng canilàng tinicmán.? Ninamnán nilà ang álac. ¿Anò ang aamoyín natin.? Aamoyín natin yaón mañga bulac-lac. ¿Ynaalaalá

mo bagá ang sinabì nang iyòng amá.? Ynaalaalà co, sa pagca,t, siyá ay
aquing iniíbig. ¿Yniíbig mo bagá nanñán ang iyòng inà.? Oo, ñga, iniíbig
co siyá. ¿Ynírog bagá niyà ang caniyàng anac. Di niyà inírog. ¿Sino ang
inaáaquit mo? Ang aquing caibigan ang inaáquit co. ¿Sino ang hinihintáy
niyà.? Ang binihintáy niyà,i, ang caniyàng asáua. ¿Sinong tinatanong
mo.? Tinatanong co ang caapid-báhay. ¿Sinong sinala mo, nóon isàng
árao.? Sinala co ang aquing anac, sa pagca,t, di niyà sinaclolò ang caniyàng capatid na lalaqui. ¿Sinong gungmibú nitòng báhay.? Sinónod.
¿Báquit di nilà hinúsay ang canilàng mañga libro? Sa pagca,t, ang mañga
libro,i, tinastás. ¿Mangyayaring pasanín mo itòng capótol na cáhoy?
Hindí, cundí mangyayaring hilahin co. ¿Caninong cuentas na tina-
tagláy mo? Sa aquing inà. ¿Anòng quiniquilic mo? Ysàng librong dasalan, sa pagca,t, ang aquing anac ay di macalácad at quinacalong co
siyá. ¿Ano,t, pinótol mo ang tinápay at guinísic mo ang cayo cong tinabás
na? Yyá,i, di co guinauá; acó,i, tungmagá nang capótol na cáhoy at
sinapol co ang mañga pono nang ságuing. ¿Tinimbang mo bagá ang bácal at
tinácal ang pálay? Aquing tinaroc ang úlac. ¿Ay anó, inaaquin mo itòng
libro? Yyá,i, quinacanilà co. ¿Yninyò bagá iyán? Oo, inaamin co iyán.
¿Minamarápat mo bagá ang guinauá nang iyòng anac? Hindí, minamasamá co. ¿Anòng gagaoin niyà niyáng mañga batò? Sisimbahanin niyà.
(gagaoin niyàng simbahan.) Báquit (inaaring amá) maamá nang caibigan
mo Si Pedro? Sa pagca,t, siyá,i, (inaaring anac) insanac ni Pedro. ¿Anòng
liliparin niyàng bánoy? Liliparin (dadaguitin) niyá ang isang sísiu. ¿Aabutan mo cayá ang iyòng caáuay? Aabutan co siyá, sa paglañgoy. ¿Anòng
sisisirin niyà? Ang sisisirin niyà.i. isàng singsing.

YCATATLONG POUO,T. TATLONG PAGSASANAY.

¿Anòng pinagotayán ypinagbilì nang mañgañgalácal? Ypinagbilì
niyàng otay-otáy ang mañga caráyom at aspiler nang aquing capatid na
babaye. ¿Anòng ytinatapon mo sa apúy? Ybig co ytapon sa apúy ang
cáhoy nang aquing amá. ¿Báquit ang pinsán mo,i. sungmasásambog nang pálay
sa caniyàng búquid? Dahil sa sungmasambúlat nang bañgo. ¿Anòng yhinalo
nang tagálog sa álac? Túbig. ¿Anòng ydinagdag nang mañgañgalácal sa
mantiquiya? Ang ydinagdag niyá,i, ang *sebo* (Sp. w.) nang aquing amá. ¿Anòng
ylinagáy nang pinsán mo sa ibúbao niyàng lamesa? Ang ynilagáy niyà,i.
ang librong dasalan nang capatid cong babaye. ¿Báquit ybinibilad mo
iyàng damit? Sa pagcat,t, basá. ¿Anòng ybinibiyaya mo sa iyòng inà.?
Ang ybinibiyaya co sa caniyà,i, salamín. ¿Anòng ysinalità niyà sa iyòng
hípag? Ytinanong niyà ang calagayan nang caniyàng alí. ¿Anòng yniáral
mo ditò sa bata? Yniáral co sa caniyà ang dasalan. ¿Aling ytinoro
nilà sa iyòng pinsáng babaye? Ytinoro nilà sa caniyà ang aquing pamay-
páy. ¿Anòng ysinasalin nang nagaáral? Ysinasalin niyà and tulá. ¿Anòng
ypinótol mo sa aquing tinápay? Ang ypinótol co,i, ang aquing *cuchiyo.*
¿Anòng ysinúlat mo sa caniyàng súlat? *Lupís* ang ysinúlat co. ¿Anòng
ysinúgat niyà sa ating caibigan? Ysàng tongcod. ¿Anò,t, di mo acó binabayaran? Sa pagca,t, ualá acó ybáyad sa iyò. ¿Anòng salapí ang ybibilì ni Pedro nang hihigán? Ang ybibilì nayà,i, salapíng tinangap sa aquin.
¿Anòng ypinagtatañgis niyàng bábaye? Sa pagca,t, namatayán siyá nang anac.
¿Anòng naytirá niyà ditò? Ang iquinatirá niyà ditò Si Ana. ¿Anòng ysinusúnod nang mañga sondalo sa canilàng pono? Ang ysinusúnod nilà,i, ang
tácot. ¿Anòng yquinayaman niyà? Ang pagbibilì nang balat siyá niyàng
yquinayaman. ¿Cailán sana darating sa dágat cung ungmalis siyá sa
capanahonan? Siyá,i, darating dóon sana bucas nang *á las diez.* ¿Sinòng
paríritohan mo? Pinaritohan quitá.

YCATATLONG POUO,T. APAT NA PAGSASANAY.

¿Anòng tinatanaoan mo sa taloctoc niyóng bondoc? Tinatanaoan co ang mañga cáhoy na may sañgà mahababa. ¿Ang úgong nang hañgin ay nararamdaman bagá niyà? Hindí niyá nararamdaman ang úgong nang hañgin, dahil sa siyá,i, biñgì. ¿Ang isdá bagá inaasnán nang alila? Ang isdá hindí pa inaasnán. ¿Tinablán bagá itòng calabáo nang sibat nang iyòng capatid? Ytòng calabáo, ay tinablán nang caniyàng sibat at caniyàng tinicmán ang dugó. ¿Anòng tinatangnán mo? ¿Ysàng sibat ang tinatangnán co. ¿Anò bagá ang pinagaralan mo? Ang pinagaralan co,i, ang uicang *inglés.* ¿Sinong pinagbabaláan nang magnanacao? Yaóng bata ang pinagbabaláan niya, binulacáan siyá mona niyá at ñgay⁰,i, dinadaya. ¿Hinatolan mo bagá at dinamtán ang bata? Dinamtán co siyá,t, hinatulan hagcán niyá ang caniyàng capatid na babaye. ¿Sinong nadingan mo nang iyòng sinabi sa aquin tungcol sa pagcalag sa bilangoin? Nadingán co,i, isang caibigan co. ¿Anòng binubucsán nang caniyang apóng babaye? Binubucsán niyà ang pinto nang halamanan. ¿Anòng guinagauá mo diyán? Pinoponan co,t, tinatacpán ang tapayan. ¿Anòng bibilhin nilà sa Americano? Siyà ang bibilhan nilà nang aquing *montequiya.* ¿Sinong quinonan mo niyàng tongcod? Ang aquing amain ang tinangapan co. ¿Sinong hiniñgán namin nitòng papel? Ang Pare ang aming hiniñgan. ¿Sáan hinánap nang alila ang inahíng manoc na naualá? Ang halamanan ang caniyàng hinalihaoan. ¿Sinong tinangapan mo nitòng salapíng báyad? Ang nacacaútang sa aquing ang siyá cong tinangapan nitòng salapí. ¿Báquit di acó binibiguián niyà nang caniyàng ibon? Sa pagca,t, ang capatid niyàng babaye, ang siyá niyàng biniguián. ¿Ytò bagá ang báhay na canilàng pinagtiponan? Hindí. ang báhay ni María ang siyá nilàng pinagtiponan. ¿Anòng ypinagtipon nilà? Ang ypinagtipon nilà,i, ang pagoósap nang tongcol sa ambaganan, (bouis). ¿Alín ang paroroonan mo? Ualá acóng paroroonan. ¿May sasabihin cang anomán sa aquin? May sasabihin acó sa iyò ¿Sáan mo ynilagáy ang aquin mañga salamín? Ang silid ang aquing pinaglaguián ¿Sinong ypinopótol (ypinagpopótol) mo niyàng cáhoy? Ang Pang-inóon co ang aquing ypinagpopótol. ¿Di co bagá sinabi sa iyo na houag ca mótol nang mañga cáhoy? Mabuti. acó,i, sungmasonod sa aquing Pang-inóon.

YCATATLONG POUO,T, LIMANG PAGSASANAY.

¿Ang pamangquín mo bagá ang pungmótol nang sañgà? Hindí siyá ang pungmótol. ¿Silá bagá ang nagsabi na acó,i, nabibilango? Ang aquing pamangquíng babaye ang siyá nagsabi. ¿Ang mañga *Italiano* bagá ang tungmuclás nang (or sa) *América?* Hindí. hindí ang mañga *Italiano,* cundí ang mañga *Castila* ang tungmuclás. ¿Sinong nagotos na ang may sala,i, patayín? Ang hari, ang siyáng nagotos. ¿Di bagá ang Hocom ang nagotos na ang iyóng pinsán lalaqui ay pagcaualáan? Hindí ang Hocom. cundí ang cápitan. ¿Ang binabasà mo, ay anò bagá? Ang binabasà co,i, ang librong ypinahiram sa aquin nang aquing caibigan. ¿Canino ca bagá

hungmihiñgi nang táuad? Hinihĩñgán co nang táuad ang aquing *Maestro*.
¿Báquit di mo íbig (ayáo) cumáin? Di acó cungmacáin. sa pagca,t, di
mangyari. ¿Ang dalá mo ritò, ay anò? Nagdadalà acó ritò nang buñga.
¿Sáan mo quinoha? Quinoha acó sa gúbat. ¿Nagsisicolate bagá ang Pare
sa touíng omaga? Nagsisicolate siyá árao-árao, pagcatapus nang misà.
¿Anòng bibilhin ni María? Bibili siyá nang tinápay at álac. ¿Di sana
lalong mabuti cun bumili siyá nang caráyom at cayo? Ualá na siyá niyóng salapíng ybinigáy mo nóong isáng árao. ¡Ay anò! Ganóon palá? Oo,
ñga. acala co,i. di pa niyà yáong guinagánit. ¿Sa alíng túbig. iinom acó?
Úminom ca sa túbig na itò, sa pagca,t, malamig at malínao. ¿Mangyayari
acóng cumuha bagá dito nang salapí? Cumuha ca lámang nang dalauàng
póuo,t, tatlòng piso. ¿Sino ang tinatauanan nang mañga bata? Ang tinatauanan nilà,i, yaóng lasing. ¿Ano ang ytinatáua nilà? Ang canilàng
ytinatáua ang caniyàng pagsusuling-suling. ¿Báquit naglalacad cayó? Dahil
sa camí ay nagmamadalí. ¿Anò,t, ang anac mo.i, sinugatan itòng aso? Sinugatan niyà, dahil sa siyá.i, quinágat. ¿Sinong sungmisintá sa capatid mong babaye? Siyá,i, sinisintá ni Pedro. ¿Sinong cungmauá nitó? Ang tauòng
naparitò niyóng lingo nacaráan ang siyáng gungmauá. ¿Sinong tungmatacbò? Ang dalaga na gungmísi nang iyóng medias ang tungmatacbò.
¿Tatauaguin co bagá siyá? Oo, tauaguín mo. ¿Anò ang sasabihin sa
aquin nang comerciante? Ang sasabihin niyà sa iyò,i, magbáyad ca nang
útang mo. ¿Magcanò ang útang co sa caniya? Nagcacaútang ca nang
tatlòng póuo,t, ánim na piso. ¿Sino pa ang nagtanong sa aquin.? Ang insic
na mañgañgalácal na naparitòng sungmisiñgil nang sa sapín. ¿Anòng
sinabi mo sa caniyà.? Sinabi cong ualá cang salapíng ycabáyad. ¿Anò,t,
hinahampás niyà ang caniyàng alila,? Dahil sa siyá,i, ninacauan nang
isàng singsing. ¿Di bagá siyá binig-uián nang gantí di pa palaláon.?
Oo, guinanti siyá, dáhil sa caniyàng pagcatapat lóob. Báquit cayá di
napariritòng hanapín ca sa báhay nang iyòng caibigan.? Quinatatacotan
niyà ang aso. ¿Anò,t. ayáo mong tangapín itòng pílac.? Sa pagca,t, di
mabuti.

YCATATLONG POUO,T, ANIM NA PAGSASANAY.

¿Sino ang pinanlilibac nang anac co.? Ycáo ang pinanlilibac niyà
¿Anò,t. nanlilibac siyá sa aquin.? Sa pagca,t, guinagamot mo ang aquing
aso. ¿Sino-sino ang pinangaliñgan nilà.? Ang pinangaliñgan nilà,i, ang
caonaonahan namayan. ¿Marúnong siyáng mangagar sa mañga pusa.?
Hindí, cundí siyá,i, marúnong mangatas. ¿Sino-sino ang pinanhahánap
nang mañga *Americano.*? Ang pinanghahánap nilà.i, ang mañga *insurrecto*
(Sp. w.) (nanhihimagsic.) ¿Nangagamot bagá si Juan.? Hindí, siyá,i,
nanhohola. ¿Anòng yquinabúhay nang mañga *insurrecto.*? Ang yquinabúhay
nilà,i, ang manghuli. ¿Sáan naninilo ang mañga bata nang ibon.? Hindí
silá naninilo, cundí nanlalambat at namiminuit. ¿Anò ang pinamimisanhan
mo.? Ang pinamimisanhan co.i, ang panlilibac at ang panunumpá. ¿Canino
nanunucsò ang bagòng tauò.? Nanunucsò siyá sa caniyàng pinsán babaye.
¿Cailán ca nañgíbig.? Pinangibigan co ang mañga dalaga cun acó,i, binata pa. ¿Anòng pinanhuhuli nang amá mo.? Pinanhuli niyà ang mañga
magnanácao. ¿Sino-sino ang pinamamahaguinan mo niyáng salapí.? Ang
pinamamahaguinan co,i, ang camaganacan co. ¿Namamahala bagá nang
halamanan ang alila mo.? Pinamamahaláan niyà ang búquid yámang
di siyá namamayan, cundí namumúquid. ¿Anòng pinañgiñgisdá naug
caapidbáhay mo.? Siyá,i, namamalós at namamalacá. ¿Anòng cagauanan
mo.? Ang cagauanan co. ang panunúlat. ¿Anòng pinaninirá nang mañga

nsurrecto. Ang pinaninirá nilá,i, ang mañga pananím at bayan at ni-ningil at nanunuñgayao dahil sa di silá manalo. ¿Sino ang pinananalanginan ino.? Ang *Dios* at ang Mahal na *Virgen* ang pinananalañginan co. ¿Pina-ñgañgaralan bagá nang Pare yaón mañga babaye nananapis.? Oo. ¿Anóng pinangagauá nang caniyáng asáua? Siyá,i, nañgiñgílao. ¿Nañgañgagat at nañgañgáin bagá nang bábuy damó iyàng asong iyán? Hindí nañgañga-gat, cundí ang mañga bábuy damó,i, nañgiñgilag at di napaábut. ¿Anóng calagayan nang mañga cáhuy sa iyóng halamanan? Hindí pa namumu-ñga, cundí namumulaclac na. ¿Anó ang pinangagauá ni Juana nang na-bubúhay pa siyá? Siyá,i, nanunulit, at nañgiñgitil nang bulaclac. ¿Anóng caniyàng paghahánap búhay.? Siyá,i, nananahi at nanunúlat. ¿Nanana-datá bagá ang mañga *Oficiales* (Sp. w.) (pono nang sondalo.)? Silá,i, nananandatà, ñguní,t, di namamalacol. ¿Nandarágat cayá ang iyóng nono? Hindí. siyá,i, nañgáhoy at nañgosa. ¿Nañgisdá bagá ang amá mo? Siyá,i, nanalabá,t, nañgapís. ¿Namíuas silá o naminuit? Silá,i, nañgílao at cun minsá,i, nanlambat. ¿Namamaril bagá ang caniyàng caibigan nang bábuy damó.? Hindí, siyá,i, nañgaso nang bábuy damó.

YCATATLONG POUO,T, PITONG PAGSASANAY.

¿Báquit di ca macalácad.? Di acó macalácad sa pagca,t, acó,i, piláy. ¿Anóng nacahahapis sa caniyà.? Ang pagcamatáy nang caniyàng iná ang sa caniyà,i, nacahapis. ¿Sino-sino ang catotouaán niyò.? Ang caniyàng mañga anac ang caniyàng catotonaán. ¿Anóng yquinalumbáy nang amá mo? Ang pandarágat ang yquinatatácot niyá. ¿Anóng yquinasamá mo nóong lingong na-caráan? Ang nacasamá sa aqui,i, ang buñga. ¿At anó ang sa iyò,i, nacagaling? Yláng gamot ang nacagaling sa aquin. ¿Nagagauá bagá niyà iyán.? Di niyà nagagauá iyán. ¿Anóng nacapañgiñgílabot sa mañga bata.? Ang culog ang nacapañgiñgílabot sa mañga bata. ¿Anóng yquinagagandà nang mañga dala-ga.? Ang yquinagagandà nang mañga dalaga,i, ang cahinhinán. ¿Anó ang nacabubusog.? Ang mañga camote nacabubusog. ¿Anóng macagagambala sana sa caniyà.? Ang caniyàng catungcolan ang nacagagambala sa caniyà. ¿Sino ang nacaguinhauá sa iyòng pagtitiis? Ang asáua co ang nacaguinhauá sa aquing pagtitiis. ¿Macalalabás siyà ñgayón? Hindí siyà nacalabás ñga-yon; cundí macaaalís bucas. ¿Nacapaglabás ca bagá nang batò? Di acó nacapaglabás nang batò. ¿Nacaaaral ca bagá nang Tagálog.? Hindí, di co macaya, ñguní,t, nacapagaáral acó niyán. ¿Nacapañgañgáral bagá siyá sa bayan.? Siyá,i, di Pare, cayá ñga di siyá macapañgañgáral. ¿Maaring conin co itòng libro? Mangyayaring cumuha ca. ¿Nacatatalastás ca ca aquin.? Hindí acó nacatatalastás sa iyò. Natatanto mo bagá ang sinasabi co? Oo, natatanto co. ¿Naririñig niyà bagá ang úgong nang hañgin.? Hindí naririñgig niyà, siyá,i, biñgí. ¿Maiísip mo bagá iyán? Hindí co maisíp, ñguní,t, aquing maalaalà. ¿Matatanto cayá niyà ang cahulogán nang uicang itò? Siyá,i, macararamdam at macaquiquita; ñguní,t, di niyà natatanto ang cahulogán. ¿Nacaamúy bagá siyà nang bañgò nang mañga bulac-lac.? Nacaamúy siyà mona, ñguní,t, ñgayó,i, hindí, at di man lámang maramdamín ang anomán sa hipo, at di rin malásap ang úlac. ¿Macapagüiuica bagá siyà? Hindí macapagüiuica, dahil sa nagagaril-garil siyá. ¿Maysasaysáy nilà bagá ang bágay? Maypahaháyag nilà sa Hocom, ¿Nacababasà bagá silà.? Silà,i, nacacaáalam. ¿Anóng guinagauá mo ditò sa baybáy? Acó,i, nacataóng naparitò. ¿Hinánap bagá nang alilà ang susì? Oo, ñguní,t, di niyà nahánap. ¿Hungmiñgi bagá nang bulac-lac ang capatid mong babaye sa ating caapidbáhay? Hindí, sa pagca,t, talas-tás niyà na di siyà macahihiñgi. ¿Anóng guinauá nang bata.? Hinábol

57

dáan.? Ypatóloy, sa pagca.t. cayó,i. malilinanagan nang bouan. figuni.t. iñgatang houag cayó maulapan.

YCATATLONG POUO,T, UALONG PAGSASANAY.

¿Pinapanhic mo ang mañga bata.? Oo, pinapanhic co na. ¿Pinapagpapanhic mo ang mañga alila nang cáhoy na ygagátong.? Oo, pinapagpapanhic co. ¿Ano ang ypinagagauá nang amá ni Jorge sa caniyà.? Pinapagaáral pa siyá niyà. ¿Báquit di mo pinapagaáral ang anac mo? Di co siyà pinapagaáral. sa pagca,t, siyà,i, may saquit. ¿Pinasisimbà bagá nang iyòng bayáo ang caniyàng mañga alila cun árao na pañgilin.? Oo, pinasisimbà niyà silá. ¿Báquit di ca nagpapatila.? Acó,i, nagpasilang (nang árao) at acó,i, nagpalamig nang árao. ¿Báquit mo pinaboboloc ang mañga halaman.? Di co pinaboboloc. cundí bageús pinahahañginan co,t, pinaaaréuan. ¿Nagpapatila bagá siyá.? Oo, nagpapatila. ¿Báquit di siyà magpaárao.? Dahil sa siyà,i, nagmamadalí. ¿Anòng ypinagauá ni Pedro sa caniyàng alia.? Sinabi niyà sa caniyà, houag ca magpatuyó nang mañga bulac-lac. ¿Báquit di mo palamiguin ang túbig.? Sa pagca,t, malamig na. ¿Báquit nagpaparaya ang capatid mong babaye.? Dahil sa siyá,i, lubháng tuso. ¿Sino ang magpapasicat nang árao,t, bouan.? Ang Dios. ¿Anò pa ang pinangyayari niyà.? Siyá ang nagpapaokán, nagpapaquidlat, nagpapaculog at nagpapaalon. ¿Siyá pa rin ang sa mañga cáhoy nagpapabulac-lac at nagpapaboñga.? Oo. ¿Sa canino nagpalimós yaóng magpapalímos.? Ang alí co ang pinagpapalimosan niyà. ¿Báquit ang mayama,i, di nagpacáin dóon sa mañga tauó? Sinali niyà sa caniyàng alilang pacainin mo silá ¿Silá bagá,i, paiinumin co.? Oo, painumín mo silá nang álac. ¿Sino cayá yaóng tauòng nagpapalimós.? Siyá,i, isàng magpapalimos na pinatolóy co cagal i. ¿Marami bagá ang pinagpapalimosan niyà.? Hindí po, di nagcacasiyà sa caniyàng ycabubúhay. ¿Báquit di mo siyá pinauútang.? Sa pagca.t. acó,i, ualáng-ualá. at pinatutubóan co ang aquing salapí. ¿Báquit di naparamit si Antonio sa caniyàng mañga anac.? Sa pagca,t, ualá siyáng maybili nang damit. ¿Sáan co palalamiguin ang túbig? Ytòng batalang itò ang pagpalamigán nang túbig. ¿Sinong Pare ang pinagcumpisalán mo? Si Pare Juan ang pinañguñgpisalán co. Báquit yaóng dalagá ay nagpapagandá? Sa pagca,t, napapapuri. ¿Napapasaán bagá ang túbig? Ang túbig ay napapasaibaba. ¿Anòng ypinarusà sa iyo nang Pareng pinañgumpisalan mo? Ang ypinarusà niyà sa aqui,i. ang acó,i, mag-*ayuno* (Sp. w.) ¿Pinainom mo ang mañga manoc? Pinainom co. ¿Anòng ang ypinacáin (ypinatucà) mo? Pinacáin (pinatucà) co nang pálay. ¿Pinabañgon bagá niyà ang caniyàng anac na lalaqui? Caniyàng pinabañgon. ¿Báquit di mo acó paraanín? Di quitá pararaanín hangán di mo acó pinaiinom nang túbig.

YCATATLONG POUO,T, SIYAM NA PAGSASANAY.

¿Anò.t, naquiquipagósap ca sa mañga matandá? Naquiquipagósap acó sa canilá dahil sa naghahañgad acóng umálam. ¿Báquit yniootos mong houag acong maquipaglaró sa mañgá babaye? Yniotos co sa iyò, sa pagca.t. mahálay ang maquipaglaró sa mañga babaye. ¿Báquit siyá naquipag-

talo sa caniyàng caapidbáhay? Sa pagca,t, ang caapidbáhay niyà,i, naquiquialam. ¿Naquiquicastila bagá ang iyòng capatid na lalaqui? Hindi, di
siyá naquiquicastila. ¿Anòng pinaquiquihiñgi mo sa caapidbáhay? Ma-
quiquibigás acó sa caniyà. ¿Sino ang ypinaquiquibigás mo? Ang ypinaquiquibigás co,i, ang aquing caibigan na may saquit, at ualáng macáin.
¿Anòng pinaquihiñgí nilà? Acó,i, naquiálac. ¿Sino ang hining–án mo?
Ypinaquihiñgí co sa mandarágat. ¿Di co bagá sinabì sa iyò na houag ca
maquihiñgí diyan sa marámot na tauò? Siyá ang pinaquihing-án co, sa pag-
cá,t, ualáng ibà. ¿Minamahal bagá siyá? Siyá,i, minamahal nang caniyàng
Pang-inóon, nang siyá,i, bata pa. ¿Gaanò ang gúlang nang anac mo? Ualá pa
halos tatlòng taón, ñguní,t, ang capatid cong lalaqui ay may labing ánim
bumiguit cumúlang, at ang bungsó ay mayróon siyam na bouan. ¿Anòng
ybinigáy mo dóon sa mañga batang yaón? Ualá acóng ybinigáy sa canilà
cahapon anomán, ñguní,t. naybigáy co na ang ypinabigáy mo nang icáo
ay dungmating. ¿Ybibigáy cayá niyà sa aquin iyáng tongcod? Hindí.
cundí ang ybibigáy niyà sa iyò ang libro na ypinagbibilin mo sa caniyà.
¿Ybig mong ypagbili iyáng cabayo? Ay anò; ¿ibig mo bagáng bilhin?
Cun mura bibilhin co. ¿Anong papel ang caniyàng sinusúlatan? Ytòng
papel na itò, ang caniyàng sinusulatan. ¿Tatauaguin bagá niyà ang Pare?
Hindí, ang tatauaguin niyà,i, ang mangagamot. ¿Anòng guinaganá niyàón
mañga bata dóon sa dalampásig.? Nañgaglalaró. ¿Anòng hihingin mo sa
iyòng amá cun dumating? Ang acó,i, bibiguián niyà nang salapí. ¿Sáan
paroróon iyáng mañga babáye? Ang paroroonan nilà,i, isàng *lugal* na
malayo ¿Bungmohos siyá nang álac sa aquing copa.? Hindí bungmohos nang álac cundí túbig. ¿Anòng iyòng guinaganá? Sinisidlán co nang
túbig ang inuman mo. na lubhàng malaqui. ¿Anòng pinagmamasdán nang
mañga tauòng yaón? Pinagmamasdán nilà ang laráuan nang mahal na
Virgen. ¿Anòng pinagaaralan nang caibigan mo? Ang pinagaaralan niyà,i.
Latín. ¿Sáan siyá nagaáral?. Sa Maynila. ¿Malíuag bagáng pagaralan
ang Latín? Oo, malíuag. ¿Báquit di ca binabati ni Pedro? Palibhasa
acó,i, duc-há ualáng lungmiliñgon sa aquin; cun acó sana,i, mayaman ma-
mahalin disin acó nang lahat. (or calahatan).

YCAAPAT NA POUONG PAGSASANAY.

¿Napasasáan ang mañga magúlang mo.? Silá,i, napapasasimbahan.
¿Napasasaescuelahan bagá ang mañga capatid mo? Silá,i, napasasadágat.
¿Alíng doòngan ang pinatotoñgohan nang sasaquian? Napapasa Maynila. ¿Di
bagá napapasa Cavite? Hindí. napapatoñgò sa ílog Pásig. ¿May paroroonan
ca bagá.? Oo, may paroroonan acó. ¿Alíng bayan ang pinatotoñgohan mo.?
Ang Maynila ang bayang pinatotoñgohan co. ¿Anòng ypinasasa Maynila mo.?
Ang ypinaroróon co,i, ang aquing capatid na lalaqui. ¿Pinaparitó mo bagá
ang alila co.? Pinaparitò co na siyá. ¿Cun pumarito ang aquing caibigan
muong sasabihin co sa caniyá? Paparoonin mo siya. ¿Napatólong bagá
siyá sa aquin.? Napatólong siyá sa iyò. ¿Anòng sinabi mo cay Juan.?
Sinabi co, acó,i, tolongan. ¿Cailán mo sasabihin sa caniyà na icáo, ay
tolongan.? Bucas, aquing sasabihin na acó,i, tolongan. ¿Báquit di mo
acó pinahahalic nang camáy.? Di quitá pahaliquin, dahil sa marumì. Báquit siyá,i, napahihipo.? Hindí siyá napahihipo sa canino man lalaqui.
¿Anòng sinabi nang Pare sa caniyàng sermón.? Ang sabì niyà,i, houag
iyó patucsò; magsua cayó sa mahal na Virgen. ¿Di bagá siyá napaáua sa iyò?
Oo, napaáua siyá sa aquin. ¿Napaano Si Pedro sa iyò.? Siyá,i, napa-
sasamà sa aquin at acó,i, napahindí sa caniyà. ¿Báquit napaayò ca.? Sa
pagca,t, ang sabì niyà, ay acó,i, isàng tacsil. ¿Napaóo ca bagá sa ñañgi-

ñgíbig sa iyò.? Acó,i, napahindí sa caniyà. ¿Báquit nagpadiablo ca.? Acó,i, di nagpadiablo, acó.i. nagpa Jesús. ¿Nararápat bagáng ygálang ang catandáan.? Dápat tayong gumálang sa matatandá. ¿Napasasáan ca.? Acó,i. napasasa Maynila. ¿Anòng ang ytinatanim nang amá mo.? Ang ytinatanim niyà itong pálay. ¿Anòng ypinaquita niyà sa caniyàng anac.? Ang ypinaquita niyà sa caniyà ay itòng libro. ¿Nag-iisà bagá siyá sa báhay.? Oo, siyá,i, nag-iisà. ¿Naquita mo bagá ang capatid cong lalaqui.? Hindí. ¿Dungmating na bagá ang panguinóon.? Di pa dungmarating. ¿Quinoha bagá niyà ang baro co.? Hindí niyá quinocoha. ¿Anò ráo ang sabí niyà? Di umanò may isàng hari nagmasaouain sa Dios. ¿Di mo bagá sasalubuñgin ang iyòng amá.? Sasaluboñgin co siyá. ¿Cailán ca babalic?. Sa lingong darating. ¿Di mo bagá íbig humarap sa Pare? Hindí, at acó,i, nahihiya. ¿Anòng inaamoyan mo.? Ynaamoyan co itòng mañga bulac–lac. ¿Anòng pinañgoñgoha diyán nang aquing amaín.? Nañgiñgitil siyá nang bulac-lac. ¿Báquit siyá ungmiyac? Dahil sa ang caniyàng inà,i, ungmalís. ¿Cailán siyá oouí.? Di co nalalaman. ¿Sungmibol cayá ang mañga sile ytinanim nang iyòng alila sa halamanan.? Hindí pa. ¿Sinong titirá sa báhay.? Ang amá natin ang siyáng matitirá. ¿Nagtirá ca bagá sa caniyà nang pagcáin.? Ualá acóng ytinirá sa caniyà anomán. ¿Guinámit mo bagá ang bihisan ypinagcalóob sa iyò nang Pang-inóon mong babaye.? Di co pa guinagámit. ¿Anòng iyòng ñginañgañga.? Mamín ang aquing ñginañgañga.

YCAAPAT NA POUO.T. ISANG PAGSASANAY.

¿Nagcacabuñga na bagá yaóng mañga cáhoy.? Oo, nagcacabuñga na. ¿Nagcasónog bagá ditò sa bayang itò.? Hindí nagcasónog ditò sa bayan. ¿Nagcasálot bagá ditò sa mañga báhay.? Oo. nagcasálot diyán. ¿Nagcacatipon bagá ang mañga tauò sa simbahan.? Oo, marami ang nañgacacapisan sa simbahan. ¿Nagcapagbacà bagá ditò sa mañga lupaíng itò.? Oo, nacapagbacà ditò. ¿May caroonan bagá ang mañga caibigan mo.? Oo, may caroonan silá. ¿Nagcacaanac bagá ang mañga anac nilà.? Hindí, cundí silá,i. nagcacapálad. ¿Nañgagcacasaquit bagá ditò sa bayán,? Oo. ang mañga taga ritò,i, nagcacabolotong. ¿Nagcacagútom bagú sa Pilipinas.? Hindí, cundí, nagcacabáguio,t, nagcacasónog. ¿Nañgagcacaguló bagá ang mañga tagálog.? Oo, silá,i, naquiquipagbacà at ang mañga búquid ay nagcacasira-sirá. ¿Alín ang pinagcacatipunan nilà.? Silá.i, nagcacatipon sa guitná nang cagubatan. ¿Nababágay bagá sa isàng tauò hubad ang lumacad-lácad sa lansañgan.? Hindí, di nababágay sa isàng tauòng hubad na lumacad-lácad. ¿Báquit di mo pinagbabágay iyáng dalauàng baro.? Ualá acóng gunting na ypagbágay. ¿Ynihandá mo na bagá ang mañga casancapang pandáy na ygagauá nang lamesa.? Hindí pa. ¿Sáan naróon ang mañga bagòng paniong sutlá.? Nasasacabán. ¿Mayróon cayóng bagòng Pañg-inóon.? Hindí. mayróon caming bagòng Pare. ¿Pinamago mo na ang bihisan.? Pinamagò co na. ¿Di mo bagá íbig humarap sa Pare.? Hindí, sa pagca.t. acó,i, natatácot. ¿Báquit linuluráan nang pinsán mo ang caniyàng capatid na lalaqui.? Sa pagca,t, siyá,i, linuráan mona niyà. ¿Sinong macaaala-alà sa aquin? Ang inà mo ang macaaala-alà sa iyò. ¿Anòng ytinanim nang amá mo diyán.? Mañga águing ang ytinanim niyà. ¿Anòng ypapásoc niyà sa silid.? Ualáng anománg ypinapásoc sa silid, sinisidlán niyà nang túbig ang vaso co. ¿Ano,t, di nila ynilalapit iyáng candilang nagnininga? Dahil sa ualá siláng tabureteng uupóan. ¿Minamabigat mo bagá ang paggauá nang cabanalan.? Di co iyán minamabigat. aquing inaala-alà ang apúy na ualáng hangán.

¿Aanhín niyà acó? Hindí ca aanhín niya. ¿Inanò ca? Di acó inanó. ¿Sino ang nagmimisa.? Ang ating Pare. ¿Báquit nagsasaya ang pinsán mong babaye.? Hindí siyá nagsasaya, siyá,i, nagtatapis. ¿Ybíg mong manabaco.? Salúmat, di acó nananabaco. ¿Báquit nagsasaquit–saquitan ang alila mo.? Ang ypinagsasaquit–saquitan niyá,i, ang di siyá parusahan. ¿Anòng ypinagaáuay nang mañga caapidbáhay mo.? Ang pagsusugal. ¿Alín ang pinagauayan nilà? Ytòng báhay na itò ang caniláng pinagauayan.

YCAAPAT NA POUO,T, DALAUANG PAGARAL.

¿Sinong naguingtauò.? Ang Anac nang Dios, ang naguingtauò. ¿Anò ang ypinaguingtavò niyà.? Ang pagsácop sa atin ang siyá niyàng ypinaguing-tauò. ¿Pinapaguingdápat bagá nang anac mo ang maguing pare.? Hindí, cundí pinapaguingdápat niyàng magcaróon nang ibàng catungcolan. ¿Na-guingtotoò bagá ang sinabi co sa iyò? Oo, naguingtotoò. ¿Maguiguing–iyò bagá acó at icáo ay maguiguingaquin.? Hindí, icáo, ay di maguiguing-aqui,t, di rin acó maguiguing-iyò. ¿Anò bagá ang naguingdahelan? Ytó ang naguingdahelan. ¿Anòng maguiguingpálad co.? Sa maguiguingpálad mo,i, ualáng nacaaálam. ¿Anò ang aquing gagaoin nang maguingdápat acó mahalín nang ibà.? Bayaran mo ang iyòng útang. ¿May gagaoin cayá anomán ang alila.? Sidlán niyà nang túbig ang tapayan. ¿Sáan ynili-bing ang iyòng asáua.? Ytòng lugar na itò ang pinaglibiñgan sa caniyà. ¿Báquit di ypinapanáog nang mananahi mo iyáng damit.? Dahil sa ualáng paglalaguián. ¿Báquit cayá siyá pungmásoc na di bungmating patoñgò.? Pagca,t, siyá,i, tauòng ualáng pinagaralan. ¿Siyá bagá,i, pungmáyag.? Pungmáyag siyáng ualáng líuag. ¿Anò ang caniyàng ypinagmamatáas.? Di niyà inaala–alà ang caniyàng pinangaliñgan. ¿Báquit cayá namimi-haçà ca mamintás sa lahat.? Di co pinamimihasanhan iyán. ¿Acó cayá,i, sasamahan mo.? Sasamahan quitá. ¿Napasaaán ca.? Acó,i, mambibíuas. ¿Anò ang pinamamahagui nang iyòng amá.? Ang pinamamahagui niyà, ay natatalastás nang aquing mañga capatid na lalaqui, na silà ang pinama-mahaguinan. ¿Sinong nagpaguingálac nang túbig.? Si Jesucristo ang nagpaguingálac nang túbig. ¿Sinong pinapaguingháyop.? Si Luzbel ang pinapaguingháyop. ¿Ang álac cayá,i, naguingsuca.? Naguingsuca. ¿Naguing-anò ang caibigan mo.? Siyá,i, naguingmarámot. ¿Napaanò cayá ang alí mo? Siyá,i, naguingbiñgi, naguingpipi,t, naguingbulag. ¿Nacacaya mo bagáng buhatín iyán.? Di co macayang buhatín. ¿Anòng iyòng hinuli.? Hinuli co, ang magnanácao. ¿Ycáo bagá cayá ang capatid ni María.? Acó ñga. ¿Arò cayá ang inaacala mong gaoin? Siyá,i, hindí naparitò, cayá ñgani hahabolin co siyá.

YCAAPAT NA POUO,T, TATLONG PAGSASANAY.

¿Anóng pinagsisigaua diyán niyàng mañga tauò.? Pinagsisipanóor nila ang laruan nang mahal na Virgen. ¿Pinagsisipanóor bagá nang maraming tauò.? Oo, pinagsisipanóor ñga. ¿Sáan siyá pinagpapancoran? Ang sim-bahan ang siyáng pinagsisipanooran. ¿Nagsisiáral bagá ang mañga maes-tro.? Lahat itò,i, nagsisiáral. ¿Sino-sino ang pinagsisiaralan nilà.? · Ang mañga batang bayan ang canilâng pinagsisiaralan. Ang lahat nang Pare bagá,i, ¿nagsisipañgáral.? Lahat silá,i, nagsisipañgáral. ¿Anòng ypinañgañgáral nilà.? Ang ypinagsisipañgáral nilà,i, ang pagtupad nang utos nang Dios. ¿Sáan silá nagsisipañgáral.? Sa pintóan nang simbahan silá nagsisipañgáral. ¿Nagsisipagáral bagá itòng mañga bata.? Nagsisipagáral silá. ¿Anòng pinagsisipagaralan nilà.? Ang *gramática* Sp. w.\ ang pinagsisipagaralan nilà. ¿Maramì bagá ang mañga nagsisipagcumpisal.? Oo. ñga. maraming maramì ang nagsisipagcumpisal. ¿Maraming mañga Pare bagá ang nagsisipagpacumpisal.? Ang lahat nang Pare, ay nagsisipagpacumpisal. ¿Nagsisipásoc bagá sa simbahan ang maraming tauò.? Hindí, ang misa,i, tapus na, at maramì ang nagsisilabás sa simbahan ñgayón. ¿Anòng ypinagsisilabás niyaóng mañga tauò sa báhay nang aquing amaín.? Ang ypinagsisilabás nilà,i, ang mañga casangcapan dahil sa cungmacálat ang apúy. ¿Nagsisitáua o nagsisitañgis bagá yaóng mañga bata.? Sila,i, nagsisitáua sa isáng lañgo na susuling-súling. ¿Sino ang nasasúloc.? Si Pedro ang nasusúloc. ¿Sáan naróon ang báhay mo.? Nasasalóob nang bayan, sa súloc nag tiangui. ¿Maramì bagáng tulisán sa bayan mo.? Oo. ñga, maramìng maramì. ¿Pungmapasáan bagá siyá.? Pungmaparóon sa labás nang dáan. ¿Gaanò ang *gagustahin* co.? Gumasta ca nang ganáng cailañgan mo lámang. ¿Ganansaaquin bagáng lahat iyáng salapíng iyán.? Sa ganán aquin cunin mong lahat. ¿Nagcacasi bagá silá.? Silá,i, nagcacasihan. ¿Anò,t, pinababayáan nang Americano ang babayeng iyán.? Dahil sa sasacáy siyáng patoñgò sa caniyàng lupaín. ¿Quinacasihan bagá nang Espíritu Santo ang mañga banal na tauò.? Quinacasihan nang Espíritu Santo ang banal na tauò. ¿Naquiquilala mo bagá iyáng tauòng napaparitò.? Dfua,i, di co naquiquilala. ¿Di mo bagá quináin ang carne.? Di co quináin ang carne, cundí ang canin. ¿May acala ca bagáng mañgalácal.? Di anòng gagaoin co, cundí ang mañgalácal ñga. ¿Anò,t, ytinatanong mo sa aquin iyán.? Sa pagca,t, cailañgan cong maalaman, cun paroróon ca dili. ¿Pungmapasáan ca? Acó,i, pungmapasasimbahan. ¿Magaanò ca dóon.? Acò.i, paroróon, at magsisimbâ. ¿Nabasà na bagá ang súlat nóong naroróon ca sa báhay.? Nabasà na ang súlat. ¿Hinànap na bagá ang manoc.? Hindí pa nahahánap. ¿Ang ating pinangaliñgan bagá ay lalong malalacás sa atin.? Ang mañga canonóang pinangaliñgan natin, ay lalong malalacás sa atin.

YCAAPAT NA POUO,T, APAT NA PAGSASANAY.

„Baquit nagtatacà ca na iyán babaye ay magsainsic.? Magtataca acò. pagca,t, di caraníuan nang mañga taga ritò ang magsainsic. ¿At naasalaman mo bagá cun sino siyá.? Di co nalalaman. ¿Di mo patatalastás na iyá,i, asana nang isàng mayamang insic na comerciante.? Di co nalaman ñgunni,t, cun gayó,i, di na acó nagtatacà na siyú,i, magsainsic. ¿Magsainglés ca bagá cun acò.i, magsatagalog. Acò,i, magsasainglés sana, cahinaa,t, di ca magsatagálog. ¿Ang nagsasamoros, ay sino-sino caya.? Ang ibàng mañga tagálog nananira sa dalampasigan nang pulong Mindanáo, ang siyáng nagsasamoros. ¿Nagsasabisaya bagá cun minsán ang mañga moros.? Nagsasabisaya silá nang cauntí. ¿Ualá bagá ibàng búlac, cundí itò.? May ibàng búlac at ibàng bácal. ¿May ibà pa siyáng pamocpoc.? May ibà pang pamocpoc siyá at catam. ¿Nag-iibà bagá nang sambalelo ang alí co.? Nag-iibà siyá nang sambalelo. ¿Pinañgiñgibahan mo bagá ang siñgao ditò? Oo, nañgiñgibà acóng lubhá. ¿Nagcaibà bagá sa dati ang anac mo? Oo, nag-ibà na. ¿Ang bácal bagá ay ibà sa patalim? Ang bácal, ay ità sa patalim. ¿Anòng pinagcacaibahan nilà? Ang pinagcacaibahan nilà,i, ang catigasan. ¿Ynaanò ca? Di acó inaanò, ¡tulong! ¿Ang caapadbahay mo bagá,i, di ibã sa iyò? Siyã,i, ibã sa aquin. ¿Nalalaman mo bagá na ang caniyàng asaua,i, di ibã sa aquin? Di co nalalaman. ¿Báquit iniicáo niyàng tauo ang anac mong babaye? Yniicáo niyà siyá, sa pagca,t, pacacasal silá. ¿Báquit mo iniicáo ang amá mo? Dahil sa caugalían nang tagálog ang ganiyán. ¿Yláng lingo mauaualá ca bagá ditò? Mañga iláng lingo lámang. ¿Na sa iyò bagá ang libro co? Ualá sa aquin. ¿Ylán catauò ang nagsiparitò? Yilán lámang. ¿Báquit di mo pinaoontí ang iyòng gasta? Sa pagca,t, ang salapí co,i, di ungmuuntí. ¿Di pa bagá niyà tinatangap ang caniyàng cabán? Di pa niyà tinatangap. ¿Báquit sungmusúlat ca nang ganiyán carahan? Sa pagca,t, di acó nagmamadalí. ¿Máy macapal bagáng pañganurin sa impapauid? Ang impapauid may macapal na pañganurin. ¿Sino iyáng batang iyán? Siyá,i. isàng tauòng mahinhín. ¿Anòng ypinagcatipon nang mañga taga bayan? Ang ypinagcatipon nilà,i, ang pagdálao nang *General* (Sp. w) (pono). ¿Sinong pinagpugayan mo? Si Gardiner, siyá,i, isàng mahal na tauò. ¿Báquit ypinagmamacahiya niyà ang caniyàng mañga magulang? Ypinagmamacahiya niyà ang caniyàng mañga magúlang, sa pagca t, duc-há.

YCAAPAT NA POUO,T, LIMANG PAGSASANAY.

¿Báquit nanhihiganti ang sondalo sa aso? Nanhihiganti siyá sa aso, dahil sa siyá,i, quinagat. ¿Panhihigantihin bagá ang tauòng bulag? Siyá,i, panhihigantihin nang caniyàng anac. ¿Sino ang paghihigantihán niyà? Panhihigantihán niyà ang bata na lungmihís sa caniyà. ¿Anò,t, nanhihimálay yaóng duc-há? Ang cagutoman niyà ang caniyàng ypinanhihimálay. ¿Nanhihilamos ca bagá arao-árao? Acó,i, nanhihilamos sa touíng aco,i, bungmabañgon sa hihigán. ¿Báquit siyá nanhihimosmós? Nanhihimosmós siyá sa pagca,t, siyá,i, mosmós pa. ¿Nagbi,i bagá ang mañga insic nang lalong murà sa ibàng mañgañgalúcal? Silà,i, nagbibili nang lalong murà cay sa canilà, sa pagca,t, ang mañga insic ay nanhihilaco. ¿Laban canino nanhimagsic ang mañga tagálog? Ang pinanhimagsican nilà,i, ang mañga Castila,t. Americano. ¿Anòng guinagauá nang anloague? Nanhihimandáy lámang siyá. ¿Báquit ang capatid mong lalaqui ay nanhihimánit sa usà? Pinanhihimanitan niyà nang maypagbili ang lamán. ¿Naanò. ang lumpò? Siyá,i, nanhimatáy cahapon. ¿Nanhihibalbas bagá ang pinsán mong lalaqui? Hindí, siyá,i, nanhihinulí,t, nanhihiniñgá. ¿Namimihasa bagá siyáng manhiñgueò? Di lámang siyá nanhihiñgueò, cundí nanhihimuta,t, nanhihilisá pa. ¿Sáan naróon ang apó niyà? Siyá,i, nasasalóob nang silid. ¿Báquit mo pinagoócol iyáng dalauàng salupan? Pinag oócol co nang aquin maalaman cung magcaparis. ¿Yoócol bagá nila ang canilàng lóob sa lóob nang canilàng amá? Oo, yoócol nilá. ¿Sino ang pono nang hochò? Ang pono nang hochò, ay ang Hari. ¿Anòng pinopónán nang alila? Ang iyòng vaso ang pinopónán niyà. ¿Sasamahan mo acó? Sasamahan catá cun pasasa Maynila ca. ¿Parurusahan mo bagá acó sa touíng hindí quitá susunorín? Parurusahan quitá touíng acó,i, do mo susunorín. ¿Sino ang tauòng lalong mabantog, mabunyi,t, marañgal nang Estados Unidos? Si Washington ang lalong mabantog. ¿Anòng quinacáin mo? Quinacáin co ang buñgang hinánap ni inà.

YCAAPAT NA POUO,T, ANIM NA PAGSASANAY.

¿Sino-sino ang mapapacagaling? Ang mañga banal lámang ang mapapacagaling. ¿Anò ang ypinapapacagaling nang tauò? Ang ypinapapacagaling nang mañga tauò, ay ang mabubuting gauá. ¿Anòng ypinañgáral nang Pare.? Ang ypinañgáral niyà,i, itò; ylagan ninyò ang casalanan bacá cayó,i, mapacasamá. ¿Anòng ypinagpacamatáy ni Jesucristo? Ang pagsácop sa tauò ang ypinagpacamatáy Niyà. ¿Sáan siyá nagpacamatáy.? Ang bundoc nang Calvario ang pinagcamatayán Niyà. ¿Anòng caraníuang gaoin nang banal? Siyá,i, nagpapacababa sa harap nang Dios, at nagpapacamahal sa harap nang tauò. ¿Anòng guinauá nang Anac nang Dios? Siyá,i, nagpacaduc-há,t, nagpacaamo,t, nagpacaapí,t, nagpacapótong nang tinic. ¿Báquit nagpapacabuti ang iyáng dalaga? Siyá,i, nagpapacabuti, nang siyá,i, purihin. ¿Pinagpasisihan mo bagá ang iyòng mañga casalanan? Oo, pinagpacasisihan co ang lahat na aquing mañga casalanan. ¿Anò,t, nagpapacamahal ang iyòng capatid na babaye? Siyá,i, nagpapacamahal sa pagca,t, palalo. ¿Báquit nagpapacarahan ang alila niyán? Dahil sa siyá,i, natatácot sa parusá. ¿Pinacaisíp mo bagá ang sinabi co sa iyo? Pinacaisíp co. ¿Anòng yniutos mo sa aquin? Pacamasdán mo ang aso, pacaiñgatan mo houag cang cagatín, magpacabait ca at magpacahúsay ca nang cuenta. ¿Nagpapacapagáral bagá iyáng binata? Siyá,i, nagpapacapagáral, nang siyá,i, pacamahalin. ¿Anòng aquing gagaoin nang acó,i, mapacagaling? Magpacahúsay ca nang ugali mo cun íbig mong mapacagaling, sa pagca,t, yaóng tungmutupad lámang nang mañga santong utonang Dios, ang mapapacagaling. ¿Napasasáan ca? Napapasaescuelahan acó. ¿Sáan naroróon ang amá mo? Ang amá co,i, nasasabáhay. ¿Saán acó paroróon? Saan ca man pumaróon, magtatrabajo ca,t, magtitiis. ¿Anòng guinauá nang mag-amá? Nang magqnita silá,i, caracaracang nagyacapan. Ang manoc mo bagá ¿sasabuñgin na? Hindí, tandang pa lámang. ¿Anòng hañgin dóon sa labás nang dágat? Símoy lámang, ang símoy ang nagpabintog sa mañga láyag nang aming sasacquián? Sinisiguid ca bagá nang mañga lamoc cun galì? Oo, sinasactán acó nang mañga lamoc at ipis. ¿May maramì bagáng paro-paro sa iyóng halamanan? Marami, at maramì namán ang langam at alit·ptap.

YCAAPAT NA POUO,T, PITONG PAGSASANAY.

¿Sáan acó napatilohod? Ang Arzobispo,i, ang pinapatilohoran co. ¿Di bagá nagpatirapá ca sa harap nang laráuan nang mahal na Virgen? Acó,i, nagpatirapá sa harap nang altar. ¿Anòng yquinapatihigá nang iyóng nono? Ang catandáa,t, ang cahináan ang yquinapatihigá niyà. Anòng guinagauá nang mañga bata? Silá,i, nagpapatitindig-tindig at napapatiopo-opo. ¿Anòng guinauá nang may saquit nang maquita niyà ang médico.? Siyá,i, nagpatiguilid. ¿Báquit nagpatihólog sa túbig and mandarágat? Di siyá nagpatihólog, ang palo,i, napatihápay at siyá,i, napatibouang. ¿Yhinápay bagá nang hañgin ang cáhoy? Hindí ang hañgin, cundí ang lintic ang nacapagpahápay. ¿Báquit siyá,i, táuag nang táuag sa canilà? Siyá.i, ualàng ibàng matáuag. ¿Anòng sinisilà nang aso,t, pusa.? Sungmisilà ang aso nang *carne*; ang pusa,i, sungmisilà nang isdá. ¿Súcat na bagá ang cayamanan nang macamtán ang caguinhauahan.? Ang cayamana,i, hindí súcat macapagcamit guinhauà. ¿Ungminom bagá siyá nang malabis.? Hindí, casiyahan lámang. Siyá na, houag mo nang salitin iyán. ¿Siyá cayá ang nagsabì.? Siyá ñga ang nagsabì. ¿Natatácot ca bagá sa caniyà? Pono man siyá di co quinatatacotan. ¿Sinúcat mo bagá ang cayong ypinadalà co sa iyò.? Hindí co sinúcat, ang insic na comerciante ang sungmúcat. ¿Ycáo rin bagá ang sungmúcat sa mañga salaual mo.? Acó ñga ang sungmúcat. ¿Súcat cayá siyáng macabáyad.? Di súcat siyáng macabáyad. ¿Anò,t, di ca nagpapatólog sa pagcatrabajo.? Súcat nang tumólog. ¿Hangán cailán matitirá sa bayan si María.? Siyá,i, matitirá ditò hangán bucas. ¿Hangán sáan mo acó sasamahan.? Sasamahan catá hangán sa ílog. ¿Daco sáan napatotoñgò ang agos nitòng ílog.? Napasasadacong hilagáan. ¿Sáan daco napatotoñgò ang sasaquián.? Napatotoñgò sa dacong lupa. ¿Sáan mo ynilagáy ang aspiler.? Ynilagáy co sa ibábao nang lamesa. ¿Nasasaitúas bagá ang capatid mong babaye.? Nasasaibaba.

YCAAPAT NA POUO,T, UALONG PAGSASANAY.

¿Sino ang pinagñgiñgisihan niyaóng bata.? Pinagñgiñgisihan niyá yaóng matandà. ¿Anòng ypinagñgiñgisi niyà. Ang calasiñgan niyà ang ypinagñgiñgisi nang bata. ¿Nagcapagcapañgisi pa bagá siyá nang napasabáhay co.? Oo, nagcapagcapañgisi pa siyá. ¿Báquit nagcapañgisi siyá.? Ang gúlat ay ang siyáng ypinagcapañgisi niyà. Sáan siyá nagcapañgisi.? Ang simbahan ang pinagcapañgisihan niyà. ¿Báquit bagá nagcapamúlat ang capatid mong babaye.? Ang balita tungcol sa pagcamatáy nang caniyàng inà,i, ang siyáng ypinagpacamúlat niyà. ¿Báquit ñgumañgañgá iyáng tauò.? Siyá.i, nacapañgañgá dahil sa bigláng saquit na dungmating sa caniyà. ¿Nacapabisaclat bagá ang magnanácao sa pagtalon niyà sa bacod.? Nacapabisaclat siyá nang tungmalon sa bacod. ¿Napatatabi bagá sa ílog ang mañgiñgisdá.? Siyá,i, napatatabi sa ílog sa pañgiñgisdá. ¿Di bagá lalong magaling ang siyá,i, manabì sa paglalayag.? Lalong madalí sana yaón, ñguní,t, di siyá manhuhuli dahil sang mañga isdá nasasatabi nang ílog. ¿Báquit tungmatabi ca sa dágat.? Nang aquing mapanóor ang mañga sasaquián. ¿Di mo bagá naalaalà ang sinabì nang iyòng amá na houag ca patatabi.? Magaling, aquing naalaalà. ¿Sáan natirá nang malaon si Santo Job.? Sa isàng tabihan. ¿Báquit di ca magpatabi nang icáo ay dumáan.? Sinabì co pong; tabì!. ¿Alín ang lupaín mo.? Ang aquing lupaí,i, ang Estados Unidos. ¿Canino mo ytinatalaga iyáng bulaclac.? Ytinatalaga co sa aquing sinisintàng babaye. ¿Pinainan mo bagá ang iyòng tagá.? Pinainan co nang uod. ¿Anòng guinagauá mo.? Tinatagá co itòng cahuy. ¿Anòng talagang hilig nang mañga Americano.? Silá,i, talagang masisípag, ñguní.t, ang mañga tagálog ay talaga matatámar. ¿Ycáo bagá,i, natatalaga tumupad nang mañga utos nang Dios? Acó,i, natatalaga diyán. ¿Anòng sabì mo.? Tambing mo tabiin ang baro co. ¿Sinong naglilo cay Jesús.? Ysá sa mañga caniyáng alagad ang naglilo sa Caniyà. ¿Anòng pinangagaliñgan niyóng banáag.? Ysàng bondoc na naniniñgas. ¿Nacaligtás si Pedro.? Cundañgan acó, namatáy sana siyá. ¿Anòng sinabì nang Pare sa bata,t, sa alila.? Sinabì niyá sa bata, hali na, anac co, at sa alilá, hali ca. ¿Anòng ypinanguiguilalás mo.? Nanguiguilalás acó sa mañga gauáng cahañgahañga nang Dios. ¿Báquit ca gungmagámit nang uicang di dápat cay Ana.? Acó,i, gungmagámit nang mahahálay na uica, dahilan sa caniyàng palácad.

YCAAPAT NA POUO,T, SIYAM NA PAGSASANAY.

¿Báquit di mo inaaliú iyáng sangol nagcacanluluha.? Di co inaaliú sa pagca,t, ang mañga pasosohín ay nagcacanluluha. ¿Anò,t, nagcacanluluha iyáng dalaga.? Ang saquit ang siyá niyàng ypinagcacanluluha. ¿Mabuti bagáng mañgáral ang cura sa iyòng bayan.? Mañgañgáral na lubhàng mabuti at sa pinanañgañgaralan ay nagcacanluluha. ¿Maanò ang lagáy nang asáua mo? Ang asáua co,i, lungmuluhá sa caniyàng saquit; siyá,i, nagcacaniihi, nagcacandudugó, nagcacanpapáuis, nagcacanláuay; cun minsá,i, naghihimatáy at nagcacantatáua. ¿Nagcanhihiya ang dalaga.? Nagcanhihiya siyá sa harapan nang caniyàng casintahan. ¿Anò,t, ganiyán carami ang mañga buñgang nagcacanlalagas.? Labis na ang cahinogan, cayá nagcacanlalag-lag sa mañga cáhuy. ¿Naglalarolaró ang mañga bata.? Ang mañga laróan ang siyá nilàng pinagcacantotouaán. ¿Anòng tinatauanan mo.? Ang pagtáua, ay, nagcacanlalabi. sa aquin. ¿Gauang tapat bagá ang magpatolóy? Ang pagpapatolóy sa ibà,i, isàng tapat na gaua. ¿Baquit di mo siyá nailagan? Dahil sa tungmapat siyá sa aquin. ¿Paanò ang pagcalagáy nang mañga cáhuy sa halamanan mo.? Nagcacatapat-tapat ang pagcalagáy. ¿Nagtapat ca nang pagparóon sa Mariquina? Yníuan co (or linisan co) ang carsada at sa tapatan acó dungmáan. ¿Pauaualán co ang nabibilango.? Yya, di natatapat sa iyò. ¿Di bagá maputí yaóng láyag na nasasadágat.? Tila madiláo. ¿Di bagá tila vapor.? Hindí tila isàng sasacyán na may láyag. ¿Matotolóy ca rin bagá nang pag-alís.? Hindí, acó,i, magpapatila mona. ¿Ay anò.? Hanapin mo ang aquing salamín at ylabás mo tulóy itòng upúan. ¿Ungminum bagá ang alila nang gatas.? Yninum niyàng patolóy. ¿Anòng gagaoin co ñga? Ypatolóy mong hampasín. ¿Saan tungmotolóy ang capatid mong lalaqui.? Ang búhay co, ang tinutuluyan niyà. ¿Anò ang catongcolan mo.? Ang catongcolan co,i, manhocom. ¿Anòng catongcolan guinaganap (or tinutupad) niyà.? Ang caniyàng guinaganap na catongcolan ay ang paníñgil. ¿Ytinongcol mona sa báua,t, isàng upahan ang caupahán naoócol sa canilà? Ytinongcol co na. ¿Anòng tinongcol nang sondalo.? Ang tinongcol niyà,i, ang magbantáy sa unahan. ¿Báquit ang babaye,t, lalaqui ay naguiisà.? Naguiisa dahil sa silá,i, mag-asáua. Ybig mong catá,i, samahan.? Hindí, acó,i, maguiisà. ¿Carampatan bagáng magcaútang at hindí magbáyad.? Hindí, hindí nararápat magcaútang, bagò di magbáyad at diri naman dápat ang mañgótang. ¿Ang caniyà bagáng panguinóon ay mabagsic o maauaín cayá.? Siyá,i, maauaín at maamong lóob. ¿Mauilihin ca bagá sa pañgañgabayo.? Hindí acó mauilihin sa pañgañgabayò.

YCALIMANG POUONG PAGSASANAY.

¿Quinauiuilihan mo bagáng paquingán ang paghuni nang mañga ibon sa omaga.? Quinauiuilihan co panoorin ang mañga ibong hungmuhuni at ang mañga sasabuñgin sa sabuñgán. ¿Caninong libro iyán? Sa batang nagaáral. ¿Nagpapaútang bagá ang insic sa nañgagsusugal.? Nagpapaútang siyá nang isàng dáan piso sa nañgagsusugal. ¿Yyúng caráyom, ay sa aquing capatid na babaye cayá.? Hindí, iyá,i, sa dalagang bungmabasà.

¿Ang pañgiñgisdá bagá ay isàng paráan.? Hindí, ang pañgiñgisdá,i, isàng paglilibang, ñguní,t, ang pagsúlat ay isàng paráan. ¿Malíuag bagá ang pamamaril sa Pilipinas.? Malíuag dahil sa casiitan (casucatan); ñguní,t, magáan dahil sa caramihan nang mababaril. ¿Ang paglilibang sa dágat ay pañgánib bagá.? Ang paglilibang sa dágat ay pañganib cun minsán. ¿Anong nasuboc mong guinagauá nang alila.? Nasubocan co siyáng ninanácao ang aquing orasán at sinosoot ang baro co. ¿Anòng bizantá niyàng togtoguín.? Binantá niyà tumogtog nang piano, ñguní,t, di natolóy. ¿Pungmoposta bagá siyá sa iyòng sasabuñgin.? Siyá,i, pungmoposta sa aquing manuc. ¿Anòng guinagauá nang Pare nang pungmasoc sa simbahan.? Siyá,i, nañgañgáral at sungmisigáo. Cun dumating camí dóon ñgayón, ¿nanhahapon cayá silá. Hindí, silá,i, di marahil nanhahapon, cundí nagsusugal. ¿Anò ang guinagauá nang mañga sastre cun silá nananahi.? Nananahi siláng nañgagsisipol. ¿Paanò ang paghuli sa mañga amó? Cun minsa,i, nahuhuli silá cun nañgañgáin (naninihi) nang lamán nang sihi sa dalampásig. ¿Anòng nacagagaling sa iyòng amá.? Ang pagpapaligo sa túbig na may *hielo* (Sp. w.) ang siyáng nacapagpapagaling sa caniyà. ¿Natotólog bagá ang mañga alila cun nagtatrabajo ang canilàng mañga panguinóon.? Ang mañga alila,i, di dápat tumólog cun nagtatrabajo ang canilàng mañga panguinóon. ¿Nagtatanim siyá nang mañga cáhoy cun (sa mantala) nagduducal nang lupa. Ytinatanim niyà ang mañga cáhoy cun (sa mantalang) nasasabúquid. ¿Cailán siyá pungmaróon sa búquid.? Siyá,i, naparóon nang icáo, ay ungmaalís na. ¿Anòng quinain niyà, nang siyá,i, nacapagáral na nang caniyàng *leccion*.? Nang nacapagáral na siya nang caniyàng *lección* siyá,i, cungmáin nang ságuing. ¿Cailán nagbabantáng umalís ang taga ibàng bayan.? Aalís pagcapanhapon. ¿Nañgañgararo bagá siyá? Hindí, siyá,i, nañgañg*arreton* (Sp. w. carreton). Anòng paquinábang sa isdá niyan. Ytò,i, mabuting pamáin. ¿Nararapat bagá acóng gumámit nang salamín, cun acó,i, bungmabasà.? Ycáo, ay nararápat gumámit nang salamín sa pagbasà t, pagsúlat. ¿Siyá bagá dadalaoin ca árao árao.? Nararápat mo dalaoin siyá lingo-lingo. ¿Sáan nadoróon ang sísiu na naualá.? Hindí nauaualá, naitò ritò. ¿Ang Dios bagá ualáng hangán.? Siyá,i, ualáng hangá,t, siyá,i, macapangyarihan. ¿Macacamtán natin bagá ang búhay na ualáng hangán.? Atin macacamtán ang búhay na ualáng hangán cun tuparín natin ang mañga otos nang Dios. ¿Siyá bagá ay ualáng sala.? Siyá,i, may sala,t, ualáng túring. ¿Anòng ating gagaoin pagcayari nitòng gauá.? Pagcayari nitò, quitá,i, magpapasial. ¿Nañgañgalisquis bagá ang cataonan niyá.? Ang cataouán niyá,i, nañgañgalisquis. ¿Pinalicpican bagá nang *cosineros* ang isdá.? Pinalicpican niyà. ¿Anò ang pagpipiritosan niyà.? Ang cauali ang caniyàng pagpipiritosan. ¿Anòng ysasamà niyà sa pagpipiritos.? Ang ysasamà niyà,i, patani,t, itò ang ating úlam.

YCALIMANG POUO,T, ISANG PAGSASANAY.

¿Naquita mo bagá ang capatid cong lalaqui.? Di co naquiquita. ¿Dungmating na bagá ang alila.? Di pa siyá dungmarating. ¿Quinoha mo bagá ang libro co.? Di co quinucuha. ¿Caniyà bagáng sinalúbong ang caniyàng hípag.? Oo, nang siyá,i, ungmaalis ay siyá namán pagdating. ¿Sino ang nagbigáy sa iyò niyáng singsing.? Ang alí co ang nagbigáy sa aquin nang si amá,i, nariritò pa sa búhay. ¿Hungmuli bagá nang paróparó ang anac mong babaye.? Hindí, nang madadampot na niyá, naualá sa caniyang matá. ¿Siyá, bagá,i, tináuag nang caniyàng inà.? Oo. nang siyá,i, papanáog na, tináuag siyá nang caniyàng inà. ¿Nacalilimot ca sa aquin.? Di acó lilimot sa iyò. ·¿Pinamamatiagan mo bagá ang sinasabì co sa iyò.?

Pinamamatiagan co ang sinasabi mo. ¿Anòng yniootos mo sa aquin.? Houag mong pababayáan ang iyòng mañga caibigan. ¿Anòng ypinagbilin niyà sa aquin.? Bago ca pa mahigá,i, magdarasal ca mona. ¿Anòng sinabi mo sa aquin.? Bago ca sumúlat ay isipin mo mona ang iyòng sasabihin. ¿Báquit di siyá cungmacáin.? Di siyá cungmacáin, dahil sa di nagogotom. ¿Báquit ca nañguñgurús.? Sa pagca,t, ang sabi ni inà sa aquin ay, mañguñgurús ca muna bago gumauá nang anomáin. ¿Báquit di ypahintólot ni amá mo cay María na basahín itòng libro.? Sa pagca,t, bago basahín ni María, ay cailañgan matanto mona niyà. ¿Sáan quitá paroroón pagcacáin.? Pasadalampásig quitá pagcapananghali. ¿Anòng gagaoin natin pagcabasà.? Pagcabasà ninyò, susúlat namán cayó. Anòng aquing gagaoin pagcabasà co nang súlat.? Pagcabasà mo nang súlat, ay ybibigáy mo sa aquin. ¿Cailán mo tinangap ang súlat co.? Tinangap co ang súlat mo nang macasúlat na acó. ¿Anòng guinauá nang capatid niyàng lalaqui.? Nang naquita niyà ang caniyang maestro, ay siyá,i, tumgmago. ¿Anòng nangyari.? Nang guinagauá co ang yniotos mo, ay ypinagbáual niyà na ytolóy co. ¿Anòng sinalíi mo sa caniyà.? Nang sasalitin co na siyà ay ayáio siyáng maquinig at ungmalís; ñguní,t, nang macamisa na tináuag acó niyà. ¿Anò,t, di ca nagaáral.? Sa pagca,t, di acó macapagáral. ¿Di bagá macasúlat ang iyòng anac.? Di siyá macasúlat, ñguní,t, macapagsasalitá. ¿Macapaguiuica bagá siyá.? Siyá,i, di macapaguica. ¿Di cayá nilà maypahayag.? Di nilá maypaháyag. ¿Maari bagáng di silá pumaróon." Di maari, di sila pumaróon. ¿Paanong mangyayari iyán.? Ganiyán ang nasacaotosán ¿Di bagá iyán guinauá sa háyag.? Hindí guinauá sa lihim. Sáan naróon ang orasán co.? Naitò. ¿Sáan naróon ang amá mo.? Nariyán. ¿Sáan ang pasimula nitòng dáar.? Ang dalampásig ang pinagsimulan. ¿Anòng nacasúgat sa pinsán mong babaye.? Ang nacasúgat sa caniyà i. ang dolo nang aspiler. ¿Sinong lungmalán sa Dios.? Ang Dios ay ualáng lungmalán sa caniyà t, uala namán Siyáng catapusan. ¿Siyá bagá,i. maauaín.? Ang áua Niyá,i. ualáng hañgán, malalaqui man ang mañga casalanan mo,i, patatauarin ca Niyà, bocod sa tinotoloñgan Niyà ang tauó sa cabanalan. ¿Sungmasáan Siyá.? Siyá,i, sungmasalahat, sáan ca man pumaróon naroróon Siyá, at anomán bágay ang gaoin mo, ay Caniyàng naquiquita. Yámang ganóo,i, gumúyac ca nang bucas macalauà macaharap sa Caniyà.

YCALIMANG POUO,T, DALAUANG PAGSASANAY.

¿May quináin ca.? Ualá acóng quináin. ¿Di bagá naquita niyà ang capatid cong lalaqui.? Di pa niyà naquiquita. ¿Di pa siyá natotólog.? Di pa natotólog. ¿Anòng ysinamà sa pañgañgalácal.? May ysinamàng báyad sa caniyàng pinacaopa. ¿Anò ang pagoosapan.? May pagoosapan tongcol sa caniyàng pagaasáua. ¿May sasabihin cang anomán sa aquin.? Oo, may sasabihin acó sa iyò. ¿May gagaoin ca bagá.? Oo, may gagaoin acó. ¿May ninanasa bagá siyá? Ualá siyáng ninanasa. ¿May sinabi ca bagáng anomán.? Acó,i, ualáng anománg sinasalí. ¿May pinatáy bagá siyáng tauò.? Siyá,i, may pinatáy na isàng tauò. ¿Sino ang may anac ditò sa bata.? Si Pedro ang may anac ditò sa bata. ¿Sino ang may gauá sa sanglibotan.? Ang Dios na atin Panguinóon ang siyáng may gauá. ¿Ycáo bagá cayá ang may ari nitòng lupa.? Hindí acó ang may ari, cundí ang bayáo co. ¿Sino sino ang may ari nitòng gúbat.? Ang caguinoohan sa bayan ang may ari nang gúbat. ¿Anó yaòng na sa may simbahan.? Yaóng na sa may simbahan. ay isàng cáhoy na lubháng mainam. ¿Sino ang may saquit.? Ang amá co ang may saquit. ¿Silá bagá ang mañga may sala.? Hindí, hindí silá ang may sala. ¿Marúnong bagá ang maestro.? Siyá,i, marúnong na marúnong. ¿Sáan gáling ang alila mo.? Siyá,i, gáling sa ílog. ¿Yarì na bagá itòng libro.? Hindí pa yarì. ¿Tapus na ang bóuan.? Tapus na. ¿Súcat bagá siyáng parusahan.? Hindí siyá súcat parusahan. ¿Ang mañga pinsán mo,i, dápat bagáng gantihín.? Dápat siláng pagcaloóban rang gantì. ¿Ybig siyá bagáng sumúlat.? Ybig niyáng sumúlat. ¿Anòng sabi niyà.? Ang sabi niyà,i, taga ibáng bayan siyá. ¿Tanoñgin mo cun siyá,i, marúnong tumogtog nang arpa.? Marúnong siyá dáo. ¿Cailañgan mo itòng bulac-lac.? Oo, po. Cun cailañgan mo,i, cunin. ¿Talastás mo ang caibigan co,i, may sintá sa iyò.? Ayauan co. ¿Di nilà ibig pumasaescuelahan.? Ayáo silá. ¿Báquit.? Sa pagca,t, ayáo co na. ¿Anòng sabi mo.? Ang sabi co,i, di maari. ¿Marúnong siyá tumahí.? Siyá,i, hindí marúnong tumahé. ¿Marúnong cang managálog.? Marúnong acó managalog. ¿May dúnong ca bagá sa pagsúlat.? Ualá acóng dúnong sa pagsúlat. ¿Marúnong cang mañgosina.? (Sp. w. *cocina*, "kitchen"). Hindí acó marúnong mañgosina. ¿Cailañgan bagáng maligo.? Hindí cailañgan maligo. ¿Cailañgan bagá.? Cailañgan. ¿Cailañgang bagáng sabihin.? Cailañgang aquing ypahayag. ¿Sáan naróon ang amá mo. Ang amá namin ay patáy na, camí,i, mañga olila. ¿Yníuan na bagá ni Juan ang sugal.? Di pa niyà iníuan. ¿Sino iyáng tauòng iyán. Siyá,i, i-àng mahírap na tauó. ¿Anò iyáng *corona*.? Pílac na tagamás. ¿Yyáng bagá ang caraníuan niyáng pagsasalità.? Yyá ang caniyáng caratihang ásal. ¿Yyán bagá,i, casiyahan na.? Hindí pa casiyahan. ¿Ano,t, di ca sungmasáyao.? Capagdinarating ang apat na pouòng taón, ang cabatáa,i, lungmipás na. ¿Anong bágay ang ynilalalo nang iyong amá. Ang caniyáng ynilalalo sa pañgañgáral.

YCALIMANG POUO,T TATLONG PAGSASANAY.

¿Anòng aquing gagaoin nang macapagcamit nang táuad sa aquing mañga casalanan.? Cun íbig mong macapagcamit nang táuad sa mañga casalanan mo, ay magcumpisal ca nang mahúsay. ¿Sungmusúlat ca bagá cun icáo,i, nagaáral.? Cun acó,i, nagaáral ay di acó sungmúlat. ¿Anòng sinasabi sa caniyá nang amá ni José.? Ang sinasabi sa caniyà,i, houag cang cacáin cun icáo,i, sungmusúlat. ¿Ypinagbilin mo sa mañga bata, na houag magsitólog cun silá,i, nagdarasal.? Oo, ypinagbilin co. ¿Báquit hungmihintó silá dóon.? Hungmihintó silá nang caniláng mapanóod ang i-àng sasaquíng naglaláyag. ¿Minamasamá mo (or inaari mong masamá) bagáng dumiñgig nang salitáng mahahálay.? Minamasamá co ñga. ¿Yuaaring magaling cayá nang pañginóon mo ang paglilingcod sa Dios.? Oo ñga. ¿Sáan ca patotoñgò.? Acó,i, lungmoloúas (or loloúas). ¿Cailán icáo babalic.? Babalic acó mameáng gabi. ¿Ayáo bagáng humárap ang anac mo sa maestro.? Nayáo siyáng humárap, sa pagca,t, nagdadalàng tácot sa parusà. ¿Cailán babasahin ang librong ybinigáy co sa caniyà.? Babasahin niyà sa lingong darating. ¿Nagaacala bagáng umalís ang mañga Americano.? Silá,i, di nagaacalang umalís. ¿Báquit ca sungmagot sa cura.? Acó,i, nagdalàng hiya. ¿Magbabalic sabi bagá siyá sa caniyàng pagmuà.? Magbabalic sabi siyá sa caniyàng uicang mahahálay. ¿Anò,t, di mo tinatalicoran ang masamáng pamumúhay.? Dahil sa nagdadalàng poot pa acó sa aquing mañga caáuay. ¿Sino ang quinatatacotan niyàng bata sa escuelahan.? Siyá,i, nagdadalàng tácot sa maestro niyà. ¿Nahilo bagá ang matandáng babaye? Siyá,i, nahilo, ñguní,t, madalíng naulían at ñgayó,i, tungmatahímic. ¿Anòng pag-iñgay iyán. Ang mañga bata, na tungmatacbò-tacbò sa lansañgan. ¿Sinabi mong silá,i, houag mag-iñgay.? Sinabi co na houag siláng mag-iñgáy. ¿Ang mañga tagálog bagá, ay nagcacatipong lihim sa paglaban sa Pono.? Oo, cun minsá,i, sa lihim, at cun minsán namá,i, sa hayagan. ¿Sino sino bagá ang maminihasang ñgumuya nang tabaco.? Ang mañga Americano, ang may ugaling ñgumuya nang tabaco. ¿Ang mañga tagálog bagá,i, ñgumañgañga.? Ñgumañgañga ang caramihan. ¿Ang quiso,i. ñginañgalot (or quiniquibit) bagá nang mañga dagá (or dinadagá ang quiso.?) Ang quiso,i, ñginañgalot nang dagá, (or quinibit, or dinagá &.) ¿Anông ñginañgatñgat nang aso.? Ñgumañgatñgat nang isáng bot-o. ¿Sinong pinagñgiñgisihan niyaóng bata.? Siyá,i, di ñgungmiñgisi sa canino man ñgungmiñgiti siyá. ¿Lungmampás bagá ang mandarágat sa tumatañgos na bundoc.? Hindí lungmampás dahil sa tinablán siyá nang tácot. ¿Anông himalang guinauá ni Jesucristo sa panahóng tinalicdán.? Gungmauá Siyá nang maraming himala. ¿Nagcacahimala bagá sa panahóng hinaharap.? Hindí pagcacahimala sa hinaharap na panahón at hindí rin marahil magcacaroón sa haharaping panahón. ¿Anông sinabi niyá.? Sasabihin co sa iyo ang sabi niyá sa madalíng uica. ¿May ilán ang naninirá sa bayang itò.? Ayon sa bílang na guinauá nóong nacaráan taón. may mañga pitòng libòng catauò.

YCALIMANG POUO.T, APAT NA PAGSASANAY.

¿Gaanò calayo ang Maynila.? Mula ritò hangán sa Maynila, ay may ánim na milla ang layo. ¿Quinusa baga niyà.? Quinusa niyà. ¿Anòng gagaoin co.? Gamagálit ca. ¿Sinong gungmauá nang lamesa.? Guinauá nang anlouague ang lamesa casabáy nang upúan. ¿Gagaoin niyàng ganitò.? Dápat niyàng gaoin ganiyán. ¿Alín ang lalong matulin sa sasaquián may láyag at sa vapor.? Ang vapor, ay siyáng lalong matulin. ¿Mabuti bagá acóng sungmúlat.? Masamá cang sungmúlat. ¿Báquit mo hinahampás nang ganiyán calacás ang iyòng alila.? Sa pagca,t, binásag niyàng tiquis ang palayoc. ¿May tauò bagá sa lóob." Ualáng tauò sa lóob; lahat silá,i, na sa labás. ¿Ang báhay niyà,i, na sa bagá nang simbahan.? Hindí, na sa licod nang simbahan. ¿Ang capatid cong lalaqui,i, na sa itaás bagá o na sa ibabá.? Siyá,i, na sa ilalim nang hihigán. ¿Sáan daco ylalagáy co ang cabán.? Ylagáy mo sa guitná nang dáan. ¿Nasáan na tayo sa ating paglalacbáy.? Nasasapaguitan na tayo sa ating lacarín. ¿Sáan naróon ang bata.? Ang bata,i, nasasapíling nang caniyàng iná. ¿Sáan naróon ang búquid niyà.? Nasasacabilá nang dáau. ¿Sáan naróon ang inyò.? Na sa sa magcabilá nang ílog. ¿Cailán mo ninanasang bayaran ang mananahe.? Ynaacala cong bayaran siyá bucas. ¿Di mo naquita bagá ang sasaquián niyóng macalauá.? Hindí. naquita cong may iláng árao na. ¿Naróon ca bagá sa teatro cagabí.? Naparóon acó ñgayó,i, may sang lingo na. ¿Ang mañga caibigan co bagá,i, naririto.? Cañgicañgina,i, nariritò silá; ñguní,t, sa acala co,i, babalic silá mameameá. ¿Anông oras babañgon acó bucas.? Bumañgon cang maaga. ¿Dungmating na bagá ang mañga alila.? Hindí pa. ¿Palagui ca bagáng bungmabasá.? Ualá acóng panahón. parati acó may guinauá. ¿Cailán co ypasosondó ang mangagámot.? Ypasondó mo capagdaca. ¿Nagaacala cang tumirá ditòng palagui.? Oo. ¿Anò ang sabi nang Pare sa caniyáng pañgañgáral.? Ang sabi niyà,i, houag na cayó magcasala cailán pa man. ¿Yláng árao mayróon mula ñgayón hangán sa catapusan nang taón.? Cúlang nang anim na póuo,t, limáng árao hangán sa matapus itòng taón. ¿Nagcacabuñga bagá itòng cáhoy nóong unàng panahón.? Oo, nagcacabuñga nóon árao, at ñgayó,i, namumuñga rin cun minsán. ¿Napasasaescuelahan bagá siyá malimit. Siyá,i, bihirang pungmapasa escuelahan. Gaanò ealimit napasasa Maynila ang capatid cong babaye.? Siyá,i, naparoróon taón-taón. „Cailán susúlat siyá? Pagcabasà niyà nitó ay susúlat. ¿Cailán nañgagúlat silá? Silá,i, nañgagúlat nang maquita nilá ang ahas. ¿Cailán ca hihigá? Acó,i, hihigá pagcapanhapon „Cailán pagaáralan nang anac mo ang caniyàng lición.? Pagcapagsimbà,i, magaáral siyá. ¿Naquita mo bagá ang *Catedral* (Sp.)? Sa touing pasasa Maynila acó, ay quiniquita co ang *Catedral.* ¿Cailán ungmiinom ang iyòng iná.? Cun cumacáin, ay ungmiinum siyá. ¿Báquit di ca bungmabasà.? Cun acó,i, sungmusúlat ay di acó bungmabasà. ¿Cailán dungmating ang iyòng bayáo.? Nang acó,i, sungmusúlat ay dungmatíng siyá. ¿Báquit di sungmúlat ang aquing pinsán.? Dahil sa ang amáin mo ay nacasúlat na nang ang iyòng capatid na lalaqui ay dungmating. ¿Cailán ungmalís siyá.? Sa pagalís nang caniyàng amá, siyá namán ungmalís capagdaca. ¿Anòng guinauá nang Conde nang (lumapit) lungmapit sa Hari.? Pagdating nang Conde sa harap nang hari, ay nagpatirapá siyáng tambíng. ¿Anòng guinauá nang Hari pagcapañgósap nang Conde.? Di pa halos natatapus ang salitá nang Conde, ay niyácap na siyá nang Hari. ¿Cailán dungmating ang capatid cong lalaqui. Siyá,i, dungmatíng pagcaalís mo. ¿Saán acó patotoñgò.? Pumasabáhay ca nang iyòng amaí,t, pag siyá,i, nabati mo na, bumalic ca. ¿Cailán quitá maliligo.? Pagcapaginisa, ay maliligo quitá. ¿Páanò ang pagyayari niyán.? Nang namumulá nang pagsasalitá ang caibigan co, acó,i, nanhimatáy. ¿Anòng gagaoin nang ahla bagò cumáin? Bagò cumáin iiguib siyá mo na. ¿Alin ditè sa mañga libro ang babasahin co mona? Iyán mona ang basahin mo.

YCALIMANG POUO.T. LIMANG PAGSASANAY.

¿Ang sastre bagá,i, maraming salapí.? Ualá, cundí caunti lámang. ¿Anò,t, di ca naparoróon sa catipunan ñgayóng gabí.? Di acó nacaparóon, acó,i, may caunting saquit. ¿Ang anloague bagá,i, may lalong maraming paco sa pamocpoc.? Ang mañga pamocpoc niyà,i, cúlang sa mañga paco. ¿Mayróon ca bagáng *mantiquiya* na labis ang damì.? Ualá acóng caramihan. ¿Anòng oras na.? Tanghali na halos. ¿Lahat silá,i, naparóon.? Lahat silá,i, naparóon liban siyá. ¿Cungmuculog bagá nang malacás.? Hindí cungmuculog: ñguní t. ungmoolán nang lubhá ¿Ycáo cayá ang capatid nang caibigán co? Oo. ¿Totoó bagáng siyá,i, nabouad? Totoó ñga. ¿Ycáo bagá i. mañgañgalacal.? Dili ¿Magsi-imbà bagá camì? Ycáo,i, hindí, at ang capatid mo,i, hindí rin dápat magsimbà. ¿Anò,t, di co itò gagaoin.? Houag mong gaoin iyán macá icáo ay masactán. ¿Ybig ninyò na siyá,i, pumaritò.? Pumaritò siyá. ¿Macásacaling may salapí ca diyán.? Ayauán co, cun sacali mayróon, ay aquing ibibigáy sa iyo. ¿Anò ang pagsampalataya.? Ang pagsampalataya, ang uica nang mañga Santo Padre, ay ang pagsampalataya sa di natin naquiquita. ¿Gaanò ang halagá nang útang ni Pedro.? Ang útang ni Pedro, ang uica nang aquing anac, ay ungmaabot sa tatlong póuong piso. ¿Nagsalitá ca sa sondalo tongcol sa bágay na yaón.? Ang uica niyà,i, mayróon na siláng pinagcasondóan. ¿Diyata,i, naquipagsalitá ca sa caniyà.? Totoòng totoó naquipagsalitá ñga acó sa caniyà. ¿Cailán tayo susulatan niyà.? Susulatan ca niyà di umanò sa bálang árao. ¿Pacacasal ca cayá sa caniyà.? Sa anò man paráan ay pacacasal acó sa caniyà. ¿Ñguní.t. may casayahan ca bagáng salapí upan matolóy iyán.? Ualá. cundí sa anò,t, anomá,i, gagaoin co. ¿Paanò.? Acó ang bahala. ¿Anòng guinagauá nang alila.? Nagaalaga siyá nang mañga búbuy. ¿Buháy pa bagá ang nono mong lalaqui.? Hindí, siyá,i, namatáy na. ¿Anòng mañga himalá ang guinauá ni Jesucristo.? Siyá,i, bungmúbuy sa maramì. ¿Binobunot bagá

ang capatid mong babaye ang bohoc niyà? Oo. binubunot niyá. ¿Diyata.?
Siyá,i. ulol. cayá maraming caulolan ang caniyàng guinagauá. ¿Ang caniyàng inà bagá, ay banal? Siyá,i, sacdal cabanalan ¿Ang iyòng alila
ay marumì.? Siyá,i, sacdal carumihan. ¿Paanò ang paggauá co nang
súlat.? Sulating mong untí–untí. ¿Matuling lumácad ang canilàng alila.?
Ynot–inot ang paglácad niyà; hungmihinto-hintó siyá sa lahat nang tindahan. ¿Nagpasalámat ca cay María dahil sa biyaya niyà sa iyò.? Pi-
nagsalamatan co siyá. ¿Sinong naririyán.? Ang caibigan natin ang na-
ririnì; salámat at dungmating ca, Ysco. ¿Pasasaán ca ñgayón.? Acó,i,
pasasasugalan upan aquing maalaman cun acó,i, pinapálad. ¿Anò ang
labás mo sa sugalan.? Acó,i, sinasamá; naypatalo co ang lahat nang
aquing salapí. ¿Di mo bagá minamabigat ang ganiyáng pagsira nang
salapí.? Di co minamatamís. ¿Saán nagmumula ang hañgin.? Hungmi-
hilaga. ¿Tungmotoñgò sa dalampasigang calonoran. ¿Sino ang pinagpupugayan niyóng bata.? Ang pinagpupugayan niyà,i, ang caniyahe maestro.
¿Piniguing bagá siyá nang iyòng amá.? Oo. ¿Mayróon ca pang sasabihin
ibá.? Ualá, acó ñgayó.i, napapaalam sa iyò. ¿Anòng guinagauá mo diyán sa silid.? Acó,i, nagsosóot. ¿Gaanò calunit nagbibihis ca.? Nagbibihís acó touíng lingo.

YCALIMANG POUO,T, ANIM NA PAGSASANAY.

¿Anò,t, Si Juana,i, laguing nanunúñgao.? Siyá,i, parating nanunúñgao
dahil sa nauiuilì siyáng manóod sa mañga dungmaráan. ¿Báquit nagbibihis ca.? Nagbibihís acó,t, acó,i, pasasasimbahan. ¿Macailán siyáng mag-
hubad árao–árao.? Siyá,i, naghuhubad lámang cun napasasahihíhan.
¿Siyá,i, may capangyarihan na acó.i. caniyàng ybilangó.? Ualá siyáng capangyarihan gumauá niyán; houag cang matácot di ca maaano. ¿Paanòng
mangyayari iyán? Hindí maarî. ¿Báquit di maari.? Sa pagca,t. hindí
mangyayari. ¿Acó bagá,i, malubhá ang saquit.? Hindí, maari pang icáo
ay gumaling. ¿Marúnong bagá siyá.? Hindí.· cundí siyá,i, maarí pang
dumúnong. ¿Anò ang ygaganti mo sa aquin.? Ualá acéng anomán may-
gantì sa iyó. ¿Anòng nangyari.? Lungmindol cahapo,t, ang aming báhay
ay lungmagpac. ¿Sungmasáan ang Pañginóong Dios.? Ang Dios ay sungmasalahat. ¿Sungmasáan Si Jesucristo ñgayón.? Si Jesucristo,i, sungma-
salúñgit sa cánan nang Dios Amá. ¿Sino ang pinapálad.? Ang tauòng
nasasa gracia nang Dios ang siyáng pinapálad. ¿Saán naroróon ang cay
Pedrong báhay.? Nasaguitná nang niogán. ¿Anò ang ytinahe niyá sa
caniyàng mañga salaual.? Tinahé niyà nang caráyom at sinúlid. ¿Anòng
ygagauá co nitò.? Ysàng licop ang ygauá mo. ¿Canino itòng mañga sasaquián.? Caná Wise. ¿Lápis bagá ang ytititic co nang súlat.? Oo, lápis
ang ytititic mo. ¿Anòng ypinatáy niyà sa bábuy damó.? Ang ypinatáy
niyà,i, isàng sibat. ¿Anòng mañga báhay sa bayan mo.? Lahat, liban sa
tatlò, ay páuang báhay na páuid. ¿Bungmilí ca bagá nang hícao na guintó.?
Hindí, ang binilì co,i, tatlòng laráuang cáhuy. ¿Saán gáling iyáng mañga
casangcapan.? Mañga casangcapang Viena. ¿Anòng capís iyán.? Capís
Cavite. ¿Ylán salop na bigás ang ypinagbili mo.? Ang ypinagbili co,i,
tatlòng salop na bigás at dalauàng boteng álac. ¿Saán naróon ang palayoc nang canin.? Ang palayoc nang cani,i, nasasúloc nang lamesa. ¿Alíng
pusa ang hinahánap nang iyòng caibigan.? Hinahánap niyà ang may
tatlòng paà. ¿Sino sa inyò ang lalong bayani.? Ang lalong bayani, ay
ang catoto ni Enrique. ¿Ybig mong sumacáy ditò sa bangca.? Ayáo acó,
isàng bangcang sinasaquián nang maramì. ¿May lalo bagáng casindacsindac na para nang lindol.? Ang lindol ay totoò ñgang casindacsindac.

¿Matáas bagá ang cay Juang báhay? Totoòng matáas. ¿Yláng báhay ang ytinindig nang iyòng amá? Ang itinindig niyà,i, tatló. ¿Báhay na pauid bagá ó batò? Ang dalauà ay batò, at ang isà,i, cáhuy. ¿Naúinili cang tumirá bagá sa báhay na páuid? Oo, ñga, caligaligaya ang matirá sa báhay na pauid. ¿Cailán ca pasasabáhay nang iyòng caibigan? Paroróon acó sa lingong darating.

YCALIMANG POUO,T, PITONG PAGSASANAY.

¿Sino ang napasaescuelahan? Si Clara ni Matilde ang napasaescuelahan. ¿Tinicmán mo bagá ang álac na aquing ypinadalà sa iyò? Oo, tinicmán co na. Ay anò, ¿minamagaling mo bagá? Hindí, minamasamá co. ¿Saán ca patotoñgò? Acó,i, pasasahalaman, cun pahihintulutan mo. ¿Pinahihintulutan mo bagá acóng paróon? Oo, ñguní,t, houag cang pipitás nang anomán buñgà; sa pagca,t, biláo pa ay bacá ca mañgiló. ¿Sáan acó uupó? Houag cang umupó sa upúang iyán, at sira. ¿Paanò ang pagcamatáy ni Lincoln? Siyá,i, pinatáy na tiquís nang isàng baliu na tauò; calunos-lunos at cahapis-hapis ang naguing camatayan niyóng bunying tauò. ¿Nagcasala bagá siyá? Siyá,i, mamamatáy mona, bagò gumauá nang casalanan. ¿Sa anò mo quinacailañgan iyáng upóan? Quinucuha co nang maupúan nang aquing caibigan. ¿Anò,t, siyá,i, nagbabanalbanalan? Nagbabanalbanalan siyá nang siyá,i, purihin. ¿Báquit di ca naghihilamos árao-árao? Dáhil sa ang túbig ay malamig. ¿Anòng yniotos mo canicañgina? Tachohín mo ang Pare at cun may masalubong cang caquilala sa lansañgan, ay houag cang humintóng maquipagósap. ¿Báquit di co siyá cacausapin? Dáhil sa ang lácad mo,i, totoòng mahalagá. Datapóua,t, acó,i, paroróon sa báhay ni Enrique. Mabutí ñga, cun paroróon ca ay houag cang malauon. ¿Namomoñgà na ang mañga cáhoy na iyòng ytinanim? Hindí pa namomoñgà, datapóua,t, namumulac-lac na. ¿Anòng sinasabi sa iyò nang amá mo? Ang caniyàng sabi ay houag cang pasagúbat, bacá icáo ay loóban nang mañga tulisán. ¿Ay anò bagá? Houag cang másoc diyán sa báhay, bacá may tauò sa itaás. ¿At anò? Houag cang tumacbò, bacá paloin ca nang iyòng inà. ¿Báquit siyá,i, natácot? Siyá,i, natácot, bacá siyá,i, mariñgig. ¿Susulatan cayá acó niyà sa touíng bouan? Siyá,i, susúlat sa iyò, houag lámang siyáng macaabala. ¿Sinong nauulol? Ang amá niyá,i, nauulol, ó siyá,i, hañgal? ¿Pariritò siyá, dili? Paritò man siyá, di man paritò, ¿anhin co? ¿Cápoua silá naparóon? Ualá sa canilà isà man caparóon. ¿Paroróon ca cayà namán? Ybig co pang magbáyad nang multa (Sp) sa pumaróon. ¿Di mo nababalitáan ang sabi na ang capatid mo,i, bulisic conó? Bagamán siyá,i, bulisic, ay di siyá insurrecto (Sp). ¿Sinaolò mo ang iyòng licsion? Cahiman pinagaralan cong mabuti, ay di co matotohan. ¿Pariritò cayá silá cun dolotan co nang salapí? Silá,i, di paparitò gani yán man. ¿Natatalagá ca bagáng maquipagbabag sa caniyà? Maquiquipagbabag acó sa caniyà, acó man ay patain. ¿Nalalaman mo na acó,i, natalo sa sugal? Di mo acó pinaquingán, manáia ñgayón ang masamáng quinasapitan. ¿Dadaláuin mo ang inà co yámang nariritò ca? Yámang acó,i, nariritò, siyá,i, aquing dadaláuin. ¿Anò,t, hindí dinalà ditò nang alila ang aquing cabayo? Dáhil sa ualá cang sinabi sa caniyàng anomán tongcol diyán.

YCALIMANG POUO,T, UALONG PAGSASANAY.

¿Sino-sino ang naririyán.? Ang mañga anac nang iyòng caapidbáhay. ¿Anò,t, pinabayáan mo siláng pumásoc.? ¡Súlung!, ang panguinóong co,i, nagagálit. ¡úrong! ¡dalí! !Abá! ¿anò...? ¡Tabi! Sasagasain quitá nang mañga calabáo. ¿Natapus na nilá ang gauá.? Tapus na. ¡Butí ñga.! ¿Naalamán mo cun anò ang nangyari,? Hindí, ¿anò? Ang cabayo nang insic, ay sungmagasa sa anac nang iyòng caibigan, at ang bata,i, namatáy. ¡Caáua-áua.! Sáyang at di co hauac ang aquing baril. ¿Sáan nañgagpapatacbò-tacbò ang mañga bata.? Sa bacooran. Cayó, mañga malilicot, ¡houag maiñgáy!, palabasín mo silá. ¡lintic!, tinutuntoñgan nilá ang aquing halaman. ¿Namamasdán mo bagáng pagcagandà-gandà ang caniyàng pinsáng babaye.? Oo,t, mahinhing-mahinhín pa siyá. ¿Ytiniric na bagá nang mañga mangagauá ang mañga tulos sa bacóod.? Pinapasán pa lamang. ¿Sáan mo ybinaón ang iyòng anac.? Ytò, ang pinagbaonán namin sa caniyà. ¿Sino-sino ang nagpasán nang cabáon.? Ang mañga caescuela niyà ang nagpas-án. ¿Anòng tinutúnao niyóng insic dóon.? Tungmutúnao nang pagquit. ¿Binucsán mo na ang iyòng cabán.? Hindí pa. Pabucsán mo capagdaca. ¿Anò ang ypinagcacatipon nang ganiyán caraming tauò.? Nagcacatipon silá, at sasalubong at babati sa Hocom dahil sa mabuting paglating. ¿Báquit binabaloctoc nang panday-bácal ang dolo niyóng sibat.? Caniyàng binabaloctot, at gagaoin pangapas. ¿Sáan nilá binili ang mañga dedal.? Canilàng binili sa isàng tindahan nang sarisari. ¿Anò mayróon ca sa iyòng halamanan.? Acó,i, mayróon sarisaring cáhoy at mañga bulac-lac na sarisaring cúlay. ¿Anòng sinisiloan mo.? Nañgiñgilo acó nang machin. ¿Anòng ypinapáin mo sa panhuhuli sa canilà.? Ang guinagámit cong páin ay niog. ¿Sino ang hinahalinhán nang iyòng anac.? Hinahalinhán niyà ang caniyàng pinsán. ¿Sinong Santo ang pinipintacasi mo sa Dios.? Si San Patricio ang pintacasi co. ¿Cailán ang piesta nang pintacasi nitòng bayang itò.? Ang Santong pintacasi, ay Si San Juan at ang capistaha,i, 24 nang Junio. ¿Nagpangap sino siyá.? Siyá,i, nagpangap oficial (Sp.). ¿Sinong dinayà niyà sa pagbabalintuna.? Maramì ang caniyàng binalintuna. ¿Nacapagbibigáy alin sa iyò ang pañgañgabayo.? Ang pañgañgabayo,t, paglañgoy ay nacapagbibigáy tóua sa aquin. ¿Niuaualáng halagá niyà siyá.? Hindí niyà siyá pinauaualáng halagá. ¿Ang mañga Pare bagá, ay pinauaualáng halagá nang lahat.? Silá,i, pinagpipitagan nang mabubuting tauò,t, pinauaualáng halagá namán nang masasamá. ¿Anò ang ypinagpapalalo nang ganiyán niyóng tauò.? Dahil sa ang caniyàng cayamana,i, naragdagan nang isáng mana. ¿Dahil bagá diyán cayá siyá nagmamatáas nang paganiyán.? Dahil ñga diyán: ñguní,t, siyá,i, nacahihiya at ang caniyàng quilos ay nacaaáua. ¿Anòng nangyayari.? May tauòng nalulúnod sa ílog. ¿Anòng ating gagaoin nang siyá,i, maligtás.? Taponan mo niyáng cáhoy, nang siyá,i, macapañgapit. ¿Nacapitan na niyá.? Hindí, ñguní,t, caniyáng cacapitan, siyá,i, tila nañgoñgolila. ¿Naaninagan na bagá ang bágay.? Hindí nañganinag. ¿Saán naróon ang usá.? Pungmásoc sa síit. ¿Anòng guinagamitan niyáng lilic.? Ypinañgañganì nang pálay. ¿Di bagá pangapas sa damó ó, guinagámit sa pagcaiñgin.? Hindí. ¿Saáng niyà dinadalà iyàng guiniican.? Hinahácot niyà sa bacooran. ¿Tinuca ca bagá nang ahas.? Hindí, cundí acó,i, siniguid nang mañga lamoc. ¿May pauican bagá ditò sa ílog na itò.? Maramì. ¿Ang mañga cala nilá,i, mayróon cayáng quinagagamitan.? Mabutì sa maraming bágay. ¿Báquit nililís ni Ana ang naguas niyá, nang siyá,i, tungmatauid sa dáan.? Dahil sa maputic.

YCALIMANG POUO.T, SIYAM NA PAGSASANAY.

¿Ybig mo acóng samahan.? Oo, sasamahan quitá. ¿Napasasáan ca.? Acó,i, mamimíuas. ¿Anó,t, iyòng tinutuyá ang mañga cababayan mo.? Di co silá tinutuyá. Ñguní,t, pinipintasán mo silá; ¿di mo natanantó pa ang mamintás sa ibá,i, pañgit na gauá. ¿Anò ang lalo mong hinahañgaán.? Ang pinaguiguilalasán co,i, ang mañga catacatacan bágay na quinapal nang Dios, at tañgi co pang tinatac-há,i, ang cariquitan nang mañga bituín sa Lañgit. ¿Mapagcacatiualáan bagá.? Di súcat siláng pagcatiualáan. ¿Di súcat bagá siláng pagcatiualáan niyaóng bágay.? Ayauán co. ¿Maari pa cayáng acó,i, gumaling.? Maari ca pang gumaling.? Macapasasa Maynila ca bagá.? Di acó macapasa Maynila at acó,i, may saquit. ¿Macapasa Maynila ang capatid mong lalaqui.? Di siyá macapasa Maynila, sa pagca,t, siyá,i, maraming abala. ¿Ytòng gamot ay macaguiguinhauà cayá sa may saquit.? Marahil, ay macaguinhauà sa caniá. ¿Sáan naroróon ang caguinoohan nitòng bayan.? Nasasasimbahan silá. Ytòng báhay bagá mayróon paligóan.? Mayróon ditò isàng paligóan nang tauòng malalaqui na, ang mañga cabatáa,i, sa ílog naliligo. ¿Anòng guinagámit nang mañga tagálog sa pag-inum.? Ang inumang pinacabaso nang mañga tagálog, ay mañga tabo (the nut of the cocoa-nut fruit when already washed clean.) ¿Sáan naróon ang paahan nitòng laráuan.? Na sa silid. ¿Sáan nagcacatipon ang mañga tagálog.? Nañgagcacatipon sa saboñgán. ¿Mayróon bagáng tubohán ang caibigan mo.? Ualá siyáng tubohán, cundí mayróon siyáng dalauàng niogan. ¿Cailán ca dungmating.? Cararating co pa. ¿Sáan naróon ang pañginóon mo.? Caális pa niyà. ¿Naquita mo ang caniyàng asáua.? Capapásoc pa lámang niyà sa báhay nang aquing maquita. ¿Ybig mo maquipananhali sa amin.? Hindí, capananánghali co pa lámang. ¿Anòng aquing gagaoin.? Caiísip ca nóon at caiíñgat ca. ¿Anòng nangyari sa iyò.? Calacalácad co pa lámang ay natísod na acó. ¿Sáan ca nadulás.? Dóon. dóo,i, mayróong quinadudulasan at acó,i, natísod sa batohán. ¿Naquita mo ang libro.? Cahahánap co pa lámang ay naquita co na. ¿Gaanò cahabá.? Casinghabá nitò. ¿Matigás bagá iyáng cáhoy.? Gabatò catigás. ¿Anò ang cauanqui nang panique.? Gaibon (or ga sa isàng ibon) cun lungmilipad. ¿Sino sino ang quinacaúsap.? Quinacaúsap co ang aquing casangbáhay. ¿Sino ang cacasamahin mo sa paglalacbáy.? Ang iyòng caáuay. ¿Mañga olila bagá silá.? Oo, cahapis-hapis ang maolila. ¿Tinicmán mo ang mañga piña.? Oo, catamis-tamís. ¿Anòng guinagauá niyóng mañga tauò sa dalampásig.? Nañgagliligo silá; cahalay-hálay panoorin nang mañga lalaqui,t, babayeng magcasamà sa pagligo. ¿Lungmañgóy ca bagá.? Oo, acó,i, lungmañgóy, catóua-tóua ang paglañgóy.

YCAANIM NA POUONG PAGSASANAY.

¿Gagaoin co bagá iyán.? Houag mong gaoin iyán macá mapacasamà ca. ¿Aalís bagá acó.? Umalís ca,t, magpacaíñgat, houag mong pabayáan gaoin ang sinabi co sa iyò. ¿Acó,i, papanhic.? Houag cang pumanhic macá mag tauò sa itáas. ¿Anòng gagaoin mo.? Acó,i, mamíminuit upan acó,i, macaby nuit. ¿Báquit di niyà binubuhat ang bayong.? Bubuhatin niyà cun caniyàni mabubuhat. ¿Pinana bagá nilá ang mañga ibon.? Pinana nilá.t, silá,i, nacapana. ¿Hinábol mo bagá siyá.? Siyá,i, hinábol co, ñguní,t, di naábot siyá. ¿Ybig mong acó.i, umalís ñgayón.? Houag cang umalís ñgayón, maca maaráuan ca,t, mainitan. ¿Malaláuon acó ditò.? Hindí, alís ca na, bacá magabihan ca sa gúbat. ¿Anòng nangyari sa canilà.? Silá,i, naglaláyag, ay inabutan nang báguio sa dágat. ¿Anong nangyari sa iyo.? Ang báhay namin ay nasónog. ¿Anòng nangyari.? Napatid ang simúlid. ¿Anòng nangyari sa iyòng bayáo.? Naualán siyá nang lacás, naualán nang díua, nabulagan siyá nang ísip, napatirán nang hiniñgá at siyá,i, namatáy. ¿Napaanò iyán.? Nabalían siyá nang tungcod, at nabalían nang paà. (buco nang paà). Báquit ca tungmatáua.? Tungmatáua acó dáhil sa yaóng tauo, ay natísod at narapá. ¿Aacayin co siyá.? Hindí, palacarin mo siyá untí-untí, bacá madulás. ¿Natatácot ca.? Oo, acó,i, natatácot. ¿Anòng quinatatacotan mo.? Ang mañga calolóua nang nañgamatáy, ang aquing quinatatacotan. ¿Anò,t, natatácot ca sa mañga multo. (Sp. muerto).? Catatacotan mo, ang Dios at houag ang mañga multo na di ca maaanò. ¿Sáan ca natísod.? Ang quinatisoran co,i, itòng batò. ¿Sáan báhay namatáy ang iyòng iná.? Sa báhay nang aming nono. ¿Anòng yquinamatáy niyà. Ang yquinamatáy niyá i, lagnat. ¿Báquit tungmatañgís iyáng babaye.? Sa pagca.t, namatayán siyá nang bungsò. Di co naquiquita ang capatid mong babaye, ¿saán narorôon.? Naróroon nacaluhod siyá sa may altar (Sp.) At ang capatid mong lalaqui, ¿saán namán naróon.? Naróon namán nacatindíg sa may haligue. ¿Di bagá yaóng nauupó sa banco (Sp.)? Hindí, cundí yaón na sa píling niyá. ¿Sino ang iyong inaama.? Ang inaamá co ay ang amá nang caibigan cong si Cárlos, at ang aquing iniiná,i, ang caniyàng capatid na babaye. ¿Yniiyò mo bagá iván.? Hindí, quinacanilà co. ¿Anò ang lagáy nang palayan mo.? Binálang. ¿Guinagalís bagá ang iyòng alila.? Hindí, siyá,i, hinihica. ¿Sinisicmura bagá siyá.? Hindí. sungmasaquit ang camáy niyà. ¿Ang amá niyà,i, tiyanín bagá.? Hindí, siyá,i, ulohan. ¿Sáan mo ynilagáy ang guiniican.? Ynilagáy co sa dacong ualisan. ¿Masunurin bagá ang iyòng alila.? Hindí, subali siyá,i, masouáin. ¿May pílac bagá sa caja (Sp.)? Oo, mapílac ang caja. ¿Mauiuica bagá itòng letra (Sp)? Magáang uicain. ¿Maiinum cayá ang túbig sa dágat.? Di mainum. ¿Ang lason ay macamamatáy bagá.? Ang lason ay macamamatáy. ¿Ang cura bagá, ay hicáin.? Hindí, siyá,i, piyohin. ¿Ang mañga quislap ay nacapapañganit bagá.? Oo, isàng quislap, ay macasosónog sa isàng báyan. ¿Macacáin bagá ang camote.? Oo, ñguní,t, cun minsá,i, macasusuya. ¿Nacasúlit ca bagá.? Hindí, di aco nacasúlit.

YCAANIM NA PÒUO T. ISANG PAGSASANAY.

¿Sino-sino yaóng dalauàng babaye.? Silá,i, maghípag. ¿Sino-sino iyáng mañga tauò.? Silá,i, ang maggúlang nitòng bata. ¿Sino yaóng lalaqui,t, yaóng babaye nacaupó dôon.? Silá,i, magasáua. ¿Magcapatid bagá yaóng dalauàng lalaqui.? Silá,i, magcapatid. ¿Yaóng tatlòng bata, ay magcacasamà bagá.? Silá,i, magcacasamà. ¿At itòng dalauà ay magcaibigan.? Silá,i, magcaibigan. ¿Napasasimbahan bagá ang magamá.? Ang magamá gayón din ang magpañginóon ay napasasimbahan cañginang umaga. ¿Naririrò cayá ang mag-iná ni Juan.? Ang mag-amá ni María ang naririto. ¿Nagpasial ca bagá cahapòn.? Maghapon acóng nagpasial. ¿Naróon ca sa báhay nang capidbáhay mo cagabi.? Magdamag acó róon. ¿Naparitò bagá ang magsasacà.? Naparitò. ¿Naquilala bagá ang magnanacao.? Hindí. ¿Magcanò ang ybabáyad co ditò sa mañga maghahabí.? Mamiso ang ybáyad mo sa canilà. ¿Gaano cayá ang ybinigáy niyà sa canilà. Manbara ang ybinigáy niyà. ¿Gaanòng bigás ang tinangap nang bálang isà.? Mañgabán ang tinangap nilà. ¿Yláin salop na bigás ang ypinagbili niyà sa báua,t isàng mangagapas.? Manalop ang ypinagbili niyà. ¿Mananahi bagá ang caibigan mo.? Hindí, siyá,i, manunúlat. ¿Sino ang manunubos nang sangcatauohan.? Si Jesucristo,i, ang manunubos nang sangcatauohan. ¿Naquita mo ang manunúlid.? Hindí, ang naquita co,i, ang manghihínang. ¿Sáan naróon ang manglalagari.? Ang manglalagari ay nasasabáhay nang mañgañgálcal. ¿Mañgiñgisdá bagá siyá.? Hindí, siyá,i, mañgañgaso. ¿Anò ang sinabi nang mangagamot.? Inotos niyà sa mandarágat na maligo sa túbig na mainit. ¿Mapagpatubò bagá itóng tauòng itò.? Siyá,i, mapagacsayá. ¿Ang anac nang ating caapidbáhay ay mapagpitagan.? Siyá,i, hindí mapagpitagan, cundí bagcús mapagpalalo,t, mapagbulong. ¿Ycáo ñga bagá,i, mapaglibac.? Di acó, mapaglibac, cundí mapagmasid. ¿Nagcacasiyà bagá diyán sa bote ang isàng gátang.? Hindí nagcacasiyà ang isàng gátang. ¿Anòng nangyari sa Pare.? Siyá,i, nagcamalí. ¿Maguiguing totoò bagá ang sinabi sa atin nang Americano.? Maguiguing totoò maráhil. ¿Báquit nanghihimásoc cang maquipagsalitá sa mañga alila nang aquing caapidbáhay.? Sa pagca,t, silá,i, táuag nang táuag sa aquin. ¿Anò,t, ang mañgañgálcal ay pasial nang pasial límang.? Sa pagca,t, siyá,i, mapaglígao. ¿Anòng ypagagauá mo sa aquin? Bumasà ca nang bumasà ¿Baquit hindí ca nagdarasal.? Dáhil sa ang pañginóon co,i, táuag nang táuag sa aquin. ¿Inanó co.? Acó,i, tinatáua nang tinatáua nitóng mañga maglílimpáy. ¿Aanhin mo 'váng aspiler.? Aquing ypanhihiñgan. ¿Maanò na ang anac na babaye nang manunulat.? Mabúti na.

YCAANIM NA POUO,T, DALAUANG PAGSASANAY.

¿Anòng parusá sa iyò nang Hocom.? Minultahan acó nang dalauàng póuong piso. ¿Anòng pamana sa iyò nang iyòng amáin.? Ang pamana niyà sa aquing ay isàng libòng piso. ¿Totoò bagá iyán.? Ytong mañga uicang itò ang napapalamán sa caniyàng súlat. ¿Aòng pagcáin iyán.? Pamáhao co itò. ¿Anòng padalá ni Couán.? Ytò ang padalà niyà. ¿Yyo bagá iyán pamutas.? Hindí, itò,i, pahiram sa aquin nang anlouague. ¿Paanò ang pagauá co.? Gaoin mong paupó. ¿Paanò ang aquing pagpótol nitò.? Potlín mong pahalang. ¿Paanò ang pagdarasal co.? Dápat cang magdasal na paluhod. ¿Patindig bagá siyá o pahigá. Siyá,i, pahigá. ¿Paanò ang panalita niyà. Ang caniyàng panalita ay útal. ¿Paano ang pagcadios nang Dios.? Ang pagcadios nang Dios ay di matingcalá nang tauo. Siyà bagá palasampalataya.? Hindí, siyá,i, palaanito. ¿Ang caibigan mo bagá,i, palainum nang álac.? Di palainum nang álac, ñguni,t, palacáin. ¿Palasintà bagá ang pinsán mong lalaqui. Siyá,i, palasintà,t, palauica. ¿Palayabang namán bagá siyá.? Siyá,i, palayabang at palausap. ¿Anò iyán nasasacamáy nang iyong manunúlat.? Ysàng panatac. ¿Di bagá isàng pamutas.? Hindí, isàng pañgáhit. ¿Sáan ynilagáy nang alila ang pamáhid.? Ynilagáy niyà casamá nang panípit. ¿Anòng gagaoin mo nitòng pangapas.? Ygagapas co nang damó. ¿Sinòng nacaquita nang pamocpoc anlouague.? Si Pedro ang nacaquita sa panhácot. ¿Na sa canino bagá ang panaroc.? Na sa mandarágat gayon din ang pañgámot. ¿Sáan naróon ang panúlat co.? Ang iyong panúlat at pañgáhit ay quinuha. ¿Ualá ca bagáng pañgúhit na ypañgúhit nitóng papel.? Mayróon acóng i.ò. ¿Sáan naróon ang panali na ytali ditò sa mañga cáhoy.? Ang pantali ay na sa bahay.

YCAANIM NA POUO.T, TATLONG PAGSASANAY.

¿Anòng pinacatinápay sa pagcáin nang mañga tagálog.? Ang canin sa canilà, paris nang tinápay sa atin. ¿Sino ang pinacapono ninyò ñgayón.? Ang Pare ang pinacapono namin. ¿Anòng pinacamalaqui sa lahat nang casamáan.? Ang pinacamalaqui sa lahat nang casamáan, ay ang sala. ¿Anòng ynilinis na pinacaualís nang alila mo sa silid.? Ang guinámit niyàng pinacaualís, ay isàng cauayan. ¿Anòng yguinagálang mo nang ga-niyáng paggálang sa iyòng amaín.? Dáhil sa siyá,i, aquing pinacaamá. ¿Anó ang pinacatenedor nang mañga tagálog sa pagcáin.? Ang canilàng mañga daliri ang pinacatenedor nilá. ¿Anòng yguinauá mo nang súlat.? Acó,i, ualáng panúlat at ang guinámit cong pinacapluma, ay itòng ba-guís. ¿Anòng calagayan sa caniyà nang caniyàng pamangquín.? Ca-niyàng pinacaalila. ¿Gaanò ang calauonan mo sa Maynila.? Ang láuon co, dóon, ay sang árao. ¿Naghintáy ca bagá sa caniyàng maláuon.? Hinintáy co siyáng sang oras. ¿Hangán cailán siyá matitirá sa atin.? Siyá,i, matitiráng sang lingo ditò. ¿Sa ganáng iláng taón ang cau-pahán pagbabayaran nang bungmobouís sa atin.? Ang pagbabayaran ni-yà,i, ang sa ganán sangtaón.? Anòng guinauá nang sang Maynila, di iilán taón ang láuon, nang silá,i, datnán nang malacás na lindol.? Ang sang Maynila,i. nanaclò sa labás nang báyan. ¿Gaanò carami ang sanganacan háyop.? Ang sanganacan, ay pitòng bilot (cubs, puppies). ¿Sáan naróon ang dáuong.? Ang dáuong ay lungmubod, at ang sangsa-sáquián tauò, ay nañgalunod. ¿Yláng casacáy sa bangca ang dungmating sa lupa.? Ang sangsasaquián tauò, ay napasaguílid. ¿Ualá bagá nani-nirá sa bayang itò.? Ang sangbayanan ay nañgagsisimbà ñgayón. ¿Uala bagáng naninirá ditò sa búhay.? Ang sangbahayán ay nañgamatáy. ¿Sino ang tungmubós sa sangcatauohan.? Si Jesucristo ang siyáng tungmubós sa sangcatauohan, at siyá,i, sinasambà nang sangcacristianohan. ¿Na-ñgálat bagá ang sálot.? Ang sálot ay nañgálat sa sangcapolóan. ¿Taga-anòng panahón catá ñgayón.? ¿Nasatag-init tayo.? Quinauiuilihan mo bagá ang tag-lamig.? Di co íbig ang tag-lamig; iyá,i, panahón maguináo na lub-há. ¿Sa anòng mañga bóuan nang taón nagtstag-amihan.? Na-tatagamihan sa Pilipinas mulá sa Noviembre hangáng Junio. ¿Anòng panahón tagbaguió sa Maynila.? Mulá sa calahatian nang Octubre han-gán sa catapusán nang Diciembre. ¿Gaanò ang caupahán ybinabáyad niyá sa tagatanod nang caniyàng cábang háyop.? Binabayaran niyá ang caniyàng tagatanod sa mañga háyop nang sang póuong piso bóuan-bóuan. ¿Tig-ilán ang pamamahagui niyà nang candila.? Tig-isà ang ybi-nigáy niyà sa lalaqui; tigalauà, ang babaye; tig-atlò ang bata. ¿Sino ang caunaunahang tauò.? Si Adán ang caunaunahan lalaqui; at Si Eva ang caunaunahang babaye. ¿Ycailáng librong iyán.? Ytó,i, ang ycatlòng *tomo* (Sp.).

YCAANIM NA POUO.T, APAT NA PAGSASANAY.

¿Anòng bibilhin co *para* (Sp.) sa caniyàng mañga bata.? Ýbili mo nang iláng laróan. ¿Pahahanapin co ang alila nang tinápay.? Pahanapin. ¿Papataín co ang sasabuñgin.? Patayí. ¿Anòng dápat niyàng gauin niyàn salapí." Ysaolí. ¿Acala mo cayá,i, may salaping casiyahan.? Acala co.i, naláng casiyahan. ¿Anòng ibig niyà.i, inúmin. ¿Maano siyá.? Tila.i, malubháng saquit. ¿Anòng sabì sa caniyà nang iyòng mañga capatid na babaye? Sinabìng, silá,i, pariritò sa á los seis. ¿Anòng ganáng cay Mr. Reynolds.? Ang sabì, magtatayó nang isàng bayuhan. ¿Anò,t, naglalácad ca.? Mabuti ang maglácad sa mañgabayo. ¿Anòng dalà mo.? Dinadalhín quitá nang aseite (Sp. aceite). ¿Abáa hunghang na hunghang itòng bata; sabì co,i, túbig ang dalhín ay aseite ang dinalà. itòng tauòng itò,i, sungmasamà,t, tila mabutìng hampasín. ¿Báquit nasira nang ganiyán iyán damit.? Dáhil sa inánay. ¿Sáan naróon ang buñgang inouac.? Ytinapon co sa mañga bábuy. ¿Anò ang linangam.? Ang mañga pananim sa aquing halamanan, ay linangam ang lahat at ang mañga cáhuy, ay inungcal nang bábuy. ¿Anòng dalà niyà sa paglalacad.? May bauon siyá sa paglalácad. ¿Anòng bihasang daguitín nang mañga láuin.? Ang mañga sísiu ang dinadáguit nang mañga láuin. ¿Anò,t, masamá ang pagcaloto sa pagcáin.? Sa pagca,t, dinali-dalí nang cosinero. ¿Binasà mo bagá ang periódico (Sp.) na ypinahiram co sa iyò cahapon.? Hinapáo co lámang (ang pagbasà). ¿Paanhín co itòng pagsasalin.? Utáy-utayin mo (ang pagsasalin). ¿Naglalámay ca bagá sa pagdarasal.? Naglalámay acó sa pagdarasal. ¿Quinusà bagá niyà.? Quinusà niyà. ¿Mabuti bagá ang pangyayari nitòng súlat.? Hindí, bagohin mo. Gungmámit baga siyá nang sangcap pandáy sa pagganá niyán.? Hindí, quinímot niyà. ¿Gungmaganá bagá ang anlouague sa arauán ó sa pacquiaoan.? Punnapacquí.io siyá. ¿Tinastás mo ang iyòng baro.? Hindí co pa tinatastás. ¿Guinisì bagá ni Pedro ang mañga dahon libro.? Guinisì. ¿Paanòng bungmiac nang buñga ang nono mong babaye.? Binibiac niyà sa ñgalot. ¿Bibigtalín bagá nang capatid mong babaye ang sing-sing.? Bibigtalín niyà. ¿Napatid bagá ang lúbid.? Oo, napatid na. ¿Sino ang tinampal niyà.? Ang tinampal niyá,i, ang caniyàng alila. ¿Báquit di pinagpag nang capatid cong lalaqui ang damit.? Siyá,i, bungmayò. ¿Anò,t, ang anac mo,i, nagtatapon nang buñga nang cáhoy.? Siyá,i, naglilíbang sa pagtatálang. ¿Anòng guinagauá niyaóng mañga bata.? Hinahaguis nilà nang batò ang cabayo mo. ¿Mahihiram co bagá iyáng libro.? Conin. ¿Sáan co ylalagáy itòng mañga papel.? Ytapon mo. ¿Nasasáan ang mañga' ibon.? Naririyán. tingnán mo. ¿Ybig mong bilhin nang iyòng caibigan ang cabayo.? Bilhin niyà. ¿Anòng tinitignán mo.? Tinitingnán co ang mañga bitouin sa lañgit na nañgagniningning na lubhá. ¿Anòng quiniquita mo rián sa bintana (Sp. ventana).? Quiniquita co ang aquing anac na canicañgina.i, naquiquipaglaró sa mañga caescuela niyà at ñgayó,i, di co naquiquita. ¿Sino ang liniliñgon ni Pedro.? Liniliñgon niyà Si María natirá sa batis. ¿Anò ang iyòng napanóod sa teatro.? Pinanooran co dóon ang pagpatáy sa Haring Ricardong ycatatlò. ¿Anòng guinagauá nang dalauàng magcaibigán.? Silá,i, nagsusuliapan. ¿Anò,t, di ca ungmaacquiat diyán sa cáhuy. Dáhil sa acó,i, natatácot na macá mo acó tiñgaláin.? ¿Mulá sa saán mo tinanáo ang sasaquián.? Tinanáo co mulá sa taloctoc niyaóng bondoc. ¿Anò,t, acó,i, tinititigan nang capatid niyáng babaye.? Sa pagca,t, icáo, ay naiibigan.

YCAANIM NA POUO,T, LIMANG PAGSASANAY.

¿Anò ang cahulugán nang "fit".? Ysàng biglàng saquit. ¿Anòng cahulugán nang aisoleiter.? Napapag-isà. ¿Anò bagá ang meison.? Ang mangagáua nang báhay na batò. ¿Anò ang Coran.? Ang Coran ay ang inaarìng Santong Súlat nang mañga Turco, sa macatouid, ay isàng librong quinapapalamnán nang mañga utos ni Mahoma. ¿Anò bagá ang isàng verhaus.? Ysàng báhay ó camálig na pinagtatagúan nang sarisaring (calácal). ¿Anò ang isàng *ocson*.? Ang pagbibili sa háyag nang pag-ari na católong at ca-alam ang *Justicia*. ¿Anò ang isàng *harang*.? Ysàng di maláuig na pananaysáy ó pahayag nang isàng Pono sa caniyàng mañga sácop. ¿Ano ang *úmnesti*.? Ysàng patáuad ó paglímot nang Hari nang caniyáng gálit sa mañga souail na tauò. ¿Anò ang *anasim*.? Ang pagtatacuil sa Yglesia sa tauòng hungmahámac nang caniyàng cautusan. ¿Anò ang *Anásomi*.? Ysàng carunúñgang naoócol sa pagcacabahagui nang cataoán. ¿Anòng cahulugán nang *ampibius*.? Ang cahulugán nang *ampibius*, ay isàng háyop na naaring mabúhay sa túbig at sa cati man. ¿Anòng cahulugán nang *antidilubian*.? Ang cahulugán nang *antidilubian* ay ang mañgoñgonà sa pagcagúnao. ¿Anò ang *Antipoup*.? Ang ungmaágao na ualáng carapatán sa pagcapapa nang Papa. ¿Anò ang isàng *antipoud*.? Ang tauòng tungmatahán sa lupang cabilá at catapat nang quinalalaguían natin. ¿Sino ang *canibal*.? Ang tauòng sungmisilà nang cápoua. ¿Anò ang isàng *uàrdrob*.? Ysàng tagúan nang damit. ¿Anò bagá ang *apendis*.? Ysàng dagdag sa isàng libro. ¿Anò ang *apóplesi*.? Ang panghihimatáy. ¿Anòng *apóstasi*.? Ang pagtalicod sa ating Pañginóong Jesucristo. ¿Anò cayá ang *apóstol*.? Ang *apóstol*, ay isàng alagad ni Jesucristo. ¿Anò bagá ang isàng *tárip*.? Upà, báyad ó halagúng túning nang mañga Pono. ¿Anò ang isàng *Arsipílagu*.? Dágat quinalalaguían nang maraming polo. ¿Anò bagá ang *arcaires*.? Ang lugar na pinagtatagúan nang mañga casulatan may halagá. ¿Anò ang *ármouri*.? Báhay ó camálig na pinagiíñgatan sa sarisaring sandatà. ¿Anò ang *hármoni*.? Ang cariquitan ó pagcacaayon-ayon nang tínig. ¿Anò ang isàng *árquitect*.? Ysàng marúnung gumauá nang mañga simbaha,t, báhay. ¿Anò ang *Astrónomi*.? Carunúñgang ócol sa mañga bituín. ¿Anò ang *áseist*.? Tauòng aayáo cumilala na may Dios. ¿Anò ang *bastard*.? Ysàng anac sa lígao. ¿Anò ang *baible*.? Ang librong quinapapalamán nang Santong Súlat. ¿Anò ang isàng *láibreri*.? Ang pinaglalaguian nang maraming libro. ¿Anò ang *bígami*.? Ang pagaásaua ulí na di dápat nang may asáua na. ¿Anò ang isàng *baiógrapi*.? Ysàng salitá nang búhay nang iisàng tauò. ¿Anò ang *boult*.? Ysàng lañgitlañgitan. ¿Anò ang *Bótani*.? Carunúñgang naoócol sa pagquilala nang mañga pananim. ¿Anò ang *brébiari*.? Ysàng librong quinatatalaán nang mañga dinadasal nang mañga Pare. ¿Anòng isàng *bula*.? (Sp.). Ysàng súlat na gáling sa Papa na quinalalamnán nang caniyàng calóob ó hátol. ¿Anò ang *leterbos*.? Ysàng butas na pinaghuhulugan nang súlat sa *correo*. ¿Anò ang *cábaldi*.? Ysàng hocbòng sacáy. ¿Anò ang isàng *compósitor*.? Tauòng nagsamà,t, naghahánay nang mañga letra sa limbagan. ¿Anò ang isàng *álmanac*.? Librong muntí na quinatataláan nang *piesta* nang mañga Santo. ¿Anong isàng *calis*.? Ysàng *copang* (Sp. *copa*) guintó o pílac na guinagámit sa pagmisa. ¿Anò ang *canon*? Ysàng capasiahan nang Santa Yglesia ócol sa pagsampalataya. ¿Anò ang isàng *cáos*.? Ang pagcacahalohalo nang lahat na bágay bagò linalang nang Dios. ¿Anò ang isàng *cárdinal*.? Ysàng matáas na Pareng casanguni nang Papa. ¿Anò ang *cháriti*.? Pag-íbig sa Dios at sa ating cápoua tauò. ¿Anò ang *chástiti*.? Ang pag-iíñgat sa cahalayan. ¿Sino ang tinatáuag na *Catéquiumen*.? Tauòng nagaáral nang dasalan. ¿Anò ang cahulugán nang *sénit*.? Ang daco nang Lañgit na natatapat sa ating ulò. ¿Anò ang *serresa*.? (Sp.) Ysàng ilac na ganitó ang ñgalan. ¿Anò ang *saians*.? Ang saians, ay carunúñgan. ¿Anò ang *siriliseshon*.? Pagcasúlong nang mañga baya,t, tauò sa carunúñgan. ¿Anò ang isàng *chimni*.? Ysàng pinagdadaanan nang asú. ¿Anò ang isàng *Coud*.? Ysàng catipunan nang mañga cautusa,t, pasià nang Hari. ¿Anò bagá ang isàng *coles*.? Ysàng bágay na gulayín. ¿Anò ang isàng *colegio* (Sp.). *colesh* (Eng. Tgz.).? Ysàng capisanan nang mañga tauòng tungmatahán sa isàng báhay na natatalagá sa pagtotoro at pagaáral nang carunúñgan. ¿Anò bagá ang isàng *cóloni*.? Capisanan nang mañga tauòng ypinadadala sa ibàng lupaín nang macapamayan dóon. ¿Anò ang *cónsiens*.? Pagcaquilala nang magaling na dápat sundín at nang masamáng, súcat pañgilagan. ¿Anò ang isàng *cónclave*.? Ang pagpopólong nang mañga *carde-*

aules sa paghalal nang Papa. ¿Anò ang isàng *cáunt.*" Tauòng may carangalan na gayòn ang tauag. ¿Anò ang isàng *conpésionery.*? Ysàng tindahan nang sarisaring matamís.

YCAANIM NA POUO.T, ANIM NA PAGSASANAY.

¿Anò ang isàng *conspírasi.*? Pagcacatipon sa paglaban sa isàng Pono. ¿Anò ang *conmemoreshun.*? Pagaalaalà. ¿Anò ang isàng *consteleshun.*? Ysàng catipunan nang mañga bitoín na hindí pabago-bago. ¿Anò ang *estrabio* (Sp.) *esmogling.* (Eng.).? Ysàng calácal na báual. ¿Anò ang isàng *convento.*? (Sp.) Tahanan nang mañga *praile* (Sp.) ó *monja.* (Sp.) ¿Anò ang isàng *coro.*? (Sp.) Ang lugar na pinagtitipunan nang mañga Pare sa pagdadasal. ¿Anò ang isàng *corus.*? Ysàng catipunan nang mañga tauòng nagaauit. ¿Anò ang isàng *coronel.*? (Sp.) Ysàng pono nang mañga sundalo. ¿Anò ang *cosmógoni.*? Ang carunuñgang nagpapaquilala sa atin nang lagáy at pagcaayari nitòng *mundo.* ¿Anò ang *cosmógrapi.*? Ysàng pagcasalaysáy nang calagayan nang ibá.t, ibàng bahagui nitòng *mundo.* ¿Anò ang isàng *cráter.*? Ang bibig nang mañga *bolcán.* ¿Anò ang isàng *criechur.*? Alin man bágay na linalang nang Dios. ¿Anò ang isàng *crusipiho* (Sp.) *crucifijo.*) Ang laráuan ni Jesucristo na napapaco sa *Cruz.* ¿Anò ang isàng *cuódrant.*? Ang ycaápat na bahagui nang mabílog. ¿Anò ang *cuaresma*" Ang panahóng nañguñgunâ sa Pascó nang pagcabúhay na sa mantala, ypinagbabáual nang *Yglesia Romana* ang pagsilà nang lamàngcati. ¿Anò ang isàng *borsdey.*? Ang úrao na caganapan nang taón mulá sa capañganacan nang isàng tauò. ¿Anò ang *Dicálongue.*? Ang sampouong utos nang Dios. ¿Anò ang isàng *déntist.*? Ysàng mangagamot, manlilinis at manghuhúsay nang ñgipin. ¿Anò ang isàng *dispensa*? (Sp.) *despensa.*) Tagúan nang mañga pagcáin. ¿Anò ang isàng *dicshionari.*? Librong parang tandáan na quinasusulatan nang lahát na uica. ¿Anò ang isàng *dínasti.*? Ang pagcacasonodsonod nang mañga Hari na iisàng lahi. ¿Anò ang isàng *Dioses.*? Lupang nasasacupan nang isàng obispo. ¿Anò ang isàng *Diríniti.*? Ang pagcadios nang Dios. ¿Anò ang *sélpisnes.*? Lábis na pagiíbig sa caniyàng catauán lámang. ¿Anò ang *imigreshun.*? Pag-alís nang tauò pasaibáng lupaín. ¿Anò ang *tu peic.*? Maglátag nang mañga bató. ¿Anò ang isàng *pòrenar.*? Ysàng tauòng tagá ibàng lupaín. ¿Anò ang *Erangelio.*? (Sp) Librong quinasasaysayan nang búhay ni Jesucristo. ¿Anò ang *pemenino.*" (Sp.) *femenino.*) Ang naoócol sa babaye. ¿Anò ang isàng *pétus.*? Batang nasasatiyán pa. ¿Anò ang *Pilántropi.*? Pag-íbig sa ating cápoua tauò. ¿Anò ang *to esmour.*? Manabaco, manigarrillo. ¿Anò ang *general.*? Ysàng pono nang hocbò. ¿Anò ang *Gloria.*? Loualhati. ¿Anò ang *gréitpulnes*" Pagquiquilala nang útang na lóob. ¿Anò ang *gramática*? (Sp.) Ang capisanan nang mañga panotong casangcapan sa mahúsay na pananalitá,t, pagsúlat. ¿Anò ang *impantri.*? Hocbòng lácad. ¿Anò ang isàng *poni.*? Ysàng cabayong muntí. ¿Anò ang *másquiulin.*? Ang naoócol sa lalaqui. ¿Anò ang isàng *pishunhoul.*? Ysàng lapati. ¿Anò ang *uomb.*? Ang búhay bata. ¿Sino ang *Papa.* (Sp.) Ang lalong matáas na *Pontipise* (Sp.) sa Roma. ¿Anòng isàng *párable.*? Ysàng talinghaga. ¿Anò ang *Paraiso.*? (Sp.) Ysàng pag-guinhauahan. ¿Anò ang *pátriotism.*? Pag-íbig sa caniyàng tinubúan lupa. ¿Anòng isàng *piedestal.*? Ysàng tontoñgan. ¿Anò ang isàng *pilar.*? Ysang haliguing bató. ¿Anò ang isàng *pulgada.*? (Sp.) Ang sangdaliri. ¿Sino ang isàng *Reina.*? (Sp.) Ysàng haring babaye ¿Anò ang isàng *Sacramento.*? (Sp.) Ysàng gamot sa calolóua. ¿Anò ang *sagrado.*? (Sp.) Ang naoócol sa Dios. ¿Anò ang isàng *siglo.*? (Sp.) Ang sangdáang taón. ¿Anò ang *síntax.*? Hánay nang pañgoñgósap. ¿Anòng isàng *taiara.*? Ysàng pótong nang Papa.

YCAANIM NA POUO,T, PITONG PAGSASANAY.

Catotohanan. Cotdín mo iyáng bata. Caalipnán. Asnán mo iyang isdá. Babhín mo ang haligue. Bathín mo ang parusà. Bay-ín mo iyáng pálay. Big-yán mo acó nang tinápay. Bilhín mo ang lañgís. Boc-dán mo acó nang dalauà. Buc-sán mo ang cubán. Di co macamtán. Ytò,i, canin. Captán mo iyáng cuchiyo (Sp. cuchillo). Dacpín mo ang magnanácao. Damtín mo itòng baro. Dantán mo iyáng bata. Dalhín mo ritò iyán. Dalhín mo sa iyòng amá. Dapán mo itòng banig. Dictán mo nitòng papel ang dingding. ¿Sino ang dininggán mo niyán? Lumohod ca at diphán mo ang harapán nitòng laráuan. Gaoin mo. Acó,i, nahalatán ni Juan nagagálit. Hapnán mo iyáng alpa (Sp. arpa). Hascán mo ang halamanan nitòng pálay. Hirmín mo itò. Higán mo ang sahig. Hinanctán mo ang iyòng caibigan. Hiñgán mo si Juan nang piso. Hintín mo ang iyòng inà. Hiñgotán mo iyáng mahírap. Ibhín mo ang uica. Igbán mo ang batis. Ihán mo itòng *orinola* (Sp.). Ibsán mo itòng alila. Limhán mo acó nang upa. Laguián mo ang lamesa niyán. Palugdán mo iyáng sangol. Lurán mo siyá. Lisán mo siyá. Mamayin mo iyán. Malán mo ang súlat. Masdán mo ang aso, macá bañgáo. Pasimúlan mo ang gauá. Nibsán mo itòng tongcod. Ulín mo ang uica. Palagyán mo ang vaso nang servesa. Palamnán mo ang súlat nang mabubuting hátol. Pañgalán mo ang iyòng inaanac. Paquingán mo acó. Patdín mo iyáng masamáng ugali. Piguín mo iyáng dáyap. Pighán mo ang ulo. Pisín mo iyáng itlog. Pislín ang aquing camáy. Ponán mo iyáng tapayan. Pinapausán siyá. Putlán mo nang isàng vara iyáng cayo. Putín mo iyáng mañga salaual. Quibtín mo ang asúcal. Quitlín mo iyáng bulac-lac. Sacyán mo iyáng cabayo. Salitín mo ang sinalitá niyà. Sanghán mo ang manga nang mamoñga nang marami. Saulán mo Si Isco nang salapí. Houag mong pagsicpín ang iyòng lóob. Sig-án mo iyáng súcal. Silín mo iyáng lamangcati. Sundín mo ang amá mo. Tac-hán mo ang cadaquiláan nang Dios. Tacpán mo iyáng pingán. Tag-ín mo iyáng cáhuy. Talicdán mo siyá. Tañgán mo ang candila. Tayán mo ang gúflid. Ticmán mo ang ságuing. Tic-sín mo iyán. Tingnán mo. Tipdín mo ang iyòng salapí. Tirán mo siyá nang canin. Tisdán mo nang suclay niyáng cuto. Tubsín mo ang iyòng sanlá. Tuyín mo iyáng damit. Ualín mo ang útang co sa iyò.

YCAANIM NA POUO,T, TATLONG PAGSASANAY.

ANG AMA NAMIN.

Amá naming sungmasalañgit ca, sambahin ang ñgalan mo; mapasaamin ang caharían mo; sundín ang lóob mo ditò sa lupa, para nang sa láñgit. Big-yán mo camí ñgayón nang aming cacanin sa árao-árao, at patauarin mo camí nang aming mañga útang, para nang pagpatáuad namin sa nañgagcacaútang sa amin, at houag mo caming ypahintúlot sa tucsò, bagcús yadyá mo camí sa diláng masamá. Amén Jesús.

ANG ABA GUINOONG MARIA.

Abáa guinoóng María, napupuno ca nang grasia, ang Pañginóong Dios ay sungmasaiyó, bucod cang pinagpala sa babayeng lahat, at pinangpala namán ang Iyòng Anac na Si Jesús. Santa María, Inà nang Dios, ypanalañgin mo caming macasalanan. ñgayón at cung camí mamatáy. Amén Jesús.

ANG SUNGMASAMPALATAYA.

Sungmasampalataya acó sa Dios amá, macapangyayari sa lahat na may gauá nang Láñgit at nang lupa. Sungmasampalataya acó cay Jesucristo, iisàng anac nang Dios, Pañginóong nating lahat, nagcatauán tauò siyá lalang nang Dios Espíritu Santo, ypinañganac ni Santa Maríang Virgen, pinapagcasaquit ni Poncio Pilato, ypinaco sa Cruz, namatáy, ybináon; nanáog sa mañga iufiernos, nang may ycatlòng árao nabúhay na nag–olí, nac–yat sa Láñgit, naloloclot sa canan nang Dios Amáng macapangyayarì sa lahat, dóon magmumulá,t, pariritòng hohocom sa nañgabúhay at sa nañgamatáy na tauò. Sungmasampalataya acó namán sa Dios Espíritu Santo, na may Santa Yglesia Católica, may casamahan nang mañga Santos; may ycauaualá nang mañga casalanan at mabubúhay na mag–oli ang nañgamatáy na tauò. at may búhay na ualáng hangan. Amén Jesús.

ANG GLORIA PATRI. (1)

Gloria Patri et Filio, et Spiritu Sancto. Sicut erat in principio, et nunc, et semper, et in secula seculorum. Amen.

ANG ABA PO SANTA MARIANG HARI.

Abá po Santa Maríang Hari. Ycáo ang cabuhaya,t, catamisan; abá pinanaligan ca namin, Ycáo ñga ang tinatáuag naming pinapapánao na tauòng anac ni Eva; Ycáo rin ang pinagbobontohang biniñga nang aming pagtañgis dini sa lupa bayang cahapishapis. Ay abá, Pintacasi ca namin, yliñgon mo sa amin ang matá mong maauaín at sacá cun matapus yaring pagpánao sa amin ypaquita mo sa amin ang iyòng Anac na Si Jesús. Abáa maauaín at maálam at matamís na Virgen María.

---

(1)   For this prayer the Latin text is preserved.

YCAANIM NA POUO,T, SIYAM NA PAGSASANAY.

ANG ACO,I, MACASALANAN.

Acó,i, nagcocompisal sa ating Pañginóon Dios macapangyayari sa lahat, cay Santa Maríang Virgen, cay San Miguel Arcangel, cay San Juan Bautista at sa mañga Santos Apóstoles, cay San Pedro at cay San Pablo, at sa lahat nang Santos ang nagcasala acó sa panimdim, sa pagüica at sa pag-gauá; acó ñgani sala, acó,i, macasalanan, sala ñga acóng lubhá. Caya ñga nananalañgin acó cay Santa María Virgen, cay San Miguel Arcangel, cay San Juan Bautista, at sa mañga Santos Apóstoles, cay San Pedro, at cay San Pablo at sa lahat nang Santos, acó,i, ypanalañgin nilá sa ating pañginóon Dios. Cahimanauari acó,i, caauán nang Pañginóon Dios macapangyayari sa lahat patauarin sa aquing mañga casalana,t, pagcalooban nang búhay na ualáng hangán. Ybiguin nauá nang Dios na macapangyayari sa lahat at lubháng maauaín ypagcalóob sa aquing acó,i, patauarin, calagán at pauian nang lahat cong sala. Siyá nauá.

UNANG PAGDALAO SA SANTISIMO SACRAMENTO.

Nariritò ang batis nang bóong cagaliñgan, Si Jesús na nasa-Santísimo Sacramento na ang caniyàng uica "Cun sino ang may oháo ay dumulog sa aquin" ¡Oh! masaganang grasiang quinamtán nang mañga Santos ditò sa batis nang Santísimo Sacramento, na dóon ypinagcacalóob nang caibig-íbig na si Jesús ang lahat na carapatan nang Caniyàng mahal na Pasion na para nang sinali nang Profeta nang daco róong panahón. "Hanapin ninyò, aniyà, nang malaquing guilio ang túbig sa mañga batis nang Mananacop (Isai. cap. 12).

Ang Condesa sa Feria naacáy sa dáan nang catotohanan nang V. P. M. Avila,i, naguintáuag sa caniyà,i, Esposa nitòng Sacramento, dahil sa palaguing nalolouatan ditò sa harapan nang Sacramento; minsán, nang siyá,i, tinanong na cun anòng guinagauá niyà nang ganóong louat, sa lagáy na yaón, ay sumagot nang ganitòng uica: "Na ang íbig co pa, aniyà,i, houag na acóng umalís dóon magpasaualáng hangán, sa pagca,t, naroróon ang bóong capangyarihan nang Dios, ay gaanò pa cayá yaón magpasaualáng haugán, na Siyáng yquinabubusog at caloualhatían nang mañga mapapálad." "¡Ah! ¿at anò cayá ang gagaoin, ang tanòng nang ibà, sa harapan nang Dios sa Santísimo Sacramento.?" "At, báquit bagá di acó tinatanong cun anò cayá ang di co guinagauá dóon.? Sintahin Siyá, purihin Siyá, pasalamatan Siyá, at amo-amoin Siyá, na para nang guinagauá nang isàng salatan sa harapán nang isàng mayaman, para namán nang isàng maysaquit sa harapán nang isàng médico at gayon din namán ang nauuháo cun macaquita nang batis na malínao.

¡Oh Jesús cong caibig-íbig, búhay at pinanaligan, cayamanan at túnay na sinisintá nang aquing calolóua' ¡Oh gaanò cayá ang ıyòng guinúgol sa paglalagac mo sa amin diyán sa Santísimo Sacramento.!

Nang macadiyán ca dóon sa aming mañga altar at nang camí ay toloñgan nang Yyòng hárap, ay súcat mo muna bathín ang pagcamatáy sa isàng crus, at sacá Ycáo ay súcat mo dalitain nang di mabílang pagalipustà sa Santísimo Sacramento.

Ang pagsintà mo at ang Yyòng nais na icáo ay sintahin natin ay nanalo nang lahat na cahirapan.

Hali na, Pañginóon co, hali na, at sumaaquin cang puso. Sarhán ang
pintóan nang aquing puso,t. magpacailán man, ay houag bigyán dáan ma-
silip ang dilâng mababaclang nang lóob co sa pagsintà sa iyo na ibig co
yháin boòng boò sa Yyò. ¡Oh! caibig-íbig cong Mananacop, ybiguin nauä
na Ycáo lámang ay ang may ari nang bóong aquing calolóua,t. cataouán,
at cun sacali acó,i, magcúlang nang pagsunod na lubós sa iyo, parusahan
mo acó nang malacás, nang acó,i, macabibigáy tóua sa haharapin panahón
sa Yyò sa lahat.

Ypagcalóob mo acó na acó,i, houag magnasa,t, humánap nang anomán
caalíuan cundí ang paglilingcod sa Yyò, madalás na pagdálao sa Yyo,t,
tangapín quitá sa pagcocomulgar. Humánap nang ibà,t, ibà ang mañga
bágay-bágay sa mundo; acó,i, ualáng iniíbig at pinagnanasáang ibàng bágay
cundí ang cayamanang pagsintà nang Yyòng puso. Ytòng biyaya lámang
ang hinihiñgí sa Yyò sa harapan nang mañga mahal na altar. Mangyari
nang limotin co ang amomán at ang houag acóng may alalahanin anò
pa man cundí ang Yyòng cagaliñgan lámang.

Mañga Serafines na mapapálad, di acó nañgiñgimbulo dahil sa cataasan
nang inyòng calagayan, datapóua,t, dahil sa pagsintà ninyó sa aquing Dios.
Turóan ninyò acó cung anò ang gagaoin co nang Siyá,i, mapaglingcoran
co,t, Siyá.i, aquing sintahin.

SEVENTIETH EXERCISE.

TRANSLATION OF THE CLOSING PART TO THE EXERCISE GIVEN
IN SEVENTIETH LESSON.

Alas,! my brethren, all these proceedings of yours are to no purpose.
If you do not direct to the Lord God your actions, if you do not make the
Lord, God, your destination, the goal of your will and the resting-place of
your earnest desires and stanch purpose, if you do not put a stop to whatever other pursuit and whatever other desire, if you do not, I say, abandon
and renounce every other pleasure here on Earth except God; alas,! all
your works are void and certainly they cannot provide the path which shall
lead you to Heaven.

Some people who earnestly desired to know the good doctrine asked
of Moses to be taught the way leading them to Heaven. Well then, that
pious and upright man, Moses. replied to them, "you know that every toil
of men here in this world has indeed an end to be attained".

There are many hardships that a soldier has to endure in time of war:
he endures hunger, thirst, weariness, and he. besides. breaks through the
enemies howeyer many, and however great may be the risk of death, and
all this only because he expects a full reward from his king.

Of little moment to the farmer is the heat of the sun, the inclemency
of the weather, the weariness, the toil and the other worries that may
render difficult his task, because it is through such troubles in his work
that he expects a good crop.

The tradesman does not fear to cross the sea, however strong the wind.
however high the billows may rise, and great and certain the risk. when
he thinks of the voyage as the means of obtaining a good and high price
for his goods.

The sick person has no pity for his body, but rather he suffers willingly the bitterness of the medicine, the pain of the caustic plaster, the ache of the sore and anything the doctor considers right to do to his body, if such treatment is to cure him and bring about some relief to his sickness.

Well then, I now ask you; whereunto do you direct your labours? Whereunto, Sir, but, (you will probably reply to me); whereto, Sir, but to our salvation in Heaven; to our attaining, of course, a happy end and the Glory which our Lord God created for us.? If so, I say to you, if so, imitate the soldier, the farmer, the tradesman and the sick person. That is to say, try to seek for what may bring health to your soul in the same manner as these people endeavour to get that which is capable of increasing their wealth and healing their bodies.

To this matter apply the questions of the holy King David who said: ¿"Quis ascendet in montem domini"? ¿"Aut quis stabit in loco sancto ejus"? That is to say, said David, "who, indeed, is the happy man who can ascend and attain to the lofty and magnificent seat of our Lord, God."? "Who, then, lodges in his sacred glory."? "Who is the happy man that can ever attain the grand end created by god for us."? And to these questions, he himself answered by these words. "Innocens manibus et mundo corde: qui non accepit in vano animam suam"; which means: "men whose hands and hearts are free from stain, and those knowing how to value their souls", of which this is the meaning: Men who are free from sin, only they will attain salvation in Heaven.

Wherefore, I now ask: are there perchance any people not knowing how to value their souls or in any way undervaluing their souls.? Yes, indeed, there are such, I say.

Your souls, you should hold above your household furniture or the tools you make use of at home or serving to earn your livelihood. What, then, if the plough is not employed for ploughing.? Is it not meanly diverted from its proper use by the employer.? The jacket, the apron, the shirt, the trousers and other similar things that you purchase, have cut in patterns and sewed by tailors and dressmakers, (experts), do you not undervalue them if, when already made, you conceal them in the chest, and do not put them on the body.? The cutlass that you get made by the smith and you intend for use at home either to split reed-cane or to meet any other want; is it not debased if you chance to keep it in the sheath or stick it in the partition-wall.?

Do I not debase this cresset in the church if, by chance, I get it not ligted by the sextons.? Alas! my brethren, it is exactly, that which I may say regarding our souls.

Does not them, man debases his soul, as it were, if he does not make use of what are called powers, memory, understanding and will, for the purpose intended by the Lord God.? Is not, I say, memory a vile thing if it is not made use of by man to remember the gifts of God.?; In a word, to remind man that he was made by God in His image and has been redeemed by Jesus Christ through His death and his precious blood on the cross only for man's sake.? Is not the understanding worthless if it is not made use of by man to know God, and to acknowledge that the wisdom, the justice and the power of God is infinite, and that He is the source from which everything flows and to which everything flows back again.? Is not the will vile if not made use of by man to love God as Father and Powerful above all things, to love also one's fellow-creatures and to honor and to practice every virtue leading the soul to Heaven, and to abhor every vice causing the eternal damnation in Hell.?

Well then, my brethren, fix in your hearts this doctrine I am preaching to you; try to realize that the reason God made you for, was just for the sake of his being remembered, loved and obeyed here on Earth that you may there enjoy eternal life

It is your giving faith to and your comprehending this teaching that will enable you to amend your wrongs, and this very same, too, will correct your long-standing bad habits. It is your believing in and comprehending this doctrine that will enable your hearts to bear with miseries for God's sake, in the same manner as the soldier bears with unutterable hardships for the sake of his king. It is through your believing in and comprehending this very doctrine that you will be capable of overcoming the enemies of your soul in the same manner as the husbandmen endeavour to overcome the difficulties in the farming of their fields, in fair weather or in foul, that they may attain a good crop.

Your believing and your comprehending of this doctrine will serve to take away from you your laziness in attending mass, in confessing, and all your excuses for not practising the commandments of God and of the Holy Church.

And finally, your believing in and comprehending rightly the main purpose and end the Lord God made you for, will enable you to employ well the powers and strength of your souls; the memory, use it to remember God and the gifts He made you a present of; the understanding, to know Him and His almighty power; and the will, to love Him here in this life that you may attain there above the eternal life. Amen.

THE END

IMPORTANT NOTICE.

Those who are acquainted with the poor press facilities Manila affords will not be surprised to find so many errata and imperfections of print in this work. The still scanty typographical ability of natives as compositors of English is accountable for most of these defects. It may be truthfully said, however, that no amount of labor or pains taken by the author would entirely eradicate the same. Fortunately, however, the errors occur for the most part in the English text and the student's knowledge of that language can safely be relied upon to prevent any misconception as to the sense intended.

As for the typographical deficiences, the student's attention is called to a very important one, reference to which has already been made in the notice appearing on the cover and first sheet; namely, the employing of *ñg* instead of *ñg*. Strange as it may appear, such Tagalog character, of the size and type suitable for this work, could not be found throughout the city, and, thus, the Spanish *ñ* had to be resorted to. The student is hereby again reminded that in writing this peculiar character he must carry the tittle above the *n* a little ahead to the right, so as to make it bear midway between the said letter and the *g*; thus, *ñg*, this two-lettered combination representing a single character in Tagalog.

The work with its manifold defects and imperfections is submitted to the fair and impartial judgment of the public. The author rests confident that whatever such judgment may be, the fact will be apparent to the reader that an earnest effort has been made to contribute something of value upon a subject that up to this time has received little more than a passing attention. Should this the first edition of the work meet with approval, the author assures the public that not only will all existing errors and defects be removed from the next edition, but that many and important additions will be made thereto.

INDEX.

PRELIMINARY STUDY.

GRAMMAR.

II.

CONTENTS.

III.

CONTENTS.

PAGES.

CONTENTS.

CONTENTS.

CONTENTS.

CONTENTS.

CPSIA information can be obtained at www.ICGtesting.com
Printed in the USA
LVOW130338280911

248199LV00003B/24/P